Inside Marketing

Inside Marketing

Practices, Ideologies, Devices

Edited by
Detlev Zwick and Julien Cayla

OXFORD
UNIVERSITY PRESS

OXFORD

UNIVERSITY PRESS

Great Clarendon Street, Oxford OX2 6DP
United Kingdom

Oxford University Press is a department of the University of Oxford.
It furthers the University's objective of excellence in research, scholarship,
and education by publishing worldwide. Oxford is a registered trade mark of
Oxford University Press in the UK and in certain other countries

© Detlev Zwick and Julien Cayla 2011

The moral rights of the author have been asserted

First Edition published 2011
First published in paperback 2012
Reprinted 2013

British Library Cataloguing in Publication Data
Data available

Library of Congress Cataloging in Publication Data
Data available

ISBN 978-0-19-965583-0

Table of Contents

Table of Contents

Acknowledgments

This book represents a composite scholarly endeavor that could not have been completed without the unwavering support of several other individuals. As an edited volume, it is a joint achievement of the editors, the authors, and the publisher. While we refrain from recognizing each author individually, we would very much like to acknowledge their tremendous efforts to turn out chapters that are innovative, challenging, and substantial. The contributors' diverse interests, disciplinary perspectives, and theoretical approaches have allowed us to put together a wide-ranging, yet focused set of viewpoints on contemporary marketing practice and theory. We hope that these chapters prompt a vigorous debate among marketing practitioners and scholars about the multifarious, and sometime nefarious, effects of the global rise of marketing practice, marketing ideology, and marketing devices. It is, we believe, a debate worth having given marketing's current and future influence on our social, cultural, and economic lives.

Furthermore, we are grateful for the support we received from Oxford University Press throughout the development and completion of this book. Special thanks go to David Musson for his constant encouragement and support for the project. We also want to acknowledge Emma Lambert, Matthew Derbyshire and Carol Bestley for all their hard work in seeing the book through its completion. We relied on a number of individuals for proofreading and copyediting at various stages of the book. In particular, we want to thank Sutapa Aditya, Yesim Ozalp, Tanvi Metha, Robert Canwell, and Mary Payne for all their careful work throughout the entire process of production. Finally, the editors acknowledge the generous support of the Social Sciences and Humanities Research Council of Canada, the Schulich School of Business, the Australian School of Business, and Euromed Management, which enabled us to make this project a reality.

Detlev Zwick, Toronto, Canada
Julien Cayla, Sydney, Australia

List of Contributors

Kalman Applbaum is an Associate Professor of Anthropology at the University of Wisconsin, Milwaukee. He is the author of *The Marketing Era* (Routledge, 2003). His current work is concerned with the making and commodification of the health care market in the United States.

Adam Arvidsson is an Associate Professor in the Department of Sociology at the University of Milan. His research examines new forms of value creation in the information economy and the economic role of brands within the contemporary information economy. His books include *The Ethical Economy: Business and Society in the 21st Century* (Columbia University Press, forthcoming) and *Brands—Meaning and Value in Media Culture* (Routledge, 2006).

Elspeth H. Brown is an Associate Professor of History and Director of the Centre for the Study of the United States, at the University of Toronto. She is the author of *The Corporate Eye: Photography and the Rationalization of American Commercial Culture, 1884–1929* (Johns Hopkins, 2005) and co-editor of *Cultures of Commerce: Representation and American Business Culture, 1877–1960* (Palgrave, 2006). She is currently working on a book concerning the history of commercial modeling in the twentieth century USA.

Julien Cayla is a Senior Lecturer of Marketing at the Australian School of Business, University of New South Wales, Sydney, Australia and a Visiting Professor at Euromed Management, Marseille, France. His work draws on anthropological theories and methodologies to study global marketing issues. His research on global marketing has been published in the *Journal of Consumer Research*, the *Journal of International Marketing*, the *Handbook of International Marketing*, and *Advertising and Society Review*.

Franck Cochoy is Professor of Sociology at the University of Toulouse and a member of the CERTOP-CNRS, France. His research is focused on the sociology of organizations, markets, and the different mediations that frame the relation between supply and demand. He is the author of *Une histoire du marketing* (La Découverte, 1999) and *Une sociologie du packaging ou l'âne de Buridan face au marché* (Presses Universitaires de France, 2002).

Daniel Thomas Cook is Associate Professor of Childhood Studies and Sociology at Rutgers University, Camden, New Jersey, USA. He is editor of *Symbolic Childhood* (2002) and author of *The Commodification of Childhood* (2004) as well as a number of articles and book chapters on consumer society, childhood, leisure, and urban culture. Cook also serves as an editor of *Childhood: A Journal of Global Child Research*.

Rita M. Denny, is an Anthropologist and a founding partner of Practica Group, where she applies an anthropological framework to consumer behavior, calling on linguistic, semiotic, and symbolic traditions for interpreting consumer attitudes, perceptions, and behavior. With Patricia Sunderland she is the author of the book, *Doing Anthropology in Consumer Research* (Left Coast Press, 2007).

Pascale Desroches is Product Manager at L'Oréal Canada working on the brand L'Oréal Paris. After finishing a master in marketing at HEC Montreal, she started in 2004 as an intern, then as a project manager in the development department for Garnier in Paris.

Robert J. Foster is Professor and Chair of Anthropology and Professor of Visual and Cultural Studies at the University of Rochester. His current research interests include globalization, corporations, material culture, and mass consumption. He is the author of *Social Reproduction and History in Melanesia* (Cambridge, 1995) and *Materializing the Nation: Commodities, Consumption and Media in Papua New Guinea* (Indiana, 2002). His most recent book is titled *Coca-Globalization: Following Soft Drinks from New York to New Guinea* (Palgrave Macmillan, 2008).

Gérald Gaglio is Assistant Professor in Sociology at the University of Technology of Troyes (France). After completing his doctoral dissertation on the social trajectory of the mobile phone in France in 2005, he worked as a market researcher in a telecom company. Since then, he has written extensively on various aspects of this experience: the place and role of writing in organizations, communication in the workplace, the impacts of qualitative studies, and the specificities of the market research profession. His most recent project deals with health on the Internet.

Catherine Grandclément is a Researcher in Sociology at EDF R&D in France. Her dissertation examines the construction of contemporary shopping through a material and historical anthropology of the supermarket. She currently works on the retailing of electricity, with a focus on how electric utilities attempt to discipline the user through the so-called "Demand-Side Integration" programs. She is interested, more generally, in the making of markets and the social and political implications of the mobilization of the category of the "consumer."

David Lyon is the Director of the Surveillance Studies Centre (http://www.surveillanceproject.org/davidlyon) and a Professor of Sociology at Queen's University. His most recent books are *Identifying Citizens: ID Cards as Surveillance* (2009), *Playing the Identity Card* (co-edited with Colin J. Bennett, Routledge, 2008) and *Surveillance Studies: An Overview* (2007). He is a founding editor of the e-journal *Surveillance & Society* and has particular research interests in national ID cards, aviation security and surveillance, and in promoting the cross-disciplinary and international study of surveillance.

Giannino Malossi is as an independent researcher and consultant in communications strategy and in economics of creative industries. He is the author of *The Style Engine: Spectacle, Identity, Design and Business* (Monacelli Press, 1998), *Volare: The Icon of Italy in Global Pop Culture* (Monacelli Press, 1999), and *Material Man: Masculinity, Sexuality, Style* (Abrams, 2000).

ix

Jean-Sébastien Marcoux is Associate Professor in marketing at HEC Montréal (Canada). He is an Anthropologist who was trained at the University College London (UCL) in the United Kingdom where he worked under the supervision of Daniel Miller. He now specializes in ethnographic research, the anthropology of consumption, and contemporary material culture studies. His research interests lie at the junction of anthropology and marketing.

Liz Moor is Senior Lecturer in Media and Communications at Goldsmiths, University of London, UK. She is the author of *The Rise of Brands* (Berg, 2007), which traces the development and impact of the branding industry. She is also the co-editor (with Guy Julier) of *Design and Creativity: Policy, Management and Practice* (Berg, 2009), which examines the commercial and political role of design and its implications for the nature of creative work.

Yesim Ozalp is a doctoral student at the Schulich School of Business, York University, Toronto, Canada. Her research focuses on commercial gentrification.

Lisa Peñaloza is Scientific Director, InteraCT Research Center, and Professor, École des Hautes Études Commerciales du Nord (EDHEC). Her research and teaching takes a cultural approach to market phenomena, with attention to interactions between consumers and marketers in consumption and marketing practice. Her work has been published in the *Journal of Consumer Research, Journal of Marketing, Public Policy and Marketing, International Journal of Research in Marketing*, and *Consumption, Markets and Culture*.

Jason Pridmore is the Senior Researcher with the DigIDeas project, a European Research Council funded project on the social and ethical impacts of digital identification systems at Zuyd University in the Netherlands. He is the author of the expert report on the surveillance of consumers and consumption, part of the report on the surveillance society commissioned by the British Information Commissioner in 2006.

John F. Sherry, Jr., an Anthropologist who studies the sociocultural and symbolic dimensions of consumption, and the cultural ecology of marketing, is the Herrick Professor and Chairman of the Department of Marketing at the University of Notre Dame. Sherry is a Fellow of the American Anthropological Association as well as the Society for Applied Anthropology, and past President of the Association for Consumer Research. His work appears in numerous journals, book chapters, professional manuals, and proceedings.

Don Slater is Reader in Sociology at the London School of Economics. His main research involvements are in economic sociology and theories of consumption; information technology, new media, and development; and visual culture (particularly photography). Publications include *Consumer Culture and Modernity, The Internet: An Ethnographic Approach* (with Daniel Miller), and *The Technological Economy* (with Andrew Barry). He is currently working on a book called *New Media, Development and Globalization*.

Patricia L. Sunderland, Anthropologist, is a founding partner of Practica Group, a consumer research and strategic consulting firm based in New York and Chicago. She is

the author, along with Rita Denny, of *Doing Anthropology in Consumer Research* (Left Coast Press, 2007). She has also contributed chapters and articles to *Advertising Cultures, Anthropological Quarterly, Ethnos, Handbook of Qualitative Research Methods in Marketing, Human Organization,* and *Consumption, Markets and Culture* as well as the trade and popular press.

Detlev Zwick is Associate Professor of Marketing at the Schulich School of Business, York University, Toronto, Canada. His research focuses on cultural and social theories of consumption and the critical cultural studies of marketing and management practice. His work has appeared in various journals, book chapters, and proceedings.

Introduction

Inside Marketing: Practices, Ideologies, Devices

Detlev Zwick and Julien Cayla

Marketing has grown into a truly global phenomenon. As professors teaching marketing in business schools, we know firsthand of the allure of working in marketing for armies of eager students from a variety of departments ranging from design and engineering to English literature and kinesiology. From this perspective of the "inside," it sometimes seems that everyone wants to learn how marketing works or how to be a marketer. Of course, what "working in marketing" means exactly is often unclear, as the label appears to describe an ever-growing and increasingly fuzzy set of job titles, tasks, and skills. The entrepreneurial work of continuous idea generation performed in a small advertising agency and the bureaucratic administration of a mature consumer brand are easily recognizable yet hardly similar examples of marketing work. The practical experiences available in these respective work environments differ significantly, but—typical of post-industrial forms of labor—they share a reliance on a common set of communicative and cognitive skills (see Ritzer, 1993; Virno, 2004).

What remains largely a mystery when looking at the prominent marketing textbooks and journals, however, is what these communicative and cognitive skills amount to (to say nothing of the effect of myriad technical devices used by marketers in their everyday work). The current, "approved" definition of marketing put forth by the board of directors of the American Marketing Association (AMA)[1] provides little more than a formal description of marketing processes: "Marketing is the activity, set of institutions, and processes for creating, communicating, delivering, and exchanging offerings that have value for customers, clients, partners, and society at large." Such a definition has very little meaning in the face of widespread agreement that its two key concepts—offerings (essentially, products and services) and value—are the outcomes of complex processes of cultural and social construction (Slater, 2002*a*, 2002*b*).

While not mentioned in the AMA's definition, a central concept of marketing is, as one would expect, the market. This term, however, when encountered in the marketing literature, suggests a universal category of exchange relations, something immutable and natural rather than historically contingent and culturally constructed. Yet marketers cannot actually define a market or a competitor "except through extensive forms of cultural knowledge" (Slater, 2002*a*: 59). For example, when Indian dairy cooperative Amul introduced very inexpensive ice cream targeting customers who live on less than two dollars a day, the market for this product was considered to be enormous because, in addition to being cheap and presumably tasty, the milk content of the ice cream made it a substitute for other dairy products (Prahalad, 2005). When the company announced plans to "enrich" its ice cream with psyllium husk, a natural laxative, concerns arose about the categorization of the product. As Prasanna Shah, the head of Amul's ice-cream business, put it: "We do not want it to be perceived as a medicine. Rather, the consumer should view it as a regular vanilla or strawberry ice-cream that additionally confers natural laxative benefits" (Damodaran, 2002). To ensure that the ice cream is not accidentally considered a substitute for other laxative products, effectively demoting it to a new and significantly smaller market, the company has vowed to promote the enriched version as a "health-cum-fun" food (Damodaran, 2002). What this example demonstrates is that marketing professionals, as well as marketing scholars, tend to think of the market as a relatively stable and objective entity, even as their own actions permanently challenge the stability of its boundaries (Callon et al., 2002; Foster, 2008). Therefore, any successful theorization of contemporary marketing practices and axioms needs to examine marketing work first and foremost as engagement in processes through which products and services come into being, acquire meaning for consumers, and obtain economic value through positioning within a competitively optimum definition of the market (Slater, 2002*b*)—in short, processes of product valorization and of constant stabilization and destabilization of market boundaries, product categories, and product features.

Marketing as Performance

Performing marketing work is a complex undertaking that involves a number of actors and tasks, including market research, product research and development, design, advertising, distribution, and pricing, among others. To unravel how market, product, and value stabilization and destabilization continually occur and are managed by various economic actors requires us to look inside the processes, conditions, and agencies of marketing performance through anthropological, textual, historical, and sociological analyses. Meaningful theorization of how marketing works—that is, to what effect it operates in various social, cultural, and economic contexts; what kind of devices marketers employ and to what end; what kind of knowledge it concerns and, hence, what kind of power it produces; and, finally, what kind of subjectivities on both sides of the exchange relationship it encourages and produces—requires a systematic and multi-methodological research effort.

Interestingly, while the work of marketing has received relatively scant attention from prominent social scientists, the "work" of the consumer and of consumption itself has been the target of meticulous academic and professional scrutiny. In the field of academic marketing, research on consumer behavior has long found a place in the laboratories of business schools and psychology departments, where throngs of undergraduate students posing as the average shopper are painstakingly probed and observed for the slightest reactions to manipulations in price, packaging, mode of distribution and display of products, music, size of advertisings, and other sometimes surprising, if not bizarre, aspects of the market environment.[2] In a desire to enrich the epistemology of capitalism no stone is left unturned; no aspect of the consumer's inner life, decision-making process, and motivation is too odd, outlandish, or negligible to preclude extensive investigation in the laboratory. In addition, a relatively smaller group of marketing scholars has adopted techniques traditionally used by anthropologists and sociologists to investigate consumers in their "natural habitat." This particular approach to studying consumer behavior was conceived in the summer of 1986, when a group of US-based marketing professors embarked on a cross-country research trip visiting swap meets, flea markets, county fairs, and other sites not only of consumption but of forms of behavior previously neglected by the laboratory approach. Touted as an attempt to generate deep cultural knowledge of consumers, this summer project ultimately gave rise to a new generation of graduate students and professors "earnestly spying on young people at the mall, or obsessively staring at them in virtual communities" (Miller, 2007: 4). Finally, there is the massive field of commercial customer research, with its own rather long and peculiar history (see e.g., Arvidsson, 2004; Miller and Rose, 1997), that ensures a constant flow of corporate knowledge production[3] of the consumer.

In comparison to the impressive amount of resources, time, and energy funneled into researching the inner life of consumers, a rather minor effort has been made to study the growing army of economic actors whose work it is to define markets and give shape to the consumer culture as we know it. Furthermore, the results of the work that marketers do are, by definition, highly visible. Indeed, we would suggest that making things visible (in the sense of bringing them forward and rendering them meaningful and

5

recognizable) through such means as product design, packaging, display strategies, commercial architecture, branding, and advertising and promotional activities is the very purpose of marketing (see e.g., Jacobson and Mazur, 1995; Ritzer, 1999). Yet the visibility of marketing activities contrasts with the relative obscurity of the inner workings of the marketing profession. Indeed, little scholarly work has been directed at "inspecting the beliefs and practices of advertising and marketing professionals, *particularly as these are enacted in organizational contexts*" (Cook, 2006: 534, emphasis added). This is particularly surprising considering that individuals have become increasingly aware of the intensification of marketing activities in their everyday lives and that many bemoan the proliferation of such social techniques as branding, promotions, solicitations, loyalty programs, and personalized product offerings (see e.g., Klein, 1999; Frank, 2000; Barber, 2007; Moor, 2007). Indeed, bracketing marketing as a profession, practice, and ideology from the critical responsibility of marketing as a social science means ignoring the key role that marketers play in driving the expansion and projecting the face of global capitalism (Applbaum, 2004).

While business researchers and marketing scholars in particular have been reluctant to study the field of professional marketing management from a cultural and critical perspective, a limited but growing contingent of social scientists have begun to turn their gaze to the behavior of this particular profession (see e.g., Dávila, 2001; Malefyt and Moeran, 2003; Mazzarella, 2003; Applbaum, 2004; Elmer, 2004). These efforts are aimed at making more transparent an industry that has come under increasing public scrutiny and finds itself often on the defensive against an increasingly informed, networked, and mobilized consumer body (Cook, 2006). However, while these authors provide analytically astute and theoretically rich accounts of various elements of the marketing profession, they generally lack a link to the material realities and managerial necessities of marketing work. They tend to be confined to a textual level of analysis rather than exploring marketing as a material social practice (Slater, 2002c), or what Callon et al. (2002) call the "process of qualification."

Through the lenses of materialization, (de)stabilization, and (re)qualification offered by Slater and Callon (and his various collaborators, see e.g., Callon, 1998; Callon et al., 2002; Callon et al., 2007), marketing comes to be seen as an amalgamation of institutional, cultural, economic, and technical processes by which goods and markets—and objects and categories—are determined, contested, and provisionally given stable forms. From this perspective, marketing work cannot be reduced to an analysis of the production and consumption of signs, ideologies, myths, and codes. For marketing professionals, both the thing and the sign matter because marketing is less concerned with the nature (physical properties) of things than with the economic effects of strategic cultural interventions (of determination and stabilization) aimed at constructing the optimal valuation and positioning, or more generally, the optimal market for a specific product, service, or symbol. And because the performance of marketing work depends on the coordination of institutional activities of a number of actors within the firm and without—including regulators, policy experts, technical devices, and consumers—to study marketing means to acknowledge what we call the political economy of marketing. It means, in other words, to look *inside* marketing.

Marketing as Governmentality

To look inside marketing does not mean that one should neglect marketing as a form of power that acts on the outside and on consumers in particular. Callon et al.'s economy of qualities and Slater's conceptual notions of stabilization, destabilization, and cultural calculation, while critical for advancing our theoretical understanding of what marketing work *does* and *is*, focus almost exclusively on the relationship between marketing and objects, or, to be precise, on the *nature* of objects and of material culture more generally in the face of increasingly globalized and complex strategies of stabilization and destabilization, qualification and requalification. In Callon's and Slater's commercial ontology, the consumer *subject* remains largely the kind of black box that these authors have so effectively opened up for the *object* of consumption. But material things and market structures are not the only entities drawn into processes of (de)stabilization and (re)qualification. The stabilization and qualification of the contemporary consumer subject, too, is a target for the sociocultural system of marketing, although the manner in which marketing acts on consumers has less to do with techniques of framing and materialization than with producing a certain culture of self-government, in the sense Foucault used the term; that is, a culture that promotes techniques of self-care, self-improvement, and self-responsibility. In short, to understand the relationship between marketing and consumption is to acknowledge an ethics of the self that links the ongoing production of lifestyle, identity, and self to consumption and the market (Finn, 2009).

From this perspective, marketing represents a perpetual questioning machine asking the modern consumer to make a project of oneself based on ongoing self-examination and querying; to look at oneself as a set of constantly multiplying problems (too fat, too wrinkly, too boring, etc.) and as yet unrealized potentialities; to translate them into personal needs and desires; and to look to the market for solutions. Marketing, as a product and producer of our contemporary obsession with a mode of existence centered on the "endless, self-creative project of making yourself and your life a work of art"

7

(Nealon, 2008: 12), positions itself as an enabler—a kind of support system and resource center—for the work of continuous self-realization and self-production (cf. Binkley, 2007). In cultivating oneself as a form of "human capital" requiring constant investment in, and updating of, one's individuality and capabilities, the responsibility for being interesting, happy, creative, healthy, and beautiful rests with the individual; marketing seeks to ensure that practices of self-problematization never cease (Jambet, 1992) and that the resulting work of self-care is channeled through the freedom of market choice (see also L. Moor, this volume).

Marketing thus understood is an art of governing that constructs the consumer subject in the image of the entrepreneur—an entrepreneur of the self: self-activating, self-responsible, and self-reliant—who embraces what Zwick and Ozalp (this volume) term "enterprising consumption." Enterprising consumption is not undertaken as an end in itself but as part of a straightforward economic calculus, a cost–benefit analysis where permanent self-problematization is required to prevent falling idle and neglecting the critical (and competitive) work of self-improvement and -investment. Under this regime of governmentality it would be irresponsible to pursue a strategy of stable identity and immutable subjectivity. Rather, individuals are urged to engage in proactive destabilization and permanent requalification of themselves. Marketing requires a self-problematizing and self-therapeutic consumer subject not only for the purpose of reproducing consumption but increasingly for the (re)production of the qualification of products (see Slater and Foster, this volume). Foster cites Callon to make this link between the creativity of the self-producing consumer and the benefits of such creative work for the work of qualification:

> In the economy of qualities consumers are thus a constant source of overflowing. And it would be counter-productive to simply suppress these overflowings, because in order to function, markets of the economy of qualities need them. (Callon, 2001; see Callon, 1998)

In his analysis of the marketing-value nexus, Foster observes that marketing has come to regard overflowings—which may come from such activities as culture jamming and symbolic resistance, creative product adaptations and hacking, open-source collaborations, or social networking—as a rich source of innovation and competitive advantage, feeding the value that is generated by the productive work of self-governing consumer subjects directly into firms' processes of value creation. Zwick and Ozalp suggest that, when marketing actively seeks to cause the production of overflowings from the process of consumer self-production (i.e., the production of consumer lifestyles and subjectivities) on the one hand and the appropriation of value generated by this process on the other, marketing becomes biopolitical by pursuing the total commodification of all human creativity—indeed all forms of human activity (see Lury, 2004; Arvidsson, 2006). Just like other forms of marketing, biopolitical marketing pursues the production of use value and exchange value, but it does so by establishing a regulatory form of power to generate and effectively channel the output of consumer self-production (Arvidsson, 2007; Bowers, 2008; Zwick, Bonsu, and Darmody, 2008). We can see biopolitical marketing at work in contemporary forms of branding (see e.g., Moor, 2003; Lury, 2004; Arvidsson, 2006) and innovation (e.g., Prahalad and Ramaswamy, 2004; Cova and Dalli, 2009), where marketers seek ways to sell the value generated *by* the consumers *to* the consumers. Hence, from a perspective of looking inside marketing, the logic of commercial ontologies sketched out by Callon and Slater, based on the temporary stabilization and qualification of markets and products, can be extended to include the consumer.

Structure of the Book

Marketing as a material social practice and global ideology is a relatively new field of inquiry without a dominant disciplinary home. A systematic and critical engagement with marketing as a field of practice, knowledge, and subjectification requires us to bring together in this volume leading scholars from various social science and business disciplines who bring to the field a rich variety of conceptual, methodological, and theoretical tools. The selections and organization of this volume are meant to reflect what we perceive to be the key concerns represented in this emerging field of study.

Toward this end, Part I, *Studying Marketing Differently*, brings together three important theoretical alternatives to the dominant view of marketing as a largely economic and sometimes psychological technique that acts *in* the world but not *on* the world. Each of the contributions by Slater, Foster, and Cochoy provides a unique theoretical perspective on marketing practice, yet the three chapters converge in their appeal to marketing scholars to study marketing at the level of its constitutive microeconomic, everyday material practices.

Slater argues that marketing has been "rendered impossible" by fundamental divisions of intellectual labor between economics and the cultural disciplines. Economics, on the one hand, has expelled all cultural logics in its analysis of formal rationality, while cultural disciplines, on the other, have focused on marketing as ideology and meaning, thus ignoring marketing as a commercial practice. For Slater, marketing—in which cultural and economic logics are inextricable—is therefore very difficult to grasp, and thus his contribution is to theorize marketing as a concurrently economic and cultural logic

9

in order to characterize the fundamental aspects of the modern division of intellectual labor.

Foster continues Slater's focus on marketing as a cultural-economic commercial practice by asking what is implied, both conceptually and politically, for the place of marketing techniques in value creation when the cultural and economic roles of producers and consumers converge. He approaches these issues through a consideration, inspired by Marcel Mauss's treatment (1967) of gift exchange, of how persons and things qualify each other. Taking up Callon et. al's (2002) idea of an economy of qualities, Foster argues that the use value of things that people realize as consumers has become a source and site of surplus value extraction. His argument invites reconsideration of the premise of Marx's political economy (1978), in which only producers (labor power in use) create surplus value. The chapter engages with recent critical work in marketing and anthropology that suggests a new role for consumers in value creation and highlights the challenges presented to marketers in managing the creativity of consumers. It emphasizes the fundamentally exploitative aspects of the consumer's new role while at the same time suggesting the possibilities for political action that inhere in marketers' efforts to put consumers to work.

In the final chapter of Part I, Cochoy describes three main avenues for understanding consumer behavior: (a) by studying consumers directly, which has been the focus of such marketing journals as the *Journal of Consumer Research* and the *Journal of Consumer Psychology*; (b) by studying consumer behavior indirectly through the practices of marketers; and (c) by attending to what Cochoy calls "market-things" (p. 60): a wide array of objects, artifacts, and devices that animate and structure consumption and consumer behavior in important ways but which, despite their significant effect on fashioning consumer behavior, remain elusive to the first two approaches. By looking at the spatial–technical transformation of grocery stores in the United States over a thirty-year period from 1929 to 1959, Cochoy is able to demonstrate how technical innovations such as the shopping cart and the turnstile were instrumental in shaping how customers navigated the store and shopped for groceries. For Cochoy, a study of market-things is able to explain some forms of consumer behavior without studying the main actors—consumers and marketers—directly. Cochoy's methodological and conceptual approach calls for future studies on the material culture of marketing, and at least one contribution in this volume, Desroches's and Marcoux's study of laboratory life at L'Oréal, has already answered this call.

The general theme of marketing as material social practice is carried over to Part II, *Marketing as Performance*, in which the authors scrutinize marketing tools and devices and the way they structure marketing work. The section starts off with a chapter by Grandclément and Gaglio, who draw on their extensive work experience in the French market research industry to present an analysis of one of marketing's central market research techniques: the focus group. The chapter analyzes this technique in great detail, from the initial marketing brief to the recruiting process to the writing of the discussion guide. During the preparation for a focus group session, the consumer persona becomes precisely defined. As a result, the moderator's challenge during the actual course of the focus group is to make the "flesh and bones" respondents in the room correspond to the consumer previously defined on paper. In addition, the focus group device, with its concealed backroom, frames the marketer, who continually trains his ear to the voice of the consumer amid the labored discourse of focus group respondents. The description of this manufactured process suggests an expedient that is quite far removed from the kind of open-ended discovery of consumer needs that is called for in the marketing discipline.[4]

The chapter by Pridmore and Lyon on loyalty programs presents another kind of market research process. The authors suggest that surveillance is at the heart of marketing practice, such that marketing has become the model for contemporary surveillance. By commanding a surfeit of personal data, marketing discerns the needs, desires, and trends of consumer behavior and shapes these behaviors by subtle and sometimes less than subtle means. Pridmore and Lyon describe this as a process of "relationship building," where detailed customer data help the marketer better understand the interconnections between consumption patterns, values, tastes, and preferences and the digital representations of consumers, thus constituting a form of commercial sociology (Ellison and Burrows, 2007: 299; see also Lyon, 1994: 142, Burrows and Gane, 2006). By focusing on loyalty marketing, the authors demonstrate how digitizing consumer information and assembling it into representations of consumers renders these consumers transparent brands.

The chapter by Sunderland and Denny offers a complementary perspective on the process of market construction discussed in the previous chapters. Drawing from their field experience as commercial anthropologists helping corporate clients understand their customers, Sunderland and Denny recount in detail a specific client project. Asked to take the client's internal customer categories—obtained through loyalty programs, customer database marketing, and other techniques referred to in the profession as relationship marketing (see e.g., Morgan and Hunt, 1994; for a brief review see Zwick et al., 2008)—and confirm them in person, Sunderland and Denny found themselves increasingly exhorted by the client to simply confirm these predefined, imaginary consumer types, rather than generate a methodologically sound and conceptually original account of the nature of the customers. Despite the occasionally comical moments of interaction between the client and the researchers—especially when Sunderland and Denny rather cautiously and in true anthropological fashion confess to the client that they simply cannot find in the field the consumers the company thought it had identified in its databases—the chapter conveys a serious message about the profession's intense emotional investment in knowing one's customer.

This section concludes with a compelling study by Desroches and Marcoux from inside one of the world's largest cosmetics companies, L'Oréal. Drawing on the work of Latour and Woolgar and evoking Howes's reflections on sensual anthropology, the chapter seeks to examine critically and reflexively the making of the sensuous consumer in and for the contemporary hypersensual marketplace. Based on ethnographic work conducted at L'Oréal's headquarters in Paris, the authors are able to expound the processes by which managers educe—through description, representation, and objectification—the sensuous consumer. This ethnography takes us beyond the typical science and technology studies, showing how the hypersensual marketplace that is taking shape at firms such as L'Oréal emerges at the intersection of practical science and an elusive sensual culture. By doing so, the chapter affirms the need to take into account the material and sensory dimensions of products often ignored by social scientists.

Taken together, the contributions in Section II reveal the inherent messiness of marketing research and invite future studies that explore how marketing techniques and marketing knowledge manifest themselves in actual practice. Such work would require a quite different approach—perhaps inspired by Latour, Callon, and others in that fold—from that of conventional marketing scholarship with its obsessive focus on the development of more effective technical tools for persuading, selling to, and knowing consumers.

In Part III, *The Political Economy of Marketing Practice*, we turn our attention to the way marketing impacts society. The chapters here do not argue that markets are political (we have known since Marx that markets and market choices cannot be independent of the state and that the economy is always a political economy), but that marketing can be thought of as a form of management (or governmentality), and perhaps exploitation, of flows of democratic consumer energies liberated by the ascendancy of consumption and the democratization of middle-class materialism following World War II.

Brown's chapter looks at the role of the black model and the invention of the US negro market in the immediate post-war era. She shows that, long before white marketers began paying attention to the US ethnic market in the mid-to-late 1960s, African-American marketing professionals invented blacks as a market in order to fashion them as a consumer demographic. Brown's essay provides a detailed and fascinating account of the history and politics of an emergent black modeling industry as an integral part of the creation of this market. To expose the linkages between race and commerce, she asks how black professionals and publishers sought to render this market visible and profitable. Trying to define a commercial space for the display of the black female body that sidestepped existing stereotypes of the asexual mammy on the one hand and the hypersexual jezebel on the other, black modeling agencies elaborated discourses of both bourgeois respectability and mid-century glamor. Importantly, Brown identifies marketers, and black marketers in particular, as key actors in parsing the twin discourses of black, class-inflected respectability and a public, managed sexuality to signify and enable blacks' full inclusion in American life through participation in the marketplace.

In another historical study, Arvidsson and Malossi examine forms of customer co-production and the role of marketing in managing the creativity of individuals as customers. Recalling the development of the Italian fashion industry in post-war Italy, the authors present two historical models according to which customers have been integrated within the value chains of the culture and creative industries: the social factory and the brand. Arvidsson and Malossi argue that in the social factory model, customers (and other external actors) are put to use in securing input for product innovation, while in the brand model the productive contribution of customers is not primarily that of developing new products, but of co-creating an environment in which certain kinds of value conventions can operate. These two models require new strategies of governance, including the promotion of a generic form of creativity as a social ideal, which can easily be confused with emancipatory developments.

Employing similar conceptual language, the essay by Zwick and Ozalp looks at the politics of marketing as value creation. The authors study contemporary condominium and loft marketing practices and discourses to illustrate two key valorization strategies of contemporary real estate marketing: lifestyle community and enterprising consumption. Situating these marketing discourses within a larger theoretical discussion of the transformation of contemporary marketing from a discipline of panoptic control to the government of consumer productivity, the authors demonstrate that, by enlisting buyers as participants in the ongoing process of production (through community, lifestyle, creative consumption, emotion, and affect), biopolitical marketing channels the emotional and creative energies of condo and loft dwellers through the logic of economic production. Such a form of marketing posits that the value of the object of consumption emerges at least partially from the anticipated value of the immaterial labor of the consumers.

While maintaining a concern with politics, Part IV, *The Diffusion of Marketing Ideology and its Effects*, shifts the focus to the processes and effects of the diffusion of marketing to an ever-increasing number of domains, from healthcare to public policy construction to advertising campaigns directed at children. In a chapter that examines why and how marketers started

13

targeting children, Cook shows that tools are never merely tools, but always operate on the theoretical level. In his contribution, Cook examines how knowledge derived in and from marketing practice—including consumer research—configures notions of the child in ways that make marketing to children not only morally palatable but, in some cases, akin to a civic duty. The child here—more precisely, the child's perspective—takes on the character of a currency or value to be leveraged so as to secure market share. Constructing children as desiring, knowing, and rational decision-makers astutely exploits and reinforces the popular discourse concerning children as savvy consumers. Such an understanding of children as competent actors in a market economy has in turn helped to further justify market research activities scrutinizing children's every want and need. Marketing, then, is establishing itself as an important player in constructing our understanding of children and of childhood in general.

Applbaum extends Cook's appraisal of how contemporary marketing configures consumers out of previously excluded groups and breaks ground into spaces of the social, the cultural, and the personal. More than forty years ago, Philip Kotler and Sidney Levy (1969) proposed that marketing's methods and concepts can and should be broadened to more than just commercial enterprises, but to schools, hospitals, museums, churches, universities, police departments, charities, libraries, labor unions, YMCAs, and even the department of defense. Applbaum finds that, four decades later, this vision has been realized. In his chapter, he addresses the implications of this broadening of marketing in light of evidence drawn from the application of marketing to the pharmaceutical industry, an industry with immense responsibility to the public interest and where a marketing-driven culture has become the norm. He describes how this industry has seen a shift in focus and spending: from research and development to innovative marketing, from investing in risky research programs to marketing blockbuster drugs, and from a long-term pursuit of meaningful health solutions to the rapid creation of meaningless product differentiations and the patenting of functionally identical drugs. Applbaum concedes that the effects of the marketing concept may be harmless in many product categories. However, his study of the socially harmful effects of the adoption of a marketing mindset in the pharmaceutical industry raises a key question: is marketing a universal tool, a technology, or even a science geared to the work of identifying and satisfying human needs and therefore unyoked to culturally particular values or implicit theories of human needs and satisfactions? In his analysis, Applbaum calls on the discipline of marketing—which for over forty years has seen little wrong with the pronouncements of two of its biggest heroes—to take a closer and more critical look at the human and social costs of universalizing marketing.

In much the same vein, Moor analyzes the infusion of marketing tools and principles into the management of public health programs in the United Kingdom. She develops a critical account of the rise of social marketing with specific reference to the establishment of the National Social Marketing Centre. Moor traces how marketing discourses and devices reconfigure health from a public matter to an individual concern, despite such phenomena as the proliferation of messages and marketing campaigns describing "flawed" individual behavior. Campaigns providing information and incentives for people to become healthier demonstrate the significance of social marketing in advancing neoliberal social philosophies of personal responsibility and calculative approaches to human welfare. The chapter goes on to consider the merits of analyzing social marketing as a performative discipline and some of the limits to its influence. Moor outlines how governments have invested significant resources in trying to understand how individuals relate to health information while at the same time neglecting to ask how the operation of markets may affect health or wellbeing.

In this part's final chapter, Cayla and Peñaloza draw from ethnographic work in the world of Indian advertising, where they investigate the diffusion of marketing through the stories marketers tell to each other about the Indian people and India's future, cultivating a discourse about opportunities on the horizon that is subject to perpetual reconstruction. The authors take us deep into the world of multinational marketing work, revealing an environment where executives are on the constant lookout for India finally becoming the great nirvana of consumer capitalism and ground zero for marketers from around the world. The authors attempt to discern the contours of a globally recognizable marketing ideology from the tools and devices used to perform marketing in the Indian context. What emerges from this fieldwork is evidence that marketing—especially in a developing consumer culture—produces highly limited and reified notions of progress and modernity, conceived exclusively in terms of consumption and access to goods and services.

In the book's concluding remarks, Sherry asks whether a more humanistic discipline of marketing is possible. He argues that any aspiration to grasp the impact of marketing on society requires a great deal of reflexivity from marketing scholars and practitioners. Such reflexivity, which has helped many other scholarly disciplines mature, will involve questioning the nature of what we know, the manner of our knowing, the values underlying our knowing, and what marketers end up doing with their knowledge. In short, it will mean extricating the cultural politics and the political economy of marketing theory and practice. Sherry's call for greater reflection on the part of marketing professionals is motivated by his observation that marketing operates as an ideological screen—rather than simply a technique—that aims to arrange the world (class, ethnicity, gender, life course, and core/periphery relations) according to a singular vision of the good life as the ability to consume commercially produced, private (rather than public) goods and services. Taming the potentially pernicious effects of rampant marketing ideology requires that the theoretical assumptions and practical consequences of marketing be inventoried, assessed, and critically examined frequently so that conventional wisdom and practices are not perpetually recycled.

In sum, this book raises critical questions and provides thoughtful answers concerning power, knowledge, politics, and ideas that marketing professionals and academics tend to ignore. In particular, the contributions refute the idea that corporate marketing is nothing more than a value-neutral organizational tool required to compete with other businesses in the age of global capitalism. Rather, they show that marketing as a technique is just as deeply political, social, and cultural as it is economic. By shedding light on the politics of market research, the targeting of children, the nefarious influence of marketing on the pharmaceutical industry, the role of marketing in the construction of race, and many other sites of marketing work, this collection raises issues that are important, timely, and hard to ignore.

This volume aims to provide researchers and policymakers with key insights into how marketing happens and the effects it has when it does happen. We encourage studying the way marketing is taught in the world's business schools relying as it does on, and actively promoting, neoliberal conceptions of human behavior, economic and social organization, and the roles of corporations and entrepreneurs in shaping public policy. Obviously, such notions are laden with ideology, feebly concealed aspirations of social engineering, and a specific political vision for how we should live our lives. Hence, it would be naïve to assume that marketing work and its enthusiastic performers—often educated in these very schools—are reducible to a set of professional skills whose execution takes place in, and is confined to, the sphere of the economic. Just as the study of the economy needs to be wrested from the grip of the economists (see Callon, 2007), the study of marketing needs to be rescued from the technocrats of marketing, who equate marketing scholarship with the refinement of a scientific and purely practical set of tools. This rescuing requires that we understand marketing as an economic *and* cultural practice (and therefore also as a political activity), which is the central argument of this book. Many of the book's contributions point to the always complex, sometimes surprising, and often negative influence of marketing practice on our lives. Collectively, they answer the call for a political economy of marketing—a need to theorize marketing as a material social practice and to disentangle its processes of reproduction, dissect its various modes of operation, and trace its profound effects in the spaces of everyday life.

Notes

1. This definition undergoes periodic updating based on the board members' assessment of the state of the discipline.
2. A look at the discipline's main journals, such as the *Journal of Marketing* or the *Journal of Consumer Research*, reveals an astonishing set of concerns studied by marketers. One can find research papers that probe how consumers react to products already touched by others; how consumers behave in "spatial confinement"; what feelings are evoked in consumers when they stand on either hard vinyl tile or carpet (as the authors point out, these are the two most common flooring types in retail); or, somewhat less comically, how to represent sex in ads so they appeal to women, not just men.
3. As Slater (2002*b*: 247) points out, "[I]t is not necessarily empirically correct knowledge (advertisers may be wrong, and infamously can never really know when they are wrong), but it must be knowledge that makes sense to the marketers [. . .] and which therefore makes sense as a strategy for marketing." This commercial form of research studies the old, the young, housewives, middle-aged men, professional women, urban basketball players, and suburban skateboarders. It examines individuals of any sexual orientation possible; any ethnic group imaginable (in a quite literal sense, but also in Benedict Anderson's sense of imagining, or "making up," such groups (see also Dávila, 2001)); and so forth. No one is safe these days from becoming part of commercial market research.
4. See for example the literature on market orientation, which defines market-oriented companies as those who are "continuously collecting information about target-customers' needs" (Narver and Slater, 1990: 63). Kohli and Jaworski (1990, p. 3) define market orientation as "the organization-wide generation, dissemination, and responsiveness to market intelligence."

References

Applbaum, K. (2004) *The Marketing Era: From Professional Practice to Global Provisioning*. New York: Routledge.

Arvidsson, A. (2004) "On the 'Pre-History of the Panoptic Sort': Mobility in Market Research." *Surveillance & Society*, 1(4): 456–74.

——(2006) *Brands—Meaning and Value in Media Culture*. London: Routledge.

——(2007) "Creative Class or Administrative Class? On Advertising and the 'Underground.'" *Ephemera: Theory & Politics in Organization*, 7(1): 8–23.

Barber, B.R. (2007) *Consumed: How Markets Corrupt Children, Infantilize Adults, and Swallow Citizens Whole* (1st ed.). New York: W.W. Norton & Co.

Binkley, S. (2007) "Governmentality and Lifestyle Studies." *Sociology Compass*, 1(1): 111–26.

Bowers, T.E. (2008) *"Bringing the 'Multitude' Back In": The Biopolitics of Marketing Affectivity*. Paper presented at the annual meeting of the American Sociological Association.

Burrows, R., and Gane, N. (2006) "Geodemographics, Software and Class." *Sociology*, 40: 793–812.

Callon, M. (1998) *The Laws of the Markets*. Oxford, UK: Blackwell.

——(2001) "Economy of Qualities, Researchers in the Wild and the Rise of Technical Democracy." Seminar (11/15/2001), Center for Theoretical Study, The Institute for Advanced Studies at Charles University and the Academy of Sciences of the Czech Republic. http:/www.sfu.ca/scolr/PDF-READINGS/callon.htm, accessed on 3/2/06.

——Meadel, C., and Rabeharosoa, V. (2002) "The Economy of Qualities." *Economy and Society*, 31(2): 194–217.

——Millo, Y., and Muniesa, F.E. (2007) *Market Devices*. Malden, MA: Blackwell.

Cook, D.T. (2006) "In Pursuit of the 'Inside View': Training the Research Gaze on Advertising and Market Practitioners." In R.W. Belk, ed. *Handbook of Qualitative Research Methods in Marketing*. Cheltenham, UK: Edward Elgar, pp. 534–46.

Cova, B., and Dalli, D. (2009) "Working Consumers: The Next Step in Marketing Theory?" *Marketing Theory*, 9(3): 315–39.

Damodaran, H. (2002) "Try Amul's New Ice-cream and—Be Relieved! [Electronic Version]." *The Hindu Business Line*. Retrieved November 29, 2009, from http://www.thehindubusinessline.com/2002/09/08/stories/2002090801530100.htm

Dávila, A.M. (2001) *Latinos, Inc.: The Marketing and Making of a People*. Berkeley, CA: University of California Press.

Ellison, N., and Burrows, R. (2007) "New Spaces of (Dis)engagement? Social Politics, Urban Technologies and the Rezoning of the City." *Housing Studies*, 22: 295–312.

Elmer, G. (2004) *Profiling Machines: Mapping the Personal Information Economy*. Cambridge, MA: MIT Press.

Finn, M. (2009) "Alimentary Ethics in the History of Sexuality and NBC's 'The Biggest Loser.'" In S. Binkley and J. Capetillo, eds. *A Foucault for the 21st Century: Governmentality, Biopolitics and Discipline in the New Millennium*. Newcastle upon Tyne, UK: Cambridge Scholars Publishing, pp. 350–64.

Foster, R.J. (2008) *Coca-globalization: Following Soft Drinks from New York to New Guinea* (1st ed.). New York: Palgrave Macmillan.

Frank, T. (2000) *One Market under God: Extreme Capitalism, Market Populism and the End of Economic Democracy* (1st ed.). New York: Doubleday.

Jacobson, M.F., and Mazur, L.A. (1995) *Marketing Madness: A Survival Guide for a Consumer Society*. Boulder, CO: Westview Press.

Jambet, C. (1992) "The Constitution of the Subject and Spiritual Practice." In T.J. Armstrong, ed. *Michel Foucault, Philosopher*. Hertfordshire: Harvester Whatsheaf, pp. 233–47.

Klein, N. (1999) *No Logo: Taking Aim at the Brand Bullies*. New York: Picador.

Kohli, A.K., and Jaworski, B.J. (1990). "Market Orientation: The Construct, Research Propositions, and Managerial Implications." *Journal of Marketing*, 54(2): 1–18.

Kotler, P., and Levy, S. (1969) "Broadening the Concept of Marketing." *Journal of Marketing*, 33: 10–15.

Lury, C. (2004) *Brands: The Logos of the Global Economy*. London: Routledge.

Lyon, D. (1994) *The Electronic Eye: The Rise of Surveillance Society*. Minneapolis: University of Minnesota Press.

Malefyt, T.D.D., and Moeran, B. (2003) *Advertising Cultures* (1st ed.). Oxford and New York: Berg.

Marx, K. (1978) *Capital* (Vol. 1). New York: W. W. Norton & Company.

Mauss, M. (1967) *The Gift*. New York: Norton.

Mazzarella, W. (2003) *Shoveling Smoke: Advertising and Globalization in Contemporary India*. Durham: Duke University Press.

Miller, P., and Rose, N. (1997) "Mobilizing the Consumer." *Theory, Culture, and Society*, 14(1): 1–36.

Miller, T. (2007) *Cultural Citizenship: Cosmopolitanism, Consumerism, and Television in a Neoliberal Age*. Philadelphia: Temple University Press.

Moor, E. (2003) "Branded Spaces: The Scope of 'New Marketing.'" *Journal of Consumer Culture*, 3(1): 39–60.

Moor, L. (2007) *The Rise of Brands*. Oxford: Berg.

Morgan, R.M., and Hunt, S.D. (1994) "The Commitment-Trust Theory of Relationship Marketing." *Journal of Marketing*, 58: 20–38.

Narver, J.C., and Slater, S.F. (1990). "The Effect of a Market Orientation on Business Profitability." *Journal of Marketing*, 54(4): 20–35.

Nealon, J.T. (2008) *Foucault Beyond Foucault: Power and its Intensifications since 1984*. Stanford, CA: Stanford University Press.

Prahalad, C.K. (2005) *The Fortune at the Bottom of the Pyramid*. Upper Saddle River, NJ: Wharton School Publishing.

——and Ramaswamy, V. (2004) *The Future of Competition: Co-creating Unique Value with Customers*. Boston, MA: Harvard Business School.

Ritzer, G. (1993) *The McDonaldization of Society: An Investigation into the Changing Character of Contemporary Social Life*. Newbury Park, CA: Pine Forge Press.

——(1999) *Enchanting a Disenchanted World*. Thousand Oaks, CA: Pine Forge Press.

Slater, D. (2002a) "Capturing Markets from the Economists." In P. du Gay and M. Pryke, eds. *Cultural Economy: Cultural Analysis and Commercial Life*. London: Sage, pp. 59–77.

——(2002b) "From Calculation to Alienation: Disentangling Economic Abstractions." *Economy and Society*, 31: 234–49.

——(2002c) "Markets, Materiality and the 'New Economy.'" In S. Metcalfe and A. Warde, eds. *Market Relations and the Competitive Process*. Manchester: Manchester University Press, pp. 95–113.

Virno, P. (2004) *A Grammar of the Multitude for an Analysis of Contemporary Forms of Life*. Cambridge, MA: Semiotext(e) and MIT Press.

Zwick, D., Bonsu, S.K., and Darmody, A. (2008) "Putting Consumers to Work: 'Co-Creation' and New Marketing Govern-mentality." *Journal of Consumer Culture*, 8(2): 163–96.

Part I
Studying Marketing Differently

1

Marketing as a Monstrosity: The Impossible Place between Culture and Economy

Don Slater

Marketing is, both for academic researchers and for practitioners, an "impossible" object—one that has been extremely difficult to stabilize into an unproblematic entity. This may appear a perverse claim, given that marketing has come to be virtually definitive of modern capitalist economies over the past century; there is evidently nothing impossible about the *existence* of marketing for practitioners, analysts, or critics. However, marketing is routinely studied and carried out despite the fact that, in a peculiar sense, it "shouldn't" exist. As this chapter will argue, largely through the case of advertising, marketing occupies a place that modern thought will not allow: a place that is both cultural and economic, and is therefore monstrous for dominant conceptions of both culture and economy. Marketing can therefore be at the same time normal, even normative, and yet somehow aberrant.

Despite being an increasingly familiar aspect of business practice over the past century, marketing in the sense that most people now identify it—branding, advertising, design, retail strategy distribution, packaging, and so on—has rarely been understood as "normal commercial practice." To the contrary, marketing has generally been defined in terms of distinctive cultural, psychological, or signifying technologies that are ancillary to normal commercial practices, or which even corrupt or displace them. Indeed, the opposition between marketing and "normal commercial practice" has been so categorical that contemporary theory seems only able to understand the increasing dominance of marketing as a revolutionary reversal of normal commerce; the rise of marketing since the 1980s is generally portrayed as an epochal shift toward, among other things, post-Fordism, postmodernity, new economy, or a dematerialized economy of signs and flows, representing a fundamental break with commerce as it once was (Slater, 2002*b*). The more plausible argument of course is not that there has been an epochal reversal of the relations between marketing and commerce, culture and economy, but rather that the definitions of all these terms have always been wrongheaded; because culture and economy have always been constructed as opposing terms, we can only conceive of their relationship as one of dominance or subordination. The "impossibility" of marketing is an artifact of what Latour (1993) has called "purification," or what Weber earlier diagnosed as "modernist differentiation": economy and culture were to be constructed and performed as differentiated, autonomous moments with disentangled logics, and in the split between them marketing has been rendered an impossible hybrid, an impure monstrosity that clearly exists but which possesses dubious conceptual rights to that existence.

The case can be advanced on two levels. First, there is a socio-historical argument: the history of advertising and marketing is dominated by legitimation strategies that logically depend on a separation between "normal commercial practice" (market practices grounded in market behaviors and calculations that are deemed normative) and "culturalist practices." Culturalist practices are those that claim to possess effective psychological, semiotic, or broadly cultural technologies for managing social meaning and experience. Advertising, for example, has long claimed the ability to produce representations that can operate on the desires and decision-making processes of consumers and has maintained that the logic of this technology is of a different order from the market logic of offering up priced goods to rational buyers whose needs are autonomously determined and whose decisions are independent of suppliers. Indeed, advertising has claimed possession of scientific psychological powers since its inception, even at the cost of heaping serious moral panic upon itself (as, e.g., in the case of hidden persuaders (Packard, 1977) and charges of subliminal manipulation (Key, 1974) in the 1950s and 1960s). The significance of these claims is not their truth or falsity but their performative value: how has modern marketing structured itself around a distinction between culture and commerce that is both consistently belied in practice and is perilous in terms of public status?

This question can also be explored on a second, more abstract level. The fault line between marketing and "normal business practices"—between commercial and culturalist practices—is indeed the line between culture and economy, two "purified" entities. It is by looking at the terms of that purification—especially the separating out of formal and substantive rationality—that we can see why marketing can appear impossible and at the same time exist as such a ubiquitous actor in contemporary consumer capitalism (as well as an object of academic study).

Marketing and Advertising as Cultural Technology

If this book or this chapter were being written at any point up to the mid-1980s, it would most likely have been about advertising, not marketing. Until the apparent rise of marketing under the neo-liberal cultural revolution of the 1980s, with its discursive reformulation as postmodernity, post-Fordism and, later, new economy, "marketing" appeared far too boring to merit academic attention in the fields of critical sociology or cultural criticism.[1] It largely lay in the domain of the rather unglamorous business historians (e.g., Chandler, 1962) who attended to such things. Advertising, on the other hand, merited the highest critical attention as psychological or ideological manipulation, as symptomatic of a modern decline into consumer or mass culture, as an incursion of economy into culture and representation. Marketing was just business as usual.

Symptomatically, pre-1980s texts generally referred to the "marketing mix" rather than "marketing" in the contemporary sense that identifies it with an overarching orientation. The term "marketing mix" is of course still in use, particularly in marketing textbooks within business education where the obligation is, precisely, to present marketing as business, but even in this case exists within a new context. The marketing mix merely groups together routine commercial functions, all of which could be regarded as normal business processes: pricing, retail distribution strategies (including transport costs, point-of-sale materials, sales force organization and motivation), packaging, PR, design, and advertising. The idea of a marketing mix—as opposed to marketing—suggests several things. First, it implies that heterogeneous practices are involved in the messy business of getting goods to the point of sale and of establishing them there on optimal terms in relation to both competitors and consumers. These need to be coordinated so that they all pull together and do not conflict (e.g., pricing decisions should be under-pinned, and not contradicted, by the stories told by sales reps, point-of-sale displays and advertisements). Hence it makes sense to regard—and manage—these ingredients as one "mix." Secondly, all components of this mix can be viewed as normal commercial practices in that they are mundane ways of getting goods to market and share in the normality of market behavior: they make goods available, identifiable, purchasable, and rationally priced; and they are in principle consistent with the market as a meeting point between autonomous buyers and sellers. Indeed, the older term, "distribution," remains generally apt for this perspective.

The very notion of a "marketing mix" was also a way of normalizing and disciplining disparate technologies under the banner of "normal business practice"; it aggregated marginal, subordinate, and even despised commercial functions into a single corporate division and chain of command. Any enumeration of the marketing mix from the last century would include advertising, PR, packaging, and design, all of which could be seen as distinctly abnormal. However, defined as part of the marketing mix, these cultural or semiotic practices were regarded in terms of their capacity to be subsumed within normal market behaviors. In this formulation, which is also that of the client marketing manager, advertising is not a specialist psychological technology but rather part of the development of the multi-divisional firm in the first half of the twentieth century. To a great extent this continues to sum up the perspective of autonomous advertising agencies that regard their clients as disciplinarian marketing directors. It also correctly emphasizes the enormous amount of mundane commercial practice involved in advertising or PR; for example, the vast majority of budgets are in very quantifiable media expenditures involving very standardized demographics and measures (such as opportunities to see ads).

Advertising's place in that mix was always contradictory, partly as a result of the (perpetually) emerging industry's own professional and institutional legitimation strategies. These involved a profound ambivalence; advertising promised to achieve normal business goals (sales volume, price premiums, profit) but not through normal business means. Advertising produced images and texts which claimed efficacious intervention in minds and cultures, and claimed to produce impacts through psychological, cultural, or semiotic knowledges that were unavailable to normal marketing practitioners, let alone to the engineers and financial figures who ruled business. That is to say, advertising defined itself in opposition to normal commercial practice while still demanding its rightful place within the marketing mix.

There is a very long-term continuity here. Particularly in the United States, advertising began toward the end of the nineteenth century as a development of media buying, which remained its financial basis until quite recently. First emerging as specialists in bulk media buying, agencies lived (as now) on the spread between discounted media space and the prices they charged clients. Their expertise centered on the emerging metrology of circulation figures and the cost of securing encounters between consumers and product messages in increasingly large and dispersed ("mass") national markets, and on their ability to profit from that measurement technology by rationalizing and exploiting price formation. The first, very small step toward what has become known as the full-service advertising agency is taken with the hiring of graphic designers and writers to draw up print ads, saving the client the expense of developing expertise in "creative" work. The surprise is that, by the turn of the century, advertising was already largely staking its claim to legitimacy and revenue on its expertise in advertisement production rather than media buying, even though its income had depended entirely on the latter. What is clear throughout is that advertising's bid for institutional autonomy isolates the engineering of the image/consumer encounter as its own special domain, and consequently the legitimacy, rationality, and professional status of advertisers depends on claims to their special knowledge of a cultural rather than commercial event: the impact of representations on desires and decisions.

The claim to an expertise in producing commercially effective representations starts with a very dramatic separation of advertising knowledge from normal business expertise. The first significant claim to a "scientific advertising" was made by Walter Dill Scott in 1903, followed by a string of books that secured his academic career as the founder of applied psychology at Northwestern (e.g., Scott, 1903, 1909, 1917). There is an avalanche of books on "scientific advertising" up through the 1950s which attempt to re-present advertising as possessing a scientific psychological knowledge of how consumer minds work and of how businesses might intervene in that working. This knowledge is entirely discontinuous from normal business practice. The claim to psychological principles is intended to construct advertising as simultaneously effective, rational, and autonomous. The scientific advertising agenda is also related to a range of contemporaneous claims to scientific management, of which Taylorism is the other paradigmatic example, and is therefore able to draw on a wider belief in modernity as knowledge-based social engineering. This legitimation strategy continues through a long line of alliances with academic psychology, high points of which include: J.B. Watson and behaviorism; Floyd Allport and the social self; Maslow and the hierarchy of needs; and Dichter, Martineau, and Chetkins's invocations of a language of depth psychology and unconscious desires. Each is an argument not only for the effectiveness of advertising but also for its radical difference and for the impossibility of securing market advantage through normal commercial practice. By the time we get to Dichter, not only is the typical client unable to respond to consumer demands through normal knowledges such as market research, but normal consumers cannot even know their own desires or behave as rational economic actors unless aided by businesses who hire psychoanalysts to reveal their preferences.

Critics of advertising have generally accepted this logical structure at face value. Critics of neoclassical economics from Galbraith leftwards believed that advertising gave the new capitalist game away: *The New Industrial Estate* argued that modern marketing produced a "revised sequence" in that now "the indifference curve reflects, at any given time, the comparative effectiveness of the sales strategies behind the products in question" rather than the autonomous preferences of consumers (Galbraith, 1972: 29). In other words, advertising is not a commercial practice at all but is rather the replacement of market processes by psychological technologies. The sovereign consumer is replaced by the corporate plan. How can we argue that market economies respond to demand when marketers can directly manipulate the demand curve through psychological technologies?

> If the individual's wants are to be urgent, they must be original with himself. They cannot be urgent if they are contrived for him. And above all they must not be contrived by the process of production by which they are satisfied.... One cannot define production as satisfying wants if that production creates the wants.... (Galbraith, 1969: 146–7)

It is quite a paradox that, despite appearing to be paradigmatic of modern capitalism, the price of advertising's legitimation turns out to be the legitimacy of capitalism itself. However, the converse is then also true: if advertising is *not* an effective psychological strategy—either because it is psychological but not effective, or because it is effective but not psychological (i.e., falls within the domain of "normal business")—then everything is fine, and capitalism is based on a rational and normative responsiveness between autonomous suppliers and consumers, mediated by free price mechanisms.

The same logic characterizes non-economic critics of the 1950s, but with an additional fear: what was at stake was not simply the consumer but the citizen. Ironically, advertising inflated its claims to possessing psychological technologies at the same moment that fears of brainwashing, propaganda, and massmedia manipulation reached their peaks. *Mad Men* met the Manchurian candidate over the prostrate figure of the new suburban housewife. This conjuncture sharply limited the terms of the debate: Like Galbraith, Vance Packard (1977) was only concerned with the "depth boys" and their capacity to hook into psychological drives that were unacknowledged by mundane market actors, whether consumer or producer. He regarded advertising as a problem to the extent that its claims to psychological power were substantiated; to the extent that they were not, advertising was neither of concern nor of interest. That is to say, as "normal commercial practice" advertising was off the political and scholarly agenda. It was, quite simply, normal.

A particularly clear example comes from an early British book on the subject, significantly entitled *Techniques of Persuasion* (Brown, 1977 [1964]), covering—as specified in its subtitle—everything "from propaganda to brainwashing," though much of the book is indeed about advertising. J.A.C. Brown revisits a case of apparent advertising success put forward by the cultural critic Denys Thompson, a collaborator of F.R. Leavis, in the 1930s (Leavis and Thompson, 1933; Thompson, 1943, 1964):

> But there is no mystery about these results, which, for the most part, would appear to be due to the informative aspect of advertising: people were told of the existence of a particular product which they needed little encouragement to want to buy at that particular time. Mothers, for some unknown reason, like their babies' hair to

be curly, and this was the first time that a product had been offered for this specific purpose. . . . (Brown, 1977 [1964]: 175)

So long as the outcome can be attributed to something other than the advertisement's independent power as a sign, no explanation of consumer behavior is considered necessary. The mothers' desire for curly-headed babies can be treated as a given, as exogenous to the process under discussion, its reason left "unknown." That it might have something to do with a commercial system broader than the operation of individual advertisements is not of concern to Brown; if the mothers' desire is independent of the causal relation under investigation, it then lies within the protected space of individual choice, which is irreducible and outside explanation. So long as the desire pre-exists the advertisement, which only "informs," Brown believes that no "social problem" exists, nor is there any need for psychological explanations: "normal" consumer behavior is taking place. All this is because Brown—like most advertising proponents—separates advertising from marketing, and through this separation, advertising becomes an isolated psychological technique (and one of dubious efficacy).

Whereas for critics such as Galbraith, Packard, or Brown the relationship between advertising and normal commerce is central to analysis, most of the critical literatures that dominated academia in the twentieth century treated that relationship as largely trivial. This is particularly true both of the long tradition of Marxist critique starting with Adorno, which merged with semiotics in the 1960s through Barthes and resulted in figures like Judith Williamson, and of the related cultural studies genealogy that stretches from Leavis to Hoggart and Raymond Williams (for an interesting recent critique of this tradition, see Wang 2008). For both traditions, advertising is important purely as a semiotic technology that produces and naturalizes ideological structures that (in the Leavis tradition) degrade cultural value or (in the Marxist tradition) construct or "interpellate" forms of subjectivity that are functional to the reproduction of capitalist economic and political order. In both cases, commerce appears as the merely "manifest" or overt function of advertising in that advertising's ostensible motive and alibi is the drive to sell. However, that function plays virtually no role in explaining the operation or social import of advertising—it is ideologically coded semiotic structures that explain how advertising works and to what effect. Judith Williamson summarizes the situation quite plainly:

Obviously, [the advertisement] has a function, which is to sell things to us. But it has another function, which I believe in many ways replaces that traditionally fulfilled by art or religion. . . . Advertisements sell us something else besides consumer goods: in providing us with a structure in which we, and those goods, are interchangeable, they are selling us ourselves. (Williamson, 1978: 12–13)

Significantly, the two functions are entirely separate, and the former plays no part in understanding the latter. Moreover, the former (commercial) function is not only trivial compared to filling the role of art and religion but it is also probably bogus: Williamson (1979: 57), apparently unconsciously replicating a whole history of advertising studies (see below, "institutional weakness theory"), simply states that advertising cannot be demonstrated to sell goods or secure any economic effects; it is therefore irrational and wasteful within capitalism's own terms, and the only important issue is its ideological and cultural impacts. This argument suggests that any research into everyday marketing practices is not only trivial but somehow counter-revolutionary because it is diversionary; advertising is not commercial practice at all, but rather an ideological state apparatus. The separation between commerce and culture is rendered complete.

This narrative has so far been restricted to claims to scientific advertising. However, not all claims concerning advertising as non-commercial expertise have been based on science; indeed, the more common strategy has been antithetical to scientistic claims. From early on, claims have been advanced that great advertising comes from creative vision, instinct, empathy experience, inspiration, and other non-rationalizable properties of special individuals; the era of Dichter is also the era of David Ogilvy (not to mention Don Draper). For many who advocated this position, claims to scientific advertising have either been wrong or (if they are accepted) undermined real advertising by handing control over to researchers and to stodgy, risk-averse clients; scientific advertising is overly rational and indeed somehow closer to client bureaucratic mentality and control than the autonomous genius of wild creatives (see Nixon, 2003).

Obviously this argument also contends that advertising is based on a logic that is discontinuous from normal commercial practice and market behavior—it just grounds this claim in a more romantic vision. Martin Mayer (1958), writing in the late 1950s, makes this connection very explicit: "Out of the hole left by the disappearance of 'scientific' advertising, [there has emerged] a large crop of advertising philosophies" (Mayer cited approvingly in Brown, 1977 [1964]: 190). Mayer's implication is that such philosophies are as fatuous as the harder claims to science, but serve a similar function in legitimating advertising expenditures and in differentiating agencies on the basis of their "principles."

In short, both scientific and "philosophical" or creative claims seek to fill advertising's underlying deficit of "rationality"—to argue for a basis for advertising that is both rational and autonomous. Again, the implication is that if advertising's claims to a non-commercial logic are unfounded, then it is not much more than a con game (and if they are true, then they undermine capitalism). This position was taken by the one brief flurry of advertising ethnographies that occurred before the 1980s. Texts by Tunstall (1964), Bensman (1970), and Lewis (1964) arguably add up to what we might call an "institutional weakness theory" of advertising. They argue that advertising seeks to sell to clients an "immaterial" and empirically unprovable effect upon consumers—the impact of media representations on consumer consciousness and behavior. Clients will only buy advertising if belief in that impact is sustained; but the claim that "advertising sells" (either in general or in any particular case) can never be substantiated. Without recourse to proof, the advertising industry's only alternative is to claim scientific principles and techniques, or a philosophy, or special (e.g., intuitive) knowledge of how to operate on consumer minds. Advertising's claims to autonomy from normal commercial logic are a clear and painful measure of their extreme institutional weakness; without clear proof of their efficacy, agencies—and the industry as a whole—are chronically insecure and vulnerable.

Tunstall's conclusion is that agencies are indeed weak and that their inflated scientistic claims are false. Moreover, he concludes—on good ethnographic evidence—that psychology plays a marginal role in actual advertising practice. Above all, he follows an older line of argument which—again correctly—sees much of the industry's scientistic language as mere re-descriptions of existing marketing practice in a scientific idiom. A nice early example is Claude Hopkins's enormously influential *Scientific Advertising* (Hopkins, 1966, 2007 [1923]), much of which simply advocates the use of returnable coupons in press ads as these allow a direct measurement of response rates and therefore impact. It is hard to see why this is "scientific" as opposed to extending advertising's historical basis in media measurement.

However, whereas figures like Packard and Brown sounded the critical "all clear" when advertising appeared to be mere marketing rather than psychology, Tunstall goes further: if it is merely marketing, then advertising must be irrational, arbitrary, and ineffective, utterly without foundation. As Lewis (1964: 131) put it, we have seen waves of "missionaries and charlatans" promoting new advertising methods and claiming "that once the new method is adopted, rationality and 'science' will govern marketing." But they are indeed charlatans: the institutional weakness approach did not consider the alternative case—that advertising is rational precisely by virtue of its subordination to marketing and not by virtue of the autonomy of the agency. Once again, the very legitimacy of advertising depends on distancing it from business as a special psychological technology, and the rationality of advertising entirely depends on it *not* being a normal commercial practice.

It no doubt seems odd to spend half of this chapter on such ancient history. However, the post-1980s story of the rise of marketing and branding can be interpreted as a simple extension of the early years described above. In the older story, the fault line between normal commerce and its culturalist other runs between marketing (and the marketing mix) and advertising as the paradigmatic technology of meanings and desires. In the post-1980s, the term "marketing" subsumes the coordination of all technologies of signification, including advertising. The term now functions and means something very close to what "advertising" meant up to the 1980s.[2] Instead of merely institutionally disciplining a mix of distribution practices, "marketing" has come to represent a transformation in the logic of commerce itself: market behavior comes increasingly to be conceptualized in terms of psychological, semiotic, and cultural expertise that can comprehend and intervene in market processes far below the level of economic rationality, and that are capable of grasping processes that are entirely unavailable to purely economic calculation. Hence value arises from forms of cultural capital (assets such as brand identity and associations); circulation is understood increasingly in terms of social or viral network connections (rather than anonymous market transactions between contracting individuals); and commodities are understood increasingly as non-material and hence infinitely malleable signs that are elaborated through cultural rather than commercial logics. These claims are increasingly associated—by both academics and practitioners—with claims about epochal shifts in the nature of markets and capitalism themselves: under numerous narratives of social transformation, we now live in a world in which these knowledges are dominant within "normal business," and this is partly because market processes themselves have shifted toward sociocultural rather than rational economic logics. The argument has been developed in many parallel forms: post-Fordist/regulationist claims that in the move to fragmented, customized, and targeted low-volume markets, the logic of the commodity is more immediately cultural; postmodern and Baudrillardian arguments about the immersion of goods, consumers, and consequently producers in the unending semiosis of sign value; and new economy and information society arguments (even claims to a "linguistic capitalism" (Poster, 2001)) in which value arises entirely from culturalist processes of information flow, network organization, innovation through knowledge production, and so on (Slater, 2002b).

This cultural turn in both academic thought and social practice is very much what worried Galbraith. He argued that marketing as cultural technology *replaces* markets and normal market behavior. This is no longer a problem for most contemporary researchers; they are rather in line with Dichter's 1950s claims that neither consumers nor firms can know desires or respond to them adequately without exogenous culturalist knowledges: it now requires cool hunters, ethnographers, and experts in memes and viral flows to bring about the response to consumer desires that rationalist markets and commercial technologies cannot accomplish. Value arises now from signs, cultural assets, and network positions, none of which is amenable to normal commercial knowledges or practices—a great market gap for many more "missionaries and charlatans" (Lewis, 1964). But what has remained virtually unchanged since the days of Walter Dill Scott is the simple impossibility of regarding marketing as simply commercial.

Purity and Monstrosity

To a great extent we can trace this "impossibility" of marketing to a fairly conventional story about modern Western thought (Slater, 1997, 2002*a*, 2002*b*; Slater and Tonkiss, 2001). In brief, since their origins in early modernity, concepts of economy and culture have always been constructed as opposing categories, the meaning of each largely established through the expulsion of the other. To the extent that marketing is clearly both economic and cultural, it also has a hybridity or monstrosity (or indeed abjection) that must be denied or contained.

Economy and culture are generally separated by a division between formal and substantive rationality. Economics has proceeded by abstracting from all substantive objects and desires in order to model a formal structure of choice. It is a "praxiology," an attempt to describe the formal properties of decision-making and calculation. In the classic utilitarian and later neoclassical formulation, economic actors are able to compare alternative qualitative choices by expressing them in a quantitative common denominator such as utility, satisfaction or—in the end—prices. By this definition, culture is expelled from economic thought: specific values, things, and desires are not within the remit of economics; the goals toward which we strive, and the values that govern our striving (other than efficiency), belong to culture, not economy. Furthermore, this formal reasoning is presumed to be a property not just of economic models but of actual social actors. Indeed, social actors can be studied as economic actors only to the extent that their decision-making is of this formal kind. This is equally true of critical political economy approaches, though for a different reason: what conventional economists treat as an invariant property of human economic action has been regarded by political economists as a historical shift into a specific regime—market-mediated capitalism—that systemically abstracts from use values and coordinates social production through exchange value.

Hence, the formal character of economic thought involves a methodological claim (that formal and substantive rationality are analytically separable and that to study them independently is a profitable research strategy, or a necessary strategy when dealing with alienated capitalist systems); and it involves a psychological claim (that human minds can indeed work this way). But for liberal economics it is also a deeply normative and political position.

33

Providing that the conditions of formal calculation are met, the myriad behaviors of autonomous actors can be socially coordinated through the price mechanism entirely without social evaluation or negotiation over the substantive content of all these actions. Individuals' evaluations of cost and utility are entirely private to them; they are sovereign over their own needs and desires. Markets (normatively) involve absolutely no social exchange concerning the moral value of people's choices, which are effectively unchallenged. Whether consumers demand guns or good schools, the market is in principle agnostic and concerned purely with the relative prices they would pay for different quantities of either.

Advertising—and post-1980s marketing—clearly offend against this regime: They represent a substantive connection between producers and consumers who should be entirely autonomous, as the above arguments of Galbraith maintain. They are interventions in consumers' substantive preferences for specific use values. They operate directly on use values—on the concrete and sensuous specificity of things, their properties both real and imagined, and on the relation between these properties and the equally concrete and specific desires and values of individuals—on "culture." Firms can therefore go around and behind the price mechanism so that market coordination is not impersonal and formal/quasi-quantitative, but rather substantive and cultural. The purely technical problems this produces have long been recognized within conventional economics (e.g., Joan Robinson, 1983): the "identification problem" suggests that economics finds it impossible to distinguish movement along a single demand curve from a shift of the entire curve in one or another direction. Textbooks deal with this by holding the latter possibility constant (i.e., they assume that any shift in price decisions represents a movement along an unmoving curve, rather than a shift of the whole structure of demand), but this is clearly no more than a methodological decision. Advertising, on the other hand, represents the everyday belief that commercial agents are constantly engaged in shifting demand curves all over the place, and that much contemporary competition is not over prices, but over the substantive preference structures that generate prices (as the earlier Galbraith quote suggested). Under these conditions, either economics or marketing must be "impossible."

At most, there have been periodic attempts based on conventional economics to define marketing, advertising, and branding as informational tools that help meet the perfect information conditions of perfect markets by telling consumers about product characteristics or by signaling the reputability of the supplier (see e.g., Nelson, 1974; Erdem and Swait, 1998). The resulting descriptions of marketing, reduced to information goods, bear little resemblance to real world marketing.

Thus advertising and marketing, which appear to be definitive of capitalism, are in fact market imperfections. This is an obviously perverse conclusion which even die-hard neoclassical economists do not generally assert. However, it does mean that economics has been constitutionally incapable of saying much that is interesting or useful about marketing; for the most part it is treated as an exogenous variable, along the lines of shifts in fashion, history, or culture, and therefore, once again, as a non-commercial, cultural intervention in commercial processes.

The exogenous logics by which this variable might be analyzed have been dealt out to disciplines that might be loosely characterized as culturalist. This does not mean that specifically cultural explanations are always supplied. For example, many accounts of both the objects and the desires that form the substantive content of markets have resorted to claims about nature: knowledge of the natural properties of things, or of the natural and basic needs or drives of humans. Similarly, most of the scientific advertising discussed above drew on psychology, and therefore referenced innate cognitive structures (e.g., associationist or behaviorist structures) that were anything but cultural, much as psychology and social psychology do today (e.g., it is astonishing the extent to which Maslow's "hierarchy of needs" is still relied upon by marketing practitioners and scholars). The argument for using the term "culturalist" is more generic: just as economics has been paradigmatic of formal analysis, so "culture" has been the term under which modern Western thought has tended to consider the substantive content of social worlds—that which fills the formal calculus of rational choice. This juxtaposition has been moral and political as much as analytical since at least the eighteenth century in that "culture" has been the term through which a vast range of social thinkers—both progressive and reactionary—have counted the cost of all that has been expelled from a market society governed by abstract and formal values. "Culture" stands for the substantive and final values, goals, and projects in the name of which people act—or should act—and for the concrete and particular material culture of objects that a society produces and which makes it an identifiable shared context for living a specific way of life. In short, culture has generally been understood as covering all that is expelled from a society that abstracts formal rationality from its concrete specificity; the very term "culture" is therefore an artifact of the early modern split in which the world is understood as increasingly governed by formal rationality and market and money calculation.

By the same token, advertising and marketing are profoundly offensive to the entire project of "culture." The idea of culture has been intended to preserve the substantive values of human life from precisely the kind of market-based abstraction that is represented by advertising and marketing. The ultimate values and goals of life, and their expression in art and ideas, have authenticity and credibility in modern terms only to the extent that they are self-determined and autonomous of material interests and motives. To be

35

properly "cultural" under modernist aesthetics is to be undetermined by material constraints or imperatives; to be "economic" is to follow formally rational algorithms of choice that are drained of all substantive cultural content. In this formulation, the very idea of a "consumer culture" is a contradiction in terms in that a culture driven by market needs is not a culture at all.

In sociological terms, we can think about the division between economic and cultural logics as a case of modernist differentiation as defined by Weber. Weber optimistically understood such projects of differentiation as progressive—it is by rationalizing different spheres of life according to their own autonomous logics that progress is secured, and the differentiation of economics and culture by assigning them to different institutional and regulatory environments is their proper mode of developing. Indeed, the normative definitions of both economic and cultural action—in terms of formal or substantive rationality—are ideal types of action against which one can diagnose imperfections, identifying where, for example, advertising as a culturalist intervention offends against economic rationalization by securing monopoly control over demand, or where formal market rationality derails the self-defined development of aesthetic practices.

Weber's diagnostic embraces modernist differentiation and deals with its "failures" as corrigible imperfections. Bruno Latour's comparable analysis (1993) of modernist "purification" offers a rather different perspective: yes, modernity has proceeded by marking out divisions or "constitutional" settlements by which pure entities—economies, cultures, society, nature—are separated out. However, Latour's claim that "we have never been modern" points to the ways in which our performance of this modernity has continuously produced unintended and unacknowledged outcomes. The very attempt to purify social moments produces overflows, externalities, or hybridities, monstrous and impure entities that belie the claim to pristine differentiation. Moreover, the public accomplishment of purification, for Latour, *requires* the unacknowledged existence of an army of these impure entities. Put simply, marketing and advertising appear as monstrous from the perspective of the modern purification of economy and culture; to accept marketing as everyday commercial practice is to acknowledge a monster (to the extent that, in the cultural turn, theorists would much rather argue that commerce has been entirely abolished by or subordinated to culture), and yet like all such orphaned hybrids, that has not stopped a very large number of people routinely carrying out marketing for over a century. To paraphrase Latour, we might say that "we have never done marketing," in the sense that the official definitions of advertising and marketing that were generated within the terms of modernist purification (they are either mundane distribution or culturalist technology, but not both at once) are perpetually at odds with the impure messiness of everyday marketing.

36

We can capture the contrast between the differentiation of economy and culture and marketing's messy hybridity by looking at the fundamental notion of "a market" (see Slater, 2002*a*; Zwick and Cayla, this volume). In order to mark out a space in which to study purely formal calculation, economics focuses on interactions within markets. So long as "the market" is a stable object that can be taken for granted, it can then proceed with studying the technical processes by which price can mediate the behaviors of autonomous agents. However, the definition of a market necessarily depends on substantive assumptions, as we know from everyday life: we routinely talk about "car markets," "markets for mobile phones," and so on. Cars and mobile phones are complex cultural entities that are constructed across assemblages of institutions, and over long histories. They may be defined differently by different people: some might see the same two mobile phone-like objects (say a "smart phone" like an iPhone and a plain old "phone") as substitutable and therefore competing, while others (including some but not all manufacturers) do not. And objects and markets can be stabilized (we "know" what a car is), or destabilized (at this moment it is unclear whether phones, GPS devices, and music players are the same or different objects).

Hence for an economist to blithely invoke "a market" as an analytical framework within which to study "economic rationality" is an act of considerable methodological violence which brackets the social effort that goes into making and unmaking use values, and all the people and practices—such as marketing—that are heavily invested in this process. Callon's discussion (1998) of the table strawberry market is still exemplary in pointing out the effort that must go into producing this condition of abstraction. To construct a market—physically or conceptually—for strawberries in provincial France required the categorization of different strawberries into grades such that substitutable goods could be identified and given uniform prices. This involved the production of a socio-technical apparatus which included the means for physically and conceptually making, displaying, and stabilizing discrete objects that were acknowledged by all as differentiated "table strawberries." The resulting device includes what has generally been taken for granted as exogenous to economic process: social agreement upon what is a strawberry, and what are the different categories of strawberry (see also Zwick and Cayla, this volume).

Callon uses this example largely to make a case for the performativity of economics, in that it was the enactment of a particular notion of free market economics that created the possibility of purely formal economic calculation and for the realization of *homo economicus*. The point here is simply that this space of formal rationality depends, on every level, upon producing and reproducing substantive assumptions about the (cultural) nature of strawberries. "The market" itself as a frame for formal economic action requires a shared substantive understanding of a strawberry; identifying competing goods, and therefore calculating pricing options, requires a shared understanding of which goods are "the same" (i.e., substitutable).

Clearly this physical marketplace is a machine for making markets into stable structures so that formally rational economic behavior can really take place; but as in many markets, there will be endless disputes, as well as historical changes, concerning the ways in which strawberries are defined, graded, eaten, and so on. The very fact that markets and competition are simply opposite faces of a coin that is made up of substantive cultural knowledges opens up the opportunity for much more complex and messy social action.

And it is precisely this space of messy, impure action that defines the impossible position of the advertiser or marketer. The advertisement, for example, is not an arcane psychological intervention in consumers' minds; it is a reconfiguration of a use value (the properties of objects and their connection to desires) that simultaneously reconfigures markets and market relations. That is to say, marketers are entirely invested in working on all the stuff that economists want to hold stable (the "cultural meanings" that stabilize markets as spaces of formal calculation) and that culturalists want to protect from the economy (the "cultural meanings" that make up ways of life and that should not be determined by commodity relations). The task of marketers is to destabilize and then restabilize definitions of objects and needs in order to reformulate markets and competitive relations to the advantage of their clients.

And *that* is "normal commercial practice." Marketing struggles over market structures, not just within them. It therefore perpetually offends against the purification on which the culture/economy divide depends; and perpetually undermines the idea that we can regard substantive objects and needs as sufficiently stable to make formal calculation possible.

Conclusion

I would like to conclude by returning to the older history of advertising one last time. It is interesting that the most common narrative of advertising history (see e.g., Pope, 1983; Leiss et al., 1986; Marchand, 1986)—one that is taken for granted in virtually all the literature—is a cyclical narrative, one in which advertising is believed to be perpetually oscillating between two poles. These poles usually define different—but eternally recurring and ever identical—eras of advertising, but they are also used to define different sectors of advertising, to differentiate various phases of an agency's biography, or to differentiate roles and power relations within agencies (e.g., they organize the incipient trench warfare between account handlers, researchers, and media buyers on the one hand and creatives and producers on the other). These poles are variously defined, but they always line up as an opposition between normal commerce and autonomous cultural logics.

In the most common story, advertising has "progressed" over the last century or so from "rational" and quasi-informational claims about products to increasingly image-based, emotional, and subjective appeals. The distinction has often been drawn as one between hard sell (e.g., USPs or "unique sales propositions") versus soft sell. This distinction maps onto numerous others: above all, hard sell is closer to normal commercial practice both in the sense that it is based on demonstrable claims presented to rational and conscious choice-making consumers and in the sense that it is treated as closer to the client's forms of knowledge and practice. By the same token, hard-sell approaches have been more closely identified with the more marketing- and client-oriented sections of the agency—account handlers, researchers, and media planners—and with more "mature" agencies (those that are older, bigger, and more integrated with client marketing departments, as opposed to creative boutiques and hot shops). Soft sell has been identified with creativity and creative personnel, and with autonomy from clients based on—to them—esoteric knowledges (scientific, empathetic, artistic, etc.) that are discontinuous with normal business.

The telling of this story has been somewhat misguided in that the storytellers have generally wanted to decide which of these two poles represents the *truth* of advertising (Cronin (2003) also suggests treating advertising claims as constitutive or performative, rather than as true or false): whether it really is, or should be, plain old-fashioned commerce or creativity or science; whether it is basically a division of the client's marketing department or an autonomous entity; whether it fulfils the informational preconditions of good markets or employs modern witchcraft to control and monopolize demand. Such a messy oscillation between purified poles demonstrates the existence of a monstrosity or hybrid, an impossible object that cannot find a voice in the confines of official language. It has oscillated between the various versions of itself offered within the terms of modernist purification, and this has had real consequences.

However, if we were to rethink marketing in terms of its hybridity rather than trying to force it back into purified distinctions, the consequences would go well beyond a better understanding of marketing. As the discussion of "the market," above, might suggest, we would need to rethink fundamental social categories as well as the foundational conceptual splits (economy/culture; formal/substantive) on which they are based. It may be that marketing really is an intellectually urgent subject because, despite its status as emblematic of modern capitalism, it actually blows apart the conceptual arrangements upon which that system has been founded.

Notes

1. The rare but still stirring exceptions to this failure to acknowledge mundane commercial life largely come from literatures that critiqued the emergent culture of salesmanship—Sinclair Lewis's *Babbit*, Arthur Miller's *Death of a Salesman*, and C. Wright Mills's great essay on the salesman in *White Collar*. Despite fine observation in all these cases, the salesman was still treated as a symptom of cultural decline in the modern wasteland, rather than as a significant socio-economic actor.

2. There is an earlier such formulation of marketing as a more general orientation or rallying point for a business philosophy which was generally summarized as "sell the consumer what they want, not what you have," and is to some extent identified with the long career of Peter Drucker from the 1950s. It is hard to resist a very early Drucker quote which shows him to be well ahead of the curve: "Because the purpose of business is to create a customer, the business enterprise has two—and only two— basic functions: marketing and innovation. Marketing and innovation produce results; all the rest are costs. Marketing is the distinguishing, unique function of the business" (Drucker, 1954: 37).

References

Bensman, J. (1970) "The Advertising Agency Man in New York." In J. Tunstall, ed. *Media Sociology: A Reader*. London: Constable.

Brown, J.A.C. (1977 [1964]) *Techniques of Persuasion: From Propaganda to Brainwashing*. Harmondsworth: Penguin.

Callon, M. (1998) "Introduction: The Embeddedness of Economic Markets in Economics." In M. Callon, ed. *The Laws of the Market*. Oxford: Blackwell Publishers/ The Sociological Review.

Chandler, A.D. (1962) *Strategy and Structure: Chapters in the History of the Industrial Enterprise*. Cambridge, MA: MIT Press.

Cronin, A. (2003) *Advertising Myths: The Strange Half-Lives of Images and Commodities*. London: Routledge.

Drucker, P.F. (1954) *The Practice of Management*. New York: Harper & Row.

——(2008) *The Essential Drucker: The Best of Sixty Years of Peter Drucker's Essential Writings on Management*. New York: Harper Paperbacks.

Erdem, T., and Swait, J. (1998) "Brand Equity as a Signalling Phenomenon." *Journal of Consumer Psychology*, 7(2): 131–57.

Galbraith, J.K. (1969) *The Affluent Society* (2nd, revised ed.). London: Hamish Hamilton.

——(1972) *The New Industrial Estate*. Harmondsworth: Penguin.

Hopkins, C.C. (1966) *My Life in Advertising and Scientific Advertising (Advertising Age Classics Library)*. New York: McGraw-Hill.

——(2007 [1923]) *Scientific Advertising*. New York: Cosimo.

Key, W.B. (1974) *Subliminal Seduction*. New York: Signet.

Latour, B. (1993) *We Have Never Been Modern*. London: Harvester/Wheatsheaf.

Leavis, F.R., and Thompson, D. (1933) *Culture and Environment: The Training of Critical Awareness*. London: Chatto & Windus.

Leiss, W., Kline, S., and Jhally, S. (1986) *Social Communication in Advertising: Persons, Products & Images of Well-Being*. London: Methuen.

Lewis, I. (1964) "In the Courts of Power: The Advertising Man." In P. Berger, ed. *The Human Shape of Work*. New York: Macmillan.

Marchand, R. (1986) *Advertising the American Dream: Making Way for Modernity— 1920–1940*. Berkeley: University of California Press.

Mayer, M. (1958) *Madison Avenue, USA: The Inside Story of American Advertising*. London: Bodley Head.

Mills, C.W. (1956) *White Collar: The American Middle Classes*. New York: Oxford University Press.

Nelson, P. (1974) "The Economic Value of Advertising." In Y. Brozen, ed. *Advertising and Society*. New York: Yale University Press.

Nixon, S. (2003) *Advertising Cultures*. London: Sage.

Packard, V. (1977) *The Hidden Persuaders*. Harmondsworth: Penguin.

Pope, D. (1983) *The Making of Modern Advertising*. New York: Basic Books.

Poster, M. (2001) *What's the Matter with the Internet?* Minneapolis: University of Minnesota Press.

Robinson, J. (1983) *Economic Philosophy*. Harmondsworth: Penguin.

Scott, W.D. (1903) *The Theory and Practice of Advertising*. Boston: Small, Maynard and Company.

——(1909) *The Psychology of Advertising*. London: Sir Isaac Pitman and Sons.

——(1917) *The Psychology of Advertising: A Simple Exposition of the Principles of Psychology in their Relation to Successful Advertising*. Boston: Small, Maynard and Co.

Slater, D.R. (1997) *Consumer Culture and Modernity*. Cambridge: Polity Press.

——(2002*a*) "Capturing Markets from the Economists." In Paul du Gay and M. Pryke, eds. *Cultural Economy: Cultural Analysis and Commercial Life*. London: Sage, pp. 59–77.

——(2002*b*) "Markets, Materiality and the 'New Economy.'" In S. Metcalfe and A. Warde, eds. *Market Relations and the Competitive Process*. Manchester: Manchester University Press.

——and Tonkiss, F. (2001) *Market Society: Markets and Modern Social Thought*. Cambridge: Polity Press.

Thompson, D. (1943) *Voice of Civilisation: An Enquiry into Advertising*. London: F. Muller.

——(1964) *Discrimination and Popular Culture*. Harmondsworth: Penguin.

Tunstall, J. (1964) *The Advertising Man in London Advertising Agencies*. London: Chapman and Hall.

Wang, J. (2008) *Brand New China: Advertising, Media and Commercial Culture*. Cambridge, MA: Harvard University Press.

Williamson, J. (1978) *Decoding Advertisements: Ideology and Meaning in Advertising*. London: Marion Boyars.

——(1979) "The History that Photographs Mislaid." In W. Photography, ed. *Photography/Politics: One*. London: Photography Workshop.

2

The Uses of Use Value: Marketing, Value Creation, and the Exigencies of Consumption Work

Robert J. Foster

Introduction: Beyond "Co-Creation" and "Customer-Made"

The influential business professor C.K. Prahalad wrote in 2004 with his co-author Venkat Ramaswamy about how the "interaction between the firm and the consumer is becoming the locus of value creation" (Prahalad and Ramaswamy, 2004a: 5; see also Prahalad and Ramaswamy, 2004b). More precisely, this interaction is the locus of *co-creating* value. That is, consumers now no longer merely purchase offerings autonomously created by the firm, but instead engage in personalized interactions with the firm with the aim of co-creating products and services that realize desired outcomes. This engagement has been identified as a trend, dubbed "Customer-Made" and defined as "the phenomenon of corporations creating goods, services and experiences in close cooperation with experienced and creative consumers, tapping into their intellectual capital, and in exchange giving them a direct say (and rewarding them for) what actually gets produced, manufactured, developed, designed, serviced, or processed."[1]

More radically, Prahalad and Ramaswamy saw the roles of production and consumption, producer and consumer converging in the co-creation of experiences that deliver *unique* value to consumers. That is, these experiences and the interactions that facilitate them necessarily vary from individual consumer to individual consumer. They vary because firms can never fully control or manage how individual consumers will go about the co-creation of their experiences. Firms that pay due attention to such variable co-creation experiences, Prahalad and Ramaswamy argue, enable consumers to co-create value that these same consumers are "by design, 'willing to pay for'" (2004a: 13). Such firms therefore put themselves in a position to defend against the "commoditization" of their products and services. By "commoditization," Prahalad and Ramaswamy mean a process by which competition renders price the only issue relevant to consumers; that is, commoditization results in consumers seeking the lowest price possible for products regarded as generic and interchangeable.

The idea that consumers as well as producers or firms participate in the creation of a product has now begun to receive critical scrutiny from academics in the fields of marketing and anthropology. In marketing, Bernard Cova and Daniele Dalli (2009) speak of "working consumers" and Detlev Zwick et al. (2008) speak of "putting consumers to work." In anthropology, I have written about "consumption work" (Foster, 2005, 2007)—a term that I have borrowed from my colleague Daniel Miller—while Adam Arvidsson (2005; see also 2006) has borrowed the idea of "immaterial labor" from sociologist Maurizio Lazzarato to describe the use of consumer goods. This critical response to co-creation poses a general question: What is at stake—conceptually and politically—when the roles of consumer and producer become blurred? And this question, in turn, poses a more specific one: What are the implications of this blurring for understanding the place of marketing techniques in value creation?

Qualified Value

Let us start with the conceptual challenge. It is not only the roles of consumers and producers that the idea of co-creation blurs. It is also the meaning of the word value. Value theory in the social sciences struggles with the knot of associations wrapped around the word value. That is, while value always implies comparison, the terms of comparison can be moral, semiotic, or economic (see Graeber, 2006).

Anthropologists usually deal with value in the first two senses. Moral values (in the plural) imply conceptions of what is proper and desirable and thus comparisons in terms of good and bad. Semiotic value—in the linguistic sense derived from Ferdinand de Saussure—implies a negative or contrastive relationship (such as that between a minimal pair of words in phonology), and thus comparisons in terms of the capacity to communicate significant difference, to make a difference that makes a difference.

Economic value, on the other hand, usually implies measurable difference, whether understood as differences in real value (classical political economy) or price (neoclassical economics). Value in this sense deals with comparisons of more or less—more or less embodied labor, more or less money—usually with the purpose of establishing commensurability or equivalence in exchange.

The moral and semiotic senses of the word value thus highlight qualitative differences; they entail an approach to value that puts to one side the question of establishing equivalence. This approach pays attention to what can be called qualified value (see Strathern, 1992). For example, when we look at the anthropology of consumption, we find an emphasis on the processes by which people and things reciprocally qualify each other. (This process of mutual qualification was first identified by Marcel Mauss (1967 [1925]) in his famous essay on gift exchange.) Anthropological discussions often foreground consumer agency (often as a response to views of consumers as manipulated, passive dupes) and render such agency as more than the expression of calculated self-interest. From this perspective, value creation appears as the activity through which people define themselves through the creative use of things.

Hence what might be called the agency of identity formation, found in the vast literature on youth subcultures. Hence, too, and more generally, the agency of objectification—what Daniel Miller (1987) has usefully theorized in his by now almost classic book, *Material Culture and Mass Consumption*. Objectification refers to the activity by which human beings fashion themselves in the external world—the activity that Marx associated with the capacity to produce or labor. Miller includes consumption in this activity, by which he means the diverse appropriations by which consumers turn impersonal, standard commodities into personal, singular possessions. This activity of appropriation is "consumption work" (see also Miller, 1988).

Use Value and Exchange Value

It would be easy to claim that while anthropology deals with qualified value, economics is all about quantifiable value—measureable differences. And indeed it is not unfair to think of neoclassical economics as largely concerned with the market mechanisms that establish relative prices between goods and services.

Classical political economy, however, distinguishes between the use value and exchange value of a commodity. In Marx's well-known formulation, all commodities have use value, physical properties that render a commodity of use in various ways. That is, use value is the material presupposition of exchange value. However, not all use values have exchange value—transferable value for others (or social use value)—and therefore not all use values are commodities.

This distinction between use value and exchange value is practically confirmed in the exchange of qualitatively different commodities, inasmuch as it is in exchange that commodities are revealed as the repositories of labor power. It is the relative quantities of labor power, abstracted from the material elements of the commodities, that are effectively compared in exchange.

Furthermore, it is not in the exchange of commodities that surplus value is created. Rather, it is in the use of one particular commodity—labor power— that surplus value is created; for it is the unique use value of labor power to produce more exchange value than it itself embodies. It would be wrong to say, therefore, that Marx gave little attention to use value. Indeed, Marx's critique of capitalism hinges on the distinction between use value and exchange value.

Can we suggest alternative ways of thinking about how use value enters the production of exchange value and surplus value? I turn first to one particular instance of the critical work on co-creation in marketing. I then adopt, with the help of anthropological approaches to the gift, the idea of an "economy of qualities" proposed by Michel Callon and his colleagues (2002). I argue that in such an economy, the use value of things that people realize as consumers becomes a source and site of surplus value extraction. I emphasize, moreover, that because such extraction presupposes the management of consumer crea- tivity (or "marketing work") it is hardly guaranteed. Marketing practitioners, in particular, must intervene in the ongoing processes whereby products (and hence persons) are qualified and requalified. In so doing, they must deal with the sometimes unruly people whom Callon (2001) calls "voicy consumers," people whose agency is the potential source of new qualifications for pro- ducts. That is, marketing practitioners must engage a tension integral to the economy of qualities: "In the economy of qualities consumers are thus a constant source of overflowing. And it would be counter-productive to suppress these overflowings, because in order to function, markets of the economy of qualities need them" (Callon, 2001; see also Callon, 1998).

Co-Creation or Theft?

The notion of value co-creation implies that consumers do more than simply purchase what a firm offers them; instead, consumers interact with the firm, often through Web technologies, assuming a direct say in what the firm designs, develops, and produces. The process is often depicted as a miracle of win/win cooperation. On the one hand, consumers get the outcome that they desire; on the other hand, firms are able to offer consumers products that command a premium price—precisely because they are what the consumers who co-created them actually want.

Value co-creation so conceived blurs the roles of producers and consumers, obviating the question of how surplus value can emerge out of cooperation.

Can the distinction between use value and exchange value afford some purchase on this question? Ashlee Humphreys and Kent Grayson (2008)—two of the recent critics of co-creation within the marketing world—have argued that this distinction is crucial for distinguishing the roles of consumers from producers. They insist that as long as a customer is producing only use value for herself—for example, in designing a pair of customized jeans on a firm's Web site—then the customer is not creating something with exchange value, something that can be sold by the firm to other consumers. By contrast, when a consumer creates something—say, a design for a T-shirt—that a firm sells to someone else, then the consumer has produced exchange value *for the firm*, that is, surplus value or profit. In effect, consumers become producers for Humphreys and Grayson *only* when they are unjustly separated from the exchange value that their labor creates. So, for example, no matter how much of the activity in a value chain is offloaded on to consumers (who, say, scan and bag their own groceries), this does not count as production. These consumers produce use value for themselves only, not use value for others and hence exchange value.

Humphreys and Grayson are surely correct in identifying theft of a consumer's creativity (her uncompensated labor) as the source of value for others. Cova and Dalli (2009) likewise describe as double exploitation the way in which Ferrero incites the fans of its Nutella brand products to post narratives and images on its "my Nutella the Community" Web site, and then stipulates that the material on the site may not be reproduced as it is copyright protected. But theft is not how Marx characterized the production of surplus value in mature capitalism. (Theft is for Marx part of the process of primitive accumulation that happened at the birth of capitalism.) On the contrary, Marx considered that the originality of his contribution to political economy consisted in explaining how surplus value was generated while the laborer was compensated fairly, that is, compensated for the real value of the labor power exchanged for a wage. From this perspective, the creation of surplus value was built right into the hidden but (formally) peaceful process of production.

I would like to inquire similarly: Is it possible to understand how consumers produce exchange value and surplus value for others as part of the ordinary, ongoing and legal process of consumption? I propose a way of thinking about the consumption or creative use of products that recognizes an element of theft, but not the sort of flagrant robbery imagined by Humphreys and Grayson. I am especially concerned with branded products and brands themselves. My proposal is meant, furthermore, to bring determinations of use value and exchange value—or, qualified value and market value (i.e., price)—into a single frame of reference: a kind of anthropological economics or economic anthropology. Both "consumption work" and "marketing work" figure largely in how this kind of economic anthropology understands value creation.

Marketing and the Qualification of Products

Michel Callon's notion of an economy of qualities is helpful here. In such an economy, products are not things in themselves; nor are they ever quite finished. Here is Callon's definition of a product:

> A product ... is an economic good seen from the point of view of its production, circulation and consumption. The concept [*producere*: to bring forward] shows that it consists of a sequence of actions, a series of operations that transform it, move it, and cause it to change hands, to cross a series of metamorphoses that end up putting it into a form judged useful by an economic agent who pays for it. During these transformations its characteristics change. (Callon et al., 2002: 197)

In other words, the product is a variable, a contingent outcome of negotiations—even conflict—around the qualification of commodities. This process of evaluation, of qualifying and requalifying, unfolds at all moments in the life or career of a product—design, manufacture, marketing, use, recycling, and so forth. But at certain moments, the qualities of a product are stabilized; the product becomes a "good," its list of qualities closed and fixed, at least temporarily.

Callon recognizes that consumers are just as active as any other economic agent—designers or advertisers, for example—in qualifying products: "There is no reason to believe that agents on the supply side are capable of imposing on consumers both their perception of qualities and the way they grade those qualities." Accordingly, the product, understood as a sequence of transformations or as a process of qualification and requalification, links consumers into the different networks coordinating all the agents involved in production, design, and so forth—agents who most likely never encounter each other face-to-face or even know of each other's existence in precise terms: "The product singles out the agents and binds them together and, reciprocally, it is the agents that, by adjustment, iteration and transformation, define its characteristics" (Callon et al., 2002: 198). Hence the product implies a dynamic "economy of qualities," an economy in which tradable goods in the market are defined by the qualities attributed to them in successive qualification and requalifications, including those enacted by consumers.

Put otherwise, products are much as Marx characterized them, namely, assemblages of properties. But these properties are not simply physical properties. They include, for example, the intangible significance (distinction) that marketers attempt to attach to products through advertising, retail display, and especially branding. Indeed, marketing is central to commercial practice in the economy of qualities, the reflexive intervention on the part of firms into the processes whereby products are qualified and materialized (see Slater, 2002). In sum, products are bundles of qualities, the interactive, recombinant outcome of all the people and processes that qualify a product. And these people include consumers and these processes include the uses—diverse and not always predictable—to which consumers put products.

Callon's view of a product as a precipitate of a network of qualifications highlights the way in which products move from one hand to another as well as how people and things reciprocally qualify each other. In this sense, his view accords with that of the anthropology of gifts and gift exchange. Let me bring in two concepts from this anthropology in order to demonstrate how use value and exchange value relate to each other in the economy of qualities. The result might be called the gift model of brands.

The Gift Model of Brands: Keeping while Giving

The first concept is what Annette Weiner called keeping while giving. Keeping while giving describes the strategies by which gift givers often keep highly valued things such as family heirlooms in their possession by giving away other things. Often, the things given away are less valuable instances of the type of thing that the inalienable heirloom epitomizes. Giving away *other* objects—"replacements"—thus functions as a means for defending what is kept; in Samoa, the retention of a fine, old woven mat is ensured by the distribution of many less fine, new mats.

Similarly, think of the *kula* exchange made famous by Malinowski (1922). A savvy man will attempt to hang on to a high ranking valuable by drawing his kula partners into preliminary exchanges (*pokala*) for lower ranking valuables. Such reciprocity does not establish social equivalence, let alone solidarity, but rather proclaims and constitutes a non-equivalent difference based on retention: "hierarchy resides at the very core of reciprocal exchange," Weiner (1992: 42) says—a point to which I will return presently.

Keeping while giving also describes the circulation of branded products. The branded product (indeed, the brand itself) is a cumulative outcome of the qualifications of many people, including many consumers in addition to marketers. But the brand itself is an owned asset, its heterogeneous sources submerged in its legally protected unitary identity. That is, branded products circulate as satellites of the brand, material tokens that consumers purchase and use for their own personal purposes. In its normal functioning, this arrangement enables consumers to incorporate branded products into their own self-definition, the creative activity or work whereby consumers objectify themselves in the external world. (I follow Miller (1987) in seeing no reason to restrict this creative activity to what is conventionally recognized as production.) But this normal functioning requires consumers to pay rent for the use of a brand that has become entangled—through this very creative activity—with their particular biographies and passions. This rent, willingly paid, allows consumers to recapture their own qualifications or at least retain continued access to them.

I have elsewhere used this notion of paying rent for the use of brands to explain what is at stake in the concept of Lovemarks developed by Kevin Roberts, CEO Worldwide of Saatchi and Saatchi Advertising (see Foster, 2007). Lovemarks are brands that are not simply respected and trusted, but *loved*. Lovemarks possess a "special emotional resonance" (Roberts, 2004: 74; see also www.lovemarks.com). They signal an emotional connection and attachment to a brand that goes beyond reason—and for which a premium price can be charged. This premium price is, in effect, the rent that consumers pay to retrieve the affect and significance that they have already invested in the brand.

I have also elsewhere used the analogy of dog stealing in Victorian London to describe this transaction (see Foster, 2008). Dog stealing constituted an artful and systematic class attack on a relatively new form of bourgeois possession, pets, whereby a terrier worth five shillings might bring fourteen pounds—the difference between the dog's impersonal market price and the ransom paid by an emotionally attached owner, typically a lady (see Howell, 2000: 38). That is, dog-stealers exploited pet owners' "dependence on animals" and their "affections and sentiments" or love, as well as a gendered ideology of the domestic sphere as a realm of "values beyond price" (Howell, 2000: 46). Dog-stealers dared put a price on that which ought to be priceless, namely, aspects of one's own personhood. Consider the words of a correspondent to *The Times* in March 1845:

> Of all the combinations of rascals which infest this mighty city, there is not one, in my opinion, more hateful than the dog-stealer. Other thieves take our property,— these rob us of our friends. . . . They make trade of our affections. They take from us one whose good qualities we should be happy to recognize in many of our human friends; and they compel us to a course of sordid bargaining with a knife at our favourite's throat. (quoted in Howell, 2000: 48)

Dog-stealers thus sought, like Kevin Roberts, to link the worlds of sentiment and the market, to expand the boundaries of the market by encompassing an economy of singularized sentiments imagined to operate on other, non-commoditized terms. Indeed, the dog-stealers respected the fiction upon which their trade rested, never actually ransoming kidnapped dogs (a brutal commodity transaction!) but instead "restoring" through concerned intermediaries "found" dogs—often the same dog over and over again. Elizabeth Barrett Browning's cocker spaniel Flush, the subject of Virginia Woolf's imaginative biography, was snatched and held for ransom no fewer than three times. Each time, Browning dutifully paid up.

The Gift Model of Brands: Partible and Composite Persons

Marilyn Strathern's landmark (1988) book *The Gender of the Gift* offers the second component of the gift model of brands: the concept of partible, composite persons. A brand's qualifications derive, as I have argued, in part from the users of branded products, yet the brand is legally attached to its corporate owners. Nonetheless, consumers practically detach the brand with their purchase and use of branded products. From this perspective, the persons of both consumers and corporations are partible. That is, we ought to think of persons much like Callon encourages us to think of products, namely, as contingent bundles of qualities or assemblages of properties.

Such persons, moreover, are not discrete unitary entities but, rather, nodes in a matrix of relations. Persons are not only partible, then, but also composite, the site of the various relations that compose them. Accordingly, the relationship between consumers and corporations appears as one based on the capacity of actors (agents, subjects) to extract or elicit from others items that become the object of their relationship. The anthropologist David Graeber helpfully explains Strathern's counter-intuitive formulation:

> People have all sorts of potential identities, which most of the time exist only as a set of hidden possibilities. What happens in any given social situation is that another person fixes on one of these and thus "makes it visible." One looks at a man, say, as a representative of his clan, or as one's sister's husband, or as the owner of a pig. Other possibilities, for the moment, remain invisible. It is at this point that a theory of value comes in: because Strathern uses the phrase "making visible" and "giving value" more or less interchangeably. (Graeber, 2001: 39–40)

What is being compared in the giving and receiving of objects, then, is the respective capacity of the actors to attach and detach parts of their own and thus other's identities. That is, the comparison is not about establishing equivalence.

Strathern argues that we should not think of the detachment of items from a partible, composite person as alienation. Detachment creates an object whose value exists both in respect of its origin (the detachee) *and* in being caused or elicited by the interest of another (the detacher). Value exists in respect of the regard of *both* parties to the exchange. Strathern's formulation thus revises the concept of keeping while giving, which emphasizes how corporate brand owners can control the activity of consumption by representing the brand as consistent with the consumer's own appropriation of it, and in so doing extracting rent. It compels us to see how this control is never guaranteed—a condition that becomes visible when consumer creativity challenges the control of the brand's attachment to the brand owner.

Consider, for example, the recent case in which Lego sued the parody rock band Spinal Tap over the in-concert use of a clever stop action digital film. The film, made by a 14-year-old boy and posted to YouTube, depicts the band as Lego minifigures performing their hit song, "Tonight I'm Gonna Rock You Tonight." It includes, among other scenes, a band member diving into the crowded audience of Lego figures and surfing atop their upraised plastic arms (see Newman, 2009). Surely a case of overflow, in Callon's sense?

> "We love that our fans are so passionate and so creative with our products," said Julie Stern, a spokeswoman for Lego Systems, the United States division of the Lego Group, a Danish company founded in the 1930s. "But it had some inappropriate language, and the tone wasn't appropriate for our target audience of kids 6 to 12." (Newman, 2009)

In such circumstances, the heterogeneity of a brand's sources become visible. The brand owner, moreover, denies the claims that consumers have to the brand; denies the claim that the brand is already owed to them, that their regard is essential to the value-definition of the brand. As Weiner might say, the hierarchy that is implicit but often disguised in reciprocity now asserts itself; keeping trumps giving. Put differently, the process of self-objectification for the consumer potentially becomes experienced as alienation; the brand owner appears as an alien actor trying to cut the consumer out of the network of relationships that produces the value of the brand. Detachment might thus well be experienced as theft.

Or maybe just as bad luck. *The New York Times* reports:

> Coleman Hickey, the filmmaker, now 16 and living outside Columbus, Ohio, says he and his eight siblings have amassed a collection of about 42,000 Lego bricks and characters. "In a way I'm disappointed that it won't be forever memorialized in a DVD," Mr. Hickey said of his video. "It's not like I was going to get any money for it, but it's too bad. Lego has the right to do that, but it's unfortunate that they don't have a little more of a sense of humor." (Newman, 2009)

Political Stakes: Destabilizing Marketing, Redefining the Corporate Person

In the economy of qualities, marketers cannot presume to stabilize and control let alone capture the qualifications (or use values) of consumers. The Lego case demonstrates the implications. Clearly, corporate brand owners should think carefully about their obligations to the consumers whose creative activity branded products elicit. It is worth noting that Lego did *not* ask the 14-year-old to remove the video from YouTube. "YouTube is a less commercial use," Julie Stern said. "But when you get into a more commercial use, that's when we have to look into the fact that we are a trademarked brand, and we really have to control the use of our brand, and our brand values" (Newman, 2009). Some of the critical marketing literature thus suggests that firms ought to compensate consumers directly for their creativity with coupons or even cash payments. Cova and Dalli (2009), for example, cite a T-shirt design competition in which the winners—from among the hundreds of designs submitted weekly by working consumers—receive 1,000 Euros and retain the copyright to their designs.

Instead of assessing the balance of power between marketers and consumers, however, I want to conclude by drawing attention to two political implications of co-creation and the economy of qualities, specifically, implications for consumer activism in contemporary circumstances of economic and cultural globalization. I take examples from my recent research on The Coca-Cola Company and its products (Foster, 2008*b*). I ask: What happens when consumers attempt to reassert their place in the economy of qualities, their relationship to the composite corporate person?

First, they reposition themselves to affect the exchange value of a corporately owned brand, that is, to contest the qualifications of branded products. In this economy, things are fragile; their integrity is threatened by the disintegration of the product networks that they—at least for the moment—hold together. Qualification is after all not the monopoly of designers and marketers. Users also qualify products—sometimes in ways that might not be compatible with the qualifications of other agents in the network. Users are capable of activating the misuse value of things; and with Coca-Cola, the possibilities are seemingly endless.

In other words, while the economy of qualities makes it possible to turn consumption into a source of surplus value, it offers other possibilities as well. Since the qualification of products is never final and always exceeds the control of product managers, then a certain kind of politics can take shape around products. When these products enjoy an almost global presence such as that of Coca-Cola, the spatial scale of such politics can expand accordingly. That is, it becomes possible for users to piggyback or hitchhike on brands, employing brand imagery to publicize oppositional messages and in so doing threatening the source of surplus value for brand owners.

For example, the Stop Killer Coke campaign—as its name indicates—has been engaged for the last several years in an attempt to hold The Coca-Cola Company accountable for its alleged complicity in labor violence in Colombia (see http://killercoke.org/). The campaign involves, among other tactics, creative misuse of the company's familiar trademarks—its advertising taglines and brand iconography. None of this would matter, I suggest, were it not for the agency that users or consumers exercise in the economy of qualities. Agency is here another word for the determination of use value—the use value that underpins the exchange value of brands. Ray Rogers, the campaign's director, could thus claim as a victory the 2007 Interbrand report that the brand value of Coca-Cola had declined three percent or about $1.7 billion from the previous year. More to the point, TIAA-CREF, the huge investment fund of teachers and other educators, excluded The Coca-Cola Company in 2006 from its Social Choice Account, the world's largest socially screened account for individual investors.

Second, and perhaps more fundamentally, consumers make visible the network of qualifications ordinarily submerged in a brand's identity; they bring into view the value-creating activity of consumption work and perforce stake a claim to this value. This visibility supplements other sorts of activism directed at exposing the composite nature of the corporate person. To take the Killer Coke campaign once more, when I interviewed Ray Rogers at his Brooklyn office in August 2007, he explained that his activist strategy involved "demysti-fying" corporations, that is, breaking down a corporation into its component elements and playing these elements against each other. For example, the Killer Coke campaign targeted Sun Trust Banks, the second largest institutional inves-tor in The Coca-Cola Company. Sun Trust has done business with and for the company since 1919 and their boards of directors are interlocked. Put differently, Rogers's strategy involved disassembling the network associated with Coca-Cola products, creating disjunctures that might redistribute agency within the network and thereby reshape the network.

Rogers's campaign not only disrupts or disassembles a product network but also reassembles or reshapes the network by enrolling new members, includ-ing college student activists across the United States. This recruitment hap-pens in two ways. First, the campaign attracts support and supporters from other issue-oriented campaigns and organizations. For example, the campaign has attempted to publicize the operations of The Coca-Cola Company in Sudan (sending syrup to a bottling plant there while indirectly purchasing gum arabic exports) despite a US trade embargo. Such publicity links the campaign against Coke with the efforts of other advocacy groups mobilized around the mass killings in Darfur. Second, the campaign establishes links with other groups arrayed against The Coca-Cola Company for reasons besides those of alleged labor violations in Colombia. Most significantly, the Killer Coke campaign has become linked with the efforts of the India Resource Center, a small activist NGO dedicated to publicizing charges that Coca-Cola bottlers in India are degrading the environment by mining groundwater supplies.

The Killer Coke campaign does not presuppose a unified body of indivi-duals; it is network-based, mobilizing and recruiting participants who do not necessarily share a single perspective on a particular product. This sort of consumer agency thus takes on the social morphology of other so-called antiglobalization initiatives and coalitions, organized in often informal and ad hoc ways through the same new media technologies of e-mail and Internet that also enable such stunning efficiencies of economic globalization as Wal-Mart's integrated transnational supply chains. Indeed, it takes on the morphology of the very networks assembled by the products that provide the focus for consumer agency (see Klein, 2000; Graeber, 2002).

The Stop Killer Coke campaign demonstrates the capacity of users not only to create (and destroy) value but also to make things public. The networks that form around products in the economy of qualities allow users to address matters of concern and thereby to constitute themselves as publics. By publics I mean affiliations performed by people's attempts to hear themselves and to make themselves heard on a particular subject. These publics emerge on an expanded spatial scale as the product networks connecting diverse economic agents extend across vast distances. So, for example, "fair trade" publics have emerged in the United States and Europe around concerns over the conditions under which farmers grow and sell tropical food commodities—coffee, bananas, and cocoa beans—in Peru, Jamaica, and Ghana. In the case of Coke, a public has come into being, linking assorted actors in India, Colombia, and the United States, with reference to a matter of concern.

Conclusion

I end by suggesting that making corporations appear as composite persons has another potentially progressive political effect. Specifically, with respect to the status—legal as well as ideological—of corporate personhood. Since the 1930s, the idea of the corporation as an exclusive association of shareholders and their managerial agents has acquired an almost unchallenged status in the courts, despite periodic attempts to include workers on the grounds that it is they who create value for shareholders. This idea achieved apotheosis in Milton Friedman's celebrated dismissal of what today is called corporate social responsibility as a violation of corporate managers' singular if not sacred duty to return value to shareholders.

Perhaps the attempt to pry open the corporation will prove more successful when it is consumers rather than workers who make claims on the basis of their role as value creators. How strange that would sound to Marx! In any case, the image of a composite person can serve the purpose of moving corporate law in the direction of public law by replacing the dominant share-holder model with a stakeholder model of the corporation (see Greenfield, 2006). In such a model not only shareholders, but a whole network of per-sons—workers and consumers, and even those affected by the corporation's "externalities"—can make legitimate claims on the value creation enabled by the legal technology of corporate personhood and expanded by the possibilities of co-creation in the economy of qualities.

Acknowledgments

Earlier versions of this chapter were presented in 2009 in seminars at the Department of Anthropology, College of Arts and Social Sciences, Australian National University; at the Department of Marketing, Schulich School of Business, York University; and in a session at the 2009 meetings of the American Anthropological Association in Philadelphia. I thank the audiences at these events for their helpful responses, and the organizers for their invitations, hospitality, and constructive suggestions. In particular, I thank Margaret Jolly for hosting me as a visiting fellow at the Gender Relations Center, Research School of Pacific and Asian Studies, Australian National University; Detlev Zwick for arranging my visit to the Schulich School of Business, York University; Julian Brash and Susan Falls for including me in the session, "Adventures in Value," at the AAA meetings; and Julia Elyachar for her thoughtful comments as discussant. My visit to the ANU was funded by a Vice-Chancellor's Travel Grant for Visiting International Academics. The chapter draws on research for which I gratefully received material support from the National Endowment for the Humanities and the University of Rochester.

Note

1. See http://www.trendwatching.com/trends/CUSTOMER-MADE.htm, accessed January 22, 2010.

References

Arvidsson, Adam (2005) "Brands: A Critical Perspective." *Journal of Consumer Culture* 5(2): 235–58.

——(2006) *Brands: Meaning and Value in Media Culture.* New York: Routledge.

Callon, Michel (1998) "An Essay on Framing and Overflowing: Economic Externalities Revisited by Sociology." In Michel Callon ed. *The Laws of the Markets.* Malden, MA: Blackwell Publishers.

——(2001) "Economy of Qualities, Researchers in the Wild and the Rise of Technical Democracy." Seminar (11/15/2001), Center for Theoretical Study, The Institute for

Advanced Studies at Charles University and the Academy of Sciences of the Czech Republic. http:/www.sfu.ca/scolr/PDF-READINGS/callon.htm, accessed on 3/2/06.

——Méadel, Cécile, and Rabeharosoa, Vololona (2002) "The Economy of Qualities." *Economy and Society* 31(2): 194–217.

Cova, Bernard and Dalli, Daniele (2009) "Working Consumers: The Next Step in Marketing Theory?" *Marketing Theory* 9(3): 315–39.

Foster, Robert J. (2005) "Commodity Futures: Labour, Love and Value." *Anthropology Today* 21(4): 8–12.

——(2007) "The Work of the 'New Economy:' Consumers, Brands and Value." *Cultural Anthropology* 22(4): 707–31.

——(2008a) "Commodities, Brands, Love and Kula: Comparative Notes on Value Creation." *Anthropological Theory* 8(1): 9–25.

——(2008b) *Coca-Globalization: Following Soft Drinks from New York to New Guinea.* New York: Palgrave Macmillan.

Graeber, David (2001) *Towards an Anthropological Theory of Value.* New York: Palgrave Macmillan.

——(2002) "The New Anarchists." *New Left Review* 13(January/February): 61–73.

——(2006) "Value: Anthropological Theories of Value." In J. Carrier, ed. *A Handbook of Economic Anthropology.* Northampton, MA: Edward Elgar, pp. 439–54.

Greenfield, Kent (2006) *The Failure of Corporate Law: Fundamental Flaws and Progressive Possibilities.* Chicago: University of Chicago Press.

Howell, Philip (2000) "Flush and the *Banditti*: Dog-stealing in Victorian London." In C. Philo and C. Wilbert, eds. *Animal Spaces, Beastly Places: New Geographies of Human–Animal Relations.* London: Routledge, pp. 35–55.

Humphreys, Ashlee, and Grayson, Kent (2008) "The Intersecting Roles of Consumer and Producer: A Critical Perspective on Co- Production, Co-Creation and Prosumption." *Sociology Compass*, 2: 1–18.

Klein, Naomi (2000) "The Vision Thing." *Nation*, July 10. http://www.thenation.com/doc/20000710/klein

Malinowski, Bronislaw (1922) *Argonauts of the Western Pacific: An Account of Native Enterprise and Adventure in the Archipelagoes of Melanesian New Guinea.* London: Routledge.

Mauss, Marcel (1967 [1925]) *The Gift: Forms and Functions of Exchange in Archaic Societies.* Transl. by Ian Cunnison. New York: Norton.

Miller, Daniel (1987) *Material Culture and Mass Consumption.* New York: Basil Blackwell.

——(1988) "Appropriating the State on the Council Estate." *Man*, n.s., 23: 353–72.

Newman, Andrew Adam (2009) "Lego Rejects a Bit Part in a Spinal Tap DVD." *The New York Times*, August 11.

Prahalad, C.K. and Ramaswamy, Venkat (2004a) "Co-Creation Experiences: The Next Practice in Value Creation." *Journal of Interactive Marketing* 18(3): 5–14.

————(2004b) *The Future of Competition: Co-Creating Unique Value with Customers.* Boston: Harvard Business School Press.

Roberts, Kevin (2004) *Lovemarks: The Future Beyond Brands.* New York: Powerhouse Books.

Slater, Don (2002) "Markets, Materiality and the 'New Economy.'" In Stan Metcalfe and Alan Warde, eds. *Market Relations and the Competitive Process*. New York: Manchester University Press, pp. 95–113.

Strathern, Marilyn (1988) *The Gender of the Gift: Problems with Women and Problems with Society in Melanesia*. Berkeley: University of California Press.

——(1992) "Qualified Value." In C. Humphrey and S. Hugh-Jones, eds. *Barter, Exchange and Value: An Anthropological Approach*. Cambridge: Cambridge University Press, pp. 169–91.

Weiner, Annette (1992) *Inalienable Possessions: The Paradox of Keeping-While-Giving*. Berkeley: University of California Press.

Zwick, Detlev, Bonsu, Sauel K., and Darmody, Aron (2008) "Putting Consumers to Work: 'Co-Creation' and New Marketing Govern-mentality." *Journal of Consumer Culture* 8(2): 163–96.

3

"Market-things Inside": Insights from *Progressive Grocer* (United States, 1929–1959)

Franck Cochoy

In 2008, after the explosion of a speculative bubble of real estate and financial markets, a time of crisis has come. And one may wonder if what happens with markets does not apply elsewhere; for instance, with marketing. Indeed, the expression "speculative bubble" has two meanings. One is restricted to financial speculation (i.e., speculation as gambling). But the other meaning is much more general: it points to the tendency of scholars to speculate at the risk of losing any connection with what they refer to (i.e., speculation as theorizing). Such speculative bubbles appear and explode like their financial counterparts when a "crash" calls the "market" back to its "fundamentals." Consider, for example, the marketing discipline. In the latter, a first crash of this type occurred in 1986, when a group of consumer researchers questioned the artificiality of marketing theories of their time. To quote W.D. Wells (1991: iii), who was among those spearheading this project:

> By the middle of the 1980s, the consumer had all but disappeared from "scientific" consumer research. In the most prestigious journals, the method of choice was the controlled experiment: college student subjects made artificial responses to artificial stimuli in situations which had none of the annoying details of real life. [...] The method of second choice was the mathematical model. Numbers replaced feelings, thoughts and actions, with no regard to whether the real life analogies ever followed the rules the numbers did. Again, the models were not about how real consumers buy gasoline, or how real audiences use television to enrich their days [...] As a result, consumers—the original and only proper focus of consumer research—had all but vanished. Worship of logical positivism had turned the discipline into a self-contained, self-reinforcing, depopulated world. [...] One consequence of all this was that "scientific" consumer research became less and less interesting to audiences outside the academe.

In order to draw the lessons from such a criticism of the marketing discipline, some scholars undertook a well-known collective project called "Consumer Behavior Odyssey." The idea was to send a team of researchers traveling through America in order to get rid of abstract thinking and study "real" consumers. As Wells put it: "Instead of looking inward at the literature, the Odyssey participants looked outward at consumers" (Wells 1991: iii). We may say that the Odyssey provoked a theoretical "crash" in the field of consumer research, which burst the theoretical bubble of cognitive psychology and brought back consumer research to its "fundamentals"—that is, "real consumers" as "the original and only proper focus of consumer research"—just like a financial crash reconnects the price of stocks to the real value of the companies they rely on.

But that was several years ago. And, much in the same way that the financial market went from one bubble and crash (1987) to another (2008), we may wonder if the "speculative" process in marketing theory that began in the late 1980s did not lead to a new type of theoretical bubble. This bubble, if it exists, is much more acceptable than the previous one because its driver, the "naturalistic/interpretive" turn in consumer research, has been very fruitful. It generated many insights about issues like "consumer identity," "marketplace cultures," "socio-historical patterning of consumption," and "mass-mediated marketplace ideologies and consumers" interpretive strategies (to quote one of the best surveys of the field: Arnould and Thompson 2005). But this stream of research nevertheless led to a new kind of speculative inflation, not by distorting its subject matter (like the previous one certainly did) but by over-emphasizing one of its dimensions only (the consumer), at the risk of overshadowing some other aspects. Indeed, consumer research quite exclusively focuses on consumers; it obsessively attempts to reveal all the aspects of consumer behavior (experiential, cognitive, cultural, anthropological, sociological, etc.). Since the subject of study is consumers, this singular fixation is of course not a problem: studying consumers by looking at consumers makes sense! But what about studying consumption? *Is studying consumption exactly the same as studying consumers? Can consumption be understood through consumer behavior only?*[1] The emphasis placed on consumers tends to neglect at least two other factors that significantly frame the consumption game. The first factor is the supply side. *Consumption is shaped by consumers, but also by marketers. As a consequence, if we want to fully understand consumption, we have to study both types of actors;* we must research marketing as well as purchasing and consuming. In other words, to get a better view of consumption we should not only look outside to consumers as Wells suggests but also "inside marketing" as the present book proposes. In short, we should invent a "marketer research" along with "consumer research."[2] The second factor is that of market objects, devices, and technologies (Callon et al., 2007). Consumption engages a triangular relationship between consumers, marketers, and a wide array of artifacts, such as the products themselves, of course, as well as packaging, credit cards, billboards, shopping carts, and so on. *If we really want to account for consumption, we thus have to study the three vertexes of the triangle: we need to supplement the study of consumers with a study of marketers, and the study of consumers and marketers with a study of what I have elsewhere called "market-things"* (Cochoy 2007). Russell Belk's idea (1988) that "we are what we have" points into the right direction, although seeing objects as part of an "extended self" classically focuses our attention on human meanings and identities acquired by *using* objects rather than on the object's abilities and properties. This contrasts with a view where objects are considered as autonomous entities that may shape consumer behavior. Consider, for example, how packaging, by bringing information about an invisible element like nicotine to the forefront, helped remake smokers previously attached to taste into new expert/chemists-like consumers conversant on the nature and effect of chemical compounds (Cochoy 2004).

Focusing on marketers and market objects is in no way a criticism of consumer research. On the contrary, they are an invitation to simply supplement the latter with new objects, in the very same way that consumer research itself focused on some additional fields in the past, as when it proposed to go beyond studying private buying behavior and to include all sorts of consuming activities (Holbrook and Hirschman 1982; Holbrook 1984). The two proposals are a positive answer to John Sherry's generous and open minded call to bring "other stuff" into consumer research (Sherry 2004: 45), provided that I can take the word "stuff" to mean not only the (speculative) "outer perspectives" Sherry implicitly favors but also in the sense of basic "material matters." To paraphrase Wells, we could say that instead of looking inward at the consumer research literature, we should look outward at consumers, and also at marketers and market-things.

In this paper, I would like to help burst the theoretical bubbles by going back to the "fundamentals." By fundamentals I mean the "naturalistic fieldwork" of the Odyssey even if, contrary to the Odyssey, I will shift the subject, the vehicle, and the direction of the journey. Instead of collectively traveling through the American "consumptionscape" on a bus, I will revisit—alone—the past of marketing and I will do so with a shopping cart (Cochoy 2009) and many other market-things. More precisely, I will focus neither on the consumer nor on marketers but on something just in between: retailing. The retailing place I will talk about is neither the department store nor the supermarket, which most analysts take as the prototypes of this sector, but the small independent grocery store. The latter is a business focused on the satisfaction of primary needs; it is the most simple and basic unit of the marketing scene. As such, it is one of the best fields to tackle the contribution of market-things to the field of marketing. As Johan Hagberg (2009) recently noticed: "Retailing is often seen as the least complex form of marketing exchange, as involving consumers (as compared to the generally believed more complex situation of business to business) and packaged products (as compared to the generally believed more complex situation of services)." In this chapter however, I will focus neither on the products sold nor on the actors who manipulate them but on the equipments, which help the products go from one hand to another. More precisely, I will trace the *technical transformation* of the grocery business from 1929 to 1959. Through an analysis of the trade press journal *Progressive Grocer* over that period, and from the perspective of actor-network theory,[3] I will show how market-things were put in motion and articulated in order to help grocers and consumers behave differently. This study intends to show that it may be worthwhile to supplement the study of consumers and marketers with a parallel description of these discreet and mundane artifacts that sometimes had the capacity to modify the very actions and identities of consumers, and of markets.

Progressive Grocer: A "Market-things" Journal

The emergence of new forms of commerce in the nineteenth and twentieth centuries—department stores, mail-order selling, consumer cooperatives, chain stores, and more recently supermarkets and malls—was a matter of moving things and people. It was largely supported by technical innovations: the mechanized warehouses of Sears that industrialized the remote distribution of products (Strasser 1989), the escalators that eased the extension of department stores and the circulation of consumers (Worthington 1989), and the automobiles and shopping carts that favored the rise of supermarkets and the development of new consumption patterns (Longstreth 1999; Longstreth 2000; Grandclément 2006; Cochoy 2009).

Did traditional shops remain passive in the face of all that? Were they pushed aside by the seductions of the new commercial spaces? Were they condemned to failure by the competition's more efficient techniques? Have they gone extinct over some larger, more attractive and innovative form of commerce? In other words, did the course of history follow the path sketched out by Zola?[4] Of course not! With the benefit of more than a century of hindsight, we know that the rise of supermarkets did not kill small retail outlets (Strasser 1989; Monod 1996; Deutsch 2001). Small, independent grocery stores were the subject of a powerful modernization movement promoted by the journal *Progressive Grocer*. This journal (launched in 1922) was targeted at independent American grocers to help them modernize their businesses as an answer to the growing competition of chain stores first (supported by the journal *Chain Store Age* from 1925) and supermarkets afterwards (led by the journal *Supermarket Merchandising* from 1936). The fact that *Progressive Grocer* was launched in 1922—that is, long before its competitors—indicates that its project was more active than reactive. *Progressive Grocer* is a professional journal which targets small independent grocers in order to show them how to transform and improve their practices. It collects a lot of testimonials, reports, and practical articles about new merchandising techniques and shop equipment. It is not a professional organization's publication, like the bulletin of an association. Rather, it is an independent publication founded by journalists who thought that the context of the progressive era (Glad 1966) and the war between chain stores and independent grocers (Haas,1979; Seth 2001) represented a double opportunity for a journal oriented toward the modernization of the retail business. At the very beginning, the journal appeared as a thick booklet in pocket format. It was published on a monthly basis and sent to American grocers as a free publication financed through advertising. *Progressive Grocer* was proud to reach 68,000 grocers by the end of the 1920s (1930, Aug., pp. 2–3). This figure represented almost one-third of the 250,000 independent American grocers at that time (1930, Feb., pp. 14–15), that is, an impressive potential readership that no other form of distribution had a chance to achieve. As I have already mentioned, I analyze this journal over the period 1929–59 in order to examine how the specialists of the "progressive grocery business" attempted to reconfigure store equipment in order to move more products and consumers. More precisely, I will show that this reconfiguration rested on four types of tightly intertwined innovations: a redistribution of furniture within the walls of the grocery, a controlled "liberation" of consumers' lines of sight and trajectories, the invention of flexible display furniture, and the implementation of devices aimed at easing the movement of the customers.

Real Estate: Playing within Four Walls

The factor that differentiates grocery stores from other types of food retailing is the nature of real estate of such stores: both forms of commerce vary based on location, form, and size of the shop. Grocery stores are cooped up in the urban space, at the bottom of buildings, often all along "mainstreet" (Longstreth 2000), where space is as precious as it is scarce and walls cannot be extended. This immutable nature of grocery stores is a characteristic that differentiates it from supermarkets. Indeed, grocers own their business and often pass them on from parents to children, as is evidenced in the many chronicles that trace the edifying evolution of the same store from generation to generation (1929, Dec., 30 sq.); 1931, Apr., 22 sq.;

1932, Dec., 16 sq.; 1939, Mar., 40 sq.; etc.). This is probably the reason why, until after World War II, the borders of the store as shown in *Progressive Grocer* (see Figure 3.1) appear as a given, unquestionable and unchangeable frame: grocery professionals organize the store space but not the limits that define it; they follow plans and maps, but within the boundaries of the given walls. The only considerations for the outdoor are aimed at showing off the store's window and front, including the store sign (1946, Oct., pp. 76–7), as if one

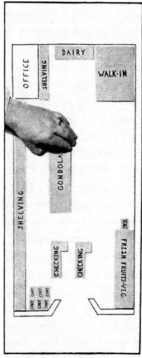

Progressive Grocer photos

5. AFTER YOU TRY a number of arrangements, you may decide this general plan meets your particular needs best. When you have made that decision, you have but to work out the details, such as whether to let the frosted-food cabinet stand as is, or square it up to the meat case, whether to move the dairy case forward, or whether you have the right size gondolas. After you have placed all the equipment items to your satisfaction, sketch them in by drawing a pencil around the cardboard blocks (or paste in), and you will have a permanent floor plan your workmen can use.

Figure 3.1 Store map (1944, May, pp. 58–9).

tried both to differentiate oneself from chain stores and to show that the identity of the independent grocer depends on the "static" real estate.

The plans exhibited in *Progressive Grocer* in the 1930s and 1940s thus take the space represented by the classical blueprint of the architect as a non-modifiable or non-discussable starting place. But inside this space, professionals try to arrange scientifically new equipment and furniture in order to modernize and transform the immutable space (see the displayed map, where the walls delineate a space on which one displaces furniture pieces cut in cardboard (1944, May, pp. 58–9)). This logic clearly supports claims for the refitting of spaces that already exist rather than for radical innovation—we can see the obsessive repetition of the theme of "modernization": *Progressive Grocer* presses its readers to modernize ("When You Modernize?" 1929, Aug., p. 29), gathers testimonies ("Shepard *Modernizes,*" 1928, Aug., p. 54), gives hard figures about the advantages of "modern" stores ("*Modern* Arrangement Boosted Sales 20%," 1929, Sep., pp. 38–9), and so on. The journal thus promoted an emblematic model of progressive, qualitative, and intensive transformation of the grocery business, which is at complete odds with the alternative model of extensive growth that supermarkets experienced at the same moment in time. Indeed, the *Progressive Grocer* concept proposes reconfiguring a limited set of square meters in a way that can hopefully speed up the circulation of consumers and goods and, ultimately, increase sales. This reconfiguration rests on a "faire laissez-faire" strategy (Cochoy 2007). This strategy encourages clients to enter the shop by putting the clerks backward and the goods forward (laissez-faire) while efficiently and discreetly organizing this new spatial and product arrangement (faire). By accepting and even favoring consumers' freedom to move, pick, and choose, "faire laissez-faire" thus fulfills the requirements of liberal ideology. But it does so in a way that reinforces managerial power over "free" economic behavior rather than handing over the control of the situation to market forces. Thus, in between the "counter service" model of the past and the "self-service" model dominant today occurred the fleeting and forgotten era of "open display," which functioned as a subtle and efficient transition between both types of systems of selling.

From Self-sight to Self-service: "Open Display"

The idea promoted by *Progressive Grocer* is to bring people and things together, to facilitate access to products, and to transform the grocery business so that clients may handle the goods themselves and without any embarrassment or obstacle, hoping that this tighter, more direct, and easier relationship between supply and demand would generate more sales. But the journal anticipates that its readers would perceive such an operation as risky.[5] It was possible that grocers, accustomed to serving clients from behind their counters with most products sheltered behind their backs, would fear that giving consumers direct access to the exposed merchandise could result in theft and damage to products (1929, Sep., 24 sq.; 1939, Jul., 42 sq.; 1941, Oct., 481 sq.; etc.). Hence, the concern of modern grocery proponents not to "release" anything without some precaution; and hence, the development of a "faire laissez-faire" strategy that can preserve the grocer's control over this more "open" type of trade. This is why "open display" preceded "self-service" or, to put it differently, this is why self-*sight* was the first step toward self-*service* (Figure 3.2).

Indeed, open display should not be confused with self-service for two reasons. On the one hand, while both techniques were aimed at introducing a more direct access to commodities, the first was meant to proceed cautiously, by limiting access to sight, thus prohibiting (more or less) customers from touching the goods. On the other hand, open display favored some gradual improvements of existing arrangements—or "agencements"[6]—rather than radical innovations because it did not remove the merchant and his sales counter like self-service did. Rather, "open display" redistributed the material

One Big Jump...

From This→

To This ↓

By arranging an "island" in the middle of the store, opening up the shelves along the sides, and locating the meat department behind a wide arch in the rear, an effect of spaciousness before almost unbelievable has been achieved

Figure 3.2 A big jump from counter service to open display (1930, Jan., p. 29).

elements of the store in novel ways, changed the qualities of some of them, and varied their proportions.

Figure 3.3 shows the situation before and after the introduction of open display (Dipman 1935, p. 12).[7] From one period to the next, the double counter, which prevented the consumer's access to the goods, was not removed but placed further away from the shelves so that the consumer gained a better view of the products. In addition, the size of the counter was reduced to a minimum and pushed to the back of the store so that consumers would see all the supplies before asking the merchant to collect the desired goods and produce the bill. The product assortment could now be increased and made more accessible by placing of a new type of furniture all along the central space. This furniture, called an "island," was made of shelves, tables of low height, or window showcases, following the concept of giving customers better lines of sight to the merchandise. As the possible journeys traced with lines and arrows in the figure clearly suggest, the island was supposed to diversify consumers' shopping trajectories and purchases. Figure 3.4 (1946, May, p. 55) shows the next stage, a decade later: the drawing is meant to represent the superiority of self-service (on the right) over counter service and open display on the left. In the self-service store arrangement the counter has disappeared. More precisely, it has been replaced by a new type of furniture: a checkout counter which is no longer placed at the back of the shop but at its entry (see in the lower part of the drawing in Figure 3.4). Until the introduction of open display, the grocery business consisted of organizing a peaceful exchange between the inhabitants of two territories—the territory of the grocer and the territory granted to the customer. The territories were separated by a border traced with some moving boundary markers: the counter and other displays. With self-service, the border was abolished. Both territories merge: one slides from the line (of the counter) to the enclosure (of the shop). The relationship between the grocer and his customer moves from an interface relationship to one of sharing the same space. Inside the common territory, the impenetrable islands disappeared. More precisely, they were replaced with a unique "gondola," which was now accessible not only to a consumer's vision but also to his or her grasp. We understand it better by looking at the circular, unique, simple, and complete journey that enables the same and single person to pick up the products he or she is looking for—a journey which starkly contrasts with the ceaseless back and forth movement encouraged by the collection of an order at the counter.

The same and single person, but who is it? From one scene to the other, the subject has not changed. Far from showing the linear wandering of the customer in the new space of self-service (as opposed to the back and forth, "beam-like" moves of the grocer in the counter service arrangement), the scenes in the figure represent the evolution of the *grocer*'s journeys. Hence

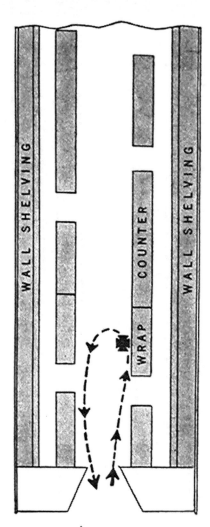 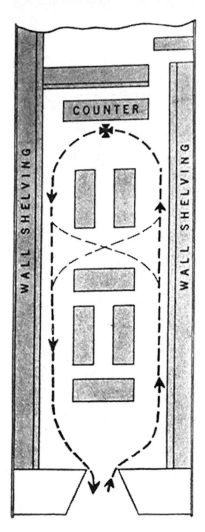

THE OLD WAY

Store No. 1—A typical layout of the old-style store. Most of the activity is in the front of the store. Long counters and show-cases separate customers from most of the merchandise. About half of the merchandise cannot be seen and less than a quarter of it can be handled. The result is that the store's sales expense is high.

THE MODERN WAY

Store No. 2—The store opposite arranged the modern way. The counters and show-cases have been removed and the side walls opened. The center of activity has been moved to the rear. The equipment and displays have been arranged into islands. Now most of the merchandise can be seen and handled. Sales will increase and expense decrease.

Figure 3.3 Situation before and after the introduction of open display (Dipman 1935, p. 12).

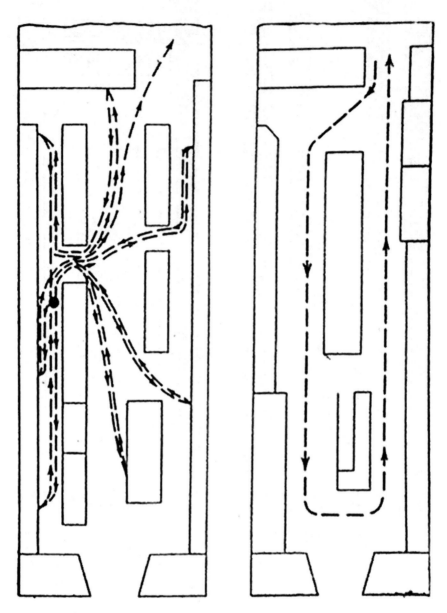

LEFT: In counter-service store assembling delivery order takes many steps. RIGHT: In self-service store but one trip (with carrier) through salesroom is necessary.

Figure 3.4 *Progressive Grocer* (1946, May, p. 55).

what we are seeing is not the evolution of the customer's journey but that of the one and the same grocer. And so the elucidation of one anomaly raises a new one: Is the offering of service in a self-service arrangement not complete nonsense? Here, because the journal is well aware of the reluctance of its public to the introduction of self-service per se, the *Progressive Grocer* relies on a trick to convince its audience. The solution is to promote the new way of selling by inverting the roles: the journal tries to show that the spatial arrangement of self-service does not in fact remove the role of the grocer and the "service" he is attached to but rather, and paradoxically, favors their further development, reinforcement, and rationalization. The message of *Progressive Grocer* is the following: "Grocers, you have to understand that the new linear and simplified journey created by the removal of the counter and the use of check-out stands, open gondolas and shopping carts will help you to prepare your orders faster and more easily!" But this journey that the journal tries to sell to the grocer as his own is also (apart from the different location of exits) the mirror image of the customer's journey. This is the very journey, of course, that the *Progressive Grocer* attempts to sell with the first one.

Furniture: Adjustable Shelves, Baskets, and Pyramids

Self-service conveys a liquefaction of commerce. This logic of flux brings more flexibility and unpredictability as it asks for constant adjustments. Like with islands or gondolas, using furniture organizes the circulation of consumers differently. At the same time, the circulation of people also affects the circulation of the objects they move.

However, channeling the mobility of objects and managing the mobility of people does not rest on the same process. On the one hand, dealing with the flux of customers is about finding a way to make them travel easily across the store space where the mandatory checkpoint of the counter has now been replaced with a checkout stand located at the very end of the shopping journey. On the other hand, handling the flux of products requires reconciling the old stocking imperative of the grocer with the new picking logic of the customer. The change is tremendous: from a synchronic position, the proper storage of goods should not only help the grocer to locate the merchandise easily but also assist customers in finding what they are looking for and, if possible, attract customers to things they do not necessarily seek! From a diachronic standpoint, it should also help the grocer to monitor closely the movement of the clientele and of products, so that in an ideal scenario the grocer is able to present customers with a visually saturated choice space without any gaps (aesthetical dimension) on a very limited space. Overcoming all of these difficulties meant finding the means to separate the products (to preserve their order and to support the "clarity" of the stock), while at the same time making the divisions between the products flexible (to optimize the storing space and to ensure the visual continuity of supply). The border logic once again proved its ability to solve these retailing problems. But this time, the solution did not come from playing with the old, unique, and fixed border of the counter, aimed at separating people one from one another. Rather, new and mobile borders aimed at sorting the products were used. In the early 1930s, *Progressive Grocer* presented some wooden shelves that could be adjusted vertically (1931, Apr., p. 26). In the 1950s, this type of system was brought into general use and improved by means of metal furniture (1951, Feb., 54 sq.) with shelves that were deprived of any lateral uprights (1951, Mar., pp. 50–5). Such improvements helped to ease the adjustment of the lateral space occupied by different groups of products on the same shelf. Moreover, it helped remove some opaque lateral obstacles, which were all the more awkward now that the consumer was moving more freely. Finally, the use of steel supported the invention of mobile, lateral divisions that proved very helpful in adjusting the display of products sold in bulk, such as the "endless display basket" of the Tote-Cart Company (Figure 3.5).

This remarkable game of abolition, resurgence, displacement, and multiplication of borders redrew the circulation spaces allotted to grocers and their customers. But when accounting for this game, we really should not forget the critical role of packaging innovations. Indeed, it could be argued that these innovations reinvented the border of the counter. Before packaging, it was the grocer who was in charge of preventing any direct contact between the customer and the merchandise. With packaging, this task was delegated to mere artifacts, but in the process the task of protecting goods was changed: it was no longer carried out at the "global" level of the store but at the "local" level of each product. See, in particular, the invention of cellophane and the generalization of cans.[8] Cellophane was invented in 1908, produced

Figure 3.5 Endless Tote-Cart display baskets (1959, Dec., p. 142).

industrially from 1917 onward, and then promoted by DuPont (1932, Feb., pp. 68–9; 1932, Dec., pp. 6–7; 1950, Aug., p. 185). The transparency of cellophane obviously supported the logic of open display. As the material's transparency improved cellophane's use extended to other products (e.g., pastas and dry vegetables previously stored in glass jars for the same reason) (1929, Aug., pp. 56–7). Also, the airtight character of cellophane and its unique flexibility (especially compared to glass) reinforced the transition toward self-service by offering the consumer the possibility to see and touch the products without facing the risk of soiling or breaking them (Figure 3.6).

Cans, which are older than cellophane (Brown and Philips, 1985), presented more or less the same advantages, with some differences: their opacity, far from contravening open display, functioned as a support for a new kind of transparency—that of product information printed on packaging. On the one hand, printing the composition and origin of the product on the packaging helps the consumer learn more about each product than would be possible through direct contact with it (Cochoy 2004). On the other hand, packaging helps the customer

CELLOPHANE DOUBLES *and* TRIPLES SALES *of*

GROCERY STAPLES –SOMETIMES AT HIGHER PRICES

Safeway Stores find visible packaging a remarkable sales stimulant even for bulk items having little eye or appetite appeal

SAFEWAY STORES are very much pleased with results from their present use of Cellophane. They find that Cellophane is a perfect medium for merchandising, particularly in a self-service store. They plan to use it in *every* store and on many additional products.

This great Western organization presents an outstanding example of the new trend in merchandising food staples which is sweeping rapidly throughout the country. It took bulk products out of bins, barrels and burlap bags and put them up in small Cellophane units. The new packages

proved ideal for displays on island counters, and were more convenient for the housewife to buy.

Overnight these homely staples in Cellophane acquired attention value. Sales increased at an almost unbelievable rate, *sometimes at higher prices*. In some cases sales were doubled, even tripled.

The sales value of Cellophane as a wrap for food products of nearly every kind has been proved by stores everywhere. A folder called "Proof" contains evidence gathered in actual retail store tests. Write for a copy to Du Pont Cellophane Co., Inc., Empire State Building, New York.

Cellophane

MADE ONLY BY DU PONT

Cellophane is the registered trade-mark of the Du Pont Cellophane Company, Inc.,
to designate its cellulose films.
In Canada the trade-mark Cellophane identifies the same products manufactured exclusively
by Canadian Industries Limited.

Figure 3.6 Cellophane (1932, Dec., pp. 6–7).

avoid the previously inescapable mediation of the vendor (Strasser 1989). Therefore, the widespread use of cans is linked inextricably to the promotion of national brands like Monarch (1929, Aug., pp. 62–3), Libby's (1929, Nov., pp. 6–7), or Gerber's (1930, Jan., pp. 74–5), or to the emergence of new preferences, like the demand for vitamins (1937, Mar., p. 10; 1941, Mar., pp. 142–3; 1942, Sep., p. 97). The great durability of cans also supported the transition toward self-service by encouraging grocers not to be afraid of letting the consumer handle the products. But, first and foremost, this quality of solidity provided cans with a decisive and proper advantage over other forms of packaging: the ability to be piled up without any risk. Piling up cans was seen as a means of building magnificent displays at low cost, as if cans were displayed on an invisible and highly adjustable type of furniture, indefinitely replaceable and adjustable. This ability of cans to be transformed into varied constructions was greeted with strong enthusiasm among the grocers of the time. Indeed, grocers undertook heroic projects of "pyramidal sales," in the literal sense of the expression (1931, Apr., p. 24). There is no doubt that pyramids of cans functioned as an important support for the evolution toward self-service (the more protected the products are by the armor of packaging the less the protection of the counter is required) (Figure 3.7).

Figure 3.7 Pyramids of cans (1931, Apr., p. 24).

Turnstiles and Magic Doors

As we can see, the art of "faire laissez-faire" involves reinstalling everywhere this general border of the counter that was supposed to be removed. New borders reappeared between the products in the form of adjustable shelves and divisions. Borders also intervened between the customers and the products in the form of envelopes and boxes designed to prevent the adulteration of any content and to clearly distinguish the moments of purchase and consumption. All these borders, even if highly efficient in channeling the legal use of self-service, were nevertheless often faulty when it came to prevent illicit behavior, especially theft (1941, Oct., 81 sq.). Here again we face the central dilemma of self-service: How is it possible to let consumers circulate as freely as possible with the hope to increase sales (because if it is not an open space, people might hesitate to walk in) while simultaneously avoiding the disappearance of products on a large scale (an open space is more inviting to theft)? On a less dramatic note, and independent of any fraudulent behavior of customers, it was necessary to organize maximum open space for the store while preserving its identity, atmosphere, and closed character.

By granting improved access to the merchandise, self-service appeared to be both the cause and the solution to the risk of theft. The recommendations of *Progressive Grocer* suggest that the best barrier against theft is paradoxically the absence of barriers: the adoption of furniture of lower height was meant to help consumers get a more panoramic view over supplies and thus gain a better access to the products; such furniture also helped the grocer control the store space and thus the consumers visually (1939, Jul., p. 43).

How is it possible to reconcile the "free entrance, free exit" principle with the necessary control of customers and the nature of the border of the store? The solution to this dilemma was found in the form of a "double reinvention" of the door. Bruno Latour (1988) showed that the age-old device of the door with hinges is the equivalent of a strange "hole-wall": on the one hand, a door is a device which exempts the one who wishes to get into a closed place to create an opening to it; but on the other hand, the same door is also a device that exempts the one who wishes to isolate himself from building a partition. Now, the equipment manufacturers for the grocery business found a way to separate and redistribute the different features of the door and to slightly modify its properties, at the entry as well as at the exit of the store.

At the entry of the store, the implementation of open display went hand in hand with the introduction of "turnstiles" (1938, Apr., p. 94). A turnstile functions as an almost invisible and asymmetric door: while it does not offer any resistance to the entry of customers, it blocks their exit. In so doing, the turnstile is a break from the perfect reversibility of the door with hinges by imposing a one-way logic to the clients.

Unlike doors with hinges and mechanical door closers (Latour 1988), the turnstile does not create any physical separation: it turns without any effort and there is no real need to even push it. It nevertheless introduces a voluntary, cognitive, and technical separation. As we will see, the target of this discrimination is the children and their supposed blundering and pilfering. The discrimination is cognitive, since the presence of the turnstile conveys a view of social control and prohibition. And if this cognitive warning is not sufficient, the components manufacturer Boston Metal Products Inc. proposes to add a technical discrimination to it, by putting an "apron [...] below the turning arms that keeps children from crawling through the gate" (1945, Nov., p. 206). This is similar to an observation made by Molotch and McClain (2008) about the New York subway entrances: variations in the design of turnstiles modify the level of social control (Figure 3.8).

In the grocery store, the reversibility of the door with hinges is abolished: the turnstile rotates in one direction only. In so doing, it attempts less to close a door (which the turnstile merely supplements: the classical door is still there, behind it) than to trap the customers in order to force them to exit another way than the one they entered. The idea is to compensate for the lack of surveillance due to the displacement of the counter in the back of the shop in the open-display era or due to the removing of the same counter after the implementation of self-service. But the idea is also to lead customers through the entire shop by having them skirt around the islands and gondolas in order to encourage them to stop more and purchase more. This idea has all the more chances of success because buying something is now the best way to exit a store that can no longer be escaped discreetly, that is, to avoid the embarrassment of passing the grocer (in the open-display era) or the cashier (in the self-service era) with empty hands on the way to the exit. In other words, the turnstile contributed to the conversion of the visitor into a buyer, thus supporting the idea that "market-things" contribute to shift people's identities.

The exit was as important as the entry since, like the entry, it was equipped with a new kind of door. In the same way as turnstiles, the idea was to set up a "quasi-barrier." A barrier was necessary to trace the borders of the property, to avoid drafts and to maintain a comfortable temperature, and to prevent undesirable intrusions like in the turnstile case. But this door was only a "quasi-barrier"—it had to let people leave as easily as possible while at the same time close behind each customer. It looked as if one tried to reinvent the door with hinges while getting rid it of its biggest flaw: the necessity to push or pull it (Bruno Latour showed, however, that no mechanical door closer is able to fully eliminate this need). In the grocery store, meeting that objective is especially important, and therefore no compromise is possible. It was not acceptable to rely on a partial solution that let only adults pass easily but neglected the weaker elderly and children. Grocers now had to let everybody

Offers New Turnstile

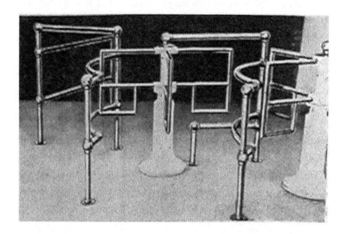

Boston Metal Products Co., Boston, Mass., announces it is now filling orders for this all-purpose turnstile. The unit features a flexible railing arrangement that can be made to fit any requirement for complete self-service or semi-self-service markets, large or small, it is said. As a consequence, any number of individual entrances can be set up. The apron below the turning arms keeps children from crawling through the gate. The turnstile works either clockwise or counterclockwise, turns at a touch, and is said to be of unusual strength and durability.

Figure 3.8 Turnstile (1945, Nov., p. 206).

leave—the strongest and the weakest, the young and the old. If everybody had to be free to go out, it is because every customer, who ever she was, went out of the store with full arms and would therefore feel affronted to find a door (again) in her path. Shopping carts could have helped to solve the difficulty of exiting with full arms by serving as a battering ram, if they were not for so long kept inside the store, thus leaving the customer alone in dealing with her overload problem as soon as she faced the door. If it was necessary to prevent customers from entering through the exit doors, it was because any form of customer circulation that could distract the vigilance of personnel and thus multiply theft had to be prevented.

It is precisely these two problems—letting people go out with full arms, and preventing them getting in through the exit door—that the invention of "magic doors" came to solve. Magic doors were able to open by themselves and did not need to be pushed by anyone (1941, May, p. 177). The door opened through the simple action of one's foot, recognized by a "Magic Carpet" (1951, Feb., p. 201), or the presence of one's body, recognized by a "Magic Eye" (Ibid.). Moreover, they do so in one direction only: from the shop to the street. The magic door managed to overcome all the flaws of its Latourian ancestor, since it succeeded for the first time in introducing a perfect "hole-wall"—a hole-wall that does not need any strong intervention from the person who wishes to pass through it, neither for opening nor for closing it. As such, it avoids any discrimination, and thus anticipates and fulfills the dreams of the "universal design" school of the 1980s well documented by Lena Hansson (2007). Even though this "hole-wall" is perfect, it is not reversible. Indeed, it copies from the turnstile the capacity to work in one direction only. As Stanley, a commercial manufacturer argued, magic doors were conceived "for greater customer convenience, for faster traffic turnover, for extra pilferage protection" (1954, May, p. 226) (Figure 3.9).

Turnstiles and magic doors are mobile devices not only from a spatial but also from a temporal point of view. Indeed, the effectiveness of their properties does not depend only on the characteristics of the technical system that the turnstile and the magic doors share. When magic doors were first implemented in the 1940s, evidence suggests that stores only used them for the exits. The entrances remained equipped with a classic door supplemented with a turnstile. Yet throughout the 1940s, some grocers began to remove the turnstile.

Why? A first reason was that the turnstile, even though more discreet and quieter than a distrustful grocer, communicated by its mere presence a suspicion which, even as it persuaded some not to do mischief, may make those with honest intentions feel subtly accused of harboring bad intentions. Not surprisingly, such surveillance devices were not too common anymore at the end of the 1940s. As a grocer committed to removing turnstiles put it: "I never liked them anyhow. They always made the store seem kind of unfriendly" (1947, Jul., p. 59).

But between the lines we can discern other reasons for removing turnstiles and these reasons were probably much more important than the first one. Hence, a second reason is connected to the introduction of shopping carts in

People talk about "the market with the Magic Doors"...in addition to the convenience these novel doors offer your bundle-laden customers, they're a super-advertising and merchandising feature. Doors open silently at a customer's approach, close after she has passed through.

The Stanley equipment is proved, dependable. It can be installed right on your present doors. Write — right now — for literature on this exclusive Stanley equipment. The Stanley Works, Magic Door Division, 193 Lake Street, New Britain, Connecticut.

STANLEY MAGIC DOORS
Require No Hand to Open

STANLEY
Trade Mark

Figure 3.9 Magic doors (1941, May, p. 177).

the grocery store universe, which began at the end of the 1930s (Grandclément 2006) and became an irresistible feature of shopping in the 1940s (Cochoy 2009). These vehicles could not cross the barrier of turnstiles and hence posed a dilemma: the grocer could either keep the turnstile and accept that the stock of carts invaded and took up usable store space or the grocer could reject the carts near the entry and thereby preserve precious selling space but give up the turnstile. The choice of the second option, when it was made, led to a third reason that called for the removal of turnstiles.

Indeed, the use of shopping carts conveys in and of itself the shift from open display to self-service. What is the use of a mobile basket if not to encourage the customer to move it all over the store without much effort and to fill it up? The shopping cart brings a predatory affordance into play: with it, the customer is no longer reduced to passively watching (the grocer) but now can take the goods him- or herself and put them into a container, thus instantly and effortlessly transforming each buying impulse into an act of immediate taking. The practice of self-service with a cart modifies the mode of paying for the wares: first, as we have seen earlier, the counter becomes an obstacle for circulating in a limited space, particularly because the consumers are not comfortable with their new vehicle which takes some extra space in stores that lack it. Second, handing over the navigation of the store to customers led grocers to quickly understand that the best place for payment was not a reduced counter at the back of the shop but a checkout stand near the exit. The reduced height and the increased storage capacity of the carts of the time (equipped with two baskets, one of them being very close to the ground) created the impetus for the generalization of a new type of furniture—checkout stands with conveyor belts or plates—that worked like a lowered counter, well suited for the unloading of shopping carts.

The cashier's task is no longer to take the products gathered in the shopping process and put them on the counter but to empty the content of a cart filled by the customer. This obliges the cashier to bend down, hence the usefulness of bringing the level of the checkout stand down to that of the cart. Checkout stands were soon equipped with two types of additions. First, they received "tunnels" (1940, May, p. 93; 1948, Apr., p. 72; 1951, Sep., pp. 96–7; 1952, Sep., pp. 78–9) or "rails" (1940, Oct., p. 98; 1941, Jan., p. 46; 1948, Dec., p. 63; 1956, Mar., p. 130; 1956, May, p. 114) in order to ensure a tidy return of the carts (Cochoy 2009). Second, they were supplemented with conveyor belts (1950, Oct., pp. 220–1) or rotary discs (1953, Feb., p. 179) in order to better cope with the growing flow of merchandise.

Now, the use of one or several checkout stands, and their location near the exit, seemed to make turnstiles redundant, especially in very small grocery stores. Indeed, these checkout stands provided the person who operated them with a site from which she could observe the incoming flow of customers and efficiently control the exits. Moreover, they allowed cashiers to perform these operations of observation and control more discreetly. The implementation of checkout stands is thus a third reason which calls for the removal of turnstiles—as the grocer who decided to remove the turnstile puts it: "Both entrances are right by the checkout counters. The checkers can see anybody trying to use them for an exit [...] What other reason is there for having a turnstile?" (1947, Jul., p. 59).

We thus see how a modification of the technical system of the grocery store brings about a spate of mutations of other elements: the introduction of the shopping cart conditions the move from open-display to self-service. Therefore, it provokes the transformation of technologies attached to each form of selling: the counter disappears with the introduction of the checkout stands and with the presence of the checkout stands the turnstile becomes a hindrance and loses its usefulness. Meanwhile, the magic door proves to be advantageous: it discreetly reinforces control while letting customers exit with their arms full of bags—bags whose number and volume tend to rise with the spread of shopping carts. Additionally, through the continuous combination and reconfiguration of these innovations and the corresponding selling system, we observe a complete transformation of the movements of the customer, who becomes both more mobile and more autonomous.

Discussion

All in all, what or who "moved," and "moved *in*," the grocery business of America from the 1930s to the 1950s? The consumer or the environment? Both shows *Progressive Grocer*. If consumers moved, and moved otherwise, it is clear that something made them move the way they did. They did not move alone, either: grocery technologies, grocers' strategies, and ordinary consumers supported one another in order to move together and differently.

The advent of self-service does not rely on the removal of obstacles in the hope of providing an open and fertile ground for the outburst of choice, as suggested by the "laissez-faire" ideology. Paradoxically, self-service rests on the displacement and renewal of borders along a pragmatic view of "faire laissez-faire" aimed at channeling practices in specific ways. Contrary to the tradition which emphasizes that the modernization of the marketplace means "more choice," it seems that the idea of self-service masks a different kind of control.[9] Inside their narrow walls—inside their "marketing laboratories"— the promoters of a modernist grocery store thus succeeded in ceaselessly reconfiguring the borders in ways that increased revenue. They also introduced more discreet orders such as adjustable shelves aimed at softly separating the products as well as cellophane and cans aimed at replacing the old border of the counter. The modernizers of grocery stores even played with the external boundaries of the store by implementing turnstiles and magic doors that proved capable of easing and controlling the movements of customers in a single gesture. Furthermore, they did not forget to introduce mobile places and partitions, like the shopping cart, which increased the mobility of customers and opened up the range of their purchases. This endeavor, which was first aimed at protecting small independent grocery stores, became so successful that the narrow and fixed walls of family groceries became too cramped for the flow of goods and customers they brought in. With time, the *Progressive Grocer* showed an interest in grocery stores that became superettes, then in superettes that became supermarkets, and so on. It thus focused on the delocalization of some businesses motivated by these transformations: the abandonment of "mainstreet" for more comfortable and advantageous locations (1931, Feb., pp. 14–15), which was quite unusual in the 1930s, became an important theme in the 1950s (1952, Jan., pp. 58, 60; 1953, Aug., pp. 48–52; 1955, Feb., 142 sq.). Small, independent grocers and their "enlightened" representatives partially joined the model of larger supermarkets, as it is often assumed in the literature on retailing history. But instead of being absorbed by a model imposed from the outside the *Progressive Grocer* conveyed a voluntary, inventive, and intensive move of modernization from "inside marketing." The transformation of grocery stores may well have contributed to setting up the attributes of the supermarkets that came after them.

Conclusion

The great paradox of this historical account is that it is possible to describe the evolution of grocery stores without focusing on the consumers, who are, after all, the store's "raison d'être," or on the grocers, who are supposed to control everything. In my account, there was nothing cognitive, nothing cultural, nothing "social"—if by social we mean embodied behaviors, norms, and values. However, there was a lot of "social" in this story—if by social we mean "association," "articulation," and "connection" between all kinds of entities (Latour 2005) such as marketers, consumers, and, in this particular case, objects.

If the analogy was not too provocative, I could say that the lesson of the *Progressive Grocer* case is very close to a Chinese proverb dear to Bruno Latour: "When the sage points at the Moon [...], the fool looks at his fingertip" (Latour 1999: 286). To paraphrase this proverb, one may take a risk and say: When a consumer or a marketer points to market-things, the analyst looks at the actor. But would it not be wiser to look at what the actor looks at? If the consumer or the grocer points at a package or at a shelf, it is indeed interesting to consider the package and the shelf in their own right. As we can see, such equipment heavily contributes to defining who the actors are and what they do.

Of course, and as suggested above, the transposition of the Chinese proverb to the case of the grocery store is too crass. On the one hand, a person's concept of what the moon is largely depends on her mental image of it. But on the other hand, this image is nevertheless heavily connected to the moon. Social meaning and social agency are thus both distributed between people and things. So if we want to fully understand consumption, we need to study marketers, consumers, and market-things at the same time. As consumer researchers have taught us convincingly for forty years now, consumer behavior is obviously a matter of consumer anthropology, psychology, sociology, and so on. But as the *Progressive Grocer* case shows, it is also a matter of logistics, technology, and "marketing hydraulics," so to speak. In fact, focusing on market-things is a good way of reconciling the two approaches, since such market-things are aimed precisely at linking people and objects, products, marketers, and consumers. As a consequence, and surprisingly, a study of "market-things" shows that sometimes a relevant study of the actors of marketing can be conducted without studying the actors directly.

Acknowledgments

This study is the result of a research mission to the University of California at Berkeley, which took place from July 14 to August 8, 2006. I thank Catherine Grandclément for the idea and the Education Abroad Program for funding the research. I am also very grateful to Jutta Wiemhoff, Martha Lucero (NRLF), Steve Mendoza (main library), and three other anonymous librarians of the Business/Economics Library and Environmental Design Library at Berkeley. I am indebted to David Vogel for his support, the Haas School of Business for its material help, Carmen Tapia for her administrative assistance, and Josephine Cocuzza and Nielsen Business Media, Inc. for granting me permission to reproduce the pictures this chapter rests upon. I also benefited from the material and intellectual support of the School of Business, Economics and Law of the University of Gothenburg while writing this chapter. I warmly thank Julien Cayla, Claire Leymonerie, Patricia Sunderland, and Detlev Zwick for their remarks and suggestions. The present chapter is an updated and adapted version of a paper previously published in the French journal *Espaces et Sociétés (Cochoy 2008b)*.

Notes

1. The fact that the leading journal in the field is called *Journal of Consumer Research* is telling. The creation of *Consumption, Markets and Cultures* was a reaction to this focus on consumers, even if "Markets" in the broad sense is still trapped between "Consumption" and "Cultures."
2. Morris Holbrook said exactly the same as early as 1984: "In my view, [the business system] differs from other types of system by virtue of the fact that a business always involves inter-relations between managers and customers or consumers. So, if we want to understand business, we had better study *both* managers *and* customers" (Holbrook 1984: 177). However, and to my knowledge, this visionary suggestion has received little attention since it was formulated. The present book, in drawing on many previous initiatives, in gathering some works looking "inside marketing" (often from its outside!) is an important contribution to this effort aimed at building a "marketer research."
3. Actor network-theory assumes that large spheres like "the market" or "society" should not be considered as the causes, but rather as the consequences of social behaviors (Latour 2005). Moreover, by "social behavior," this theory does not

mean "human behavior" only, but rather all the processes engaged in the *association* of a wide array of human (e.g., consumers, marketers, retailers, advertisers, regulators...) and non-human resources (e.g., money, management theories, shopping carts, shelves, and so on). These resources are combined into an "actor-network," that is, a hybrid collective where agency is distributed among all the involved entities. In such a network, some actors (e.g., marketers and retailers) attempt to control the others (e.g., consumers) by means of arguments, tools, ideologies, devices, and so on, in an effort to stabilize the network along some given objectives (e.g., increasing sales and profits in the marketing case) (Callon 1986). But the resources and the targets of manipulation often act in their own way and take some unexpected directions; they even may try to gain their own control over the situation. For further references about the relevancy of actor-network theory for the understanding of business issues, see Araujo et al. (2008) and Woolgar et al. (2009).

4. In his famous novel *Ladies' Delight*, Zola stages the mutant department store of the modernist entrepreneur Mouret, while relegating to the backstage of history the immutable ancient store of the poor Baudu, who seals his death by saying: "Since almost a century now, the Vieil Elbeuf is well-known, and it does not need to have such trickery [like the department store Le Bon Marché] at its door. As long as I'll live, the shop will remain like I took it, with its four pieces of swatch, on the right and on the left, no more!" (Zola, Émile, *Ladies' Delight*, my translation).

5. See, for example, the various studies on how retailing professionals implemented self-service in the American, English, and Swedish cases: Rachel Bowlby (2001), Paul du Gay (2006), and Hans Kjellberg and Claes-Fredrik Helgesson (2007), respectively.

6. This term, borrowed from Callon (2005), has the great advantage of pointing at the links between agencies (be they human or non-human) and arrangements (social, technical, organizational), which enable action. For an excellent presentation of the concept and its interest for economic sociology, see McFall (2008).

7. This illustration is not borrowed from *Progressive Grocer* but from a book written by its main editor, Carl Dipman, and published by the journal as a kind of special edition.

8. Cardboard boxes combine the properties of cellophane and cans, since they borrow from the former a kind of softness and from the latter their opacity.

9. I thank Julien Cayla for suggesting this idea.

References

Araujo, L., Kjellberg H., and Spencer, R. (2008) "Market Practices and Forms: Introduction to the Special Issue." *Marketing Theory*, 8(1): 5–14.

Arnould, E.J. and Thompson, C.J. (2005) "Consumer Culture Theory (CCT): Twenty Years of Research." *Journal of Consumer Research*, 31(4): 868–82.

Belk, R.W. (1988) "Possessions and the Extended Self." *Journal of Consumer Research*, 15(2): 139–68.

Bowlby, R. (2001) *Carried Away: The Invention of Modern Shopping*. New York: Columbia University Press.

Brown, M., and Philips, P. (1985) "The Evolution of Labor Market Structure: The California Canning Industry." *Industrial and Labor Relations Review*, 38(3) (April): 392–407.

Callon, M. (1986) "Some Elements of a Sociology of Translation: Domestication of the Scallops and the Fishermen of St. Brieuc's Bay." In J. Law, ed. *Power, Action and Belief: A New Sociology of Knowledge?* London: Routledge & Kegan Paul, pp. 196–229.

——(2005) "Why Virtualism Paves the Way to Political Impotence: A Reply to Daniel Miller's Critique of *The Laws of the Markets*." *Economic Sociology: European Electronic Newsletter*, 6(2) (February): 3–20 (available online at http://econsoc.mpifg.de/archive/esfeb05.pdf).

——Millo, Y., and Muniesa, F. (eds.) (2007) *Market Devices*. Oxford: Blackwell.

Cochoy, F. (1998) "Another Discipline for the Market Economy: Marketing as a Performative Knowledge and Know-How for Capitalism." In Michel Callon, ed. *The Laws of the Markets*, Oxford: Blackwell, pp. 194–221.

——(2004) "Is the Modern Consumer a Buridan's Donkey? Product Packaging and Consumer Choice." In K. Ekström and H. Brembeck, eds. *Elusive Consumption*. Oxford and New York: Berg Publisher, pp. 205–27.

——(2007) "A Sociology of Market things: On Tending the Garden of Choices in Mass Retailing." In Callon et al. eds. *Market Devices*. Oxford: Blackwell, pp. 109–29.

——(2008a) "Calculation, Qualculation, Calqulation: Shopping Cart's Arithmetic, Equipped Cognition and Clustered Consumers." *Marketing Theory*, special issue on Markets Forms and Marketing Practices, 8(1): 15–44.

——(2008b) "Progressive Grocer, ou la 'petite distribution' en movement. États-Unis (1929–1959)." *Espaces et Sociétés*, 135(4): 25–44.

——(2009) "Driving a Shopping Cart from STS to Business, and the Other Way Round: On the Introduction of Shopping Carts in American Grocery Stores (1936–1959)." *Organization*, 16(1): 31–55.

Deutsch, T.A. (2001) *Making Change at the Grocery Store: Government, Grocers, and the Problem of Women's Autonomy in the Creation of Chicago's Supermarkets, 1920–1950*. University of Wisconsin-Madison.

Dipman, C.W. (1935) *The Modern Grocery Store*. New York, NY: The Progressive Grocer.

du Gay, P. (2006) "Le libre-service. La distribution, les courses et les personnes." *Réseaux*, 24(135–6): 33–58.

Glad, P.W. (1966) "Progressives and the Business Culture of the 1920s." *The Journal of American History*, 53(1) (June): 75–89.

Grandclément, C. (2006) "Wheeling Food Products around the Store . . . and Away: The Invention of the Shopping Cart, 1936–1953." Food Chains Conference: Provisioning, Technology, and Science, Hagley Museum and Library, Wilmington, Delaware, November 2–4.

Haas, H.M. (1979) *Social and Economic Aspects of the Chain Store Movement*. New York: Arno Press.

Hagberg, J. (2010) "Exchanging Agencies: The Case of NetOnNet." In L. Araujo and H. Kjellberg, eds. *Reconnecting Marketing to Markets: Practice-based Approaches*. Oxford: Oxford University Press.

Hansson, L. (2007) "The Power of Design—Allies Fighting Design Exclusion." In H. Brembeck, K.M. Ekström, and M. Mörck, eds., *Little Monsters, (De)coupling Assemblages of Consumption*. Berlin: Lit Verlag, pp. 15–28.

Holbrook, M.B. (1984) "Belk, Granzin, Bristor, and the Three Bears." In P.F. Anderson and M.J. Ryan, eds. *Scientific Method in Marketing*, 1984 AMA Winter Educators' Conference, Chicago, IL: American Marketing Association, pp. 177–8.

——and Hirschman, Elizabeth C. (1982) "The Experiential Aspects of Consumption: Consumer Fantasies, Feelings, and Fun." *Journal of Consumer Research*, 9 (September): 132–40.

Kjellberg, H., and Helgesson, C.-F. (2007) "The Mode of Exchange and the Shaping of Markets: Distributor Influence in the Swedish Post-war Food Industry." *Industrial Marketing Management*, 36(7) 861–78.

Latour B. [Johnson J.] (1988) "Mixing Humans with Non-Humans: Sociology of a Door-Closer." *Social Problems*, 35(3): 298–310.

——(1999) *Pandora's Hope: Essays on the Reality of Science Studies*. Cambridge, MA; London, UK: Harvard University Press.

——(2005) *Reassembling the Social: An Introduction to Actor-Network Theory*. Oxford: Oxford University Press.

Longstreth, R.W. (1999) *The Drive-in, the Supermarket, and the Transformation of Commercial Space in Los Angeles, 1914–1941*. Cambridge, MA: MIT Press.

——(2000) *The Buildings of Main Street: A Guide to American Commercial Architecture*. Walnut Creek, CA: AltaMira Press.

McFall, L. (2009) "Devices and Desires: How Useful is the New Economic Sociology of Market Attachment?" *Sociology Compass* 3(2): 267–82.

Molotch, H., and McClain, N. (2008) "Things at Work: Informal Social-Material Mechanisms for Getting the Job Done." *Journal of Consumer Culture*, 8(1): 35–67.

Monod, D. (1996) *Store Wars: Shopkeepers and the Culture of Mass Marketing, 1890–1939*, Toronto: University of Toronto Press.

Seth, A. (2001) *The Grocers: The Rise and Rise of the Supermarket Chains*. Dover, NH: Kogan Page.

Sherry, J. (2004) "Culture, Consumption and Marketing: Retrospect and Prospect." In K. Ekström and H. Brembeck, eds. *Elusive Consumption*. Oxford and New York: Berg Publisher, pp. 45–64.

Strasser, S. (1989) *Satisfaction Guaranteed: The Making of the American Mass Market*. New York: Pantheon Books.

Wells, W.D. (1991) "Preface." In R.W. Belk, ed. *Highways and Buyways: Naturalistic Research from the Consumer Behavior Odyssey*. Provo, UT: Association for Consumer Research, i–iii.

Woolgar, S., Coopmans, C., and Neyland, D. (2009) "Does STS Mean Business?" *Organization*, 16(5): 5–30.

Worthington, W. Jr. (1989) "Early Risers." *American Heritage of Invention and Technology*, 4(3) (Winter): 40–4.

Part II
Marketing as Performance: Tools and Devices

4

Convoking the Consumer in Person: The Focus Group Effect

Catherine Grandclément and Gérald Gaglio

Introduction

For more than fifty years, the legitimacy of marketing in the world of business has been grounded in the capacity to orient production toward the desires of consumers while simultaneously fulfilling a profitability constraint. Such is the power of the marketing concept, the cornerstone of the profession, which places the consumer at the center of an organization's production activities (McKitterick, 1957; Hirschman, 1983; Cochoy, 1999). One implication of such a consumer orientation has been the development of a whole body of knowledge about consumers giving birth to an entirely new branch of academic research: consumer research. In the business world, this knowledge about consumers and the corresponding ability to appropriate consumers' point of view and share their universe are considered mandatory for marketers. Consumer knowledge involves more than the mere use of socio-economic descriptors. It is the ability of marketers to "step into consumers" shoes[1] to create an intimate familiarity with them, the kind of intimacy that is a product only of repeated and meaningful interactions. How is this closeness obtained? How can marketers become intimate with mobile, elusive, uncertain creatures like consumers?

Conducting focus groups remains the most common way by which marketers build that intimate understanding of the consumer. The technique occupies a place of quasi-absolute supremacy among qualitative methods in market research. For getting acquainted with consumers and evaluating whether or not a brand name, product, or advertisement will suit their tastes, the focus group is often the ultimate answer of the market research industry, an answer often expected and eagerly agreed upon by clients desiring to consult the consumer in a reliable, expeditious, and safe manner—not to mention their desire to maintain control over the process.[2] Although regional variations remain,[3] focus groups have become a real industry, with rules and routines ensuring that the daily flow of communication between market researchers who run focus groups and the marketing professionals who commission them proceeds easily.[4]

One reason why the focus group is so revered is that it provides marketers with the unique opportunity to observe their consumers "in the flesh" while enjoying the privacy of the facility's back room. Focus groups also help marketers grasp the very interiority of consumers through projective techniques that are meant to provide access to the participants' inner selves. For marketers to gain their core expertise and to exert their professional competencies means to commission and periodically attend an endless series of encounters with "real consumers" through the two-way mirror of the focus group facility. The very absurdity of an encounter that is characterized by prevention of interaction by way of a physical obstacle, namely the obscured or mirrored window, sheds a telling light on the paradoxical "reality effect" of the device of the focus group, which we will explore in the present chapter.

As a research method, the focus group is at odds with the ethnographic and in-depth methods praised for naturalistic inquiry in consumer research (Belk, 1991). A typical focus group session consists of putting inside a room eight strangers and asking them bizarre if not nonsensical questions like: "if Allianz (the insurance company) was a meal, what meal would it be?" or "notwithstanding the price, would you buy that service?" Soon after the end of the focus group, statements in the form of "how consumers see" things begin to circulate. Not only is this highly artificial and constrained discourse taken as genuine evidence of the true opinion of people in the room, but these people are also endowed with the capacity of "consumers." In our view, however, an individual is hardly ever a consumer, at least not substantially. Among "worker," "citizen," "parent," "militant," "voter," "victim," or "member" of a church, political party, or any other group, "consumer" is one of the many identities—or rather positions—that an individual can momentarily endorse depending on the socio-technical network he is inserted in (Akrich, 1992, 1995). The possibility to nevertheless convoke the consumer in the isolated room of a focus group facility is the result of the cumulated work of social scientists (most prominently psychologists, sociologists, and marketing researchers) who have sought over years to chart the territory of consumers from their minds to their practices. In doing so, they have developed further the socio-technical network that makes up the consumer (Rose, 1996; Miller and Rose, 1997; Callon, 2007a, 2007b, 2008). Marketing practitioners inherit from but also contribute to this endeavor in producing their own description of the consumer of which focus groups exhibit specimens—individuals endowed with a potent imaginary who feel more than they think—thus advancing further the construction of the consumer.

The objective of this chapter is to analyze the construction of this encounter between marketers and consumers in the focus group setting. We will extend our inquiry beyond the single moment of the focus group session itself to analyze the preparatory phases that make it possible. We will thus show that this encounter brings with it a series of very choreographed, routinized processes that permit physically "convoking" the consumer in the focus group facility and endowing her or him with a character, specific features, and expressive qualities. Our approach considers the focus group within the wider context of the market research process itself, a process without which the consumer could not be convoked in the first place. In not limiting ourselves to the very moment of the focus group as such, but rather extending our analysis to the process that precedes it, we show how the consumer is framed in such a way as to allow marketers to "recognize" him or her while attending a focus group.

Our approach positions itself within two recent and convergent bodies of literature: the ethnography of marketing and the sociology of markets. First and foremost, our research contributes to the emerging trend of research that examines marketing practices from an ethnographic or near-ethnographic viewpoint (Cayla, 2002; Barrey, 2006; Gaglio, 2007 and 2010; Araujo et al., 2008; Simakova and Neyland, 2008; and the present volume). In a move quite similar to that of the social studies of science about thirty years ago (Latour, 1987), this new trend of research has broken away from grand interpretive schemes about marketing and consumer society, as well as from normative statements about how marketing ought to be done. Although radically opposed in their appreciation of marketing, both grand schemes and normative efforts rejoin in their lack of factual attention to actual marketing *practice*. Instead, ethnographers and sociologists of marketing focus on the everyday practices of marketing as they unfold. Researchers thus go into advertising agencies, marketing departments of various organizations, and marketing consultancy offices to report at length the everyday activities of workers in order to study "marketing in action." Our approach is also connected to another stream of research centered on the study of empirical markets and their relationship with market theories (Callon, 1998; MacKenzie et al., 2007). Drawing extensively on innovation studies, the sociology of markets has shown the ubiquity of the schematic personage of the consumer in the everyday activities of marketing professionals (Cochoy and Dubuisson-Quellier, 2000; Callon et al., 2002). This stream of research explores how consumers are personified differently across the different nodes of an organization (Barrey et al., 2000), making intensive use of a variety of representational techniques (Hennion, 1989; Akrich, 1995; Denis, 2008). On the one hand, these personas are not consolidated into a single unified representation of the consumer for whom the product would be carefully designed (Hennion and Méadel, 1989; Dubuisson-Quellier, 2003). On the other hand, actual users of a product or service are much more diverse than the target and segmentation profiles used to market the product or service (Akrich, 1995). Our contribution follows this path in focusing on one type of representational technique favored by marketers—the focus group—and on the kind of consumer it elicits. Although based on different research material and methodology our work is also very much in line with recent and illuminating inquiries into the inner mechanisms of focus groups (Puchta and Potter, 1999, 2002; Lezaun, 2007). Puchta and Potter use conversation analysis of actual market research focus groups in order to show how focus group talk is produced in practice. Lezaun relies on a careful reading of textbooks to uncover the underlying political epistemology of focus groups. Drawing on our experience as market researchers, we rejoin these authors' analyses, albeit by different means, replacing the conduct of a focus group in its larger framework: that of marketers' and market-researchers' collaborative venture to make the consumer express himself or herself.

The data we use to support our reflection were collected and assembled by the two authors during two parallel stints as participant observers in the market research industry in France. One of the authors draws from her experience as a freelance contractor from 2005 to 2006 and as a senior market researcher in 2007 at Marketocom,[5] a multinational market research company. The other author draws from his experience as a market researcher in 2005 with mobile service provider Telecomob[6] and from a set of twenty-five semi-structured interviews with market researchers and product or project managers conducted in 2007. At our fieldwork sites, focus groups were part of an industrialized production process characterized by time pressures, a large number of research studies, and standardized formatting of results.

We consider our methodological standpoint to be that of observing participation rather than participant observation; not only were we deeply immersed in lengthy fieldwork where participation was often more important than observation but the act of observation was a product of genuine engagement with colleagues on a professional basis. Our research was not a covert ethnography, wherein researchers infiltrate a social milieu that is opaque or esoteric to them. Our position within our research sites was one of active professional commitment, motivated by the potential, later use of accumulated experiences, materials, notes, and recollections for social–scientific analysis. In a sense, the idea of observing participation requires replacing the assessment habits of purposeful ethnographic missions (methodological adequacy, informed consent) with that of reflexive examination of one's collectively shared professional experience.[7]

Our argument proceeds chronologically. In the first section, we examine the decision to conduct a qualitative market research study as well as its justification and the rather vague representation of the consumer at this stage of the process. This representation will rapidly be absorbed into a routine process wherein the consumer will have to be defined as the target. In the next section, we observe how research managers prepare for the arrival of and encounter with consumers in the flesh. This requires a precise definition of the identity of the consumers to be met so that suitable respondents can actually be recruited for their participation in the group. Finally, during the focus group itself, an important task is to produce consumer talk, that is, to try and match the way respondents speak with the pre-established persona of the consumer they are supposed to represent. We hypothesize that the back room (behind the two-way mirror) is an important node in the marketer's construction of consumers.

Preparing the Encounter with the Consumer

In this section, we look at the very reasons for meeting the consumer through a qualitative methodology. These reasons are mostly linked to marketers' prior experience with market research. Next, we look at how writing a short outline of the study's layout supposes an initial formulation of the consumers to be interviewed (called targets), which circumscribes the choice of methodology. During these first two phases, marketers have to translate their problems and questions—problems and questions which are always specific and dependent on the situation—into conventional and standardized devices internal to the company, such as the "marketing brief." An interrogation that, at its inception, is either vague or too limited in scope comes to be rapidly absorbed into the routine processes of the market research organization. The ability to successfully align an encounter with the company's research needs and the consumer is highly dependent on these routine processes, implying that the identity of the consumer is specified quite early on in the process.

Motives for launching a qualitative study

One might ask why consumers are brought onto an organization's premises in order to talk about and reflect on (and even provide directions regarding) the organization's internal affairs. One of the first reasons for bringing consumers in, so to speak, can be found in the corporate manuals for market research (Blankenship et al., 1998). The view of qualitative research exhibited in these manuals is very formal, presenting it as a method for the evaluation of consumer acceptance of a new product or as a way to understand the flaws of an unsuccessful product offer. From the normative and prescriptive point of view found in these marketing textbooks, qualitative methodology comes to be thought of as merely a node within a rational decision-making process. It is used to augment an organization's effectiveness in response to the supposed needs of consumers in order to improve profits and seize market share.

In reality, however, the initiation of a qualitative study is conspicuously linked to a set of rather ambiguous reasons and opportunities, chief among them being that of permitting marketers to appear objective without actually having to defend (or even to make) a decision. Arbitrary judgments are a plausible and perhaps common reality in marketing life, and the effect of objectivity that a standardized methodology provides can serve well the purpose of timely justification. Seasoned marketers we met during our participant observation and in our interviews often tended to downplay the claim that the results of a qualitative study can help an organization to make relevant decisions about a product or service. This, of course, does not mean that the market research process is useless. Some marketers explained that the main reason for them to conduct qualitative studies was to be able to "see consumers," especially since their daily activities (meetings, writing e-mails, and so forth) drew their attention inward and away from the sphere in which their products were consumed. Qualitative studies are often presented by marketers as a way to connect with and gain an understanding of the (reportedly distant) world of the consumer. These research apparatuses can also help in bringing ideas out into the open, fostering dialogue about strategic topics, and pushing agendas forward within the organization, especially when decision-making runs the risk of proving to be uninformed (Courpasson, 2006). The use of focus groups can thus arise from the need to establish rationality as a value (with focus groups as part of a decision-making process that is supported by data), or even as a way to legitimize marketing as a meaningful professional activity (to be a marketer is to be close to consumers, which entails meeting them frequently).

One PowerPoint slideshow used during a training session for marketing interns at Telecomob entitled "Marketing issues and survey design" described "faulty uses" of market research in a very revealing manner. These faulty uses included commissioning a survey in order to justify a decision that had already been made or commissioning a survey out of cowardice to pass on a choice that was to be made by the professional in charge to the vague and distant consumer. Such straightforward instructions do, in our view, evidence that faulty uses occur frequently enough to warrant didactic attention.

At this stage, the clients to whom the qualitative study is addressed (e.g., product managers at Telecomob) do not yet rely on specific consumer profiles. The general idea is that consulting consumers is basically about asking them to express their views—for example, on a new product concept.

The representation of the consumer-to-be-interviewed is relatively vague at this stage. He or she is supposed to act cooperatively inasmuch as, in return for a little economic compensation, he or she will talk about topics of interest to the client, answer unanticipated (sometimes clearly odd) questions, imagine himself or herself in fictional future situations and, of course, show at least a little interest in the themes covered by the study (Gaglio, 2007). At this stage, the characterization of consumers who are suitable for the focus group is not yet a matter of urgency. It is the launch of the study itself which most concerns the protagonists, and getting the study underway is very much at the heart of the action.

Expectations in relation to the study are strongly linked to a preliminary understanding of its potential usefulness as a resource in organizational disputes. We find, on the one hand, marketers who are inexperienced or who pay little attention to studies—either who expect too much of them and think that they will easily obtain the desired results, or who expect little of them and are simply carrying out an order given from above—delegating the studies in their entirety to internal market researchers. On the other hand, we find marketers who are very much "study-based" and who soak them up in order to "speak consumer" within the organization. They carefully monitor the study as it unfolds (screener, discussion guide, focus groups, validation of the final results, and so forth). These marketers use studies to their advantage, often shifting the mechanism into high gear when they have something at the back of their minds—that is, when they want to substantiate an orientation that they already like, albeit discreetly.

Specifying the consumer: the brief

Once the decision has been made to carry out a study, the internal market researcher turns the product manager's concerns into a practical study project. This involves channeling the numerous and sometimes elliptical demands of the marketing team. For example, a marketing manager at Telecomob provided the following message as the sole brief for a study on the mobile Internet: "I want to know what people want for two euros in the "Sport," "News," "Games" and "Music" sections." A precaution at Telecomob, however, consisted in sending a template called the "Marketing study brief" to marketers for them to use in preparing a first draft. A meeting would then be organized with the internal market researcher to translate the language of marketing (the commercial offer) to that of the study (considerations likely to affect consumers) and to complete and improve the brief. The document would be co-written by the internal market researcher and the marketer in order to provide a framework for their relationship. The brief also serves to develop concise specifications for the market research companies who will be competing during the tender process, constituting a basis for their offers. Figure 4.1 shows the brief which resulted from the demand mentioned above.

Before finalization, this document is sent back and forth several times. Its particularity is that it incorporates further details to support an oral request,

---

MARKETING STUDIES BRIEF

DATE: 08-31-2005	REQUESTING DEPT.: Mobile Internet/Services Dept.
	CONTACT(S) NAME(S): XXXX
	DEPARTMENT MANAGER: XXXX

➢ **CONTEXT OF THE STUDY**

The results relating to the mobile Internet offering in terms of unique visitors, levels of subscription to editor services and subscription duration are below objectives. More to the point, subscription duration shows a high level of churn for several portal themes.

This said, the price for a monthly subscription with automatic renewal must now be considered the only one viable for the ecosystem (client-operator-content editor).

➢ **MAIN OBJECTIVES OF THE STUDY**

The objective of this study is to achieve results that enable us to increase the number and length of subscriptions within the mobile Internet offering and help us understand the reasons of the churn (subscription cancellation). To do so we closely examine use of three product areas:

- Downloading of Music and Ring tones
- Games
- News-Sport

The study will therefore have three parts. To achieve the objectives (increase in volume and length of subscriptions, reasons of churn) the study pursues specific questions:

- What are the drivers for purchase and renewal of subscriptions? In other words, what are the reasons for satisfaction and dissatisfaction, which are rarely the same?
- Is the range of product offerings a viable avenue for increasing volume of subscriptions and renewal rates? Sub-questions to explore here:
  - What products do customers expect to find and how does up-selling look like? (e.g. does buying a song for a ring tone lead to buying the full album of a concert ticket?)
  - Do our section titles make sense to customers?
  - Do customers know what they are entitled to under the subscription and how to get the most value from it?
- Do customers expect an ongoing conversation with the service provider? If so, what kind?

What can we learn from previous customer studies?

Customer Awareness Study on subscription lifetimes, Editors management chart, studies on the services of the portal.

➢ TARGET

- People to be surveyed (prospects/ equipped/ pre-paid/ package/ competition/ age/ geographical spread/ SPC)
  - Current subscriber of the products explored / one time buyers / inactive subscriber / switcher (former customer)/ non-customer attracted to mobility services
  - Trendy youngsters, techno-pragmatic, chatty: under 20, 20-30, 30+
  - Recruiting in Paris and in the Paris region
- Specific readings

The questions for each products will be processed independently (Music / Ringtones, Games, News-Sport). The methodology of the study (groups, individual interviews) remains to be decided.

➢ DESIRED DATE FOR FINAL RESULTS

ASAP. Details of the individuals to be recruited nevertheless involves extracting a customer file from Telecomob's databases, which takes a minimum of 3 weeks following the request.

➢ BUDGET

Planned budget: XXXX

Cost centre to be charged to: XXXX

Name of manager: XXXX

Figure 4.1 The marketing brief.

making it more explicit. We note that an effort is made to describe the "context" and to set out the "objectives" in the specific vocabulary of market research professionals. One can measure the difference compared to the first informal request, which was sent by email. The internal market researcher writes the final draft of the document prior to validation by the marketer. In certain cases, marketers might delegate the writing of the draft entirely to the internal market researcher, either due to a lack of experience among more novice marketers or, for more experienced marketers, because confidence has been built up over time.

Certain sections of the forthcoming study nevertheless remain in limbo, as the specifications constituted by the brief are only partial. Indeed, the budget has not been determined and the date for the results to be handed in is "ASAP." Above all, the creation of this document involves fitting it into a preconfigured framework, even though the demands are in fact always circumstantial. It denotes a standardized mechanism for the production of studies but opens up a path between the "consumer in general" and the characteristics of specific individuals to be met. In this respect, one notes the targets listed in the brief (Figure 4.1). First of all, the "trendy youngster," "techno-pragmatic" and "chatty" categories, with details of age and geographical location, are convoked within the study because they are considered relevant to the questions to be asked. These ideal types remind us of the socio-styles which were made popular in France in the 1960s by the CCA (Centre de Communication Avancée, a renowned market research institute in France) and were intended as an alternative to the socio-professional categories used by the INSEE (Institut National de la Statistique et des Etudes Economiques, the French national institute for statistics and economic studies) and to the vision of a social space divided into relatively stable classes. These opened the way for simplification and made it possible to invent denominations by which to characterize groups with evocative ad hoc names that sometimes sound overtly crazy ("the off-the-wallers," "the adventurers," etc.), particularly by referring to marketing trends in fashion at the time. The scientific legitimacy of socio-styles has been heavily criticized (Georgakakis, 1997). Nevertheless, this manner of classifying consumers through reference to segmenting attitudes and lifestyles has spread considerably, to the extent that it now influences several corporate marketing segmentations. It is clearly this flexible (theme-based groups instead of fixed categorical boundaries) and changing (it is updated as required) cartography of consumers that has been inherited by the market researchers and marketers we studied.[8] Marketers can thus characterize publics with such sets of salient traits and turn them, accordingly, into "their consumers."

The segmentation in use at Telecomob during the period of observation was concocted by marketing consultants to meet the needs of a mobile Internet commercial offer. However, this segmentation did not constitute the sole grid of consumer classification in use at Telecomob. The consumer types which are put forward in the brief ("techno-pragmatic," "trendy youngster," "chatty") indeed come from the mobile Internet segmentation. But the more concrete criteria also mentioned in the brief ("switchers," "unique visitors") come from the vernacular, practical consumer categorizations typical of marketing professionals and they need to be integrated into the "official" segmentation format. They will then be transformed into "profiles" that make it possible to recruit flesh-and-blood individuals and bring these categories to life by making them talk, literally. As a matter of fact, in this particular case, it will be easier to find a "techno-pragmatic" who also happens to be a "switcher" than a "techno-pragmatic" only defined by his "techno-pragmatic" quality, which is vaguely defined as having an "attraction to new technologies."

The methodology for the forthcoming study has not yet been decided at this stage, however. It has only been decided that the methodology ought to be qualitative instead of quantitative. The client wanted to get results quickly and then duplicate the study for several sections in the range of services for which he was responsible. The manager also wanted to "involve" the content producers for Telecomob's mobile Internet offer (a sports magazine for the Sport section, a television channel for the News sections, etc.) in these studies. Involvement was meant to include help with the financing of the study, ideas to develop the screener and discussion guide, and attendance of the focus groups. His underlying aim was "to make them aware of the problems with the mobile Internet offer." We observe that the ideation of the study is less directly motivated by a desire to know what consumers want (or may want) than by a determination to signal to the marketer's partners (the content editors, in this case) the problems posed by the construction of the commercial offer. In a sense, this veteran marketer, who was deeply acquainted with these types of methodologies and their effects, was almost able to predict how focus group participants might react in one configuration or another—to predict or indeed to frame in accordance with the configuration that he was pushing for.

We identified in our ethnography a marked preference for focus groups over one-on-one interviews within the overall domain of qualitative methods. This tendency stems in part from the plasticity of group interviews, which can meet different objectives (e.g., testing a new product or establishing a brand diagnosis) and which can be run in different ways (creativity, confrontation groups, and so forth). But the generalized resort to focus groups is also the result of an economic rationalization of the manufacture of the consumer's voice and of its processing, something which finds favor with both clients and market research companies. It is indeed less costly in terms of both time and energy to organize a few roundtables with consumers than to ask one or more market researchers to carry out a dozen one-on-one interviews. Furthermore, each focus group requires an audio recording lasting approximately three hours, whereas an individual interview takes roughly one hour. Transcription and analysis are more rapid, especially as clients do not expect detailed reporting. What they require above all is to be handed the results as quickly as possible. Highly industrialized division of labor allows market research companies to hand over the final results of a qualitative study involving four to six groups within about six weeks of the date on which the client accepts the quotation. The preference for focus groups also certainly has to do with the very lively experience of enacting a close encounter with flesh-and-blood consumers, watching them talk "naturally" from behind the two-way mirror.

Introducing the Consumer in Person

Let us shift now to the market research company's side of the fence. When a market research company gets a request for a study from a client, a set of routines is triggered that includes, in particular, "recruiting" focus group participants (a field in which a myriad of small companies specialize), thus ensuring the conversion of the consumer as imagined on paper into a flesh-and-blood person who is expected to act as a valid surrogate. Such a process partakes of the commercialization of response to surveys and, by extension, of the commercialization of the consumer's persona, which has become a mass-produced ware of the market research industry.

Fixing consumer persona

When a request for a study was received from a future client at Marketocom, attention was essentially focused upon three elements: the targets, the methodology to be used, and the timetable. The choice of targets is very much at the heart of the study mechanism of the consumer encounter. Even when a client's brief included the targets' specifications, market researchers at Marketocom proposed alternative or additional targets as a means to appropriate the study and challenge the client (arouse its interest). During our fieldwork, targets often appeared as stereotypes: "trend-setters," "charentaises,"[9] "switchers" (those who have ceased to use a service), "intentionists" (those who intend to buy), "technophiles," "technophobes," "experienced users," and so forth. These stereotypes are common knowledge within the market research milieu, neither formalized (there is no ready-made "catalog" of consumers' profiles) nor made explicit in Marketocom's study proposal (except for "novice" marketers who are unfamiliar with these stereotypes). More empirically grounded elements are sometimes added to describe the targets (taken from quantitative studies or from the company's current segmentation criteria). Generally speaking, these consumer types are in fact types needed for the study, that is, ad hoc personas—relevant to the questions asked, as stated earlier—which only last as long as the study itself. The aim here is to characterize the consumer's persona for the purposes of the study, defining the salient traits of the supposed identity of the consumer who must then appear with these same traits in the focus group room.

In contrast, to leave the consumer type undetermined is to threaten the success of the study. Respondents who are too different, too idiosyncratic, or who lack the salient characteristics which ought to attune them to the commercial offer being tested will most likely hamper the production of a credible consumer opinion. At Marketocom, one brief for a study on an energy-saving home-automation service stated that the targets for the study remained "to be determined." On the phone, the client systematically avoided the study director's requests that the type of interviewee be made explicit. "It's Mr. and Mrs. Joe Bloggs who run a household and who are careful with their electricity bills," said the client, repeating this several times and even talking about "Mr. and Mrs. Michu."[10] Irritated by this uncooperative and evidently novice client, the study director then gave instructions on how to write the study proposal regarding targets:

> So, the targets. . . . We are doing an interface test, so we remove skilled people, which means experienced Internet users. And then, well, then we remove all the extremes, we eliminate novices and web professionals, extreme incomes, we take average socio-professional categories, average age, pffff. . . . Well, okay, what about targeting 35–50 years-old, essentially home-owners? Couples, with and without children. All of them concerned by energy saving, not against the principle of remote management of household appliances.

Faced with the client's refusal to choose consumer types, it is an "average consumer" who will be used by the researchers. This idea of an average consumer, which makes the study director sigh because it relates to nothing in particular, nevertheless ends up being defined, as we see above, by a fairly long list of criteria. Yet this list of criteria does not characterize respondents with a consumer profile because nothing is truly discriminatory: "everyone is careful with their electricity bills" and "everyone is concerned by saving energy," says the study director. From these untargeted respondents (in the sense that they are "non-typified," or not characterized by any salient trait), the study director thus expects "woolly," "disinterested" responses from individuals who "don't care" and who "will say yes, whatever" to everything because they simply feel "not concerned." It will consequently be very difficult to produce a consumer's persona from them during the course of the focus group.

As far as professionals familiar with qualitative studies are concerned, there is no doubt that target characterization is a vital step. It allows them to ensure that they are going to meet the right people, the "real consumers." Such is the paradox: that, to meet "real consumers," one has to invent them (by typifying them). The more specific marketing professionals are about the types of consumers they wish to meet—which involves making strong hypotheses about their identity—the more likely it is that they will in effect meet "the consumer" and not just see some random assortment of nonchalant guys in a focus group facility. Carried out by market researchers both from inside the client company and from the market research company, the work of defining targets constitutes an extremely crucial consumer-framing operation, an operation through which the consumer can be given a concrete form. It is through this work that one moves from invoking the consumer as a distant entity to convoking flesh-and-blood individuals who will represent specific consumer profiles.

Ordering consumers: the logistics of recruitment

As soon as the client has agreed to go ahead with the study, field development falls under the responsibility of project managers who take charge of the planning, catering, travel, reservation of rooms, recruiting of respondents, and incentives. In order for the right respondents to come to the right place at the right time, project managers work with companies specializing in consumer recruitment.[11] This is where the list of criteria such as the one mentioned above for Mr. and Mrs. Joe Bloggs is important, because this is what will allow project managers to develop the screener, a questionnaire for the selection of participants. As with target definition, writing the screener does not involve reaching into a ready-made catalog of consumer types. Project managers rely on their experience and take inspiration from other screeners in previous studies, but also improvise, imagining for example which criteria might adequately portray the "advanced mass-market customer" in banking and meditating on how many banks one must be a client of in order to qualify as "dynamic," bank-wise. Some characteristics of the desired consumer persona add up during the screener-writing phase of the study process. At the end of the questionnaire, for instance, a sort of an impressionistic question that is unrelated to the topic at stake is asked: "If tomorrow you were to win millions of euros in the lottery, thus allowing you to take your dream holiday, what type of holiday would you choose given that money would be no object?" This is to assess the person's capacities for verbalization and imagination, which are qualities required for focus groups.

The screener is then forwarded to the recruiting company. Questionnaires are passed to potential respondents picked from the recruitment company's own pool or from a file provided by the client. Appointments are made with the individuals who match the requirements put forward throughout the process. An entire industry thus exists to make consumers available for interrogation that is meaningful to marketing. The massive process of consumer framing which took place during the target definition phase is fed into a standardized system for respondent ordering. The list of criteria on which the screener is based is often referred to by market researchers and study directors as the "recruiting order." Consumers become tradable. It is possible to order some of them in the same way that one orders meal trays, meeting rooms, and the other raw materials needed for a study. This process of commodification of respondents' performance is partially responsible for the emergence of what is often referred to as "professional consumers" in market research parlance: people who regularly propose their services as consumer representations. They are market researchers' pet hate on the grounds that their repeated experience translates into a lack candor.[12] They are also overtly suspected of cheating in order to be enrolled in the study. Such professional respondents could actually be blacklisted at Marketocom. One, for instance, reportedly presented himself as driving a Peugeot one month and a Renault the next month when, in reality, he did not have experience with either brand. Market research companies have introduced control procedures, such as asking respondents to show their car registration papers prior to access to the focus group room and maintaining up-to-date databases on respondents. Recalcitrant professional consumers often try to counter these control procedures with even greater professionalism, playing for instance on all possible versions of their names (maiden or married, as well as variations in spelling) and contact details (different telephone numbers) in order to cloud the issue.

Seeing the Consumer behind the Mirror

After everything has been carefully put into place comes the realization of the focus group itself. In this section we examine how the practice of the focus group achieves two crucial effects: bringing the persona of the consumer to life in front of the clients, and providing marketers with an experience of acquaintance with it.

The discussion guide as script

Marketing has in a sense followed in the footsteps of the social sciences. It now characterizes individuals in terms of the diversity and mobility of their facets; the idea of the "ever-changing consumer" is widespread and echoed in the notion of the hyper-segmentation of the marketplace (Corstjens and Corstjens, 1995). But focus groups seem to follow a rather opposed path. They rely most centrally on presenting individuals who remain entirely faithful to their identities: they may be "achievers," "successful," or "technophiles," for instance, and they are those things in an exclusive and unambiguous manner. In this sense, this is what focus groups actually "focus" upon: maintaining profiles that must be meaningful and recognizable in relation to the ideas put forward by the marketer regarding what a consumer opinion or a consumer perception could be.

How is the "achiever" brought in front of the marketer when respondents, although selected, are only recruited in relation to a small number of relatively general criteria? The achiever came in as a target at Marketocom in the context of an international segmentation study for a finance and insurance company. The description of this category was: young adults (25–35 years old) who were ambitious, with career prospects, motivated by money, and attentive to their personal finances. Although these criteria can indeed provide a meaningful representation of a person, the truth is that different people meeting them can (and most likely do) think and behave in totally different ways. It is the configuration of the focus group device which nevertheless makes it possible to present consumers who correspond to the envisioned targets. The traits that caused respondents to be recruited thus need be brought to the fore throughout the practice of the focus group.

Here, the discussion guide plays a crucial role. As its name suggests, this document is intended to help steer the discussion toward particular topics and toward a particular form.[13] The achievers study took place in the context of a brand repositioning. Consultants who were advising Marketocom's clients were selling the idea that the relationship between the brand and its consumers had always been approached in terms of trust and promise, but now it was about keeping these promises and shifting the terms to acts and evidence. As a consequence, Marketocom's focus groups needed to make consumers appear highly critical of finance and insurance companies, and worried because they had not obtained what they were expecting. Participants could subsequently be asked to imagine the types of concrete evidence that three prospective brands might provide in order to build their relationship with their customers. The discussion guide included a whole series of directions (in a form similar to that of stage directions) to ensure that the moderator would stress negative aspects:

> Focus on the main negative images and preconceptions [...]. Presentation of the concepts must be based as much as possible on what participants have previously said. Especially, introduce this part of the group with a recap of participants' perceptions and expectations. "You have told us (repeat what they have said: that the customer doesn't feel like he is well-treated or taken care of; that customers don't know what they are buying, etc.)." (Instructions in the discussion guide)

This framing clearly favors the idea that respondents are indeed highly negative, perceive themselves to be poorly considered, and ignore the technicalities of the products they bought. The discussion guide constitutes a sort of scenario, a "script" (Akrich, 1992) which in this case serves to produce a critical consumer. This theatrical dimension became even clearer when the moderators were briefed at Marketocom; it was about "rehearsing" the right way to orient the focus group. Examples were given of expected responses to each question, with moderators being frequently reminded of the purpose of the study, so that they had a clear idea of what they were looking for and what they wanted the respondents to talk about. Here is an example of the types of comments about the discussion guide that were provided to moderators by a Marketocom research executive during one of these briefings:

> *How do I feel in this universe? What words, adjectives, images, feelings?* They will answer things like: complicated, uncertain, competition, security, small print. You write it down on the paper board and then you can say something like: "There are many negative things in all this. *Are they valid critiques or are they only preconceptions?*" They will say yes, of course, that these are valid critiques, that they have had terrible experiences with insurance companies. So you go on with: "Could you tell me about these bad experiences you have encountered?" You let one person tell her story. Remember that our client wants proof, evidence, he wants concrete details. So we want the respondent to explain what happened to him. After each experience, you ask the others if they have had similar experiences. This is so we know if it is the general case or if it is infrequent. And then you ask for other types of bad experiences. And you go on like that for approximately ten minutes. (Italicized questions are as they are written in the discussion guide)

During the briefing, the scenario configured by the discussion guide is staged for the first time. This was a multi-country study, which throws up many additional difficulties. For example, local moderators in Germany were being briefed in English by a French research executive. Hence, the "rehearsal" was also a test of the ability of everyone involved to cope and communicate with each other despite the low level of mastery of the English language displayed by most. One of the implicit rules in such situations was for the "briefed" moderator to rephrase what the "briefer" had said in order to make sure that the message had been properly understood. Short scenarios for responses to each of the questions were thus elaborated during the briefing phase.

Moderators become ready to select and highlight certain responses in order to give critical coloring to what the group says. They also use a whole series of standard moderation techniques in order to guide what is said and thus obtain a series of speech excerpts (later to be reported verbatim) which "arrive" in the desired manner. For example, when participants are expected to reply with a single word, as in the first part of the above exercise, moderators will generally repeat and sometimes rephrase what participants say so as to train them to answer with a single word.

The scenario is not only a useful device for organizing the relationship with respondents; it is a key element in handling relations with clients. The discussion guide is agreed upon with them. Market researchers explain to the client how the devised series of questions meets the "study objectives," objectives which were themselves a careful translation of the expectations, which the client voiced during the study's preparatory meetings with Marketocom's market researchers. In the empirical example considered here, the group went as planned, in line with the scenario that was agreed upon by the parties. The client was provided with the feeling of having seen and heard relevant consumers answer the right questions—his own. These questions were defined and stabilized upstream when agreement on the moderation guide was reached.[14] This agreement activated a process of recognition of the elements looked for in the focus group event. In other words, the preparation of the study constitutes at the same time a period of preparation of the client, who becomes more accepting of preconfigured information.

The focus group as performance

The sanction for the moderator's success or failure in making the consumer's voice heard is immediate: clients, located in the back room, assess the *performance* of the group and of the respondents that they are observing. They will state that they have seen "a good group" or, alternately, that the session "was limp." The running of a focus group comes across as a performance in two senses of the word: as a staged play and as an exploit. A focus group has all the traits of a scenic device: a monitoring screen, an invisible public, a backstage area, and a moderator. Behind the mirror, steeped in darkness, with the sound piped in from the room in front, the team from the client company does indeed watch a sort of show. The moderator also gives a performance; his success (or failure) in "animating" the consumer's persona before the eyes of the client is at stake.

As we observed in multiple occasions throughout our fieldwork, this scenic device is quite powerful and constitutes the crux of what we term the "focus group effect." This is an effect of the experience of direct access to consumer reality. This effect stems from a space being split in two by a two-way mirror (video feedback is sometimes used but does not have the same power)—a frame within which one can see an artificially constructed (though extremely lively and thus plausible) sample of the social world. Placing a pane of glass between two sets of people creates, in a sense, a type of distance analogous to the apparatuses of objectivity in the natural sciences, but which is somehow at odds with an interpretive stance in the social sciences (Rabinow and Sullivan, 1988; Latour, 2005). We of course all live with "real people" and with "real consumers" (as we ourselves are). But through a most curious combination of closeness and remoteness, the focus group device produces the surprising effect of exhibiting "real people" as a rare and unique experience. Focus groups are thus literally spectacular; their scripted nature, their theatrical display—all these elements are there to provoke the thrilling experience for a marketer of watching a consumer without being seen.

However, the focus group effect is not produced solely by the way the equipment is arranged. The framework cut in two by the two-way mirror is prepared by a series of preliminary framing operations: construction of an agreement on what must be shown (targets and scenario), selection of the participants, orientation of opinions, and management of respondents. This latter point takes us to the second meaning of performance: that of the moderator's success in making the device work.

What is a "good group"? Essentially, it is an "animated" group, a lively and productive group which will generate fruitful responses from the participants in a balanced manner (as opposed to permanent consensus, "flat answers," or one or more people monopolizing speaking time). It is thus a group which is animated in terms of the role played by the moderator, who is in fact termed in French the "animateur" with all its connotations—both vital (to stimulate, to put into movement) and theatrical (to create drive and interest, both on stage and in the audience, the entertaining nature of the focus group being crucial for both respondents and observers). In a sense, the meaning of the word animateur is quite spot on for the focus group; it is not merely about moderating or facilitating, but rather about bringing to life a spirit—hence the consideration that a good moderator receives, almost as the "author" of the focus group.

A group is a good group when its collective dynamics work: opinion circulates and the participants "spring to life." And yet there can be no group effect, in the sociological sense, in a good group (Puchta and Potter, 2002; Lezaun, 2007). Leadership, collusion, connivance, and influence (typical sociological phenomena to be found in groups) are totally prohibited. A situation in which a "leader has drawn the group [in this or that direction]" constitutes a bitter failure for any moderator. The latter must maintain the individuality of the participants despite the group situation in which they find themselves. The very idea of "moderating" a group is indeed one of restraining it, of keeping it at a low intensity, of preventing the effective development of any actual "group" as such. The focus group is about using the group situation as a way to foster participants' emulation, that is, the creation of a dynamic. But nothing would be more contrary to its objectives than the emergence of a novel entity conveying new identities. In short, participants brought together to form a focus group must not form a group. They must instead remain a collection of individuals, in such a way as to maintain their identities as, say, achievers.

Moderating techniques (a complex topic that we will not tackle in detail here) are crucial in constructing a group performance. Let us focus on one quite simple, highly generalized ingredient of these techniques: respondents are prohibited from arguing. They must not speak among themselves. While members of a focus group must of course listen to what the others say, they must not reply, but rather must address the moderator to deliver their reactions. Lezaun (2007) aptly describes this series of requisites governing the way to talk as the "moral epistemology" of focus groups. A focus group is not about convincing or persuading. "It is not a political meeting," as a market researcher at Marketocom put it, "you're not here to come to an agreement or to find out who is right and who is wrong." The aim is to produce individual opinions under the form of "freestanding opinion packages" (Puchta and Potter, 2002), which are elicited through a group situation while not being influenced by it (Lezaun, 2007). This is why participants must provide a reaction rather than a response that would stimulate dialogue. When putting forward a point of view, respondents should not be developing new positions out of their ongoing exchange with others, nor should they generalize or adopt any positions other than their own. "We don't care what the French think, that's not what we are here for, tell me what you think, you personally," replied a moderator to a respondent who was elaborating on the idea of the "French character." Excluding debate from the space of the focus group is a way to maintain individuality in the face of the collective situation—a way, in short, to prevent the creation of a group.

Some interesting effects of this careful (and paradoxical) management of the interplay between the individual and the group can be observed in the dual judgments heard in the back room, behind the two-way mirror: clients' remarks on the group's performance in general might differ from judgment on the particular individuals comprising the group. For example, during one focus group session at Marketocom, a female participant was deemed to be particularly interesting because she fit the target well and was coming out with short and striking speech sequences that "spoke" to the clients. Conversely, during the first group meeting for the aforementioned banking and insurance study, clients felt that one of the respondents was not a fine representative of the target—"that one is not an achiever," they said. Yet the respondent in question met the criteria defining the target as set out in the screener: socio-professional category, holding several financial and insurance products with different companies, and positive attitude toward risk and money. These criteria came directly from a quantitative segmentation study, but this was the first time the study's clients were seeing their segments in "flesh and blood." As stated earlier, the achievers segment was one composed of young and ambitious persons. But the clients felt that this particular respondent was a bit conservative, less of a winner and less daring than the others, his assessment of the concepts being tested tending to differ from those of the other respondents. This was not, however, a "recruiting error" in the classic sense (loophole or ambiguity in the screener, being less strict about certain criteria when recruiting becomes difficult, presence of a professional respondent). Clients did not consider the group to be a failed group; they liked the group and felt they had seen achievers.[15] They simply did not recognize an achiever in this particular respondent—this very possibility having been opened by the construction of individuality in the group, making the presence of a non-achiever discernible. Through the comparison, in situ and in real time, of what the different group members say, observers in the back room can refine their representation of achievers or, more exactly, their ability to recognize through the two-way mirror the personification of one of their market segments.

The moderator's performance ultimately serves to effect the consumer's expression. We use the idea of "expression" in a strong sense: that of drawing out of a person (here, the respondent) something which has already been prefigured. It is about bringing out, through the voice of the respondent, the opinion of the consumer, in this case that of the achiever, so as to unfold from within the expressed opinion the deep characteristics of the target.[16] The focus group is not only a discussion without debate, it also requires the respondents to abandon reflexivity. They must respond "without thinking" with "whatever comes to mind." Study professionals call this abandon "spontaneity." Combined with the other aspects of group moderation mentioned above, the so-called spontaneity that the device produces allegedly makes it possible to reach the authentic consumer behind the social mask. Within the focus group device, the effect of spontaneity is a truth effect. Withheld reflection, reactions to a word thrown out into the room, and the speed at which the respondents take turns voicing their opinions are combined in an attempt to short-circuit consciousness and provide access to the inner consumer. The group circumstance stimulates production of this non-reflective opinion, following a principle loosely derived from the psychoanalytical technique of free association. The questions themselves—let us not forget that the discussion guide "guides"—do not invite argument. Indeed, the guide proposes projective games to lead respondents toward non-rational opinion. In the

"If it was..." game, for example, respondents are asked what a given brand would be if it were a plant, an evening out, or a famous person. A participant who is being too "rational" will be redirected with a "we are not talking about reality, we are imagining." In short, respondents are encouraged to forget about thinking excessively.

All these aspects (consumer target stereotyping, preparation of clients, opinion guidance, management of respondents' response) contribute to the achievement of the focus group effect, a truth effect whereby clients sometimes come to immediate conclusions and decisions.

Standing backstage: the behavior of marketers

To account for the successful course of everyday interactions, Goffman developed an extended theatrical metaphor that likens social life as a whole to a continuous performance. Individuals are actors who manage the impressions they make upon others through playing parts in accordance with a given situation (Goffman, 1959). Goffman's theatrical metaphor met with great success in the social sciences, despite Goffman's own efforts to undermine and re-elaborate the idea (Goffman, 1974; Manning, 1992). Our own account of focus groups as performances obviously partakes of an analogous dramaturgical idea. Our use of the notion of performance, however, is closer to that of the performativity program in the anthropology of markets (MacKenzie et al., 2007). To perform something is for us about making the thing happen for real; it is about provoking material realities and not merely about staging a play or accommodating collective representations. We depart from a Goffmanian dramaturgical theory of social life, but we nonetheless observe that professionals in market research are often informed by a somewhat Goffman-like view of social life in their quest for the "real consumer." That view puts forward the basic postulate that the authentic self is buried under a social posture. The true individual is therefore not within easy reach, save for specific tools of social and psychological investigation, of which the interviewing techniques of the focus group (projective interrogations, rapid pace of exchanges between compatible social types, and so forth) are a clear example.

The device of the focus group—the material setting and the interviewing techniques—does indeed prevent some participants (the consumers) from behaving à la Goffman, but it also enables a Goffmanian conduct for some other participants (the marketers). Since it claims to reach the consumer's true self behind his social mask, the focus group actually prevents respondents from engaging in a truly Goffmanian performance, the idea of a substantial self not quite belonging to the Goffmanian repertoire anyway. Incongruously enough, however, this authentic self is also supposed to correspond to a social type, that is, a role, like that of the "achiever," the "successful," the "deal

seeker," or the "life is a struggle"—all roles in the "play" of insurance consumer segmentation. Actors performing in the discussion room may not be
genuinely Goffmanian, but those who stand behind the glass are definitely
placed in a Goffmanian situation. The back room of the focus group facility
indeed resembles the two interrelated properties of backstage regions
described by Goffman (1959: 112): "a place in which to relax out of public
view, but also to spend time with peers and prepare for one's own role."

Insofar as we have been able to witness it, focus group observers—marketers,
project managers, or other workers from the client's organization—feel in most
cases entertained by the group, at least during part of it. The entertaining value
of the focus group is sometimes openly constructed by the moderator as he or
she displays showmanship. Food and wine may also contribute to the focus
group enjoyment. Placed in unusual circumstances and attending a relatively
pleasant event, focus group observers may drop for a moment the mask of their
professional identity in noticeable symmetry with the respondents' expected
conduct. "Here the performer can relax, he can drop his front, forgo speaking
his lines, and step out of character," writes Goffman (1959: 112).

The entertainment of a focus group session includes making fun of the
respondents. Why exactly observers jest, mock, and scoff at respondents is
not absolutely clear to us. Derision might be a means for observers to differentiate themselves from respondents, to reinstate the difference between oneself
and the "consumer other" that the two-way mirror has established. Perhaps
focus group observers are just taking advantage of the situation, the unique
privilege of being able to see without being seen, and adopting the general
posture—also described by Goffman (1959: 170)—of teams who ridicule one
another when one is absent, the special enjoyment here being that the other
team is both present and absent. Either way, the very fact that observers are
able to make fun of participants proves that they are considering them seriously, taking them as valuable specimens of consumers. Were this not the
case, if indeed the back-room observers doubted the quality and veracity of
what was happening in the front room, it would seem rather pointless to
laugh, mock, and snigger. The relaxing behavior backstage also includes such
activities as getting bored, resting, daydreaming, chatting, eating, and so on,
and even completely distracting activities such as writing e-mails.

As well as relaxing, the actor backstage takes advantage of standing out of
public view to fabricate, openly and painstakingly, his role. Backstage behavior is mostly about doing marketing, which here means gaining knowledge of
the consumer that is being presented to him. Goffman points to the "stor[age]
in a kind of compact collapsing of whole repertoires of actions and characters"
that happens backstage (1959: 112). Behind the glass, marketers are indeed
acquiring and accumulating repertoires of consumer characters, language, and
insights that they incorporate into their own repertoires so as to enable them

to communicate effectively the consumer's voice to their organization. "They just repeat what I kill myself explaining to colleagues!" a product manager once told us during the course of a focus group in a revealing role reversal, as if he wanted us to bear witness to his profound and empathic understanding of the consumer.

Getting acquainted with consumers through focus group attendance happens, we argue, through critically listening to respondents. What we call "critical listening" here is a mode of active attendance, of putting into perspective and of mentally confronting the present consumers in terms of those already integrated by the marketer, thus being able to confirm a trait, to challenge a statement, or to discern a novelty. The difference in approach between novice and experienced marketers is salient here. Novice marketers—often called "beginners" in Marketocom's "treatment of the absent," to follow suit with Goffmanian notions—found it difficult to make sense of respondents' discourse. They were either taking a respondent's statement at face value and jumping to conclusions or being bemused by the focus group effect, unable to dig beneath the lively and entertaining surface of focus-group-produced consumer talk. What we observed of experienced marketers, in contrast, was their real-time processing of information as the group unfolds. They were continuously assessing the credibility of the individuals in front of them, weighing a specific piece of discourse against what they already knew of consumers, challenging focus-group-produced ideas and insights, drawing and updating implications for their current projects from respondents' answers—new product ideas, advertising copy, sales strategies, and so on—and otherwise establishing links with the organization's current concerns and constraints. This is what is at play when clients judge that a respondent is not enough of an achiever or reject a respondent's comment as irrelevant. For instance, in a Marketocom test of an online lottery with a soccer theme, one female respondent said that she would prefer a more womanly sports theme than soccer. The marketing director of the company, subsequently reacting on the other side of the mirror, dismissed the point on the grounds that, after similar opinions emerged from previous studies, a quick survey which had been conducted on the market potential of such a game had found none. This is how, in our view, marketers cultivate consumer intimacy: not through a conversation with the consumer, but through a critical listening of strictly framed, focus-group-produced consumer talk.

Concluding Remarks

Noticeably enough, marketers are more often absent than not from behind the mirror. As a rule, marketers only attend the "pilot," or the first focus group in a series (note the entertainment industry connotation of the word). The lack of hidden observers, however, does not inhibit the performance aspect of the focus group. A focus group always is a fragile event, an event that needs to be performed, regardless of whether or not someone is behind the mirror. For their part, experienced marketers are able to compensate for their absence. They have participated in preparatory phases and may ask market researchers for a quick summary (called a "debrief") about each group. Marketers' familiarity with the focus group process allows them to "understand the consumer" from their reading of qualitative market research reports. Familiarity with the consumer indeed stems first and foremost from familiarity with the study process. It is the result of monitoring dozens or hundreds of groups and reading countless reports embellished by consumer quotes, which are expected to pass along some of the group's life.

Fragmented and non-argumentative as it is, focus-group-produced consumer talk needs to be put back into narrative form so that the marketer can assimilate the consumer's point of view. Marketing professionals' participation in a focus group often includes a follow-up discussion with the moderator, referred to as debriefing. Debriefing is a little like re-enacting the group and, in that sense, reminiscent of the rehearsal dimension of the moderator's briefing. The moderator and the clients discuss the main outcomes of the group, reminding each other what respondents have said in connection to one thing or another. Reviewing the group afterwards is essential to building a common understanding of what has happened during the group. These discussions indeed help reconcile the views of the clients and of the market research company executives. During the post-group debriefing, marketers begin to translate consumer opinions into marketing concerns (typically on product development and profitability). They reverse the process that led to launching the study, going from the convoking of the consumer that has happened during the study process to the invoking of the consumer, albeit this time with circulable quotes to sustain their claims.

As Cayla and Penaloza (this volume) strikingly put it, market researchers are not really interested in the private lives of focus group respondents as much as they are in fulfilling marketing and market research objectives. The focus group device—which includes a series of conditional steps taken beforehand, from the brief to the recruiting process to the writing of the discussion guide—is dedicated to presenting marketers with strictly framed consumers who are able to answer their calculated (marketing) questions. It would be going too far, however, to simply dismiss focus group market research on the grounds of its manufactured nature. Our inquiry into the study process brought us behind the mirror—not only into the back room of focus group facilities, but also into the preparatory phases of focus group sessions. There, we discovered skilful marketers who, being well aware of this manufactured nature, know how to handle the device so as to produce valuable outcomes. In addition, the manufactured nature of focus-group-enabled marketer–consumer encounters does not apply only to the consumer side of the encounter. Marketers themselves are shaped during the study process because they have to develop a special relationship with consumers. Convoking the consumer indeed requires that marketers define who their consumers are. The back room of the focus group facility thus takes the form of a place in which to become a marketer—a place to incorporate the consumer into the marketer's world. Examining the device of the focus group is indeed examining a range of techniques (from the translation of clients' expectations and interests into the discussion guide to the material setting of the focus group facility) that work together to produce the reality effect of naturalistic consumer talk, and to transform the client into a consumer-connected marketer.

Acknowledgments

We thank Mathieu Brugidou, Julien Cayla, and Fabian Muniesa for many insightful comments on an earlier version of this text. We are also grateful to Tanvi Mehta and Chris Hinton for their invaluable help in translating the text from the French. The final result and possible errors remain, however, our own.

Notes

1. We use double quotation marks when we refer to direct quotes from marketing professionals interviewed during our ethnography. For the sake of readability, we only signal professional language with double quotes at its first occurrence in the text.
2. Marketing professionals are well aware of the limitations of the focus group method and of its artificial character (see Malefyt (2009) and Desroches and Marcoux (this volume)), although popping up at someone's bathroom—as Desroches and Marcoux suggest—to contemplate his or her hair-coloring process is no less an artificial method than putting him or her in a laboratory-like setting.
3. See for instance Cayla and Penaloza (this volume).
4. In what follows, we use the words "marketer" or "client"' to refer to actors from company marketing departments commissioning market research, and "market researcher" to talk about professionals in charge of studies and surveys inside company marketing departments (internal market researchers) or in dedicated market research companies (external market researchers).
5. We use a pseudonym to protect the identity of this company.
6. Same note as above.
7. From a biographical viewpoint, this research's fieldwork phase corresponds to a period of career uncertainty (job opportunities intermingled together with scientific

concerns in a rather contingent, uncoordinated manner), while the analytical phase takes place at a later stage of stabilization of academic perspectives.

8. In the United States, the use of sociocultural criteria for consumer segmentation purposes from the 1950s onwards marked a turning point in marketing practices and the shape of markets. See Tedlow (1990) and Cohen (2003: ch. 7).

9. "Charentaises" in France are a traditional type of winter slippers, originated in the Charentes region. They stand as a symbol of anti-fashion, unattractive tradition oriented toward the home (versus the outer world). By extension, the "charentaises" target designates unadventurous and home-oriented individuals.

10. In the telecommunications sector in France, "Madame Michu" pejoratively designates a housewife under 50 years old, who is relatively unskilled in the use of new technologies. In the meetings we attended, this imaginary character was often used to examine how easy a new service was to use: "Would Madame Michu be able to use it?"

11. External market researchers concern with consumer profiling also entails a budgetary concern—narrow targets being more costly to bring to a focus group room. On the consumer recruitment activities, see also Sunderland and Denny (this volume).

12. For an analysis of this aversion, see Lezaun (2007: 136–7).

13. Claudia Puchta and Jonathan Potter (1999, 2002) give an accurate demonstration of the way in which the moderator manages to elicit the type of responses he or she is looking for—not so much in their content but in their form and theme.

14. Of course, the client may (and actually quite often do) want to change the questions or to introduce a concept to be tested during the study.

15. A group does not fail simply because one respondent is not corresponding well to the target. The opinion produced by the seven other respondents can be used, while that of the "unsuitable" respondent is excluded. This group in question did succeed in presenting seven achievers to the clients.

16. On this topic, see also Puchta and Potter (2002).

References

Akrich, M. (1992) "The De-scription of Technical Objects." In W.E. Bijker and J. Law, eds. *Shaping Technology/Building Society*. Cambridge, MA: The MIT Press, pp. 205–24.

——(1995) "User Representations: Practices, Methods and Sociology." In A. Rip, T.J. Misa, and J. Schot, eds. *Managing Technology in Society: The Approach of Constructive Technology Assessment*. London: Pinter, pp. 167–84.

Araujo, L., Kjellberg, H., and Spencer, R. (2008) "Market Practices and Forms: Introduction to the Special Issue." *Marketing Theory*, 8(1): 5–14.

Barrey, S. (2006) "L'épreuve des collections dans la mise en marché des produits alimentaires. Le cas de la grande distribution." *Réseaux*, 24(135–6): 193–219.

——Cochoy, F., and Dubuisson-Quellier, S. (2000) "Designer, packager et merchandiser: trois professionnels pour une même scène marchande." *Sociologie du Travail*, 42(3): 457–82.

Blankenship, A., Breen, G., and Dutka, A. (1998) *State of the Art Marketing Research* (2nd ed.). New York: McGraw-Hill.

Belk, R.W. ed. (1991) *Highways and Buyways: Naturalistic Research from the Consumer Behavior Odyssey.* Provo, UT: Association for Consumer Research.

Callon, M. ed. (1998) *The Laws of the Markets.* Oxford: Blackwell Publishers/The Sociological Review.

——(2007*a*) "What Does It Mean to Say That Economics Is Performative?" In D. MacKenzie, F. Muniesa, and L. Siu, eds. *Do Economists Make Markets?: On the Performativity of Economics.* Princeton, NJ: Princeton University Press, pp. 311–57.

——(2007*b*) "An Essay on the Growing Contribution of Economic Markets to the Proliferation of the Social." *Theory, Culture & Society,* 24(7–8): 139–63.

——(2008) "Economic Markets and the Rise of Interactive Agencements: From Prosthetic Agencies to Habilitated Agencies." In T. Pinch and R. Swedberg, eds. *Living in a Material World: Economic Sociology Meets Science and Technology Studies.* Cambridge, MA: MIT Press, pp. 29–56.

——Méadel, C., and Rabeharisoa, V. (2002) "The Economy of Qualities." *Economy and Society,* 31(2): 194–217.

Cayla, J. (2002) A Passage to India: An Ethnographic Study of the Advertising Agency's Role in Mediating the Cultural Learning and Adaptation of Multinational Corporations. Doctoral thesis. Department of Marketing, University of Colorado.

Cochoy, F. (1999) *Une histoire du marketing: discipliner l'économie de marché.* Paris: La Découverte.

——and Dubuisson-Quellier, S. (2000) "Introduction. Les professionnels du marché: vers une sociologie du travail marchand." *Sociologie du travail,* 42(3): 359–68.

Cohen, L. (2003) *A Consumer's Republic: The Politics of Mass Consumption in Postwar America.* New York: Knopf.

Corstjens, J., and Corstjens, M. (1995) *Store Wars: The Battle for Mindscape and Shelfspace.* Chichester: John Wiley & Sons.

Courpasson, D. (2006) *Soft Constraint: Liberal Organizations and Domination.* Copenhagen: Business School Press.

Denis, J. (2008) "Projeter le marché dans l'activité: les saisies du public dans un service de production télévisuelle." *Revue Française de Socio-économie,* 1(2): 161–80.

Dubuisson-Quellier, S. (2003) "Goûts des produits et goûts des consommateurs. La pluralité des épreuves de qualification dans la mise en marché des produits alimentaires." In S. Dubuisson-Quellier and J.P. Neuville, eds. *Juger pour échanger. La construction sociale de l'accord dans une économie des jugements individuels.* Paris: INRA Editions, pp. 47–74.

Gaglio, G. (2007) "Recours aux études marketing, nouveaux services et rationalité." In C. Caron and G. Gaglio, eds. *L'organisation à l'épreuve: autour du temps, de la sociabilité, de la rationalité et du métier.* Rennes: Presses Universitaires de Rennes, pp. 179–201.

——(2010). "Le marketing au concret: le drame social du travail des chargés d'études marketing dans de grandes entreprises." *Recherches sociologiques et anthropologiques,* 41(1): 125–41.

Georgakakis, D. (1997) "Une science en décalage? Genèses et usages des 'socio-styles' du Centre de Communication Avancée (1972–1990)." *Genèses,* (29): 51–72.

Goffman, E. (1959) *The Presentation of Self in Everyday Life.* Garden City, NY: Doubleday.

Goffman, E. (1974) *Frame Analysis: An Essay on the Organization of Experience*. New York: Harper & Row.

Hennion, A. (1989) "An Intermediary Between Production and Consumption: The Producer of Popular Music." *Science, Technology, & Human Values*, 14(4): 400–24.

——and Méadel, C. (1989) "The Artisans of Desire: The Mediation of Advertising between Product and Consumer." *Sociological Theory*, 7(2): 191–209.

Hirschman, E.C. (1983) "Aesthetics, Ideologies and the Limits of the Marketing Concept." *Journal of Marketing*, 47(3): 45–55.

Latour, B. (1987) *Science in Action: How to Follow Scientists and Engineers through Society*. Cambridge, MA: Harvard University Press.

——(2005) *Reassembling the Social: An Introduction to Actor-Network-Theory*. Oxford: Oxford University Press.

Lezaun, J. (2007) "A Market of Opinions: The Political Epistemology of Focus Groups." In M. Callon, Y. Millo, and F. Muniesa, eds. *Market Devices*. Oxford: Blackwell Publishing, pp. 130–51.

MacKenzie, D., Muniesa, F. and Siu, L., eds. (2007) *Do Economists Make Markets?: On the Performativity of Economics*. Princeton, NJ: Princeton University Press.

McKitterick, J.B. (1957) "What is the Marketing Management Concept?" In F. M. Bass, ed. *Proceedings of Frontiers of Marketing Thought and Science*. Chicago: American Marketing Association, pp. 71–92.

Malefyt, T. de Waal (2009) "Understanding the Rise of Consumer Ethnography: Branding Technomethodologies in the New Economy." *American Anthropologist*, 111(2): 201–10.

Manning, P. (1992) *Erving Goffman and Modern Sociology*. Stanford, CA: Stanford University Press.

Miller, P., and Rose, N. (1997) "Mobilizing the Consumer: Assembling the Subject of Consumption." *Theory, Culture and Society*, 14(1): 1–36.

Puchta, C., and Potter, J. (1999) "Asking Elaborate Questions: Focus groups and the Management of Spontaneity." *Journal of Sociolinguistics*, 3(3): 314–35.

———(2002) "Manufacturing Individual Opinions: Market Research Focus Groups and the Discursive Psychology of Evaluation." *British Journal of Social Psychology*, 41(3): 345–63.

Rabinow, P., and Sullivan, W.M. (1988) *Interpretive Social Science: A Second Look*. Berkeley, CA: University of California Press.

Rose, N. (1996) *Inventing Ourselves: Psychology, Power, and Personhood*. Cambridge, Cambridge University Press.

Simakova, E., and Neyland, D. (2008) "Marketing Mobile Futures: Assembling Constituencies and Creating Compelling Stories for an Emerging Technology." *Marketing Theory*, 8(1): 91–116.

Tedlow, R.S. (1990) *New and Improved: The Story of Mass Marketing in America*. New York: Basic Books.

5

Marketing as Surveillance: Assembling Consumers as Brands

Jason Pridmore and David Lyon

Introduction

Marketing is the "exemplar par excellence" of contemporary surveillance. It is perhaps the most efficient and productive realm for surveillance, defined as the "purposeful, routine, systematic and focused attention paid to personal details, for the sake of control, entitlement, management, influence or protection" (Ball and Murakami Wood, 2006: 3). Marketing practices make use of technologies and methods that increasingly render consumers as both known and knowable entities, resulting in the emergence of the "glass consumer" (see Lace, 2005) whose identity (or identities) is fluidly connected to the sets of categories to which they are deemed to belong. These transparent consumers are increasingly the focus of marketing initiatives and evaluations, used to prod and manage consumer behavior in desired directions. Yet the production of "glass consumers" is only possible in so far as everyday routines of consumption have been digitized.

Contemporary marketing is embedded in systems of data gathering that are used to better discern the needs, desires, trends of consumer behavior as well as to shape these behaviors by subtle and less than subtle means. This chapter focuses on the specific practices of loyalty marketing as a means of digitizing consumer behavior and assembling this information into digital representations of consumers whose everyday lives are rendered transparent. Loyalty marketing seeks to reward consumers that regularly patronize a particular corporation's offerings by providing incentives for this behavior in terms of service, recognition, or financial advantages. Loyalty marketing is often hailed as one of the best examples of one-to-one or relationship marketing, touted as an excellent example of corporate–consumer "relationships" in action (Hart et al., 1999). Loyalty programs, which usually entail reward cards and the collection of "points" or "miles" by consumers, are the most tangible manifestation of loyalty marketing. These programs are used to engage consumers in an ongoing relationship with a corporation. Yet this relationship is predicated on the collection of personal data, the means by which corporations are able to identify, maintain, and increase "the yield from best customers through interactive, value added relationships" (Capizzi and Ferguson, 2005: 72). It is a clear form of surveillance.

At first blush, surveillance may seem to be about something entirely other than processes of marketing and consumption. Surely surveillance is what police, intelligence agents, borders guards, and, possibly, public health professionals do. This is true, but for a number of important reasons many other processes and practices must be considered under the rubric of surveillance. Most significantly for our purposes, and in common with policing and intelligence practices, marketing depends increasingly upon collecting and categorizing personal data (Gandy, 1993). These activities are enabled—and sometimes constrained—by new softwares and protocols for digital data processing. The data are used for analysis and for assessment, such that groups and individuals, placed in different categories, may be treated differently. We must be clear here, and note that surveillance is not, nor has it ever been, total or all-encompassing, rather we argue that surveillance, as a means for analysis and assessment, is now the basic building block, the defining practice, of modern organizations of whatever type (Lyon, 2007; Haggerty, 2009).

Surveillance provides a critical framework for thinking about how loyalty marketing is both the impetus for and the final result of consumer surveillance. The consumer becomes "known" in the compartmentalization of their data, "assembled" in the production of a consumer "brand," and all of this is made possible by forms of commercial sociology that operate as complex and effective surveillance systems. This notion of commercial sociology describes the kinds of analysis done by contemporary marketing companies. Customers are reduced to datasets, as information about purchasing preferences and proclivities is detailed to provide marketers with useful profiles. Such commercial sociology thus simulates consumers for analysis. But it also interprets these behaviors and normalizes them as a part of the surveillance process and, in addition, incorporates further information on the activities and preferences of consumers as feedback. In this way, commercial sociology echoes other sociologies, which always exhibit a "double hermeneutic" (Giddens, 1987). This happens when the concepts and categories used by sociologists are re-appropriated through lay readings, and help to alter the original findings, creating an ongoing dynamic. Similarly, consumers accept some categories from commercial sociology, but also make choices that themselves contribute to the categorization process, in a persistent hermeneutic circle.

In order to understand this in more depth, a number of interviews were conducted with the top executives in a dozen of the largest loyalty programs in Canada, ten of which use reward cards to better understand their consumers' behaviors. These executives each had oversight into their respective programs and how the "loyalty component" fit into the overall business models of their company. All of the major loyalty "brands" in the "mature" Canadian loyalty marketplace (see Capizzi and Ferguson, 2005) are represented in these interviews. They yielded valuable data for analyzing marketing practice in its contemporary form. In what follows, we first examine the genesis of loyalty marketing, to see where today's practices originate. Interviews with marketing executives give unique insights into the aims of loyalty-maintaining strategies. However, what began, more humbly, as a means of holding onto customers for the long haul was steadily transformed into a means of finding out more and more about them, ironically, under the pre-computer banner of "knowing your customer." Secondly, the effect of this was to enable the process described as "assembling the consumer brand." As consumer information is analyzed and systematized, so the consumers themselves become "subjects of consumption" with specific "performance expectations" attached to each category and profile. Consumers are constructed through this process and loyalty marketing acts in a sense to program consumption in a particular way.

However, the story must then be rounded out, thirdly, by looking more closely at the notion of consumer sociology as surveillance. Feedback loops are generated, which constantly involve the customer as she or he engages in consumption practices. A "double hermeneutic" operates here as elsewhere. So if the prophecies are self-fulfilling it is because those prophesied about are actively contributing to the prophecies. Or so we shall argue. We conclude by indicating how the consequences of loyalty marketing as surveillance raise both analytical and ethical questions.

"Know thy Customer"

One of the key concepts in contemporary marketing literature is that the better a corporation knows and understands its consumers and then orients its business practices toward this knowledge, the better it is able to meet the needs of those consumers and to create a "sustainable competitive advantage" (Narver and Slater, 1990: 20). Though started as incentives for continued patronage (see Pridmore, 2008), loyalty programs have developed to become an informational portal for this information, allowing an unprecedented accumulation of information on individual and collective consumer consumption behavior, preferences, geo-demographic information, and more. These have also, to differing extents, become a key source for the development of market segmentation strategies, a means for a very direct form of relationship marketing, and mechanisms for customization.

Loyalty programs contribute to definitions of consumers as statistically relevant sets of data—consumers that are quantified and measured—and can then be manipulated and moved in statistically relevant ways. It provides an optimal means for the consistent monitoring and codification of consumer "biographies" (see Evans, 2003), biographies that are reassembled into digital representations of consumers and upon which "scientific analysis" can be done. As Patricia Sunderland and Rita Denny make clear (this volume), this is never a straightforward process and the connection of these digital representations to the "real lives" of the consumers they are intended to replicate is tenuous at best. However, these digitized representations are "what counts" (Lyon, 2001: 26); they are how the consumer is understood. Regardless of accuracy or of disconnects with the "actual" customers, digital representations serve to define marketing practice and are set in the context of a conglomeration of individuals with similar digitized biographies—differentiated clusters of consumers with similar neighborhoods, purchasing patterns, life stages, age, gender, income levels, and other characteristics. These are the segmentation distinctions that Sunderland and Denny point out "too easily become self-fulfilling tenets" in the eyes of marketers.

These segmentation distinctions, the categories or clusters to which a given consumer may belong, are important because they represent the potential marketing offers made to that consumer, the differing levels of service, the amount of required fees, the accumulation of loyalty program points, and the opportunities for special rewards and more. One of the executives interviewed for this research, "Paul," described the number of categories that might be used when integrating consumer data into marketing campaigns:

> ...[T]here is a whole list [of segments]...there is a value segment, there is a campaign history segment, there is category history segment, there is genre segment,...there is frequency score, there is RFM [recency, frequency, monetary] score...there is mosaic demo[graphics], there is the life stage segment, and there is age. So in any given campaign we may use all or some of those....And within the value segment, there are ten possible groupings, and in different campaigns we include whether the consumer has or has not received or responded to other particular campaigns.

Consumers may find themselves in many of these segments or their subdivisions.

> Paul: A typical segment might be...50 to a 100 thousand consumers. Our narrower segmentation is...2000 to 5000.
> R: How many different categories might a particular person [be] in?
> Paul: Very many.

It is in the accumulation of these segments that each consumer is rendered as increasingly "known." Their buying habits, income levels, familial status, among numerous other categories of "belonging," are readily apparent to marketers with access to these systems. Digital representations become indicative of a consumer as a "retiree," a "garden enthusiast," and living in an "up-scale suburban neighborhood." The added data from loyalty programs allows for highly specific and targeted micro-marketing. Likelihoods for receiving specific corporate offers, from discounts to new product offerings, depend upon whether the data that constitutes the digital representation fits within the objectives of a particular marketing campaign. Associations with segments may also influence the speed at which a consumer's call to a call center is answered and whether or not a service fee is waived or not (see, for instance, Winnett and Thomas, 2003; Bibby, 2006).

The use of categories—enumerating personal biographies into database segments—allows corporations "to capture information on customers in a useful and accessible fashion" (Evans, 2003: 668). The categories become "a sort of surrogate for the type of tacit knowledge of customers that the "corner shop" of old, would possess" (Ibid.). Capturing data to use as a substitute for tacit knowledge is precisely the point of loyalty programs and a primary objective for CRM (customer relationship management) practices; it enables corporate–consumer interactions that are seen as more intimate. Though the degree to which an intimate corporate–consumer relationship is possible is debatable (see, for instance, Millard, 2003 and Payne and Frow, 2005), understanding the consumer in terms of their digital representation is central to personalized interactions with consumers. Another interviewee, William, makes this very clear: "... [T]he whole program was built on the idea of understanding our customer better. So how we use it and work with data is a very important part of our program." Despite differences in the interpretation of data, as well as its potential uses, William's comment indicates an unquestioning perspective on the use of and measurability derived from consumer data. Data is seen as paramount. It defines consumer behavior and guides marketing practice.

The main benefit in loyalty marketing is its ability to produce information on consumers more consistently, efficiently, and more accurately. In a study of European loyalty programs in retail locations, an interviewee put it this way:

> Customers will always tell you something that they think you want to know. A customer that is less affluent is not going to admit that they go in and buy [the] cheapest possible products, because they have a personal image and they don't wish to say that. You have to interpret that data. Whereas [with] our data, we know exactly what they have bought, therefore it's a lot more accurate, a lot more valuable, and there's a lot more in it. (Cuthbertson and Laine, 2004: 293)

Of course this data, while both accurate and plentiful, has to be interpreted in some way. The data such as is gathered through loyalty programs allows for the production of financial measures, such as return on investment (ROI) or corporate profitability, to be produced with relative ease. Marketing that is "customer centric," however, seeks to understand the implications of these measurements beyond short-term financials. The loyalty marketing executive at a major retail business put it this way:

> [I]f you don't understand the consumer performance measures you need to learn them. If you are going to a meeting with the President or to some people that are very influential in an organization and you don't know those, you better learn them quickly. And if in your job you cannot prove you have moved those measures the consumer measures, there is a problem. Those drive the financial measures; that's the difference.... It's the consumer measures that drive the financial measures and in our corporation there is a real desire now to put them together.

In the context of this quote, she contends that corporate profitability increases by placing consumer information, what she refers to as consumer measures, as the driver for financial practice. The emphasis in marketing literature, especially in loyalty marketing, is increasingly on having a customer-focused business strategy rather than seeing the management and analysis of data as a technological integration issue (Payne and Frow, 2005). Yet invariably, the value of marketing is inextricably connected with profitability and the analysis of increasingly detailed data about consumers. This data is segmented and sorted into categories related to metrics for a consumer's potential lifetime value (LTV)—a profile that indicates their current or presumed economic worth (Danna and Gandy, 2002). The LTV is used to manage future transactions, and serves as an indicator of risk, signifying the likelihood that a corporation will recoup its expenditures (described in terms of an investment) in developing and maintaining an ongoing relationship with a particular consumer.

Loyalty programs, though often starting mainly as a means for increasing consumer retention, have become crucial mechanisms for gathering data to determine a consumer's LTV. The programs serve to create measurable and meaningful knowledge of consumers and prescribe the means by which a corporation engages in corporate–consumer relations.

> Well, obviously this whole getting a single view of a client is sort of like the backbone. How can you provide a good service to a client if you don't know the client? So, it's sort of [that] you have to adapt if you know that [a consumer] is 50 plus, he likes to have a peace of mind when he travels and this and that. Well, then you design that service and the product accordingly.

It is this creation of a "single view" of the consumer as an aggregate collection of data that has "revolutionized the way capital assesses, values and relates to the customer" (Green, 1999: 34). Databases now "play a central role in the production of consumer identities" (Zwick and Dholakia, 2004*b*: 32). They create the means by which consumers become organizational artifacts, "owned and controlled" by the company (Beckett, 2004: 46). Increasingly the social and consumptive ties that serve as the basis for the expression of personal identity in our society (see Bauman, 2001; and Zukin and Maguire, 2004) are intimately connected to the digital representations corporations maintain. In this process, and despite the fact that corporations cannot act directly upon a particular consumer, the created digital image of the consumer "effectively stands in for the real consumer. It becomes the consumer's identity" (Zwick and Dholakia, 2004*b*: 34). Once consumers are constituted digitally, they can be engaged with and acted upon strategically, further subjecting them to the mechanisms under which they have been made. They are marketed to in accordance with their digital representation, or in certain cases the "wrong customers" are subject to a process of "demarketing" in which service, products, and opportunities are designed specifically as disincentives for further patronage (Gordon, 2006: 3).

Marketing campaigns are considered successful in relation to the percentage of consumers known to respond to a given campaign. The response or lack of a response by each individual consumer can then be integrated back into the system as yet another part of their digital representation, creating more refined representations of consumers and their likelihood to respond to different marketing stimuli. Consumers then are continually reproduced as a collection of data within infrastructures that represent a world "out there" in the form of categories that depict everyday consumption and consumption behaviors. The digital representations of consumers allow marketers the ability to break down consumer behavior into measurable and manageable bits that can be reassembled and deemed as significant for future marketing practice. It is this consumer, in a digital form, that has become the priority and goal of marketing.

Assembling the Consumer Brand

These digital representations of consumers are collections of data deemed somehow significant. An individual consumer is an assemblage of meaningful data with which corporations are able to work—each does not exist on its own, rather each consumer is logically assembled and made comprehensible as an object for marketing (see Miller and Rose, 1997). In other words, "knowing about" subtly translates into "re-shaping" customers in specific ways, desirable to the corporation. As Moisander and Eriksson see it, this process is intimately connected with: "making up or assembling a particular subject of consumption and orchestrating the little rituals and practices of everyday life in a way that links up a particular complex of subjective tastes and allegiances with a particular product or brand" (Moisander and Eriksson, 2006: 259).

With the amount of data increasingly available on consumers, specifically in relation to their tastes, allegiances, income, and location, these "particular subjects of consumption" are set into typologies that are best understood in terms of branding—a process by which a complex set of relations is reduced into a singular concept (see Lury, 2005). Database marketing in general and loyalty marketing in particular act as "identification programs," allowing the corporation the opportunity to individually know buyers, in a "manner somewhat symmetrical with what branding offers to products" (Deighton, 2005: 233). Consumer "brands" are mediated and flexible; they are dynamic and digitally malleable; they can be configured and reconfigured into marketing forms that map likely trajectories for consumption; they are indicative of response levels to campaigns; and they can indicate costs associated with corporate marketing interventions.

By digitizing consumer information and then assembling from this consumers as brands, the parameters of expectations for consumer "performance" becomes set. The database serves to constitute "the customer subject as a known and knowable object upon which the marketer can now act strategically" (Zwick and Dholakia, 2004b: 32). In the process, consumers are increasingly seen by corporations in terms of the reputations "ascribed to them" (Deighton, 2005: 233). In the case of loyalty marketing, evaluating the routine practices of consumption allows these corporations to "calculate how many people there are in a home by the number of toilet rolls that are purchased, whether you have just had a child, and when you are about to go on holiday" (Rowley, 2005: 123). These analyses indicate how dynamic typologies of consumers are created with certain values and aesthetics attached to them. In the case of loyalty marketing, this may allow for more personalized marketing practices, as corporations search for: "marketing strategies that will improve their offer, in such a way that they achieve an increased level of shopping. In short, in exchange for modest rewards and incentive points the customer is granting implicit permission [for the company] to use their data, to enhance business success and profitability" (Ibid.: 123).

The production of consumer "brands" enables marketers to "understand their customers better" and determine the degree to which they want to pursue a particular relationship with these "brands" of consumers. It is connected to the multiplicity of ways in which the digital representations of consumers are segmented. These segments were described in a bit more detail by one of the loyalty program executives:

> We have a number of ways we segment our customer base, based on recency of shop, frequency of spend, and how much they spend. . . . We also look at them in terms of their deciles, so we divide the entire customer base into 10, with the top 10 percent of our customers in decile one and then the next 10 in decile two, etc. This allows us to see them from a profitability perspective. We also look at them from the life-stage point of view. We've identified, I believe 12 different life-stages that our customers are at, at any given time. This is largely inferred based on what they are buying, so if we know customers are buying diapers and baby powder we [categorize them] as parents with young kids.

While life stages are often connected with age, other corporations use age itself as an important and useful means for marketing to their consumers. In the case below, generational groupings are a key component in the set of relations that make up a particular consumer brand:

> We have a general kind of cultural segmentation we have broken into . . . generational groups, the traditional kind of boomer, family, careerist, young adult, gen 'Y'ish, tweens, etc. We then cross that with the mosaic data [third party lifestyle demographics] on which kind of mosaic groups they fall into. And that gives us about five times twenty groups potentially and we tend to use about 15 to 20 of those of groups as they seem to be responsive to communications and are the core of our business.

Both of the above quotes indicate how particular associations become categorized as important. Depending on the marketing objectives for different campaigns, loyalty programs assemble consumers in ways that "engages the central life themes" of the consumer and that shapes the consumer's tastes by presenting him or her with products and opportunities designed to fit with their digitally presumed, prescribed, and branded "life" (Deighton, 2005: 237). As corporations have increasingly become able to brand consumers in terms of statistically relevant characteristics, they are able to prefigure the consumer by identifying likely consumption patterns of current and potential consumers. This also allows them the opportunity to decide, by means of customer lifetime values and other measures, in precisely which consumer brands they should invest.

In the process of assembling consumers as a branded object for marketing, loyalty programs provide particular services to consumers and fulfill their expressed or constructed needs. It is not that these mechanisms of behavioral analysis simply produce "false needs" within consumers, though that may be part of this process (see Miller and Rose, 1997). Instead, the technological processes that render consumer data meaningful also serve to rearrange practices of consumption to fit its own objectives for measurability (see Ellul, 1990). Loyalty marketing produces self-fulfilling prophecies because they guide consumers into particular transactions that occur within fixed limits and automate consumption into a "cybernetic-like system of reproduction" (Elmer, 2004: 141). The database and its analysis dictate how a corporation will engage with particular consumers. This is evident in the context of another interview: "We measure and decide what the right investment is for different customer groups. We do this according to their value segmentation, their category orientation in terms of which categories they purchase in, and their frequency behaviour." By discursively assembling consumers on the basis of layers of data about them, future marketing engagements are able to be simulated (or mapped out) in a way that ensures corporate efficiency and profitability (Elmer, 2004: 88). The process continues a trend Miller and Rose identified as occurring within marketing research in the 1950s: "[j]ust as one could identify 'product images', so too could one identify 'personality images'. Clearly, what was necessary was to map the one onto the other" (Miller and Rose, 1997: 19).

For loyalty marketers, mapping the trajectories of consumer behavior onto product offerings is fundamental to their existence. Yet as the layers of data are assembled together to "make up" consumers, to brand them as a collective set of socio-economic relationships, those same socio-economic factors implicit in the production of these consumers form the very basis for their mapped-out consumption patterns. This inevitably reinforces the social structures from which loyalty marketing is drawn and to which the assembled consumer is mapped.

Commercial Sociology and Surveillance

The digitization of consumers, and the subsequent reassembling of them as identifiable consumer brands, has accomplished something that marketing has long sought to achieve. For years, market researchers trained in fields of psychology and anthropology have attempted to make connections between product choices and socio-economic characteristics from class to income to education (Zukin and Maguire, 2004). However the perceived problem with these processes was that they were "unable to make visible individual con-sumers" (Zwick and Dholakia, 2004a: 217). While researchers were able to make relatively detailed accounts of shopping behaviors historically, they made few attempts to make these swaths of description specific. Certain institutions may have set out to create or "assemble" subjects of consumption through a complicated means of psychological engagement that "mobilized" certain consumption practices (see Miller and Rose, 1997), but these were never individualized. At best, they connected a general knowledge of the consumer with advertising practices in an attempt to direct consumers choices by "forging intricate, intimate connections between specific product attributes...and human passions, fears, and values" (Zukin and Maguire, 2004: 183).

In order to understand the individual consumer better, "psychographic" analyses of consumers in the form of surveys about "self concepts and their preferences on a broad array of topics—e.g., spouses, household arrangements, pets, leisure time" were employed (Ibid.). Though this information may not have had a direct connection with particular products, the data was refined into "clusters of attitudes," which could stand in as proxies for more specified consumer product choices. It was through the expansion and increased capabilities of information and communication technologies (ICTs) that more specified engagements with consumers began. Personal data is increasingly integrated into these systems of knowledge, improving the degree to which individual consumer habits are understood by placing them against a backdrop of consumer segments: "The hitherto 'massified' consumer [understood only in terms of large scale segmentations] who remained epistemologically absent while anonymously slipping in and out of markets, can now be inscribed, recorded, and classified according to attributes, capacities, and conducts and finally differentiated against other individual data profiles" (Zwick and Dholakia, 2004a: 217–18). The digitization of consumers and their being reassembled as significant makes them absent no longer—they are rendered visible as a collection of data points that allow marketers to create and maintain meaningful one-to-one relationships with the consumer.

This attempt to develop these relationships based on data and to better understand the interconnections between "consumption patterns, tastes, values and preferences" and the digital representations of consumers can be described as a form of "commercial sociology" (Ellison and Burrows, 2007: 299; see also Lyon, 1994: 142 and Burrows and Gane, 2006). Through the use of a multiplicity of data-gathering techniques—the same as those employed by the social sciences—and by placing digitized representations of consumers in relation to sets of other consumers similarly defined and clustered, marketers are able to anticipate trajectories of consumption. These are based on the assumption that these consumers will replicate the patterns of other similarly classified consumers. "Birds of a feather," recall these marketers, "flock together." The collection and analysis of data is gathered to make connections between everyday consumption, individual consumers, and social contexts in order to increase marketing efficiency and effectiveness. Essentially, commercial sociology practices are forms of "for profit" sociology. The routine processes of these forms of sociology involve the gathering, sorting, and evaluation of data to establish social patterns and subsequently assigning these patterns degrees of worth (financial, in this case) or potential risk (whether corporate investment in marketing to certain consumers will "pay off" in this context). This commercial sociology forms the basis for marketing as a rather robust and intricate form of contemporary surveillance. That is, the means by which commercial sociology allows marketers to know consumers at an intimate level exemplifies what surveillance is—the systematic and focused attention to personal details in order to variously influence, manage, protect, entitle, or control its subjects (Lyon, 2001).

This conception of marketing as surveillance focuses attention on the notion that consumption, while offering an abundance of opportunities and choice, also very much directs consumers down particular predetermined routes for this consumption (Miles, 1998). The surveillance employed here can be seen to operate in several different ways. First, these digital representations serve to constitute consumer simulations that are subject to "forms of hypersurveillant control" (Bogard, 1996: 4). Second, the databases that underpin commercial sociological practices can be seen to normalize certain individually prescribed consumption patterns through systems of rewards and punishments. Last, marketing prompts consumers to produce certain forms of discourse about who one is as a means of constituting oneself in a consumer society.

The digitization of consumer information to predict and anticipate consumer behaviors serves to create reassembled consumers as profiles that can be used to model consumer behavior. These digitized profiles replace "'actual' with 'virtual' processes" and "'real' consumers with electronic representations," forming the basis for consumer simulation (Bogard, 1996: 3). It is the simulation of a consumer's behavior that allows collected data to become useful—a process in which the "real" consumers have projected, through their monitored and analyzed habits and preferences, a digital profile that subjects the consumer to particular corporate expectations. The "avid" score for consumers of one particular loyalty program is one such example of how a simulated consumer is used. These scores are used to determine the offerings consumers receive and is the measurement by which consumers are corporately understood. The loyalty program executive described the score this way:

> [W]e have gone out and built what we call an avid score—that is, a propensity to be highly responsive to Advantages as an offering. The avid score is based on a series of 5 questions that we ask about the consumer. Depending on the scores that come back, we then compare that back against behavioural data. This is called an attitudinal and behavioural response and then what we have done is model a sample base. I can't remember how big it was, 5 or 6 thousand consumers that we collected the core . . . qualitative and quantitative data on. We [then] built a predictive model off of that and . . . scored the entire data base against . . . the model that was developed. [W]e could then say you might have a 0.65 avid score and . . . draw a line somewhere in the mix to say above this line we consider you avid, below that line in the score we consider you an average consumer.

Later in the interview, he also indicates that these avid scores are broken down into several segments, from deciles of top tier best customers to a final tier simply labeled "demarket"—consumers with whom the corporation has "deselected" as optimal customers. The avid score—a digital demarcation of marketing responsiveness—is taken into consideration for any and all future transactions, from marketing campaigns to service interactions. It is a crucial factor in how the offerings of the program are made, from whether something will be offered at all to what type will be marketed to what types of specific consumers.

Avid scores are not imposed upon "false images" of the consumer. Rather, they are connected with simulated representations of consumers that exist "at the intersection of actual and virtual worlds" (Bogard, 1996: 27). At issue is not how these simulations resemble their corresponding subjects, but how in this instance consumers increasingly start to resemble their profiles (Ibid.; see also Lyon, 2001: 117). As consumer behaviors are deemed significant only in so far as they are observable through corporate metric, it is the metrics that become the focal point of corporate marketing. The intentions of simulation within commercial sociology is clear—to predict consumer behavior. The simulated consumer is quantified, measured, and statistically categorized, and allows marketers to trace future outcomes by means of modeling (see Stivers, 2004). These surveillance practices cannot uncover deep knowledge about consumers—the surface tends to suffice (Bogard, 1996: 21). Simulations are predictive projections on consumers that do not seek to discover the underlying attitudinal dimensions of consumer behavior. It allows a consumer to be rendered known and knowable in terms of their behavior only, specifically as they come to fit the self-fulfilling prophecies of their digital profile.

The layering of consumer data—connecting multiple levels of categories to a particular digitized consumer—and linking these to specific consumer transactions as "simulations," "afford a particular diagnostic and . . . governmental capacity" for the corporation (Elmer, 2004: 88). They serve to control offerings and interactions with specific consumers, interactions that are always carefully versed:

> For any given segment of customers you can [do] general marketing [for] those segments. . . . [I]f interest rates are going to creep up those that [we can assume] have highly leveraged mortgages are going to have less disposable incomes and may actually look at switching out of their house. You could get a geodemographic view of who those customers might be and . . . talk to them about mortgage opportunities. [Y]ou wouldn't say 'I'm highly leveraged' [or that we know this], or 'my job is on the border and I am having triplets,' [or other things we might be able to] know. . . . But you can start to look at it in terms of the conditions being right, there might be likelihoods or a high probability or a propensity for something increases and therefore we should put offers and marketing in front of these folks. . . . So, we

combine all kinds of the four pieces of that data...your personal information, behavioural, attitudinal and then market information and in one block [to determine our engagement with the consumer].

Simulations, as in this case are often intentionally subtle, but they should not be seen as either illusory or without material effects. In fact, the "better a simulation, the less awareness there is an artifice that identifies itself *as* a simulation" (Bogard, 1996: 31). This is made clear in a discussion with another program executive named Peter:

> Peter: I would hope that in two or three years time a consumer would open a package and have that eerie feeling that Advantages is a little bit like their best friend that seems to know everything that they do—but in the best friend kind of feel. And that it is trusting,—yeah it is a trusting, "they really help me out" type of relationship. This would be as opposed to "the big brother is watching" and "creeping me out" kind of relationship. So we are very careful on the language we use in the communication. You know it's never a "Hey! We've," you know...
>
> R: "We have seen you do this before."
>
> Peter: Right. That is exactly right. It is not the... "we've noticed you haven't been in our store recently."
>
> R: That might drive more people away than back in.
>
> Peter: Yeah. And that is not the intent. I mean the intent is to provide a service.

By simulating consumers, loyalty programs demonstrate that they "know" consumers—they know what she likes, know where he lives, know what kind of people she hangs out with. But, perhaps most importantly, loyalty programs expect consumers to act in certain ways. In positioning consumers this way, they are approached, advertised to, and generally "marketed to" differently. Equally, they receive different levels of service, are given differing commercial opportunities, are afforded differing degrees of flexibility in their transaction, pay different prices, and their interactions with the corporation are interpreted through the social and economic positioning of their data.

In addition to the simulation of consumers, commercial sociology operates from a position of relative informational power. It is this informational power that increasingly renders consumption meaningful, producing consumer behaviors, sorting consumers into particular categories, and becoming the means for shifting consumer behavior in accordance with corporate desires. The intentions for data collection and its use were described by one loyalty program executive this way:

> [F]rom our group's standpoint, you look at things from a relationship side of things and with the purposes of growing the purchase activity of our consumers. We call this 'share of wallet'. Make no mistake about it; we want to find ways to ensure that

our customers choose Emporium over one of our competitors, and we also want to migrate them to certain products and offerings that they may not have tried before.

These offerings are always connected to relevant digital categories intended to entice consumers with a "preset familiar world of images" and new opportunities in line with their digital representation (Elmer, 2004: 49). However, this same process can be seen to "disciplines consumers that actively seek out the unfamiliar, the previously unseen, purchased, or borrowed" (Ibid.). The classificatory power of the database serves to constitute and normalize individually prescribed consumption patterns.

Data is central to this process. As one interviewee said very clearly,

> If you want to do [Customer Relationship Management (CRM)] then a loyalty program is one way to collect data, so you see a loyalty program as a means to an end—the end is CRM. It is understanding who your customers are, how valuable they are, what they are doing, what they are not doing and managing them. It is in shifting their behaviour to different channels introducing them to new products and all that .... So a loyalty program doesn't necessarily get to CRM, particularly if you are not collecting and using data .... The difference is what you do with the data.

The use of consumer data is the means by which the consumer can be "managed." It allows for the behavior of consumers to be shifted by means of producing particular forms of marketing discourse. Cuthbertson and Laine's study on loyalty programs quotes a loyalty program executive indicating the means by which another loyalty program was able to promote and influence purchasing patterns through the use of a database:

> X manufacturer wanted to promote product Y .... We then [identify] people who bought children's clothes (the size suggesting the age of their children) that would like to look at Y. We worked out the population of who could buy Y. We then promoted to them and we sold more Y than any other retailer in the country. We continue to enjoy enhanced sales. That was a very cost effective promotion. (Cuthbertson and Laine, 2004: 294)

The database is crucial for objectifying individual consumers, feeding them into "cybernetic triages" that sort consumers according to presumed economic value—what Oscar Gandy calls the panoptic sort (1993: 1). These digital representations of consumers are reassembled in relation to previously categorized "lifestyle groups," allowing marketers to selectively engage with certain clientele on the basis of their being deemed desirable.

Clearly, these conclusions resonate with Foucault's arguments, such that customers could be seen within a system of consumer government(ality) in which they freely and voluntarily place themselves within lifestyle groups and categories that are themselves partly the product of their purchasing behaviors. The loyalty program is in this view the conduit through which ongoing consumer behaviors are channeled in ways that profit the program manager, the corporation, and its shareholders, but that are never felt by the consumer to involve any kind of constraint let alone coercion. But the imbalance of benefits becomes apparent over the longer term.

In the process of being filtered like this, many consumers benefit because their commendable consumer behavior is recorded and they can reap the rewards. Others, however, may suffer from what Gandy has referred to as "cumulative disadvantage" in which certain consumers are precluded from economic opportunities and by extension the social and political possibilities they entail (2006: 319). Data from consumer behaviors make their way into credit-reporting databases and data brokerage companies, and these may be used by government departments to make judgments on eligibility for claimed benefits (Gandy, 2009). So-called rational discrimination thus has social results that are veiled by consumer processes that are in turn read by consumers only in terms of positive promotion—the rewards of loyalty. The penalties of loyalty remain obscure.

Yet these sorting practices are ones with which people have seemingly become increasingly comfortable. They are seen as natural, and as both "descriptive" and "operative"—defining the possibilities for action and consumer behavior (Bowker and Star, 1999: 236). These corporate expectations of consumers are integrated into the discourse of everyday life just as other bureaucratic measures pervade the consumer's sense of identity. Value conscious consumers, consumers with bad credit, high-end consumers, or consumers labeled with geo-demographic profiles all come to understand their own shopping habits in both explicit and implicit ways along the expectations of the corporation. Consumers are rewarded for behaviors that fit with their categorization—they are actively engaged with targeted marketing, loyalty program currencies, and promotional campaigns. Yet they are also "punished" by the system through mechanisms such as reduced service, increased fees, and limited exposure to corporate marketing. These "demarketing" practices are intended to reduce expenditures on "the wrong customers" (Gordon, 2006: 3). Over time, marketers anticipated that consumers will alter their behavior toward preferred corporate trajectories that follow the "natural" classificatory schema embedded in the "configurations of language" that flow from the database.

In a society in which consumption has become paramount (see Bauman, 2001), there is little consumer choice regarding the integration of their data into these systems of surveillance. Data are continually gathered and used for systematic sorting, and each bit of information in the database is important:

Information that has little value in isolation gains value to the extent that it becomes part of an extensive database. Thus, the ability of consumers to choose whether or not they enter into what might be described as the "digital enclosure"— a realm of monitored interactivity wherein they surrender information about themselves—increasingly comes to resemble the forced choice [within capitalism of having to sell ones labour for financial remuneration]. Consumers may be "free" not to interact, but they increasingly find themselves compelled to engage in interactive exchanges (and to go online) by what [has been] described as "the tyranny of convenience." (Andrejevic, 2003: 139)

Loyalty programs can be seen as a "tyranny of convenience" as the discourse surrounding these programs is designed to make enticement into the program difficult to resist. These programs are presented as "partners" or "solution providers" for consumers, and are based on the premise of having consumers reward themselves for the consumption that they do on a regular basis. Consumers who choose to remain outside of the system by not participating in these programs end up implicated nonetheless: similarly situated others in their social networks serve as proxies for their participation. Non-participation may limit unique and personalized offerings, but these consumers are still clustered together with similarly conceived digital peers. Commercial sociology provides the means for sorting and segmenting consumers, objectifying them and implicating them in patterns of consumption practices based on the classificatory powers of surveillance. This not only creates and enumerates categories by which consumers are defined, but it also creates a consumption framework around which consumers begin to understand and articulate their lives.

Things cannot be left there, however. While commercial sociology both simulates consumers and normalizes interpretations of their behaviors as a form of surveillance, it also incorporates "feedback technologies" (Elmer, 2004: 38). Consumer engagement and interaction is continually sought, and any new data gained from these interactions is appended to the digital representation of the consumer. This produces more "robust" profiles that allow consumers to be known and marketed to more efficiently and effectively, and it creates more accurate clusters for micro-marketing. Consumer data is constantly updated and modified, and each encounter, from purchases to service contacts, is added to consumer profiles. These digitized interactions can be seen to incrementally render the socio-economic worlds of the consumer more visible, and the dynamic nature of systems of consumer evaluation indicates that the simulation and categorization of consumers is supplemented by consumer feedback mechanisms. That is, through the surveillance techniques of commercial sociology, consumers serve to define their own categorization by self-identifying with particular products, brands, lifestyles, life stages, interests, and more.

Consumers are increasingly solicited to divulge personal information—to self-identify with consumer classifications and produce knowledge that serves to refine those categories:

> We would like to know them so that we can serve them better, so we can recognize their worth and that kind of thing.... [T]he purpose of knowing a customer is about knowing the culture that they ascribe to and participate in, and whether or not [the company] can be a part of that and help solve problems within that.... [B]y letting us know you, we are going to learn more about you and be better at solving your problems.

In the process of allowing a corporation to know its consumers by monitoring the most mundane of activities—everyday shopping—these transactions become an indication of the needs, desires, and uses of particular products and services by an individually identifiable human being. By their very nature these transactions inform the corporation about individual consumers, making visible ordinary daily practices as well as personal aspirations. This is then further supplemented by numerous surveys, focus groups, and interviews with consumers designed to draw out social meanings behind consumption practices and how products are integrated into their lived experiences.

Commercial sociology uses data gleaned from both more intimate (in the form of personal surveys and focus groups) and less intimate (transactions) interactions to improve its predictive and prescriptive capabilities. These data are readily drawn into a technological system programmed to evaluate this information in order to more accurately classify, target, and personalize interactions with consumers. Corporations use knowledge obtained from consumers to produce relevant marketing for the consumer and others deemed similar. In the case of loyalty marketing, one executive states that a: "... loyalty program is simply a device that creates an action that allows you to get consumers to identify themselves. [It] allows you to create segmentations, and differentiate and categorize whatever you want of that consumer base so that you can have a much clearer view of what is really happening [with consumers]." This information serves to modify corporate marketing practices, their directions, and promotions (though the motivation for profit does not change), by the continual surveillance of consumers. Databases do not maintain a singular flow of information collection (from the consumer to the corporation). Rather databases "speak" or engage with individual consumers in a variety of formats through the use of feedback technologies (Elmer, 2004: 77). These feedback technologies are an attempt to use data to "foster, automate and network the act of consumption" (Ibid.: 71) by modifying and improving the technological systems of marketing practice, as well as the simulations and categorization of consumers.

The discussion of loyalty programs demonstrates how major corporations engage in marketing practices that penetrate deeply into the everyday life-worlds of contemporary consumers. The programs are common, widespread, and increasingly taken-for-granted as the way today's marketing and promotional initiatives work. But this inward reach into what Foucault might call the capillary level of the social organism is far from inconsequential. It is a means not only of consumer government, but through such government of reordering those lifeworlds and of redistributing advantage and disadvantage. As marketing practices interact with intimate social life, so patterns classically theorized in terms of class, gender, and race will increasingly have to be re-thought.

Conclusion

Marketing, then, and especially loyalty marketing, qualifies as a form of surveillance. With loyalty marketing, purposeful, routine, systematic, and focused attention is paid to personal details, in this particular case to manage or influence consumers. Immense amounts of data are collected on customers in order to "know," brand, and construct them as consuming subjects. Examining loyalty marketing as surveillance both indicates what sort of process is under consideration—and thus connects with various other kinds of digitally enhanced surveillance, for monitoring workers (Ball, 2003), entitling citizens (Lyon, 2009), or enhancing the in/security of travelers (see Aas et al., 2008)—and at the same time showing how its purposes and mechanisms may also differ from these. In particular, we have shown how the feedback loops inherent in loyalty programs render this as a type of commercial sociology in which a dynamic process is generated, such that consumers contribute to the very categories that create them. This does not lessen the surveillant quality of loyalty marketing, but it does help to distinguish it from some other forms of surveillance—such as that for "homeland security"—where feedback loops of this kind are a less prominent feature of the process.

Two related areas are opened for further analysis by this study of loyalty marketing as surveillance. One is that seeing loyalty marketing as part of a more general turn toward anticipatory or pre-emptive surveillance opens the way for extended comparative analysis of the similarities and differences between the various burgeoning forms of surveillance that are apparent across the spectrum of organizational life. If the theorem is sound, that surveillance has become *the* preferred mode of organizational practice, then this will prove a fruitful way forward for studying loyalty marketing and related phenomena.

The second implication, given the socially varied consequences of loyalty marketing as surveillance, is that new opportunities for ethical analysis are opened up. If, as we have suggested, an unintended consequence of loyalty marketing is subtly to reinforce already existing socio-economic differentials between conscientious and what Bauman calls "flawed consumers" (Bauman, 2004), then it can no longer be viewed as a supposedly neutral means of maintaining profitability or market shares. This, of course, is where the surveillance mode of analysis points up the political dimensions of practices such as loyalty marketing. But if marketers really "knew" their consumers, they would also be aware that market "fairness" is also valued highly by many (see e.g., Oliver and Sawn, 1989). How far this expectation works within impersonal forms of consumer-courting such as loyalty marketing is an empirical question. And one that—either way—still has vital ethical ramifications.

References

Aas, Franko, Katja, Helene Oppen Gudnhus, and Lomell, Heidi Mork (2008) *Technologies of Insecurity: The Surveillance of Everyday Life*. New York: Routledge-Cavendish.

Andrejevic, Mark (2003) "Monitored Mobility in the Era of Mass Customization." *Space & Culture*, 6: 132–50.

Ball, Kirstie (2003) "Categorizing the Workers: Electronic Surveillance and Social Ordering in the Call Centre." In David Lyon, ed. *Surveillance as Social Sorting*. London, Routledge, pp. 201–25.

——and Wood, David Murakami (2006) "'A Report on the Surveillance Society' for the Information Commissioner (UK), by the Surveillance Studies Network." Available at http://www.ico.gov.uk/upload/documents/library/data_protection/practical_application/surveillance_society_full_report_2006.pdf.

Bauman, Zygmunt (2001) "Consuming Life." *Journal of Consumer Culture*, 1: 9–29.

——(2004) *Work, Consumerism and the New Poor*. Buckingham: Open University Press.

Beckett, Anthony (2004) "From Branches to Call Centres: New Strategic Realities in Retail Banking." *The Services Industry Journal*, 24: 43–62.

Bibby, Andrew (2006) "Big Spenders Jump the Queue." *Mail on Sunday*, March 13.

Bogard, William (1996) *The Simulation of Surveillance: Hypercontrol in Telematic Societies*. Cambridge: Cambridge University Press.

Bowker, Geoffrey C., and Star, Susan Leigh (1999) *Sorting Things Out: Classification and its Consequences*. Cambridge, MA: MIT Press.

Burrows, Roger, and Gane, Nicholas (2006) "Geodemographics, Software and Class." *Sociology*, 40: 793–812.

Capizzi, Michael T., and Ferguson, Rick (2005). "Loyalty Trends for the Twenty-First Century." *Journal of Consumer Marketing*, 22: 72–80.

Cuthbertson, Richard, and Laine, Arttu (2004) "The Role of CRM within Retail Loyalty Marketing." *Journal of Targeting, Measurement and Analysis for Marketing*, 12: 290–304.

Danna, Anthony, and Gandy, Oscar H. (2002) "All That Glitters is Not Gold: Digging Beneath the Surface of Data Mining." *Journal of Business Ethics*, 40: 373–86.

Deighton, John (2005) "Consumer Identity Motives in the Information Age." In S. Ratneshwar and David Glen Mick, eds. *Inside Consumption: Consumer Motives, Goals and Desires.* London: Routledge.

Ellison, Nick, and Burrows, Roger (2007) "New Spaces of (Dis)engagement? Social Politics, Urban Technologies and the Rezoning of the City." *Housing Studies,* 22: 295–312.

Ellul, Jacques (1990) *The Technological Bluff.* Grand Rapids, MI: W.B. Eerdmans.

Elmer, Greg (2004) *Profiling Machines.* Cambridge, MA: MIT Press.

Evans, Martin (2003) "The Relational Oxymoron and Personalization Pragmatism." *Journal of Consumer Marketing,* 20: 665–85.

Gandy, Oscar H. (1993) *The Panoptic Sort: A Political Economy of Personal Information.* Boulder, CO: Westview Press.

——(2006) "Quixotics Unite! Engaging the Pragmatists on Rational Discrimination." In David Lyon, ed. *Theorizing Surveillance: The Panopticon and Beyond.* Portland, OR: Willan Publishing, pp. 318–36.

——(2009) *Coming to Terms with Chance: Engaging Rational Discrimination and Cumulative Disadvantage.* London: Ashgate.

Giddens, Anthony (1987) *Social Theory and Modern Sociology.* Stanford, CA: Stanford University Press.

Gordon, Ian (2006) "Relationship Demarketing: Managing Wasteful or Worthless Customer Relationships." *Ivey Business Journal,* March/April: 1–4. http://www.iveybusinessjournal.com/view_article.asp?intArticle_ID=625.

Green, Stephen (1999) "A Plague on the Panopticon: Surveillance and Power in the Global Economy." *Information, Communication and Society,* 2: 26–44.

Haggerty, Kevin (2009) "'Ten Thousand Times Larger': Anticipating the Expansion of Surveillance." In Daniel Neyland and Benjamin Goold, eds. *New Directions in Surveillance and Privacy.* Cullompton: Willan.

Hart, Susan, Smith, Andrew, Sparks, Leigh, and Tzokas, Nikolaos (1999) "Are Loyalty Schemes a Manifestation of Relationship Marketing?" *Journal of Marketing Management,* 15: 541–62.

Lace, Susanne ed. (2005) *The Glass Consumer: Life in a Surveillance Society.* Bristol: The Policy Press.

Lury, Celia (2005) "The Objectivity of the Brand: Marketing, Law and Sociology." In Andrew Barry and Don Slater, eds. *The Technological Economy.* London; New York: Routledge, pp. viii, 204.

Lyon, David (1994) *The Electronic Eye: The Rise of Surveillance Society.* Minneapolis: University of Minnesota Press.

——(2001) *Surveillance Society: Monitoring Everyday Life.* Buckingham, UK; Phildelphia, PA: Open University.

——(2007) *Surveillance Studies: An Overview.* Cambridge; Malden, MA: Polity.

——(2009) *Identifying Citizens: ID Cards as Surveillance.* Cambridge; Malden, MA: Polity.

Miles, Steven (1998) *Consumerism—As a Way of Life.* London: Sage.

Millard, N.J. (2003) "A Million Segments of One—How Personal Should Customer Relationship Management Get?" *BT Technology Journal,* 21(1): 114–20.

Miller, Peter, and Rose, Nikolas (1997) "Mobilizing the Consumer: Assembling the Subject of Consumption." *Theory, Culture & Society*, 14: 1–36.

Moisander, Johanna, and Eriksson, Päivi (2006) "Corporate Narratives of Information Society: Making Up the Mobile Consumer Subject." *Consumption, Markets and Culture*, 9: 257–75.

Narver, John C., and Slater, Stanley F. (1990) "The Effect of Market Orientation on Business Profitability." *Journal of Marketing*, 54: 20–35.

Oliver, Richard J. and Swan, John E. (1989) "Consumer Perceptions of Interpersonal Equity and Satisfaction in Transactions." *Journal of Marketing*, 53: 21–35.

Payne, Adrian, and Frow, Pennie (2005) "A Strategic Framework for Customer Relationship Marketing." *Journal of Marketing*, 69: 167–76.

Pridmore, Jason (2008) Loyal Subjects?: Consumer Surveillance in the Personal Information Economy. Ph.D. Dissertation, Department of Sociology, Queen's University.

Rowley, Jennifer (2005) "Customer Knowledge Management or Consumer Surveillance." *Global Business and Economics Review*, 7: 100–10.

Stivers, Richard (2004) "The Role of Statistics in Management Magic." *Bulletin of Science, Technology & Society*, 24: 99–106.

Winnett, Robert, and Thomas, Zoe (2003) "Are You a Second Class Consumer." *Sunday Times*, October 19, p. 9.

Zukin, Sharon, and Maguire, Jennifer Smith (2004) "Consumers and Consumption." *Annual Review of Sociology*, 30: 173–97.

Zwick, Detlev, and Dholakia, Nikhilesh (2004a) "Consumer Subjectivity in the Age of Internet: The Radical Concept of Marketing Control through Customer Relationship Management." *Information and Organization*, 14: 211–36.

——(2004b) "Whose Identity Is It Anyway? Consumer Representation in the Age of Database Marketing." *Journal of Macromarketing*, 24: 31–43.

6

Consumer Segmentation in Practice: An Ethnographic Account of Slippage

Patricia L. Sunderland and Rita M. Denny

Consumers, too, are invented, displaced, translated, through fine chains of inter-est. (Latour, 1996: 42)

Our goal in this chapter is to illuminate some of the inherent messiness, in essence the effervescence of humanity, embodied in consumer research and consumer segmentation. To do so we focus the lens on a particular study in which, as a commercial project, not much went right. Slippage was the order of the day—slippage in the segment criteria, in time, in the willingness of research participants to partner with us in the process. As anthropologists employed as consultants for business clients, the majority of our work entails ethnographic or semiotic cultural analyses carried out in the United States. From a research point of view, the study in question was mundane, almost quotidian. We were contracted to carry out an ethnographic, cultural analysis of entertaining. The research task was to illuminate how people prepared and shopped for their "at home" entertaining events. The ultimate client, a large retailer, was interested in developing customized messages (in terms of direct mail, online/e-mail communications, print, and in-store marketing) for increasing entertainment spending targeted to their customer segments: Exec-utive Manager Moms, Buoyant Boomers, Experience Demanders, and Bargain Hunters, as well as Competitive Store Shoppers and three of their business customer segments, for example, Small Retailers and Resellers.[1]

Admittedly, the slippage in this project was extreme to the point of comedy. Yet we see this case as illustrative, not exceptional. Our goal is both quite general and serious: to show how consumer research grounded in consumer segmentation practice is realized in real time and in terms of real lives. Cru-cially, our goal is to highlight how consumer segmentation, founded in the collection of consumer information, is, in practice, not always the manipulative, controlling, iron caging of consumers as it is often framed to be (Turow, 1997, 2006; Elmer, 2004; cf. Zwick and Knott, 2009; Pridmore and Lyon, this volume). Rather, we want to show that, if anything, the practice is more manipulative, controlling, and an iron caging of those closer in, that is, the people whose work is focused by these databases and segmentation schemes.

Our additional purpose of highlighting the human element infused in and around consumer segmentation and consumer research practice is to show that while consumer segmentations as abstractions are real, and thus as objects, as things, as reifications have a Latourian life and material agency of their own, in the practice of their use these schemas are also infiltrated by the messiness of human life. For researchers and clients, carrying out the research involves matters of agency, personal and political agendas, and just making it all happen with the material realities of US life as lived—geographic dispersal and mobility, digital devices, and relentless busyness. Likewise, for research participants, personal and political agendas, agency, and the matrix of contemporary life are also crucial. We want to show how human relationships and the messiness of human life as lived are in the end the engine and medium that animate consumer research and that keep the restrictive glue of consumer segmentation schemas from actually sticking.

In the presentation of this case we have tried to retain some of the small facts and the details of language, for instance in the reprinting of actual e-mails exchanged. Providing this ethnographic detail speaks to our muses in the theoretical traditions of ethnomethodology and linguistic anthropology; we are interested in the ways social practices and ideologies are co-constituted by language-in-use (Schieffelin et al., 1998; Hanks, 2005; Silverstein, 2006; see also Callon, 2007). We envision our approach and analysis as aligned with the social and critical analyses of marketing worlds by the other authors in this volume, as well as aligned with social and ethnographic studies of science, technology, finance, and financial worlds (e.g., Latour, 1996; Callon, 1998; Ong and Collier, 2005; Fisher and Downey, 2006; Ho, 2009; Holmes, 2009).

Portals of Entry, Portals of Engagement

The catalyst for our involvement in this project was a telephone call at the end of April 2007 from Kim, who had been a client of ours since 2001. She was the portal to our interactions with the retailer as well as to members within her own organization.

Kim's company was a large producer of consumable packaged goods. Her company had agreed to organize, and pay for, the research. Their interest in carrying out consumer research for the retailer was grounded in desires to sell more of their products to the store's customers—but only indirectly. This research entailed understanding the preparation and purchase processes for home entertainment events more generally, well beyond the purchase of this producer's goods. The results were going to be incorporated in the retailer's overall marketing plans, without necessarily taking the producers' products into account. Kim's company's proximal purpose in undertaking the research was to strengthen their relationship with the retailer.

As the detailed analyses of Malefyt (2003), Mazzarella (2003), and Moeran (1996) regarding advertising agency practices have made clear, even if consumer research is often framed as "knowing the consumer" or "the voice of the consumer," one of its pragmatic values resides in the relationships it forges between concerned parties. Just as consumer knowledge is a strategic resource in the relationship-building between advertising agencies and their clients, so it is between manufacturers and retailers. At least in the United States, amidst an atmosphere of stiff competition and payment for shelf space as well as aggressive delisting of slowly selling products, retailers have gained positions of power in bringing goods to the marketplace. Without a viable relationship and partnership, which leads to the retailer's shelf space and attention, manufacturers have no sales. As we have frequently witnessed, the producers of goods will therefore provide research on the retailer's customers and business as a way to foster their own relationship and the resultant placement and sales of their goods with the retailer. Manufacturers pay for and organize the research and deliver it to the retailer. As important as end users are for packaged goods manufacturers, their crucial "customer," as the appellation generally goes, is the retailer of their goods.

In this case, Kim's contact with the retailer, her portal to conversations with that company, was Bill, who, like Kim, was a senior member of his company's research department. Before contacting us, Kim and other members of her company's team had discussed with Bill the possibility of a joint research project focused on entertainment purchasing. Their original telephone conference call had then been followed-up with a number of clarifying e-mails from both Bill and Kim. Based on these discussions, Kim had agreed that her company would organize both a qualitative and quantitative study focused on the retailer's predefined consumer segments.

Kim contacted us to carry out the qualitative portions. She knew us. If the formal protocol for contracting consumer research would be to send out a competitive request-for-proposal (RFP), to preselect a small group for further winnowing, and perhaps to meet with individual "suppliers" (as we are often called), this no longer applied. In 2001, it had. At that time, Rita had taken a plane in order to meet with Kim and her director face-to-face, to discuss the research, and to have lunch. It was successful, we got that first job. Rita has always felt that it was not only the feeling of security regarding our ethnographic skills but a particularly enjoyable repartee about baseball which had sealed the deal. Whether "baseball talk" was the crucial initial factor could be debated, but without question, over the years, beyond establishing ourselves as a reliable (and insightful) research partner, we had evolved a client–research supplier relationship of great respect and liking for one another. Clients go to the field with us and the bonds between us are strengthened by interesting field experiences. In interactions with Kim, the impromptu time she and Patti had spent together at a tattooing and piercing conference had created an especially memorable bond. As in the relationships between advertising agencies and clients, and between manufacturers and retailers, and as in other realms of life, business clients call us back because of strategic interests as well as established relationships. In essence then, in their framing, and in their initiation, commercial consumer research projects are a partnership and collaboration: a collaboration of interests among many parties in the research question and project at hand as well as a collaboration of other strategic interests and agendas. And, in the situations where things tend to work well, liking one another, human sympathy (in the French sense), affection, whatever word one wants to use, is involved. At the least, life and work is made more pleasant with a relationship partner with whom one enjoys interacting.

In this instance, as important as relationship-building with this customer was for Kim's company, Kim's own internal budget constraints necessitated being extremely cost conscious. It was a shoestring budget, but we wanted to make it work. Thus, we devised a way that we could conduct an ethnographic project—and still keep the costs minimal. Between that first phone call and then one other, we jointly agreed that we would carry out the qualitative research with a mix of ethnographic diaries and four to seven mini-focus groups, conducted within the particular store of interest in order to have people actually interact with the merchandise as well as to save money. In between the ethnographic diaries and the focus groups, Kim would organize and carry out a quantitative online survey. We were not to be involved in this quantitative portion except to give input into issues to cover based on the ethnographic diaries. Then, the groups were planned to take place after the completion of the online research—so that we could use the group and in-store encounters to explore in vivo any issues that had risen to the top in this quantitative portion as well as matters that were still unclear based on the diaries. Then we would complete our analysis and write a report based on the iterative combination of diaries, groups, and in-store observations.

We actually liked this method and iterative format. Over the years ethnographic diaries have become one of our favorite research modalities, as we see video and audio diaries as not only a means of extending the reach of ethnographic inquiry in time and space, but also as a key means of involving those with whom we conduct research in the research process, in essence in engaging them in a relationship of collaborative partnership and conversation (Sunderland and Denny, 2002). Doing focus groups in the store also allowed a chance for in vivo research that is so close to our anthropological hearts, and would get us out of the focus group room and away from the inherent tensions of a behind-the-glass back-room audience (see Grandclément and Gaglio in this volume; Lezaun, 2007; Sunderland and Denny, 2007).

We did not write a formal research proposal for Kim at that time. When she called we were very busy with other projects. The calendar notes indicate two client debriefs; Rita in Tampa doing fieldwork and Patti starting a report for a major automotive client as well as working on the accompanying edited video—all between the Friday of the phone call and Kim's go-ahead message the following Wednesday. Not writing out our plans in a proposal was okay with Kim. In fact, she did not even ask for a proposal from us at that time. She knew from prior experience that we would carry out what we had agreed. Kim did, however, have to write a proposal for Bill. On May 2, she sent us an e-mail which implicitly and explicitly evidenced her sense of partnership and trust with us regarding this project. She asked for our opinion on study design as well as for us to just correct anything we thought incorrect in the proposal for Bill. Details and tone of the e-mail also evidenced her situation of tightly booked, ferociously speeding time.

> Patti,
> Can you take a look at the correspondence below as well as the proposal (I need to finish Phase 3, but you'll get the gist of it). Could you provide your thoughts as to how we can re-design to incorporate the business segments too? He's wanting to include 3 Business segments. I would need this soon—later today even—if possible, since I'd like to get this proposal to him tomorrow. I just can't do it this afternoon since I'll be tied up in a meeting. Please correct anything that I've mis-stated in the proposal.
> Could you also provide a rough timeline as you see it?
> BTW, we're officially awarding you this project . . . .
> Thanks!
> Kim

Time was of the essence in this project. We needed to get the research moving so that we could ask participants to complete diaries focused around preparations and events for the last weekend in May, the Memorial Day holiday. Widely celebrated, Memorial Day is the holiday in the United States that marks the start of summer fun. In the abstract, this holiday held the promise of lots of home backyard, poolside, and beachfront entertaining. With Kim, we further planned that the Memorial Day-focused diaries would be completed and returned to us by June 4, the online survey would be completed and analyzed by July 31, and we would carry out the focus groups during the first or second weeks of August, just in time to inform Bill's company's upcoming third-quarter marketing plan.

Organizing the research around the Memorial Day holiday also held the promise of being able to find consumers who were entertaining. We did know that we would need to ask a number of people before we were likely to find people who: (*a*) fit the target segment criteria; (*b*) were actually hosting a home entertainment event in our window of time; and (*c*) would agree to document that process during a ten-day to two-week period. If one stops to think about it, all of these needle eyes could be relatively small, and we needed to thread all three simultaneously and as soon as possible.

Within our own organization, the call from Kim catalyzed a series of e-mails and calls to Elke, our recruiting coordinator. In the carrying out of consumer research in the United States, the actual recruiting of participants for a study—the contacting of people by telephone or e-mail—is generally done by geographically local recruiters. Elke is our portal to conversations with these local organizations. She garners their agreement to contact people on our behalf. As a rule, Elke also writes the recruiting questionnaire, "the screener," which is basically a series of questions to make sure participants meet client-specified demographic or other (e.g., segment) criteria, and if they do, then an invitation to take part in the study, routinely sweetened by the offer of a financial incentive. Local recruiters generally request at least a week to recruit participants for a study. In a more complicated ethnographic study that necessitates greater participant involvement and time commitment, at least two.

Immediately after the project was approved, Elke began preparing the basis of a screener, as well as contacting local recruiters in some of the cities that we had discussed with Kim as good potential "markets" for this research. So now, we were standing ready and local recruiters were also standing ready, but we had to wait on information from Bill, via Kim, on specifications of their consumer and business customer segments as well as final agreements on the markets for the research in order to finalize the recruiting materials.

On the morning of May 3, Kim had received a return message from Bill, thanking her for the proposal and indicating that he was going to share it internally for "some additional commentary" and would get back to her with feedback as soon as possible, "ASAP." He also included some clarifications regarding numbers and segments to be included in the qualitative and quantitative portion, and then ended his message with a promise to be back in touch shortly and the assurance with exclamation mark: "I think this project will be valuable to both our organizations!"

As it turned out, Bill's "as soon as possible," his ASAP, was not in time for a Memorial Day focus. In fact, it was barely in time for a July 4, Independence Day holiday focus. Not until June 13, at 10:52 pm, with July 4th rapidly approaching, did we get the go ahead from Kim to begin recruiting. On June 14, Elke sent the recruiting materials to recruiters. The goal was to recruit thirty-two participants (split among the segments) in the metropolitan areas of Los Angeles, Dallas, Orlando, and New York, and we wanted recruiters to find them almost immediately.

Time, and its slippage, was a continuing force in this project, but what we felt even more acutely was the landslide of problems unleashed by the segmentation scheme.

Slippery Slopes

It certainly was not in Kim's control to make decisions about geographic locations for the research nor was she in the position to tell us the specifications we would need to recruit participants. This was Bill's purview. Bill needed to have a say in the geographic markets researched—so that the research would be perceived as valuable within his company. Moreover, he needed to inform Kim, and Kim in turn us, and us in turn Elke, and Elke in turn the local recruiters regarding the recruiting specifications for each target segment. We did not and could not know what constituted an Executive Manager Mom, Bargain Hunter, Experience Demander, Buoyant Boomer, or even Competitive Shopper. What ages, what attitudes, what type of purchasing? What would be our criteria? Obviously, one could conjure up some ideas of the ages and attitudes that might seem to correlate with each of these segments. But, really, that was not up to us to decide. Past experience had taught us, too many times, that one must take client's target specifications very seriously. If we recruited "the wrong people" for a study, clients were likely, at best, to dismiss the findings, and most likely, also to dismiss us. As Flynn (2009) noted at Microsoft, findings can be dismissed if the assumptions a client group makes about their customers' distinctiveness are not honored. Further, the dismissal can be emotionally heated, in part because the client group takes on the unique distinctions of "my customers" as their own mandate and field of action.

Moreover, we had learned the hard way that not only do clients have an emotionally vested interest in their consumer segments, but that the finer points of the consumer segment differentiations often reside in implicit or unsaid attitudinal distinctions. A number of years ago, Patti was conducting in-home interviews and shop-alongs for Target, a mass merchant branded with a touch of cachet. Accompanying her was a planner from Target's advertising agency. One of the first interviews was with a woman who talked about how she especially liked going to Target to pick up small stylish birthday gifts, for example. We went to a local Target store with her, she certainly knew the store; she, without question, had experience shopping at Target. Yet, after the interview, deeply upset and deeply concerned, the planner continuously reiterated that she was not a Target shopper. Rather, he said, she was a Walmart shopper. While it seemed almost an absurd statement to Patti given that clearly this was a woman who shopped at Target, for him, this interviewee was a Walmart shopper because her attitude (and lack of income) made her consistently focus on saving money and that was not the attitude (nor income situation) of a (real) Target shopper. Yes, Patti agreed, she had told us she shopped at Walmart and she was very conscious of her spending, yet she also shopped at Target and she did seem to think about Target in a way that appeared in line with Target's brand image. There was tension in the back and forth which included Patti arguing that it was okay anyway as the information from the interview did provide relevant details regarding the question at hand. He was not pleased; he thought we had recruited the wrong person for the study, a "mis-recruit" in industry jargon. He was worried. We only had a handful of interviews and suppose we did not get any Target shoppers? As the study progressed, Patti herself observed this attitudinal difference and could appreciate the perceived differences as he saw them. Still, in the world of actual shopping, the notion that people who are shopping in Target are not Target shoppers, but rather Walmart shoppers borders on the absurd. These differences, like the assumed differences in the practices of IT professionals by server type based on Microsoft's own internal organization, do not make any sense in terms of an ethnographic analysis of how products and services are enmeshed in everyday life (see Flynn, 2009). Moreover, segmentation distinctions too easily become self-fulfilling tenets. This self-fulfillment is one of their vulnerabilities in terms of an inductive approach to understanding the realities and opportunities based on what people are really doing in the marketplace, the ostensible reason for which we are usually engaged.

Nonetheless, we knew, without question, that we had to be conscious of recruiting in terms of Bill's company's target definitions. Within the world of commercial ethnography, we must work within and negotiate the consumer segmentation matrix whether we like it or not. And, at some level, Elke feels that pressure even more—because Elke is responsible for writing the screeners that contain the criteria that recruiters are required to use, and when we hear from our clients that a participant does not fit the criteria (or is in any way a "phony" respondent), Elke is the first to hear it from us.

In the end, the recruiting screeners that we sent out for this entertainment study did not contain many questions. They were very thin, largely assuring that the person was going to be purchasing for an entertainment event sometime in the next three weeks and that they did, in general, purchase the category of products produced by Kim's company when entertaining. These screeners were thin because beyond the Competitive Store Shoppers, a segment of customers whose names and numbers were not in the retailer's database, the criteria for other consumer segments were not given to us. Instead, Bill's company supplied us with customer lists for each segment. The recruiters' task was simply to find people from those lists who were going to be involved in a home entertaining event and who were also willing to complete a diary of their activities for us during that time.

Customer lists worry us. They do not work well as recruiting tools. Such database lists, generated from sources such as store membership or credit cards, product warranty registrations, or other producer–consumer interactions, contain people's names, addresses, and phone numbers. But, it's a mobile, changing world and people are people. Thus, we have always found it true that on any list a very significant number of the phone numbers are no longer valid, that many of the names and addresses are simply wrong (both do change), and that even if the information is correct, many people—whether out of fear or annoyance of how their name got to a "telemarketer"—simply hang up. We also know that many times people on a list did not actually fit the recruiting criteria—even if, per the list, they should. There are frequently a number of people who are not actually consumers of the product, service, or store in question. Thus, in car studies, we might have a list which indicates that a certain person owns a particular car. But we prefer to ask this question in the screener. It would not be good to arrive at the door to find out that the person had purchased that car for her cousin, who in fact lives in another state. If a customer has a store card, and seems to be a big purchaser of lawn products, perhaps that's because he is buying for the neighbor. Or, perhaps someone was convinced by a spouse to get a store credit card, and the now estranged spouse is the one who is actually using it. One can imagine the endless permutations of complicated human situations which would subvert the intended purposes of the lists. And so, we almost literally begged, "just in case," for some criteria to use to be sure that those we recruited fit the desired segment. But none were forthcoming.

Customer lists as recruiting tools also inspire fear in us because we know that when they do not work, we have to be the ones who let clients know that their customer information is problematic. Clients tend to love and live by their customer lists. The lists are artifacts and cultural capital, they represent consumers, are proof these *are* the consumers for a company (see Zwick and Knott, 2009; Pridmore and Lyon, this volume). Feeling that one has an accurate database undoubtedly provides feelings of control: These people are my customers, the database constitutes my knowledge resource, I am in control. And so when we must tell clients that much of their consumer information is inaccurate, or that many of the people simply cannot be found, these are not generally words that go down smoothly or easily.

Prophylactically, we warned Kim about the problem of lists. As a consumer goods manufacturer without a credit card, warranty, or other form to easily keep track of consumers, lists were not the norm for their own typical consumer research projects. Before it happened, we wanted her to hear from us that we were concerned about the lists. We reiterated that it really would be good to know the target criteria and for recruiters to be able to recruit from the lists as well as their own resources, or, at least, be able to be sure that the people we did recruit from the lists fit the target criteria. Kim responded in an e-mail with what she had been told:

> Bill is going to provide a list of 1000 per segment to choose from. These will be the "best fit" members for each segment; in other words, those that are most tightly matched to the segment criteria. He said that they refresh the data so often that we should not encounter problems with someone not being in the segment to which they're coded.

We held our breath. Not for long. The lists quickly proved problematic.

Elke sent the lists to recruiters on June 14. By noon of the next day, a Friday, problems had begun to surface. At 12:06 pm, Elke sent Kim and Bill an e-mail, cc'ing Patti (the e-mail portal had been opened up so that Elke now had direct e-mail contact with Kim and Bill to keep things moving), reporting what she had been informed by the recruiters:

> On the Executive Manager Mom list, there are men. Since we never received actual definitions of each Segment, should I stay away from the men on this particular list? Or is it OK to call them?
> The recruiters have started the list today, but already have had a few disconnects and wrong numbers....
> I'll have a better update next week.

In just over an hour, Bill responded to Elke, cc'ing Kim and Patti:

> It would be possible to have men on that list since it is based on transaction behavior and not straight demographics. That being said though...I think we should try to go with females on the list who are truly moms.

> Thank you for bringing that up. If there are any other questions, please feel free to let us know.

So, within less than twenty-four hours, the "disconnects and wrong numbers" on the lists had begun to surface, and the Executive Manager Moms, even if there were men on that list, needed to be females who were "truly" moms. And while the tone of Elke's e-mail to Bill and Kim was measured, there was frustration. As Elke expressed this frustration in a private e-mail to Patti, approximately five minutes after her "official" e-mail:

> You know – this is what I hate!
> Do you think Bill could have actually told us what each segment meant, so I could have incorporated that in the screener?

I mean, yes, it sounds obvious that Executive Manager Moms are actually Moms, but still we did not put in the screener any requirements for demographics.
I hope nothing else comes up, or I'll be pissed.
I mean, should we now assume that Buoyant Boomers are people in their 50's and 60's?

Elke's message that "we did not put in the screener any requirements for demographics" spoke to the implicit understandings of the recruiters' commitment. Local recruiters know that they must recruit in terms of the screener criteria (or tell us when they cannot). The screener acts as a kind of sacred document—if they recruit someone who fits those criteria, we accept them and pay for that recruit. If the person does not fit, we can complain. Recruiters and Elke were becoming concerned because of the segment names. Hence Elke's question about whether we should also define Buoyant Boomers as people in their fifties and sixties.

Just before 4 pm on the same Friday, Elke sent a follow-up e-mail to Bill, again cc'ing Kim and Patti, which incorporated a further update regarding the list problems local recruiters had encountered and another polite plea for the information that would allow us to recruit in line with their segment criteria.

Bill,
I was just wondering, would it be at all possible to provide me with the "specs" for each of the segments—what they are supposed to be?
On the Executive Manager Mom's list—two of the women were over 70 years old. Obviously, we terminated on this, but if there is something else we should watch out for when recruiting anyone that is interested, it would really be helpful. for example, do the Moms have kids under a certain age? Are all the Buoyant Boomers supposed to be 50–60 years old?
Thank you!
Elke

On the following Monday, shortly before 6 pm, Bill responded requesting a telephone call as it was becoming clear that e-mail exchanges were not sufficient to clarify the issues. The problems recruiters were encountering in recruiting the segments had to do with slippage between the actual means by which segments were determined and the names that were attached. As Bill wrote:

Could we have a quick call about this tomorrow by chance? The problem is that our segmentation is transaction based and then married to attitudinal research. It is almost absent of basic demographics. The basis is what you purchase and how your purchase behavior manifests itself in the store. That is why you can have men in the Executive Manager Mom or 20 year olds in the Buoyant Boomer segment.
Let me know availability please.
Regards, Bill

Shortly before 8 pm, after clarifying with both Kim and Patti that we would, in fact, not be available the next day, Elke sent a reply to Bill, in which she finessed the fact of Kim and Patti's unavailability into a positive for the project, provided her phone number, and requested an early in the day call. By shortly before noon, Elke still had not heard and sent Bill another e-mail, reiterating that we "just want to make sure that we are recruiting the correct type of respondent" and that to keep things moving we needed to know "today or tomorrow." There was considerable back and forth, delay and disruption in the time organization of that call, but they were able to arrange a 10 am call for the following morning. Their conversation and negotiations are what allowed the project to move forward, with a bit of clarification regarding people to recruit within segments and a new screener. While Buoyant Boomers were in fact supposed to be over fifty, we were allowed to retain a forty-five-year-old who had already been recruited. As Elke happily pronounced in an e-mail to Patti and Kim:

> I spoke with Bill. He and his assistant called at exactly 10am this AM! Very prompt!
>
> Anyway, he did say that if we had other questions, to contact Gustav since he is traveling and also dealing with 21 other projects. . . .
>
> So—the only thing that he specified regarding the Consumer segments are the Executive Manager Moms . . . must be Female and have 1+ child under 18 at home and Buoyant Boomers must be 50–62 years of age.
>
> We had already recruited an Buoyant Boomer who was 45, but he said we could keep her (thank goodness).
>
> The other segments are based on shopping habits and didn't need demographic info attached to them.
>
> I have attached the revised screener (all changes are highlighted)
>
> I am expecting an update later on today and will forward that once it has been received and I have checked it over.
>
> Thanks!

So now in the recruiting we were applying demographic recruiting specifications, on top of their lists which comprised the "best fit members" for each target segment. We were assuring that the Executive Manager Moms were actually female and had a child under eighteen living at home and that the Buoyant Boomers were between fifty and sixty-two years of age. But if these demographic criteria did not actually adhere to their shopping-habit, transaction-based target segmentation, why were they then applied? Clearly, it had to do with their naming and the assumptions that were ushered in by the linguistic fact of those names (see Silverstein, 1985). Executive Manager Moms conjures up the notion of a middle- or upper middle-class mother who organizes her household and family life like a business. Buoyant Boomers evokes images of 50+ adults who are actively engaged in life. Experience Demanders and Bargain Hunters are built on the notion that consumption and shopping is a quest for experience for some, while primarily a matter of attending to price for others. While Executive Manager Moms, Buoyant Boomers, Experience Demanders, and Bargain Hunters are, in fact, pseudonyms we are using in this chapter in the interest of client confidentiality, the actual names of this retailer's segments conjured up the same types of notions—we have chosen them for that reason. Moreover, that name changing in itself makes the point, there is conjuring and slippage involved in consumer segmentation efforts, not least of which occurs through their naming.

And if this case's examples seem extreme (where 70-year olds and men become members of the Executive Mom segment and 20-year olds can become quasi-retirees), we would also argue that its conceptual assumptions are no more absurd than more sophisticated segmentation algorithms. As anthropologists and consumer researchers, coming to grips with client assumptions about their customers and being able to negotiate beyond imposed boundaries is a task oft repeated. Nonetheless, the client's interest in this case, as it is in many, was in developing customized messaging and our study had thus to be carried out in terms of their predefined consumer segments. Such consumers may not exist except as an abstraction, but the parameters of that abstraction are also the conceptual cage in which we are incorporated as anthropologists in the business world.

The problems of segmentation categorizations (and other caging practices) do often come to light in the recruiting of participants. In this case even as the naming of the segments was rendered absurd in light of the actual demographics of the people falling into those segments, the naming of segments nonetheless required recruiters and researchers to not accept certain people as "the right respondents." In other cases the in vivo absurdity of segmentation criteria is illuminated when recruiters cannot find people who meet the specified criteria. We have repeatedly encountered this particular problem in studies for automotive manufacturers. The use of a persona, an image of a particular kind of person for whom a given car model is created, may be a powerful device to align the efforts of diverse teams within an organization (Patton, 2009; see also Flynn, 2009). Yet when ethnographic researchers are asked by marketers to flesh out the lifeworlds of this persona in real life, problems ensue. We can be asked, for instance, to find someone of a particular age; with a particular kind of job; who drives a particular kind of car; who is single, or married, or with or without kids (of specified ages); who exhibits a certain set of attitudes; who finds art (or something else) very important in their lives; lives in a certain city; and is planning to buy a car in the next three years. At 1 percent incidence, what is the point? And, of course, the person must also agree to let us videotape them in their home and while driving, on a particular day of a particular week.

So, we frequently end up in polite standoffs and then negotiate a "loosening" of target criteria once recruiting has begun. In the current US climate of pervasive busyness, where it is difficult to have any sustained conversations, this is no mean feat. In between and in the background of the messages between Elke and Bill reprinted above were a number of communications between Elke, Patti, and Kim. In these interactions, the actual amount of effort, anxiety, and the life disruptions, the real work that managing these conversations entailed was more apparent. On the day on which Bill had suggested we all speak the next day, Kim had let us know that it was going to be difficult for her because she was going to be in out-of-town meetings all day and then heading back to the airport. When by noon of that next day Elke had still not heard from Bill, despite her request to speak in the morning, we actually wanted to call him rather than e-mail; however, we did not have his phone number. Thus, Patti tried to contact Kim, even knowing that she was likely in transit, to obtain Bill's number. Kim had quickly responded, via her Blackberry, that she was on the way to the airport, but would be able to give us Bill's phone number within the hour. This led to some back and forth messages of "thanks" and "no problem." The issue getting in the way of quick resolution was, as Kim framed it: "Usually these blackberries do the trick but for some reason his number isn't coming up. I need to fire up my pc when I get to gate!" One can visualize Kim racing through security, trying to get to her gate, meanwhile trying to turn on her computer and get the number to us, while also trying to insure that she boarded the plane and had the devices turned off by the time the cabin door closed. In addition to these efforts on Kim and Patti's part to secure Bill's number for Elke, there were the emotional costs for Elke. There was annoyance, anxiety, and life disruption. As she intimated her feelings and the situation in a background e-mail to Patti:

> Well, of course, I've been friggin' sitting by the phone all day waiting for this guy to call, and his counterpart—Gustav, sends me an e-mail wanting to do it at 5:30pm my time tonight, and I have my five-year-old's friends over now and can't take the time to talk on the phone! So now I told him it either has to be later or first thing tomorrow AM. . . .

In the e-mail to Gustav and Bill, she had simply and politely glossed her reply in terms of "sorry" and that she could do it after 6:00 pm but not at 5:30 pm. And if, in this case, Elke's back channeling to us versus her professional replies to Bill helped release and lessen some of the personal tension felt, this did not fully overcome the problems of these categorizations; it only managed to manage them in the moment. We had to wait for the humanity of the actual participants to render the adhesive power of the conceptual caging moot.

Participant Intervention

This study's recruiting problems did not end with the clarification of the recruiting criteria to use in further screening people on the lists. Later in the same day, Elke was again e-mailing Gustav, requesting permission for recruiters to tell business owners that the study was being done on behalf of the retailer. Despite three days of calling people from the business segment lists, none would agree to take part. Our hope was that by identifying the retailer, the business owners would have a greater understanding of how their name appeared on the calling list as well as a better rationale for their own interest in participating. We also decided on the same day to increase the monetary incentive for the business participants, hoping that offering more money to complete the diary might also increase our recruiting success. Neither intervention worked.

Four days later, on June 25, at 11:11 pm, in an e-mail with the subject line of "the recruiting dilemma," Patti, cc'ing Elke, explained the issues to Kim:

> kim,
> now we're having recruiters saying they've gone all through lists, no more to call, lots of disconnects...elke has already asked bill for more lists. just wondering before we give up the whole ghost...can't we just recruit the demos from people (or shopping habits as seems to be the segmentation criteria), and let the recruiter pull from database and just make sure people are the store's shoppers? We'd just need to know the criteria from bill and we'd be good.

In the middle of writing this note explaining that there was no longer even a pool to call upon, as well as alerting Kim that we had already intervened to get more lists and once again "begging" for the retailer's segment criteria (this time so that the recruiter could just call from their own "database" basically a shorthand for a list of people who have pre-stated interest in participating in consumer research studies as well as their own "snowball sampling" interventions), a thought had occurred. If the thought had mostly been generated in an attempt at humor in order to lighten the emotional toll of the situation, it took on value as a seriously good idea by the end. As Patti continued her late night note:

> or, we just forget their whole segmentation thing and recruit people who are 1) having a party; 2) shop at the store at least 4x/year; 3) buy your product, including for get-togethers; 4) are at least 21.
> do you think that would work?
> i started off just kidding when i wrote the latter, but why not?
> best, patti

At 7:02 am, Elke intervened with an informal addition to the conversation, just an in-between "FYI" message minus any salutations which indicated not simply a tacit acceptance of the segmentation criteria, but an appreciation of Bill's subject position. On her call with Bill and Gustav, enough intersubjective understanding must have been achieved to forge a bond of sympathy, if not camaraderie. Perhaps, in particular, it was the amount of work commitments and constraints in which Bill was operating with "21 other projects" that had won Elke's heart.

> fyi—not sure we would be able to get the whole segmentation thing.... After talking to Bill, it sounded like it's a big deal—based on their shopping habits, exactly what they buy, how much they buy each time, etc.

In response to both messages, Kim ushered in the voice of reason and realism just after 8:00 am. She took up Patti's suggestion of forgetting the need to be concerned about recruiting in line with the desired segmentation as well as reduced the recruiting goal in half. Kim now suggested sixteen participants, instead of the planned thirty-two.

> Actually I was thinking more along the lines of Patti's "latter" suggestion if we didn't have any more luck over the weekend. I am willing to live with fewer respondents at this point; don't think we could or should get to the 32. Do we have seven now (the 8 you sent minus the guy who dropped out)? What would you think about trying to recruit maybe 6–8 more if possible using the criteria Patti outlined? Seems 16 would be a good number, but I could live with fewer.

Truly, with July 4 as the holiday of focus, we were in trouble if by June 25 we had no more names on the "1000s of best fit customers" lists to call and had only recruited seven willing participants plus an eighth who called to decline when he received the diary instructions (as Kim called him, "the guy who dropped out"). Time and list possibilities clearly had run out. So, by the end, we were just trying to find people who were going to be entertaining, whether on or off the list, and beyond gender, age, and shopping at a certain store, we were not concerned about any kind of segmentation. We just needed people. We did finally finish recruiting on July 5, one day after July 4, with twenty-four recruited participants, not thirty-two as originally planned. Elke sent us an e-mail, with the title "done." Patti's one word response: "Bravo!"

Yet little did we know at that time that Kim's claim of being able to live with fewer than sixteen, her newly revised goal for the number of completed diaries, was prescient. Of the twenty-four diary assignments sent out, only fifteen were sent back to us, with the last straggling in at the end of August (when even the final phase focus groups should have been completed). We ended up with diaries from two business owners and thirteen diaries from individuals, eight of whom were store customers and five who were shoppers of competitive stores.

So why were people not even willing to agree to take part, despite the multiple hundred-dollar incentive? And if twenty-four people had actually agreed to take part and been sent diary materials, why were only fifteen diaries returned? It would be too easy to simply discuss typical response rates and leave the issue there. It would also be deceptive. Even if we do have to loosen target criteria, we are typically able to recruit the number of research participants that we set as a goal. Moreover, just using our own typical diary completion rates as a metric, we would have expected to receive at least twenty-two back. What happened here?

As we noted above, diaries presuppose collaboration and conversation between us and participants; they presuppose engagement with us as researchers and commitment with the research task at hand. When the diary task works as a mode of ethnographic inquiry, participants' motivation goes well beyond money. As a rule we like to first meet and interact with those doing diaries by way of an interview or focus group. In this way participants can have a greater understanding of the research interests as well as an image of the person they are speaking to in their diaries. They become our partners in researching the issue at hand. We also like to believe that they do the assignments, at least in part, because they like us. Other times, we ask participants to complete a diary and then we meet with them, individually or in a group. We have noticed that this method also tends to produce "good" diaries. The thoroughly institutionalized, emotionally disciplined matter of doing a good job on an assignment which carries the promise of evaluation and the potential for face-to-face shame clearly plays a role. We see this phenomenon in play when we assign collage assignments as "homework" (which is, in fact, what we call it) prior to meeting us. The collages that people create are shockingly good. And as they present to us what the images they have included on their collages represent, they often apologize for not doing a better job, express worry about whether they did the right thing, and the like. Clearly, people in the United States often like to please others, at least when confronted face-to-face, and as a rule, if paid for something, accept that doing a good job is part of the implicit contract.

In this study, where time and financial constraints were salient variables at its inception, we let the step of a first meeting go. Spending the time and money to fly to varied geographic locations—to meet just a few participants— did not seem worth it in anyone's eyes, including our own. The original plan had been to carry out the focus groups with the same people who had completed diaries, but then as time and geographic markets slid and the numbers just did not add up (difficult to do four to seven groups with such a small number of respondents scattered in multiple geographic locales), we also let this go. We told ourselves, in fact, that recruiting would be easier because people only had to agree to keeping a diary, not to do that plus attend a focus group.

Still, cognizant of the potential problem of assigning diaries without meeting respondents, and motivated ourselves to make this study work, we attempted to assure that the diaries would contain the volume and type of details we needed. We tried to create an introductory instructional document that would engage participants' interest and would align their diary efforts with the research questions at hand. As we had noticed in the last few years that participants often failed to read the printed instructions we provided, we were concerned. If participants did not read—and we were not there to tell them—they might just do a diary on the day of a party rather than all the shopping and other preparation leading up to the event, hence negating much of the purpose of the inquiry.

Given these concerns, we decided to shift from providing instructions in a fairly densely packed Word document to a less wordy, more visually appealing PowerPoint document. We thought that if we wrote shorter instructions, the likelihood that they would be read might just be higher. We framed our relatively spacious and large-font instructions with colors and shapes taken from PowerPoint's palette and we took pains to find just the right photographs for the top cover pages, using different photos for the consumer and the business customers. We thought we were making improvements. We thought we could engage research participants in a research relationship with this document. We were mistaken; many participants did not become partners in the ethnographic quest.

Perhaps the diary just seemed another task not worth adding to an undoubtedly busy life, despite the multiple hundreds of dollars we were offering them to do it. Even the raising of the incentive for business customers obviously did not lead to much in terms of results. Clearly money was not enough of a practical or emotional reward for the task—it was not motivation enough. We would argue also that there was not "relationship" enough; not enough emotionally and morally charged human pressure. The visually engaging format made little headway against a disembodied request.

Moreover, if more than one out of three did not send anything back at all, of the diaries we did receive back very few provided the real time, in-the-moment, in situ details that inspire. Rather, too many were what we tend to label "worthless." These "worthless" diaries contained too much haphazard, thin, after-the-fact reporting, or some coverage of events, but with little/no in-the-moment and/or after-the-fact reflection on the events for us—in other words, the "unsaids" and the "unseens" that would help us to understand what was going on. Too few were like the one where a mother and a teenage daughter were in their car, caught in the rain, in which we could sit and watch along with them as the windshield wipers wiped the rain, back and forth, back and forth...and wait, long minute after long minute, and then hear the sigh which we took as such a meaning saturated utterance, followed (basically) by, "forget it, we won't go to that store because it's too far to go in the rain, let's just go to the one right here," a statement that told us something about the interchangeability of retail outlets. These are the kinds of diaries that make us feel secure that we are garnering the kind of ethnographic detail we need to produce a cogent anthropological analysis.

From business owners we received only two diaries back, and interesting here was the implicit, in fact, virtually explicit frame that both of them used in creating these documents. As we have discussed elsewhere, how research participants create diaries, especially video diaries, are clearly influenced by the frames of popular culture (see Sunderland and Denny, 2007: ch 9). Most notable in this study was the video diary from an owner of a catering company. He clearly capitalized on the diary assignment as a tool for marketing his own business. Rather than being a diary that truly documented the day-to-day planning and shopping activities as we had asked, he created one that was reformulated as something that might interest others in hiring him. It was his own edited version, replete with a telltale editing mistake of showing his face, clearly in need of a shave, then panning to the street, and upon returning to show his face, it had miraculously become clean shaven. His hat and sunglasses had also magically transformed. The sales video frame was a new one for us.

At least his editing errors, built on his agentic repurposing intervention, gave us a laugh amidst the overall chagrin of the diary output. Still, at first, we were not overly concerned about the ethnographic thinness of the diaries—there was enough in them to provide input to Kim for her quantitative online survey. We planned to mine the in-store group component that was to take place after the completion of the online component for as much of our analysis as we could. Unfortunately these groups did not happen before we needed to write a report. From the end of the summer through the fall, the start of the online kept being delayed and thus the date for the in-store groups was always floating. Finally in November 2007, we sent an e-mail to Kim—our fiscal year was coming to an end—and we assumed theirs was too and what should we do? Kim decided to have us write a report as in January 2008 they had a meeting with Bill and his team, and it would be good for us to present the diary report along with the results from the online survey, which they hoped to field before the end of the year.

On December 26 (which can only mean that we were working right up to and right after, even if not including, Christmas day), we submitted our report. We could not help but feel that this report, which we titled, "Entertaining Today: Ethnographic Cultural Analysis," was based on thin rather than thick description, so clearly trying to retain our integrity as researchers; we also subtitled it with "Preliminary Analysis: Phase 1 Diaries." Most critically, given the small number of participants who had actually agreed to take part, we did not refract any of the thirteen diaries submitted by the non-business owners through the lens of segmentation, but instead mined them for a more general explication of entertaining, exploring what get-togethers, parties, and celebrations meant within the context of everyday lives—before, during, and after entertainment events. We implicitly assumed the situational context as the unit for analysis, not the individual person as the unit of concern, and were able to write our report using that framework. In our report we allowed ourselves rather promiscuous anthropological bricolage, not calling on Lévi-Strauss for more than this general orientation, but definitely channeling a bit of Durkheim with notions of reinforcing social solidarities in entertainment events. We also drew on notions of linguistic marking to discuss ways in which entertainment events were marked as outside the boundaries of the everyday. From the overall analytic framework, which did not segment or individualize consumption, we were able to draw a number of strategic implications which, if implemented, did hold the promise of making the retailer significantly more attractive as an entertainment event shopping venue. So, if the human messiness that seeped into the database list was a solvent that began to loosen the glue of the segmentation schemas, it was the participants' unwillingness to take part that completely unstuck the segmentation schema for us, and thus via the analysis and report unhinged them for Kim and Bill, at least in terms of this report and its implications.

Kim was pleased with the report and asked us to make only minor tweaks and revisions, among them to change the cover photograph. The cover photo, of people at a yard party, showed a man looking off at something in the distance, a woman clearly in the midst of talking while also holding a beer in her hand, and in between them, in a stroller, a baby drinking milk from a bottle. The concern from a person in Kim's company was something along the lines of, "he's mad, she's bored and bitching about something with a beer in her hand, and nobody's paying attention to the baby who's dazed and slumped over in the seat." We had thought that the baby looked really happy holding on to his bottle and that the photo was a nice illustration of the intergenerational aspect of in-home entertaining. Despite annoyance at losing this illustration of this ethnographic insight, we did change it—if "drunk and bored people who do not pay attention to their kids" was the way it would be read when we were not there, it was not a good choice. We replaced it with other photographs of attractive spreads of food and drink, tweaked the other few minor things Kim had requested, and submitted another version on January 14, almost nine months from the time of Kim's first, relatively urgent, telephone call.

The Tyranny and Irony of Segmentation Practices

While it is tempting to think that business practices have monolithic power, what we hope to have shown is that the tyranny of segmentation practices is most exquisitely felt by those most involved in sustaining them. In the present example, this would include the recruiters who are paid to abide by screening criteria, by researchers who grapple with the outfall in "right" and "wrong" research participants in fieldwork and analysis, managers who plan marketing strategies according to the boxed distinctions, and business partners who tacitly accept a schema's legitimacy in order to move other agendas forward.

We also hope to have shown how both human action and the messiness of humans and artifacts have the power to subvert grand schemes. In this case, the messiness seeped in from corporate practices (lack of accuracy in the database, naming conventions, ASAPs that were later than when necessary to move things forward); research participants' actions (unwillingness to participate, i.e., complete diaries, in the absence of emotional and practical ties of a human relationship, repurposing the assignment to suit one's own agenda); and the time slippage (of deadlines, in communication) ironically generated by the fact of densely scheduled, geographically mobile, relentlessly busy lives aided and abetted by the use of mobile digital and communication devices (which are themselves constitutive aspects of busyness, see Darrah et al., 2007).

If in this case the strictures and limiting boundaries of consumer segmentation were ultimately transcended, it was not an easy process. Consumer segmentation schemas are sticky due to their embeddedness in work practices; they are the terms in which things get done. Consumer segments also come to have a life of their own as they further other forms of practice—political maneuvering, jockeying between divisions or brand groups, divvying resources. "My customer" takes on a different cast in this light, that is, "not your customer." Segments are something to possess and be possessive about, something "owned" by a brand group (see Flynn, 2009). Clearly these abstractions live on not only due to the virtues of their schemas (their ostensible reason for being) but because they are a material reality of work life and relationships, one that often organizes work practices (see Lury, 2004).

The use of consumer segmentations is also pervasive. Consumer segments are models, whether we consider them as an example of virtualism (Miller, 2002), or as manufactured (Zwick and Knott, 2009), or in the terms of "dividuals" (Deleuze, 1992). Segments are managerial models of "consumers" and "consumers" are not (living, breathing) people, yet segments quite literally are brought to life by virtue of naming and psychological profiling (in this case in the "marriage" of transaction-based data with attitudinal research and the assumptions attached to the segment names). As "quasi-people," target segment characterizations afford intimacy; they offer a façade of verisimilitude for actual consumption. From these personalized parameters comes deep attachment. We would contend that such abstractions also adhere because they mesh with reigning ideas of personhood, individual control and personal choice, and corresponding notions that consumption is best understood as a single individual making a choice. Such intuitive models of behavior and consumption are thus also likely to persist because such models offer fewer surprises and therefore accrue greater buy-in from managers (Zaltman and Deshpandé, 2001). Of course these individually oriented models of consumption grate in the context of our own allegiance to anthropological modes of analysis. If consumer segmentation annoys us as researchers, it is not only because of the recruiting dilemmas; it is also because of the analytic frame in which they tend to push our work. They do not facilitate an examination of how consumption actually happens in everyday life. They do not allow for an analysis of consumption that would consider processes that involve more than an individual; they close down the possibilities of examining consumption in other terms, for instance in terms of "market-things" (see Cochoy, 2007, this volume). Hence, also part of the reason we were, in fact, not unhappy that the entire segmentation scheme came unglued in this particular study (see Sunderland and Denny, 2003).

We take our clients' research questions seriously—just as here we took to heart the question of how the retailer could be made more attractive as an entertainment shopping venue. Yet one of the challenges of clients' fervency in laying claim to the significance of segment differences is their subsequent disincentive for discovery. Here, the tyranny of "right" and "wrong" consumers and finding what one seeks (vs. exploring and discovery) is felt in the field. However ironic, we are often asked to bring a particular segment to life because decontextualized information proves too thin for the task of humanizing. Yet if in the attempt to humanize we wander into boxes other than those of personality or make the acquaintance of other personas we are often bid to make a quick retreat. As we work amidst such frameworks we are challenged to devise new forms of research inquiry that come to terms with and bridge the realities of business practices and consumer lives (and meanwhile stay sane). As in this case, it is the effervescence of humanity that helps dissolve irritating glue. It is the relationships with clients and research participants that sustain, and the sheer Malinowskian emotional and intellectual pleasure of being engaged in figuring something out while being set down in the middle of it that gives heart.

If in this chapter we have also sought to challenge notions of the inherent power of consumer segmentation practices, our goal was not to minimize the problems and surveillance possibilities of evermore sophisticated and seemingly inexorable information gathering processes made possible by technology. We are not trying to equate problems one can have in using customer lists in the recruiting of research participants with the kinds of alterations that can be achieved, for example, via loyalty marketing practices (Pridmore and Lyon, this volume). Nonetheless, we cannot help but also ponder the discursive performance of descriptions of marketing's control and marketing's power. If we consider these discursive formulations as genres and ways of talking, one could gloss them as "marketing control talk" and "marketing power talk" (see Silverstein, 2006). Are the discourses of "marketing control talk" and "marketing power talk" themselves an insertion of marketing talk into the discursive space of everyday life? Are "marketing control talk" and "marketing power talk" as critiques from within the discipline also extending marketing as a discipline? (see Cochoy, 1998). Or, is it speculative inflation? (see Cochoy, this volume).

In essence we are suggesting that it can be difficult to slip out of marketing's control and marketing's power while simultaneously utilizing its discursive machinery. But what we hope also to have suggested with this chapter is that in paying attention to the actual messiness of artifacts and everyday life and through involvement with the humanity of actual people (be they "marketers" or "consumers"') one can, sometimes, render the conceptual caging moot.

Note

1. Names of consumer segments, clients, and some details in reprinted e-mails have been slightly altered to protect confidentiality. We would like to thank George Hunt, fellow partner at Practica. George played a lead role in the analysis of diaries and report writing for the project described. We would also like to thank Julien Cayla, Detlev Zwick, and Franck Cochoy for their thoughtful comments on an earlier draft of this chapter.

References

Callon, Michel (1998) "Introduction: The Embeddedness of Economic Markets in Economics." In Michel Callon, ed. *The Laws of the Markets*. Oxford: Blackwell, pp. 1–57.

——(2007) "What Does it Mean to Say that Economics is Performative?" In Donald MacKenzie, Fabian Muniesa, and Lucia Siu, eds. *Do Economists Make Markets? On the Performativity of Economics*. Princeton: Princeton University Press.

Cochoy, Franck (1998) "Another Discipline for the Market Economy: Marketing as a Performative Knowledge and Know-How for Capitalism." In Michel Callon, ed. *The Laws of the Markets*. Oxford: Blackwell, pp. 194–221.

——(2007) "A Sociology of Market-Things: On Tending the Garden of Choices in Mass Retailing." In Michel Callon, Yuval Millo, and Fabian Muniesa, eds. *Market Devices*. Malden, MA: Blackwell, pp. 109–29.

Darrah, Charles, Freeman, James, and English-Lueck, J.A. (2007) *Busier than Ever!: Why American families Can't Slow Down*. Stanford: Stanford University Press.

Deleuze, Gilles (1992) "Postscript on the Societies of Control." *October* 15: 3–7.

Elmer, Greg (2004) *Profiling Machines: Mapping the Personal Information Economy*. Cambridge, MA: MIT Press.

Fisher, Melissa S., and Downey, Greg, eds. (2006) *Frontiers of Capital: Ethnographic Reflections on the New Economy*. Durham: Duke University Press.

Flynn, Donna (2009) "'My Customers are Different!' Identity, Difference, and The Political Economy of Design." In Melissa Cefkin, ed. *Ethnography and the Corporate Encounter: Reflections on Research in and of Corporations*. New York: Berghahn, pp. 41–57.

Hanks, William F. (2005) "Pierre Bourdieu and the Practices of Language." *Annual Review of Anthropology*, 34: 67–83.

Ho, Karen (2009) "Disciplining Investment Bankers, Disciplining the Economy: Wall Street's Institutional Culture of Crisis and the Downsizing of 'Corporate America.'" *American Anthropologist*, 111: 177–89.

Holmes, Douglas R. (2009) "Economy of Words." *Cultural Anthropology*, 24: 381–419.

Latour, Bruno (1996) *Aramis or the Love of Technology*. Cambridge: Harvard University Press. Translated by Catherine Porter.

Lezaun, Javier (2007) "A Market of Opinions: The Political Epistemology of Focus Groups." *Sociological Review*, 55: 130–51.

Lury, Celia (2004) *Brands: Logos of the Global Economy*. New York: Routledge.

Malefyt, Timothy (2003) "Models, Metaphors, and Client Relations: The Negotiated Meanings of Advertising." In Timothy Malefyt and Brian Moeran, eds. *Advertising Cultures*. Oxford: Berg, pp. 139–63.

Mazzarella, William (2003) *Shoveling Smoke: Advertising and Globalization in Contemporary India*. Durham: Duke University Press.

Miller, Daniel (2002) "The Unintended Political Economy." In Paul du Gay and Michael Pryke, eds. *Cultural Economy*. London: Sage, pp. 166–85.

Moeran, Brian (1996) *A Japanese Advertising Agency: An Anthropology of Media and Markets*. Honolulu: University of Hawaii Press.

Ong, Aihwa, and Collier, Stephen J., eds. (2005) *Global Assemblages: Technology, Politics, and Ethics as Anthropological Problems*. Malden, MA: Blackwell.

Patton, Phil (2009) "Before Creating the Car, Ford Designs the Driver." *The New York Times*, July 16, Automobiles: 1.

Schieffelin, Bambi, Woolard, Kathryn, and Kroskrity, Paul, eds. (1998) *Language Ideologies: Practice and Theory*. New York: Oxford University Press.

Silverstein, Michael (1985) "Language and the Culture of Gender: At the Intersection of Structure, Usage, and Ideology." In Elizabeth Mertz and Richard J. Parmentier, eds. *Semiotic Mediation*. Orlando, FL: Academic Press, pp. 220–59.

——(2006) "Old Wine, New Ethnographic Lexicography." *Annual Review of Anthropology*, 35: 481–96.

Sunderland, Patricia and Denny, Rita (2002) "Performers and Partners: Consumer Video Documentaries in Ethnographic Research." In *Qualitative Ascending: Harnessing its True Value*. Amsterdam: ESOMAR, pp. 285–303.

————(2003) "Psychology vs. Anthropology: Where is Culture in Marketplace Ethnography?" In Timothy Malefyt and Brian Moeran, eds. *Advertising Cultures*. Oxford: Berg, pp. 187–202.

————(2007) *Doing Anthropology in Consumer Research*. Walnut Creek, CA: Left Coast Press.

Turow, Joseph (1997) *Breaking up America*. Chicago, IL: University of Chicago Press.

——(2006) *Niche Envy*. Cambridge, MA: MIT Press.

Zaltman, Gerald, and Deshpandé, Rohit (2001) "The Use of Market Research: An Exploratory Study of Manager and Researcher Perspectives." In R. Deshpandé, ed. *Using Market Knowledge*. Thousand Oaks, CA: Sage, pp. 31–80.

Zwick, Detlev, and Knott, Janice (2009) "Manufacturing Customers: The Database as New Means of Production." *Journal of Consumer Culture*, 9: 221–47.

7

The Making of the Sensuous Consumer

Pascale Desroches and Jean-Sébastien Marcoux

> To feed the flow of innovations, perfect knowledge of hair, expert mastery of oxidation dye techniques and above all creative scientists are required in order to imagine new colourings.[1]

Hair coloring products are a common feature of the consumer goods marketplace. They represent a commodity that entails a particular relationship with technology. Indeed, it rests upon the domestication of know-how long possessed only by professional hairstylists.

As a beauty product, hair coloring pertains to the realm of experiential consumption as it is usually defined in marketing (Kotler, 1973; Holbrook and Hirshman, 1982; Pine and Gilmore, 1998). It is a product with sensual appeal designed as a sensuous experience. As the above quotation from the L'Oréal Web site implies, it also belongs to an activity sector characterized by intensive research and development. Innovation in hair coloring not only involves the marketing department and the laboratory, however, it also contributes to the social construction of the senses. As such, it raises new questions.

Our research deals with creativity and innovation management in the late-capitalism sensory economy.[2] In particular, it analyzes the making of the sensuous consumer in the contemporary "hypersensual marketplace" (Howes, 2005) from the standpoint of the managers who are involved on a day-to-day basis in creating hair coloring products. It analyzes how marketers conceive, design, and seek to expand the range of consumers' sensations. As will be demonstrated here, the senses are not only valorized as perceptual captors, as described in traditional marketing literature—they are objectified. Colors and smells are branded (Howes, 2005; Moeran, 2007) and become *products* themselves.

This chapter is based on the ethnography of the *Direction Marketing Internationale* (DMI) of L'Oréal at the company's headquarters in Paris between

June and December 2004. Follow-up was conducted in 2005, 2006, and 2009. The fieldwork was done by one of the authors of this chapter, who acted as an observant participant (Moeran, 2006) at the DMI. She first joined the organization as a trainee and later became a project manager. The second author supervised the fieldwork but remained outside the field. For ethical purposes, all the people encountered in the course of the project were informed at the outset of the double role of our researcher/project manager and of the existence of this ethnography.

Marketing is a key activity at L'Oréal. The company also draws upon a strong scientific tradition. L'Oréal was founded in 1909 by Eugène Schueller, a French chemist who had developed an innovative, safe hair coloring formula and who instilled the beauty company with a scientific mindset. L'Oréal is now the world leader in coloring, with annual sales in 2008 of 17.5 billion euros.[3] Hair coloring has traditionally been L'Oréal's core business activity. Today, the firm has five divisions. Besides the consumer division and the professional division, which both develop hair coloring products, the firm also has a luxury division, a cosmetics division, and a body shop division. L'Oréal's Paris DMI offers a particularly interesting opportunity for fieldwork because it is the source of most, if not all, of the company's innovations. The DMI has worldwide reach because peripheral markets—other countries—adapt these innovations. For example, fifty-two people were working at the DMI in 2004 on Garnier, one of the major hair coloring brands, with seven members of the brand's marketing department (one director, three project managers, two junior project managers, and one intern) working on coloring. The five women and two men were aged between 25 and 35 and the majority were French. A laboratory with a staff of five served the hair coloring department, as was the case with each of the marketing sectors.

Our discussion takes as its starting point the ethnographic analysis of Latour and Woolgar (1979) that opens up the "black box" of the laboratory and analyzes the socio-technical process of the construction of science. While Latour's work (1983, 1987) has been highly influential primarily in the field of science and technology studies, it has also had a significant impact on contemporary material culture studies. An example can be found in Lien's work (1997) on the commodification of convenience food, which extends Latour's laboratory studies to the marketing department. Our discussion goes beyond the laboratory studies, however, and explores the intersection between the socio-technological construction of knowledge as popularized by Latour, and the anthropology of the senses advocated by sensory anthropologists such as Howes (2003a, 2005), whose research examines the sensory dimensions of culture. Howes's approach to the study of the senses takes us beyond the textual turn in anthropology to the heart of the sensual turn.

We believe that our discussion has a broader relevance for researchers interested in better understanding the construction of consumers and the logic that prevails inside the marketing department. While Lien (1997) approaches the marketing department with the expectation of studying a food culture in the making, we did so with the expectation of understanding the sensory economy in the making. The chapter is structured as follows: The first section describes the marketing people's search for the "real" consumer. The second section analyzes the tensions between the marketing department and the laboratory, with particular emphasis on the divergences that exist between the two over the construction of reality. The third and fourth sections describe the tests performed in the laboratory and the concomitant reification of the consumer. In the fifth section, the findings are examined in relation to the existing literature on sensory anthropology. The implications for marketing research and consumer culture theory (CCT) are discussed in the conclusion.

Looking for the "Real" Consumer in the Field

When young managers join the DMI, they learn that the creation of new products and new brands involves a process commonly called a "creative spiral" (to use L'Oréal's own terminology). It is important for the managers to observe and decode the market's "signals," listen to consumers, and use their own intuition.[4] Empathy is a key part of their ethos. In other words, they are constantly encouraged to try to see and experience the products just as consumers will.

Innovations are often based on analysis of consumers' usage and attitudes, as well as on trend analysis. Focus groups (the DMI term for them is "qualis," short for qualitative tests) are also conducted in order to understand why consumers color their hair, what they like and dislike about the products available, and so forth. For example, qualis have revealed that consumers are sometimes scared to use hair coloring products partly because of their smell. Indeed, consumers usually associate the odor of ammonia with chemical and harmful aspects of hair coloring products. Some consumers even complain about having problems breathing when applying such products. Qualis are also used to test the concepts, stories, and ideas developed to promote a brand or a new product. They are used to verify whether the "average" consumer identifies with a brand's story: whether she likes the visual components of a new brand and whether the packaging successfully conveys the brand story. In short, managers use qualis to *test* the words, the codes, and the signs that will be used to embed the brand or product in a web of cultural meanings.

In some instances, managers are requested to move beyond qualis. On one particular occasion during the fieldwork, the brand's general manager expressed dissatisfaction with the project managers' presentations. He complained that they understood neither the consumer nor the market and he invited his team of project managers to delve deeper in order to understand both. The marketing people had to develop a different research approach. They were asked to go native and accompany consumers from the time they shopped for the product to the moment they actually used it, that is, in the intimacy of their own environment. In other words, they had to infiltrate the consumers' private lives. The objective was to innovate in terms of understanding consumers, in bringing them to life, and in trying to experience what they were really experiencing. The brand's general manager hoped that this experiment would broaden his managers' horizons and that new product ideas would be the outcome.

One of the authors of this chapter was assigned to a consumer who used hair coloring products and who agreed to spend a morning being scrutinized as she carried out her usual consumer activities. The consumer was met at her apartment. She seemed intrigued but also embarrassed by the idea of allowing a professional into her bathroom. Yet this was precisely what the DMI managers sought to do. One of us accompanied the consumer to the supermarket where she usually purchased her hair coloring products. Back at the apartment, we followed her into her small, pink bathroom. Just like the other project managers involved in the experiment, we paid attention to the bathroom's aesthetic. We observed the consumer as she managed to perform such a complex coloring ritual in a space designed to accommodate only one person, and to do so in the presence of a professional. We also noted the numerous hair care, skin care, beauty, and hygiene products in her bathroom. But, as project managers, our main attention was focused on the consumer as she opened her hair color box. We listened to her as she commented on each step of the coloring process, and then as she blow-dried her hair and remarked on the coloring result. After going through a questionnaire with her, we discussed the results of our observations with other colleagues who had been asked to do the same thing with other consumers.

Considerable informal testing goes on in the marketing department. For example, one of us tried several of the new shampoo formulas designed by the laboratory. When the new cool brown collection was launched, we tried the color on our own hair. Trying the new formulas in our capacity as project managers became a way of asserting our expertise and showing a commitment to the brands. As mentioned earlier, it is important to feel, touch, and smell the products as consumers do (or as we think they do). Or, as Grandclément and Gaglio (in this volume) put it: it is important to "speak the consumer's language."

The infiltration experience took managers a step further. It was meant to provide access to the consumer's reality as happens in a naturalistic inquiry.

However, unlike anthropologists going out into the field, managers were sent out without any preparation. We were sent out with the "candid" expectation that observing a consumer in her "real" environment would provide insights and create new opportunities. It was as if the managers' presence in the natural context of consumption could, in itself, generate new ideas. The value of this experiment rested mainly on its being conducted in a "real" bathroom with a "real" consumer and on being able to administer a question-naire immediately afterwards. The aesthetic of the bathroom, its smallness, and the multitude of other brands found there all acted as indices of authen-ticity (Grayson and Shulman, 2000).

Even if focus groups are a frequent, almost essential part of the innovation process, managers have often expressed doubts about such research initia-tives. We were told by DMI managers that qualis cannot be the sole recourse for testing products before they end up in consumers' hands. As one project manager put it: "One needs to take a step back from qualitative tests." It was not unusual for managers observed during the fieldwork to challenge a quali-tative study's results. The general opinion was that sometimes a "dominant" consumer can have an undue influence on the focus group and a determinant effect on the outcome of the test. It was also commonly argued that, during a focus group, everything depends on how a concept is presented to consumers; even slight changes can affect the outcome of the test, either positively or negatively. We heard people complain that they often came out of qualitative tests feeling "empty-handed." One informant mentioned that qualis results cannot be presented in meetings if the goal is to convince the VP of some-thing. Indeed, when managers are looking for a more definitive validation—evidence that a new product is going to work better than old ones—what is needed is a series of other tests such as concept use tests (CUTs) that provide the best arguments for proving the "superiority" of a given product. CUTs involve a significant number of consumers (more than one hundred) and combine study of the concept (the brand's meanings) with the formula's performance. CUTs are conducted when the budget is available. They are similar to the consumer tests described by Grandclément (2006) and Trebu-chet-Breitwiller (2007) in the food and perfume industries in France.

Interestingly, even though the infiltration experiment is distinct from the ethnography practiced in the corporate world (Malefyt and Moeran, 2003; Moeran, 2006; Sunderland and Denny, 2007), it clearly shares with corporate anthropology a fascination with the field as a reservoir of knowledge. Both field research and focus groups are designed to glean consumer insights and must be distinguished from the research that is done to convince managers. Indeed, neither in situ observations nor qualis are seen as sufficiently scientific since they rely on a small number of consumers and pertain to subjective matters. CUTs are necessary, but these can usually only be elaborated after a consensus has been reached inside the firm between the marketing and laboratory personnel. In such circumstances, a scientific technological apparatus is mobilized through the aura and authority of laboratory experiments.

Marketing Reality versus Laboratory Reality

L'Oréal has developed a science of color. It is used to estimate, analyze, measure, and quantify the colors involved. The firm also uses a scientific coding that accounts for three dimensions of color: hair color level, lightening level, and reflects (or highlights). The coding is used on a daily basis and, as an essential tool for managers and scientists, it is a means of asserting expertise. This coding also provides a basis for communication—a common language—between the marketing department and the laboratory.

For example, during the fieldwork, the marketing department needed a new cool brown for the *100% Color* brand. A mid-level brown called *châtain glacé* ("frosty deep brown") was designed. The new color was considered to have ashy reflects. It also possessed a red reflect. It was coded 4.15 by the laboratory. The same color was translated into marketing vocabulary as "glamorous brown," an elegant color similar to dark leather. The color was not exuberant and was perceived by consumers as a "safe choice." It had cool color reflects and proved extremely popular. Focus groups revealed that it provided consumers with a sense of daring and of standing out. In 2006, the dark, cool brown was in fact the top-selling color in France.

The example of color coding brings to light significant differences between the marketing department and the laboratory at the level of language, representation, and metaphor (Lien, 1997). The relationship between a marketing department and a laboratory is a complex one. The two entities deal with different time frames. Each year, a marketing department must reinvent existing brands and create new ones. For their part, the laboratories devote a considerable amount of their time to developing coloring technologies that might take up to ten years to be implemented. They work primarily in the context of a long-term vision. They also work on various projects simultaneously. At the DMI, the laboratories have the power to initiate projects they believe could lead to an innovation or help achieve a competitive advantage in the marketplace, but the marketing department must approve these projects before they take shape.

Marketing people and laboratory people work well together, but there are almost no close relationships or friendships between them. Many marketing colleagues see each other on weekends, but these encounters never include laboratory people. During our fieldwork, we never saw anyone from the marketing department having lunch with people from the laboratory.

Significantly, when marketing people invited the laboratory director to a brainstorming session, she was surprised by the invitation and felt out of place, thinking she could add nothing to such a session.

There is an important cultural gap between the marketing department and the laboratory personnel, which could be described in terms of different tribes in this context. Both have their proper space. Their offices are located in separate buildings. Each has its own aesthetic. While the marketing department is full of colors, images, brands, models, and magazines, the laboratories are all white and full of machines and tools. It is an example of Baudrillard's opposition (1968) between the world of values and that of colors, where the "escape in white" attests to a denial of impulse, intuition, and subjectivity.

During our fieldwork, we also often observed disagreements, if not actual "controversies" (in the Latourian sense of the word), between the two groups. They were not examples of some simple anomaly within the system. Rather, they were ethnographically revealing moments. One case of the development of a new hair color for *100% Color* is noteworthy. After identifying a market opportunity in the blonde market, the marketing department asked the laboratory to develop a new *irisé-doré* (coded 0.23) to fill this gap. The laboratory people did not share the marketing people's optimism, however. Louise,[5] the person in charge of relations between the marketing department and the laboratory, confided to us that the golden effect sought by the marketing people would only fully appear on white hair, not on dyed hair: "On dyed hair, the golden effect will always come closer to a 0.32 than a 0.23. They [the marketing people] want to see a 0.23 here, but they lack the proper understanding of the products. . . ." Whereas the laboratory people argued that it would be more realistic to present the new shade as a "golden blonde," the marketing department contended that the *100% Color* portfolio already contained such a color. They had faith in the consumers' capacity to see the difference. The new shade was finally developed according to the marketing department's request, but the laboratory ensured that the packaging clearly mentioned that better results would be obtained if the product were used on a light-colored base.

Disagreements and controversies between the marketing department and the laboratory are frequent during the product development process. The result of these differences is evident in product packaging, over which the laboratories' influence remains paramount. The technical color codes occupy as important a place as the colors' marketing names (see Figure 7.1). A section of the packaging is devoted to explaining the technology and demonstrating its technical "superiority." Marketing integrates this technical language with respect to the color and attempts to utilize it in communicating with consumers who normally do not use such codes or even understand them. The gap between the marketing department and the laboratory, however, is nowhere more evident than in the way each of them perceives authenticity

Figure 7.1 Haircolor box of *100% color*, shade 415 Dark cool Brown.

and constructs what it claims to be real. The marketing department and the laboratory talk about the consumer's experience and the "real" effects of colors or scents in radically different ways. If indices drawn from the field are understood as legitimate indices of authenticity for the purposes of marketing, as far as laboratory people are concerned, "reality" is something that can only be assessed in a controlled, disciplined setting. Whereas marketing people see the technical improvement of a chemical formula as an opportunity to renew a brand's story, laboratory people consider the new formula as a valid, meaningful sales argument only when clinical tests have demonstrated its "superiority."

The culture clash between marketing people and creative people, scientists, or engineers has been documented elsewhere (Workman, 1993; Miller, 2003*a*; Moeran, 2006). In contrast to Workman's description (1993), tensions, conflicts, and controversies are considered to be not only normal or inevitable but elements of a climate of confrontation that is highly valued at the DMI. In other words, the marketing department and the laboratory exist in a "structural tension" (Miller, 2003*a*) intended to produce value. Indeed, despite their differences, marketing people and laboratory scientists pursue a similar goal: the creation of high-quality products. The synergy of the two groups is their driving force.

169

It is mostly through concrete experimentation that differences are negotiated, if not resolved. It is thus appropriate to look at the tests supervised by
the laboratory, since these tests are at the heart of the innovation process.
They mobilize consumers, but not as informants. The tests use consumers as
stimuli.

Assessing the Color of Reality

In most countries where the brand was launched, 100% Color has quickly become
a must on bases with intense highlights, which represent more than one-third of
the market. Having succeeded in this first stage, we must now attack and put 100%
Color into a commanding position in the two segments that make up more than
half the market: brunettes and blondes. (Étienne, *100% Color* Project Manager).

As project manager, Étienne put it, *100% Color* was doing well in the purple,
red, and black segments, all of which are characterized by intense color highlights. These segments are usually made up of young people. Significantly, this
contributed to producing a young brand image and positioning. The brand
was weaker, however, in the blonde and brown segments, occupied by more
mature consumers, with these two segments accounting for 50–60 percent of
sales in the industry. *100% Color* faced a challenge. The brand enjoyed strong
positioning in intense color segments, but needed to tap into the more
"natural," mature segments and do so without compromising the brand's
positioning. Managers identified market opportunities for new shades, leading to the suggestion of *châtain glacé*.

In some cases, such as that of *100% Color*, new formulas are subjected to
head tests. A head test is an experiment performed using real consumers. Head
tests allow for de visu observation of the effects of new colors. They precede
the launch of *every* new product and constitute key moments of the product
development process. They may even be considered ritual moments in the life
of socio-technical innovations. Head tests are designed to provide access to
what Pinch (1993) calls the "pure technical realm" that reveals the immanent
logic of a technology. The difference, however, is that these tests are aimed at
accessing the "pure sensual realm" of the future formulas.

On the very first day that one of the authors spent at the DMI, the marketing
director for hair coloring brought the project managers to the laboratory
where hair coloring products were tested. We understood how important
this place was. It was used by marketing managers to make decisions and
provide feedback on the colors developed by the laboratories. Head tests are
essential to grasping the exact color of a chemical formula. They take place five
minutes away from the offices of the marketing managers in a laboratory

containing black seats, deep sinks, large mirrors, and hair dryers—everything found in a hairstyling salon. However, in this space, which is dominated by white-tiled floors, white walls, and white cabinets, the hairstyling materials create a rather unusual—even destabilizing—atmosphere. Whether due to the absence of decoration or to the minimalist aesthetics, this place is all about work, containment, and control. The environment is not conducive to checking one's appearance or indulging in the chit-chat typical of a hair salon. It is a laboratory as Latour (1983) describes it: a place of absolute artificiality. The laboratory is not intended to reproduce the consumers' real environment. It is built along radically different codes. For instance, the white walls do not simply signal the absence of color; the laboratory's whiteness becomes the perfect expression of the "construction of neutrality" (Young, 2004).

Laboratory scientists use head tests to assess a formula's effects. They detail the changes in the color of the hair roots, in the percentage of grays, and in the hair's shininess. They also test the new formula's tactile properties. They check its viscosity by making sure it is neither too liquid nor too solid. The formula must be pleasant to use. It should be easy to apply evenly. A new formula should also be easy to rinse out. Sometimes, the subjects are asked to return after a week or two so that changes in hair color can be assessed. The objective is to develop color that will remain as shiny and vibrant two weeks after the application as it was on the first day. Usually, two models (a term employed by the head-testing personnel) are used to test each color. Three shades of color per model are tested and three sections are delineated on each model's head: one on the front of the head and two on the back. As with conventional experimental protocol, the shades are tested on the different sections. The subject is then asked to sit under a neon light, which provides clearer, sharper lighting, for an expert examination of the results. The consumers who take part in head testing are volunteers—women from various age groups and occupations. Even if a significant proportion of the participants are older women who do not work full time, there are no stringent selection criteria for head testing. The only requirements relate to the condition of the person's hair. Socio-demographical factors, cultural and ethnic differences, and the consumers' perceptions and interpretations are *unimportant* here. Only the hair's biography—its condition and its reaction—matters. As a matter of fact, Marie-France, the woman in charge of head testing, takes great pride in talking about the quality of hair of her models. She prefers to test colors on "healthy" hair whose color and shine are at their full potential.

Head tests are especially important for managers because consumers have different perceptions of any given color depending on how healthy their hair is and on their past usage of hair coloring products. Head tests are used to determine the variations of the color to make sure that it will be as close as possible to the result the consumer will obtain. In other words, while for marketing people perceptions are usually more important than reality, the laboratory attempts to understand what the true color is in reality.

Head tests are also used to try and resolve the disagreements and tensions that arise between the marketing department and the laboratory. Interestingly, the scientific appearance of this procedure is what makes it convincing. Using consumers as stimuli, performing experiments on *real* people's scalps, and dividing the scalps into sections (so as to obtain a basis for comparison) are all measures that evoke the positivist construction of reality. The laboratory's lack of aesthetic (or functional aesthetic (Baudrillard, 1968)) and the atmosphere of artificiality that prevails there attest to the capacity to control, as in an experiment, the procedure's outcome. As such, despite the small number of observations made during head tests, these are taken to be more reliable than focus groups and closer to reality.

Making the Smell Visible

> We hadn't touched Movida for 10 years.... Movida is the brand of choice to lead women into colouring owing to its non-permanent, softer, less radical technology. This technology can have a worldwide appeal.... It's a highly advertising-sensitive brand; it stimulates a desire. Creating new ad copy to support a brand requires telling another story. (Elizabeth, Garnier hair colour director)

As Garnier's hair color director, Elizabeth explained during our interview, in attempting to increase *Movida*'s sales and reach new consumers, the brand needed to tell a new story. The brand visuals needed to be rejuvenated, but it was also clear that such a cosmetic change would not be enough. Managers contended that they had to give consumers another "reason to believe" in the brand. They decided to adjust the chemical formula and give it a more hedonistic character by altering its smell. At the time of the fieldwork, *Movida* was the entry brand in hair color. Because the formula had no permanent effects, it allowed consumers to cover their first gray hairs and to do it softly, without any long-term commitment. The target consumers for the rejuvenated brand were women in their thirties who had noticed their first grays and wanted to cover them without giving the impression of having had their hair colored. They were women who wanted to regain their natural hair color.

Movida therefore needed a perfume that users would find soft, fruity, and creamy, these being the characteristics corresponding to the brand's positioning. The advertising and packaging depicted an apricot, conveying the brand's soft, natural image. The marketing people wanted to use the apricot's scent to reinforce the connection with the brand's visual positioning. Sensory anthropologists have revealed synesthesia between the two senses. The sense of smell becomes a means of short-circuiting what Howes (2005) calls the "conventional five-sense model" that divides them. As such, the scent establishes cross-linkages with color, becoming a means of "experiencing" colors.

The marketing department asked the laboratory to develop a new perfume to fit with the brand's more modern image. The inspiration for the new advertisement came from Brazil, where the brand had enjoyed a strong market share. From the marketing people's perspective, the advertisement was soft, shiny, and sensual. It successfully conveyed the brand's positioning. The model that was selected had long, curly, auburn hair that draped her body. The new visual also presented an apricot with a pink and orange butterfly perched on it. The claim read: "0% ammonia, 100% softness. Say goodbye to first greys." The general manager also wanted the packaging to express the novelty of the product and its formula. "New formula, rich cream, fruity perfume" was printed on the packaging.

From an ethnographic point of view, it is important to mention that the technology available at that time did not allow adding scents to oxidation formulas. A hair coloring product comprises an oxidant and an after-care lotion. The after-care lotion was already perfumed with apricot milk. When the laboratory achieved a breakthrough and developed a means of adding perfume to the oxidant base, it became clear to the marketing people that *Movida* needed such a perfumed oxidant. If the apricot smell asserted itself as an obvious choice, the ethnography reveals that the making of the smell was more complex.

In response to the marketing department, the laboratory produced two different perfumes. While agreeing that the scents proposed by the laboratory resembled that of an apricot, the marketing people were dissatisfied. They contended that the scents did not really convey the *spirit* of the brand. For them, the scent had to evoke an apricot, even if this required slight changes in the proposed fragrances. From their standpoint, the banana tone of the first option was too intense for consumers, while the second option's scent was not fruity enough. In attempting to resolve the disagreement over the assessment of the two fragrances, the laboratory director asked that the new formula's scents be tested in what she called the consumer's "actual environment"—a confined bathroom. Her point was that when the hair color process is activated, the scent is different. A sniff test was thus required.

Sniff tests take the form of an experiment in which consumers become the stimuli. They take place in a controlled environment. On the day of the sniff test, project managers went to the laboratory offices, where they met the laboratory director and her team. Each wore a white blouse. Attending the test were the marketing director, the laboratory director, and the L'Oréal perfume specialist, who worked on everything related to perfume within the group. The laboratory assistant and a hair colorist also attended the test. As with experimental protocol, it was necessary to test both formulas and to make multiple observations. The laboratory assistant explained to the participants (the project managers) that some consumers' scalps can generate more heat than others. On a warmer scalp, the perfume would be stronger. Since hair coloring could produce different effects on different people and also smell differently, four rooms were needed to test the two formulas. Managers would have to go into each of the rooms immediately after the hair color had been applied, again after ten minutes, and once again after twenty minutes. Each project manager received a comment sheet with four rows (one for each room) and three columns pertaining to the instances of observation during the experiment: T0, T10, and T20. One by one, they were asked to walk through a different door, smell the perfume contained in the room and record their comments on the sheet so as to translate, as Trebuchet-Breitwiller (2007) puts it, scents into scores and words.

As the sniff test proceeded, project managers entered the cubicles. In each of the four rooms sat a real consumer. Managers were required to enter the cubicles quickly and close the door behind them immediately to prevent the scent from escaping. They usually greeted the consumer who was sitting there. In one case, a subject mentioned that she found the odor of her coloring pleasing, that it was not as strong as was usually the case, but that she had trouble making comparisons with her usual product. It was not the woman's impressions that mattered, however, but rather those of the managers. The test continued until the sheet was completed, though the rules were not always fully respected; the managers taking part in the experiment found it difficult not to discuss their findings with each other. At times the differences in smell were so striking that the project managers felt the urge to share their thoughts immediately. After the completion of the test, the laboratory assistant revealed which perfumes had been used in each of the cubicles. The project managers were then invited to a debriefing where they shared their impressions and made recommendations.

In contrast to Trebuchet-Breitwiller (2007), who analyzes how sniff tests are conducted to assess consumers' preferences in the perfume industry in France, here the tests are used to assess the managers' perceptions. Scientists accept that, in the case of hair coloring products, consumers might decide whether or not they like a new scent, but nothing more. Unlike a quali or a focus group, only a sniff test can provide an accurate description of scents. A sniff test becomes a means of affirming expertise and, more importantly, a means of moving beyond the realm of consumers' own interpretations.

Interestingly, even though the significance of the consumers' participation in the experiment is minimized as if to control for distortion, subjectivity, or the consumers' lack of expertise, the laboratory people's own perceptions and prejudices pervade the whole process. Those who design sniff tests start from the premise that the average consumer exists. They assume that consumers color their hair in their bathrooms and remain there throughout the process. But even if (as marketing people well know) it is common for consumers to leave their bathrooms and perform other tasks during the coloring process, it is essential for the people in charge of the sniff tests to remain with the consumer in the enclosed place where the scent is contained. During an interview, the laboratory director explained that, because the tests need to simulate what happens in a bathroom, they have to take place in rooms small enough to avoid diluting the scent of the perfume, thereby producing a high concentration of the scent that allows it to be correctly assessed.

Testing the formula on living hair is crucial—hence the need for the consumer's physical presence to allow full impregnation of the coloring's scent and to offset the coloring variations due to the heat generated by the model's scalp. Nonetheless, laboratory people keep the consumers at some distance. It is no coincidence that scientists generally refer to the models who take part in sniff tests as *"Madame Michu"* (a popular term in the marketing industry in France. See Grandclément and Gaglio in this volume). The vocabulary is deliberately depersonalized. By assigning a generic name to the model, they emphasize the distance between the inside of the laboratory and the outside world. Once they are selected for the experiment, the consumers are reduced to the hair on their heads. They are reified.

The transformation of the consumer into a living subject and the reduction of her into hair take on their full meaning in the context of Latour's analysis (1983) of the laboratory as an iconic cultural setting and a place in which a framing effect is both possible and required. For Latour (1983), the laboratory is a place where the scale of social phenomena is changed. It is an artificial environment that is designed to enlarge what is small or invisible so as to better control it. In the present case, the experiment creates an environment where high concentrations of scents are present, thus providing an interesting contrast to a field inquiry where everything can potentially run out of control.

If, as Latour (1983) describes it, Pasteur's laboratory was a setting where invisible molecules were made visible for both scientists and the general public, the laboratory we describe is a place where "real" colors and scents become material. The technological apparatus of the laboratory and the ritualized performance of the experiment conducted in this setting are fundamental. They give managers the opportunity to translate their perceptions and impressions into empirical evidence—irrefutable proof of the "superiority" of a given scent. As such, they are instrumental in resolving conflicts, disagreements, and controversies between marketing people and scientists. As a matter of course, marketing managers always comply with the decisions taken during an experiment.

Whereas head tests are used to assess the color and shininess of new products, sniff tests serve to evaluate the scent of hair coloring products and to assess new perfumes. They also help define an olfactory signature, even an olfactory territory (or *smellscape*) for a brand. As such, the different products that constitute a brand like *Movida*, that is, all the different shades that the brand includes (ranging from blonde to black), have a "common" smell and come to be recognized as belonging to a greater whole. Applying Grayson and Shulman's work (2000) on the semiotics of authenticity, one could go as far as to say that a given smell becomes an "olfactory" index: it serves a factual or evidentiary function and signals that a formula belongs to the brand in its entirety.

Through a complex technical apparatus, sniff tests seek to control a sense as elusive as smell. The need to domesticate smell and to subsume it to a practical, scientific logic is related to the difficulty of studying it as both a theoretical and practical tool (Moeran, 2007). Indeed, Moeran finds that there appear to be no inborn olfactory preferences (besides instances of aversion) with respect to smell. But more importantly, the lack of inborn preferences regarding smells results in "apparent anarchy" (Moeran, 2007) when individual smell associations are considered. In this context, the construction of colors through smell (i.e., the synesthesia) is relatively arbitrary. Even though the laboratory people were convinced that they had managed to capture the "real" apricot's scent in the first instance, the marketing people required them to change the proposed scent slightly so as to improve the connection with the brand's values. Scents can be modified—either emphasized or attenuated. If marketing people wish to capture the essence of an apricot, they can have the laboratory emphasize certain features of the aroma and soften others. Indeed, what marketing people really seek to capture is the spirit of the brand. Just as Howes (1988) talks about the "odor" of the soul in Indonesia and Western Melanesia, we note how scents must embody the brand's spirit in the "hypersensual marketplace" that characterizes late-modern capitalist societies.

While they enable managers to gain important information that consumers could not provide them, head tests and sniff tests do contribute to the decontextualization of the coloring experience. They erase socio-demographic differences, such as age, social or ethnic group, class and lifestyle, in the process of reducing people to the properties of their hair. From the point of view of laboratory people, the reification of consumers is a necessary concomitant. It is part of the framing process that Latour (1983) argues is fundamental to any laboratory's efficacy; only by reducing the consumer to her scalp can the laboratory isolate the smell from other factors, enlarge its power, and make it "visible."

Senses Beyond Words

Considerable effort has been made in modern marketing departments to reduce uncertainty and to acquire knowledge regarding consumers (Lien, 1997; Grandclément and Gaglio, in this volume), but most particularly their responses to sensory marketing (Howes, 2003b; Trebuchet-Breitwiller, 2007). Head tests and sniff tests are two examples of the tests carried out in the sensory marketing industry. The concern for truthfulness that drives these tests, the desire to observe the impact of new formulas on live subjects, and the possibly illusionary endeavor to gain access to real consumer experience combine to produce a particular understanding of the senses and the sensuous consumer. Head tests and sniff tests are carried out to improve each part of the consumption experience: the scent when the product is applied on the hair, its texture as it is being applied, its smell and the color that results a few days (or a few weeks) after the product has been applied. These tests leave little place for the consumers' interpretations. The focus is on a formula's technical effects, not on the meanings attributed to it.

We can consider these observations through the lens of sensory anthropology. The research of Classen et al. (1994) and Howes (1988, 2003a, 2005) on the *sensorium* (i.e., the cultural construction of the variety of sensory combinations (McLuhan, (1962)) is particularly relevant here, as it reveals the complexity of the senses in cultural life.

Howes's work (2003a) is important. It distances itself somewhat from the interpretive anthropology (in which Geertz's analysis (1973) is prominent) that conceives culture through the metaphor of the text that an anthropologist can read. His critique of anthropology can be extended to such disciplines as consumer research, in which the conception of culture as a text, or a discourse, has prevailed since the textual/linguistic turn in the 1980s (Sherry, 1991; Arnould and Thompson, 2005). Much like such material culture theorists as Latour (1991, 1995) or Miller (1987), sensory anthropologists like Howes seek to uncover the sensory cultural life that cannot be reduced to words and that is entailed, permitted, or produced by interactions with objects. Indeed, Howes questions the primacy of the text over the realm of sensations and sensuality. He invites us to "come to our senses" and engage the senses fully in our understanding of the world. In this light, the chemical formulas developed by the DMI are not only signs of success, repositories of meanings, or instruments involved in the consumers' construction of identity; they also allow the people who use them to expand the range of their sensations and engage their senses fully.

In many respects, the senses that are imagined, designed, and created by the DMI are diametrically opposed to the way Howes conceives them. Indeed, Howes (2003a, 2005, 2007, 2008) questions the instrumentalization of the senses in the sensory economy and the marketing tendency to isolate the senses, to treat them metaphorically as "silos," and to conceive of them in a universalist, a-contextual fashion. He also questions the hegemony of laboratory methods of sensory analysis in marketing. The measures implemented by the DMI to assess colors and smells in order to test the "superiority" of new colors and new perfumes and to brand them attest to a growing objectification of consumers' sensorial experience and to a lack of sensual relativism. The implementation of research protocols by which consumers are used as stimuli is another example of reification in that the person is reduced to the single element of her hair. This is particularly evident in the description of consumer segments in terms of hair colors: "blondes," "browns," etc. Values, perceptions, and cultural and ethnic differences cease to be important. What matters is the hair's history, its "condition," and its "health."

In other respects, however, just like Howes, the DMI implicitly or perhaps indirectly questions the pre-eminence that is given to discursive knowledge. By using a complex technical, technological, and scientific apparatus, the DMI seeks to move beyond what consumers say about colors and scents, what they can articulate, and what they are *willing* to articulate during a quali or a field experiment. The company has put in place a procedure that seeks to overcome some of the difficulties posed by smell, scents, and perfumes. It seeks to avoid the evasive, subjective, uncontrollable—almost "anarchical" (Moeran, 2007)—nature of smells. It seeks to move beyond the discourse, the words, and the meanings by which the senses come to make sense.

While this ethnography attests to a growing objectification of the senses, the empirical evidence presented also demonstrates the meticulous construction of the sensuous consumer through the design and development of products intended to perform, act, and work beyond both the realm of words and consumers' consciousness. Consumers who use hair coloring products are often skilled. Many of them show mastery, even *meastra*, but very few are actually aware of (i.e., knowledgeable about) the technical properties of the products they use. The sensory products developed by the DMI embody practical knowledge, expertise, and intentions, as Gell (1996) or Latour (1994) might put it. They are programmed to produce a given shine, impart a particular scent, and instil a new synesthesia. These products *can* act independently of consumers because every formula developed by the DMI incorporates the work of a multitude of scientists and objectifies the results of numerous laboratory tests. Hence, *Madame Michu* is not alone in a bathroom. She mobilizes dozens of invisible chemists, perfume specialists, and other scientists.

The case of L'Oréal reveals that colors and scents are created through much trial and error and experimentation. The search for the "right" scent—the scent that will embody the *spirit* of the brand, the one that will assert itself as "superior," and that will seduce consumers—is marked by doubts, ambiguity, and negotiations. In one way, companies like L'Oréal stand at the vanguard of the sensory economy.

The question now arises whether L'Oréal truly avoids subjectivity and interpretation by implementing such a scientific apparatus. Despite the sophistication of its experimental protocols, even if the firm has been able to maintain control of its consumers and domesticate senses as elusive as smell, color assessment and scent evaluation ultimately rest upon the managers' personal interpretations.

Conclusion: Engaging Latour to the Sensual Turn

Bruno Latour and his followers opened up the "black box" of the laboratory and exposed how science is fabricated. They have demonstrated the framing effect of the laboratory, which can be taken as a context of absolute artificiality.

In line with Latour's work, this ethnography unveils the complex relationships between the marketing department and the laboratory. As we have seen, DMI managers constantly do research on consumers. We observe that a significant portion of the research effort is devoted to resolving disagreements, tensions, and controversies that arise between the marketing department and the laboratory, for instance, over the construction of reality. We also observe how the two entities coexist in a climate of tension—if not one of confrontation—that is intended to be productive.

This ethnography takes us beyond the science and technology studies, however. It shows how the "hypersensual marketplace" that is taking shape in the DMI as sensory products continue to be developed and tests are repeated lies at the junction between the practical science described by Latour (1983, 1987) and an elusive, often "primitive" (Howes, 2005), and sometimes undisciplined (Moeran, 2007) sensual culture.

We propose to use the laboratory to generate new theoretical insights on consumer culture. Ironically, while in the last twenty years "the field, rather than the laboratory, became the natural context for CCT" (Arnould and Thompson, 2005: 869, 870), the artificial context of the laboratory asserts itself as a context with a larger theoretical interest. Indeed, we can draw from this ethnography important conclusions on the making of the senses, sensuality, and the sensuous consumer. For instance, in contrast to the essentialist vision of the senses that prevails in marketing (Kotler, 1973; Holbrook and Hirshman, 1982; Pine and Gilmore, 1998), this ethnography shows that the senses are not a given. They are socially and technologically constructed. This ethnography also shows how the consumers' sensual experience cannot be reduced to words. It takes shape through, and is made possible by, a complex technological and material apparatus. Hair coloring products have the potential to convey cultural meanings. But they are more than that.

By analyzing the performance of chemical formulas rather than the meanings that the brand conveys, a firm like L'Oréal delves into the material and sensory dimensions of products in a way that remains unexplored by most interpretive researchers in CCT. These products embody practical, technical, and scientific knowledge. They are intended to perform independently of the consumers' awareness. This shows the need to distinguish between what objects, products, and commodities mean, and what they do. It stresses the need to look at what commodities achieve for the consumer, how they act, and how they come to matter. It also points to the need for us to broaden our understanding of the consumer.

We hope that our research has demonstrated the need to look more closely and more reflectively at sensory-based culture and the importance of understanding the material culture that makes sensory experience possible. It is obvious that a thorough understanding of consumer behavior can no longer be based on a study of consumers seen solely as human individuals, groups, tribes, or communities. It becomes essential for CCT researchers to provide a better account of the production of commodities. It also becomes essential to integrate the actors such as the marketing managers, the scientists, the chemists, and the perfume specialists whose work is crystallized in the commodities, but who remain silent, invisible, or "fetishized" (as Miller, (2003b) would say) if we look at brands only as symbolic resources or if we focus solely on consumers even when observed in such intimate environments as their bathrooms. In other words, we need to take consumer research beyond the consumer.

Acknowledgments

The authors would like to thank Julien Cayla for his advice. They also want to thank Catherine Grandclément, David Howes, and Brian Moeran for their critical comments and suggestions concerning an earlier draft of this chapter.

Notes

1. L'Oréal.com/research/colour/dye innovation Rubilane/L'Oréal innovation and hair dyes, June 8, 2009.
2. We use this term in place of "experience economy" because the defining feature of the latter is its engagement with the senses—or better, its attempt to manipulate the senses. The works of Lindstrom (2005) is an example of this.

3. L'Oréal.com/finance/company overview/Key figures, June 8, 2009.
4. We use quotation marks to highlight the informants' own words and expressions.
5. Pseudonyms are used.

References

Arnould, Eric J., and Thompson, Craig J. (2005) "Consumer Culture Theory (CCT): Twenty Years of Research." *Journal of Consumer Research*, 31(March): 868–82.

Baudrillard, Jean (1968) *Le système des objets*. Paris: Gallimard.

Classen, Constance, Howes, David, and Synnott, Anthony (1994) *Aroma: The Cultural History of Smell*. London: Routledge.

Geertz, Clifford (1973) *The Interpretation of Cultures: Selected Essays*. New York: Basic Books.

Gell, Alfred (1996) "Vogel's Net: Traps as Artwork and Artworks as Traps." *Journal of Material Culture*, 1(1): 15–38.

Grandclément, Catherine (2006) "Le marketing des similarités: les produits à marque de distributeur." *Réseaux*, 1–2(135/136): 221–52.

——and Gaglio, Gérald (2011) "Meeting the Consumer in Person: The Focus Group Effect." In Julien Cayla and Detlev Zwick, eds. *Inside Marketing*. Oxford: Oxford University Press.

Grayson, Kent, and Shulman, David (2000) "Indexicality and the Verification Function of Irreplaceable Possessions: A Semiotic Analysis." *Journal of Consumer Research*, 27 (June): 17–30.

Holbrook, Morris B., and Hirshman, Elizabeth C. (1982) "The Experiential Aspects of Consumption: Consumer Fantasies, Feelings, and Fun." *Journal of Consumer Research*, 9(September): 132–40.

Howes, David (1988) "On the Odour of the Soul: Spatial Representation and Olfactory Classification in Eastern Indonesia and Western Melanesia." *Anthropologica: Bijdragen Tot De Taal-, Land- en Volkenkunde*, 144: 83–113.

——(1990) "Les techniques des sens." *Anthropologie et Sociétés*, 14(2): 99–115.

——(2003a) *Sensual Relations: Engaging the Senses in Culture & Social Theory*. Ann Arbor, MI: The University of Michigan Press.

——(2003b) "Évaluation sensorielle et diversité culturelle." *Psychologie Française*, 48(4): 117–25.

——(2005) "Hyperaesthesia, or, the Sensual Logic of Late Capitalism." In David Howes, ed. *Empire of the Senses*. Oxford: Berg, pp. 281–303.

——(2007) "Multi-Sensory Marketing in Cross Perspective (part I): From Synergy to Synaesthesia." *Percepnet*, January 22, 2007.

——(2008) "Multi-Sensory Marketing in Cross Perspective (part II): Making Sense of the Senses." *Percepnet*, May 15, 2008.

Kotler, Philip (1973) "Atmospherics as a Marketing Tool." *Journal of Retailing*, 49(4): 48–64.

Latour, Bruno (1983) Give me a Laboratory and I will Raise the World." In Karin Knor and Michael Mulkay, eds. *Science Observed: Perspectives in the Social Study of Science*. London: Sage, pp. 141–70.

Latour, Bruno (1987) *Science in Action: How to Follow Scientists and Engineers through Society*. Cambridge, MA: Harvard University Press.

——(1991) *Nous n'avons jamais été modernes: essai d'anthropologie symétrique*. Paris: La Découverte.

——(1994) "Une sociologie sans objet? Remarques sur l'interobjectivité." *Sociologue du travail*, 36(4): 587–607.

——(1995) "Lettre à mon ami Pierre sur l'anthropologie symétrique." *Ethnologie française*, 26(1): 32–6.

——and Woolgar, Steven (1979) *Laboratory Life: The Construction of Scientific Facts*. Beverly Hills, CA: Sage.

Lien, Marianne Elisabeth (1997) *Marketing and Modernity*. Oxford: Berg.

Lindstrom, Martin (2005) *Brand Sense: How to Build Powerful Brands through Touch, Taste, Smell, Sight and Sound*. New York: Free Press.

McLuhan, Marshall (1962) *The Gutenberg Galaxy*. Toronto: University of Toronto Press.

Malefyt, Timothy Dewaal, and Brian Moeran, eds. (2003), *Advertising Cultures*. Oxford: Berg.

Miller, Daniel (1987) *Material Culture and Mass Consumption*. Oxford: Blackwell.

——(2003*a*) "Advertising, Production, and Consumption as Cultural Economy." In Timothy Dewaal Malefyt and Brian Moeran, eds. *Advertising Cultures*. Oxford: Berg, pp. 75–89.

——(2003*b*) "Could the Internet Defetishise the Commodity?" *Environment and Planning D, Society & Space*, 21(3): 359–72.

Moeran, Brian (2006) *Ethnography at Work*. Oxford: Berg.

——(2007) "Marketing Scents and the Anthropology of Smell." *Social Anthropology*, 15 (2): 153–68.

Pinch, Trevor (1993) "Testing—One, Two, Three... Testing: Toward a Sociology of Testing." *Science, Technology, & Human Values*, 18(1): 25–41.

Pine, Joseph II, and Gilmore, James H. (1998) "Welcome to the Experience Economy." *Harvard Business Review*, 76(July/August): 97–105.

Sherry, John F. (1991) "Postmodern Alternatives: The Interpretative Turn in Consumer Research." In Harold H. Kassarjian and Thomas S. Robertson, eds. *Handbook of Consumer Behaviour*. Englewood Cliffs, NJ: Prentice-Hall, pp. 548–91.

Sunderland, Patricia L., and Denny, Rita M. (2007) *Doing Anthropology in Consumer Research*. Walnut Creek, CA: Left Coast Press.

Trebuchet-Breitwiller, Anne-Sophie (2007) "Comment le marketing saisit les goûts: le cas des tests de jus dans la parfumerie fine." In Olivier Assouly, ed. *Goûts à vendre: Essais sur la captation esthétique*. Paris: Institut Français de la Mode/Regard, pp. 185–206.

Workman, John P. Jr. (1993) "Marketing's Limited Role in New Product Development in One Computer System Firm." *Journal of Marketing Research*, 30(November): 405–21.

Young, Diana, J.B. (2004) "The Material Value of Color: The Estate Agent's Tale." *Home Culture*, 1(1): 5–22.

Part III
The Political Economy of Marketing Practice

8

Black Models and the Invention of the US "Negro Market," 1945–1960

Elspeth H. Brown

Historians usually conceptualize the segmentation of the US consumer market in the immediate post-war era as a development instigated by mainstream merchandisers seeking new markets. Though this is often the case for some demographics, such as the youth market, the opposite was the case for black consumers in the rising prosperity of the late 1940s and 1950s. Long before white marketers began paying attention to the "ethnic" market in the mid-late 1960s, African American marketing professionals invented blacks *as a market* in order to become visible as a consumer demographic. Visibility as a market, addressed through consumer research and the focused hail of advertising's interpellation, emerged as a goal for not only black industry insiders, but civil rights leaders as well. As Charlie McGovern (2006: esp. 62–95) and Lizabeth Cohen (2003) have argued, a twentieth-century US history of equating the market with society had led to the imbrication of consumption and political belonging; in the context of post-war abundance, market visibility signified citizenship. Paradoxically, then, precisely at the historical moment when blacks were fighting against segregation in housing and education, market segregation—or, segmentation—proved an important route toward visibility and inclusion, key aspects of a liberal, market-based, civil rights politics. This chapter of *Inside Marketing* historicizes marketers' invention of African Americans as consumers in the 1945–60 period, before civil rights activists began focusing on the US advertising industry as a site of symbolic apartheid. More specifically, I examine the history and politics of an emergent black modeling industry in the creation of a "Negro market" in the post-war years. How did black professionals and publishers seek to render black Americans visible as a profitable market, and what strategies did they use to transform how whites represented and addressed this demographic within the period's duplicate advertising campaigns? What were the politics of representation in this particular moment, a period of rising prosperity for all Americans, including blacks, but before the radicalism of the civil rights movement after 1966? This chapter explores these questions through a discussion of the birth of the Negro market in the World War II years, and a brief survey of the archive of racist advertising imagery against which Negro modeling agencies sought to construct a progressive counter-archive. The post-war black modeling agencies, such as New York City's Brandford Modeling Agency and the Grace Del Marco Agency, elaborated discourses of both bourgeois respectability and mid-century glamor to define a commercial space for the display of the black female body that sidestepped older stereotypes of the asexual mammy on the one hand, and the hypersexual jezebel on the other. Marketers elaborated the twin discourses of black, class-inflected respectability and a public, managed sexuality—what the historian Peter Bailey has called "parasexuality"—to signify and enable blacks' full inclusion in American citizenship, through consumption.

The Birth of the Post-war Negro Market

The emergence of black modeling agencies in the late 1940s signified a renewed wave of efforts by Negro market experts and civil rights groups to both render visible a black consuming public and to change how blacks were depicted in white advertising. Model agents' efforts to land jobs for Negro models were successful in direct proportion to the Negro market's visibility to national, white-owned businesses and their advertising agencies. Underwriting this post-war focus on the Negro market were two significant shifts: the rise of a black, urban population and the increase in their disposable income (Weems, 1998: 7–30; Walker, 2007; Chambers, 2009: 20–44). Tracking the size and purchasing power of the post-war Negro market became an essential survival strategy for black newspapers and magazines, which needed reliable data to convince white businesses to advertise in these media outlets. As a result, the period saw a series of research studies into the Negro market, usually either commissioned or produced by black newspaper and magazine publishers. These market research investigations both insisted on the viability of a black consuming public and, at the same time, provided white advertisers with their only window onto black purchasing habits. They had important precedents, such as Paul K. Edwards's important 1932 study, *The Southern Urban Negro as a Consumer* and David J. Sullivan's work in the early to mid 1940s. Sullivan, in particular, worked tirelessly to convince reluctant white marketing professionals that urban blacks represented an ignored market demographic. Writing in 1945, for example, Sullivan argued "it is the general opinion of advertisers and marketers that a majority of Negroes live on the other side of the railroad tracks, or resemble something closely akin to a sharecropper" (Sullivan, 1945: 68). In making the case that there is "such as thing as a Negro market," Sullivan (1945: 68) showed that the gross annual income among the US Negro population more than doubled between 1940 and 1943, jumping from 4.67 billion to 10.29 billion. "Here then is a market bigger in size than the entire Dominion of Canada by approximately 10 per cent, and with over $1,250 million more income in 1943" (Sullivan, 1945: 68), he concluded—a claim which later found its way into black modeling agency founder Edward Brandford's public pronouncements concerning Brandford Modeling, Inc. (see also Sullivan, 1943, 1944, 1950).

Tracking the size and purchasing power of the post-war Negro market was an essential survival strategy for black newspapers and periodicals, which needed reliable data to convince white businesses to advertise in these media outlets. Black newspapers and magazines needed reliable market data in order to convince white businesses to advertise in the black press. The results of these later studies were reported on heavily in the black press, however, with less attention paid in the white press until the early 1960s when articles on the "ethnic market" and the "Negro market" appeared with increasingly regularity in the business trade press.[1] One of the early post-war studies into the northern, urban "Negro market" was conducted by Edgar A. Steele of the Research Company of America, and commissioned by the Afro-American chain of newspapers in cooperation with the Urban League. Steele was commissioned to conduct the study of more than 3000 Negro homes in Washington, Baltimore, and Philadelphia in order to provide "much more complete and dependable facts than had previously been collected and analyzed" (Steele, 1947: 401). The study, conducted in 1945 and published in 1947, summarized findings concerning income and educational attainment but focused more specifically on consumer brand choice. The study demonstrated which brands had leading market shares in which cities in a variety of categories, including packaged coffee, flour, pancake mix (where 70.6 of all pancake mix purchasers preferred Aunt Jemima), laundry soap, toothpaste, alcoholic beverages, cola, cigarettes, and cars—among other products. Steele (1947: 401) concluded that "the Negro is very brand conscious." "More importantly," Steele argued, "he is unusually 'brand loyal.' Sales executives should take note" (Steele, 1947: 401; see also Cohen, 2003: 323 and Dates, 1990: 421–54).

In general terms, these research endeavors produced a consistent narrative concerning the Negro market in the ongoing effort to win more lucrative advertising in black media. Studies emphasized the relative growth of Negro incomes after the war; the growing urbanization of the black population, which increased the number of blacks who could be reached by mass media; the numerical size of this market (as large as Canada at first, and by the late 1950s, as large as the total US export market, some studies claimed); the tendency among Negroes to spend a larger percentage of their income on consumer goods than whites in the same income bracket; this group's especially high degree of brand loyalty; and Negro women's important role in making purchasing decisions for white households, as so many black women were employed as domestics.[2] The studies addressed as well the two main reasons cited by white advertisers for not marketing directly to the black community: the assumption that Negroes lacked the necessary purchasing power to make investment in the market worthwhile and the fear that catering to Negroes would alienate white consumers and adversely affect sales, especially in national marketing campaigns.[3] As Robert E. Weems, Jr. (1998: 54) has pointed out, one manifestation of corporate America's interest in African American consumers is the first appearance of the term "Negro Market" in volume 19 of the *Readers Guide to Periodical Literature*, covering April 1953–February 1955.

The entry of John H. Johnson into the post-war publishing and advertising world radically altered the relationship between white businesses and the "Negro market." As Jason Chambers (2009: 43–9 on Johnson and *Ebony*, see also Green, 2007) has argued in his excellent study of Madison Avenue's color line, "Johnson's importance in generating corporate interest in black consumers can scarcely be overestimated." Already a successful publisher of *Negro Digest*, a *Readers Digest*-like magazine that focused on African Americans, Johnson launched *Ebony* in November 1945 as a middle-class magazine for blacks, modeled on *Life*, which eschewed the political focus of most black newspapers in favor of the "happier side of Negro life." *Ebony* was an instant success. Circulation numbers reached over 200,000 in a few weeks, bringing a new challenge for Johnson: how to secure additional advertising revenue to meet rising production costs. Most ad agencies, however, refused to place ads in black periodicals, citing client resistance; as a result, in 1947, Johnson bypassed the agencies and went directly to their clients. This strategy bore spectacular results when Zenith Radio's Commander Eugene McDonald not only agreed to an advertising schedule in *Ebony*, but also agreed to assist Johnson in securing advertising commitments from other white-owned businesses.[4] By the early 1950s, with advertising revenues securely in place, Johnson developed a market research arm of Johnson Publications in a successful move to become the premier interpreter of the Negro market for white advertising and marketing directors.[5]

Advertising's Minstrelsy Archive

The success of Johnson's publications as well as that of his competitors, such as New York-based monthly *Our World*, created the post-war market for Negro models. As researchers constructed and sold the "Negro Market," they underscored the relationship between winning black consumer loyalty and the presence of black models within the advertisements themselves. However, the issue for blacks contemplating the brandscape of twentieth-century America was not simply the relative dearth of blacks as advertising models. There were black models in mainstream advertising before the post-war period, of course: it is just that these models were confined to scripted roles that reinscribed racial hierarchies. By the early post-World War II (WWII) period, a longer history of racism and representation had become condensed into a few recognizable stereotypes that had increasingly become the focus of both civil rights politics and the emerging Negro modeling industry (Ruffins, 1998). For African American men, the most persistent representations were that of the Pullman porter, cook, or waiter, sometimes called the "Uncle Tom" or "Uncle Mose" type; for African American women, the ubiquitous and only advertising model was that of the "mammy," or "Aunt Jemima," who populated the ads as cook, laundress, and housekeeper.[6]

The archive of racialized stereotypes in advertising illustration is exemplified by the work of two black models, whose work for Madison Avenue in the 1920s–1950s represents the racist advertising archive against which Negro modeling agencies sought to construct a counter-archive of bourgeois respectability. Maurice Hunter was the single most photographed Negro in American advertising from the 1920s through WWII. Born in South Africa and adopted by American missionaries, Hunter emigrated to Brooklyn as a child.[7] His sole support throughout his life was as a model, for both fine artists and commercial illustrators, including Robert Henri, Daniel Chester French, Walter Biggs, and James Montgomery Flagg. Most of Hunter's work, however, was in advertising illustration where he was the ubiquitous model for nearly every stereotype of African American masculinity in interwar advertising.[8] As a *Talk of the Town* reporter in the *New Yorker* wrote in 1935, "You can be pretty sure that any darky waiter you see in a cigarette or whiskey ad is Hunter, or any dusky pirate, sheik, Moor, African, South Sea native, or Negro cotton-picker, convict, or crap-shooter you see in the magazine illustrations."[9] In the 1920s, Maurice was both of the two crap-shooting "darkies" startled by a red-nosed Irish police office for a Fisk Tire ad (1927) and the obsequious porter carrying a white lady's luggage as she stepped off the train into her husband's arms in a 1925 ad for Palmolive soap. In the 1930s, Hunter's visage appeared in the pages of *The New Yorker* as a smiling waiter exclaiming "Yes, Suh, Boss, I's Got

De Best!" while holding a tray of Laird's Apple Jack brandy. By 1947, an article in *Ebony* began, "the next time you see a Negro's face on a cigarette or whiskey ad, the odds are 1000 to 1 that it will be Maurice Hunter" (Figure 8.1).[10] He sold, to quote *Ebony*, "beer, whisky, clothing, oil, gasoline, soft drinks, radio, and cigarettes," often (though not always) as a waiter.[11]

Hunter considered himself a successful artist whose work in posing and expression allowed him to both pay the bills and to express himself creatively (Figure 8.2). "I just like to model," he told a reporter, "It makes me feel free and good."[12] According to both his own reports and those of his artists he posed for, his popularity as a model stemmed from his ability to assume a variety of convincing emotional expressions in rapid succession, such fear, mirth, pathos, guilt, and rage; this ability to pantomime emotional expression made him invaluable as a model for white commercial illustrators. The

Figure 8.1 Maurice Hunter, model, in an advertisement for Paul Jones Four Roses whiskey, *c.*1940s, clipping in Maurice Hunter Scrapbooks, Schomburg Center for Research in Black Culture, The New York Public Library, Astor, Lenox and Tilden Foundations. Reproduced with permission.

Figure 8.2 Maurice Hunter, model, headshot sheet, in Maurice Hunter Scrapbooks, folder 1, Schomburg Center for Research in Black Culture, The New York Public Library, Astor, Lenox and Tilden Foundations. Reproduced with permission.

representation and commodification of emotion has been central to American advertising since the early twentieth century, and Hunter was especially adept at producing, instantaneously, the range of expressions required of him. As commercial illustrator Karl Godwin testified about his work, "Maurice Hunter has been working for me for 10 or 12 years and has great ability to get character in his work. He has always given me just what I wanted in the spirit and action of the pose which is wanted by the magazines in their pictures."[13] Hunter's expertise, in other words, was his versatile ability to pantomime white racist stereotypes of Africans and African Americans to an implied white audience.[14]

Hunter's work performing the range of male stereotypes was complemented by that of female models, whose representations of black femininity were similarly narrow in range. Regardless of the talents of those who posed for advertising illustrations, black women were cast exclusively as variations of the "mammy" stereotype—never the "Jezebel," whose hypersexual promiscuity might compromise the brand for the ad's implied white reader. The persistence of these casting requirements in mid-century advertising can be seen in the career of actress and chorale singer Virginia Girvin (1902–75). Although a lifetime member of the Negro Actors Guild, a community activist, and a member of SCLC (Southern Christian Leadership Conference), her commercial modeling for print advertising was strictly typecast. In 1941, a plump, smiling, and be-aproned Girvin stands behind an ironing board while the white mistress places a Goodrich ironing pad over the board (*Time* magazine). In a 1946 *Collier's* illustration, Girvin as faithful mammy holds a frightened white woman in a protective embrace. In an ad for Heisey tableware (Figure 8.3), a uniformed and smiling Girvin polishes crystal wine goblets while exclaiming to the white child looking on, "It's Heisey honey! And this has

Figure 8.3 Virginia Girvin, model, in a advertisement for Heisey tableware, *Bride's Magazine*, c.1940s, Virginia Girvin Collection, MG 639 Box 1, folder 11, Manuscripts, Archives and Rare Books Division, Schomburg Center for Research in Black Culture, The New York Public Library, Astor, Lenox and Tilden Foundations. Reproduced with permission.

been a 'Heisey family' since I was as young as you!" Girvin's spectacles signify her advanced age; the mammy figure here is as loyal to her employer as the family has been to the brand. Her phrase "It's Heisey, honey" suggests the longevity of Aunt Jemima's popular catchphrase, first popularized at the 1893 World's Fair in Chicago, "I'se in town, honey."[15]

As numerous scholars have shown, the "mammy" figure appeared within nineteenth-century US culture as a white romanticization of slavery's gender and racial politics (Bogle, 1973; Kern-Foxworth, 1994; White, 1995: 27–61; Manring, 1998; McElya, 2007). In contrast to the "Jezebel" figure, whose lustful sexuality was invented as the cause of white men's sexual transgressions across the color line, the mammy represented an ideal of how black women behaved when under proper white authority and control. A strong, asexual figure, the mammy's unwavering devotion and loyalty to the white plantation family soothed white guilt over slavery and uplifted white women by making it unnecessary for them to enter the kitchen, empty chamber pots, or perform other everyday domestic labor. She was, in Deborah Gray White's view, the "personification of the ideal slave, and the ideal woman" for antebellum Southerners, a product of both the nineteenth-century cult of domesticity and white racism (White, 1995: 58). In the 1880s and 1890s, the slaveholding Old South became invented as a romantic fable of racial reconstruction that allowed white Northerners and white Southerners to reconcile sectional differences through the segregation and disenfranchisement of actual blacks. The mammy played a key figure in this popular romanticization of the plantation South. Clearly, one of the most enduring representation of the mammy has been the invented spokesperson for boxed pancake mix, Aunt Jemima—first a secular slave song, then a minstrel figure from the 1870s, then a pancake mix trade name from 1889 (Manring, 1998: ch. 3). By the early twentieth century, as actual memories of the Old South dimmed, invented memories of loyal black houseslaves preventing the "rape of the South" became more sharp: mammies proliferated on stage and screen to protect southern virtue and feed pancakes to tired confederate soldiers and (eventually) middle American families. By the 1920s, the visual and verbal features of the mammy figure became codified through a national discourse of product advertising, as admen such as J. Walter Thompson's James Webb Young drew on the racial stereotypes of the Old South to provide the visual props that anchored middle-class consumption. She was always heavyset in size; almost always wore some aspect of clothing that signified domestic service or southern origins, such as an apron, bandana, or head wrap; her features conformed to the two acceptable emotional expressions of happy or sassy; when she spoke, it was almost always in dialect.

Blacks, who regularly read not only their own press but also major white magazines, were painfully aware of the minstrelsy stereotypes that dominated

American advertising. When Paul K. Edwards conducted his market survey of southern Black urban consumers in the late 1920s, he asked respondents to comment on a series of J. Walter Thompson advertisements featuring Aunt Jemima. Respondents disapproved of the ad, citing their objections to the mammy figure in particular. A respondent for example commented he disliked "pictures of Aunt Jemima with a towel around her head," while another remarked "I am prejudiced intensely against any picture of former slave mammy." The great majority of interview subjects saw the handkerchief as a symbol of subservience and ignorance; some were mystified at the mammy's resilience within popular culture, commenting "Don't see why they keep such pictures before the public." Importantly, many respondents commented on the disparity between the representation and what they saw as their own lived experience. One commented that the advertisement was "not lifelike," while another told Edwards that she did not like "coloured characters in advertisements" because they are "always shown as menials" (Kern-Foxworth, 1994: 82–3; Manring, 1998: 157).

The print illustration modeling performed by Maurice Hunter and Virginia Girvin in the interwar years constitutes an archive of racist stereotypes that shaped the dominant discourse of Negro modeling in the early post-war years. Of course, blacks had long constructed photographic counter-archives to combat the visual violence of racist representation, from public exhibitions (such as W.E.B. DuBois' showing of Negro portraiture at the 1900 Paris Fair), to photojournalism within the pages of the Negro press, to the ubiquitous framed family portraits within black homes (Hooks, 1994; White and White, 1998; Smith, 2004). But within mainstream, white-dominated commercial culture, the color line's visual iconography remained virtually unchanged between the dawn of Jim Crow in the 1880s and the end of WWII. To be Negro and a commercial model at the dawn of the post-war era meant to be (in representation) a mammy or an uncle tom: there were no alternatives in the white advertising pages.

The Founding of Negro Modeling Agencies, 1946–1960

When black marketing professionals and media buyers sought to package and sell the Negro market in the mid-1940s, these racial stereotypes emerged as a specific list of what advertisers needed to avoid when approaching black consumers. In a 1943 article in *Sales Management*, marketing pioneer David J. Sullivan outlined the racist advertising and marketing practices that continued to demean and belittle blacks. His list of marketing "don'ts" includes several of the racist tropes that shaped Hunter's and Girvin's work in this period: "Don't picture colored women as buxom, broad-faced, grinning mammies and Aunt Jeminas," he admonished his readers. "Avoid incorrect English usage, grammar, and dialect" such as "'Yas, suh,' 'sho,' 'dese,' and 'dem.'" Sullivan recommended that advertisers avoid the "Uncle Mose" stereotype, the southern male counterpart to Aunt Jemima, whose northern migration had resulted in the innumerable waiters and porters for which Maurice Hunter was Madison Avenue's most popular model (Sullivan, 1943: 47; Weems, 1998: 32–4; Chambers, 2009: 69–74).

The first Negro modeling agencies were founded in the immediate post-war years as a means of providing Negro models for advertisers seeking to reach the Negro market through less overtly racist sales appeals. As the "Negro market" moved from a discursive construction championed by African American marketing professionals to a multimillion-dollar sales opportunity for white businesses seeking to reach urban, black consumers, the question of who modeled these consumer goods, and how, emerged as a central marketing concern. Although the small literature on the growth of black modeling in the civil rights era emphasizes fashion modeling, the initial destination for these Negro models was not in fact the fashion industry, where the color barrier seemed insurmountable in 1945, but in print advertising.[16] In the context of a booming post-war economy and increased discretionary spending in the growing black middle class, black entrepreneurs were optimistic that white businesses would need Negro models to win brand loyalty among Negro consumers for household consumer products. In the context of a Jim Crow modeling industry, where the dominant modeling agencies such as John Powers or Harry Conover barred blacks from bookings, a duplicate Negro modeling industry emerged to provide models for duplicate advertising directed at black consumers.

Although numerous Negro modeling agencies were founded in the late 1940s and 1950s, the two most nationally visible agencies were both founded in New York, the center of the nation's advertising industry, in 1946.[17] The Brandford Model agency (after 1954, Barbara Watson Models, Inc.) was founded by three partners: commercial artist Edward Brandford, stylist Mary Louise Yabro (the only white member of the business), and Barbara M. Watson, a Columbia University graduate who had worked in radio broadcasting for the Office of War Information (OWI) during the war. Born in Jamaica, Brandford was educated at Cooper Union Art School in New York, where he graduated in 1930. He opened a successful commercial art studio at 55 W. 42nd Street, and became one of the very few blacks working in marketing in any sort of professional capacity; *Advertising Age* mentions Brandford as the nation's "foremost Negro commercial artist." In 1948, two years after the modeling agency opened, Brandford founded his own advertising agency, Brandford Advertising, Inc.; the new agency was the first black advertising agency that included merchandising, public relations, art work, production, and model services.[18] In a very highly segregated business and city, Brandford was one of the few black professionals whose commercial expertise promised access to the big money of post-war consumption: white-owned businesses and advertising campaigns.[19] Mary Louise Yabro brought her experience as a stylist at the Arnold Constable & Co. department store to the new business; her later position as fashion editor for the black middle-class New York-based magazine *Our World* helped ensure a venue for Brandford Models.[20]

Barbara Watson, the third founder, basically ran the business as of 1949, as Ed Brandford played less and less of a role; by 1954, Watson renamed the company Barbara Watson Models, Inc., and had established new offices in the fashion district 505 Fifth Avenue, at 42nd Street.[21] Watson was the daughter of Judge James S. Watson, a West Indian immigrant and New York's first black municipal court judge. During the war, she worked for the United Seaman's Service and also did broadcasting in French and English for the OWI. Using her experience at OWI, Watson launched her own radio dramatic program designed to promote improved race relations on WNYC called "I'm Your Next Door Neighbor."[22] Watson continued to direct the agency until 1956, when she closed both the modeling agency and its affiliated modeling school on 35th Street and Park Avenue. In 1962, Watson graduated third in her class at NYU's law school; she eventually became the first African American Assistant Secretary of State, serving in the Johnson, Nixon, Ford, and Carter administrations, and also served as US Ambassador to Malaysia in 1980–1.[23]

The other main agency to attract national coverage in the late 1940s and early 1950s was the Grace Del Marco Modeling Agency, also founded in New York in 1946. This agency, eventually headed by Ophelia De Vore when her partners pulled out due to the new industry's erratic cash flow, eventually distinguished itself from the Brandford Models by focusing on the fashion industry. The mixed-race De Vore, passing for white, attended the Vogue school of modeling in New York in the late 1930s and landed some jobs as a "northern European" model. In 1946, tired of advertising stereotypes depicting blacks "hanging from a tree or scrubbing floors," she started Grace Del Marco Modeling Agency to sell "the idea of Black models to the advertising industry." She saw her models as the products she was selling to advertisers; to "develop the product, and then create a market for it," she founded a modeling school (Devore School of Charm), became a fashion columnist for the *Pittsburgh Courier*, produced fashion shows, and eventually expanded into public relations (she developed a promotional campaign for Nigeria, for example, in 1969).[24]

Agency founders for both Brandford and Grace Del Marco emphasized the centrality of the growing black consumer market to the founding of the new agencies, as well as the central role of non-stereotypical Negro models in reaching black buyers. Their initial efforts focused on getting advertisers to use Negro models in sales campaigns directed at retail consumers of household goods, not the apparel industry. When asked by *Labor Vanguard* magazine why he opened the agency, Brandford declared "Negroes in America represent buying power equal or greater to that of the people of Canada. Until fairly recently, this market has been pretty much neglected or entirely ignored by the manufacturers of nationally known products."[25] Mary Louise Yabro told the *Afro-American* newspaper that the idea of starting a "colored agency" was sparked when 300 advertisers at a May 1945 Chicago meeting told her that they would be willing to "do something about the colored market" if they had "colored models" to work with. The main purpose of Brandford Models, Yabro told the interviewer, "is the strong drive to aid advertisers who wish to get the colored market to use colored models in a glorious, dignified, human fashion . . . we will not release an 'Aunt Jemima' or 'Uncle Tom' type because we believe this is not a true picture of the colored people."[26]

Despite the widespread recognition that fashion would not provide many employment opportunities for newly minted Negro models in the early post-war years, however, the fashion show played a central symbolic role in announcing a new chapter in race progress. When Brandford Models opened as an agency, it was launched to advertisers and the press via a fashion show at New York's elegant Hotel Astor in Times Square, with actor and civil rights activist Canada Lee as the master of ceremonies. At this initial launch, the models were students, artists, and dancers for Katherine Dunham's company, who had taken classes with Yabro and Watson on deportment, posture, clothes, and grooming. As Yabro recalled,

> we got an immediate response. The majority of calls were not about models at first. But the advertisers saw the value of going after the Negro market, and they called to ask "how can we get to this market to sell our products?" We started to tell them not only to use Negro models, but also to change the tone of their ads from emphasizing a Negro laundress, for example, to using a "very attractive Negro matron as a model" washing clothes for her own family.[27]

The fashion show was a familiar spectacle by 1946 to both black and white audiences, with varied meanings resulting from the history of racist represen-tations of American beauty. Racially segregated, all-white fashion shows were the descendants of *haute couture* mannequin parades, which were popularized in the US in the years just before WWI through department store spectacles. The term "fashion show" migrated from the trade term used to describe the still-life display of goods and (non-human) manikins in the department store show window; after 1910, "fashion show" described the animated parade of living models who demonstrated clothing designs within the store itself.[28] In African American communities, although fashion shows were used as sales vehicles as well, their more important function was to construct and display a sartorial discourse of black bourgeois respectability, a necessarily political intervention in the context of white racism. As a result, fashion shows produced by and for black audiences bore a close relationship to other social formations of the black upper class, such as sorority events and debutante balls (Higginbotham, 1993; White and White, 1998; Wolcott, 2001). By launching the Brandford Modeling Agency as a fashion show at the elite Astor Hotel, the principals tied disparate historical meanings into a new, post-war formula that effectively linked black bourgeois respectability to the politics of the market.

Race, Parasexuality, and the Commodification of Bourgeois Femininity

By the mid-1950s, efforts by black publishers, marketing experts, and modeling agency personnel had succeeded in changing the advertising landscape of black periodicals—especially the weekly magazines, whose advertising revenues surpassed those of the older newspapers. Readers of *Ebony, Jet,* and *Our World* found large, often full-page advertisements featuring Negro models enjoying a range of consumer products in advertisements whose visual rhetoric represented a marked departure from mammy and uncle tom stereotypes. Most, though not all, advertisements were for personal care products (hair, cream, sanitary napkins, toothpastes, and deodorants), tobacco, and alcohol. Brandford model Dorothy McDavid relished a smoke for Lucky Strike (Figure 8.4), while two other Brandford Girls, as they were known, discussed the merits of Lysol for "intimate use."

As black models made their way into advertising campaigns directed at black consumers, the rhetoric used by Negro market entrepreneurs to describe the cultural work of black models shifted accordingly. Rather than emphasizing the history of racist stereotypes while arguing for the importance of the invisible "Negro market," those involved in the new Negro modeling agencies elaborated on a pre-existing discourse of black femininity that combined glamor with a wholesome sexuality that while appealing, lacked the aggressive overtones of the interwar "vamp." The wholesome appeal of the glamorous Negro model was closely tied to two related developments in the 1940s modeling industry more generally: John Powers' successful efforts to mainstream and sanitize the model's public image, and the transformation of the pin-up model after WWII from an assertive, sexually aware woman to a more passive ingénue. Both developments involved the containment of female sexuality through the discourse of the natural girl. Marketers of consumer goods borrowed heavily from this form of commodified sexuality, which the historian Peter Bailey (2002), in another context, has described as

198

Figure 8.4 Dorothy McDavid, model, in an advertisement for Lucky Strike, Barbara M. Watson Papers MG 421, Box 9, folder 4, Schomburg Center for Research in Black Culture, The New York Public Library, Astor, Lenox and Tilden Foundations. Reproduced with permission.

"parasexuality": a deployed, but contained, sexuality that straddles the divide between public and private, and which has emerged as a central element of capitalist leisure and, I would argue, marketing. In the early-mid 1950s, the Negro modeling industry positioned itself as offering a black equivalent of this sanitized and commodified version of female sexuality, which had become so central to the marketing of goods within white-dominated advertising agencies and campaigns. In doing so, marketers drew on shifting ideas of post-war gender and sexuality as a whole in order to commodify black female sexuality for the purpose of creating consumer desire, while at the same time sidestepping the other stereotypical pole of black female representation: the Jezebel. The market emerged, in other words, as a route toward inclusion in the American dream through consumer citizenship while also

199

performing hegemonic labor toward twin contradictory projects: elaborating a counter-archive of non-racist representations with commercial culture while embarking on the assimilation of marketing and advertising agencies while, at the same time, reinscribing the color, class, and gender hierarchies of the black bourgeoisie.

In 1946, when the Brandford and Grace Del Marco agencies opened, the gold standard of the modeling industry was John Robert Powers. Although Powers' position would soon be usurped by Eileen and Gerry Ford, who started Ford Models in 1946, Powers had not only founded the industry but was so equated with American glamor that Hollywood made an unsuccessful movie based on the agency in 1943, entitled *The Powers Girl*. Powers, an unemployed actor who modeled for commercial photographer Lejaren à Hiller in the early 1920s, began his business as a theatrical agent for actors; by 1930, his agency had moved away from representing actors to theaters and film companies, in order to focus specifically on photographic print advertising (Brown, 2000, 2005, 2009). Powers' market here was the growing advertising industry, which after pre-war innovations such as Hiller's moved *en masse* to commercial photography as the industry's main medium (Marchand, 1985: 149; see also Bogart, 1995: 171–96). But while the camera offered a clear view of the product, it also showcased the model; marketers became increasingly concerned about the specific look of their product's model in the larger project of manufacturing desire and selling goods. As Powers (1941: 27) pointed out, "advertising, as everyone knows, is directed at women who do most of the nation's purchasing." He needed a new type of female visage to be represented in these print advertisements: pretty, to be sure, but not "artificial," stagey, or vampish; models with whom potential American consumers would identify and emulate. "My job," Powers wrote, "was to find models with whom the women of the buying public would be willing to make that identification: models who possessed not only beauty, but breeding, intelligence, and naturalness." He sought what he called "the natural girl" (Powers, 1941: 27).

By the 1940s, the magazines regularly featured stories that betrayed marketers' understanding of female consumers' identification with advertising models. Magazine stories on well-known white models routinely distanced their subjects from any suggestions of moral impropriety, emphasizing instead "beauty and breeding" safely contained within the familiar roles of wife and mother. A 1944 article feature in *Life* entitled "Model Mothers," for example, pointed out that half of all models were married, and half again were mothers; Powers, the article states, believes that "being a mother usually improves a girl's disposition."[29] A 1947 *Life* article explicating "myths" and "realities" of the model's life disputed, as did Powers in his work, the model's public image as a "luscious creature" with "low morals and not very much in the way of a brain"; instead, the article detailed how the era's well-known models had smarts, Ivy League educations, and business acumen. "Indeed," the article concluded, "the only characteristic left to bear out the popular notion of models is that they are beautiful."[30] The rhetoric of beauty and allure, reworked in the 1930s as a version of glamor, were still central to the model's public image, and to the sale of goods she facilitated; but Powers and his popularizers successfully contained any potential threat from the model's public performance of sexual appeal through a discourse of domesticity and middle-class propriety.[31]

This sanitization of the model's sexuality was part of a larger transformation within American popular culture in early post-war America. As Maria Elena Buszek has shown, during WWII, mainstream pin-up iconography was emblematized by Alberto Vargas' work for *Esquire*, whose illustrations depicted models as "sexualized yet pointedly active women usurping and clothed in the accoutrements of male power, learning drills and semaphore" (Buszek, 2006: 209). As the war ended, and soldiers returned from overseas, white middle-class women were, in Elaine Tyler May's terms, "homeward bound"; conservative gender roles became the norm, and popular culture's representation of an idealized femininity shifted from an assertive, if not aggressive, sexuality of the pre-war years to a contained, domesticated sexuality.[32] At *Esquire*, the Varga Girl was replaced in the post-war period by new illustrations that, in Buszek's words, "eschewed the working woman and sexual dynamo for the bobby-soxer and cuddly coed" (Buszek, 2006: 236). By the late 1940s, white models were represented as beautiful, to be sure, but their glamor was also safely contained within the familiar, and unthreatening, roles of wife and mother.

This shift from vampish chorus girl of the 1920s to the natural, well-posed coed of the late 1940s was a public relations triumph for Powers, who headed an industry that has always been haunted by accusations of moral and sexual improprieties. In the context of African American modeling, however, where Powers also represented the epitome of the industry, his rebranding of the model from vamp to collegiate/mom illuminated a path between the twin abysses of the mammy's asexuality and the Jezebel's promiscuity. Powers' discourse of middle-class respectability for white models found its parallel in the Negro modeling industry, where a discourse of glamorous African American womanhood as an exemplar of race pride replaced the early post-war year's emphasis on the Negro market. The discourse of African American beauty, elaborated most fully in beauty contests but also closely tied to the emergence of the Negro modeling industry, was central to a liberal civil rights discourse that tied racial uplift to both the accomplishments of the "talented tenth" and the commodification of sexuality. As Maxine Leeds Craig has shown, the black beauty contests of the late nineteenth through mid-twentieth centuries were one of several methods through which the black middle class constructed and displayed racial pride during an era when de facto and de jure segregation was the norm (Craig, 2002; see also Kinloch, 2004). By the post-war era, these beauty contests, working in dialog with an overlapping history of black beauty culturists, had elaborated a rhetoric of race progress and middle-class propriety to define new meanings for the public display of, and sanctioned looking at, black female bodies.[33] Black marketing entrepreneurs inserted the "Negro model" into this cultural space, thereby explicitly tying the display of the female form to the market of goods—but through a discourse of respectable femininity.

The black models featured in product advertising directed toward the emerging "Negro market" exemplified a specific class and gender-inflected ideal with long roots in African American discourses of respectability. As Evelyn Brooks Higginbotham (1993) has shown, black Baptist church women in the early twentieth century, working to oppose white supremacist social structures and symbolic representations, elaborated what she has called a "politics of respectability" to shepherd blacks toward middle-class, assimilationist ideals concerning the body and its comportment. The politics of respectability emphasized "manners and morals," while at the same time asserting traditional forms of protest such as boycotts, petitions, and verbal appeals to justice (Higginbotham, 1993: 187). In the same period, discourses of respectability and racial uplift were tied to ideals of exemplary beauty, as images of black women designed to "Exalt Negro Womanhood" became regular features in African American publications such as the *Messenger*, *Crisis*, and *Opportunity* (White and White, 1998; see also Gill, 2006). By the post-WWII period, the visual signifiers of this middle-class politics of respectability were readable both at sites of African American commercial culture, such as beauty contests and salons, and also on the female body itself, signified through deportment, skin color, clothing, and (straightened) hair.

The advertising and marketing work featuring black model Sarah Lou Harris exemplifies how post-war African American models helped construct a discourse of glamorous beauty that nonetheless adhered to a class-inflected politics of black respectability. Harris, along with Sylvia Fitt Jones, was the period's most famous black model; in 1954, unlike most of the underpaid and underemployed black models in the fledgling industry, both Harris and Jones earned the going rates of $10–25 per hour and had their pick of assignments.[34] In this 1952 advertisement for Remington adding machines, Harris appears as a clerk leaving her desk at the end of the workday (Figure 8.5). Dressed for departure in a well-fitted outdoor coat with a tasteful scarf tucked around her neck, she smiles at the camera while pulling on a pair of fitted ladies' gloves. The understated makeup, clothing and accessories, light skin, straightened hair, and elegant deportment signify the discourse of middle-class respectability which had long eluded the representation of black women in American

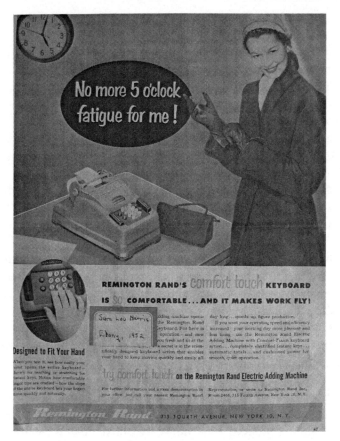

Figure 8.5 Sarah Lou Harris, model, 1952 advertisement for Remington adding machines, Barbara M. Watson Papers, MG 421, Box 9, folder 4, Schomburg Center for Research in Black Culture, The New York Public Library, Astor, Lenox and Tilden Foundations. Reproduced with permission.

media. In contrast to this carefully crafted image of the black model's respectability, however, in 1951, *Ebony*'s cover featured a buxom vixen clothed only in a leopard skin bikini to accompany their featured story "Is it True What They Say About Models?" The article opened with the stereotypes of the model's loose reputation as "a loose, reckless party-girl" only to argue, as did *Life* in the 1940s in their stories on white models, that the new black models were college-educated career girls with husbands and children. The article introduces nationally famous black model Sarah Lou Harris as a wife and mother: "Most of us are family girls who are simply doing a job," she says. "We are seeking a decent life and some security . . . we have ideals too."[35] These protestations worked to contain the otherwise explosive sexuality of Harris as a glamorous beauty, a necessary element to her marketability, and one that was featured in other coverage, such as her pin-up profile on the cover of *Jet* magazine as the "cover girl of the disc jockeys."

The model's sexuality was a central element of marketing goods in these images for consumer products targeted to the new "Negro market." But how might we further understand the specificities of this particular deployment of mid-century glamor, when sexual appeal represented both a libidinous enticement yet at the same time a threat to post-war narratives of domestic togetherness? This middle ground of deployed, but contained, sexual appeal is the terrain of what the historian Peter Bailey has called "parasexuality": the ensemble of sites and practices that capitalists and managers have constructed to enable the circulation of an "open yet licit sexuality," a commodified form of sexuality that bridges public and private, is commercialized in its expression, and is familiar to us most often through the largely unexamined arena of "glamor."[36] In Bailey's analysis of the Victorian barmaid, the management of sexuality emerged as a key element in an increasingly commercialized world, where in the pub, the music hall, and the popular theater sexuality emerged as, in his words, "a natural resource rather than a natural enemy." Parasexuality, in Bailey's formulation, "is sexuality that is deployed but contained, carefully channeled rather than fully discharged."

Black marketing professionals were, like others in the industry, well versed in the sales appeal of sex appeal. The deployment of a sanitized version of female sexuality had long marked the history of American advertising, where the comely charms of Kodak and Coca-Cola girls had beguiled consumers since the late nineteenth century. Yet racism within the American advertising industry had also produced what might be called a parasexuality color line: only white women had been cast as sanitized sirens in advertising's pageant of consumer cornucopia, and only white men became Arrow Shirt or Gillette models (West, 2000; Kitch, 2001; Reichert, 2003). The invention of the Negro market, and the marketing strategies that ensued, joined for the first time the visual representation of black models with the commodified sexuality that had long been the signal elements of modernity's imbrication of the market and gender. With the visibility of blacks as an economically attractive demographic, African Americans won recognition and inclusion into American life through their role as consumers. The advent of the black modeling agencies in the 1940s, and the duplicate marketing strategies of which they were part, marked a breakthrough in the longer politics of race and representation. For the first time, both black men and women were depicted in national advertising campaigns in the visual vocabulary of black middle-class respectability: as career women, for example, or as whiskey-sipping (rather than whiskey-serving) men at leisure—rather than, solely, as mammies or uncle toms. Blacks used the market as a means to rewrite the visual rhetoric of black bodies in commercial representation: from the hyper- or hypo-sexualized discourses of jezebels and bucks, or mammy and toms, to the middle ground of commodified sexuality, the parasexuality of commercial discourse. At the same time, however, marketers codified the color, gender, and class hierarchies of the black bourgeoisie.

Conclusion

This rapprochement between the advertising industry and the black middle class was short-lived, however. Even while black businessmen were succeeding in establishing duplicate advertising campaigns suffused with the politics of black respectability, the sociologist E. Franklin Frazier was writing what emerged as a devastating critique of the complacency of what he termed the "black bourgeoisie." Published in Paris in 1955 as *Bourgeoisie Noire* (and translated in 1957 as *Black Bourgeoisie*), Frazier critiqued college-educated, middle-class blacks—and the black business class in particular—for abandoning social justice for conspicuous consumption. In Frazier's view, the post-war shift in the black press to celebrate black "achievements," as in the pages of *Ebony*, insulated the black leadership class from the real problems facing all black Americans, creating a world of "make believe" that compensated for blacks' inferiority complex without changing it (Frazier, 1957). While the book was immediately controversial within the black community, Frazier's critique found a sympathetic audience with many student activists, including one of Frazier's undergraduates at Howard University, a young Stokely Carmichael. As president of the Student Non-Violent Coordinating Committee (SNCC), it was Carmichael who would lead civil rights activism away from King's liberal integrationist politics toward the radicalism of the black power movement, with its critique of both racism and capitalism. The black middle-class student rejection of their parents' commitment to bourgeois respectability and its visual signifiers necessitated a response among marketers seeking to reach this demographic. The market is a malleable formation, however: though it took a few years before the new signifiers of pan-Africanism and black militancy made their way into the visual rhetoric of American advertising, it was not long before marketers had rewritten the codes of black parasexuality to conform to a new historic moment.[37]

Notes

1. See for example Claude H. Hall's regular feature in *Printer's Ink* in the early 1960s, "The Negro Market." For a brief discussion of this history of cultivating the black consumer, see Marilyn Halter, *Shopping for Identity: The Marketing of Ethnicity* (New York: Schocken Books), 43; see also Kathy M. Newman, "The Forgotten Fifteen

Million: Black Radio, The 'Negro Market,' and the Civil Rights Movement," *Radical History Review*, 76 (Winter, 2000): 115–35.

2. Marcus Alexis, "Pathways to the Negro Market," *The Journal of Negro Education*, vol. 28, no. 2 (Spring, 1959), pp. 114–27. For reporting on these studies, see Felicia Anthenelli, "Negro Market," *The Wall Street Journal*, February 23, 1952, p. 1; "See Negro Market of $30 Billion," *The Chicago Defender*, July 24, 1954, p. 21; "Abramson Lauds Negro Market Gains," *The Chicago Defender*, July 25, 1953, p. 4; "Wall Street Feature Cites Importance of Negro Business," *Atlanta Daily World*, January 17, 1954, p. 4; Albert Barnett, "Big Business Courts Negro Market: Indolent South Finally Wakes Up," *The Chicago Defender*, February 6, 1954, p. 9; for additional studies, see Joseph T. Johnson, *The Potential Negro Market* (New York: Pageant Press, 1952). On blacks' brand loyalty, see "The Forgotten 15,000,000 . . . Three Years Later," *Sponsor*, 6: 76–7, July 28, 1952, cited in Marcus Alexis, "Pathways to the Negro Market," *The Journal of Negro Education*, vol. 28, no. 2 (Spring, 1959), pp. 114–27, p. 121; Albert Barnett, "Negro Business a 12 Billion Dollar Market," *The Chicago Defender*, February 5, 1949, p. 7; John H. Johnson, "Why Negroes Buy Cadillacs," *Ebony* (September, 1946), p. 34.

3. See for example "The Negro Market: An Appraisal," *Tide*, vol. 21, March 7, 1947, p. 15; "The Negro Market," *Tide*, vol. 26, July 25, 1952, p. 47; "Fourteen Million Negro Consumers," *Management Review*, 36, June 1947, p. 338.

4. Cite ad from Watson papers; Chambers (2009: 43); Weems (2000: 73); Johnson, *Succeeding Against the Odds* (1993).

5. *Ebony and Jet Magazines Present the Urban Negro Market for Liquors, Wines and Beers* (July, 1953 study no. 1; study no 2: 1954; 1957); John H. Johnson, "Does Your Sales Force Know How to Sell the Negro Trade? Some Dos and Don'ts," *Advertising Age*, 23, March 17, 1952, pp. 73–4; for sales films, see Chambers, *Madison Avenue and the Color Line*, p. 43 and John H. Johnson, with Lerone Bennett, Jr., *Succeeding Against the Odds* (New York: Amistad, 1989), 230.

6. The term "Uncle Tom" comes from Harriet Beecher Stowe's *Uncle Tom's Cabin* (1851), the work that more than any other helped crystallize Northern antislavery feeling in the antebellum period. Stowe's character was meant to embody the gentleness and capacity for forgiveness central to the perfect Christian character; over time, the term became synonymous with white representations of black docility and subservience. See George M. Frederickson, *The Black Image in the White Mind: The Debate on Afro-American Character and Destiny, 1817–1914* (New York: Harper and Row, 1971), 110–11.

7. "A Statue? Arabs? That's Mr. Hunter from Zululand! Ad Men's Favorite Dusky Model a Good Actor," *New York Post*, November 30, 1935, clipping in Maurice Hunter Scrapbooks (hereafter MHS), Schomburg Center for Research in Black Culture, New York Public Library (hereafter Schomburg); Maurice Hunter, "I Pose . . ." *Design Magazine*, January 1951, clipping in MHS; Mel Heimer, "Men's Whirl," *Social Whirl* December 27, 1954, p. 14 in MHS.

8. MHS; see also these scrapbooks for numerous examples of the illustrated fiction for which he posed. For a history of African stereotypes in Western popular culture and the relationship of these stereotypes to European and US imperialisms, see Jan Nederveen Pieterse, *White on Black: Images of Africa and Blacks in Western Popular Culture* (New Haven: Yale University Press, 1992), esp. 113–22 on the cannibal, 124–31 on

the "black moor" as servant, and 152–5 for the US stereotypes of Uncle Tom and Aunt Jemima.

9. *New Yorker*, "Talk of the Town," November 16, 1935, in MHS/Schomburg.

10. "The Man in the Ads: Maurice Hunter Pops Up on Billboards All Over U.S.," *Ebony*, 1947, 35, article in Maurice Hunter Collection, folder 1, Schomburg.

11. Ibid., 35. For the ads, see MHS; for the obituary, see *New York Times*, March 4, 1966, in Maurice Hunter Collection; for the Pennsylvania Railroad mural, designed by Raymond Loewy, see Drix Duryea, "The Biggest Heads in the World," *Popular Photography*, February 1944, pp. 40–1, 92–3.

12. *Musical Advance*, May 1943, clipping, MHS/Schomburg.

13. MHS/Schomburg, scrapbook three, card from Godwin.

14. Hunters' commercial clients appeared oblivious to the long history of black protest against white racist representations, while Hunter himself believed his was creative work that furthered "the race": see Frieda Wyandt, "I Became a Model to Help My Race, Says Negro Made Famous by Artists," *New York Evening Graphic*, Magazine Section, April 16, 1926, p. 6, MHS/Schomburg. For a history of protest against Aunt Jemima stereotypes, see Manring (1998) and McElya (2007), esp. 116–69; for a discussion of the NAACP (National Association for the Advancement of Colored People) protests against *The Birth of A Nation*, see Melvyn Stokes, D. W. Griffith's *The Birth of a Nation: a History of "The Most Controversial Motion Picture of All Time"* (New York: Oxford University Press, 2007). Although television offered more varied roles for black actors, J. Fred MacDonald describes the persistence of the Uncle Tom and Aunt Jemima stereotypes in his *Blacks and White TV: Afro-Americans in Television Since 1948* (Chicago: Nelson-Hall Publishers, 1983), 22–4.

15. (*Bride's Magazine*, 1940s, n.d.) and other ads cited here in Virginia Girvin Collection, folder 11, Schomburg; see also *Slave in a Box*, 75.

16. See for example Janice Cheddle, "The Politics of the First: The Emergence of the Black Model in the Civil Rights Era," *Fashion Theory*, vol. 6, issue 1, 2002, 61–82; an exception is Laila Haidarali, "Polishing Black Diamonds: African American Women, Popular Magazines, and the Advent of Modeling in Early Postwar America," *Journal of Women's History*, vol. 17, no. 1, 2005, 10–37, whose work ties modeling to the emergence of the "brownskin" ideal of African American femininity.

17. Some of these other agencies in the 1946–50 period, in the New York area alone, included Sepia Art Models, based in Harlem, which provided Negro models for Ivel furs and ran an annual "If I Were a Model" contest, c.1947–50; the Thelma May models; the Hat Box Models; the Gynlo Models; and the Newark-based Belle Meade School of Charm and Modeling. In 1950, *Ebony* reported Negro modeling agencies in New York, Chicago, Cleveland, and Los Angeles. See "Ivel Seeks Model In Glamour Test," *New York Amsterdam News*, August 30, 1947, p. 19; *New York Amersterdam News*, October 11, 1947 p. 2; "Ivel Furs Third Contest Begins," *New York Amsterdam News*, November 8, 1947, p. 21; Gerru Major, "Fashionettes," *New York Amsterdam News*, April 8, 1950, p. 23; "Model Schools: Racket or Business," *Ebony*, September 1950, 73–7; for the Belle Meade School, see Barbara Summers, *Black and Beautiful: How Women of Color Changed the Fashion Industry* (New York: Amistad Press, 2001), 25.

18. "New Advertising Agency to Service Negro Market," *New Journal and Guide*, January 31, 1948, p. 3; see also Jason Chambers, *Madison Avenue and the Color Line*, 74–7.

19. "First Negro Model Agency Opened in New York," *Printers' Ink*, August 9, 1946, reprinted from *Advertising Age*, August 5, 1946, in Barbara Mae Watson Papers, Box 9, folder 10, New York Public Library, Schomburg Center for Research in Black Culture (hereafter Watson Papers); "Brandford Models: Rated with the Best," clipping from *COLOR*, n.d., Watson Papers, Box 9, folder 10; "Tan Model Agency May Change Ads," *The Pittsburgh Courier*, October 19, 1946, p. 1.

20. "Negro Model Agency Opens in New York," *Philadelphia Tribune*, August 10, 1946, p. 3.

21. "Barbara Watson's Brown Skin Models: Judge's Daughter Has Idea, Makes it Work," *The Chicago Defender*, February 20, 1954, p. 12; see also Jessie Carney Smith and Shirelle Phelps, *Notable Black American Women*, vol. 2 (Detroit: Gale Research, 1992–2003), 691–3.

22. "J.S. Watson, N.Y. Judge, Dies at 59," *The Chicago Defender*, May 17, 1952, p. 1; "Career Woman at Home," *The New York Age*, March 5, 1947, clipping in Watson Papers, Box 9, folder 10; "Barbara Watson's Brown Skin Models: Judge's Daughter Has Idea, Makes it Work," *The Chicago Defender*, February 20, 1954, p. 12.

23. Barbara Watson papers, Schomburg, finding aid.

24. Ophelia DeVore, "Figure, Voice, Make-Up, Breeding, Lead to Charm," *New York Amsterdam News*, September 5, 1953, p. 10; Melissa Sones, "The Secret to Inner Beauty," *American Legacy*, vol. 9, no. 3 (Fall, 2003): 20–32; Barbara Summer, *Black and Beautiful: How Women of Color Changed the Fashion Industry* (NY: Amistad, 1998), 25–38; Laila Haidarali, "Polishing Black Diamonds: African American Women, Popular Magazines, and the Advent of Modeling in Early Postwar America," *Journal of Women's History*, vol. 17, no. 1, 2005, 10.

25. "Ed Brandford: The Guy Who Created Brandford Models," *Labor Vanguard* clipping, n.b., Watson Papers, Box 9, folder 10.

26. "No Uncle Toms or Aunt Jemimas," *The Afro-American*, November 30, 1946, clipping Watson Papers, Box 9, folder 10.

27. "Harlem's First Professional Glamour Girls," newspaper clipping, Watson Papers, Box 9, folder 10; "Modeling Agency Opens in N'York At Hotel Astor," *Atlanta Daily World*, August 17, 1946, p. 1.

28. "The Easter Show," *Dry Goods Economist*, March 17, 1906, 101.

29. "Model Mothers," *Life*, vol. 16, May 22, 1944, 65; for a similar article, with nearly identical references to Powers, see Betty Hannah Hoffman, "The Model Mother," *Ladies Home Journal*, October 1945, 159–62, 174–5.

30. "Notions about Model," *Life*, vol. 22, May 12, 1947, 16.

31. For a wonderful history of glamor in the 1920s–1940s era, see Liz Willis-Tropea, "Hollywood Glamour: Sex, Power, and Photography, 1925–1939," Ph.D. dissertation, University of Southern California, 2008.

32. Elaine Tyler May, *Homeward Bound: American Families in the Cold War Era* (New York: Basic Books, 1988); for a critique and complication of May's argument, see Joanne Meyerowitz, ed., *Not June Cleaver: Women and Gender in Postwar America* (Philadelphia: Temple University Press, 1994). See also Patricia Vettel-Becker,

"Female Body: Artists, Models, Playboys, and Femininity" in *Shooting From the Hip: Photography, Masculinity, and Postwar America* (Minneapolis: University of Minnesota Press, 2005).

33. For a discussion of the relationship between discourses of racial progress and the work of African American beauty culturalists during Jim Crow, see Kathy Peiss, *Hope in a Jar: The Making of American Beauty Culture* (New York: Holt, 1998), 203–38; Gill (2006); Walker (2007).

34. Harris, a graduate of Bennett College in North Carolina, also pursued graduate work at Columbia; she had an active career as a singer and actress. In 1963, she married her second husband, John Carter, a Guyanese barrister who was knighted by Queen Elizabeth in 1966. Carter was Guyana's ambassador to many countries during his career, including the United States, Canada, and England. Smith and Phelps, *Notable Black American Women*, vol. 2, 87.

35. "Is It True What They Say About Models," *Ebony*, November 1951, pp. 60–4; for other coverage of Sarah Lou Harris, see "Ebony's Girls," *Ebony*, November 1950, 23–4 and "New Beauties vs. Old," *Ebony*, March 1954, 50. See also "Model Schools: Racket or Business," *Ebony*, September 1950, 73–7 for a similar themed article that also includes a discussion of Sarah Lou Harris.

36. Since Bailey's article, historians have begun writing about glamor as a category of commodified femininity central to modern capitalism. See Kathleen Barry, *Femininity in Flight: A History of Flight Attendants* (Durham, NC: Duke University Press, 2007) and Liz Willis-Tropea, "Hollywood Glamour: Sex, Power, and Photography, 1925–1939," Ph.D. dissertation, University of Southern California, 2008.

37. For a case study of just one example, that of hair care products, see Robin D.G. Kelley's incomparable "Nap Time: Historicizing the Afro," *Fashion Theory*, vol. 1, issue 4 (1997): 339–52.

References

Bailey, Peter (2002) "Parasexuality and Glamour: The Victorian Barmaid as Cultural Prototype." In Kim M. Phillips and Barry Reay, eds. *Sexualities in History: A Reader.* New York: Routledge, pp. 222–46.

Bogart, Michele H. (1995) *Artists, Advertising, and the Borders of Art.* Chicago, IL: University of Chicago Press.

Bogle, Donald (1973) *Toms, Coons, Mulattoes, Mammies, and Bucks; an Interpretive History of Blacks in American Films.* New York: Viking Press.

Brown, Elspeth H. (2000) "Rationalizing Consumption: Photography and Commercial Illustration, 1913–1919," *Enterprise and Society*, 1(December): 715–38.

——(2005) *The Corporate Eye: Photography and the Rationalization of American Commercial Culture, 1884–1929.* Baltimore, MD: Johns Hopkins University Press.

——(2011) "The Emergence of the Model in the Early Twentieth Century United States." In Joanne Entwistle and Elizabeth Wissinger, eds. *Fashion Models: Modeling as Image, Text, and Industry* (forthcoming in Berg).

Buszek, Maria Elena (2006) *Pin-up Grrrls: Feminism, Sexuality, Popular Culture*. Durham, NC: Duke University Press.

Chambers, Jason (2009) *Madison Avenue and the Color Line*. Philadelphia, PA: Penn Press.

Cohen, Lizabeth (2003) *A Consumers' Republic: The Politics of Mass Consumption in Postwar America*. New York: Knopf.

Craig, Maxine Leeds (2002) *Ain't I A Beauty Queen: Black Women, Beauty, and the Politics of Race*. New York: Oxford.

Dates, Janette L. (1990) "Advertising." In J.L. Dates and W. Barlow, eds. *Split Image: African Americans in the Mass Media*. Washington, DC: Howard University Press, pp. 421–54.

Edwards, Paul K. (1932) *The Southern Urban Negro as a Consumer*. New York: Prentice-Hall.

Frazier, E. Franklin (1957) *Black Bourgeoisie*. Glencoe, IL: Free Press.

Gill, Tiffany M. (2006) "'The First Thing Every Negro Girl Does': Black Beauty Culture, Racial Politics, and the Construction of Modern Black Womanhood, 1905–1925." In Elspeth H. Brown, Catherine Gudis, and Marina Moskowitz, eds. *Cultures of Commerce: Representation and American Business Culture, 1877–1960*. New York: Palgrave Macmillan, pp. 143–70.

Green, Adam (2007) *Selling the Race: Culture, Community, and Black Chicago, 1940–1955*. Chicago, IL: University of Chicago Press.

Higginbotham, Evelyn Brooks (1993) *Righteous Discontent: the Women's Movement in the Black Baptist Church, 1880–1920*. Cambridge, MA: Harvard University Press.

hooks, bell (1994) "In Our Glory: Photography and Black Life." In Deborah Willis, ed. *Picturing Us: African American Identity in Photography*. New York: The New Press, pp. 42–53.

Kern-Foxworth, Marilyn (1994) *Aunt Jemima, Uncle Ben, and Rastus: Blacks in Advertising Yesterday, Today and Tomorrow*. Westport, CT: Greenwood Press.

Kinloch, Valerie Felita (2004) "Beauty, Femininity, and Black Bodies: Challenging the Paradigms of Race in the Miss America Pageant." In Elwood Watson and Darcy Martin, eds. *"There She is, Miss America": The Politics of Sex, Beauty, and Race in America's Most Famous Pageant*. New York: Palgrave Macmillan, pp. 93–109.

Kitch, Carolyn L. (2001) *The Girl on the Magazine Cover: the Origins of Visual Stereotypes in American Mass Media*. Chapel Hill, NC: University of North Carolina Press.

McElya, Micki (2007) *Clinging to Mammy: The Faithful Slave in Twentieth-Century America*. Cambridge, MA: Harvard University Press.

McGovern, Charles F. (2006) *Sold American: Consumption and Citizenship, 1890–1945*. Chapel Hill, NC: University of North Carolina Press.

Manring, M.M. (1998) *Slave in a Box: The Strange Career of Aunt Jemima*. Charlottesville, VA: University Press of Virginia.

Marchand, Roland (1985) *Advertising the American Dream: Making Way for Modernity, 1920–1940*. Berkeley, CA: University of California Press.

Powers, John Robert (1941) *The Powers Girls: The Story of Models and Modeling and the Natural Steps by Which Attractive Girls are Created*. New York: E.P. Dutton.

Reichert, Tom (2003) *The Erotic History of Advertising*. Amherst, NY: Prometheus Books.

Ruffins, Fath Davis (1998) "Reflecting on Ethnic Imagery in the Landscape of Commerce." In Susan Strasser, Charles McGovern, and Matthias Judt, eds. *Getting and Spending: European and American Consumer Societies in the Twentieth Century*. Washington, DC: German Historical Institute, pp. 379–406.

Smith, Shawn Michelle (2004) *Photography on the Color Line: W.E.B. Du Bois, Race, and Visual Culture*. Durham, NC: Duke University Press.

Steele, Edgar A. (1947) "Some Aspects of the Negro Market." *Journal of Marketing*, 11 (April): 399–401.

Sullivan, David J. (1943) "Don't Do This—If You Want to Sell Your Product to Negroes!" *Sales Management*, 52(March): 46–50.

——(1944) "The American Negro—An 'Export Market' at Home!" *Printer's Ink*, 208 (July): 90–4.

——(1945) "The Negro Market Today and Postwar." *Journal of Marketing*, 10(July): 68–9.

——(1950) "Why a Handful of Advertisers Dominate the Negro Markets." *Sales Management*, 65(September): A.

Walker, Susannah (2007) *Style and Status: Selling Beauty to African American Women, 1920–1975*. Louisville, KY: University Press of Kentucky.

Weems, Jr., Robert E. (1998) *Desegregating the Dollar: African American Consumerism in the Twentieth Century*. New York: NYU Press.

West, Nancy Martha (2000) *Kodak and the Lens of Nostalgia*. Charlottesville, VA: University Press of Virginia.

White, Deborah Gray (1995) *Aren't I a Woman: Female Slaves in the Plantation South*. New York: Norton.

White, Shane, and White, Graham (1998) *Stylin': African American Expressive Culture from its Beginnings to the Zoot Suit*. Ithaca, NY: Cornell University Press.

Wolcott, Victoria (2001) *Remaking Respectability: African American Women in Interwar Detroit*. Chapel Hill, NC: UNCP.

9

Customer Co-production from Social Factory to Brand: Learning from Italian Fashion

Adam Arvidsson and Giannino Malossi

In recent years, academic marketing discourse as well as actual marketing practice has focused on customer co-creation. Traveling under a number of different names, "value co-creation," (Prahalad and Ramaswamy, 2004) "user-led innovation," (von Hippel, 2006), "open innovation" (Chesborough, 2006), a "service-dominant logic of marketing" (Vargo and Lusch, 2004), or even "wikinomics" (Tapscott and Williams, 2006), the basic idea is the same: In an age of heightened connectivity and generalized creativity, consumers can (and want to) take a more active part in the co-production of the products and services that they consume. As Henry Chesborough claims, such "Open" practices are premised on the idea that "useful knowledge is now widespread," and not the scarce property of companies and their R&D departments.[1] Having thus internalized the notion—long under way in cultural studies and the sociology of consumption (McGuigan, 1992), and in what in academic marketing circles is known as "Consumer Culture Theory," or CCT (Arnould and Thompson, 2005)—that the distinction between consumption and production is becoming increasingly blurred; the co-creation paradigm posits consumers, not as the passive recipients of marketing efforts, but as partners in productive relationships, and as subjects whose "voluntary" and "spontaneous" co-creation can be even posited a form of labor (Arvidsson, 2006). Co-creating consumers constitute a positive externality for business and a significant, albeit difficult to measure, source of economic revenue. Indeed, the point of business practice, and marketing practice in particular, becomes not so much to sell the stuff that one can produce, but to "unlock the productive potential of relationships" (Prahalad and Ramaswamy, 2004: 10; see also Zwick and Ozalp, this volume).

The arrival of customer co-creation can be viewed as yet one step in a long process of opening up brands and marketing practices, and of shifting the strategic focus away from products to relationships (Gronroos, 2006). Within marketing theory (as well as management guides) this event has often been celebrated as a progressive step away from the repressive realities of a (mostly imagined) industrial order where consumers where "not free," and marketing was obsessed with control and dominance, toward a new era of mutually beneficial and much more egalitarian relations. (These arguments are very similar to the celebration of the "active consumer" within cultural studies in the 1990s, cf. Arvidsson, 2008.) Gathering momentum, perhaps, from the contemporary hype about Web 2.0 this celebratory attitude has, until recently stood virtually unchallenged, within marketing debates as well as within other fields (cf. Zwick et al., 2008; Bonsu and Darmody, 2009). What is more, the contemporary talk around customer co-creation is fundamentally ahistorical. Customer co-creation is presented as something radically new, caused by the arrival of new networked information and communication technologies, and hence as a harbinger of radical transformation. But even a cursory look at how consumers have been conceptualized by marketing theory in the past, as well as how actual marketing practices have positioned them, reveals that customer co-production has a long and complex history within marketing, going back, in certain sectors (such as fashion), as far as the beginnings of the last century (Arvidsson, 2003; Sassatelli, 2007). In light of this it is less clear whether contemporary practices can be simply conceived as an emancipatory achievement with respect to the past.

This chapter will attempt to clear up some of the confusion within present debates around customer co-production and its relationship to the contemporary consumer economy. Drawing on the empirical case of the development of Italian fashion, we will present two historical ideal types (in the Weberian sense of that term[2]) of how customers have been integrated within the value chains of the culture and creative industries. Taking inspiration in the Italian tradition of post-*autonomia* thought on the one hand (Lazzarato, 1997; Hardt and Negri, 2000, 2004; Virno, 2004), and contemporary theories about brands and creativity (Arvidsson, 2006, 2007; Currid, 2007) on the other, we will call these modes of integration, respectively, "social factory" and "brand." Our claim is that in the "social factory" model, customers (and other external actors) are mainly used to supply input for *product* innovation (see also Zwick and Ozalp, this volume). In the "brand" phase on the other hand, customer contribution (and contributions form the social more generally) is rather channeled into the sorts of practices that can supply the cultural conventions that serve to establish the value of brands on consumer and financial markets. In other words, the productive contribution of customers becomes not primarily that of developing new products, but of co-creating an environment in which certain kinds of value conventions can operate. This entails different strategies of governance, such as the marketing of a generic form of "creativity" as a social ideal, which can easily be confused with emancipatory developments.

We have chosen the case of Italian fashion, not only because the fashion sector was one of the first to systematically rely on productive customer input (see below), but also because this case provides an excellent example of the passage from social factory to brand as modes of integration of customer co-production, or, to use a more precise term, socialized productivity. What we know about other sectors of the creative industries (and about the creative industries in other countries), as well as what we think we know about contemporary "informational" capitalism in general, leads us to suppose that this development is fairly representative for the ways in which socialized productivity is generally positioned vis-à-vis the capitalist accumulation process in the contemporary economy (although such a hypothesis requires further and more detailed substantiation). Given this hunch of ours, we will conclude by outlining the beginnings of a critique of the contemporary discourse of creativity, particular to the brand phase, as not only a form of ideological misrepresentation but as an important tool of governance in relation to a very real socialized productive power.[3] Before we begin describing our two ideal types, however, we would like to offer a number of more general theoretical coordinates to help us better locate the phenomenon of customer co-production.

Customer Co-production, Immaterial Labor, and General Sentiment

The phenomenon of customer co-production reflects a growing importance of socialized and autonomous productive processes to the capitalist valorization process (autonomous in the sense of beyond the command of the wage relation through which the Fordist accumulation process was principally organized). Customer co-production is but one of many concepts by means of which contemporary managerial discourse is struggling to come to terms with this transformation, and even within instances of customer co-production, *strictu sensu*, the productive practices of interest are generally not limited to those created by customers. The online public in general, for example, is also an important actor that often figures in these initiatives. Other instances are the reliance on autonomous public opinion in Corporate Social Responsibility initiatives (Orlitsky and Benjamin, 2004), the role of trust and social capital in coordinating complex production chains (Lane and Bachmann, 1996), and the reliance on the capacity for self-organization among knowledge workers (du Gay, 2007).

Alongside the managerial discourse, reflections on the socialization of production and the concomitant growing autonomy of many productive practices has a long history within the Italian tradition of post-*autonomia* thought. Departing from Marx, and in particular from the *Grundrisse* (Marx, 1973 [1939]) and drawing on experiences from the labor struggles that accompanied the restructuring of Italian industry, first to Fordist mass production in the 1960s, and then on to more diffuse post-Fordist forms in the 1980s, this tradition has produced a number of reflections on the new role of socialized production (Wright, 2002). More recently these reflections have been developed by Maurizio Lazzarato (1996, 1997) in his theory of "immaterial labor." With "immaterial labor," Lazzarato refers to those practices that produce the "ever more important immaterial content of commodities," such as, principally, innovation and brand. This can be the matter of paid work, like the practices of knowledge workers (Drucker, 1993), symbol analysts (Reich, 1992), or the creative class (Florida, 2002). More importantly it is a matter of unpaid autonomous practices that unfold outside of the direct control of firms and organizations, such as, in this case, customers and members of the networked public co-producing aspects of a brand, product, or service.

Lazzarato uses Paolo Virno's term (2004) "mass intellectuality" to refer to these socialized productive processes. It is worth examining this term in some detail. Mass intellectuality refers to two theoretical traditions: the Gramscian conception of the intellectual and Marx's concept of the General Intellect. Gramsci argued that all people have the potential to act as intellectuals, but within a given historical condition only some are positioned to exercise this function. In the Fordist regime of industrial capitalism the function of the intellectual was restricted to the educated elites, whether managerial elites or party cadres, who were positioned to "speak for" everybody else and to articulate goals, visions, and ideologies that "the masses" were to follow. The masses, in turn, were supposed to be silent. Such a division of labor was applied in both the Taylorist factory and the Leninist party (Gramsci, 1971). Today, according to Virno (2004), the function of the intellectual to articulate identities, goals, and ideologies has become a mass condition bringing about a state of mass intellectuality (popular sociological concepts like "reflexivity" refer to the same process, cf. Giddens, 1991; Beck, 1992). The reasons for this generalization of the condition of the intellectual have to do with the Marxian concept of General Intellect. This concept is tied to a complex and interesting line of argument that can be summarized as follows. In the so-called "Passage on Machinery" in the *Grundrisse*, Marx (1973) argues that as the complexity of productive processes grows direct labor becomes less important to value creation in relation to generally available skills and competences—General

Intellect—that grow more or less organically out of processes of productive cooperation. Marx suggests that the remediation of productive cooperation, via assembly lines, factory systems, and ultimately a world market, links together and puts into communication individual actors in such a way that what was once individual and individualized skills and competences become transformed into generally available knowledge, or into a General Intellect. Virno, Lazzarato, and the others in the post-*autonomia* school argue that the growth of the culture industries, the emergence of a consumer culture, and the rise of networked information and communication technologies have vastly expanded the scope of the remediation of productive cooperation by extending it outside the factory gates (so to speak) to a growing share of ordinary social relations. The result of this remediation of social relations is that the General Intellect becomes a feature not just of productive interaction on the factory floor but of social interaction in general. In fact, Virno (2004) argues that if Marx conceived of General Intellect as embodied in machines and productive technology, today it is best understood as embodied in language and other generally available tools for the construction of social relations (such as pop culture and the Internet). Indeed, immaterial labor as mass intellect produces as its most valuable resource social relations (or what Lazzarato calls an "ethical surplus"), identities, lifestyles, and trends that can be used as input for an ever more "culturalized" production process.[4] These forms of life, or the "ethical raw material" to use a twist on Lazzarato's terminology, become strategically important to capital because they remain untouched (so far) by the processes that have automatized and standardized other forms of production and cannot, consequently, be "commoditized" (to use a marketing expression). Given the new productive role of social relations it becomes important to understand the raw material from which such relations are built—affect—and the relation of affect to modern forms of mass mediation. In order to articulate such an understanding from a historical perspective it is useful to revisit the writings of French sociologist Gabriel Tarde, whose thoughts represent an important theoretical resource for Lazzarato.

Gabriel Tarde, a long forgotten but recently rediscovered (see Latour, 2002) French sociologist offered an interesting and strikingly contemporary critique of both Marxist and mainstream economics. Tarde (1902) argued for the importance of what he considered to be the essential modern social form—the public—as a factor in producing what Lazzarato calls the immaterial content of commodities, namely the perceptions of "truth, beauty and utility" that largely determine their market price. Tarde argued that the emergence of a new industrial culture and a circulating public opinion served to socialize the production of such immaterial values.[5] The new role of public opinion as a new source of immaterial production was evident also to other early observers of the emerging consumer economy like Georg Simmel (1900) and Torstein

Veblen. In *Theory of the Leisure Class* (1994 [1899]), Velben showed how the production of stylistic innovation in modern society had effectively been socialized, located within an ongoing dynamic between the "trend setting" elites and their imitation on the part of the masses. In his *Psychologie économique* (1902), Gabriel Tarde took this line of argument even further. He argued that with the formation of modern mass publics the value of commodities would increasingly depend on their ability to trigger and sustain processes of public communication. In the absence of traditional value systems the public establishes "truth, beauty and utility" of a good, which in turn determines its monetary value. This process is not entirely autonomous. There are "elites" that attempt to influence the public, like politicians, advertisers, opinion makers, and so forth. But contrary to his contemporaries in the emerging field of advertising psychology (see Arvidsson, 2001), Tarde did not grant these elites much power. Rather the public retains its autonomy; it becomes an uncontrollable element to the (immaterial) value chain that has to be taken into account, managed, and controlled rather than simply silenced with powerful propaganda or even ignored.

Tarde thus offers a conception of what we could call customer co-production as endemic to a modern consumer economy. He also sheds some light on the important role of affect and sentiment in this process of social co-production, as well as on the link between affect and mass mediation. For Tarde a public value—a common and sustained notion of the aesthetic value (*valeur-beauté*) of a fashion garment, for example—is the result of an *affective communion* (however temporary), which contains far more dimensions than mere consumer rationality.[6] With the advent of a modern public, the value of goods thus comes to depend increasingly on their ability to sustain such "affective communions," which, in deciding "truth, beauty and utility" of objects, also determine what we would call the experiential values of these goods.

Tarde thus draws our attention to the important link between the remediation of social relations and the emergence of the immaterial as an important dimension of economic value. We can illustrate this with the case of fashion garments. Fashion begins to find a market beyond the nobility once the expansion of a money economy creates more widespread purchasing power and, more importantly perhaps, a breakdown of traditional cultural barriers. The erection of a number of sumptuary laws prohibiting the use of particular garments for particular social groups beginning in the fourteenth century is instructive in this case. These laws represent a reaction against the possibility for certain social groups to use specific garments to signify a symbolic membership to a social group of which they were not traditionally a part. With the dual arrival of mass production and mass culture and the concomitant recomposition of the labor force, specifically the migration of rural workers to the cities where they formed an urban proletariat, and the emergence of a white collar middle class as a distinctly modern formation, the accompanying remediation of social relations becomes a tangible fact. Consequently culture, or "the immaterial," acquires a distinct use value as a way to construct a personal (class) identity through consumption. But remediation should also be understood in a different sense: it constitutes a new and important "becoming public" (and hence potentially "becoming productive") of affect. Similarly, Friedrich Kittler's work on discourse networks (1990) suggests that rather than being experienced as something entirely interior (as in the nineteenth-century romantic tradition), the formation of affect and sentiment is now partially externalized, guided by the flow of public opinion and the catalytic role of celebrities and *divae* as (momentary) containers of affective investment. Just as, according to Marx, the remediation of productive cooperation through assembly lines, factory systems, and, ultimately, the world market makes individual skills and competences commonly available as General Intellect, so the remediation of affect, through the industrialization of culture and the emergence of a mass public, renders individual affect generally available as what we could call General Sentiment (cf. Illouz, 2007; Hearn, 2008).

The Designer and his Social Factory

The concept of the social factory, as developed by Negri (2007), is used to denote extended networks of value production that involve the autonomous practices of consumers and other members of the public and that are, in Gabriel Tarde's description, characteristic of a modern consumer economy. In many ways, the fashion garment as commodity anticipates this arrangement of value networks, thus making it the original hybrid product by fusing the material and the immaterial.

In Italy, the emergence of fashion can be traced back to the Renaissance when a vibrant tradition of high-level, local craftsmanship was joined with the emerging cultural centrality of the court as a source of immaterial innovation.[7] Since that time, fashion has been a core component of the cultural economy of Italian cities with the provincial bourgeoisie giving much weight to a fashionable appearance as a sign of local distinction. Until World War II, the production of fashion garments remained a largely artisan business. Although the textile industry was rationalized in the late 1800s, industrial production was concentrated on cloth production while garments were still made at home or in tailor shops, especially for the urban bourgeois market.[8] Even though Puccini, D'Annunzio, and other stars of early Italian mass culture did become important stylistic referents for the development of fashion, the connection between industrial production and industrial culture necessary for creating the extended networks of immaterial production that characterize the social factory had to wait until after World War II. In the 1950s, the arrival of a developed Fordist consumer society in Europe gave rise to a substantial rationalization of production and distribution. Supermarkets, market research, and integrated advertising campaigns were all attempts to integrate public opinion and general sentiment as much as possible into the sphere of managerial control (see also Cochoy, this volume). At the same time the remediation of social relations continued and intensified. Urbanization and labor migration created a new urban working class with a strong presence in the geographic and cultural make-up of the city and with a growing political consciousness. Rising prosperity, prolonged schooling, and access to new consumer goods and media technologies enabled the youth to emerge on the social scene as a distinct subject endowed with a particular, generational cultural politics and style of consumption that, to some extent, cut across class distinctions. For the working- and middle-class youth of the time, consumer goods and consumption practices—ways of dressing and forms of leisure— became natural avenues for the development and expression of identities and world-views with often political and ideological connotations. As contemporary observers like Guy Debord (1967) and Jean Baudrillard (1968) emphasized, consumption, and in particular the consumption of garments, acquired meanings that went far beyond mere questions of style and aesthetics. This way, consumption became a form of symbolic production. In particular garment consumption became intricately tied up with the formation of subjectivity. The emergence of youth as a social subject of cultural importance combined with the rise of consumerism as a means to articulate personal and social identities produced a new urban bohemia that engaged in creative experimentation with emerging consumption styles. While bringing together youth of mixed class backgrounds, this countercultural scene was dependent on the presence of a strong, urban working class. The availability of well-paying, industrial work provided a kind of personal autonomy and economic freedom encouraging and enabling the experimentation with different lifestyles and expressions of the self. In addition, working-class neighborhoods were a crucial source of cheap housing, canteens, and drinking holes (Martin and Moroni, 2007). The emergence of such an urban bohemia at the fringes of the working class, constituted the first sedimentation of the networks of immaterial production that formed the basis of the social factory. Concentrated in particular neighborhoods like Carnaby Street in London or Brera in Milano, the production of urban "cool" relied on an institutional framework made up of the quickly growing number of boutiques, art galleries, and coffee shops. Such cultural effervescence gave birth to a new generation of entrepreneurs— ranging from artists like Andy Warhol and Richard Hamilton to designers like Mary Quant to an army of small boutiques owners—that became central actors in a highly dynamic consumer culture by enabling the production and rapid circulation of innovations in fashion, music, and design. The famous boutique Cose opened shop in Milan's Via della Spiga in 1963. Cose sold Nuccia Fattori's London-influenced designs as well as imported fashions from designers like Emanuelle Khan, Paco Rabanne, Zandra Rhodes, Karl Lagerfeld's Cloé, and other names from the emerging international fashion movement. In 1966, Cose added another store, Altre Cose, that stayed open late and was located in Milan's club district. Cose and similar boutiques were tightly connected to the intellectual, artistic, and political milieus of the city and the emergence of street fashion was part and parcel of a cultural effervescence where ideas, identities, music, celebrities, and affective configurations emerged and circulated easily through the city.

These new boutiques formed an institutional framework able to concentrate the diffuse networks of immaterial production that formed the basis of the emerging social factory. This function was visible in the forms of social interaction that developed on these premises. The shops were conceived not only as points of sale but as spaces for social interaction with a deliberate focus on innovative interior designs and choice of in-store music. Altre Cose, for example, was made entirely of glass and steel and the merchandise was displayed in transparent cylinders hanging from the ceiling and suspended in mid-air. Warehouse stores that mushroomed in big cities during the 1960s were more affordable but put a similar weight on music and interior design. This new breed of fashion stores also changed the way salespeople related to customers by transforming the dominant commercial paradigm of service and sales into a kind of youthful sociality. When Fiorucci opened stores in Milan in 1967 and nine years later in Rome, they featured halogen lights, steel and glass shelves, pounding rock music, and young personnel without the traditionally subservient attitude of regular store clerks. People entered the store not necessarily to buy but to have a chat, or to just walk around and try on clothes while socializing. As sociologist Ragone (1985: 43) observed about the Rome store:

> There is a certain communitarian climate that tends to homogenise, socially and culturally, who buys and who sells. This commercial universe is deeply marked by a particular ideology, to hide, to negate as far as possible the economic and productive conditions on which it rests. Indeed, one feels rather like in a refuge; an almost magical place where the act of selling merchandise is only an excuse for meetings, little breaks, exchanges of sociability.

Even as parts of the 1960s counterculture acquired strong, anti-capitalist connotations, it also articulated a clear vision of commercial practice, albeit smaller, more entrepreneurial and ideologically opposed to the bureaucratic rigidities of big business. The circulation of consumer goods had remediated a significant share of social relations into a particular affective communion centered on specific consumer practices and characterized by specific tastes and sensibilities that produced a General Sentiment of consumerist experimentation. In other words, the institutional framework of the city provided a platform for a continuing consumer effervescence, which, because of its ontological compatibility with commodity culture, could quite easily be appropriated as a source of product innovation. The new store and boutiques became particularly important as a meeting point between entrepreneurs and the networks of immaterial production of the social factory. The fact that this meeting occurred on "commercial ground"—so to say—left it open to appropriation by Big Capital. This was accomplished via the figure of the designer, as illustrated by the story of Elio Fiorucci.

The first marque designer was Elio Fiorucci. He had opened up a small store in Milan in 1967 where he designed and sold fashion influenced by hippie culture.[9] Featuring a significant variety of different garments at affordable prices, customers were encouraged to play with different looks and creatively combine various styles in a display of countercultural masquerade. Fiorucci's clothes served to create "a generalized, yet personal image that expressed the wish to stay young and not to be sucked up by that great devil, 'the system'" (Malossi, 1987: 12). Institutionalized creativity was crucial to Fiorucci's philosophy of fashion as free and creative self-expression rather than imposed standards or cannons. As the women's magazine *Amica* commented in 1974:

> The age of imposed fashion is over, Fiorucci says. "Why does someone have to wear beige if he doesn't like beige? No, let everyone dress as they want." That's why you'll never find one single trend in Fiorucci's stores, you find hundreds. Negozio Fiorucci: A Bazaar where you'll feel younger. "Tonight I'll be a Geisha and bring you some tea." "Why not try a green watermelon bath tonight."[10]

The reliance on general social creativity was central to Fiorucci's way of working. His design studio was organized non-hierarchically and based on loosely connected project teams whose members were often only temporarily employed and came and went as needed. Fiorucci also harbored a famous "graphics department," which could be described as a sort of cool hunting bureau *ante litteram*, where designers worked on styles together with intellectuals and young radicals picked up from the student movement. Members of the graphics department were encouraged to travel and keep up with an increasingly global cultural effervescence. A lot of time and money was spent on books and magazines. Fiorucci's management style, in many respects anticipating contemporary ideas of "project management," was intended to keep in touch with a highly fluid street culture and configured for a quick turnover, producing a new collection every six months.[11] His implicit business model was to extend the networks of the brand as far as possible into the informal productive networks of the surrounding social factory, in order to maximize its productive potential as a source of product and brand innovation.

In 1974, Fiorucci was acquired by the retail chain Standa, and Fiorucci stores quickly spread across Italy. With the backing of Standa, Fiorucci expanded internationally and launched a successful campaign in the American market where his clothes were inextricably connected to the 1970s disco era. While ultimately unsuccessful commercially, Fiorucci's design factory left behind a significant cultural legacy. When Standa left Fiorucci in 1980, the company ran out of money quickly and finally went into receivership in 1989. But Fiorucci had created a radically new model of design and innovation, where the external productivity of the social factory was rationally and systematically deployed as a source of innovation. This model was subsequently followed by many other large companies chief among them the Italian textile conglomerate GFT (Gruppo Finanziario Tessile). Established in 1930, GFT started out as a textile producer but began to manufacture men's apparel in the 1950s. In 1971, in an effort to reorganize industrial production at the company, the new CEO of GFT, Marco Rivetti, developed a production model that relied on freelance fashion designers paid through a royalty system. Because of this restructuring of production, a generation of (then) young designers including Giorgio Armani, Ungaro, Louis Feraud, Valentino, Massimo Osti, and Chiara Boni, suddenly found themselves with access to the creative command center of the largest and most powerful industrial producer of fashion garments in Europe. Marco Rivetti's successful business model became the hegemonic mode of production and innovation in the Italian fashion industries during the 1980s and 1990s. It was finally challenged by new trends in financialization, globalization, and fast fashion.

During the 1980s and 1990s, the material production of Italian fashion garments was still located in the famous-to-be Italian industrial districts, where dynamic networks of small factories with a strong artisan component allowed flexible response to a quickly shifting market demand (the standard practice for the fashion industry had by now become a least two collections a year), and a vibrant innovative tradition in which new cloths and cuts could be elaborated in close cooperation with the designer and his staff. On the other side, the fashion designer represented a new figure with deep roots in the General Sentiment of the time, in particular through the urban effervescence of the city of Milano, which throughout the 1980s remained a center for arts and design, as well as the intellectual center of Italy. The role of the stylists—like Fiorucci or Versace, or later Armani and Trussardi—was not to impose their own taste on consumers. Rather it was limited to interpreting what went on "around them" in the cultural effervescence of the city. As sociologist Francesco Alberoni described this new phenomenon in 1976:

[The stylists] are no longer part of the elite, and they do not pretend to control anything. Often, they are marginal figures, without roots, in continuous movement. [They do not aim at controlling] collective sentiments, imposing their own symbols or values. Rather they act more as a resonance case, amplifying events and collective sentiments that occur among different ethnic groups, social strata or peoples: sentiments that are in continuous mutation in response to different situations and different social and political conflicts. (Alberoni, 1976: 135–6)

In the Milan of the 1960s and onwards, fashion designers and the fashion economy in general had been deeply integrated in the cultural and political life of the city. Fashion design was considered a vital part of a vibrant art scene and of a general urban "movida" (the famous *Milano da bere* of the 1980s). In addition, the cultural economy of fashion and design was closely linked to a booming communications and advertising sector (with a growing private television sector dominated by Silvio Berlusconi) and even to the political entourage of the dynamic socialist leader Bettino Craxi. In short, fashion had become an integral element of a new "postmodern," "post-political" national culture.

In the 1970s and 1980s, the figure of the designer and the institutional arrangements that developed around him reinforced the connection between industrial production and social effervescence typical of the extended value chain described by Negri and others as a "social factory." While the 1960s consumerist effervescence was built on the presence of a large and powerful urban working class, it contained very few traces of the ontological opposition to capital typical of the pre-War urban proletariat.[12] Rather, this effervescence played out within the contours of a public constituted by the circulation of consumer goods, and it was marked by a particular form of General Sentiment that fostered attitudes and innovations that, although often framed within a countercultural imagery, could be relatively easily appropriated by business. Seen this way, the emergence of a social factory represents one additional step in the movement toward the subsumption of the value-creating potential of the public under the managerial control of capital. As we shall see below, the model of the brand represents an additional step in this direction.

Brands and "Creativity"

Since the 1980s brands—rather than products—have come to occupy a central stage in marketing discourse as well as business practice. The new centrality of brands can be linked to two significant aspects of the global economic restructuring that has been under way for the last couple of decades: globalization and financialization. First, the globalization of production and the concomitant diffusion of technology and know-how have generalized the ability to engage in high-quality material production. This means that, with the exception of a few exceptional luxury products, material production and quality is no longer a source of strategic advantage. As a consequence, immaterial qualities like experience, identity, and community—in short the brand—have become relatively more important (Pine and Gilmore, 1999). Second, and perhaps most importantly, the rising significance of brands has been linked to the expansion and growing role of financial markets vis-à-vis the productive economy. The expansion of financial relative to non-financial profits means that financial markets have become the key mechanism for distributing a globally produced surplus within contemporary capitalism.

Because of this development the goal of management has shifted from maximizing the long-term productivity of the firm to maximizing the (often short-term) value of stocks. However, since a growing portion of the financial value of stocks and other corporate assets are composed of so-called "intangible" assets for which there are no precise measurements, financial values become increasingly a function of public conventions that can be established as to the value of a firm. In other words, in the absence of commonly accepted measurements and standards for evaluating such intangible assets, their value becomes in many respects a cultural construct, an effect of the ability of a company to use its media and communicative strength to establish a credible and accepted narrative about its own value. Seen this way, a brand, such as Nike, not only motivates consumers to pay a premium price for its product, but it also motivates investors to pay a "premium price" for company stock, far above the book value of the company. In the new, increasingly finance-oriented economy that has emerged since the 1980s, brands increasingly fulfill these dual functions: Brand management is about organizing public communication and affect so that a shared convention as to the value of a product, above and beyond its material function, can be established. This convention subsequently translates into two related aspects: consumers' willingness to pay a premium price for branded goods and investors' willingness to endow a company with a market valuation that far exceeds its book value. Seen this way, a brand is essentially a mechanism that organizes and translates public communication into value conventions that have relevance for investor decisions. Within such an analytical model, the social effervescence posited by Lazzarato and others as a significant productive externality still exercises a valuable function. But the value of social effervescence lies less with its function as a source for product innovation and more with its ability to craft and support the kinds of branded narratives that provide the important conventions that are influential in determining financial values (Marrazzi, 2008).

Italian fashion clearly exemplifies this development toward a greater strategic importance of brands, in particular during the most recent, post-dot.com phase of financial expansion (between 2004 and 2008, Interbrand's valuation of a Gucci, Armani, and Prada increased by 75, 40, and 35 percent, respectively[13]). Corporate investments in fashion designers with strong brands attached to their names, like Armani or Versace, gradually transformed business models that prevailed within the industry. Because of the growing financial importance of brand names, it became crucial to impose brand consistency in new and powerful ways.[14] The result was a rationalization of the immaterial aspects of the value chain of the fashion industry where activities like product innovation and the creation of trends and lifestyles, which had formerly been left to the (relatively) autonomous practices of the social factory, were now internalized as new professional practices in communication and retail design. As a result of this development toward a brand-centered "experience" economy, the share of communication and related marketing activities like the creation of events and the design of retail spaces increased significantly (Marchetti and Gramigna, 2007).

Of these developments, the transformation of the retail environment was perhaps most important. Globalization, the creation of global brands, and the resulting homogenization and democratization of global consumer tastes, along with deregulation and the corresponding growth of chain stores, shopping malls, supermarkets, and outlets led to a declining importance of the traditional fashion store dealing in many different brands. Instead we can observe rapid growth in experiential brand temples like the Prada store in New York, designed by star architect Rem Kolhaas, and their less spectacular imitations that have come to populate shopping malls the world over. The transformation toward a more homogenized supply of experiential consumption spaces had the effect of further distancing brands from the risk of fluctuations in consumer demand while increasing the value of high street locations. Even if the bulk of actual sales occurred in shopping malls, chain stores, and outlets, the high street store fulfilled the symbolic function of signaling the inclusion of the brand into the luxury market segment worthy of the aspirations of the global middle classes. Beginning in the 1990s, Italian fashion brands pursued a consistent investment strategy toward acquiring high street presence in European, US, and, increasingly, Asian markets. The resulting "branditization" of city centers contributed to a significant increase in urban real estate prices: in Milano the price per square meter in the central fashion street, via Montenapoleone, doubled between 2000 and 2006 (Cietta, 2006: 105).

With the strengthening of the brand-centered business model and the ensuing phase of financialization, the Italian fashion industry morphed from a consumer industry to one that focuses on the industrial production of image, dreams, and spectacle geared to substantiate, in the form of brand equity, largely conventional valorizations of financial assets. The industry's core logic shifted from connecting the productive potential of General

225

Sentiment to material production to linking this productive asset directly to financial valorization.

However, the surrounding urban environment still provided an important source of value, albeit now in more controlled ways. Quite paradoxically, the reconfiguration of the productive role of the urban environment has been conceptualized, in Italy as well as elsewhere, under headings such as "creativity," "creative industries," or "creative cities." The discourse of creativity refers to two important transformations. First, the urban environment itself is increasingly conceptualized as symbolic capital to be managed rationally and capitalized on in the form of events like the important Milan Fashion Weeks (Power and Janson, n.d.). Consequently, local administrations invest in architecture, gentrification, and other public amenities in order to provide the appropriate "creative" atmosphere. However, such policy decisions alter radically the geographies of the city. In Milan, the area around Via Montenapoleone and Via della Spiga used to be a diverse inner city district combining upscale stores and aristocratic and bourgeois residences with back streets frequented by residents from the nearby "bohemian" neighborhood of Brera. The push toward a "more creative" city has transformed this neighborhood into a "Fashion Quadrant," quite remote from the ordinary life of the metropolis, populated by branded stores, luxury hotels, and luxury restaurants that mainly cater to an international clientele of luxury shoppers and professional fashion buyers (plus Japanese and, lately, Russian tourist groups). As a result, fashion brands shift their alliance from a "real," material city made up of embodied effervescence and cultural innovation to an imaginary "luxury city" made up of fashionable, yet preprogrammed and pre-packaged experiential shopping spaces.

Second, the discourse on creativity supports the marketing of "creativity" itself as a desirable lifestyle (see also Zwick and Ozalp, this volume). On the one hand this translates into a profusion of a brand-centered "creative" middle-class consumption style (à la Richard Florida, 2002). Fuelled by design magazines and consumer-oriented television programming, the marketing of creativity establishes originality, authenticity, and individuality as overarching consumer ideals. On the other hand, the marketing of creativity translates into a proliferation of design and media degrees and a general emphasis on creativity and entrepreneurship in secondary education arts and social science curricula. The establishment of creativity and the creative industries as an important career destination for middle-class university graduates has created a structural overproduction of university graduates eager to enter into the creative sectors, hence causing a persistent underemployment within the creative sectors of the city.[15] Between 2001 and 2005, the number of people employed on short term, "precarious" contracts increased from 25 to 61 percent in the fashion sector (the transformation accelerated after the change in Italian labor law in 2003). Our own survey of workers in the fashion and communications sectors (which in practice often coincide, see Arvidsson et al., 2010) show similar results: 70 percent of the respondents work on short-term contracts, 65 percent earn less than 1,500 Euros a month, and 45 percent less than 1,000 (the median income is 1,150 Euros a month). Sixty percent claim to not have the necessary means to meet their needs and 67 percent depend economically on their families. At the same time salaries at the top end of the fashion business have grown enormously and our qualitative interviews reveal almost feudal conditions of hierarchy and inequality within the industry. The impression is that big fashion houses ever more resemble Renaissance courts where a small inner circle rules arbitrarily over a mass of underpaid and overworked personnel. Yet, we also find in our interviews evidence that creative workers are ready to endure many years of underpaid, hard work for the satisfaction of belonging to the "world of fashion," albeit only vicariously as the consumption style associated with such an identification is far beyond their reach. The hope that such work experience will improve one's personal vita sufficiently to one day participate more fully, and in less precarious conditions, in the glamorous lifestyle of the select few proves to be a powerful motivating force (Arvidsson et al., 2010).

The successful marketing of "creativity" as a desirable lifestyle—a complex discursive operation worthy of a study in its own right—has transformed the young urban bohemia, the main source of autonomous forms of effervescence that fuelled the social factory of the 1970s, into a docile, "creative" workforce prepared to endure harsh working conditions and low pay. Today, the creative workforce is used in two principle ways. First, its members represent elite consumers that populate hip stores and nightspots of the city, thus providing a sort of living lab for the controlled experimentation with, and "seeding" of, new trends and fashions. Second, members of the creative workforce provide a massive pool of inexpensive and highly motivated workers to take on the communicative aspects of fashion work and to produce and maintain the complex web of relations and events that make the world of fashion possible.[16] The construction of such a creative lifestyle has proceeded through a detournement of the collective countercultural values of autonomy and self-realization that marked the "artistic" counterculture of the social factory (Boltanski and Chiapello, 1999). These values have been individualized and depoliticized as for workers in the fashion industry, individual self-realization is the goal. The modernist artistic ideal of pure creativity has become the guiding principle for the productive pursuits of mass intellectuality.

Seen this way, the brand phase represents a further subsumption of mass intellect under the controlled value chains of the fashion business. This is accomplished in two ways: first, through a rationalization and internalization of large parts of the immaterial value chain, which combined transform the autonomous construction of lifestyles of the social factory into the planned production of "experiences"; second, through an internalization of the productive dynamics of the urban environment enabled by the complex web of practices that is connected to the discourse on "creativity." The result of strategies of subsumption of creativity is, on the one hand, the rational management of the cultural capital contained in the urban environment through gentrification and new forms of experience-oriented urban planning. On the other hand, it promotes an ideology of creativity that individualizes and depoliticizes the ideals of autonomy and self-realization that have prevailed in the social factory over the past decades and transforms them into the ideal of individual self-realization.

Conclusion

What lessons can we draw from the ways in which customer co-production has been positioned by the Italian fashion industry? First, we can state that practices of co-production have quite a long history, reaching back to the beginnings of the century and acquiring institutionalized and rational forms of management already in the 1970s. Furthermore, we argue that contemporary forms of customer co-production, which are deeply intertwined with managerial attempts to encourage and cultivate a "creative" consumer and worker subjectivity, actually represent a more far-reaching subsumption of the productive potential of social effervescence within the value chains of capital. Indeed, the emphasis on the emancipatory potential of customer co-creation that prevails in the contemporary managerial discourse is deeply connected to a well-established tradition of conceiving of work as emancipatory and creative and of consumer goods as providing authentic experiences (du Gay, 2007; cf. Pine and Gilmore, 1999). Both these discursive traditions presuppose non-conflictual forms of self-realization that naturally occur through work, consumption, and other practices that are directly compatible with the needs of capital. What these discourses forget, and what our example shows, is that the emergence of such non-conflictual ideals of self-realization are premised on a development where the commercialization of culture, of the urban environment, and of the whole biopolitical context of life has altered the very foundations for the formation of subjectivity. The external, non-capitalist environments, like working-class cultural spaces and not yet themed urban spaces, which permitted the creation of countercultural subjectivities that could act as a source of both social critique and consumer innovation, are gone. In their place we have an "ideology of creativity" (in the Althusserian sense of that term, cf. Althusser, 1971), which, through a number of very material and concrete ideological apparatuses—chiefly the marketing of creativity in education and in popular culture—produces subjectivities that naturally conceive of their own self-realization as an entrepreneurial, competitive pursuit unaffected by the political context in which it takes place. Indeed, arguments about the emancipatory potential of customer co-creation as well as of new managerial and consumer practices ignore the fact that the modality of power, as exercised by the most advanced factions of contemporary capital, is no longer premised chiefly on a disciplinary repression of the freedom of individuals. Rather, it works through that freedom, constructing a biopolitical environment where such freedoms tend to take quite naturally the right direction. The paradoxical conclusion we can draw from our historical case study of the Italian fashion industry is that in contemporary forms of customer co-creation, the mass intellect of the public has become at the same time more empowered (particularly through the diffusion of networked information and communication technologies), more "free," and much more controlled in its freedom.

Notes

1. Morris, R., Interview: Henry Chesbrough, Examiner.com, July 12, 2009, available at www.examiner.com/x-14678-Dallas-Business-Commentary-Examiner-y2009m. htm, accessed July 30, 2009.
2. An "ideal type" in the Weberian sense of the term is an abstraction from reality that helps us interpret reality. It refers, in Gerth and Mills terms, to the "*construction of certain elements of reality into a logically precise conception*" (1948: 59). For our purposes this means that while we can abstract the two models of "social factory" and "brand" from the empirical history of the Italian fashion industry, we will have to use some combination of both abstractions to describe its dynamics at a particular historical moment.
3. For a similar line of argument, albeit in a different context, see Moor's chapter in this volume.
4. This overwhelmingly cultural conception of mass intellect might need some qualification in view of recent trends toward increasingly socialized forms of technological innovation, such as Free/Open Source Software and emerging Open design movement trends. It is corroborated, on the other hand, by the growing economic importance of social networking sites.
5. If a new industrial culture and a circulating public opinion were previously concentrated on particular institutions, like the courts or the church, the public extends the networks in which such values were constructed.
6. Indeed, for Tarde, the social is composed of such "affective communions" or mental unions in which one mind affects the other in a multiplicity of ways. That is why he kept arguing for a social psychology and against a Durkheimian sociology.

7. Or even earlier as suggested by Ambrogio Lorenzetti's 1340 painting "Allegory of Good and Bad Government" in the Palazzo Comunale in Siena, where the refined and fashionable elegance of the city girls stands out noticeably against the blander dress of the country folks.

8. In 1954, industrial garment production finally surpassed industrial cloths production.

9. The store was also selling garments brought back by Italian hippies from their trips to India, Nepal, and Afghanistan.

10. "Fiorucci Story," *Amica* 18/8, 1974, as cited in Arvidsson, A. (2003) *Marketing Modernity: Italian Advertising from Fascism to Postmodernity*. London: Routledge, p. 168.

11. Malossi (1987): 73.

12. Such attachments to traditional working-class struggles were expressed elsewhere such as in the more politicized part of the counterculture, where what Boltanski and Chiapello (1999) call the "social critique of capital" grew stronger after 1968 as part of the movement against the Vietnam War.

13. Data elaborated from Interbrand's annual surveys of the world's most valuable brands, 2004–8, www.interbrand.com

14. It can be argued that the very choice of resorting to strong brands through long-term strategic alliances between financial capital and designers was in itself a reaction to the increasing volatility of consumer demand that marked the fashion market in the 1980s and 1990s. The share of fashion garments on sale, a good indicator of the unpredictability of demand, grew from 7 percent in 1970 to 35 percent in 1995 (cf. Ricchetti, 2006: 35). This development was further fueled by the speeding up of turnover time and the development of a new kind of fast-fashion aimed at an almost continuous turnover of collections. Such an accelerated design innovation model became possible within the controlled market segments that strong brands could create. More recent successes brands like Zara or H&M perfected the fast-fashion model by reducing the shelf life of garments and other articles to a couple of weeks, or even days.

15. In Milano there were 11,000 graduates from design and fashion schools, compared to 3,000 new jobs created in this sector between 1991 and 2001 (Bonomi, 2008).

16. It is significant that in our interviews most fashion workers had only a very vague conception of the value of their labor. We can interpret this as an indication that their contribution lies more in the realization of the collective project of the "world of fashion," made up of events and relations, than in easier-to-measure efforts of value creation for individual firms. They create a controlled and planned form of social effervescence that remains commonly available to firms in the fashion business to appropriate and valorize individually.

References

Alberoni, F. (1976) *Italia in Trasformazione*. Bologna: il Mulino.

Althusser, L. (1971) "Ideology and Ideological State Apparatuses." In *Essays on Ideology*. London: Verso.

Arnould, E., and Thompson, C. (2005) "Consumer Culture Theory (CCT): Twenty Years of Research." *Journal of Consumer Research*, 31(April): 868–82.

Arvidsson, A. (2001) "Between Fascism and the American Dream: Advertising in Interwar Italy." *Social Science History*, 25(2): 151–18.

——(2003) *Marketing Modernity: Italian Advertising from Fascism to Post-modernity*. London: Routledge.

——(2006) *Brands: Meaning and Value in Media Culture*. London: Routledge.

——(2007) "Creative Class or Administrative Class? On Advertising and 'the Underground'." *Ephemera*, 7(1): 8–23.

——(2008) "The Function of Cultural Studies in Marketing: A New Administrative Science?" In M. Tadajewski and D. Brownlie, eds. *Critical Marketing: Issues in Contemporary Marketing*. Chichester: Wiley, pp. 329–44.

——Malossi, G., and Naro, S. (2010) "Passionate Work? Labor Conditions in Italian Fashion." *Journal for Cultural Research*, 14(3): 295–309.

——and Peitersen, N. (forthcoming, 2010) *The Ethical Economy: Business and Society in the Twenty-First Century* (to be published with Columbia University Press).

Baudrillard, J. (1968) *Le système des objets*. Paris: Gallimard.

Beck, U. (1992) *Risk Society*. London: Sage.

Boltanski, L., and Chiapello, E. (1999) *Le nouvel esprit du capitalisme*. Paris: Gallimard.

Bonomi, A. (2008) *Milano ai tempi delle moltitudini: Vivere, lavorare, produrre nella città infinita*. Milano: Bruno Mondadori.

Bonsu, S.K., and Darmody, A. (2009) "Co-creating *Second Life*: Market–Consumer Cooperation in Contemporary Economy." *Journal of Macromarketing*, 28(4): 355–68.

Chesborough, H.W. (2006) *Open Business Models: How to Thrive in a New Innovation Landscape*. Boston, MA: Harvard Business School Press.

Cietta, E. (2006) "Il punto vendita." In M. Ricchetti and E. Cietta, eds. *Il valore della moda: Industria e servizi in un settore guidato dall'innovazione*. Milano: Mondadori, pp. 89–142.

Currid, E. (2007) *The Warhol Economy: How Fashion, Art and Music Drive New York City*. Princeton, NJ: Princeton University Press.

Debord, G. (1967) *La société du spectacle*. Paris: Gallimard.

Drucker, P. (1993) *Post-capitalist Society*. New York: Harper Collins.

du Gay, P. (2007) *Organizing Identity*. London: Sage.

Florida, R. (2002) *The Rise of the Creative Class*. New York: The Free Press.

Frank, T. (1997) *The Conquest of Cool*. Chicago: University of Chicago Press.

Giddens, A. (1991) *Modernity and Self-Identity*. Cambridge: Polity Press.

Gerth, H.H., and Mills, C.W. (1948) "Introduction: The Man and his Work." In H.H. Gerth and C.W. Mills, eds. *From Max Weber: Essays in Sociology*. London: Routledge, pp. 3–74.

Gramsci, A. (1971). "Americanism and Fordism." In Q. Hoare and G. Nowell-Smith, eds. *Selections from the Prison Notebooks*. New York: International Publishers, pp. 277–320.

Gronroos, C. (2006) "On Defining Marketing: Finding a New Roadmap for Marketing." *Marketing Theory*, 6(4): 395–417.

Hardt, M., and Negri, A. (2000) *Empire*. Cambridge: Harvard University Press.

——(2004) *Multitude*. London: Penguin.

Hearn, A. (2008) "Meat, Mask and Burden: Probing the Contours of the Branded Self." *Journal of Consumer Culture*, 8(2): 197–217.

Illouz, E. (2007) *Cold Intimacies: The Making of Emotional Capitalism*. Cambridge: Polity Press.

Kittler, F. (1990) *Discourse Networks 1800/1900*. Stanford: Stanford University Press.

Lane, C., and Bachmann, R. (1996) "The Social Constitution of Trust: Supplier Relations in Britain and Germany." *Organisation Studies*, 17(3): 365–95.

Latour, B. (2002) "Gabriel Tarde and the End of the Social." In P. Joyce, eds. *The Social in Question: New Bearings in History and the Social Sciences*. London: Routledge, pp. 117–33.

Lazzarato, M. (1996) "Immaterial Labor." In P. Virno and M. Hardt, eds. *Radical Thought in Italy: A Potential Politics*. Minneapolis: University of Minnesota Press, pp. 133–50.

——(1997) *Lavoro immateriale*. Verona: Ombre Corte.

McGuigan, J. (1992) *Cultural Populism*. London: Routledge.

Malossi, G. (1987) *Liberi tutti: Vent'anni di moda spettacolo*. Milano: Lampi di stampa.

——(1987) *Liberi tutti: 20 anni di moda spettacolo*. Milan: Mondadori.

Marazzi, C. (2008) *Capital and Language*. New York: Semiotext(e).

Marchetti, A., and Gramigna, E. (2007) *Produttori di stile: Lavoro e flessibilità nelle case di moda milanesi*. Milano: FrancoAngeli.

Martin, J., and Moroni, P. (2007) *La luna sotto casa: Milano tra rivolta esistenziale e movimenti politici*. Milano: Shake.

Marx, K. (1973 [1939]) *Grundrisse*. London: Penguin.

Negri, A. (2007) *Dal operaio massa al operaio sociale: Intervista sul operaismo*. Verona: Ombre Corte.

Orlitsky, M., and Benjamin, J. (2004) "Corporate Social Performance and Firm Risk: A Meta-analytic Review." *Business and Society*, 40(4): 369–96.

Pine, J., and Gillmore, J. (1999) *The Experience Economy*. Cambridge: Harvard Business School Press.

Power, D., and Janson, J. (n.d.) "Fashioning a Global City: Global City Brand Channels in the Fashion and Design Industries, the Case of Milan." Working paper, CIND, Center for Research in Innovation and Industrial Dynamics, Department of Social and Economic Geography, Uppsala University, Sweden.

Prahalad, C.K., and Ramaswamy, V. (2004) "Co-creation Experiences: The Next Practice in Value Creation." *Journal of Interactive Marketing*, 18(3): 5–14.

Ragone, G. (1985) *Consumi e stili di vita in Italia*. Naples: Guida.

Reich, R. (1992) *The Work of Nations: Preparing Ourselves for 21st Century Capitalism*. New York: Vintage.

Richetti, M. (2006) "Economia della moda: Un'introduzione." In M. Richetti and E. Cietta, eds. *Il valore della moda: Industria e servizi in un settore guidato dall'innovazione*. Milano: Bruno Mondadori, pp. 21–54.

Sassatelli, R. (2007) *Consumer Culture: History, Theory, Politics*. London: Sage.

Simmel, G. (1900) *Philosophie des Geldes*. Leipzig: Duncker & Humblot.

Tapscott, D., and Williams, A.D. (2006) *Wikinomics: How Mass Collaboration Changes Everything*. New York: Portfolio.

Tarde, G. (1902) *Psychologie économique*. Paris: Félix Alcan.

Vargo, S.L., and Lusch, R.F. (2004) "Evolving to a New Dominant Logic for Marketing." *Journal of Marketing*, 68: 1–17.

Veblen, T. (1994 [1899]) *The Theory of the Leisure Class*. New York: Dover.

Virno, P. (2004) *A Grammar of the Multitude*. London: Verso.

von Hippel, E. (2006) *Democratizing Innovation*. Cambridge, MA: MIT Press.

Wright, S. (2002) *Storming Heaven: Class Composition and Struggle in Italian Autonomist Marxism*. London: Pluto Press.

Zwick, D., Bonsu, S.K., and Darmody, A. (2008) "Putting Consumers to Work: 'Co-creation' and New Marketing Govern-mentality." *Journal of Consumer Culture*, 8(2): 163–96.

10

Flipping the Neighborhood: Biopolitical Marketing as Value Creation for Condos and Lofts

Detlev Zwick and Yesim Ozalp

Introduction

The market for condominiums and lofts (hereafter CaLs) located in transitional urban neighborhoods and targeted at the upwardly mobile, educated, and relatively young population of urban professionals has been a profitable and vibrant business for real estate developers across many North American cities. In Toronto, Canada, for example, tens of thousands of new CaL units were built and sold just over the last few years and while the recent economic crisis has caused both the speed of construction and the volume of sales to decrease significantly, the market for this type of real estate remains impressive at a total of 14,522 units and a record high fourth-quarter sales (McIsaac, 2010). In many large cities across the globe, CaLs represent one of the main drivers in what Zukin (1982: 175) calls "the reconquest of the downtown for high-class users and high-rent users." Often built, or converted in the case of traditional lofts, in urban terrain undergoing gentrification, these clusters of exclusivity and relative affluence compete for space with other urban groups, especially small business, social service agencies, and individuals that depend on the availability of low rents in the downtown core. For large property developers looking to drive the value of space to the highest possible level the continued presence of low-end retail outfits, inexpensive living space, social service institutions, and their associated populations in the terrain represents an obstacle, especially when the selling of CaLs relies on the promise of entering an attractive, middle-class pattern of life. Conversely, property located in an area that indicates to the potential buyer a clear promise for further gentrification benefits from expectations of future increases in demand and price for living space located in this area. Of course, a more pronounced and confident anticipation of rising future property values drives up the selling price today. From the developer's point of view, then, the objective has to be to strengthen the perception of a quick and successful gentrification process and to "capture" as much of the future increase in property value in today's sales price. The question we therefore want to ask in this chapter is: What strategies do marketers of CaLs pursue to maximize the value of their product? Or, put more abstractly, what are the valorization strategies of contemporary CaL marketers and what can we learn from these strategies to generate more general theoretical insights about the nature of marketing practice and ideology in contemporary post-Fordist capitalism?

The Market for CaLs

As residents of Toronto, Canada, our interest in studying CaL marketing is not particularly surprising. Before the current financial crisis brought the development market all over North America to a grinding halt, Toronto had experienced staggering growth in the construction and sales of condominiums. Indeed, by November 2008, Toronto was one of the biggest condominium markets in North America with approximately 34,000 (Thorpe, 2008) condominium units under construction. In 2007, a record number of such apartments—in excess of 22,000—had been sold (*Condo Boom is Ending, Report Predicts*, 2008). CaLs represent a significant share of the overall housing market. One out of four single family housing sales in the general metropolitan area and almost four out of five in the central downtown district are now condominiums (*Market Watch January*, 2009).

As one of the most competitive markets for this product in the world, marketing practices have become increasingly aggressive, ubiquitous, and creative. From a narrower product perspective, amenities such as the 24-hours security concierge, a fitness center, and the party room are now must-haves of CaL projects and no longer provide differentiation between the many competitive offers on the market. Therefore, developers have gradually shifted the emphasis of their sales messages, which tend to stress relatively sober price–space ratio and the inventory of product features but increasingly include visions of lifestyle and community.

When these tactics "work" and as neighborhoods and their associated lifestyles become "hot," sales numbers and property prices often skyrocket very quickly in these parts of town. In 2008, for example, developer CanAlfa was able to sell a group of newly built townhouses in one of Toronto's recently turned trendy, west-end neighborhoods for five times the price of almost identical houses released as part of the same development just three years earlier (Condo Profile, 2008).

For our study of CaL marketing in Toronto, we chose to investigate the practices of a few prominent developers active in a more fashionable and "artistic" neighborhood of the city, known as West Queen Street West.[1] The neighborhood represents an ideal setting for our investigation of CaL marketing practices because the area, especially the west-end part of it, has seen significant development, both residential and commercial, since 2004. Between 2006 and 2008, a total of eleven condominium applications has been submitted to the city for the so-called "West Queen West Triangle"[2] area, and as of December 2008 six of these applications had been approved for a total of 1,813 condo units.[3] An additional 646 units are under consideration (West Queen West Development Update—Fall 2008). Moreover, two popular boutique hotels and eleven bars have opened up shop over the last few years in the same area, turning this part of the neighborhood into what locals sometimes resentfully call "an entertainment district."[4]

Marketing as Valorization Strategy

It is the task of marketing to make sense of and shape the market, to understand the motivations of consumers, and to find ways and means for connecting the product with a buyer. In other words, marketers of products and services must find a path to ensure that consumers perceive the offer presented to them of sufficient value. Marketing, then, is a particular mode, or strategy, of valorization.[5] Marketers of CaLs employ a range of valorization techniques among them what we would call the traditional sales pitch based on product attributes such as number, quality, and design of bedrooms, bathrooms, kitchen appliances, and amenities, the age and location of the building, and so forth. While these sales tactics remain important and have not changed very much over the years, we are witnessing the rise to prominence of what we call biopolitical strategies of CaL marketing. Put simply, the goal of biopolitical marketing approaches is to shift the buyer's focus away from the physical characteristics of the object for sale (i.e., the stuff of the traditional sales pitch) and instead draw attention toward the dwelling's symbolic, emotional, communal, and affective potential for facilitating the production of specific forms of life and subjectivities aspired to by the buyers of the product. Of course, the lifestyles and subjectivities imagined by the developers and presumably desired by the buyer are not simply waiting "out there" like a service to be consumed. They have to be *produced* within the existing urban space by the buyers themselves. And this production of lifestyle and self is central in the valorization of space. Specifically, the transformation of space "to a higher use" (Zukin, 1982: 175), which increases its value and in turn the value of the CaLs, becomes linked to the performance of middle-class, consumerist lifestyles. From this perspective, it would be naïve to interpret all those prominent magazine advertisements and oversized billboard ads for condominiums and lofts as simple communication efforts equating CaL ownership with access to the good (city) life. Rather, such depictions represent a form of political and economic rationality that places middle-class condo living in direct competition with forms of life of the current population, which does not possess the economic and social capital to "upscale" the neighborhood.

Drawing on Foucault's notion of govern-mentality and the concept of biopolitical production developed in recent autonomist reinterpretations of Marx (see e.g., Dyer-Witheford, 1999, 2005; Hardt and Negri, 2004; Virno, 2004), we use the term biopolitical marketing to conceptualize the kind of valorization strategies that rely on the mobilization and extraction of value from the production of consumer lifestyles and subjectivities. We argue that biopolitical marketing strategies aim on the one hand to free the productive powers of the CaL buyer to self-produce as an enterprising, self-interested consumer subject (consumption as subjectivation[6]) and on the other to govern others (consumption as subjectification) as subjects of "ethical deficiency"[7] and economic incompetence. These strategies of marketing rely and indeed require a subject that exercises considerable agency and autonomy in the production of him- or herself as a uniquely economic subject—the entrepreneurial self—who governs himself as an economic enterprise (Binkley and Capetillo Ponce, 2009). Biopolitical marketing is thus a strategy of governing the conduct of populations—in this case the population of CaL developments—in a way that maximizes their productivity from a perspective of market-based values such as self-interest, rational choice, and cost–benefit calculation. It is, hence, a form of neoliberal governmentality that exhorts the potential CaL dweller to regard his or her lifestyle decisions and consumption practices *as a CaL owner* as an investment. Therefore, marketing becomes biopolitical marketing when it attempts to valorize and subsume the productive value of self-production, of life itself, under capital.

Thus understood, biopolitical marketing is not a form of collective command and control. On the contrary, its strength is that it encourages each member of the population to fashion him- or herself as an autonomous and voluntary agent in the production of economic value. The individual is made responsible for the performance of a particular style, behavior, aesthetics, and way of life in the neighborhood and for bringing this performance into competition with existing but "less valuable" forms of life. Thus, by encouraging the self-production of specific consumerist lifestyles and entrepreneurial subjectivities that act on each other and on the surrounding space and its

237

people, valorization through biopolitical marketing depends on affecting (i.e., transforming it and elevating it "to higher-class use") all aspects of neighborhood life.

Similar to other forms of marketing, biopolitical marketing pursues the production of exchange value. But it does so by attempting to insert the object for sale deeply into the social fabric of life itself, and, thus, to make the production of lifestyle and self contribute to the continuous and dynamic reproduction of exchange value. By pursuing strategies that attempt to mobilize and subsequently appropriate the creative, entrepreneurial, competitive, and cooperative capacities of condo dwellers, contemporary CaL marketing follows a recent trend visible in other spheres of modern marketing such as branding (see e.g., Moor, 2003; Lury, 2004; Arvidsson, 2006) and innovation (e.g., Prahalad and Ramaswamy, 2004; Cova and Dalli, 2009), where marketers are looking for ways to generate, channel in productive directions, and appropriate the labor power of consumers as economic value (Arvidsson, 2007; Bowers, 2008; Zwick et al., 2008). The goal, in other words, is to sell the value generated *by* the consumers *to* the consumers through their collective production of social communication, lifestyle, social relationships, community, and so forth. And as CaLs in most urban centers across North America develop into an increasingly standardized mass market, looking for economic value in the productive capacity of a population of buyers becomes an attractive valorization strategy for marketers.

In CaL marketing, the biopolitical turn manifests itself in two overarching valorization strategies—selling lifestyle communities and promoting enterprising consumption. We will discuss these strategies in much detail below. For now, suffice it to say that despite their many differences, both strategies share in common a fundamental reliance on the willingness of the CaL buyers and dwellers to conduct themselves as self-interested and self-responsible market actors eager to maximize the return on their investment. Hence, marketing lifestyle communities and enterprising consumption could be considered as strategies that exhort the CaL population to perform the strenuous, daily work of transforming features of the neighborhood (including populations, retail choices, leisure options) deemed to be problematic. By configuring CaL buyers as agentive, decisionistic, and dynamic entrepreneurs of specific forms of middle-class life (Binkley, 2007, 2009) and by encouraging this population to act as a community despite individualized life politics (Bauman, 2001), CaL marketers envision the building and its inhabitants as a "social factory"[8] whose productive output can be reconnected back to the value of the building itself, as well as its individual units. In short, *marketers of CaLs endeavor to put the very buyers of their product to work and to appropriate the future value of this labor by feeding it back into the sales price of the CaL unit.*

The first strategy, selling CaLs as a lifestyle community, poses a more complicated challenge than appears to be the case at first glance. Certainly, the dream of a community that protects against loneliness, ensures meaningful personal encounters, and holds the promises of authentic and lasting social relations may appeal to many potential CaL buyers. Yet, the frailty of each member's social, professional, and personal relationships means that for most "members" community constitutes hardly more than a fragile network of personal contacts. More importantly, given the increasing unpredictability of professional and personal biographies in liquid modernity, the upwardly mobile condo dweller cannot well afford belonging to a community made up of lasting, committed relationships to a group, a person, or a place. Social responsibilities and emotional dependencies are considered a liability for mobility, a drag on personal freedom, and a potential barrier to a life of enterprise (Beck and Beck-Gernsheim, 2002; Bauman, 2003). Hence, marketers must be careful not to present an unfashionable, traditional version of community when what their particular clientele is seeking is a deliberately patched-together set of active, consumerist, pleasant, and affluent individuals "just like them"—what Dean (2003: 124) calls "enterprise community"—that allows for safe, enjoyable, and cooperative exchanges while guaranteeing a non-committal and always temporary association with others characteristic of neoliberal individualism.

A second biopolitical strategy of CaL marketing pursues what we term enterprising consumption. It aims at stirring the desire of the aspiring middle-class CaL population to maintain a mode of existence centered on the "endless, self-creative project of making yourself and your life a work of art" (Nealon, 2008: 12). The marketer asks the CaL buyer to consider the dwelling together with the large and always-changing universe of consumption opportunities as a resource for the work of continuous self-realization and self-production (cf. Binkley, 2007). Enterprising consumption is, hence, presented as a form of self-government that pushes the buyer of the condo or loft to cultivate him- or herself as "human capital" employed toward the maximization of her own creative potential and investment. However, this pursuit of lifestyling as a practice of continuous self-formation is not to be viewed by the consuming subject as an end in itself. Rather, enterprising consumption is to be undertaken as part of a straightforward economic calculus where the right kind of local consumption is positioned as a key practice in the transformation of the neighborhood and thus of economic value creation; for example, attracting and supporting a more high-end retail environment in turn increases the neighborhood's desirability more generally thus ensuring a rise in value of the real estate investment. Put differently, by urging the buyer of a condo or loft to consider every act of consumption as a matter of entrepreneurial judgment—as a cost–benefit calculation that can ultimately be tied back to the value of the acquired real estate—CaL marketers hand the responsibility of future value creation (through the transformation of the immediate and extended vicinity of the CaL development) over to the autonomous choices of each individual owner.

Our study of contemporary condo and loft marketing practice and strategies uses data from different sources, including newspapers, trade publications, marketing materials, and extensive on-site visits and observations in the Queen West neighborhood of Toronto. In the remainder of this chapter we first illustrate in more detail the two main valorization strategies of CaL marketing: lifestyle community and enterprising consumption. In the second part we situate these marketing discourses within a larger theoretical discussion of the transformation of contemporary marketing from a discipline of panoptic control to the government of consumer productivity (Lury, 2004; Arvidsson, 2006; Moor, 2007), or what Hardt and Negri (2004: xvi) call "biopolitical production." In the final analysis, we argue that by enlisting buyers as participants in the ongoing process of production (*qua* community, lifestyle, creative consumption, emotion, and affect), biopolitical CaL marketing techniques aim to subsume social and cultural forms of condo life under the logic of economic production, thus allowing the value of the CaL to emerge from the anticipated value of the immaterial labor of the inhabitants rather than from the object itself.

Selling Lifestyle Communities

Developers that manufacture expensive, chic living spaces for the upwardly mobile, professional class of the post-Fordist metropolis aspire to deliver, at least according to the accompanying marketing material, fashionable and exclusive lifestyle communities. The promise made to the prospective buyer lies in the slightly magical transformation of dilapidated industrial structures and empty urban spaces into contemporary utopias of the good life shared with neighbors who understand the importance of abiding by good rules of living closely together and of working out an enduring modus co-vivendi (Bauman, 2001). Moreover, CaL living invites practices that encourage the production of a specific, self-consciously present-day locality full of vitality and community. Built into CaLs is the assumption that the predictability of the apartment design is accompanied by some degree of certainty about the nature of the building's population. After all, the population brought together in ownership represents an *exclusive* community because admission is limited to those relatively few individuals that possess sufficient economic capital to buy a unit and the "right" cultural capital to appreciate its contemporary design and urban location. By bringing together a relatively homogenous set of residents, CaL marketers promote the possibility of forming social bonds no longer easily available elsewhere. But as Bauman explains (2008: 103), the construction of such communities "is a task that, unless confronted, consciously embraced, and resolutely seen through, would not start, let alone be completed, on its own momentum." Thus, like other amenities of condo and loft buildings, lifestyle community is included by design but it requires a productive and voluntary effort of the CaL population to materialize.

> Rivaling suburbia for its community ambience, these urban condominiums are like small tows within the city. Neighbours meet each other while walking, bicycling, inline skating and enjoying the raft of shops and services within easy reach. The sense of community in a condominium however, goes much deeper—to the interior design that nurtures neighbourliness among residents. A condominium is really a *vertical* community where residents enjoy privacy in their homes and interaction with others in the wonderful amenities today's condominiums include. It's a real luxury to be able to hop on the elevator to go to an aquafit class in the pool or join neighbours in the theatre room to watch grey cup or super bowl. Condo residents have a lot of fun mixing and mingling with other home owners in the fitness centre, on the roof top patio and in the landscaped courtyards and beautiful lobbies that help to make their condominium feel like home. These built-in social gathering spots are places where they feel like they belong—which community is all about. (Sarrapociello, 2009: 16)

The strategy of creating lifestyle communities provides an antidote to the alienating and individualizing forces of modern life with its relentless demand for flexibility, mobility, and need to leave even the most immediate past behind to clear the path forward (Eriksen, 2001). Between the glossy representations of happy condo living found in magazine advertisements, oversized billboards, and chic websites as well as the architectural integration of "common spaces," potential buyers are faced with more than just a faint promise of communal bliss and social unity, of course without the danger of having it encroach on one's individual autonomy (Bauman, 2001). In sociospatial terms, CaLs represent a form of private and gated community, what Rosen and Razin (2008) refer to as neoliberal enclave, that have sprung up in response to the post-welfare, market-driven demand "for prestige, lifestyle, privacy, and security, isolating affluent dwellers from widening disparities, social tensions, nuisances, and hazards of the outside world" (Rosen and Razin, 2008: 2898). Indeed, in this well-protected, self-enclosed space that brings together like-minded cohabitants while keeping out the *strangers of urban life* (Jacobs, 1993), a certain version of community is within reach.

CaLs represent a form of transplanted population, to be imprinted on a place of already existing communities. For the privileged lifestyle of the condo population to unfold efficiently within and without the boundaries of the building, a competitive stance against less "productive" forms of life and communities is required including physical security systems and the policing of undesirable social behavior in public spaces (Davis, 2006). The presence of the "other," however, accentuates a sense of commonality and common purpose among members of these lifestyle communities who recognize and acknowledge each other not only on the inside of the building but also on the outside as part of the desired, legitimate, and productive population of the neighborhood. This way, the constructed community is tied to, and realized through, a sense of a common purpose.

> Sales centers are designed to promote what White calls "atmosphere amenities," the intangibles like luxury, social acceptance, access to the in-crowd, that carry a more powerful emotional wallop than any workout or party room ever could. "We want to make people feel like they are that [fantasy] person," says Lamb, "that they are living a hip, cool, downtown lifestyle by being in that space—even if they are not."
>
> It's about creating an environment that tells people that, by buying this tiny piece of property in the sky, you are investing not in a couple of rooms, but in a fully realized, designer-sanctioned, fully catered lifestyle. (George and Maich, 2007: 29)

The task of performing lifestyle community begins with the individual condo owner and it is a daunting challenge to instill a sense of collectivity into an otherwise entirely individualistic pursuit of life: the buying of a private space and the act of living in it. The developer as well as the mortgage broker, the legal counsel, and the utility company address him or her only as a single consumer of services. The act of purchasing a CaL, hence, interpellates the buyer as an individual market actor embroiled in the autonomous pursuit of the good life through competitive acquisitiveness and the administration of private choice. Yet, while the notion of community hardly features in such dynamic and competitive expressions of market agency, the expectation that the individual inhabitant make use of his or her personal freedom, creative energy, and emotional sustenance to join a *collective* effort targeted at the production of consumerist lifestyles and the "securing" of urban space merges effectively with neoliberal aspirations of self-interested consumerism as political activism (Beck and Beck-Gernsheim, 2002; Harvey, 2005; Clarke, 2007). As Dean (2003) puts in, "[L]iving alone means living socially."

In the end, CaL marketers propose a dreamt-up community of enterprising individuals who never have to make the dreaded trade-off between personal freedom and self-interest on the one hand and collective interest on the other. Akin to Maffesoli's postmodern (1996) neo-tribes, the community form of liquid modernity is maintained for only as long as it provides use value (emotional surplus, security, economic return, sense of belonging, affect, etc.) to the individual member; and it can easily be exited when its usefulness is spent, or, more accurately, when one's input for the reproduction of use value exceeds the return on the investment. Hence, while the logic of a lifestyle community as a means for mobilizing human emotions represents an important valorization strategy, marketers need to balance buyers' desire to belong with the undesirability of belonging too much. In other words, marketers must ensure that the imagined configuration and performance of the community subject does not clash with the self-fashioning neoliberal subject who prefers the vitality of market agency over the inertia of social dependencies (Binkley, 2009).

Enterprising Consumption

The complications of selling an object that is physically immobile to a population of potential buyers for whom being mobile—socially, culturally, and physically—is no longer a choice but a necessity of life are addressed in CaL marketing by integrating the object into a flexible network of activities and sensations whose individual parts are dispersed throughout the urban space and can be rearranged according to the consumerist wishes of the actor. Put differently, the marketer invites the prospective condo owner to consider the living space as the hub from which to embark on an exploration of a rich, spatially dispersed, and always-changing universe of experiences. The practical work of exploration is depicted as an autonomous, individualistic, and highly voluntaristic activity where the expression of consumptive vigor becomes the means to a continuous reproduction of identities, lifestyle, and social relations. The message is clear: while you own a dwelling, you do not dwell.

> If windows could talk, what stories they'd tell. Food, fashion, furniture, fabric... and fetishes—Queen West retailers have been satisfying the needs of their ever-changing clientele for decades. Rolling with the times, stores that once catered to hard working immigrants now cater to the artists, fashionistas, photographers, filmmakers, designers and other urbanites that call this avant-garde community their home. If windows could talk, what would they say about you? Be part of the continuing story. Move on west to Bohemian Embassy. (*Bohemian Embassy*, 2009 [Not available in the current version of the website])

For marketing, the task at hand is to make sure that the buyer comes to regard him- or herself as responsible for making life in and outside the condo or loft and work through the active use of resources and exploitation of opportunities. From this perspective, marketing represents a not so subtle attempt to govern culture in ways that constitute the class of apartment owners as the new and legitimate agent of (local) history charged with the creative process of authoring life as a work of art. Rather, life in the CaL demands a reflexive process of self-actualizing and of choosing and performing a personalized style of existence based on self-directed acquisitiveness and dynamic consumerism (Beck and Beck-Gernsheim, 2002).

> At West Side each loft is a masterpiece waiting to happen; a blank canvas ready to come alive. From the first stroke to the last, your loft will exude your personality from every corner and every wall. 10' ceiling heights, exposed concrete ceilings and floors, open kitchens, translucent glass sliding room partitions—these and other features let you decide how to define and finish your space, whether it's with sleek and modern finishes, shabby chic accessories or nothing at all. (West Side Lofts Sales Brochure, 2007)

> Bohemian Embassy Lofts is all about "being." Various rooms of the apartment invite the resident to "be creative" (the kitchen), "be inspired" (living room), "be outside" (balcony), and "be expressive" (the closet). (*Bohemian Embassy*, 2007 [Not available in the current version of the website])

> Hidden between mom and pop shops, appliance stores, greasy spoons and other quirky fixtures, are some of the city's most spectacular bars, restaurants, galleries and boutiques. (West Side Lofts Sales Brochure, 2007)

> Though locals will tell you that West Queen Street West extends all the way down to Gladstone Street, where the oh-so-hip Gladstone Hotel opened in late 2006, walking any farther than the intersection of Ossington and Queen Street West is an exercise in diminishing returns—with appliance stores more numerous than trendy cafes. This part of this street, it seems, is still waiting for its own renaissance. Maybe they'll call it Western West Queen Street West. (Emmrich, 2007: TR4(L))

These texts speak directly to consumer subjectivities of liquid modernity, "[C]hoosing, deciding, shaping individuals who aspire to be the authors of their lives, the creators of their identities, [emerge as] the central characters of our time" (Beck, 1999: 9). Interestingly, by cheering buyers to self-produce as active and autonomous (consumer) subjects, marketers subtly push onto the individual the responsibility for making this process of self-production work. CaL subjectivities are portrayed as the ideal type of Florida's creative, urban dweller (2002), who designs cutting-edge advertising campaigns during the day and attends a jewelry design course at night before heading west on Queen Street where a retailscape still populated by convenience stores, cheap appliance depots, and plain eateries offers an increasing number of one-of-a-kind fashion boutiques, designer showrooms, modern furniture stores, art galleries, organic food shops, and cool restaurants and bars to the discerning shopper.

CaL marketers use significant parts of their promotional material to stage the neighborhood and its "vibrant" community in very selective and specific ways to further fuel the narrative of middle-class commercial culture inescapably taking hold in and around new condo and loft developments. In this geography of rapid "becoming," the incumbents have to be on their toes as the competitors move in and threaten to displace existing forms of consumer culture. Hence, in the non-gentrified urban settings of Toronto, living in a CaL becomes closely tied to the willingness of the dweller to navigate, explore, seize, and occupy the larger geography of consumption surrounding the building; to frequent "sanctioned" locales; and to support newly emerging venues in the competitive struggle toward neighborhood lifestyling, "hipification," and gentrification. In this sense, the individualized performances of active and transformational lives characterized by entrepreneurial and self-responsible dispositions imply not only a productive mode of existence but also, "paradoxically, a collective lifestyle" (Beck, 1999: 9).

Enterprising consumption represents a conception of the individual full of enterprise and vitality, an individual, in other words, capable of working on the ongoing transformation of space, population, and culture. Interpellating the CaL buyer as a source of productivity transfers the onus of population control and improvements of the business and leisure climate from the city, developers, and the police to the culturally produced self-policing dwellers. Thus, the government of the development and the neighborhood increasingly comes to operate, in the words of Nikolas Rose (1990), through the "soul" of the individual entrepreneurs of life acting in unison.

Toward a Theory of Biopolitcal Marketing and the Production of Value

Lifestyle community and enterprising consumption represent two broad cultural marketing strategies that, first, aim at shifting the buyer's attention away from the apartment's physical characteristics toward its potential as a lifestyle enabler. Second, however, these marketing strategies are strategies of valorization that hope to subsume the generative force of everyday life performed by a CaL population filled with the "exuberance and vitality of market agency" (Binkley, 2009: 61). It is precisely this productive capacity of the individual to constantly self-produce, to work on oneself and on others—often through specific modes of consumption—that biopolitical marketing tries to encourage and control.

With Foucault we would then characterize biopolitical marketing as a form of government, or "the conduct of conduct" that brings together the government of one's self (subjectivation) and the government of others (subjectification). Biopolitical marketing is a strategy of subjectivation by encouraging consumers to cultivate themselves as autonomous and self-interested individuals who regard their performance of a specific consumerist lifestyle, based on a particular set of economic, cultural, and social resources, as a form of investment, which can generate a return (see Binkley, 2009). It is a strategy of subjectification in that it seeks to govern a population of consumers, or a community of buyers, as a form of "human capital" whose effects produced at the level of everyday life are pitched against other forms of human capital, thus framing all forms of life in economic value and making *every* individual— including, as in the case of CaL marketing, populations not directly targeted by biopolitical marketing—morally responsible "for navigating the social realm using rational choice and cost–benefit calculation to the express exclusion of all other values and interests" (Hamann, 2009: 38).

Attempts by capital to enlist consumers as producers of surplus value are not new (see e.g., Ritzer, 1993; Dyer-Witheford, 1999) and recently a number of analyses have emerged that try to unpack the variegated processes by which companies encourage, rely on, and appropriate value from the active work of their customers (Arvidsson, 2007, 2008; Foster, 2007; Humphreys and Grayson, 2008). Sociologist Michel Callon (2002) goes as far as to suggest that the communication and sharing of ideas, feelings, approval and disapproval of what he calls the "voicy consumer" is in fact a crucial element in the complex process of a product's "qualification" as this interaction between consumer and company ensures an alignment, at least temporary, of the consumers' needs and the product's features. Voicy consumers, by virtue of their agency and ongoing production of new identities and dispositions, also destabilize any momentary alignment of qualities and needs, a process that makes consumers, according to Callon, a constant source of "overflowing" (Callon, 1998). As Foster points out (2007: 714), "[C]onsumer overflowings, then, are sources of innovation and competitive advantage for a firm as well as sources of uncertainty and challenges to expertise and authority." In the business literature, such processes of customer–company collaborations have been discussed in similar ways—albeit less theoretical and more celebratory—by prominent business scholars C.K. Prahalad and Venkat Ramaswamy (2000, 2004), who have popularized the belief that close, cooperative relationships between customers and companies, based on respect, equality, and emotional attachment, will become a central source for value creation in the future. In other words, economic value materializes out of a process of value "co-creation" that appropriates the labor of consumers.

Biopolitical marketing shares with these concepts of overflowing and co-creation the notion that valorization strategies increasingly rely on the appropriation and subsumption of the creativity, knowledge, and what the autonomists call, following Marx, general intellect of consumers. What differentiates biopolitical marketing from these strategies is that its target of intervention is not the object of consumption (commodities and services) but its subject. In other words, it aims at configuring the consumer subject in a way that allows for its productive capacity to emerge and deploy. From this perspective, biopolitical marketing represents an "indirect" valorization strategy because the co-creation of economic value (through overflowing and customer creativity) becomes a function of the prior production of a personal ethic of voluntaristic sociality and enterprising consumption—a prior fashioning of the "inner life of the neoliberal subject" (Binkley, 2009: 61).

Marketers' attempts to cultivate and profit from consumers' self-production of neoliberal subjectivities is not without difficulties. Because the work consumers perform in producing enterprising communities and lifestyles is "free" (in the sense of being unpaid *and* autonomous), it is a form of labor that is at once economically attractive and managerially problematic (Zwick et al., 2008). Put differently, while it is the creative and entrepreneurial autonomy of consumers that generates valuable and productive forms of life, as a "workforce," consumers are beyond the direct control of any company (cf. Terranova, 2004). Therefore, biopolitical marketing must identify and promote among consumers common interests that can serve as a suitable platform for promoting "collective" forms of subjectivation; interests that, in the spirit of neoliberal governmentality, provide sufficient impetus for the individual consumer to do the work of self-construction, self-modification, transformation of others, and the reorganization of local power relations (cf. Lemke, 2002). The creation of community and the vitality of its inhabitants' individualized consumption styles as productive labor represent a fundamental increase in the scope of economic rationality because this kind of work eradicates traditional boundaries (rooted in time and space) of employment, leisure, production, and consumption. In the case of the condo and loft population, biopolitical marketing represents the uncompromising pursuit of valorizing and comparing—on the singular dimension of "return of investment"—every aspect of everyday life in the city (see also Keil, 2002).

Contrary to disciplinary forms of marketing and their technologies of domination and subjection (see e.g., Pridmore this volume; Zwick and Dholakia, 2004*a*, 2004*b*), biopolitical marketing wants to govern consumer conduct as a technology of the self, not through force and coercion but through "autonomous" processes by which the self constructs and modifies him- or herself in ways desired by the marketer (Arvidsson, 2006; cf. Foucault, 1993). Biopolitical marketing relies on a form of power that is primarily about the *guidance* of consumer behavior, "i.e. governing the forms of self-government, structuring and shaping the field of possible action of subjects" (Lemke, 2002: 52). It is not, and cannot operate like, sovereign or disciplinary power as both of these forms of power undermine and even disallow for an "autonomous" individual's capacity for self-control, self-interest, and self-modification, which are all considered to be central characteristics of market agents. Biopolitical marketing conjures up a homo economicus that is structured by principles and motivations of self-government and any technique of domination (as behavior control) must also be a technique of the self. The operating principle of this form of marketing is no longer curtailment of individual freedom but its expansion and to allow, or more accurately *force*, the consumer subject to choose constantly between competing strategies according to the rules of exchange, investment, interest, and return.

From the perspective of the marketer, what emerges from the free and self-producing actions of the CaL population is an aggregate of economic activity—a sort of commons—which, in absence of any programming, could evolve in undesirable or unprofitable directions (Callon, 1998; cf. Lury, 2004). Control of the productivity of the common cannot easily be accomplished without the intervention of some rationalizing force. Biopolitical marketing's role, hence, is to provide a specific rationality that manages to channel and attach the benefits produced by a mass of autonomous individuals across an unstructured urban space to a clearly defined target of common interest. In other words, by appropriating the surplus value generated by the consumers who perform lifestyle communities and entrepreneurial consumption to increase the value of the real estate, capital turns mass creativity, affect, and social communication into a direct force of production (see Virno, 2004). In its most sophisticated form, biopolitical marketing manages to bestow a sort of property right (i.e., economic value) on the social production of a self-producing consumer subject, as can be seen when brand valuations benefit from the unpaid social communication of permanently self-modifying consumers (see Lury, 2004; Arvidsson, 2006) and when the speed of innovation increases by tapping into the cognitive, creative, and communicative capacities of the masses (Prahalad and Ramaswamy, 2004; Tapscott and Williams, 2006; Li and Bernoff, 2008).

Conclusion

Despite their various differences, strategies of lifestyle community and enterprising consumption are both employed for erecting what Negri (2008) refers to as "biopolitical space," which structures as cooperative, and then captures the value of, relatively autonomous processes of social, communicative, and cultural production that unfold in the urban environment (Arvidsson, 2007). Because top-down control of consumers can neither be legitimized nor reconciled with an ideology of the homo economicus, biopolitical marketing is about creating an ambience for participation that allows for the population of autonomous and free buyers to conduct itself in similar ways, and to do so in the absence of disciplinary power (Dean, 1994). The selling of the CaL, in other words, is not primarily an attempt to describe the physical attributes of the product but that of asking the buyer, in fact the multitude of buyers, to put themselves to work and produce a specific mode of existence that collectively translates into economic benefits for all owners. Having examined and analyzed these emergent marketing innovations, we formulate a theory of contemporary CaL marketing as a biopolitical practice that aims at valorizing and appropriating the labor that goes into the production of community, emotion, affect, and lifestyle. In short, the biopolitical turn in marketing is an attempt to erect a specific space of power that produces self-producing and self-governing subjects; and to manage and channel the processes of self-production and self-governance into profitable avenues.

As a consequence, biopolitical marketing turns conventional marketing on its head by positing what would be considered a desirable *outcome* of a purchase such as community, social communication, and lifestyle as an *input* for a new mode of surplus value production. In the case of CaL marketing, the need for mobility of identities, social networks, careers, life partners, and consumption habits becomes the basic condition for the continuous reproduction of enterprise community, enterprising consumption, and flexible subjectivities. Put simply, then, biopolitical marketing represents a valorization strategy where the exchange value of the product is a function of the amount of labor that goes into the *production of continuously self-producing* consumer subjects.

There are a number of reasons why the use of biopolitical marketing may be particularly effective in the context of CaL marketing. One factor, already discussed above, is the restless search of increasingly atomized and urbanized populations for some form of community. Marketers are therefore able to rely on a common disposition of CaL buyers to produce social cooperation and communication and, more generally, to put the work in to establish a community, no matter how fleeting its specific composition. Another crucial one is the efficiencies that can be obtained in the mass production of social communication, affect, emotion, and community; by providing the relevant social, physical, and cultural infrastructure in a compact local setting (Scott, 2008). Put simply, the urban density provided by CaL developments facilitates social interactions, attracts high-end consumer amenities, and accelerates gentrification and the homogenization of the area's population (Glaeser and Gottlieb, 2006). However, it is not only the effectiveness of the spatial conditions that matters here. Equally important is the increased ability of marketers and buyers (for both parties ultimately share this objective) to effectively appropriate the surplus value generated by the production of enterprising community, consumerist lifestyle, emotional attachments, and affective performances when the working population is concentrated in such a limited geographical area. In the final analysis, biopolitical marketing—as a technique to generate and subsume all of consumer life under capital and to erect, as it were, a social factory where "work processes have shifted from the factory to society" (Terranova, 2000: 33)—is likely to prove particularly successful in the case of the market for condominiums and lofts because money, knowledge, and communication, the main forces of biopolitical value production, flow in this newly manufactured spatially agglomerated activity system forcefully and expeditiously (cf. Scott, 2008).

Notes

1. The area is also known to have the largest concentration of art galleries in the city.
2. This area is enclosed by Queen Street West to the north, Dovercourt Road to the east, and Sudbury Street to the south.
3. Of these 1813 approved units, 515 have been set aside for the rental market and 70 for affordable housing space for artists.
4. Taken from our interviews with residents and store owners.
5. To be distinguished from the general strategy of valorization that concerns the planning process of the entire corporation including labor relations, personnel policies, and wages, profit allocation, and corporate-level strategic decisions (see e.g., Aglietta, 1987).
6. We follow the distinction made by Rosenberg and Milchman (2009) on Foucault's term "assujettissement." Rosenberg and Milchman distinguish between "subjectification" and "subjectivation," where the former refers to the mode of constituting others as subjects through processes of power (which often but not always include processes of subjugation and discipline) and the latter refers to the manner by which individuals are produced by power as self-producing subjects (see also Binkley, 2009).
7. We expand on this term below. In brief, ethical deficiency is used in Foucault's sense of the term to refer to the individual's failure to fashion him- or herself as a productive and competitive agent.
8. This term was introduced by Tronti (1973) and has since become a central concept in the work of so-called autonomist Marxist such as Virno, Hardt, Negri, and Lazzarato (see e.g., Terranova, 2004; Dyer-Witheford, 2005; Gill and Pratt, 2008). From the perspective of the social factory, labor is conceived of as geographically deterritorialized, socially dispersed, and organizationally decentralized. When labor is longer confined to the walls of the factory or corporation, all of life can be posited as value-creating and "the whole society is placed at the disposal of profit" (Negri, 1989: 79, cited in Gill and Pratt, 2008: 7).

References

Aglietta, Michel (1987) *A Theory of Capitalist Regulation: The US experience*. London: Verso.
Arvidsson, Adam (2006) *Brands—Meaning and Value in Media Culture*. London: Routledge.

——(2007) "Creative Class or Administrative Class? On Advertising and the 'Underground.'" *Ephemera: Theory & Politics in Organization*, 7(1): 8–23.

——(2008) "The Ethical Economy of Customer Coproduction." *Journal of Macromarketing*, 28(4): 326–38.

Bauman, Zygmunt (2001) *The Individualized Society*. Cambridge: Blackwell.

——(2003) *Liquid Love: On the Frailty of Human Bonds*. Cambridge, UK: Polity Press.

——(2008) *Does Ethics have a Chance in a World of Consumers?* Cambridge, MA: Harvard University Press.

Beck, Ulrich (1999) *World Risk Society*. Malden, MA: Polity Press.

——and Beck-Gernsheim, Elisabeth (2002) *Individualization: Institutionalized Individualism and its Social and Political Consequences*. London and Thousand Oaks, CA: Sage.

Binkley, Sam (2007) "Governmentality and Lifestyle Studies." *Sociology Compass*, 1(1): 111–26.

——(2009) "The Work of Neoliberal Governmentality: Temporality and Ethical Substance in the Tale of Two Dads." *Foucault Studies*, 6: 60–78.

——and Ponce, Jorge Capetillo (2009) *A Foucault for the 21st Century: Governmentality, Biopolitics and Discipline in the New Millennium*. Newcastle upon Tyne, UK: Cambridge Scholars Publishing.

Bohemian Embassy (2007) (cited January 23, 2007). Available from http://www.bohemianembassy.ca/

—— (2009) (cited March 3, 2009). Available from http://www.bohemianembassy.ca/

Bowers, Todd E. (2008) "Bringing the 'Multitude' Back In": The Biopolitics of Marketing Affectivity." Paper presented at the annual meeting of the *American Sociological Association*. Hilton San Francisco & Renaissance Parc 55 Hotel, San Francisco, CA.

Callon, Michel (1998) "An Essay on Framing and Overflowing: Economic Externalities Revisited by Sociology." In M. Callon, ed. *The Laws of the Markets*. Malden, MA: Blackwell.

—— Meadel, Cecile, and Rabeharosoa, Vololona (2002) "The Economy of Qualities." *Economy and Society*, 31(2): 194–217.

Clarke, John (2007) "Unsettled Connections: Citizens, Consumers and the Reform of Public Services." *Journal of Consumer Culture*, 7(2): 159–78.

Condo Boom is Ending, Report Predicts (2008) (cited April 19, 2009). Available from http://network.nationalpost.com/np/blogs/toronto/archive/2008/08/19/krejhtkrjhtkrjetertret.aspx.

Condo Profile (2008) *Condo Guide*. September 29–October 13, 2008, pp. 30–1.

Cova, Bernard, and Dalli, Daniele (2009) "Working Consumers: The Next Step in Marketing Theory?" *Marketing Theory*, 9(3): 315–39.

Davis, Mike (2006) *City of Quartz: Excavating the Future in Los Angeles*. London and New York: Verso.

Dean, Mitchell (1994) *Critical and Effective Histories: Foucault's Methods and Historical Sociology*. London: Routledge.

——(2003) "Culture Governance and Individualization." In H.P. Bang, ed. *Governance as Social and Political Communication*. Manchester: Manchester University Press.

Dyer-Witheford, Nick (1999) *Cyber-Marx: Cycles and Circuits of Struggle in High-technology Capitalism*. Urbana, IL: University of Illinois Press.

Dyer-Witheford, Nick (2005) "Cyber-Negri: General Intellect and Immaterial Labor." In T.S. Murphy and A.-K. Mustapha, eds. *Resistance in Practice: The Philosophy of Antonio Negri*. London: Pluto Press.

Emmrich, Stuart (2007) "Go West, Young Hipsters." *The New York Times*, September 2, 2007, TR4(L).

Eriksen, Thomas Hylland (2001) *Tyranny of the Moment: Fast and Slow Time in the Information Age*. London: Pluto Press.

Florida, Richard L. (2002) *The Rise of the Creative Class*. New York, NY: Basic Books.

Foster, Robert John (2007) "The Work of the 'New Economy': Consumers, Brands, and Value Creation." *Cultural Anthropology*, 22(4): 707–31.

Foucault, Michel (1993) "About the Beginning of the Hermeneutics of the Self: Two Lectures at Dartmouth (translation by Mark Blasius)." *Political Theory*, 21(2): 198–227.

George, Lianne, and Maich, Steve (2007) "A 'Hip' Lifestyle of One's Own." *Maclean's*, 120(51/52): 38–40.

Gill, Rosalind, and Pratt, Andy (2008) "In the Social Factory? Immaterial Labour, Precariousness and Cultural Work." *Theory, Culture & Society*, 25(7–8): 1–30.

Glaeser, Edward L., and Gottlieb, Joshua D. (2006) "Urban Resurgence and the Consumer City." *Urban Studies*, 43(8): 1275–99.

Hamann, Trent H. (2009) "Neoliberalism, Governmentality, and Ethics." *Foucault Studies*, 6: 37–59.

Hardt, Michael, and Negri, Antonio (2004) *Multitude: War and Democracy in the Age of Empire*. New York: The Penguin Press.

Harvey, David (2005) *A Brief History of Neoliberalism*. Oxford and New York: Oxford University Press.

Humphreys, Ashlee, and Grayson, Kent (2008) "The Intersecting Roles of Consumer and Producer: A Critical Perspective on Co-production, Co-creation and Prosumption." *Sociology Compass*, 2(3): 963–80.

Jacobs, Jane (1993) *The Death and Life of Great American Cities* (Modern Library ed.). New York: Modern Library.

Keil, Roger (2002) "'Common-Sense' Neoliberalism: Progressive Conservative Urbanism in Toronto, Canada." *Antipode*, 34(3): 578–601.

Lemke, Thomas (2002) "Foucault, Governmentality, and Critique." *Rethinking Marxism: A Journal of Economics, Culture & Society*, 14(3): 49–64.

Li, Charlene, and Bernoff, Josh (2008) *Groundswell: Winning in a World Transformed by Social Technologies*. Boston, MA: Harvard Business Press.

Lury, Celia (2004) *Brands: The Logos of the Global Economy*. London: Routledge.

McIsaac, Nicole (2010) "Q4 Condo Sales up 36%: Report." *National Post*, January 30, 2010.

Maffesoli, M. (1996) *The Times of the Tribes* (Translated by D. Smith). London: Sage.

Market Watch January (2009) Toronto: Toronto Real Estate Board.

Moor, Elizabeth (2003) "Branded Spaces: The Scope of 'New Marketing.'" *Journal of Consumer Culture*, 3(1): 39–60.

Moor, Liz (2007) *The Rise of Brands*. Oxford: Berg.

Nealon, Jeffrey T. (2008) *Foucault Beyond Foucault: Power and its Intensifications since 1984.* Stanford, CA: Stanford University Press.

Negri, Antonio (2008) "The Labor of the Multitude and the Fabric of Biopolitics." *Meditations,* 23(2): 9–24.

Prahalad, C.K., and Ramaswamy, Venkat (2000) "Co-opting Customer Competence." *Harvard Business Review,* 78(January–February): 79–87.

——(2004) *The Future of Competition: Co-creating Unique Value with Customers.* Boston, MA: Harvard Business School.

Ritzer, G. (1993) *The McDonaldization of Society: An Investigation into the Changing Character of Contemporary Social Life.* Newbury Park, CA: Pine Forge Press.

Rose, Nikolas S. (1990) *Governing the Soul: The Shaping of the Private Self.* London and New York: Routledge.

Rosen, Gillad, and Razin, Eran (2008) "Enclosed Residential Neighborhoods in Israel: From Landscapes of Heritage and Frontier Enclaves to New Gated Communities." *Environment and Planning A,* 40: 2895–913.

Rosenberg, Alan, and Milchman, Alan (2009) "The Final Foucault: Government of Others and Government of the Self." In S. Binkley and J. Capetillo, eds. *A Foucault for the 21st Century: Governmentality, Biopolitics and Discipline in the New Millennium,* Newcastle upon Tyne, UK: Cambridge Scholars Publishing.

Sarrapociello, Mirella (2009) "Condo Matters: Community, Important on All Levels." *Condo Guide:* March 16–30, 2009, p. 16.

Scott, Allen John (2008) *Social Economy of the Metropolis: Cognitive-Cultural Capitalism and the Global Resurgence of Cities.* Oxford and New York: Oxford University Press.

Tapscott, Don, and Williams, Anthony D. (2006) *Wikinomics: How Mass Collaboration Changes Everything.* New York: Portfolio.

Terranova, Tiziana (2000) "Free Labor: Producing Culture for the Digital Economy." *Social Text 63,* 18(2): 33–58.

——(2004) *Network Culture: Politics for the Information Age.* London and Ann Arbor, MI: Pluto Press.

Thorpe, Jacqueline (2008) "Toronto's Condo Kings: Is Their Boom Sustainable?" *Financial Post,* June 2, 2008.

Tronti, Mario (1973) *Operai e capitale.* Torino: G. Einaudi.

Virno, Paolo (2004) *A Grammar of the Multitude for an Analysis of Contemporary Forms of Life.* Cambridge, MA: Semiotext(e) and MIT Press.

West Queen West Development Update—Fall (2008) (cited March 12, 2009). Available from http://www.adamgiambrone.ca/downloads/WQW_newsletter.pdf.

Zukin, Sharon (1982) *Loft Living: Culture and Capital in Urban Change.* Baltimore: Johns Hopkins University Press.

Zwick, Detlev, Bonsu, Samuel K., and Darmody, Aron (2008) "Putting Consumers to Work: 'Co-creation' and New Marketing Govern-mentality." *Journal of Consumer Culture,* 8(2): 163–96.

——and Dholakia, Nikhilesh (2004a) "Consumer Subjectivity in the Age of Internet: The Radical Concept of Marketing Control through Customer Relationship Management." *Information and Organization,* 14(3): 211–36.

——(2004b) "Whose Identity is it Anyway? Consumer Representation in the Age of Database Marketing." *Journal of Macromarketing,* 24(1): 31–43.

Part IV

The Diffusion of Marketing Ideology and its Effects

11

Commercial Epistemologies of Childhood: "Fun" and the Leveraging of Children's Subjectivities and Desires

Daniel Thomas Cook

James McNeal, pioneer of children's consumer research, noted once that he received hate mail after the publishing of "The Child Consumer—A New Market" in 1969 in the *Journal of Retailing* (McNeal, 1987: xv). His detractors—some of whom were marketers—according to McNeal did not concern themselves with the content of the argument where he discusses the size of the market of children aged 5–13, the satisfactions children gained from purchasing, the kinds of consumer knowledge that arise at different ages, and the ways companies were already marketing to children. The complaint, rather, centered on the *fact* that he identified and named children as a market, thereby rendering childhood a legitimate site for commercial exploration. It was the act of defining and thus conceptualizing children as consumers, that triggered the intense response.

Four decades hence, concerns about children's consumer involvement both have expanded and fragmented in publicly voiced complaints about "spoiled brats," unscrupulous marketers, and/or inattentive parents in the United States and elsewhere. A significant, vocal segment remains vigilant against any kind of marketing directed at children (Linn, 2004; Schor, 2004). Public discourse on the whole, however, tends to accept the existence of children consumers as a social inevitability, with the focus on sorting "good" from "bad" consumption and marketing.

The change from hate mail for identifying children as a market to the contemporary situation where there exist entire television networks, brands, and stores developed to cultivate and serve this market entails a transformation that extends beyond a simple growth in "demand." The historical rise

and contemporary significance of the children's market involves, in a fundamental way, new conceptualizations of "the child" as a social actor and being
(Cook, 2004; Cross, 2004; Jacobson, 2004). The new view of the child was not
brought about entirely by marketing alone; I contend, however, that it would
not have taken hold absent the actions of marketers.

In the course of plying their trade, market practitioners—that is, marketers,
researchers, designers, manufacturers, and other market actors—actively con-
figure notions of markets, consumers, and consumption. When conceptualizing and executing research, contemplating the audience to whom to direct a
promotion, conjecturing about the impact of a design, or developing a brand
strategy, market actors utilize and rely upon culturally based and historically
specific ideas about who consumers are, their motivations, and the manner in
which they engage with what one might call the marketplace. Ideas about the
make-up of consumers and their actions underlie and inform virtually the
whole of marketing practice as many scholars have demonstrated (Davila,
2001; Mazzarella, 2003; Sender, 2004). One can no more develop a product
or test a brand concept without imagining a "consumer," as one could purchase
advertising space without data on the breakdown of potential audiences.

The perspective put forth here understands ideas—in this case, the idea of
the child consumer—as occupying a reality on a par with "concrete" things.
Ideas have this status because they have consequences. McNeal's act of naming children as a market serves as a case in point about the power of definition.
It also brings to the fore issues regarding the moral dimensions of markets
and market behavior in terms of who and what can be deemed appropriate
subjects for commercial action.

In the following discussion, I delve into some of the contours of what I call
"commercial epistemologies" of children's consumption. An epistemology,
put simply, refers to a theory of knowledge and of the sources and structures of
knowledge in a particular domain. I intend the term to highlight the socially
constructed nature of commercially relevant knowledge about children's
consumer identities, particularly as it pertains to marketing practices and
discourses of market actors. Commercial epistemologies are ways of "knowing" about children and childhood that arise from the interested positions of
those whose livelihoods revolve around ascertaining the marketability of
goods and ideas. One might think of commercial epistemologies as lenses
through which market actors see and apprehend children and childhood for
specific purposes and toward particular ends.

Drawing mainly upon published trade materials, I discuss how knowledge
derived in and from marketing practice, including consumer research, config-
ure notions of the "child" in ways that make marketing to children not only
morally palatable but, in some cases, akin to a civic duty. The significant point
to be gleaned from this mainly theoretical–conceptual treatment revolves

around they ways in which this "child"—more specifically, the child's perspective—takes on the character of a currency or value to be leveraged so as to secure market share. After laying out some of the ways the "child" is leveraged, I delve into examples and discussion of how fun and playful food serve as particularly useful entrée points into the commercial forms of knowledge about childhood.

To Know is to Sell: Leveraging the Child's Perspective

Marketers know, or come to learn quickly, that promoting and marketing products intended for children's use and consumption takes place within a highly surveilled, emotionally charged moral context. At its heart, the moral question surrounding children's participation in consumer life concerns itself with determining the extent to which the target market (usually specified by age and gender) can be said to be able to behave as knowing consumers. Such determinations encode judgments regarding the appropriateness of the product or promotion in terms of age or developmental stage. If the child consumer is imagined as willful, even savvy, then suspicion of exploitation on the part of the marketer can be obviated to some extent because the child can be said to have the ability to make decisions on some fundamental level that can be recognized as legitimate. Put simply, the more children appear or are construed as more or less competent social actors, the more directly they can be addressed and acted upon as a primary, non-derivative market without intense moral approbation.

Conceptualizing children as knowing consumers extends beyond providing moral cover for marketers. It makes practical sense to be able to consider children as having desires and preferences of their own who in some way are able to act upon them, even as these are mediated by parental gatekeepers, lawmakers, and consumer watchdog groups. Prior to the 1980s, most of the usable knowledge about children's consumer and media behavior was derived less from direct research on children and more from the application of general developmental psychology to specific age–gender categories and matched with income and spending data (Cook, 2000). In the ensuing decades, direct market research on and with children has arisen as an industry in its own right, with a significant number of firms specializing in children, replete with innovative and proprietary methods and measures. Having the (moral) right-of-way to focus on children as consumers in their own right—to research and "know" them directly—allows market researchers to discern the particular contours and details of children's perspectives and attitudes toward products and campaigns and thus tailor these accordingly. The more marketers, retailers, designers, and manufacturers can know, or claim to know, what children themselves want, the stronger their moral and strategic position to serve the child market.

Hence, it is not surprising that the exponential growth in the children's market since 1990 has been accompanied both by increased efforts to research and "know" the child and by the advent of sustained rhetoric about the "savvy-ness" of the contemporary child consumer (Banet-Wiser, 2007; Cook, 2007; see Schor 2004: 180–1). An important component of children's market research centers on garnering the child's view of goods, promotions, and experiences. Market research firms leverage "the child" and, more particularly, the child's perspective as a form of symbolic currency that can be exchanged for monetary currency. The more a firm can demonstrate that it knows how to elicit and translate children's expression into actionable insights better than other firms and certainly the client, the better its market position in the child knowledge trade.

Just Kid, Inc., for instance, founded in 1994, necessarily positions themselves as experts in understanding what kids "really think": "We know how to design questionnaires and surveys that reveal what kids are really thinking, not what they think you want to hear. And our only view of the world is seen 'through a kid's lens.'"[1] The Geppetto Group promotes their expertise in understanding the "underlying motivations of childhood"—which they call "Kid Why"—and in "decoding the discreet and powerful dimensions of kid humor," among other things.[2] KidzEyes, an online survey panel, makes children's responses to questions available to participating companies and boasts that its only goal is to "gather kids" opinions and views so that companies can see their products, services, and trends through kids' eyes.[3] In this powerful and well-positioned belief system, to "know" the child (through research) is to, in a sense, respect the child by seeking her or his views, tendencies, and preferences in the effort to tailor goods and purchasing opportunities in light of this knowledge. Paco Underhill (2001), retail anthropologist and President and CEO of Envirosell, Inc., discusses how observations made of children in retail stores can inform the placement of goods on shelves. "If it's within their (children's) reach, they will touch it, and if they touch it there's at least a chance that Mom or Dad will relent and buy it." Here retailers, armed with research on the "child's perspective," encourage children to assert their preferences by either requesting an item (often repeatedly) or by putting the item in the cart without permission until discovered later, perhaps at the checkout counter, which is then either purchased or discarded by the parent. McNeal (1999: iv) notes that conducting research on children can offer insights into their views on goods, packaging, the layout of stores, and on whether they feel welcomed or not in such environments. He points to a drawing by a child depicting herself reaching in vain for the M&M's candy on a top shelf as evidence of children's understanding of their potential disempowerment in retail settings (p. iv).

The "respect" marketers demonstrate for children by seeking out their voices and views through research, according to Sutherland and Thompson (2001), is simply following the model set by contemporary, "liberal" parents who have "bi-directional" relationships with their children where influence flows both ways (p. 17). "Families who do not confer with their children about purchases... deny their kids an opportunity to develop important life skills" (p. 18). Market discourse—which is a form of practice—here extends beyond a strictly commercial relationship to encompass beliefs about how children's participation in consumer decisions relates to children's "development." Market research, in this way, does not simply uncover actionable "truths" about consumer behavior; it both draws upon and contributes to larger understandings of childhood, parenthood, and their relation to the world of commerce.

Two recent and persistent marketing truths have to do with the oft-repeated notion of the "savvy" child consumer, almost regardless of age, and how marketing contributes to children's empowerment. A number of scholars, including myself, have written on the emergence and importance of these ideas since the 1990s (Buckingham, 2000; Schor, 2004; Cook, 2004, 2007). One argument, again offered by Sutherland and Thompson (2001), centers on the extensive choices children now have in the marketplace which lead to "media conscious kids": "Instead of transmitting the idea that self-worth is something kids buy at the mall, our marketing-driven culture and multimedia world mean that kids learn early on how to interpret and react to a society that is falling over itself to cater to them" (p. 71). Marketing makes contemporary kids more intelligent, a view recently echoed by others (Johnson, 2005). The variety of goods and media now available to savvy children and their liberal parents do more than offer choices and "developmental" opportunities; for some, these market-based choices are positively empowering to the extent that they allow children to exercise options and hence to realize, in some measure, dimensions of their own selves (Schor, 2004: 181–3; Cook, 2007). Indeed, from these statements, it would seem downright negligent to refrain from marketing to children.

Marketer discourses enact commercial epistemologies of children's consumption to the extent that they define, analyze, and conceptualize children and their relationship to adults/parents in reference to the world of goods. Market research serves as the practical vehicle through which the model of the knowing, desiring child consumer becomes enlivened, given dimension and, as well, infused political and social purpose. "Knowing the child" in a particular, proprietary way, as claimed by the research firms mentioned above, provides a competitive edge; as well, it brings the child in as a partner against counterclaims about inappropriateness in terms of level of development (Linn, 2004) or concerns about materialism (Schor, 2004).

"Fun": A Portal into Children's Perspectives

Market research often seeks the child's perspective as a way both to tailor messages and goods to specific audiences and as a way to address children as legitimate consumers in their own right. In recent years, marketers increasingly have come to recognize, research, and utilize "fun" as a particularly child-relevant lens through which one can know and speak to children's interests.

One market researcher, for instance (Poris, 2005: 14), considers fun and play as "absolutely vital" to brand awareness and success and as an "essential cost of entry to the kids" market. Her study conducted for Just Kid, Inc. found ten different kinds of fun[4] unevenly distributed over a variety of age, gender, and racial–ethnic characteristics. In an article written to publicize the study, the author concludes that "(u)nderstanding the ten distinct dimensions of fun will allow marketers and advertisers to connect with kids on the type of fun that matters most to them and will increase their likelihood of successfully developing products and messages that resonate with kids" (p. 22). "Fun" here stands as a form of instrumental knowledge, a way of making entrée into children's worlds so as to develop products that "connect" marketers with kids. The study (The FUNdamentals Study) positions itself as the "first syndicated quantitative research tool to provide a "deep dive" on kids' definitions of fun" (from a Just Kid, Inc. promotional brochure, no date or title). It offers marketing professionals a "richer, more granular" understanding of kid fun so they may better position advertising, have more successful new products and programs, and produce more effective promotions.

Play and fun, for marketers, have long served as portals into children's subjectivities and hence as avenues to discern and act upon their desires. It is in the realm of food and eating where fun and play have taken hold most decisively as marketing strategy, particularly since the 1990s. The historical examples of the fun-food-child connection are varied and long, and cannot be discussed here with the kind of attention required, but well-known examples abound—for example, candies (James, 1982), the prizes in Cracker Jack boxes, McDonald's Happy Meals, tie-ins with radio, television, film and sports, character licensing, among others. I focus the remainder of the discussion on some ways market practitioners have sought to promote edibles and related packaging as forms of entertainment, or what has become known popularly as "eatertainment."

"Eatertainment": Shapes, Colors, Packaging, and Containers

Eatertainment makes fun and amusement the point of food and meals and is often associated with themed restaurants (Gottdiener, 2001) intended for children and adults alike, but now found in many forms associated with the supermarket and supermarket foods. In the world of children's grocery foods, the shapes, colors, containers, and textures of foodstuffs intended for children have made many items identifiable as belonging to "kids," intended to "involve" the child with the food beyond the activity of eating. Often the "interaction" of the child with the food item resembles grade school arts-and-crafts activities such as painting or manipulating shapes, further solidifying the connection of the food with "fun."

Identifiable, even trademarked, shapes of foods transport the item out of the everyday, generic world of mundane eating. Animal Crackers is perhaps the longest standing and best-known brand that use shapes in this way. Pepperidge Farm products have aggressively branded and promoted Goldfish snacks—small, cheese-flavored crackers in the shape of fish—through advertisements, its website,[5] and by publishing children's storybooks using the fish as the main characters (McGrath, 1999a; Kirkpatrick, 2000).[6] A number of other companies, such as Kellogg's Fruit Loops, Cheerios cereal (McGrath, 1999b), Oreo cookies, and SunMaid Raisins (Weir, 1999), have also published children's storybooks where the personified food brand serves as the protagonist. Food shapes need not be iconic to be fun, only an intervention into the ordinary. Miniaturization is one tactic. VDK Frozen goods introduced minipancakes and French toast sticks under the Aunt Jemima brand that can be eaten as finger foods and dunked into syrup for kids "on the go" (Supermarket Business, 1999). Whimsical shapes also indicate fun. Children's cold cereals for decades have had characters, shapes, and colorful food bits associated with them. Dole, the canned fruit company, extended this practice with its line of fruits shaped like moons, stars, sea creatures, and seashells to sell the "mother snack food market" with appeals to nutrition (McGrath, 1999b). In 2001, Fran's Healthy Helpings, an upstart company, introduced Socceroni and Cheese with soccer ball shaped pasta—perhaps taking the "soccer mom" demographic a bit too literally—and Dino Chicken Chompers made of chicken pieces in the shape of dinosaurs (Cioletti, 2001).

Food shapes execute several commercial functions. For one, they can help make the product and/or brand recognizable outside of the container. Grape-Nuts, traditionally an "adult" health cereal, began marketing Grape-Nuts O's (with added sugar) in a "fun and contemporary new shape that a younger consumer can relate to" (Toops, 1999), according to a company spokesperson. Fruit Loops and Lucky Charms are among the cereals that, according to two British brand consultants, put a "3D equity in the brand" thus enhancing its "pester power." To get children to say "I want one that looks like..." can sometimes be enough if the name is forgotten, they maintain (Brand Strategy, 2002). For another, they "speak" to children's subjectivities, their perspectives, by "playing" with the ordinary, making it fun and thus properly in the realm of things that belong to "kids."

The marketing of fun serves as a portal into children's subjectivities also through the colors, containers, and packaging of food. Heinz foods famously introduced E-Z Squirt in 2000, an easy-to-grip squeezable bottle which was filled with green-colored ketchup. According to Dave Siegel of Wondergroup, Inc. (November 4, 2005 interview with the author), a market research firm, the idea of an off-colored condiment that could be treated as paint arose from observing children playing in a research setting with arts and crafts. The success, he believes, lay not so much in the novelty of the color of the ketchup but with the ability to play with their food. The bottle design allowed children to draw with the food on their buns or plates. The color and design of the product "talk" to children "so that they form a lifelong relationship with Heinz," according to the managing director of Heinz USA's ketchup, condiments, and sauces division (Thompson, 2000).

Package design is integral to creating and maintaining the fun-sales-food nexus. A product and packaging executive offers four important principles of "kid packaging" to marketers (Sensbach, 2000). First, kids are "savvy" consumers who thereby require that the package message and market segment be clear because "fun" means different things to children of different ages. Second, a good package must use their language which is visually oriented. Third, it capitalizes on the power of media by allying with popular licensed characters. Finally, for kids, "the package is the product." It is what they see first on the shelves. Breakfast cereal boxes, which can be "veritable amusement parks," are prime sites for children's attention and involvement. "Because kids will read a cereal box five or six times before the product is used up, it's a perfect venue for cross promotions, premiums, games, puzzles, collectibles such a as trading cards and educational opportunities" (Sensbach, 2000: 14). Note how the marketing discourse operates within "the child's" perspective by lauding their agency and knowledge (i.e., "savvy" consumers), all the while unproblematically invoking children's desires as having a natural or essential affinity with the unspecified product to be carefully packaged accordingly.

"Kid sizing" of meals and containers further moves the idea of food and meals in the direction of making them child specific. The "grab and go" appeal to busy parents and over-scheduled children has made headway into such areas as Yoplait brand Go-Gurts, a child-sized squeezable tube of yogurt, replete with personified, exciting graphics of a youthful, slightly crazed boy on the container, and, of course, its own website.[7] Mini-sized juices, puddings, bags of potato chips, containers of apple sauce, and bite-sized frozen foods help to delineate a specifically designated child world of foodstuffs. These miniatures carry out a kind of "double talk" of appealing both to children (via images of fun, amusement, and a sense of cultural ownership of the product) and to mothers with the convenience of prefigured serving sizes and disposable containers small enough to fit into school lunch bags. Fun works in and for kids' marketing in large part because shared, contemporary beliefs position children as inhabiting something of a parallel world to adults—one where play and fantasy form (or hopefully form) a protective barrier from the vile, everyday world of drudgery and unchecked self-interest. The Disney Corporation has built and empire on just this notion. This "magic" now extends to adults who may seek to re-live a time of "protective innocence" by delving into "wondrous innocence," to use Gary Cross' (2004) terms.

Martha Wolfenstein (1955) pointed out over five decades ago that parents in American culture, especially mothers, tend to feel it a duty to have fun with—and perhaps "be" fun to—their children. Since that time, market efforts have helped transform the fun imperative of parenting and of childhood into something akin to a child's right—most certainly into a marker of recognition of children's desires and perspectives. When marketers and designers deploy whimsical images, bright colors, and out-of-the ordinary names and shapes to the packaging of food products, they are indicating to children and adults alike that certain foods are meant "for kids."

Such a gesture distinguishes child from adult and provides for a sense of propriety, of cultural ownership, on the part of children. When a product "speaks" to children in visual, verbal, and design languages—when something cajoles fun and play—it gives an indication that someone or something recognizes them and that they have a place in and among the world of goods. This strategy, which has been utilized perhaps most globally by the Nickelodeon television network (Banet-Wiser, 2007), calls out and favors the kind of enterprising self-privileged in neoliberal capitalism theorized by Foucault (1982, 1991) and Rose (1990). "Fun," in this way, enacts contemporary (adult/parental) wishes for a benign childhood, addresses children as social and market actors, and, at the same time, provides a bridge to the world of commerce without which the fun—and the self that accompanies it—could not arise and be made manifest on their own.

Final Thoughts

Marketing ideology in itself is not mysterious. The point is to secure workable knowledge for clients so that both realize financial benefit. When children are at issue, however, the interested and instrumental nature of gathering and using this knowledge becomes problematic. Hence, great effort is expended to garner the perspective of the child, to seek out her or his expressions of preference, and thereby to reconfigure the consumer research act as something of an altruistic one that entails listening to children and responding to their needs and wants.

In the act of executing research and subsequent product development and advertising campaigns, market practitioners at once draw upon, help create, and ultimately disseminate images and conceptions of children as knowing, desiring consumers. In the process, this marketing labor thereby re-legitimates children *as* consumers—that is, as an identity necessarily tied to the commercial world. Marketing ideology in this way feeds back on itself as when commercial constructions forged in the act of attempting to capture market share reappear as naturalized and given characteristics of consumers. The child consumer persists, in part because commercial epistemologies—ways of knowing—assist in creating morally appropriate social identities which children can inhabit and parents can find provisionally acceptable. The knowing, desiring child does not simply live in the marketer's dream, but also in the parent's kitchen.

If we are, or seem to be, distant from the mindset that produced hate mail for McNeal's understandings about children and consumer markets, it is due in significant part to the diffusion of general and specific beliefs about consumption and marketing and the place of goods in everyday life. Childhood itself transforms and has been transformed by marketing practice—a practice that can never confine itself to its target—and hence will continue to mutate into forms in the future perhaps unrecognizable from those we accept today as given and natural.

Notes

1. Just Kid Inc. Website, http://www.justkidinc.com/kid_research.html (accessed December 10, 2009).
2. Geppetto Website, http://www.geppettogroup.com/ (accessed December 10, 2009).
3. Kidzeyes Website, http://www.kidzeyes.com/faq.htm#1 (accessed December 10, 2009).
4. These are: friend-orientated fun, empowering fun, creative fun, silly fun, sports-orientated fun, competitive fun, family-orientated fun, surprising/adventurous fun, relaxing fun, and rebellious fun.
5. Pepperidge Farm Website, http://www.pfgoldfish.com/ (accessed December 10, 2009).
6. Also available at Advertising Educational Foundation Website, http://www.aef.com/ (accessed February 24, 2004).
7. Yoplait Website http://www.yoplait.com/products_gogurt.aspx (accessed December 10, 2009).

References

Banet-Wiser, S. (2007) *Kids Rule! Nickelodeon and Consumer Citizenship*. Durham, NC: Duke University Press.

Brand Strategy (2002a) "Entertainment Puts Brands on the Plate." January 9: 26.

——(2002b) "A Fruity Brand Extension." July 26: 24.

Buckingham, David (2000) *After the Death of Childhood*. Cambridge: Polity.

Cioletti, Jeff (2001) "Kid-venience." *Supermarket Business*, May 15, 2001 (on-line, accessed January 10, 2003).

Cook, Daniel Thomas (2000) "The Other 'Child Study': Figuring Children as Consumers in Market Research, 1910s–1990s." *Sociological Quarterly*, 41(3, Summer): 487–507.

——(2004) *The Commodification of Childhood: The Children's Clothing Industry and the Rise of the Child Consumer*. Durham, NC: Duke University Press.

——(2007) "The Disempowering Empowerment of Children's Consumer 'Choice.'" *Society and Business Review* 2(1): 37–52.

Cross, Gary (2004) *The Cute and the Cool*. Cambridge: Harvard University Press.

Davila, Arlene (2001) *Latinos, Inc.* Berkeley: University of California Press.

Day, Sherri (2003) "The Potatoes Smile: The Fries are Blue." *New York Times*, March 13, 2003., hhttp://www.nyt.com, accessed March 13, 2003.

Foucault, Michael (1982) "Afterword: The Subject and Power." In H.F. Dreyfus and P. Rainbow, eds. *Michel Foucault: Beyond Structuralism and Hermeneutics*. Brighton: Harvester Press.

——(1991) "Governmentality." In G. Burchell, C. Gordon, and P. Miller, eds. *The Foucault Effect: Studies in Governmentality with Two Lectures by and an Interview with Michel Foucault*. London: Harverster Wheatsheaf.

Gottdiener, Mark (2002a). *The Theming of America*. Boulder: Westview Press, 2001.

Hunter, Beatrice Trum (2002a) "Marketing Foods to Kids: Using Fun to Sell." *Consumer Research*, 85(3, March): 16–20.

——(2002b) "Marketing Foods to Kids: Using New Avenues." *Consumers Research*, 85(4, April): 23–36.

Jacobson, Lisa (2004) *Raising Consumers*. New York: Columbia University Press.

James, Allison (1982) "Confections, Concoctions and Conceptions." *Oxford Anthropological Journal*, 10(2): 83–95.

Johnson, Steven (2005) *Everything Bad is Good for You*. New York: Riverhead.

Kirkpatrick, David D. (2000) "Snack Foods Become Stars of Books for Children." *New York Times*, September 22, 2000 (on-line) also available at http://www.aef.com/,accessed February 24, 2004.

Levine, Jane (2000) "Junk-Food Marketing Goes Elementary." *Educational Digest*, 65(5, January): 32–4.

Linn, Susan (2004) *Consuming Kids*. New York: Random House.

McGrath, Barbara Barbieri (1999a) *Pepperidge Farm Goldfish Funbook*. New York: HarperCollins.

McGrath, Barbara Barbieri (1999b) *The Cheerios Counting Book*. New York: Scholastic Books.

McNeal, James U. (1987) *Children as Consumers: Insights and Implications*. Lexington, MA: Lexington Books.

——(1992) *Kids as Customers*. New York: Lexington Books.

——(1999) *The Kids' Market: Myths and Realities*. Ithaca, NY: Paramount Market Publishing.

Mazzarella, William (2003) *Shoveling Smoke: Advertising and Globalization in Contemporary India*. Durham: Duke University Press.

Poris, Michelle (2005) "What Fun Means to Today's Kids." *Young Consumers* 6(4): 14–22.

Rose, Nicholas (1990) *Governing the Soul*. London: Routledge.

Schor, Juliet (2004) *Born to Buy*. New York: Scribners.

Sender, Katherine (2004) *Business, Not Politics: The Making of the Gay Market*. New York: Columbia University Press.

Sensbach, Paul R. (2000) "Don't Kid around with Kid Packaging." *Marketing News*, 34 (24) (November): 14.

Supermarket Business (1999) "What's New Around the Store." April 1, 1999, accessed through http://progessivegrocer.com/, July 2003.

Sutherland, Anne, and Thompson, Beth (2001) *Kidfluence: Why Kids Today Mean Business*. Toronto: McGraw-Hill Meyerson.

Thompson, Stephanie (1999) "Gen'l Mills Taps into Craze with Pokemon Rolls Treat." *Advertising Age*, October 4, 1999.

Turscik, Richard (2002) "Category Captains 2002." *Progressive Grocer*, November 15, http://www.progressivegrocer.com/, accessed February 5, 2003.

Underhill, Paco (2000) *Why We Buy: The Science of Shopping*. New York: Simon and Schuster.

Weir, Alison (1999) *The SunMaid Raisins Play Book*. Little Simon: New York.

Wolfenstein, Martha (1955) "Fun Morality." In Margaret Mead and Martha Wolfenstein, eds. *Childhood in Contemporary Cultures*. Chicago: University of Chicago Press, pp. 168–78.

12

Broadening the Marketing Concept: Service to Humanity, or Privatization of the Public Good?

Kalman Applbaum

Hindsight allows us to see today why social reforms proposed in the 1960s enjoyed the unique possibility of adoption: Both the political right and left were suing for change in existing arrangements of public administration. The watchword of the age was freedom. For the left, freedom meant from the authority of institutions such as schools, families, legal codes, and cultural norms. For the right, freedom meant the liberation of commerce from regulation. (Laissez faire was not a new idea; however, it had fresh wind at its back because of the communist threat. The "command economies" of the Eastern bloc were seen as a conduit to tyranny, a "road to serfdom," as Friedrich Hayek put it.) The common goal was to break the domination of impersonal forces in society.

Academic marketing participated in the new synthesis that emerged from the coalition against impersonal authority. The discipline was a hybrid of social–cultural and economic–commercial thought. Its charter was to mediate the gap between individuals and their needs on one hand and producers and their capabilities and requirements on the other. Seen from the point of view of its champions, marketing was on both the individual's and the corporation's side in the battle against the forces of the impersonal. In the view of marketing humanists, if I can suggest this term to mean those who see marketing as a wholly positive force in society, the success of marketing's most consequential discovery, the brand, signaled the triumph of the personal, particular, expressive, meaningful, unique, identity-endowed, and humanized over undifferentiated mass commodities. Brands, like other elements of marketing, succeed by virtue of a concurrence between corporations and their public that needs are satisfied in the cooperative venture between the two. The prevalence of marketing humanist optimism was based on this accord and contributed to the profession's view of itself in the 1960s as "a societal force" (Bartels, 1974).

It was into this context that two marketing academics—who themselves represented the formerly contrasting sides (Philip Kotler was an economist, Sidney Levy a hybrid psychologist/anthropologist)—framed a proposal to extend marketing ideas gleaned from business enterprises to the non-market domain of public administration. The authors depicted a confrontation between the forces of the impersonal and the personal:

> Modern marketing has two different meanings in the minds of people who use the term. One meaning of marketing conjures up the terms selling, influencing, persuading. Marketing is seen as a huge and increasingly dangerous technology, making it possible to sell persons on buying things, propositions, and causes they either do not want or which are bad for them. The other meaning of marketing unfortunately is weaker in the public mind; it is the concept of *sensitively serving and satisfying human needs*. This was the great contribution of the marketing concept that was promulgated in the 1950s, and that concept now counts many business firms as its practitioners. The marketing concept holds that the problem of all business firms in an age of abundance is to develop customer loyalties and satisfaction, and the key to this problem is to focus on the customer's needs. (Kotlera and Levy, 1969: 15; italics in the original)

In the public imagination, particularly following the publication of Vance Packard's book, *Hidden Persuaders*, marketing epitomized an impersonal, threatening force, "a huge and increasingly dangerous technology" (Kotler and Levy, 1969). The view of marketing Kotler and Levy wished to promote, by contrast, was of a human, personal, and sensitive discipline working in humanity's interest. Under the influence of the marketing concept, they averred, corporations had left behind their self-centered production orientation and assumed the lofty purpose of sensitively serving and satisfying human needs. Now it was time for public sector enterprises to follow suit so that they too would at last serve the needs of their constituents and clients.

Posing marketing as leverage for the personal against the impersonal was a strategic reframing of the more traditional opposition between those forces held to exist in the service of the pubic good and those organized for the pursuit of private gain, namely, capitalist firms or corporations. Viewing marketing as a handmaiden to greedy corporations, Kotler and Levy wished to tell us, was an erroneous view of marketing. The marketer's true calling is to serve mankind, and marketing is a tool, a technology, even a science geared to the work of satisfying human needs. As such, it could be transferred, or "broadened" to all areas where human needs required attending to, not just commercial consumer products.[1]

The extensive privatization and commercialization Western economies underwent in the three decades following the 1960s (Carrier, 1997; Gray, 2000) helped bring marketing managerial models increasingly into wider spheres of relevance. State-run sectors of the economy were recast as private enterprises and governmental and nonprofit organizations that could not be privatized because profit was not extractable from their operations came under increasing pressure to nevertheless think like businesses (Williams, 2006). Marketing models gained standing as just one component in the effort to disabuse public sector enterprises from non-market driven models. General management, finance, governance, as well as marketing were all broadened to the social sector at the same time. Eventually the pretense of "personal good, impersonal bad" was dropped. The claim—indeed under America's first MBA president, George W. Bush, the marketing byword—became "private good, public bad." This extended in every conceivable direction: Social security bad, private investment good. Public health care bad, private health care good. Regulation bad, free market good. Government bad, corporations good. The supposed autonomous workings of the market and the expertise of business managers, if only we were to turn our wealth and our institutions unquestioningly over to them, would bring universal prosperity and, trickling down from that, Social Good.

Marketing, again, purports to span the two camps. On one hand, the discipline owes its existence to the insight that the untouched mechanism of supply and demand does not directly provide people the satisfactions they need and want; the role of marketers is to translate across the demander/supplier divide. Peter Drucker says, "In marketing... we satisfy individual and social values, needs, and wants—be it through producing goods, supplying services, fostering innovation, or creating satisfaction.... Marketing is thus the process through which economy is integrated into society to serve human needs" (1958: 252). For Drucker and others with a humanist view, marketing's beneficent contribution is to act as a bridge to a utopian future when the visible hand of marketing can recede from the scene, having performed its worldly function, after which the market can take over the role of providing for human needs without human interference.[2] On the other hand, the staunchly individual, self-interested, maximizing, rational decision-taking homo economicus of neoclassical theory has survived more or less intact as a model for human nature underlying most marketing research and practice (Applbaum, 1998, 2004)—a point of view also reflected in Kotler/Levy's article.[3]

It is not my central purpose here to explore these philosophical antinomies, but only to point out that between 1969, when Kotler and Levy published their treatise, and today, much of what once fell under the category of public interest, whether in the social or the private sector, yielded either to private ownership or to thinking like businesses. Marketing contributed ideas and practices to this broadening. Our question therefore is not whether the marketing concept has been broadened (it has), but (a) What particular addition has marketing made to the privatization model? (b) Has this effect been significant (c) In what ways has it been salutary and in what ways deleterious to society's interest?

The example I explore is from health care, and in particular the creation and distribution of pharmaceuticals, which constitutes roughly 18 percent of the global health budget, and is growing faster than health expenditure overall.[4] In the United States, annual per capita spending for pharmaceuticals in 2008 was nearly $850. If we add in expenditures for medical device industry, these numbers are much larger.

Beyond the magnitude of private and public spending devoted to it, health care is an ideal example to discuss for two reasons. First, whether it is mainly privately held, as it is in the United States, or publicly administered, as in most of the world, health care is at heart an enterprise in the public interest. Prescription pharmaceuticals are called ethical drugs because, unlike most other goods, their distribution is vital to human welfare, and violation of that welfare, either through intentional compromises made to the safety of drugs or through the attempt to unnaturally limit or expand their distribution in the interest of profits, is considered unethical. The degree of oversight of pharmaceuticals, even in the United States where regulation has been greatly attenuated, is evidence that they are considered social goods of a unique kind. At the same time, pharmaceuticals are first-order commercial entities. Because of the cost and esoteric process of development they are heavily proprietary. Pharmaceutical pills are branded products, objects of trust and hope, intimate, compact, and transportable. They circulate widely if not effortlessly on the wings of medical science, and are thus also vehicles of globalization. If we had to select among all objects the best symbol to represent the meeting of public interest and private commodity, a pill would be it.

Another reason that health care is the ideal sector in which to measure marketing's contribution to public good—the claim at the heart of the broadening concept—is because marketing proposes that its unique contribution to both humanity and to the scientific study of it lies in its expertise in assessing and meeting human needs. Medicines and health care constitute a final frontier for marketing application because our needs in that province of experience are, in result of our mortality, infinite. Good health is the very template upon which the concept of need might rest. However, it is not just our mortality at stake in health care, but the quality of our lives while we live them. Marketing concerns itself with this "unmet need" facet of health and health maintenance, while biomedicine has lately paid less attention to this aspect of health care, focusing instead on disease-specific interventions. Pharmaceuticals and health care thus lie precisely at the juncture between private and public administrative methods, motives, and conceptual models of service to humanity, such that we can estimate whether the application of marketing principles to it is appropriate and useful.

Pharmaceuticals: From Sales to Marketing

Preface—Rival views of the history of pharmaceutical marketing

The historiography of marketing is replete with minor disputes over when modern marketing concepts took root. A similar debate in miniature may be taking shape in the history of pharmaceutical marketing. On one side are those who claim, as I do, that the late 1980s and early 1990s marked a break with what preceded it, insofar as at that time marketing became a total institutional fact in the industry. Marketing and R&D (research and development) were largely combined under the direction of marketing; the driving orientation became the pursuit of product/brand/patent equity through strategies of extension and control; and the application of customer segmentation (in which physicians rather than end users were the main target) became routine. The reintroduction of direct-to-consumer (DTC) advertising coincided with this periodization, contributing further to the marketing focus of firms.

The fruit of this application of marketing principle was the emergence of blockbuster drugs, designated as drugs whose annual sales exceeded $1 billion. The profits from blockbusters came to rival that of all the other drugs combined in a pharmaceutical company's product line. Blockbusters accounted for 6 percent of the overall pharmaceutical market in 1991. This figure tripled to 18 percent by 1997, and in 2001 occupied fully 45 percent of the market.[5] The top ten drugs alone, constituting less than a quarter of 1 percent of drugs available in a growing pharmacopeia, accounted for over $60 billion in annual sales in 2006.[6] The rise of the blockbuster focus in the industry, in my view, reflects and drives the current competitive and organizational structure of the industry.

The counter to the theory that something new had occurred around the year 1990 is held up by examples of modern marketing techniques having been employed in the industry already in the 1950s. There are several engaging accounts of this (Healy, 1997, 2002; Rasmussen, 2004; Greene, 2007). One persuasive notion is that a conceptual development in medicine and public health prepared the ground for a new approach to expanding the market for pharmaceuticals. The conceptual development in question was the shift in focus from the treatment exclusively of visible disease (old medicine) to the management of risk (new medicine). In keeping with the growing faith in the scientific superiority of quantitative measurements, in medicine too epidemiological studies changed how medicine was practiced. Practitioners became reliant on statistical tabulations of risk and on the use of

273

guidelines and rating scales with which to evaluate the patient sitting in front of them.

The initial impetus behind this shift, according to Jeremy Greene, was the detection of the relationship between hypertension and cardiovascular disease. The relationship was discovered not in clinical or laboratory investigations, but by epidemiological studies. Or rather, not even quite epidemiological studies as actuarial ones. It was insurance companies that originally invented the annual checkup, which they did to screen risks and to help set rates. They discovered that elevated blood pressure was a risk for cardiovascular disease. The competitive pursuit of pharmacological agents to treat high blood pressure, the development of sales organizations to convince doctors to prescribe these medicines, and the pressure exerted by the industry on public health authorities to set treatment guidelines are, regardless of how we choose to evaluate the medical outcome of these activities, classical tales of marketing evolution in the industry.

The saga of "prescribing by numbers" (Green, 2007) rather than by symptom (since hypertension is not felt by the individual), and the marketing edifice this gave birth to, begins as early as the 1940s. By the 1970s, with the addition of "pre-diabetes" and hypercholesteremia to the list of health risks measured by epidemiologists rather than clinicians, the opportunity for unprecedented expansion of drug use came into full view. Greene describes the editor of *Drug and Cosmetic Industry* magazine, Milton Moskowitz, arguing the potential for infinite expansion of drug use based on the examples of Diuril (the antihypertensive) and Orinase (for management of type II diabetes) already in 1961:

> Diuril and Orinase, Moskowitz argued, were two examples of a new form of pharmaceutical marketing that refused to accept the incidence of disease as a fixed market or a zero-sum game. Any disease was a potential market for a drug, but chronic diseases such as diabetes and hypertension were growth markets that could continue to expand—as long as the screening and the diagnosis could be pushed further outward to uncover more hidden patients among the apparently healthy. In the infinitely expandable universe of chronic conditions, in the logic of preventive pharmacology, Moskowitz saw unlimited growth capacity for the pharmaceutical industry. (Greene, 2007: 87)

Therein lay the start of a trend that would reach full realization much later: expansion strategies based on the deployment of scientific evidence as a marketing tool for convincing physicians and consumers that increased consumption of pills would lead to improved health.

The resolution of the two historical views lies in the recognition that when the marketing concept is properly applied, its realization is actualized simultaneously in a formulation of consumer need as well as an institutional structure that reflects that need so to best be able to meet it (Kohli and Jaworski, 1990). For readers unfamiliar with marketing theory, this may seem a bit abstract. In fact, it is not very different from what can be explained by means of a simple example. If the need in question is a fast meal, the restaurant serving that meal has to be organized in such a fashion so as to deliver it. The kitchen, the skills of the chef, the layout and atmosphere of the dining area, the ingredients, the size and training of the restaurant staff, the location and access of the restaurant, and so on must all mirror or conform to the product being delivered. Try to serve fast food to a line of people at a five-star restaurant, or a five-star meal out of the kitchen of Burger King, and you get the idea.

The case of pharmaceutical markets and companies is similar. The needs of the consumers of the company's products and the organization to deliver it must be matched. The difficulty of accomplishing this harmonization in an industry where consumer needs, distribution channels, stake-holding constituencies, and products are as complex as they are is one of the most important reasons why the adaptations I speak of below become necessary. Since I am speaking of consumer needs on the one hand and institutional arrangements to meet them on the other, I split these into two separate discussions.

PART I: ABSTRACTION OF CONSUMER NEEDS

Why should prescribing by numbers have been uniquely suited to fostering the growth of marketing activities in the firm? Prescription by numbers conforms loosely to a pattern I have elsewhere called the abstraction of needs and the mining of presumed latent needs. This abstraction helps globally expanding firms overcome the problem of the specificities of consumer preferences:

> Successful expansion depends upon the power to standardize one's product and marketing.... The need to respect individual and cultural differences through marketing adaptation—the ultimate factor at stake in customer orientation—is resolved by a practical consensus to incorporate higher and therefore more inclusive levels of abstraction in the consideration of consumer needs.... The application of this *customer need abstraction*, in which rather than listening to what customers say they want, the marketer determines by his or her own means what the customer would actually like, is effected by means of marketing-inspired models of consumer behavior. (Applbaum, 2004: 81)

As a material aside, we can see from Kotler/Levy's own work that expansion through abstraction is a standard formula in marketing thought. In Kotler/Levy's broadening program, there were two needs being abstracted. The first was the service component of public administration. If museums, churches, universities, police departments, charities, libraries, labor unions, YMCAs, and the defense department were to drop the narrow version of their missions Kotler/Levy say (e.g., universities = "to educate the three Rs"; churches = to "produce religious services," etc.) and instead promote more abstract goods (e.g., universities = "to serve the social, emotional and political needs of young persons"; churches = their "basic product . . . is human fellowship") with the use of marketing tools, then they would be more successful at serving their consumers and constituencies.

The hazard of the above recommendation to the specific goals espoused by those organizations aside, Kotler/Levy's article can as readily be taken as a treatise of marketing advocacy, for in it the attempt to reposition marketing itself into a more abstract provider of services is only thinly veiled. This is the second need that could use a makeover by means of an abstraction. They cite Levitt (1960) to bemoan the failure of the marketing imagination due to literalism. The exemplar is a cosmetics company that should see its basic product "as beauty or hope, not lipsticks and makeup." With the broadening of marketing application to nonprofit sectors, we can infer, its practitioners would get a makeover: Marketers would be purveyors of beauty and hope, not lipstick and makeup. That the authors had marketing advocacy (or the promotion of marketing) and not just marketing humanism on their minds is evident from the vehemence with which they wish to negate "the indictment in Vance Packard's *Hidden Persuaders* and numerous other social criticisms, with the net effect that a large number of persons think of marketing as immoral or entirely self-seeking in its fundamental premises" (Kotler and Levy, 1969: 15). Broadening the application of marketing to the social sector, the authors hoped, would defuse the growing negative public image of their profession.

In the case of pharmaceutical marketing, the abstraction of symptoms to invisible markers that would be measured at a distance from patients and clinics allowed the industry to redefine their work as being not just the treatment of disease but the management of risk associated with becoming sick. More importantly, from a commercial point of view, curative treatments tend to be of short duration, whereas the management of risk is ongoing. The goose that lays blockbuster eggs is not cure, but maintenance and prophylaxis. Antihypertensive medications are forever; premenstrual dysphoric disorder and hormone replacement therapies are intended to blanket the individual's lifetime; cholesterol-lowering medication, with the incipient endorsement of the American Academy of Pediatrics, may soon be successfully marketed as a cradle-to-grave protection against cardiovascular risk. Slowly this logic overtook the rationale for drug development in many sickness categories: osteoporosis, gastritis, arthritis, type II diabetes, irritable bowel syndrome, insomnia, allergies, and pretty much all psychiatric disorders including ADHD, bipolar disorder, depression, obsessive compulsive disorder, and dementia. Many of these are measured abstractly either because they conform to epidemiological rather than medical inspirations to diagnosis (i.e., you do not feel sick when your triglycerides are high), or because the symptoms are calculated against a rating scale that objectifies the patient from a distance, as when a patient who reports to her primary care physician that she tends to blush, or has experienced poor appetite lately, or is low on energy, or is simply not feeling as fun-loving as she used to is prescribed an antidepressant (Currie, 2009).

David Healy, psychiatrist and pre-eminent historian of psychopharmaceuticals, says:

> Rating scales are increasingly being imported into clinical practice, based on the argument that they will reduce variability in the clinical encounter and make that encounter more scientific. Healthcare practitioners are encouraged to administer depression or other behavioral rating scales when seeing patients. As a result pharmaceutical companies now run symposia at major professional meetings aimed solely at introducing clinicians to rating scales.... For example, at the 2007 American Psychiatric Association meeting Pfizer supported the symposium "From Clinical Skills to Clinical Scales: Practical Tools in the Management of Patients with Schizophrenia." The practical tools discussed were rating scales, the use of which would draw attention to how the company's drug was superior to others in the field. (Healy, 2009: 26)

Through the abstraction of risk numbers and rating scales, pharmaceutical marketers have found undreamt of reserves of unconscious and invisible signals that they have appointed themselves to construe as "unmet needs" that they are appointed to meet.[7] Few people today question the validity of this paradigm of discovering and treating sickness, much less notice that the incidence of most of the above-named sicknesses has mysteriously expanded manyfold in recent decades. Often, where we find lifelong or maintenance therapy risk management, the research that resulted in discovery, estimation of prevalence, and then treatment was not inspired by medical, scientific, or epidemiological curiosity but by "condition branding," a subset of pharmaceutical marketing devoted to heightening consumption for one's drug (Angelmar et al., 2007).

Condition branding may sound technical or innocuous. We have become convinced, not coincidentally through industry propaganda, that disease awareness campaigns might do much good, in that sick people previously untreated might thereby go to the clinic and get treatment. What a growing critical health studies literature has shown, however, is that condition branding quite often does not begin with the determinations of medical science, after which marketing conveys information and purveys solutions. Instead, the industry builds its expansion platform on small truths—that some people have clinically significant premenstrual dysphoric disorder (PMDD), restless leg syndrome, or social anxiety, for instance; or that some people are at particular risk for cardiovascular disease and should be treated prophylactically with medicines; or that some populations at large are undertreated for depression. These instances become the kernel of truth on which multibillion dollar forays in tendentious science is launched, packaged, and promoted by "key opinion leader" (KOL) doctors to their peers and to the public as being far more prevalent, indeed blockbuster, truths.

Critics call this practice "disease mongering," described as:

> ... the effort by pharmaceutical companies (or others with similar financial interests) to enlarge the market for a treatment by convincing people that they are sick and need medical intervention. Typically, the disease is vague, with nonspecific symptoms spanning a broad spectrum of severity—from everyday experiences many people would not even call "symptoms," to profound suffering. The market for treatment gets enlarged in two ways: by narrowing the definition of health so normal experiences get labeled as pathologic, and by expanding the definition of disease to include earlier, milder, and presymptomatic forms (e.g., regarding a risk factor such as high cholesterol as a disease in itself). (Woloshin and Schwartz, 2006)

The logic of the abstraction of consumer medical needs as a vehicle for disease mongering reaches its pinnacle in relation to fields of medicine, such as psychiatry, where the nosology and treatments available remain ambiguous and emergent (Hacking, 1999; Applbaum, 2009). In these cases, marketers are free to market needs and position products to serve them without having to obey the strictures of scientific determinations. As Healy pointed out over a decade ago, "Although there are clearly psychobiological inputs to many psychiatric disorders, we are at present in a state where companies can not only seek to find the key to the lock but can dictate a great deal of the shape of the lock to which a key must fit" (Healy, 1997: 212). A more recent empirical investigation by Healy and Lenoury (2007) of bipolar disorder appears in Box 12.1.[8]

Analogously, in a study called "Alzheimer medications and the anthropology of uncertainty," Annette Leibing traces the expansion in Brazil of the use of pharmaceuticals for treatment in dementia. This expansion is not based on the demonstrated efficacy of existing drugs for halting cognitive deterioration, which they cannot do, but on redefining the disorder to include "non-cognitive symptoms and notions like quality of life or functionality" (Leibing, 2009: 188). There may be little evidence that the drugs provide benefit on these important but nevertheless non-scientific measures either, but this does not affect the marketing-stimulated trend toward increased prescriptions. FDA warnings of the lethality of one common class of these drugs (atypical antipsychotics—in

---

Box 12.1 HEALY/LE NOURY'S CASE STUDY IN STRATEGIC MEDICALIZATION: BIPOLAR DISORDER*

Early 1990s: Abbott Laboratories meaninglessly differentiates the compound sodium valproate, an anti-convulsant in use since the 1960s, to semi-sodium valproate.

This trivial distinction was sufficient to enable the company to gain a patent on the new compound. Depakote was approved by the FDA on the basis of trials that showed this very sedative agent could produce beneficial effects in acute manic states. Any sedative agent can produce clinical trial benefits in acute manic states but no company had chosen to do this up till then, as manic states were comparatively rare and were adequately controlled by available treatments. Depakote was advertised as a "mood stabilizer." Had it been advertised as prophylactic for manic depressive disorder, FDA would have had to rule the advertisement illegal, as a prophylactic effect for valproate had not been demonstrated to the standards required for licensing. The term mood stabilizer in contrast was a term that had no precise clinical or neuroscientific meaning. As such it was not open to legal sanction. It was a new brand. In addition to branding a new class of psychotropic drugs, the 1990s saw the rebranding of an old illness. Manic-depressive illness became bipolar disorder. Lilly, Janssen, and AstraZeneca, the makers of the antipsychotic drugs, olanzapine (Zyprexa), risperidone (Risperdal), and quetiapine (Seroquel), respectively, sought indications in this area, and the steps they have taken to market their compounds as mood stabilizers illustrate how companies go about making markets.

First, each company has produced patient literature and website material aimed at telling people more about bipolar disorder, often without mentioning medication.... Among the claims are "that bipolar disorder is a life long illness needing life long treatment; that symptoms come and go but the illness stays; that people feel better because the medication is working; that almost everyone who stops taking the medication will get ill again and that the more episodes you have the more difficult they are to treat."

A second aspect of the marketing of the drugs uses celebrities such as writers, poets, playwrights, artists, and composers who have supposedly been bipolar. Lists circulate featuring most of the major artists of the nineteenth and twentieth century intimating they have been bipolar, when in fact very few if any had a diagnosis of manic-depressive illness.

A third aspect of the marketing has involved the use of mood diaries [Eli Lilly, AstraZeneca]. These break up the day into hourly segments and ask people to rate their moods.... Most normal people will show a variation in their moods that might be construed as an incipient bipolar disorder.

A fourth aspect of the current marketing of all medical disorders involves the marketing of risk. In the case of bipolar disorder, the risks of suicide, alcoholism, divorce, and career failure are marketed.

Fifth, direct-to-consumer advertising.... Viewers are encouraged to log onto bipolar-awareness.com, which takes them to a "Bipolar Help Center," sponsored by Lilly Pharmaceuticals. This contains a "mood disorder questionnaire." No drugs are mentioned. The advert markets bipolar disorder.

The sixth strategy involves the co-option of academia and is of particular relevance to the pediatric bipolar domain. Satellite symposia linked to the main American Psychiatric Association meeting could cost a company up to $250,000. The price of entry is too high for treatment modalities like psychotherapy. There can be up to forty such satellites per meeting. Companies usually bring hundreds of delegates to their satellite. At the 2003 meeting, an unprecedented 35 percent of the satellites were for just one disorder—

bipolar disorder. Fifty-seven senior figures in American psychiatry were involved in presenting material on bipolar disorder.

Until recently manic depressive illness was a rare disorder in the United States and Canada involving 10 per million new cases per year or 3,300 new cases per year. Bipolar disorder is now marketed as affecting 5 percent of the United States and Canada—that is 16.5 million North Americans, which would make it is as common as depression and ten times more common than schizophrenia. Clinicians are being encouraged to detect and treat it. They are educated to suspect that many cases of depression, anxiety, or schizophrenia may be bipolar disorder and that treatment should be adjusted accordingly. And, where recently no clinicians would have accepted this disorder began before adolescence, many it seems are now prepared to accept that it can be detected in preschoolers. Where one might have thought some of the more distinguished institutions would bring a skeptical note to bear on this, they appear instead to be fueling the fire. Massachusetts's General Hospital (MGH) has run trials of the antipsychotics risperidone and olanzapine on children with a mean age of 4 years. A mean age of 4 all but guarantees 3- and possibly 2-year-olds have been recruited to these studies.

* Based on Healy and Le Noury (2007).

which the term "atypical" is itself apparently a marketing brand and not a scientific term (Tyrer and Kendall, 2009)), in combination with the mounting evidence that their use provides no advantage to non-pharmacological therapies, did not dissuade Leibing's physician informants from adopting the medications as the first line of long-term treatment. She explains the influence of pharmaceutical marketing in bringing this change about:

> One of the best-known atypical antipsychotics in the treatment of Alzheimer's disease is risperidone—produced by Janssen Pharmaceuticals, which has been actively involved in the creation and promotion of the new category BPSD.... Janssen provided an unrestricted grant for a consensus conference organized by the International Psychogeriatric Association (IPA) in Landsdowne, VA in 1996, the event that was central to the development of the new category BPSD. "The development of the Consensus Statement on Behavioral and Psychological Symptoms of Dementia (BPSD) represents a first step towards recognizing that *these are core symptoms of dementia* and that it is as essential to study and treat them as it is to study and treat any other aspects of dementing disorders," wrote one of the organizers (Finkel, 1996, emphasis added). A second conference followed in 1999, resulting in more publications (IPA, 1996a, 1996b, 1996c, 2000, 2002). Afterwards updated educational materials were regularly mailed to all IPA members, in an effort which gradually changed the way health professionals understand and define dementia. (Leibing, 2009: 191)

One of the interesting features of Leibing's case is the contradictory combination of increased backing of and reliance on bioscientific treatments of Alzheimer's disease at the same time that the drugs are promoted to treat less neuroscientifically specifiable aspects of dementia. "There is a lack of definitions and validated measurements of functionality, and their relation to drug efficacy," she says (Leibing, 2009: 192). The drugs have dubious efficacy in preventing cognitive deterioration, so they are promoted to treat behavioral problems associated with dementia. On one level there is the truth of scientific evidence; on another, competing level, there is marketing rationale.

This is not to say that drug companies invented BPSD, or that it is an unimportant dimension of Alzheimer's, or that the promoted drugs will never show an effect in relation to BPSD. The question rather is whether the manipulated push for scientific validation of the drugs for use in BPSD is resulting in drained budgets and enthusiasm for non-pharmacological thera-pies that may be much safer and more important for helping to manage people suffering from the disease, or for affording them palliative care that at the same time helps reduce the burden to their family members. Pharma-ceutical companies are always competing for share of pocket (i.e., of private and public health budgets) against non-pharmacological approaches to treat-ment, and they have at their disposal staggering budgets with which to promote their point of view.

Pharmaceutical marketers concern themselves with two activities: Deter-mining unmet needs and making profits by selling drugs that meet those needs. In many cases, the products available are inadequate to the task because the science is undeveloped. Investor and executive greed for profit, however, operates by a different clock than medical progress. The show must go on. If drug companies are to prosper even in scientifically lethargic times, a rationale for sale must be found and pushed through the system. Broadening the definition of a disorder to focus drugs on more abstract needs (quality of life vs. cognitive function, in the case of dementia) enables the selling to continue. For dementia, as for many psychiatric disorders, the measures for improvement in social function are subjective, placebo effect rich, and non-specific. Most of us can be mystified in this process, because we do not understand what the FDA's actual function is and how drugs are approved. For present purposes, Healy can again be our guide:

> A difference between active drug and placebo that is statistically significant is taken to indicate that the drug "works." Regulators approve such drugs, drug companies market them as effective, and clinicians prescribe them. But if the trials are suffi-ciently large, even a minor difference of one or two rating scale points can be made statistically significant. As a result of this, a drug, which is a little bit sedating or tranquilizing, will show up as "working for depression" if the rating scale includes sleep or anxiety items. On this basis it would be possible to prove nicotine, benzodiazepines, anti-histamines, methylphenidate, or other treatments for ADHD, and most of the antipsychotics, and a number of anticonvulsants, to be "antidepressants." Indeed, many of these diverse agents have RCT evidence of benefit in depression. (Healy, 2009: 18)

It is unsurprising that the unmet need should surround quality of life issues (for the sick person as well as his family), since this is a marketing specialty. The abstraction of customer needs in this way is normative to marketing thought, and many of the marketers and sales personnel at Janssen may have no perception that they are denuding public health budgets and acting against both private and public interests.

Where the marketing concept is applied correctly, as I suggested earlier, the consumer model finds its correlate in the institutional involvement of the firm. In the conventional view of marketing development, there are several differences between the marketing-led and the sales-led organization: sales executives tend to think in terms of sales volumes rather than profits, short-run rather than long-run objectives, individual consumers rather than market segment classes, and fieldwork rather than desk work. Marketers, by contrast, think of long-run trends, threats and opportunities; customer types and segment differences; and how to institute effective systems for market analysis, planning, and control (Kotler, 1991). Let us see how this contrast is reflected in the organizational orientation of the contemporary pharmaceutical firm.

PART II: INTEGRATION OF MARKETING AND R&D

In pharmaceuticals, the sales-led organization would be one in which products are developed in the lab, and sales personnel would take these to the field, a process that would be drawn as: **Research → Development → Sales**. Later, perhaps, one might substitute "marketing" for sales. Finally, in a more marketing-enlightened age, the process would evolve into: **Market Research → Research → Development → Marketing**.

In this later model (like the first, an idealization), market researchers gather data at clinics, hospitals, and among consumers and then use this data to select among research proposals for drugs with the greatest market potential. The laboratory personnel need not be bothered with marketing considerations per se. They might take their orders from those who have the market's needs clearly in mind, but their scientific work would not otherwise be affected. This was apparently the model employed in the case of many historical cures, and it remains the image the pharmaceutical industry projects to the public about how it operates. But this species of process has in fact ceased to apply. For in the current time crunch, this model is not commercially sustainable.

Today, as the most cursory glance in the trade literature reveals, all attention is fixed on length of time under patent during which a firm can exclusively sell and accrue profits for a drug. Since a patent is taken out upon the formulation of a molecule, and several years stand between then and when the drug is developed, approved, and brought to market, companies seek to shorten the time between patent registration and product launch. The clinical research phase and the approval process can hardly be made shorter than it has been already.

The new thinking is that if marketing is started prior to the launch itself, the non-sales time of the drug can be leveraged to improve profitability during the commercial phase of the drug. This is described as "pre-commercial planning and marketing." Pre-commercial planning and marketing is the attempt to compress the sequence by involving scientists and incorporating their research capacities directly into the marketing process. This is where the institutional integration of marketing and R&D comes in.

Beginning in the 1990s, pharmaceutical marketing executives began speaking obsessively about the integration of marketing and R&D. The first may have been William Steere Jr., who was promoted from marketing to the CEO-ship at Pfizer in 1991. Greg Critser quotes Steere's priorities for the company upon assuming command. There were three. "The first one was get marketing and research closer together. The second one was get marketing and research closer together. And then he said the third one was get marketing and research closer together" (Critser, 2005: 91).

The procedural details of this transformation—and a transformation clearly was what was entailed—would have to be worked out by the cooperation of teams at various locations in the company. A typical management consultant to the process explains, "Pre-commercial marketing requires the collaboration of multiple brand stakeholders, including clinical affairs, preclinical, regulatory, legal, medical affairs, and marketing. Everyone involved should have an understanding of the broad commercial issues that will or are likely to affect the product when it reaches the market, as well as the elements that create value for a product."[9]

In 2002, at a round table entitled "When Worlds Collide: The Unleashed Power of Marketing/R&D Collaboration," one executive said,[10] "At Takeda we believe that the opportunity is integrating early and through target product development profiles, making sure that everyone is going in the same direction." He offered the example of Trovan as an ideal case when such integration was achieved.[11] Another executive said, "At AstraZeneca R&D people started to embrace more of the entrepreneurial mindset and understand customer needs better"—in other words, the institutional reorganization under the direction of marketing. "We struggled initially, but it eased once the R&D folks truly understood what we were all working toward, which is 'value enhancement.' We were all trying to figure out how to have an impact on the bottom line." And an executive from Wyeth pharmaceuticals concluded, "You can't have a blockbuster without [integration]."

In these and many more comments we hear that integration of marketing and R&D is the first important step toward what marketers in many consumer goods industries call *value creation*. Since the internally created value has to mirror what external stakeholders will value also, its counterpart is *value demonstration*. Value creation/demonstration therefore mirrors the distinction between the internal/external stakeholder divide. In other words, if *creating* value is the focus of the pharmaceutical company team, with implications for how therapies are identified and researched, the complementary task is *demonstrating* that value to the world outside the company.[12] This distinction is more analytical than practical. The organizational approach to creating value internally in fact bears a strong resemblance to demonstrating value to external stakeholders. These include regulators, physicians, and insurers who must be brought "on board" in the drug-marketing process. In theory and practice, value creation and demonstration work best when they are absolutely simultaneous and perceptually coincident in the minds of all stakeholders, internal and external. Management consultants speak of the collaboration of internal team members and external experts. Insofar as the internal and external actors both need to be convinced of the value of the gestational product so as to maximize its commercial potential, the responsibility of marketing extends similarly across this divide. The internal team, which includes sales, "regulatory," "publication planners," and in-house physicians employed as marketing personnel, extends seamlessly into the non-company public.

The practical implications of this is that even from the outset the entire team, including lab researchers, is devoted to demonstrating the efficacy and safety of the product yet to be born. The new flow chart becomes: **Value creation/ demonstration (Marketing Research) → R&D → Marketing Control**.

In a prelaunch strategy map drawn by Francoise Simon of the SDC Group consulting company and, coincidentally, Philip Kotler, already before Phase I trials, "thought leaders," meaning influential doctors, are identified and developed. Simon and Kotler estimate that thought leader development accounted for 20 percent of marketing costs and was rising (2003: 147). By comparison, direct-to-consumer advertising in 2004 accounted for only 14 percent of pharmaceutical spending. Thought leaders can, in the preclinical stage, "communicate unmet medical needs and shape the design and endpoints of Phase I and II clinical trials." Thus, depending on how successful the thought leaders are at generating interest among doctors and people at large, and accounting for consumer (to include physicians') attitude information, the clinical trials can be altered accordingly. Thought leader participation in successive trial phases is itself part of the procedure aimed to ensure awareness and adoption at the time of launch.

Simon and Kotler continue: "Opinion leaders drive the second-most crucial premarketing component, that is, publications. There is a close correlation between successful launches and aggressive publication programs" (2003: 147). This is referred to as "value through data." In this procedure, publications are "brought out" to begin the awareness campaign and to initiate a

---

Box 12.2 MERCK CORPORATION: REORGANIZATION FOR MARKETING CENTEREDNESS*

Merck is a good example for showing the changeover in the industry to marketing predominance both because of the company's size and reputation, and because Merck appears to have been reluctant to relinquish its traditional science-directed organizational culture for one directed by marketing.

Until about 1990, Merck was considered the most research-driven company in the industry. They had a 70 percent drug approval rate at the FDA, as against the industry average of about 50 percent. They were hardly strangers to aggressive sales; however, marching orders came from Merck Research Labs (MRL), and the divisions were separate, with sales and marketing where they belonged: in the field, away from the laboratories.

Profits in the pharmaceutical industry have traditionally been far higher than industrial averages, and because pharmaceuticals are vital to the public interest, special regulatory attention has been focused upon pricing and competition in the industry since the late 1950s. In 1984, the Hatch–Waxman Act permitted generics to cut into patented drug profits. At the same time competition, including from smaller start-ups, reduced the amount of time successful drugs could enjoy cash cow status. Managed care organizations became wiser at restricting their formularies and bargaining over the price of drugs purchased in volume. Most importantly, competitors such as Pfizer were stepping up their investments in sales and marketing. To keep profits high, Merck felt it had to do the same.

The intrusion and then market-share triumph of Pfizer's me-too cholesterol drug, Lipitor, over Merck's Zocor (Merck had pioneered the category with Mevacor), was a compelling signal to the company that marketing was king. Sales forces throughout the industry more than doubled during the 1990s. Also in the 1990s, restrictions on direct-to-consumer advertising were lifted. This positively affected the firm's possibilities for expanding its market base, and brought marketing considerations to higher status in the company.

In 1994, Merck's new CEO, Ray Gilmartin, scrapped the executive vice president of human health position and replaced it with three marketing presidents. Fond of brandable acronyms, Gilmartin introduced PACE, the Product and Cycle Time Excellence model for drug development. In this new structure, marketers were allotted dedicated budgets for Phase V, or post-marketing research. Marketers could now design and conduct their own trials, or "label change studies," with more or less only advisory input from Merck Research Labs, the traditional R&D executives and firm leaders. Basic research is said to have fled the company. Like many of its competitors, Merck was reduced to being a commercializing agent for research conducted outside the firm.

* Much of the above sketch is derived from Gilbert and Sarkar's discussion (2005) in *Merck: Conflict and Change*.

---

paper trail for future citations. Company sponsored and ghostwritten publications have lately become the centerpiece of public debates over conflicts of interest between pharmaceutical manufacturers and medical research (Healy and Cattell, 2003; Moffat and Elliott, 2005; Smith, 2005; Healy, 2006a, 2006b; Sismondo, 2007). A substantial portion of the content of leading medical journals originates in corporate publication-planning offices and subcontractors

(Blumsohn, 2006; Lexchin and Light, 2006; Sismondo, 2009*a*), a fact that has resulted in so many instances of malfeasance that Washington lawmakers on both sides of the aisle (Henry Waxman, D-California; Charles Grassley, R-Iowa) have taken up the cause of fighting it. As I was writing this chapter, Merck was discovered to have produced an entire journal (*The Australasian Journal of Bone and Joint Medicine*) mimicking or posing as an independent peer review publication but whose sole purpose was to promote Fosamax (for osteoporosis) and Vioxx.[13]

The point is, Simon and Kotler are not speaking the language of cooperation between marketing and science but of the strategic integration of the two at every step *under the direction of marketing*. Marketing must *own* the pipeline, not react to its outcomes. As one of the executives from the aforementioned pharmaceutical roundtable said, "The companies that do it right don't talk about R&D and marketing. If you can get the key people to all be brand managers—to look for brands rather than just compounds.... Branding is about the ownership of ideas. The Cox-2 inhibitors are the most recent examples of owning the science from day one." (Cox-2 inhibitors, of course, refer to Vioxx, Celebrex, and Bextra, all three of which have been associated with unethical marketing practices.) Box 12.2 describes the reorganization of Merck to accommodate marketing integration.

Forms of Value: Consequences of Marketing's Aim to Control the Process

Clinical trials are the most credible and powerful form of marketing in the pre-launch period. (Simon and Kotler, 2003: 147)[14]

Each time I have explained the integration process, or even shown the above quote to physicians and independent scientists, my audience has been aghast. Why? Simon and Kotler might be amazed to hear this report, as might the pharmaceutical marketers they advise, since they see themselves as being involved only in clever and virtuous business—doing good while doing well, as the saying goes. The explanation lies in the astonishing gap that has opened up between two ways of looking at medicine, representing two mutually exclusive or even opposed systems of value. The distinction is between how medical science views research and how marketers do.

I have spoken of value. Value is the most loaded cultural referent in the world. It is because of its ability to signify all that is important and good to one cultural community and the exact opposite to its neighbor. What is meaningful to marketers, in this case, may be useless or meaningless to science and vice versa. Medical scientific value is not ontologically variable; value consists in a discovery's capacity to explain phenomena verifiably and then be applied impartially to reduce human suffering from the diseases that afflict us. Marketing value, by contrast, is fluid, relative, and contingent upon perceived utility. Brands are a pure example of marketing value in so far as a brand's importance lies first in the realm of consumer perception, and not in the tangible benefits of the product itself. Marketing value is measured in accordance with its ability to achieve product differentiation, which refers to the process of making one's product offering appear unique and superior to those of one's competitors in the marketplace. In pharmaceuticals, product differentiation means as against other options available in the treatment market, whether these are other drugs, diet and exercise, behavioral therapy, or just waiting.

In the wake of integration of marketing and R&D across the entire face of contemporary commercialized medicine, scientific innovation has suffered. In the words of a 2006 US Government Accountability Office Report to Congress, "Innovation in the pharmaceutical industry has become stagnant." Merrill Goozner, head of the Center for Science in the Public Interest, says, "Three out of every four drug applications involve drugs that either replicated the action of medicines already on the market or were new formulations that at best added minor conveniences for patients and doctors." Another study revises the estimate of non-breakthrough applications to 92 percent (see also Martin et al., 2006).[15] The terms "innovation" and "therapeutic breakthrough" have themselves been aggressively negotiated and compromised in regulatory contexts to accommodate the marketing objectives of blockbuster-driven applicants. Immoderate use of the terms likewise conforms to the public's faith in the industry's inclination and capacity to produce life-saving drugs on a broad, which is to say blockbuster, scale (Abraham and Davis n.d.).

And yet, the relationship between industry and scientific (as against marketing) innovation is more tenuous than ever. In his book, *The $800 Million: The Truth Behind the Cost of New Drugs*, Goozner argues that there has been a misperception about the sources of scientific creativity in the pharmaceutical and biotech industries.

> By recounting the history of several of the most significant new drugs of the past two decades, this book shows that the inception of drugs which have truly made a difference in recent years and which will make a difference in the twenty-first century can almost always be found in the vast biomedical research enterprise funded by the federal government. (Goozner, 2004: 8)

In effect, Goozner is telling us that the public pays three times for pharmaceutical invention. First, through taxes we pay for the primary research conducted mainly in universities and National Institute of Health (NIH) labs. Second, as consumers we pay through insurance and other prescription plans for the commercialization, synthesis/manufacture, and (especially) marketing of the drug. Third, through a scheme of in-advance public underwriting for what

Goozner calls "biohype" research, the public pocket is picked by the influence of six hundred pharma lobbyists on Capitol Hill who secure high prices for their drugs through the ironically specious claim that "without high prices, the innovation that led to new medicine would dry up" (2004: 7).

For pharmaceutical marketers, as we have seen to especially great effect since the early 1990s, pharmaceutical value has often been a marketing proposition, not a scientific one. The high proportion of lifestyle and "me-too" drugs (plus new molecular entities offering no improvement over prior ones), which describes derivatives or salts of existing compounds, being proposed to and approved by the FDA is in my view a direct outcome of the integration of marketing and R&D. The sense of the very expression "me too" is telling. Marketers regard the pursuit of me-toos (and line extension products) as a positive marketing option associated with sub-segmentation of existing markets and the pursuit of brand values. In medicine, me-too products are trivial variations of drugs already on the market, imitative, and therefore the opposite of innovation. There is little evidence for the argument that me-toos offer significant therapeutic options in most classes of medicines (to accommodate different patients' tolerance and receptivity, for instance) (see e.g., Rosenheck et al., 2008; see also Angell, 2004; Avorn, 2004), and the economic arguments that they increase competitively borne innovation and result in lower prices appear at this point to be groundless. Drugs that by design are "meaninglessly differentiated" (Carpenter et al., 1994), such as those in which a molecule is altered to create a new product or to extend a patent but the functional properties of the drug remain unchanged, are valid marketing entities but empty medical ones.[16] This may be a harmless marketing trick in most consumer goods areas, but in medicine the societal and scientific opportunity costs need to be accounted for, including the upward drive of health-care costs resulting from artificially stimulated demand for health-care products.

While the public seems not to question the notion that any product that succeeds in the market must be innovative indeed, the reality is that the most successful pharmaceutical products today bear the mark not of scientific innovation but of effective marketing. Pfizer's Lipitor was the sixth statin (cholesterol-lowering medication) on the market, for instance, but with an estimated $1.3 billion invested by Pfizer in 2002 alone (one hundred times the health budget for Haiti in the same year,[17] or roughly the equivalent of the NIH budget for research into Alzheimer's disease, arthritis, autism, epilepsy, influenza, multiple sclerosis, sickle cell disease, and spinal chord injury combined) toward increasing the public's awareness of the dangers of hypercholesteremia, the entire market enjoyed double-digit growth for half a decade.[18] Sales of Lipitor topped $14.3 billion in 2006.

Marketing is designed specifically to further excite people's hopes. In the all-out push to create blockbusters, me-too drugs are billed as breakthroughs and modest advances are overblown. Thus do we have in the United States an "Overdosed," "Overtreated," "Rx Generation", to refer to the titles of three recent bestsellers. Even for new drugs that do offer improvements, excessive marketing results in inappropriate prescriptions and the consequent deterioration of the drugs' benefit/risk profile in the population. Public safety, health budgets, innovation, and the integrity and autonomy of the medical profession suffer simultaneously even while profits soar and the power of marketers occludes that of the scientists, ensuring the continuation of the current predicament.

In short, in the midst of a teeming sea of new products surrounded by enough hype to raise hopes for the dead, we find fewer and fewer expressions of scientific value—an outright cure for dread disease X, or a frank evaluation of the many-sided approaches to delaying the onset of grave diseases or managing the ones for which our science has not yet discerned a path to cure. Instead, we find in increasing abundance the promotion of marketing-created values and the gargantuan effort to demonstrate these to the different stakeholders whose cooperation is required for the successful launching of the product (Healy, 2006a; Applbaum, 2009, 2010)—a procedure Mr Kotler elsewhere advocated under the term "megamarketing" (1986). Marketing and scientific concepts of value can overlap, but they do not necessarily have to. We have watched this split open up precisely in the era of integration. For what is meaningful to marketers in terms of value and usefulness has become often meaningless, sometimes dangerous, and always costly to everyone else.

The widespread contravention of ethics in the industry should be regarded as a symptom of decay that has accompanied marketing's triumph at broadening its definition of value to this domain. Fresh wrongdoings are being called out with disquieting regularity in regards to every stage of drug development and promotion. The briefest list includes campaigns to "ghost manage" the conduct of basic science; to rig clinical trials and to run trials in poor countries where ethical oversight is weak; to conceal safety data from the FDA, the public, and from doctors; to knowingly market medical conditions far beyond their natural incidence; to sway public health criteria for the threshold of disease risk; and to lure some of the nation's most respected doctors into risky off-label promotion schemes (see e.g., Antonuccio et al., 2003; Healy, 2003, 2006c, 2007; Elliott, 2004, 2006, 2010; Fishman, 2004; Medawar and Hardon, 2004; Oldani, 2004; Sismondo, 2004, 2009b; Ferner, 2005; Lacasse and Leo, 2005; Moynihan and Henry, 2006; Phillips, 2006; Brody, 2007; Lane, 2007; Petryna 2009).[19] Because clinical trials have become the gatekeepers as well as the advertising tools with which drugs are now sold (per the Simon/Kotler epigram), ownership of trials and control over their data are vital to drug companies. The broadness of label indications for a drug is its source of wealth. As a senior executive at Merck comments, "In the past, the molecule was the product, but

289

now the label is the product" (Gilbert and Sarkar, 2005: 6). For this reason, Healy cautions,

> Clinical trial data are increasingly linked to pharmaceutical companies and this data appears shot through with problems stemming from the non-reporting of trials or ghostwriting of those that are published. [B]ecause of these ambiguities, it is not inconceivable that an ever-closer adherence to what may appear to the best evidence could lead to a deterioration in the health of patients. (Healy, 2009: 18)

Put otherwise, the substitution of scientific truths for marketing ones has profound consequences for public health, because of its reliance upon disinterested scientific data and analysis.

Pre-commercial planning and marketing is one policy among others one could cite to demonstrate how the marketing-driven outlook in pharmaceutical companies today pushes these enterprises toward fulfilling their own efficiencies at the expense of public health. What emerges is a system in which the scientific search for cures and the marketing-led pursuit of meeting unmet medical needs stand not in cooperative tandem one with the other, but in direct competition—a competition that reaches directly into companies such as Merck and drains their once exceptional research prowess. That there is an incompatibility between medical scientific and pharmaceutical marketing-defined medical values may be intuited by the magnitude of the push with which marketing versions of science have to be promoted. In addition to all the publication planning (i.e., ghostwriting), key opinion leader cultivation, and guidelines symposia, there is today in the United States approximately one drug rep for every six physicians.

Reformers focus on the implications for drug costs of this statistic; less commonly is it pointed out that breakthrough drugs that work would hardly need that much marketing. They would, as in Peter Drucker's optimistic scenario, sell themselves. The process describes a vicious cycle: The less innovative the product, the more marketing push becomes necessary. The more marketing there is, the more its budget competes with that of R&D, the less innovation is nurtured. Marc-André Gagnon and Joel Lexchin conclude that the US pharmaceutical industry spends nearly twice as much on marketing as on R&D (2008). The foregoing analysis suggests that this figure must be revised sharply upward because much of what is classified as R&D spending (including competitive drug trials, publication planning, and post-marketing surveys) is devoted to non-exploratory efforts to improve market share or to maintain a hold on profits associated with impending patent expiries. These can be labeled "adjunct-to-marketing" R&D as opposed to "exploratory" R&D activities. Together with me-too drug research, adjunct-to-marketing R&D greatly overshadows the conduct of exploratory science in all the major pharmaceutical companies. Indeed, quibbling over the relative investment numbers of marketing vs. R&D may be beside the point, because, realistically the two have already been integrated under the direction of marketing.

As an "inside marketing" project, discussion of contrasting forms of value brings us closer to seeking an understanding on the level of system and norms rather than motivations in evaluating contemporary pharmaceutical industry actors. One should dwell less on ethical violations than on the conditions that have given rise to these. Excessive competition, the patent system, and marketing norms each play an integral role. The fact that the instances of pharmaceutical industry corruption that are at present being exposed almost weekly represent legal and ethical violations but not contraventions of good marketing practice alert us to the divergence of value systems. This is why one fails to come across any meaningful self-examination in the industry trade literature. Internal critics agree that misconduct contributes to a poor industry image, which they fear will lead to shrinking pharmaceutical profits in the future. But is this genuinely an ethical argument?

One marketing scholar who purports to be taking an ethical stance argues that the solution to the drug industry's dismal public image and to "the imperfect alignment of private profit-maximizing objectives with public health needs" (Santoro et al., 2005: 4) is more, not less, marketing involvement. "[T]o repair their relationship with society in a sustainable manner, drug companies must learn to think of diverse groups as active partners in the process of drug development and sales" (Santoro et al., 2005: 5). In other words, only once all external stakeholders are acquiescent with the intended program, when even the industry's natural opponents are brought unwittingly "on board," criticism will be neutralized and the industry will be able operate in a frictionless world of limitless drug sales. The tactics for greater inclusion of the drug industry's publics are familiar to students of marketing as "relationship marketing" and "value co-creation" programs, which are extensions of the promotional efforts of the companies to convince the public that the drug company's truth is their truth. The goal is not to bridge the private maximizing vs. public health divide through ethical reform and compromises to corporate power, but to bring back into "alignment" the public's misapprehension of the actual compatibility of the two domains. The problem, in sum, boils down to an image issue that can be corrected through an industry-wide public relations campaign. The incipient arm of the campaign is "industry branding"—a term critics can well be forgiven for seeing as an ominous sign of oligopoly. At the least, it is fair to say that we are witnessing in this approach another instance of marketing advocacy that would drive us further from rather than toward a humanistic outcome.

Jerome Kassirer, former editor of the *New England Journal of Medicine*, offered this simple review of Santoro's volume (2007):

There is virtually no mention of the pharmaceutical industry's major ethical lapses, such as hiring ghostwriters to write favourable journal articles, rigging study designs to produce favourable results, hiding unflattering results, failing to publish negative findings, promoting off-label drug use, giving bribes and kickbacks in return for promises to prescribe, and intimidating researchers whose results counter a company's interests. There is also little mention of shameless attempts by manufacturers to extend their monopolies, to block the production and sale of generic drugs, to put undue influence on the US Food and Drug Administration (FDA), to buy off large cadres of doctors, to promote drugs to treat social conditions, and to spend more money on marketing than on research—and, at the end of the day, to produce a shrinking list of truly innovative, clinically useful drugs. Inexplicably, with minor exceptions, most of the chapters have little relevance to the ethics of pharmaceutical companies.

The absence of attention in Santoro's volume to the industry's ethical lapses appears less inexplicable once one observes that marketing values are distinct from those of medicine and public health, and that ethics, which for present purposes might be classified under humanistic values, are subordinated to marketing advocacy. It is difficult in this case to see how humanistic and marketing goals can coincide.

Is Marketing Humanism Possible?

In pharmaceuticals, ethical violations, decline in innovation, and skyrocketing costs are combined symptoms of the institutionalization of an overly keen and insufficiently monitored adoption of marketing-driven culture in the industry. Marketing has broadened itself in an uncontrolled fashion and the result is the opposite of what a marketing humanist might hope for.

Can there be a valid marketing humanism? Can the marketing concept be applied to the public interest? Perhaps it can in a limited way, but not as marketing theorists to date have tended to conceive of it. Marketing humanists seem to want to say that marketing is just a tool, unyoked to culturally particular values or theories of human needs and satisfactions. Marketing, they say, is like fire that can be put to use in both creation and destruction. Under shelter of the fire analogy, even the marketing humanist who is willing to concede that pharmaceutical marketing practices have lately not exerted a salubrious influence, will nevertheless say, "Yes, marketing has run amok in this case, like a fire out of control, but it is not the fault of marketing theory but of certain marketing practitioners. Marketing is still nothing more than a conceptual tool."

Conceptual tools, however, *are* theories, if by theory we mean how we exclude unfitting elements in our explanation of reality. No tool can be universally applied to all tasks, just as there can be no theory or model of everything that is not reductive to nonsense. For instance, only a map that is the exact size of the United States can represent the United States exactly. When you reduce the map to the size of a blackboard or a sheet of paper, you are performing both an act of symbolization, since symbols on the map "stand for" things that are not physically present, and you are imposing one cartographic model or another to achieve your purpose—the criteria by which you exclude data constitutes your theory. Marketing-as-tool is no different, even in the absence of professional self-reflection on that point.

The limitation of marketing-as-universal-tool, and with it the possibility to be broadened to humanistic ends, lies in the discipline's implicit core theory of the human experience. Few marketing theorists and practitioners conceive of the human being in broader terms than that which is signified by the construct of "consumer." Yes, we may all now be consumers of the fruits of capitalist production, but that is not the sum of who we are, nor is it an adequate model for explaining how people have satisfied even their creaturely requirements in other times and places.

Though it should hardly require saying, the point is that not all of our needs, hopes, wishes, fears, beliefs, imaginations, creativities, affections, dislikes, curiosities, greeds, passions, sympathies, values, loyalties, prejudices, traditions, . . . , etc., are reducible or even translatable to that one component of our experience described by the word "consumer" so as to be properly served by a marketer's methods of evaluating and meeting us on those terms alone. The variegated conditions and possibilities of human experience have given birth to a matching range of cultural, social and moral institutions, and traditions, not nearly all voluntary or reducible to lifestyle, choice, and the pursuit of satisfactions in a consumer logic. When marketing humanists come to grasp the true limitations of the consumer model for explaining and satisfying human needs, when they stand prepared, in other words, to recognize the hazards of "broadening the marketing concept" too far, they may cease to appear to the rest of us to be marketing advocates, and may join the ranks of true humanists.

Notes

1. The authors were addressing themselves to an audience of marketing specialists. The paper was published in the *Journal of Marketing*, which in 1969 may have had a broader readership among marketing practitioners than is true today, but it was essentially trade talk, not a forum for philosophy and public affairs. The "marketing insider" orientation is reflected in the split I see in their paper between a

marketing humanist program, on the one hand, and the subtext of self-promotion of the field of marketing itself (or marketing advocacy) on the other.

2. Drucker says: "The aim of marketing is to make selling superfluous. The aim is to know and understand the customer so well that the product or service fits . . . and sells itself." (1973).

3. This is what Kotler and Levy have to say, for instance, about why people give charity—a point of view they hoped would be installed in charities with the broadening of the marketing concept to this domain: "Fund raisers have learned that people give because they are getting something. Many give to community chests to relieve a sense of guilt because of their elevated state compared to the needy. Many give to medical charities to relieve a sense of fear that they may be struck by a disease whose cure has not yet been found. Some give to feel pride. Fund raisers have stressed the importance of identifying the motives operating in the marketplace of givers as a basis for planning drives" (Kotler and Levy, 1969: 14).

4. Organisation for Economic Co-operation and Development web site http://www.oecd.org/dataoecd/46/2/38980580.pdf, accessed March 18, 2009.

5. MCOL website http://www.mcareol.com/mcolfree/mcolfre1/visiongain/blockbuster.htm, accessed June 17, 2008.

6. This estimate is based upon reports published by IMS Health and available at IMS Health Website www.imshealth.com, accessed June 28, 2008.

7. That people may come to identify closely with or feel the reality of abstract measures of their health, such as high cholesterol, is testament to human suggestibility, not evidence of unconscious needs, as some consultants would like us to believe (e.g., Zaltman & Zaltman, 2008).

8. The juvenile studies conducted at MGH spoken about at the end of the text box were conducted by Joseph Biederman (and his colleagues) who is currently under investigation for the $1.6 million in fees accepted from the pharmaceutical industry during the course of these researches. See, for example, http://www.nytimes.com/2008/06/08/us/08conflict.html.

9. L3 HealthCare Marketing Website http://www.l3hm.com/documents/L3_PreCommercialWhitepaper0508.pdf, accessed June 30, 2008, p. 1.

10. PharmExec.com website http://pharmexec.findpharma.com/pharmexec/Current+Issue/When-Worlds-Collide/ArticleLong/Article/detail/29963, accessed October 13, 2008.

11. Trovan later became infamous for the ethical research abuses associated with its testing practices in Nigeria (Petryna, 2005).

12. The emphasis in contemporary marketing theory on "marketing value chains" and on "value co-creation" with consumers is one more iteration of the free will/determinism-like tension between the effort to retain control over defining product value at every stage of the marketing process at the same time—or even by means of—encouraging consumer participation in the value creation process. See Zwick et al. (2008) for a thoughtful discussion of this complex subject.

13. Bob Grant (2009) "Merck Published Fake Journal" TheScientist.Com website http://www.the-scientist.com/blog/display/55671/, accessed July 25, 2009. Ross et al. (2008) explore the consequences of other ghostwriting activities surrounding Vioxx.

14. Simon and Kotler (2003), Free Press, p. 147.
15. Gooznews on Health website www.gooznews.com/archives/000573.html, accessed June 20, 2008. http://yaleglobal.yale.edu/display.article?id=5678, accessed August 7, 2008.
16. Examples of this include Prilosec → Nexium, all of the isomers of antidepressants—desvenlafaxine (Pristiq), escitalopram (Lexapro), and the metabolites—paliperidone (Invega), and numerous others.
17. ImpactAIDS website http://www.impactaids.org.uk/lancet363.htm, accessed June 23, 2008.
18. Sharon, Reier "Blockbuster Drugs: Take the Hype in Small Doses." *International Herald Tribune* March 1, 2003. http://www.iht.com/articles/2003/03/01/mdrug_ed3_.php?page=2, accessed June 20, 2008.
Kolata, Gina. 7/13/2004. "Experts Set Lower Low for Levels of Cholesterol." *New York Times* http://query.nytimes.com/gst/fullpage.html?res=9C00E5DE1F3BF930-A25754C0A9629C8B63, accessed June 23, 2008.
19. A growing library of news reports and other mass publications are available at the Healthy Skepticism library: http://www.healthyskepticism.org/library.php

References

Abraham, J., and Davis, C. *Deconstructing Pharmaceutical "Science", "Innovation", and "Therapeutic Breakthrough": A Case Study in the Ideologies and Realities of Drug Regulation in the US and the Supranational EU.* Manuscript.

Angell, M. (2004) *The Truth About the Drug Companies: How they Deceive us and What to do About it.* New York: Random House.

Angelmar, R., Angelmar, S., and Kane, L. (2007) "Building Strong Condition Brands." *Journal of Medical Marketing,* 7(4): 341–51.

Antonuccio, D.O., Danton, W.G., and McClanahan, T.M. (2003) "Psychology in the Prescription Era: Building a Firewall between Marketing and Science." *American Psychologist,* 58: 1028–43.

Applbaum, K. (1998) "Sweetness of Salvation: Consumer Marketing and the Liberal-bourgeois Theory of Needs." *Curent Anthropology,* 39:323–49.

—— (2004) *The Marketing Era: From Professional Practice to Global Provisioning.* New York: Routledge.

——(2009) "Getting to Yes: Power and the Creation of a Psychopharmaceutical Blockbuster." *Culture, Medicine and Psychiatry,* 33(2): 185–215.

——(2010) "Shadow Science: Zyprexa, Eli Lilly and Globalization of Pharmaceutical Damage Control. *BioSocieties,* 5: 236–55.

Avorn, J. (2004) *Powerful Medicines: The Benefits, Risks, and Costs of Prescription Drugs.* New York: Knopf.

Bartels, R. (1974) "The Identity Crisis in Marketing." *Journal of Marketing,* 38: 73–6.

Blumsohn, A. (2006) "Authorship, Ghost-science, Access to Data and Control of the Pharmaceutical Scientific Literature: Who Stands behind the Word?" *AAAS Professional Ethics Report,* 29(3): 1–4.

Brody, H. (2007) *Hooked: Ethics, the Medical Profession, and the Pharmaceutical Industry.* New York, NY: Rowman and Littlefield.

Carpenter, G.S., Glazer, R., and Nakamoto, K. (1994) "Meaningful Brands from Meaningless Differentiation: The Dependence on Irrelevant Attributes." *Journal of Marketing Research*, 31: 339–50.

Carrier, J., ed. (1997) *Meanings of the Market: The Free Market in Western Culture.* Oxford: Berg.

Conrad, P., and Leiter, V. (2004) "Medicalization, Markets and Consumers." *Journal of Health and Social Behavior*, 45: 158–76.

Critser, G. (2005) *Generation Rx.* New York: Houghton Mifflin.

Currie, J. (2009) "The Marketisation of Depression: Prescribing Ssri Antidepressants to Women." Women and Health Protection Website, http://www.whp-apsf.ca/pdf/SSRIs.pdf, accessed August 2009.

Drucker, P. (1958) "Marketing and Economic Development." *Journal of Marketing*, 22: 252–9.

——(1973) *Management: Tasks, Responsibilities, Practies.* New York: Harper and Row.

Elliott, C. (2006) "The Drug Pushers." *Atlantic Monthly* (April): 2–13.

——(2004) "Pharma Goes to the Laundry: Public Relations and the Business of Medical Education." *Hastings Center Report*, 34(5): 18–23.

——(2010) "Making a Killing." *Mother Jones* (September/Ocotober): 55–63.

Ferner, R.E. (2005) "Wide Ranging Report Identifies Many Areas of Influence and Distortion." *BMJ*, 330: 855–6.

Fishman, J. (2004) "Manufacturing Desire: The Commodification of Female Sexual Dysfunction." *Social Studies of Science*, 34(2): 187–218.

Gagnon, M.A., and Lexchin, J. (2008) "The Cost of Pushing Pills: A New Estimate of Pharmaceutical Promotion Expenditures in the United States." *PLoS Medicine*, 5(1): e1.

Gilbert, C., and Sarkar, R.G. (2005) *Merck: Conflict and Change.* Boston: Harvard Business School Publishing.

Goozner, M. (2004) *The $800 Million Pill.* Berkeley: University of California Press.

Gray, J. (2000) *False Dawn.* New York: New Press.

Greene, J. (2007) *Prescribing by Numbers.* Baltimore: Johns Hopkins University Press.

Hacking, I. (1999) "Madness: Biological or Constructed?" In I. Hacking, ed. *The Social Construction of What?* Cambridge, MA: Harvard University Press, pp. 100–24.

Healy, D. (1997) *The Antidepressant Era.* Cambridge: Harvard University Press.

——(2002) *The Creation of Psychopharmacology.* Cambridge: Harvard University Press.

——(2003) *Let Them Eat Prozac.* Toronto, ON: James Lorimer & Co.

——(2006a) "Manufacturing Consensus." *Culture, Medicine and Psychiatry*, 30: 135–56.

——(2006b) "The New Medical Oikumene." In A. Petryna, A. Lakoff, and A. Kleinman, eds. *Global Pharmaceuticals: Ethics, Markets, Practices.* Durham, NC: Duke University Press, pp. 61–84.

——(2006c) "The Latest Mania: Selling Bipolar Disorder." *PLoS Medicine*, 3(4): e185.

——(2007) "The Engineers of Human Souls & Academia." *Epidemiologia e Psichiatria Sociale*, 16(3): 205–11.

——(2009) "Trussed in Evidence? Ambiguities at the Interface between Clinical Evidence and Clinical Practice." *Transcultural Psychiatry*, 46(1): 16–37.

——and Cattell, D. (2003) "Interface between Authorship, Industry and Science in the Domain of Therapeutics." *British Journal of Psychiatry*, 183: 22–7.

——and Le Noury, J. (2007) "Pediatric Bipolar Disorder: An Object of Study in the Creation of an Illness." *International Journal of Risk & Safety in Medicine*, 19: 209–21.

Kassirer, J. (2007) "Pharmaceutical Ethics? Open Medicine 1(1)." Open Medicine Website http://www.openmedicine.ca/article/view/16/2.

Kohli, A.K., and Jaworski, B.J. (1990) "Market Orientation: The Construct, Research Propositions and Managerial Implications." *Journal of Marketing*, 54(2): 1–18.

Kotler, P. (1986) "Megamarketing."*Harvard Business Review*, vol. 81, 3 (March/April).

——(1991) *Marketing Management: Analysis, Planning, Implementation and Control.* Englewood Cliffs, NJ: Prentice-Hall.

——and Levy, S.J. (1969) "Broadening the Concept of Marketing." *Journal of Marketing* 33(1): 10–15.

Lacasse, J.R., and Leo, J. (2005) "Serotonin and Depression: A Disconnect between the Advertisements and the Scientific Literature." *PLoS Medicine*, 2(12): e392.

Lane, C. (2007) *Shyness: How Normal Behavior Became a Sickness.* New Haven, CT: Yale University Press.

Leibing, A. (2009) "Tense Prescriptions? Alzheimer's Medications and the Anthropology of Uncertainty." *Transcultural Psychiatry*, 46(1): 180–206.

Levitt, T. (1960) "Marketing Myopia." *Harvard Business Review*, 38: 45–56.

Lexchin, J., and Light, D. (2006) "Commercial Influence and the Content of Medical Journals." *British Medical Journal*, 332: 1444–7.

Martin, P., Abraham, J., Davis, C., and Kraft, A. (2006) "Understanding the 'Productivity Crisis' in the Pharmaceutical Industry: Over-regulation or Lack of Innovation?" In A. Webster, ed. *New Technologies in Health Care.* Basingstoke: Palgrave Macmillan.

Medawar, C., and Hardon, A. (2004) *Medicines out of Control? Antidepressants and the Conspiracy of Goodwill.* Amsterdam: Aksant Academic Publishers.

Moffatt, B., and Elliott, C. (2005) "Ghost Marketing: Pharmaceutical Companies and Ghostwritten Journal Articles." *Perspectives in Biology and Medicine*, 50(1): 18–31.

Moynihan, R., and Cassels, A. (2005) *Selling Sickness: How the World's Biggest Pharmaceutical Companies are Turning us all into Patients.* New York: Nation Books.

——and Henry, D. (2006) "The Fight against Disease Mongering: Generating Knowledge for Action." *PLoS Medicine*, 3(4): e191.

Oldani, M. (2004) "Thick Prescriptions: Toward an Interpretation of Pharmaceutical Sales Practices." *Medical Anthropology Quarterly*, 18: 325–56.

Petryna, A. (2005). "Ethical Variability: Drug Development and Globalizing Clinical Trials." *American Ethnologist*, 32(2): 183–97.

——(2009). *When Experiments Travel: Clinical Trials and the Global Search for Human Subjects.* Princeton: Princeton University Press.

Phillips, C.B. (2006) "Medicine Goes to School: Teachers as Sickness Brokers for ADHD." *PLoS Medicine*, 3(4): e182.

Rasmussen, N. (2004) "The Moral Economy of the Drug Company–Medical Scientist Collaboration in Interwar America." *Social Studies of Science*, 34(2): 161–85.

Rosenheck, R.A., Davis, S., Covell, N., Essock, S., Swartz, M., Stroup, S., McEvoy, J., and Lieberman, J. (2008) "Does Switching to a New Antipsychotic Improve Outcomes?" *Schizophrenia Research*, 107(1): 22–9.

Ross, J.S., Hill, K.P., Egilman, D.S., and Krumholz, H.M. (2008) "Guest Authorship and Ghostwriting in Publications Related to Rofecoxib: A Case Study Of Industry Documents from Rofecoxib Litigation." *Journal of the American Medical Association*, 299(15): 1800–12.

Santoro, M.A., and Gorrie, T.M., eds. (2005) *Ethics and the Pharmaceutical Industry*. New York: Cambridge University Press.

Simon, F., and Kotler, P. (2003) *Building Global Biobrands*. New York: Free Press.

Sismondo, S., ed. (2004) *Social Studies of Science* Special Issue on Intersections of Pharmaceutical Research and Marketing, Vol. 34, p. 2.

Sismondo, S. (2007) "Ghost Management: How much of the Medical Literature is Shaped Behind the Scenes by the Pharmaceutical Industry?" *PLoS Medicine*, 4: 9.

——(2009*a*) "Ghosts in the Machine: Publication Planning in the Medical Sciences." *Social Studies of Science*, 39(2): 171–98.

——(2009*b*) "Medical Publishing and the Drug Industry: Is Medical Science for Sale?" *Academic Matters*, May: 8–12.

Smith, R. (2005). "Medical Journals are an Extension of the Marketing Arm of Pharmaceutical Companies." *PLoS Medicine*, 2(5): e138.

Tyrer, P., and Kendall, T. (2009). "The Spurious Advance of Antipsychotic Drug Therapy." *Lancet*, 373. DOI:10.1016/S0140-6736(08)61765-1.

Williams, A. (2006) *A Women's Nonprofit Organization in Crises: An Ethnography of Volunteerism*. Ph.D. dissertation, University of Wisconsin-Milwaukee.

Woloshin, S., and Schwartz, L.M. (2006) "Giving Legs to Restless Legs: A Case Study of how the Media helps make People Sick." *PLoS Medicine* 3(4): e170.

Zaltman, G., and Zaltman, L. (2008) *Marketing Metaphoria: What Deep Metaphors reveal about the Minds of Consumers*. Boston: Harvard Business School Press.

Zwick, D., Bonsu, S.K., and Darmody, A. (2008) "Putting Consumers to Work: 'Co-creation' and New Marketing Govern-mentality." *Journal of Consumer Culture*, 8(2): 163–95.

13

Neoliberal Experiments: Social Marketing and the Governance of Populations

Liz Moor

Introduction

Although social marketing is a well-established sub-specialism of both academic marketing research and professional marketing activity, it has rarely attracted attention from critically minded scholars in other disciplines. Perhaps because marketing that is oriented to social ends appears to be the least controversial aspect of marketing practice, discussion of its precepts, methods, and applications has been largely confined to specialist journals in the areas of health promotion and non-profit sector marketing. Yet there are a number of reasons why social marketing should be of interest to a wider audience: firstly, there are a significant, and growing, number of commercial marketing, advertising, and design agencies doing work for non-profit or public clients;[1] secondly, social marketing often draws heavily on commercial marketing techniques (such as customer research, market segmentation, and analyses of price, competition, and exchange) and thus raises important questions about the diffusion of marketing concepts and the extension of market models to ostensibly non-commercial spheres; thirdly, more and more of the marketing for *commercial* organizations incorporates "social" values in its efforts to build brands and command customer loyalty, further blurring the boundaries between public and private interests. Finally, social marketing is explicitly concerned with the refashioning of publics and populations, and thus relates directly to an analytical tradition interested in modes of governance. From Foucauldian analysis to more recent debates about the governance of consumption or the performativity of markets and economics, the discipline of sociology in particular has long been concerned with the discourses and techniques deployed to govern behavior and shape publics. Social marketing, so I want to claim, is an important contemporary example of such a technique.

In what follows, I develop a critical analysis of social marketing that emphasizes the ways in which particular philosophies of government and models of the individual combine with the use of specific materials and techniques to establish social marketing as a legitimate method of intervening in the governance of populations. I begin by outlining briefly the history of social marketing as a discipline, its relationship to commercial marketing, and its early role in lending legitimacy to commercial marketing while expanding the territory of marketing as a discourse and practice. I also consider some of the key practical and ethical issues that have thus far occupied scholars in social marketing and related areas such as health promotion.

I then move on to consider the diffusion of social marketing more concretely, by outlining the means by which it has been adopted within the UK's National Health Service. Using the case of the National Social Marketing Centre (NSMC) as an example, I describe the effort to turn key concepts and ideas from the literature on social marketing into reality, to promote social marketing as a systematic way of conducting welfare campaigns and interventions, and to devise ways in which this area of practice can reflect upon its own effectiveness. In doing this, I seek to position social marketing as a form of governance involving the deployment and coordination of a variety of actors, representations, techniques, and objects. I go on to suggest that social marketing in Britain has been formulated primarily as a behavioral technique—that is, as an intervention designed not to work on "deep" levels of the human psyche nor upon the social structure in which individuals and groups are enmeshed, but rather on the manifest behaviors of aggregates of individuals. Similarly, I argue that the NSMC's methods for identifying and describing populations, and for working on and measuring them, are also grounded in a market model in which populations are considered above all as consumers rather than, for example, citizens or patients. I explore how this model has worked in practice, briefly outlining a number of small-scale interventions in which participants were invited to "exchange" one form of behavior for another, choose knowledgeably from a variety of alternatives, and track or reflect upon their own behavior over time.

I then outline a variety of ways in which social marketing—as one instance of the diffusion of marketing concepts and ideology—might be understood analytically. I begin by considering the extent to which social marketing can be considered to be a "performative" discipline that brings certain types of social action into being, or whether instead it should be considered as a more limited, contingent, and experimental form of action; this is followed by a consideration of the ways in which social marketing's focus on manifest behavior allows its interventions to be brought more squarely within the frame of economic calculation. I then consider how social marketing might be understood as part of a more general "economization of the social" (Shamir, 2008), before finally outlining some of the ways in which social marketing might be reconceived in the future.

History of Social Marketing

The history of social marketing, both as a part of the academic discipline of marketing and as a set of practical interventions in the social, can be traced to North America in the 1960s and 1970s. As a number of commentators (e.g., Lazer and Kelley, 1973; Desmond, 1998) have pointed out, while early discussions of the subject were concerned with what social marketing could contribute to society, they were also very much interested in what the extension of the "marketing concept" could do for the discipline of marketing itself. At a time of perceived shifts in social values, and widespread skepticism about the activities and effects of big business, social marketing emerged in part as a project with the potential to assuage public fears about the selfishness of business by highlighting its potential social contribution.[2] Social marketing was seen, at least by some of its early theorists, as able to contribute to business success through the social shaping of markets (a happy and healthy population would mean "better" markets), by avoiding negative judgment from the government and citizens, and through extending its own power and jurisdiction relative to that of governments.

Early theories of social marketing also set out a more pragmatic or "common sense" rationale for the extension of marketing concepts and analysis to noncommercial domains. The main thrust of Philip Kotler's early articles (see e.g., Kotler and Levy, 1969; Kotler and Zaltman, 1971) was that sophisticated forms of marketing-like behavior were *already* widely practiced outside of the commercial realm (e.g., in trade unions, government departments, charitable foundations, and educational institutions). In this way, Kotler and others were able to claim that marketing—or at least something like it—must in some sense be a generic concept or "category of human action" (cited in Morgan, 2003: 114). In this context, surely it would be better for society if these diverse but important non-business areas of activity were able to benefit from the insights of academic marketing and market research in a more systematic way. As Kotler and Levy (1969: 15) put it, "the choice facing those who manage nonbusiness organizations is not whether to market or not to market, for no organization can avoid marketing. The choice is whether to do it well or poorly." This formulation of the rationale for social marketing did not go unchallenged (see e.g., Luck, 1969; Laczniak et al., 1979),[3] but by drawing attention to the fact that a variety of "promotional" activities were routinely undertaken by key American institutions such as universities and police forces, Kotler and his co-authors succeeded in raising questions—that persist to this day—about the scope and nature of marketing itself.

These writers were not especially interested in examining *why* such an array of non-market institutions were engaged in promotional activities, or what the effects of their activities might be; rather, their analysis was aimed squarely at establishing and extending the legitimacy and the territory of marketing as a discipline. In its extended form, a small sub-discipline called social marketing would morally underwrite the existence of a much larger discipline of commercial marketing which, by the late 1970s, was already well established as the servant of large corporations (Morgan, 2003). Nonetheless, questions about the appropriate objects of marketing and market analysis were not unprecedented; after all, marketing had not always existed to solve the problems of managers and reproduce the assumptions of laissez-faire economics. In an earlier incarnation, some of the key marketing departments in American universities had played a much more interesting, critical, and socially engaged role of analyzing the functioning of markets and the ways in which they might be distorted by powerful individuals and corporations to the detriment of consumers, workers, and smaller businesses (Desmond, 1998; Morgan, 2003). Yet by the time of these more focused critical discussions in the early 1970s, much of academic marketing had long since moved away from such a role, a shift facilitated in part by the colonization of academic marketing by neoclassical economics, which had little interest in the social constitution of markets, and in part by the influence of experimental psychology, whose conception of human needs was similarly dehistoricized and decontextualized (Morgan, 2003: 124). What this meant, paradoxically, was that the tools and concepts imported from commercial to social marketing lacked a robust *social* basis right from their inception. Their conception of the social, as we shall see, was one that simply involved scaling up from the individual to the mass, construing the objects of social marketing interventions as aggregates of individuals and types.

Social Marketing as Ethical Problem

These early formulations of the "marketing concept" have shaped discussions of social marketing right up to the present day. Much of the scholarly literature on social marketing continues to be concerned with debates about the practical value of extending the "marketing concept" into the social field— that is, with questions about whether the language and concepts of marketing accurately *describe* what those working in charities, health organizations, or other types of social welfare organizations are trying to do and the problems they face (see e.g., Peattie and Peattie, 2003). In particular, authors in this area have repeatedly questioned whether the notion of "market orientation" and the "4Ps" of commercial marketing theory can be meaningfully applied to the social realm, and whether it is useful to think about social marketing campaigns as types of "exchange," offering "products" to "customers" and facing "competition" from other actors.[4] As part of these debates, the scholarly literature on social marketing has also been concerned, virtually since its inception, with the ethical issues raised by adopting such techniques and concepts. Thus writers have considered how the use of the language of marketing impacts upon health workers' relationships with clients, whether the focus on "exchange" will lead to unethical forms of incentivization or manipulation, and whether the adoption of commercial marketing techniques and concepts will replace socio-political rationales for social welfare interventions with a more technical and economistic set of logics (see e.g., Buchanan et al., 1994).

Perhaps most importantly, scholars in this area have raised questions about how far social marketing engages with issues of social and political context, how it understands cause and effect, and the position it adopts, implicitly or explicitly, on the location of responsibility for social problems. As Buchanan et al. (1994) point out, one of the most problematic aspects of the translation of traditional marketing terminology into the social realm (and the field of health promotion in particular) may be its implicit assumption that people's health and well-being is poor either because they lack information or, more typically, because they are not seen as sufficiently "motivated" to change their behavior. This in turn implies that the social context in which they are embedded is not *in itself* a sufficient barrier to explain their poor health. This, the authors claim, represents a betrayal of the ethical foundations of public health promotion, which is often marked—sometimes explicitly in charters and codes of conduct—"by its recognition of the critical effect that environmental conditions create in supporting or undermining health" (Buchanan et al., 1994: 53). In a similar vein, Goldberg (1995) argues that the focus on individual behavior within social marketing imports the biases of commercial marketing and its experimental psychological tradition, and that this makes it "inherently conservative in that it implicitly endorses the status quo with regard to factors associated with the social structure" (Goldberg, 1995: 357). As Wallack et al. (1993) suggest, "downstream" interventions, targeting individuals or small groups, are often made not because they are the most effective ways to act on social welfare issues, but because they are the most acceptable—and the least controversial—to business and the media.

These debates are important and ongoing and, as I suggest below, may turn out to be important in the future development of social marketing theory and research. On the other hand, forms of social marketing that borrow directly from commercial marketing techniques and terminology have already become well established in many countries. This is not simply because these versions are the ones that dominate business schools and marketing departments but also because they sit very neatly with prevailing political philosophies and modes of governance across a range of national contexts. Understanding the diffusion of "marketing ideology" therefore involves tracing the connections and disjunctions between intellectual debates about what social marketing should be and the specific political context through which it takes hold in policy documents, institutions, and forms of practice. In what follows, I try to trace this process in the United Kingdom, focusing firstly on the way in which social marketing has come to occupy a formal role in government health policy, and secondly how it has become involved in the making up of populations.

The Institutionalization of Social Marketing in Britain

The ascendance of social marketing in Britain is closely linked to the context of a broader political rationality—prevalent since the 1980s—emphasizing an expansion of the role of the market and a curtailing of direct state responsibility in the sphere of welfare. Public sector reform under successive governments has been characterized by an emphasis on the creation of markets and "customer choice" in public service delivery and by the assumption that "best value" for taxpayers and users will be delivered by competition between established public providers and private or voluntary sector agencies for contracts (Martin, 2002). In this context, the figure of "the consumer" or "user" of public services has become much more central to government discourse. This figure mirrors the image of consumers in commercial transactions; in place of the supposedly "passive" and "dependent" public service users of the past, the new consumers are seen as "self-directing and self-possessing individuals . . . exercising choice in pursuit of self-realizing lift projects" (Clarke, 2007: 160–1). Their ability to exercise choice is presumed to drive greater efficiency and responsiveness among providers competing to deliver services; at the same time, their more active role is also supposed to remake consumers themselves, as active participants in their own welfare. Indeed it has been made clear that expansion of welfare services cannot continue indefinitely, and that while such services must be made more "efficient" (through the market mechanisms outlined above), individuals must also take on greater responsibility for their own welfare. This process of "responsibilization" (Rose, 1999; Shamir, 2008) is a distinctive feature of neoliberal regimes of government.

These broad political themes have taken on more concrete and programmatic form in various policy documents outlining goals and objectives for health and other public services. And it is here that the evolution of social marketing into a more formal part of government strategy can be seen. A British government white paper from 2004, *Choosing Health*, explicitly positioned the health of a population as, at least in part, the outcome of choices people make *as consumers*, with the role of government correspondingly seen as one of working on consumer demand. In one chapter, the report describes the government's role as one of "promoting health on the principles that commercial markets use," in order to make health into "something people aspire to." This in turn, the report claims, will "create a stronger demand" for health and "influence industry to take more account of broader health issues in what they produce" (Department of Health, 2004: 19). In order to take on this more promotional role, the government sought advice from commercial marketers. One of the commitments of the *Choosing Health* white paper (Department of Health, 2004) was to conduct a national-level review of social marketing and health-related campaigns in England, and to establish an independent body to institute the more systematic use of social marketing principles in British health and health-related campaigns. In the same year, the UK government set up the National Social Marketing Centre (NSMC) as a collaborative venture between the National Health Service (NHS) and National Consumer Council (NCC).

Part of what makes this case so interesting is that it was an explicit effort to apply social marketing principles in a relatively pure form. In order to do this, social marketing had to undergo a process of formalization in which new institutions were created, key personnel identified and trained, principles and theories codified, and materials and technologies assembled and deployed in particular ways. A second report, *It's our health!* (National Consumer Council, 2006), outlined twenty-two operational principles, and established a further fifty-six operational objectives for social marketing in Britain, including the setting up of institutions, the development of models, theories, materials and technologies, the establishment of knowledge centers and training facilities, and the institution of particular types of evaluation and measurement techniques. Thus the NSMC began to identify a series of partner agencies, including a roster of social marketing consultancies and a university network of researchers and practitioners. It also began to develop a set of materials and technologies to support social marketing, including an "e-calendar" of health-related programs and events, a national health communications guide, an archive of exemplary social marketing-based health campaigns, and various other techniques and mechanisms for facilitating coordination between agencies. It also sought to develop and consolidate a knowledge base for social marketing through a series of training projects to build capacity, including resources to develop academic research, the setting up of seminars and conferences, the use of information and communication technologies, and the integration of social marketing training into the "core skills and competencies" frameworks for NHS staff.

As these developments suggest, the diffusion of marketing concepts and ideology is not a straightforward matter, but rather is a process, which, like other forms of governance, involves a "complex assemblages of diverse forces—legal, architectural, professional, administrative, financial, judgemental—such that aspects of the decisions and actions of individuals, groups, organizations and populations come to be understood and regulated in relation to authoritative criteria" (Miller and Rose, 2008: 63). Indeed although the extension of the marketing concept is partly an effect of the discipline's own ability to attach itself to new areas, it is also facilitated by trends in contemporary governance, which increasingly relies on the expertise and administrative capacities of external authorities—which in this case include not only marketing professionals, but also academics, researchers, and health service staff.

Looking at social marketing in this way also reveals the sense in which it is not simply a body of knowledge *about* the world, but also a form of action that is *constitutive* of the spheres in which it seeks to intervene (see e.g., Slater, 2002; MacKenzie et al., 2007). This is especially clear in the case of the NSMC, which, as I have suggested above, was given the authority to constitute itself as a source of knowledge and expertise, to construct various populations (including health-care professionals as well as unhealthy populations) as legitimate objects of that authority, and to seek to remake those object-worlds in its own image. This project does not simply involve human actors but also makes use of materials and technologies—such as electronic archives, guideline booklets, and tracking methods—which may also be said to have agency in the sense of the capacity to intervene in the construction of particular sites of expertise (Muniesa et al., 2007).

Social Marketing and the Making up of Populations

In its early stages, then, social marketing in Britain has involved a process of formalization in which new institutions were created and invested with authority, and in which those institutions, in turn, have been able to influence the activities of other actors such as academic researchers and health-care professionals. Yet for social marketing to play an active role in the reshaping of populations, it must produce a systematic way of identifying and describing those populations, and then outline a set of ways for working on them and for measuring the effectiveness of such interventions. In the case of the NSMC, this has been organized through the use of fixed criteria in the planning and conduct of social marketing campaigns. These criteria were established in the NSMC's founding report, and adapted from Alan Andreasen's original guidelines (2002), and all social marketing campaigns must demonstrate use of all eight criteria in order to be entered into the NSMC's "archive" of social marketing projects. They include: a "customer orientation" in the research and planning of interventions; the development of "deep insights" into behavior and motivation; a focus on "actionable and measurable behavioural goals"; a grounding in one or more behavioral-based theories; an analysis of the intervention in terms of the "exchange" being proposed; an analysis of the "competition" for the program (i.e., what "competes" for the time and attention of the proposed audience); a segmented and targeted approach based on psychographic and lifestyle data as well as demographic information; and finally a "methods mix" oriented to some combination of informing, supporting, regulating, or adjusting the environment.

Thus, for example, in a campaign aimed at promoting healthy eating among young children, the "exchange" element of the program involved giving small tokens such as stickers and certificates as rewards for "good behavior" and trying new foods, while the "competition" was understood as "peer pressure" and the fact that children had a "brand allegiance" to unhealthy foods.[5] An intervention based on sexual health screening involved forms of "customer orientation" through the use interviews and questionnaires and the testing of logos and websites in focus groups. Similarly in a campaign aimed at raising awareness of alcohol-related health risks and encouraging people to take "ownership" of those risks, segmentation was based on psychographic categories such as "depressed drinker," "conformist drinker," and "macho drinker," while the "methods mix" included telephone helplines, self-help manuals, and websites for identifying risk levels. Finally, in a campaign aimed at increasing people's levels of physical activity, the "behavioral goals" were to increase the numbers of people who exercised for thirty minutes five times a week, and the underlying "theory" was that of goal setting.

Clearly some of these examples are open to the types of criticism that have already made by writers in the field of health promotion. Using an exchange-based system of rewards to encourage young people to eat certain foods, for example, raises ethical questions about manipulation and largely ignores the social and economic context in which families make food choices. Similarly, positioning major fast food brands as simply another form of "competition" does nothing to address their substantial and disproportionate power and resources, and indeed normalizes that power by positioning it as simply part of the "market context" in which social marketing takes place. In almost all of the interventions described here and in the NSMC archive, the focus is "downstream" on the behavior of individuals, with little or no reference to possible "upstream" interventions aimed at government policy or regulation. And although some "upstream" interventions have been made elsewhere by government, it is significant that the social marketing projects created under the auspices of the NSMC have not themselves been concerned with such matters, and have restricted their conception of marketing to interventions aimed at consumers, rather than at the supply side or government regulation of markets. Indeed as I have suggested above, the setting-up of the NSMC was itself based on a policy paper, *Choosing Health* (Department of Health, 2004), in which "health" had already begun to lose some of its public qualities, and taken on more and more the qualities of a private consumer good—something that people should "aspire to" and something that promotional techniques could create a "demand" for, and precisely not simply a matter of state or public provision.

So how far do these projects represent a systematic way of conceiving and acting upon the social? Although the materials included in the NSMC's archive are varied, they do involve distinctive ways of identifying and acting upon target populations. Firstly, and most obviously, these populations appear as discrete but potentially overlapping groups who can be identified and described through research, whose behavior is in some sense maladaptive, but which is also open to adjustment through the use of appropriate insights and techniques. Like classic behavioral therapies, the focus for both description and action remains primarily on manifest behaviors rather than the "hidden depths of the soul" (Rose, 1989: 234). This means that while the social marketing interventions described above may sometimes have a theoretical basis in ideas about social learning or "social norms" (and indeed the use of a *variety* of theories has been actively encouraged), they are, more often than not, underpinned by behavioral ideas about goal setting and reinforcement.

More striking, however, is the fact that where earlier behavioral techniques identified their target populations through psychometric indices of personality (Rose, 1989), the objects of social marketing are identified through the demographic, psychographic, and lifestyle measures of commercial market research. This is particularly clear in the segmentation techniques used for identifying problem drinkers, who were categorized according to nine psychographic or lifestyle profiles including "boredom drinker," "macho drinker," "de-stress drinker," "re-bonding drinker," "depressed drinker," and so on. Equally important is the fact that all target populations, regardless of psychographic or other characteristics, are understood as consumers. They are assumed to be living in a fully fledged market society in which *all* choices and decisions (and not simply those associated with household provisioning or discretionary spending) can be understood in terms of products, exchanges, and competition, and indeed in which the "competition" for their adoption of healthier practices is rarely seen in terms of social or economic deprivation or problems, and more often seen in the form of competing products, brands, sites of consumption, or other promotional techniques.

These ways of describing populations also have implications for the ways in which they are to be worked upon, and for the ways in which interventions are to be measured. As consumers, they are understood—notwithstanding insights about social norms and networks—to be relatively free to choose alternatives given the appropriate incentives and/or information. They are also understood as people who are routinely influenced or engaged by the efforts of commercial marketers, and correspondingly seen as open to the use of such techniques in matters concerning their health and well-being. Thus all projects begin with a period of market research and "customer insight" generation, and many include focus group activities in which the target population is involved in the choice of a name and logo for the project. In a number of the case studies from the archive, there is a strong emphasis on the building of "iconic brands" with which people might identify, as well as on the use of experiential or ambient forms of promotion, such as outdoor advertising, "chillout" cabins in city centers to promote alcohol awareness, interactive features on websites, and so on. There is, in short, a strong belief in the appropriateness of treating target populations as market actors. This is true both in the sense that their health and well-being is conceived as directly linked to *freely chosen* consumption behaviors, and in the sense that those market behaviors may be influenced by forms of non-price competition such as branding and marketing.

Measuring the effectiveness of these interventions is, however, an altogether trickier matter, since it depends mostly upon self-reporting through questionnaires and interviews. Unlike commercial marketers, social marketers are unable to access objective evidence of success through sales figures, and if parents report that their children have eaten more fruit and vegetables in the three months following an in-school intervention, then social marketers must take their word for it. On the other hand, it is a significant, if mostly implicit, part of the behavioral focus of such campaigns that they sometimes involve forms of self-monitoring that extend the intervention beyond its original site into, for example, the home, school, or workplace. This is especially common in campaigns aimed at children, where parents and teachers can be recruited to use wall charts and stickers to measure progress, or workbooks to track behavior. As Miller and Rose point out, these forms of inscription can be seen as a type of "action at a distance," enjoining people to "work out 'where they are', calibrate themselves in relation to 'where they should be', and devise ways of getting from one state to the other" (2008: 67). For the most part, however, the tracking and measurement of outcomes involves comparing self-reported behavior or attitudes at the start and end of a project, perhaps with a follow-up questionnaire among a restricted sample three or six months down the line. While such tracking processes may prompt a change in the subject, by encouraging reflection upon practice, the significance of these behavioral measures lies mostly in the *new* reality they are given when they are put into circulation elsewhere (see Barry, 2001). For reports of success can be used to confirm the legitimacy of social marketing techniques as effective interventions in the social, while the ongoing effort to identify "costs per user" or return on investment (ROI) represents an effort to bring social marketing within the realm of auditability and to compare the value for money delivered by different approaches to the same problem. In this way, social interventions are brought into the frame of economic calculation, even while the validity of particular measurement techniques remains secured by their legitimacy (their acceptance by other actors) rather than their accuracy (see Arvidsson, 2006).

The Implications of Social Marketing

What are the implications of this diffusion of marketing language and techniques into the social realm? Clearly the application of marketing language to a new field of practice does not necessarily mean that that field has *become* a market, or that the people and institutions that make up that field have come to see themselves as market actors. As Colin Williams (2005) points out, it has been a characteristic problem of recent commentaries on commodification to confuse the advent of a marketized language for describing the world (e.g., referring to people as "consumers") with the process of commodification itself. At the same time, for governments to think about parts of their populations as markets, and to think about working on them in terms of the shaping of consumer demand or market provision does represent a shift from earlier models of welfarism or liberalism (Miller and Rose, 2008). In any case, the developments described here are not simply a matter of a change in language but also involve a redirection of considerable material resources. How, then, should we think about the rise of social marketing?

Performativity

A performative approach to markets and economics is useful here because its point is precisely to examine the ways in which such disciplines may not, *contra* Williams, be simply ways of describing the world, but also ways of producing it. And in this context, what is at stake is not whether those ways of describing the world are "right" or "wrong" —that is, whether it is *accurate* to think of target populations as markets—but how far those descriptions are able to transform that world (MacKenzie et al., 2007: 2). A number of writers have argued that this ability to transform the world does not rest solely with the power to describe, but is also connected to the power to shape behavior through the design of the environments, institutions, and technologies in which it takes place (MacKenzie et al., 2007). In this respect, an idea or a discipline can become influential without actually having to have a "psychological" effect or to persuade people of its veracity. In the case of social marketing, one might say that interventions in which people are made to act in market-like ways (participating in focus groups, exchanging goods, choosing among competing alternatives) make the discourse of marketing influential—and give it the ability to transform the world—without any need for those people being targeted to conceive of themselves as "market actors" at all. Insofar as social marketing provides a material infrastructure (e.g., through websites, children's workbooks, nutritional guides, and so on) through which the behavior of target groups may be channeled into market-friendly forms, it may institute a more durable disposition to seek out information and take responsibility for choices in the "consumerist" manner envisioned by government. It may also facilitate ongoing forms of self-monitoring, encouraging people to see their health and well-being as matters of personal responsibility, or at least as the outcome of a relationship between themselves and the market, rather than themselves and the state. All of these behavioral forms are consonant with a neoliberal desire to encourage individuals to equip themselves with the capacities to participate in market-oriented social institutions.

Yet clearly there are limits to the performative powers of a discipline. In the case of social marketing, a huge variety of resources were devoted to the project of turning a disciplinary framework and set of ideas into a set of institutions and techniques capable of remaking part of the world in its image. And while those resources have made social marketing the dominant national framework for health promotion in Britain at the time of writing, its future may not be so secure, since it has depended for its effectiveness on its relationship to particular political rationalities, economic circumstances, and programs of government. It is not clear that this relationship will last indefinitely.[6] What is more, the performative power of a discipline may be linked to issues of time and scale. Almost all of the "exemplary" social marketing interventions described above were limited in space and time, and their ability to influence, track, and measure behavior may arguably have been directly linked to those narrow parameters. As social marketing campaigns are scaled up to the regional or national level, the sheer cost of interventions means that elaborate strategies based on experiential marketing, the provision of new spaces and environments, or self-monitoring through workbooks and diaries may become less viable. These may diminish the effectiveness of such schemes, while their measurement techniques must presumably also move from the recording and tracking of specific consumption behaviors to a more general set of indicators of overall health outcomes. In this respect, social marketing may not be a fully performative discipline, in the sense of bringing a certain (new) reality into being through its interventions. Instead, it may be better construed as a more limited and contingent intervention, based on a "theory testing" or experimental approach to marketing (MacKenzie et al., 2007). As such, the NSMC might be seen as a type of laboratory for modeling and testing new approaches to the molding of human behavior—experiments which, I would suggest, are increasingly common in neoliberal regimes of governance.

The politics of calculation

Another approach to the diffusion of marketing might be to consider what kind of politics is made possible or impossible by its calculative approach to human behavior. From this perspective, the apparently "consumerist" focus and the emphasis on manifest, measurable behaviors in the NSMC may be thought about less in terms of its creation of a market or a consumer mentality, and more in terms of its connection to a wider sphere of political debate about health and welfare. Writing about the use of particular measurement techniques in the monitoring of pollution, Andrew Barry (2002) argues that the increasing importance of information and measurement to both the economy and government is linked to a specific "politics of calculation." Typically, he argues, it is through measurement that "a whole range of objects and problems is brought into the frame of economic calculation" (Barry, 2002: 273). And once they become calculable, it is assumed that political contestation over the nature of the problem has ended. In Barry's own example, the establishment of standardized techniques for measuring exhaust emissions from cars "frames" debates about the causes and consequences of pollution and may reduce the space for political contestation. Thus measurement techniques and standards become "anti-political," even while they also have beneficial effects.

It may be useful to think about social marketing in this way too; the interventions of the NSMC may have short- or longer-term benefits for the populations they target, but they may also—through their institutionalization, standardization, and focus on calculation and measurement—have the effect of stifling debate about the causes of social problems and the best ways to address them. Indeed part of the point of the early part of this chapter has been to show that while debates over the ethics of social marketing have continued in scholarly journals, the institutionalization of social marketing has proceeded in part by fixing or bracketing those debates, and acting as though they had already been resolved. In Barry's analysis, standardized or established measurement techniques may serve the additional function of acting as "relays" between the economic and political spheres, connecting them but also helping them to retain their semblance of purity and distinctiveness. In the case of social marketing, the sphere of "welfare" and the social is preserved as a separate domain in which governments still have a responsibility to act (although that responsibility is diminishing and is increasingly devolved to external agencies), yet the focus on behavioral outcomes and the tracking and measurement of "effectiveness" allows that sphere to be connected to an economic rationality elsewhere. At the same time, Barry points out that regimes of measurement and calculation are not invulnerable; from time to time, political events open them to public scrutiny and new ways of measuring may come into view. When measurement becomes re-politicized, debates about the nature and causes of particular problems may be put back on the table. Ongoing debates about the costs and value of social marketing[7] hint at such a re-politicization.

The economization of the social

A final but related approach to the diffusion of marketing concepts is to consider how social marketing, as a relatively new source of authority, relates to the broader "market" of authorities and expertise that characterizes contemporary governance (see Miller and Rose, 2008; Shamir, 2008). For social marketing is not the only discipline that uses marketing techniques to act on the social; commercial organizations are increasingly involved in social initiatives through mechanisms such as cause-related marketing or corporate social responsibility, and while these practices may be distinguished from "proper" social marketing by their self-interest and focus on corporate reputation (Peattie and Peattie, 2003; Littler, 2008), they are nonetheless an important part of the context in which social marketing takes place. More specifically, they contribute to a situation in which government-sponsored forms of social marketing do not only "compete" with, for example, alcohol advertising or fast food manufacturers, but also with the social initiatives of corporations. As I have suggested in the preceding section, social marketing in Britain has proceeded as though this competition is entirely normal. There has been little or no attempt to consider how marketing expertise might explore the ways in which the operation of markets *itself* impacts upon health or well-being. Rather, social marketing has restricted its role to the attempt to influence consumer choice *within* an already-established market.

To understand this orientation, it is again useful to consider how the institutionalization of social marketing in Britain and elsewhere connects to a broader political rationality. Describing the new prominence of corporate social responsibility initiatives and other techniques for the "moralization of economic action," Ronen Shamir (2008) suggests that such configurations of the economic, the social, and the political are part of a general neoliberal drive to ground social relations in the economic rationality of markets. As he puts it, "no longer satisfied with conceiving the rationality of the market as a distinct and limited form of social action, [the neoliberal imagination] posits the rationality of the market as the organizational principle for state and society as a whole" (Shamir, 2008: 6). Under neoliberalism, "top-down" models of state authority are replaced by a more distributed form of "governance," which includes this effort to export the logic of the market into other domains and to facilitate what Shamir calls "private forms of authority." And although social marketing in Britain has been a state-sponsored, rather than private, form of authority, it does nonetheless compete in the "market of authorities" that Shamir describes. This market of authorities is not so much regulated as *facilitated* by governments. And it contributes to a situation in which socio-moral concerns are no longer seen as "public" goods, but rather are reframed within the instrumental rationality of markets—as the outcome of choices made by citizens from a variety of competing options. As Shamir and others (e.g., Rose, 1999; Miller and Rose, 2008) have argued, the effects of this are an ongoing tendency toward the responsibilization of individuals, in which the consequences of citizens' actions are to be borne by them alone on the basis that government has already discharged any responsibilities it may have through the provision of information and, increasingly, through marketing campaigns.

Conclusion

In this chapter I have described the gradual development of social marketing in Britain as one example of the diffusion of marketing techniques into new spheres. I have tried to avoid seeing this diffusion as the inevitable outcome of marketing's own ideological power, or as the simple implementation of that ideology in a new context. Instead, I have sought to show that its development has depended upon its connection to an ascendant political rationality and the deployment and coordination of a variety of socio-technical devices across time and space. At the same time, I hope I have made it clear that the development of the National Social Marketing Centre—which was charged, in effect, with coordinating the roll-out of social marketing in Britain—did depend quite heavily on concepts and frameworks adopted more or less directly from an existing literature on social marketing developed elsewhere. In this sense at least, the British government's experiment with social marketing may be seen as an instance of political "virtualism," that is, an explicit effort to make the world conform to the structures of the conceptual, with little attention to variations in social context (Carrier and Miller, 1998).

In trying to assess the significance of social marketing, I have also drawn selectively from a related set of arguments made by proponents of a "performative" view of markets and economics. In this view, academic disciplines such as marketing are not seen simply as providing accounts or descriptions of the world, but are also, at the same time, implicated in constituting that world *through* their descriptions and actions. There is, I think, some justification for approaching social marketing in this way, for it has been quite evangelical since its inception—not only making claims about the world (that non-business institutions routinely engage in a form of marketing activity) and describing or analyzing it, but also actively seeking to create a world that conforms to those descriptions. This effort has involved developing sites of expertise, organizing conferences, formulating tools, techniques, frameworks and benchmark criteria, and explicitly seeking to influence policy makers and health-care professionals. In addition, specific campaigns have sought to reorganize citizens' perceptions of their health in more "market-friendly" ways, deploying materials and resources to encourage them to take responsibility, to seek out information, to make informed choices, to monitor their own behavior, and so on.

At the same time, I have argued that there are limits to a performative understanding of social marketing, whose potential to shape the world in its own image is limited both by fluctuating levels of political support and by practical constraints on its ability to shape citizens' behavior in widespread or durable ways. Furthermore, although social marketing flourishes in political regimes animated by neoliberalism, those same regimes may also force social marketing to compete within a broader "market" of authorities. In this situation, its own interventions and expertise, despite being state-sponsored and sanctioned, are still just one "authority" among others, and lack the more expansive power associated with more fully "performative" disciplines.

Finally, I have tried to consider how the growth of social marketing is connected to the expansion or contraction of various forms of political contestation in the sphere of welfare. Drawing on Andrew Barry's analysis (2001) of the relation between political and "anti-political" activity, I have suggested that the formalization and institutionalization of social marketing, accompanied by the development of various benchmark criteria and techniques for measuring effectiveness, may have the effect of halting or bracketing political conflict over the nature, causes, and treatment of social problems, while also bringing those problems within the frame of economic rationality and calculability. Yet as Barry notes, this bracketing of political debate—as one of the "anti-political" effects of formal measurement regimes—is rarely permanent, and may be overturned by new data and information, or a new turn of events, which reopen, or reframe, political problems.

Taking this one step further, we might consider, finally, how social marketing itself might be reconceived in the future, and how it might be able to engage more productively with political debates about welfare. As I indicated toward the start of this chapter, scholars within social marketing and related disciplines such as health communication or marketing research have for a long time expressed concerns about the dominant ways in which social marketing has been conceived. They have questioned its reliance on commercial marketing techniques and on concepts derived from approaches to markets grounded in experimental psychology and neoclassical economics. They have also raised ethical concerns about its methods of incentivization and its apparent lack of social or political engagement. As part of this, some scholars have begun to develop more nuanced models based on a more selective engagement with marketing concepts (e.g., Peattie and Peattie, 2003), or even proposed new ethical frameworks for the discipline. Goldberg (1995), for example, argues that an ethically engaged form of social marketing should attend to environmental and policy factors as well as individual ones, and that research into individual decision-making should be explicitly designed to feed into policy and "close the loop" between "upstream" and "downstream" variables. While Goldberg acknowledges that "truly upstream" variables such as housing and employment may be beyond the scope of marketing researchers, he suggests that there are a number of intermediate, or "second order," upstream variables that are both amenable to market research and structured toward policy interventions. These might include testing the elasticity of demand for cigarettes as a function of price, which has direct implications for taxation policy, or assessing the impact of alcohol packaging, which has implications for product development and regulation.

While such interventions may appear limited in scope, their advantage would be to provide forms of data that reframe social problems as demanding a political or institutional rather than individual response. This in turn returns us to a point raised at the beginning of this chapter, that marketing research and analysis was not always organized to serve business interests, but instead had a more critical and socially engaged role of monitoring markets and analyzing the ways in which their operation—and in particular their distortion by powerful corporations—could lead to negative social outcomes. The challenge for social marketing is therefore to restructure its own research agenda—and rethink its relationship with practitioners—so that it does not simply become a laboratory for neoliberal policymaking. This must surely involve a shift of focus from eye-catching branding and advertising campaigns aimed at altering individual behavior within an existing market to examining how the operation of markets—and, increasingly, marketing itself—impacts upon social concerns and public goods.

Notes

1. These include dedicated "social marketing" agencies and consultancies, but such work also makes up a substantial proportion of the work done by more established agencies, particularly design consultancies.
2. In an early review of the literature on social marketing, Lazer and Kelley (1973) high-lighted three ways in which its contribution to society could equally serve the interests of marketing itself; first, if marketing is able to contribute to the solution of social problems, they suggest, this would have knock-on effects on business through "better satisfied customers, better markets, and an improved environment" (1973: 10). Second, if marketing fails to devise and implement "social actions that are acceptable," "the reactions of society may be rather severe"; and third, in such a scenario "government will be forced to do that which marketing has not been willing to do voluntarily, thereby circumscribing the boundaries of marketing management" (1973: 11).
3. For example, Luck (1969: 53–4) argued that Kotler and Levy's proposals were so broad that, if one followed their definition, anything that resembled marketing would in fact *be* marketing, even if it did not result in a market transaction. He went on to suggest that business was socially beneficial through its contribution to Gross National Product, and that marketers should leave additional "social needs" to other institutions. Laczniak et al. (1979), in a survey of marketing practitioners and "professors of ethics," expressed unease at the asymmetries of power involved in governments using marketing techniques to influence a population's opinions. See also Arndt (1978) and Houston (1986) for further discussion of the scope and limits of the marketing concept.
4. Peattie and Peattie (2003), for example, question whether social marketing actually involves any type of "exchange," whether what is offered is in fact a "product" (rather than, say, a "proposition"), and whether the concept of "price" is as useful as that of "cost." They propose instead a more selective and critical engagement with commercial marketing concepts.
5. The fact that children have "brand allegiances" was not, in itself, considered to be a problem.
6. For example, in 2009, the British Conservative Party criticized the amount spent by the Labour government on social marketing and advertising, accusing it of being wasteful and paternalistic. Since its election in 2010, the coalition government has placed greater emphasis on behavioral economics than Social marketing, although it has promised to publish Marketing Strategy in 2011.
7. See note 6, above.

References

Andreasen, A. (2002) "Marketing Social Marketing in the Social Change Marketplace." *Journal of Public Policy and Marketing*, 21(1): 3–13.
Arndt, J. (1978) "How Broad Should the Marketing Concept Be?" *Journal of Marketing*, 42(1): 101–3.

Arvidsson, A. (2006) *Brands: Meaning and Value in Media Culture*. London and New York: Routledge.

Barry, A. (2001) *Political Machines: Governing a Technological Society*. London: Athlone.

——(2002) "The Anti-political Economy." *Economy and Society*, 32(2): 268–84.

Buchanan, D., Reddy, S., and Hossain, Z. (1994) "Social Marketing: A Critical Appraisal." *Health Promotion International*, 9(1): 49–57.

Carrier, J.G., and Miller, D., eds. (1998) *Virtualism: A New Political Economy*. Oxford and New York: Berg.

Clarke, J. (2007) "Unsettled Connections: Citizens, Consumers and the Reform of Public Services." *Journal of Consumer Culture*, 7(2): 159–78.

Department of Health (2004) *Choosing Health*. London: The Stationery Office.

Desmond, J. (1998) "Marketing and Moral Indifference." In M. Parker, ed. *Ethics and Organizations*. London, Thousand Oaks, and New Delhi: Sage.

Goldberg, M.E. (1995) "Social Marketing: Are We Fiddling While Rome Burns?" *Journal of Consumer Psychology*, 4(4): 347–70.

Houston, F. (1986) "The Marketing Concept: What It Is and What It Is Not." *Journal of Marketing*, 50(2): 81–7.

Kotler, P., and Levy, S.J. (1969) "Broadening the Concept of Marketing." *Journal of Marketing*, 33(1): 10–15.

——and Zaltman, G. (1971) "Social Marketing: An Approach to Planned Social Change." *Journal of Marketing*, 35(1): 3–12.

Laczniak, G.R., Lusch, R.F., and Murphy, P.E. (1979) "Social Marketing: Its Ethical Dimensions." *Journal of Marketing*, 43(2): 29–36.

Lazer, W., and Kelley, E.J., eds. (1973) *Social Marketing: Perspectives and Viewpoints*. Homewood, IL: Richard D. Irwin, Inc. and London: Irwin-Dorsey International.

Littler, J. (2008) *Radical Consumption: Shopping for Change in Contemporary Culture*. Buckingham: Open University Press.

Luck, D. (1969) "Broadening the Concept of Marketing—Too Far." *Journal of Marketing*, 33(3): 53–6.

MacKenzie, D., Muniesa, F., and Siu, L., eds. (2007) *Do Economists Make Markets? On the Performativity of Economics*. Princeton and Oxford: Princeton University Press.

Martin, S. (2002) "Best Value: New Public Management or New direction?" In K. McLaughlin, S.P. Osborne, and E. Ferlie, eds. *New Public Management: Current Trends and Future Prospects*. London and New York: Routledge.

Miller, P., and Rose, N. (2008) *Governing the Present: Administering Economic, Social and Personal Life*. Cambridge and Malden, MA: Polity.

Morgan, G. (2003) "Marketing and Critique: Prospects and Problems." In M. Alvesson and H. Willmott, eds. *Studying Management Critically*. London, Thousand Oaks, and New Delhi: Sage.

Muniesa et al. (2007) "An Introduction to Market Devices." In M. Callon, Y. Millo and F. Muniesa, eds. *Market Devices*. Oxford and Malden, MA: Blackwell.

National Consumer Council (2006) *It's Our Health! Realising the Potential of Effective Social Marketing*. London: National Social Marketing Centre/National Consumer Council. Available at http://www.nsms.org.uk/public/default.aspx?PageID=16, accessed April 10, 2009.

National Social Marketing Centre (2006) "Social Marketing National Benchmark Criteria." Available at http://www.nsms.org.uk/public/default.aspx?PageID=20, accessed March 20, 2009.

——(n.d.) "ShowCase: Social Marketing Case Studies." Available at http://www.nsms.org.uk/public/default.aspx?PageID=32, accessed March 19, 2009.

Peattie, S., and Peattie, K. (2003) "Ready to Fly Solo? Reducing Social Marketing's Dependence on Commercial Marketing Theory." *Marketing Theory*, 3(3): 365–85.

Rose, N. (1989) *Governing the Soul: The Shaping of the Private Self.* London and New York: Routledge.

——(1999) *Powers of Freedom: Reframing Political Thought.* Cambridge, New York, and Melbourne: Cambridge University Press.

Shamir, R. (2008) "The Age of Responsibilization: On Market-Embedded Morality." *Economy and Society*, 37(1): 1–19.

Slater, D. (2002) "Capturing Markets from the Economists." In du Gay, P. and M. Pryke, eds. *Cultural Economy: Cultural Analysis and Commercial Life.* London, Thousand Oaks, New Delhi: Sage.

Wallack, L., Dorfman, L., Jernigan, D., and Themba-Nixon, M. (1993) *Media Advocacy and Public Health: Power for Prevention.* Newbury Park, CA, London, and New Delhi: Sage.

Williams, C.C. (2005) *A Commodified World? Mapping the Limits of Capitalism.* London and New York: Zed books.

14

Mapping the Future of Consumers

Julien Cayla and Lisa Peñaloza

Marketing will transform us into modern beings. Or at least that is the underlying assumption that lurks behind many conversations occurring in corporate boardrooms. Underlying the academic texts of international marketing and embedded in the everyday practices of marketing departments are the same fundamental ideas: that exposure to more market choices emancipates individuals and that the unavoidable development of markets worldwide will transform us all into modern consumers. This paradigm, which places Western consumers at the end of history and people from non-Western nations at the beginning, is at the core of marketing's social imaginary—that is, the set of values, institutions, and symbols that animate the practice and teaching of marketing. Yet this social imaginary is rarely examined or questioned. This is all the more problematic because of the increasing reach of marketing discourse, tools, and techniques all over the world.

An essential dimension of marketing's social imaginary that we question here is a vision of history and development that exists not only in the marketing literature but also in the way marketers think about the historical trajectory of Western and non-Western countries. Key questions about the way we map the future of consumers, about how we trace the trajectory of non-Western nations, or about the way we define modernity lie largely outside the intellectual debate in marketing. Marketing theory has somehow avoided fundamental questions about the relationship between marketing practice and modernity by celebrating the creative resistance of non-Western consumers facing the hegemony of the West, or postmodernity as a form of re-enchantment (Firat and Venkatesh, 1995). Yet in the boardrooms of Colombo (Kemper, 2001), Bombay (Mazzarella, 2003), Kathmandu (Leichty, 2002), and Tbilissi (Manning and Uplisashvili, 2007), executives are constantly discussing what it means to be modern. In this paper, we focus on the conceptions of modernity that circulate in India's advertising world. We study marketing and advertising executives as cultural intermediaries brokering ideas and images about what it means to be a modern person. Drawing from ethnographic fieldwork in an Indian advertising agency, we examine the ideology of marketing as it is diffused in the non-Western world.

Our approach is to consider alternately the vision of history that is presented in foundational marketing texts and the stories marketers tell us about the future of consumers. We want to examine the way marketing practice diffuses and reflects assumptions about the future and about modernity, which are at the core of academic marketing discourse. We go from the micro level of particular advertising campaigns and stories to the macro level of marketing's imaginary—that is, the conception of the world and the future that dominates marketing academia and spills over into the professional marketing world. By attending to the details of everyday life in an advertising agency and examining the tools marketing and advertising executives use to map the future of Indian consumers, we seek to unearth the values and ideals that permeate marketing practices. We end by arguing that the vision of history that exists in marketing hinders our ability to imagine multiple trajectories for the evolution of market cultures.

Fieldwork and Analysis

In 2001 and 2002, the first author spent nine months at a Bombay advertising agency, a subsidiary of a large multinational advertising agency that we call Lorton in this chapter. The offices of Lorton were located in South Bombay, a few hundred feet away from Salman Rushdie's childhood mansion at the bottom of Malabar Hill, one of the poshest neighborhoods of the city. As a participant in the everyday activities of the agency (Lofland and Lofland, 1995), the first author regularly helped with small projects and tasks in the planning department (e.g., the analysis of focus group data). In exchange, the agency gave him access to meetings, archives, and employees who shared their experiences in selling products and services to Indian consumers. Advertising executives were managing campaigns for brands of ketchup, scooters, motorcycles, life insurance, cake mixes, or breakfast cereals, and in their meetings the most pressing questions were: "Who is the Indian consumer we are talking to? What are his dreams and aspirations?" The answers to these questions, which often took the form of stories about Indian men and women, are what form the basis of our analysis.

Storytelling is one of the main ways humans make sense of the world. It is also one of the oldest forms of communication and is pervasive in every area of business. Consider these examples: Procter and Gamble trains managers to create brand stories that will appeal to consumers (Zaltman, 2003), screenwriters advise companies on the best way to raise money by telling compelling stories (McKee, 2003), and marketing academics rely on case studies of what has happened to companies to teach students and executives. Narrative approaches have received considerable attention not only in strategy, organizational management, and public policy literature (Morgan, 1989; Boje, 1991; Wade, 2003), but also in such disciplines as history (Cronon, 1992), anthropology (Rosaldo, 1989), and psychology (Polkinghorne, 1988). Yet, even though management researchers have discussed strategy as a key *sensemaking* device (e.g., Weick, 1995), marketing researchers have not yet turned to narrative concepts and analytical tools for the rich insights they yield regarding marketing managers' views of themselves, consumers, and processes of market development. Because strategic intent and planning are often made and implemented discursively as a series of explicit, sequential events (Barry and Elmes, 1997), we suggest that narrative analysis is particularly useful for researching international marketing strategy.

We have not realized the full benefits of narrative approaches in marketing. The field has digressed from early insightful studies that revealed what marketers do and why to a current emphasis on producing formulas for individual customer satisfaction. Yet the stories managers tell about what they do and why are important to understanding how markets develop. In this chapter, we turn to these stories as data for examining managers' explicit and implicit understandings of market development. We look at a range of stories in interviews, creative briefs, meetings, and presentations, but focus more specifically on the stories managers and advertisers tell about consumers, their organizations, and their products and services. We see stories as a way to study the greater narrative of marketing as it is diffused in different parts of the world.

Drawing from semiotic and rhetorical approaches to studying narratives (Boje, 1991), we emphasize both structure and process in the analysis—structure in the sense of the elements and relations between them, and process in terms of the way the story is used, told, and received. We distilled the following fundamental elements for analysis: characters, voice, temporality, oppositions, interpretations, and audience (Barry and Elmes, 1997; Feldman et al., 2004). For the purposes of this chapter, we will concentrate on the characters that emerge across stories, the plots and timing of stories, and the perspective from which managers told these stories about Indian consumers. We argue that such stories imply a hierarchy where consumption of and access to new commodities is placed at the very top, and where other ways of being and living are deemed to be on the lower rungs of the modernization ladder.

The Frame of the Stories

Work on a new advertising campaign often starts with a focus group. We would travel from South Bombay, where elite Bombay residents lived and where the agency was located, to the north of the city and its sprawling suburbs of Andheri and Malad and study what Indian middle-class[1] consumers aspired to buy and how they were responding to the influx of new products on the market. Auto-rickshaws driving on dirt roads replaced the black-and-yellow taxis of South Bombay, with women wearing saris instead of the jeans and salwar kameez[2] of South Bombayites. We would typically hold focus groups in the homes of Indian families recruited for their connections in the neighborhood and the convenient location of their houses. Members of the agency team would sit in the family's bedroom, observing on a television monitor the development of the focus group, while in the living room a moderator would talk to the group of recruited consumers.

After familiarizing informants with the idea of the focus group and the tasks they were to perform, a large portion of the focus group was designed to develop ideas for new campaigns. For example, consumers would have to personify the brands of the specific category we were working on. For work on a new motorcycle, male informants, all in their late twenties and early thirties, were given a two-page leaflet of thirty-five pictures depicting Western men in a variety of situations: a young couple in the bath, covered in foam and in a sensuous embrace; a man in the snow, seated by a fire, nuzzled by his faithful husky and dressed in snow gear; and a picture of the American actor Mark Wahlberg, standing bare-chested. Sitting in another room with executives of the agencies and the clients watching the group, the first author observed these men examining and pondering these images while trying to decide which of these Western men best embodied the brand of motorcycle studied and which of these situations they could relate to. In one of the groups, when the moderator asked them which of the men was more like them, one man remarked in Hindi: "Hum nahi hain, gore hain" ("this is not us, these are white people"). When the first author asked one of the planners at the agency why it kept pictures of Western men despite most of the interviewees being Indian, and despite the agency being asked by clients to create ads that would resonate with the Indian middle class, his answer was: "We could not find enough variety in the Indian photographs we found to get a really good focus group going."

His answer could be interpreted in a number of ways, but the main point we want to make here is that the reality of the marketplace often takes backstage in the development of marketing research because the primary goal of the focus group is to establish a common language with clients. The structuring language of those interactions and of the group was the language of aspiration. Studies of advertising have long shown how images and ads are produced to create the kind of distance that resonates with consumer desires while remaining close enough to the realities of their lives to avoid alienating them. In the context of Indian advertising, however, the language of aspiration needs to be contextualized and understood in relation to India's increasing economic liberalization. The opening of the economy to foreign companies and foreign trade has helped promote individualism and the primacy of individual needs. To sell new forms of consumption, companies and their ad agencies have had to emphasize the figure of the cosmopolitan consumer in touch with his desires, willing to embrace new commodities and services.

Hence these images of Western men were particularly relevant not because ad executives wanted to create ads that appeared Western, but because such images reflected a world of individual consumer desire that suited the products Indian executives were trying to sell. These images and the stories circulating in the agency emphasized the ability of individuals to become modern through the consumption of new goods and services, and for India as a nation to modernize by celebrating such individuals. These were specific notions of modernity imagined as individual choice and as the ability to consume the way people in wealthier countries do. The frame in which consumer stories had to fit was predetermined and reflected a vision of modernity that the agency executives could work with.

Other chapters in this book explore focus groups and other tools of market research as framing devices. What we want to consider here is the ideology of the frame. More specifically, what we seek to detail is the hierarchy that lurks behind these stories and consumer representations. As Applbaum pertinently argues in his chapter, the tools that we use to represent the world are never merely tools. The maps, the creative briefs, and the stories we tell about consumption and consumers always involve choices. These choices are structured by the constraints under which corporate actors operate, but they are also always embedded in cultural and institutional frameworks. As with any other human endeavor, marketing operates in a context of both insight and blindness. Market research devices provide a perspective—a way of seeing the market—that is simultaneously a way of not seeing the market, of discarding an alternative future for consumers. For example, when some of these Indian men refused to recognize themselves in pictures of Western men, they were asked to take a leap of imagination ("just imagine what character the brand would be"). The fact that the realities of these men's lives had little to do with images of a carefree couple taking a bath together had little relevance. First, the primary objective of the focus group was to generate new ideas for the campaign. They were not that interested in understanding the lives of the Indian men they were studying. Rather, the imperative was to devise a new positioning for the brand. Second, when they talked about their lives, this information had to be reinterpreted and fashioned in the language of aspiration and in adherence to the narrative of marketing as an agent of progress and emancipation. In the following section, we detail a campaign for Grainberry's cake mixes that describes this story of marketing as emancipation and empowerment.

Cake Mixes as Modernization

In the choices that are made to represent consumers in the world of Indian advertising, there is also a hierarchy at play that positions consumption as a superior and more modern way of being, and paints the switch to new commodities and services as a journey toward modernity. Campaigns for Grainberry, an American company selling a range of time-saving products such as cake mixes and refrigerated dough, illustrate how this hierarchy structures the way Indian women are represented.

In the United States, Grainberry is positioned as the "brand of baked goods that makes it easy to provide physical and emotional warmth for your family" (Grainberry Brand Manual). At the time of fieldwork, Grainberry's brand volume was highly concentrated in the United States, with less than 12 percent of sales outside of its home market. But the company was increasingly looking to the Chinese and Indian markets to fuel its growth.

Grainberry faced daunting cultural challenges in India. In the United States, Grainberry defined its products as being "modern and more efficient," helping women save time with convenient products. In India, however, market research revealed that convenience, while attractive to housewives, was not compelling enough to trigger consumption. Most Indian women perceived processed foods as expensive, unhealthy, and unappealingly foreign. Baking is not common in Indian cooking and, while the *tandoor* oven has been part of Punjabi cooking for centuries, its purpose is more akin to grilling. Urban Indians often buy cakes for birthdays and office parties, but baking at home is still unusual in India. A market research report revealed that, in the early stages of Grainberry's entry into the Indian market, the company was perceived by Indian women to be like an "NRI [non-resident Indian] woman; a foreigner with an alien lifestyle and upscale tastes."

Grainberry's managers decided to deal with this issue in two main ways. First, Grainberry addressed the lack of oven penetration in India by developing a cake mix to be prepared in a pressure cooker, a much more common appliance than ovens in urban India. Second, marketing executives decided that they have would would have to move the definition of their company to a higher level of abstraction, from convenience to empowerment. In an internal report, a branding consultant summarized the findings of a brand essence workshop where Grainberry's managers articulated the core of the Grainberry brand essence as warmth, togetherness, and empowerment:

> EMPOWERMENT—Grainberry liberates the housewife and puts her in control of her life. The effect of Grainberry's rational and emotional benefits is to liberate the housewife from drudgery, to create time "to do", to reinforce her role as a good mother and cook, to promote her self esteem, to invite appreciation and gratitude from her family, "and to deliver quality time for SELF...in short, the housewife feels EMPOWERED". (Brand Essence Report, 2001)

The objective, in the words of Grainberry's marketing manager, was to give Indian women "modern means to express traditional values." In interviews, Mrs Mishra declared that she wanted her brand and the Grainberry woman to be "sociable, young, modern, progressive, empowered." The Grainberry woman was to "look forward" without renouncing traditional values.

There is a process of selective modernization in the way Grainberry's essence was formulated: Indian women could adopt new commodities as long as they kept an Indian core of values and traditions. Here we are reminded of Chatterjee's discussion (1993) of the role of women as custodians of Indian tradition. In Grainberry's campaign and others, the Indian woman is treated as the custodian of tradition, defending Indian homes and Indian identity in the face of foreign contact. But what is never questioned in this and other stories that assume India would resist the invasion of foreign influences is the essential narrative line of marketing as progress—of foreign companies arriving on Indian soil as an illustration of India's modernization process, even if this modernity came in the shape of cake mixes. The idea not just of modernity as an ineluctable wave, but of new products and brands as the expression of that modernity was never really contested by the Indian executives working on such brands. For example, in creative briefs, the advertising executive working on the Grainberry account described the "Grainberry woman" in the following way:

> Kamini Malhotra is the mother of two school-going children. Her home and her kitchen play the central role in her life. Baking is synonymous with western style of cooking and modernity and is thus aspirational. She would like to be considered as "prescribing to the modern school of thought" and this is the way she deludes herself as doing that. She looks traditionally homely yet contemporary [...] Baking is alien to her because she does not own an oven and was never taught baking by her Mom. Baking being associated with "modern Western-style cooking" is considered to be difficult but aspirational.

It is important to note that such representations are often infused with the emotions and identity of the executives who craft them. Contrary to the story of Kamini Malhotra as aspiring to bake, focus group research revealed that baking cakes was not really perceived as aspirational. The market research company working on the account quoted Indian women saying about cake consumption: "Roz ki baat nahin hai" ("it's not an everyday thing"); "It's chuma consumption.... It's not very definite the way you plan it." Yet to justify the sale of cake mixes or other relatively new products, advertising and marketing executives had to take a leap of faith and imagine that middle-class Indian women would eventually buy such products. The identity and professional position of Indian marketers has become that of modernity brokers. They are active in diffusing that narrative line of progress and modernity because it gives meaning to their work and the presence of foreign multi-nationals in India.

When we claim that the character of these stories, the traditional yet modern housewife Kamini Malhotra, is constructed, we do not imply that these descriptions have no relation to the reality of Indian women's lives. The Grainberry campaigns do resonate with the Indian middle-class desire to experiment with a variety of food items. At the end of the 1980s, Appadurai (1988) talked about a growing class of Indian families using regional Indian dishes to position their identity as squarely middle class. The description of the target for Grainberry's cake mix as "scouring through recipes" does reso-nate with the reality of wealthier urban Indians curious to taste new food items. Rather, we argue that there is a process of selection and construction that goes into the consistent representations of consumers that aspire to a modern future with a Western allure.

Characters: From the Cosmopolitan Man to the Dutiful Daughter-in-Law

Many of the multinationals that worked with the advertising agency decided early on that they would expand in India progressively. They would start with the upper-middle class, the "transnationally oriented" member of the middle class that Derne (2008) mentions, before moving on to the much larger but also poorer "locally-oriented" (p. 203) middle class. As in other models of market development, they would start with more familiar consumers—In-dians who understood the language of multinational companies. Characters from the Indian upper and middle classes were prevalent in stories that circulated at Lorton. Discussions centered on the Westernized elite, the "cos-mopolitan man," and the "contemporary woman" that were most likely to buy the new types of products and services on the Indian market: cake mixes, powder detergents, health insurance, credit cards, ketchup, packaged flour, and canned vegetables.

For global brands of vodka, cars, and clothing, the ad executives would discuss the life of the cosmopolitan man: an English-speaking, well-educated Indian man who is linked to global networks of production and consumption. In a meeting, Lorton's advertising executives described him as a "global manager, somebody who wants to show his position in society; dressed in Van Heusen, smart clothes, international style"; "he watches the BBC or the National Geographic channel." The cosmopolitan man is connected to the outside world. His car, his bank, and the whisky he drinks are all taken to be signs of an international culture of success that India has successfully assimilated since the liberalization of its economy.

The feminine counterpart of the cosmopolitan man is what Indian executives would call the "contemporary woman." Similar to the cosmopolitan man, in a print ad for breakfast cereals she is addressed as a global consumer with the headline, "the world over, a good breakfast lesson begins with V-I-R-L-O-G." She is constructed as connected to a larger sphere of consumption (cf. "the world over") and is reassured that, despite the claims on her time, she is doing what is best for her family. In an Indian ad for chocolate, the young contemporary woman wears Western clothes and teases her boyfriend with a chocolate bar. The executives working on the chocolate campaign describe her in the following terms: "She is urban, she knows what she wants, she is not too serious about things." The contemporary woman is constructed as more individualistic, more Western, than her locally oriented middle-class counterparts. In a campaign for Virlog, she is described as "more like an NRI," a woman who is able to navigate both India and the Western world.

A few rungs down the social ladder are people executives described as "traditional" and "vernacular." One of the directors of the agency explained that, as one goes down the social-class ladder, "consumers become more cultural." For example, the housewife appearing in advertisements for Grainberry and Hansel retains enough tradition to appear authentically Indian while having some of the contemporary woman's freedom. In Grainberry's cooker-cake advertisement, she is portrayed as enjoying a fun and loving relationship with her children, whom she surprises with her cakes. She is not only a mother but also a friend. Cake mixes allow her to go beyond her traditional role and establish a warm relationship with her children.

The male equivalent of the traditional yet modern housewife is the character of the "cosmopolitan-local man." Fried Burger executives would exchange stories about this character when they tried to devise the best ways to attract the Indian middle class to their restaurants. After three years in the Indian market and despite many local adaptations such as buffalo (instead of beef) burgers, cheap eating options (ice cream cones priced at seven Indian rupees), and advertisements broadcast in Hindi, Indian middle-class consumers still saw Fried Burger as largely inaccessible and foreign. In the words of the ad executive working on the campaign: "For them Fried Burger is like taking a trip abroad."

For Fried Burger, expanding the consumer base from upper-middle-class to middle-class Indians then amounted to creating a zone of comfort, both in their restaurants and in the commercials they broadcast on Indian television, that middle-class Indians could enter. In this context, the character of the cosmopolitan yet local father featured in Fried Burger ads becomes reassuring: he is a man from the locally oriented middle class who enjoys a special relationship with his son and takes him to Fried Burger to forget his worries. Most importantly, this reassuring and friendly father is a way for Fried Burger's executives to represent a figure the middle-class Indian can identify with. In the advertisement, the character speaks Hindi and, though he wears Western clothes (pants and a shirt), is far from the image of the cosmopolitan man equipped with a briefcase, a mobile phone, and a foreign car. The father's modest and gentle manners contrast with the aggressive desire of the cosmopolitan man to get ahead. To create a more vernacular type of Indian masculinity, advertising and marketing executives endow male characters with a humility that contrasts with the materialism of the cosmopolitan man.

All of these characters are more than representations of the market; they reflect and reinforce a cultural hierarchy. Discussions revolving around questions such as "who is the modern Indian housewife?" and "how is she different from the traditional Indian housewife?" mirror and solidify deep-rooted assumptions about what it means to be modern. Through these discussions, ad agencies produce a system of oppositions and relations between consumers. We recall here the structuralist insight about difference (Saussure, 1966): that meaning is not in the signifier itself, but only exists in a network of relations between signifiers. In stories about consumers, the figure of the cosmopolitan man only has meaning through its relation to such characters as the vernacular man or the cosmopolitan-local man. These oppositions are also rife with assumptions about market development: for most executives interviewed, many Indians were becoming more like the character of the cosmopolitan man or the contemporary woman.

Plots and timing

The plot that is implicit in many of these stories about Indian consumers is that they would eventually upgrade to new commodities, and that this switch to cell phones, sachets of shampoo, and powder detergents would be an expression of their latent modernity. Stories about Indian lives needed to conform to a metanarrative about the relationship between an increase in consumption choices, the availability of products depicted as modern, and their own modernity: the modern consumer buys modern products.

The case of Hansel, an American company selling a variety of household and personal-care products, illustrates this narrative of progress that Indian consumers were supposed to be following. Hansel entered India in the late 1980s on the platform of bringing superior products to middle-class Indians living in large cities. But in the mid-1990s, lured by the promise of a vast rural market, Hansel decided to penetrate the Indian heartland by selling detergent to consumers living in medium-sized towns and rural areas. Hansel's main challenge was to convince Indian women to switch from their more traditional oil-based bars of soap to synthetic powder detergents.

The challenge of selling powder detergents is similar to that of selling cake mixes. It involves convincing Indian housewives that their work won't be replaced by convenient products. In the following quote, an ad executive describes how grueling the process of washing clothes is in India, yet how little enthusiasm convenient laundry products generate:

> In the Indian context, washing laundry means you soak clothes then scrub it with a detergent cake then scrub it with a brush, rinse under water, check for stains and then do it all over again. Even people using washing machines would also scrub clothes. Collars and cuffs would be treated with a detergent cake, then a brush and then put it in the machine. More than anything, what's important is the feeling of involvement, that what she is doing cannot be replaced by a machine; "it needs my rigor, it needs my elbow power then only I can get satisfactory results." Even though she was offered a convenient product she was very reluctant to accept that. (Pradnya)

Similar to cake mixes, discussions about powder detergent revolved around notions of convenience, efficiency, modernity, and progress: how can Indian women be convinced to upgrade to more efficient products without emphasizing their convenience?

As they researched habits of consumption, Hansel and Lorton executives discovered that Indian women paid special attention to clothes that were to be worn outside. A memo details the importance that clothing worn outside the home appear very clean: "There is a category of 'important' clothes which is given special care while washing e.g. husband's office/'outgoing' shirt, children's school uniform, costly saris." (Lorton archives, July 1995). The same memo emphasizes that, for rural housewives, getting very clean clothes might not be that important: "It is not important to get very clean clothes which will be dirtied in the fields the next day." However, she will want her children "to go into service where clothes are important because of our standing in society." The cleanliness of clothes becomes associated with social status and the aspiration to enter the middle class through employment in the Indian administration.

There is a large amount of research emphasizing the boundaries between the outside and the inside, between the public and private spheres in India (e.g., Chatterjee, 1993). By traversing both spheres, clothing becomes an extension of the household's identity, its purity, and social status as its wearer goes outside. The distinction between the private and the public is also evident in the Western clothes that urban Indian men will wear in public (pants, shirts) and the Indian clothes (kurtas,[3] pyjamas) they typically wear inside the house. The outside is the domain of work and contact with things that are impure and foreign. It is also the domain where men can rise through the social hierarchy by being more professional and by understanding Western practices of professionalism, hygiene, and cleanliness. Hence, clothes worn outside are doubly important: they are to be cleaned because the outside is impure but also because it is necessary on the path to professional achievement.

But while Hansel and Lorton executives agreed that Indian women would buy a premium detergent like Hansel for special clothes to be worn outside, they disagreed about the profile of Indian women Hansel could sell to. In rural areas, the ad agency argued, people would look for the cheapest alternative—Indian brands such as Nirma or regional contenders like Ghadi—not foreign detergents like Hansel, which command 25 percent higher prices for the same quantity. At the core of discussions between Lorton and Hansel is the notion that, as they become richer, consumers advance to better, premium products that are more efficient, a notion Lorton's Managing Director Rajeev refers to when he says, "The assumption is that if consumers are given better quality products, they will run to buy them." This assumption surfaced in briefs that Lorton and Hansel executives devised for the "hinterland" campaign: "We believe that there is a distinct psychographic group of consumers whom we can target. These are upwardly mobile women who aspire for a better life for their children and husband and want to be recognized as belonging to a more progressive social class." (Lorton Creative Brief, 1997).

The use of "we believe" suggests that, rather than being based on data, the construction of this consumer representation stems from the *hope* that Indian women from the middle class will eventually be more like upper-class Indian women and Western consumers in their willingness to pay premium prices for quality detergents. None of the market research indicated that consumers were really unhappy with their detergents. One of the reports rationalized that Indian women just did not know the kind of cleanliness and whiteness Western consumers are used to. They would need to be shown that superior cleanliness, described by one executive as higher "standards of cleanliness," was possible and desirable.

The assumption that Indian consumers would eventually become more like their Western counterparts is not specific to Hansel, but is corroborated repeatedly for many companies in fieldnotes and archives. For example, an underlying assumption that circulated at Virlog was that Indians would adopt breakfast cereals at the same pace as in other countries, and that one needed only to map the penetration of cereals in Mexico to determine how far behind India was. When asked about the challenges the company faced in India, one of Virlog's managers revealed that the speed at which India was moving along that imaginary axis of development was not as fast as had been predicted.

> In India, successes have been mainly to create a market for breakfast cereals. Challenges have been related to the fact that maybe the pace of market expansion has not been as fast as we thought it would be. We thought that for example our generation would be more receptive to change and more likely to adopt products like breakfast cereals. But that has not really happened; lifestyles and habits are much more entrenched than we originally thought they would be.

While upper-middle-class Indians were consuming an increasing amount of cereals, Virlog faced the same problem as other foreign companies in India: convincing Indian households from the middle class to switch to more efficient and expensive forms of consumption had proven to be more difficult than expected. Market research showed that Indian consumers enjoyed their Indian breakfasts. They were also not keen to consume cereals with cold milk because milk is usually delivered hot every day to urban Indian households. Despite this resistance to foreign habits of consumption, marketing executives at Virlog and other multinationals still believed that Indian consumers would eventually become more like Western consumers. They accepted that the pace at which different cultures would reach that point varied, but the nature of cultural change was never really questioned; more Indian consumers would eventually become more global, more like their Western counterparts, and the apex of these changes was considered to be more modern.

In discussions about the future of Indian consumers, the executives at Lorton would often play the role of cultural broker, emphasizing their understanding of Indian market culture. After all, their very existence depended on the necessity to localize advertisements for the Indian market. As Mazzarella (2003) describes in his monograph, Indian advertising agencies use this purported expertise on Indian market culture to fashion advertisements and ad characters they see as resolutely Indian. They were quick to point out that India would resist the arrival of foreign companies, reflecting Nehru's description of India's integration of foreign influences: "She was like some ancient palimpsest on which layer upon layer of thought had been inscribed, and yet no succeeding layer had completely hidden or erased what had been written previously" (Nehru, 1946: 39). But it would be naïve to assume that Indian ad agencies always resisted MNCs' narrative of Indian consumers becoming more like their Western counterparts. While part of the agency's position of being a cultural broker is predicated upon this resistance and preservation of Indian cultural difference, agency executives are also adamant that Indians are becoming more consumerist and global and hence modern. It would be a misleading approximation to equate Indian advertising agencies with the local and MNCs with the global. Rather, the stories organizational actors were telling showed they were always operating along the same axis of development, from traditional to global consumers and from vernacular to global and Western languages. Debates between the agency and MNCs only revolved around the pace at which the change would occur and what strata of society would be involved. The ineluctable path of development and the nature of development were never really questioned by agency or MNC executives.

Voice

To understand the stories managers tell, it is important to understand the perspective from which they are telling them. The overwhelming majority of executives working in advertising agencies in Bombay come from the upper-middle class. They have often benefited from the liberalization of the Indian economy, enjoying access to better-paying jobs in the service sector. These are men and women in their late twenties who are often able to buy their own cars, expensive clothes, and holidays abroad.

One of the most difficult challenges for the executives was to empathize with and relate to a locally oriented middle class whose lives and aspirations seemed quite distant from their own. The women working on the Grainberry account would often tell stories about the fact that, while they have to advertise food products, they are hardly ever involved in the preparation of food in their own households (servants would do most of the cooking). Other executives often told stories about other executives' lack of knowledge about Indian culture. In a client meeting, executives on the Virlog marketing team expressed concern that Indian women would pour warm milk over their cereal, making it soggy. They would use the milk that had been delivered at their doorsteps early in the morning and which they had boiled to preserve it longer. A creative director revealed her lack of knowledge about middle-class consumer behavior by asking, "Why doesn't she pick up a carton of milk in the refrigerator?" An account planner told me: "The executives working for the client, Virlog, were kind of startled, looking at her. I mean, how many people have milk cartons, Tetra Paks, in their house in India?"

Examining the background of advertising executives helps in understanding the types of identities that they fashion for Indian consumers. As in the case of other cultural producers (Dornfeld, 1998), Indian advertising and marketing executives project many of their own contradictions and desires onto the advertising characters they create. The aspirations of the characters Lorton executives created probably had more to do with their own aspirations and vision of the good life than the consumers they were trying to advertise to.

Many of these executives had global dreams and talked of future plans of "getting away" to Western countries: Nestor related to me his plans to move to Canada, Tasneem aired her frustrations after being refused an American visa, and Kaushik spoke of plans to move to London. While at work they emphasized their ability to speak in the language of the local man, while outside of work they watched television channels broadcasting in English, talked of their desire to go to Western business schools to get their MBAs, and avidly read management and marketing textbooks. A popular character who came to the agency every other week was the young salesman selling marketing and business textbooks to ad executives. He would open a big suitcase, replete with new editions of David Aaker's books on branding (e.g., Aaker, 1996) or Jean Marie Dru's *Disruption* (1996). The salesman knew little English, but knew the names of the marketing gurus necessary to elicit attention and make a sale. Outside the agency, at one of the busiest intersections of the city, they could pick up the latest edition of the *Harvard Business Review* collections of articles. Young boys would swiftly pass between air-conditioned cars on the street to sell the latest management books alongside novels and magazines to Indian executives stopped in traffic. On the street corner, a small news-stand carried myriad Indian marketing magazines as well as foreign publications. For Indian executives, these were important points of access for mastering what they saw as sophisticated forms of marketing knowledge, models of consumer behavior, and ways of understanding marketing systems that came from the West. Those who were quick to point out that India was different and that the Indian market required a tailored approach were the same who regarded marketing as a universal language they had to master in order to progress in their careers. It is from this intersection of the world of Western brand gurus and the reality of the Indian marketplace that advertising executives construct their stories of market development. As advertising executives imagine Indian consumers, they devise a story of resistance to global pressures, yet in their conceptions of progress and development, they are not only embracing but also diffusing a Western-centric, teleological view of development as essentially consumerist and populated with global brands.

The Imprint and Enduring Legacy of Modernization Theory

Here we use the data collected in India to reflect upon the assumptions about history that already exist in marketing textbooks and articles. Rather than being an oddity, the account of history that is found in Indian boardrooms reflects a view of the world that is ubiquitous not only in international marketing practice but also in academic scholarship. The repeated criticisms raised against modernization theory (see Mehmet, 1999) should have relegated this model of development to a footnote. Yet one can find the influence of modernization theory in numerous marketing articles and books.

The most popular modernization theorist was Walter Rostow. Originally published in 1960, Rostow's seminal work, *The Stages of Economic Growth*, was tellingly subtitled a "Non-Communist Manifesto" because it offered a capitalist alternative to Marxist theory. It was also a specific vision of the world which saw development as a civilizing process, a singular and universal path that involved individual emancipation, technological advancement, and human mastery of the environment; if America was a first-world country, and if first-world countries were advanced and third-world countries were traditional and backward, then third-world countries would inevitably seek to emulate them. Like much marketing scholarship, modernization theory emerged during America's economic domination in the 1950s and its ideological battles against communism. In modernization theory, the model of the modern man (Inkeles and Smith, 1974) is that of an individual ready for new experiences and open to change but also punctual, regular, orderly, and confident in his ability to dominate his environment through the exercise of careful planning. The modern man, as conceptualized by modernization theorists, is the Western man.

Modernization theory still carries a great deal of influence in marketing and is still taught in many business schools as though this model of development were devoid of ideological underpinnings. Early on, marketing scholar Coskun Samli (1965) explained that the terms "underdeveloped" and "developing" applied to countries "whose inhabitants desire some of the modern facilities and comforts of Western life" (p. 42). The work of Rostow is still reported, though not critiqued, in major international marketing textbooks which sell thousands of copies all over the world. For example, Cateora and Graham (2002) use Rostow's five-stage model of economic development and his idea that less developed nations have fewer needs for symbolic goods. In his classes and lectures, Philip Kotler regularly uses Rostow's stages of development to explain how nations progress through different stages of economic growth, from traditional societies to societies of high mass consumption (Applbaum, 2009). Marketing scholars also use modernization theory to develop managerial recommendations. For example, Ramarapu and her colleagues (1999) suggest that companies can recycle technologically dated products in less developed countries such as China and India because their level of development lags behind that of the United States. In fact, modernization theory has become so naturalized in marketing that discussions of Rostow and modernization theory in international marketing often fail to mention the conditions of its emergence (see e.g., Luqmani et al., 1994).

Even more dangerously, modernization theory creates a pernicious hierarchy which puts Western countries at the pinnacle of development.

As Ferguson (2005) puts it, the narrative of modernization employs a temporalized historical sequence in which poor countries are not simply at the bottom, but also at the beginning. What is left unspoken in this development metanarrative is the fact that the economic gulf between the richest and poorest countries is actually growing, and rapidly. As an illustration of this growing divide, Easterly (2000) has noted that most African countries are much further from the promised economic parity with the third world than they were twenty years ago. Linear models of development such as the ones that exist in international marketing or in corporate boardrooms mask the uneven and unequal way in which the global economy is evolving. Many scholars have in fact insisted that the wealth of developed economies depends on absorbing the resources of less wealthy nations.

Several researchers have started to question the Western-centric view of the world that is prevalent in business research (Boyacigiller and Adler, 1991; Usunier and Lee, 2005). They have turned their attention to Western underpinnings of management and marketing concepts and criticized the Western-centric view of the world that endures in many multinational companies. For example, Prahalad and Lieberthal (1998) point out that the first wave of MNCs simply exported the products they were already selling in the West, assuming that middle-class consumers in China and India would favorably respond to this influx of new products and services. As Prahalad and Lieberthal point out, after many blunders and efforts to grapple with the reluctance of "underdeveloped" consumers to buy obsolete products, many MNCs have started to think differently about emerging markets. Turning to other emerging markets, they have enjoyed some success in transferring knowledge, personnel, and other resources from one third-world country to another. In his work on what is called the "bottom of the pyramid," management researcher C.K. Prahalad (2004) has gone further and encouraged companies to address the needs of the poorest consumers on the planet and to turn the bottom of the socio-economic pyramid into an economic opportunity for companies.

However, it is our sense that much of this work on the "bottom of the pyramid" never really questions the ideas about development and modernity that are the core of business research and business practice. The idea that "underdeveloped" nations follow in the footsteps of "developed" ones is never really questioned. In addition, the stories that are told in this literature about companies addressing poorer consumers (see Prahalad and Hammond, 2002; Prahalad, 2004) are almost always stories about consumption of and access to better, more efficient commodities. Of course, there is no denying that some of these commodities, such as mobile phones, provide better access to jobs or facilitate commerce. Prahalad (2004) recognizes that development is more than increased access to consumption choices, but most of the case studies he cites only illustrate development through examples of increased consumption and choice. For example, Prahalad argues that the ability of poor people to buy sachets of shampoo and detergent empowers consumers by improving their dignity and self-esteem. But one has to wonder what ideology allows marketing and management researchers to equate access to cheaper, more efficient detergents with emancipation. This is not a far cry from the idea circulating in Indian boardrooms that cake mixes are tools of empowerment. What do we miss if we only frame development and human emancipation as a story of more and better consumption?

A different vision of history, an alternative to this ineluctable temporal evolution of societies and consumers, can be found in the idea of "alternative modernities"—the idea that third-world nations are on parallel tracks, inventing their own forms of modernity as they go via diverse and creative cultural practices that simultaneously coexist with variations in modern consumption and marketing practices (see Gaonkar, 2001). This stream of literature in the social sciences finds resonance in the consumer research literature examining the creative ways through which non-Western consumers have adopted, transformed, and resisted foreign cultural influences (see Ger and Belk, 1996).

However, even this romantic story about agency, plurality, and cultural difference fails to question basic assumptions about economic progression and development. For many people in third-world nations, the hope of development has been replaced by "a game of chance, a lottery in which the existential temporal horizon is colonized by the immediate present and by prosaic short-term calculations" (Mbembe, 2002: 271). Talk of consumer agency will often highlight individual consumers at the top of Prahalad's pyramid in their respective countries and ignore the worsening of global inequality and the inadequacy of these development metanarratives to explain it (Ferguson, 2005), to say nothing of dealing with it strategically.

The boardrooms of Indian advertising agencies are humming with creative adaptation, the types of alternative modernity that scholars have talked about at length. They often emphasize respect for traditional values and the fact that Indian consumers will not buy into the Western vision of the good life. Yet the equation of modernity with the increase of consumption choices and the availability of more efficient products is never really questioned in corporate boardrooms. Of course, that the advertising world operates with such conceptions of modernity is not very surprising.

Conclusion

In this chapter, we have documented how the everyday practices of marketing—the crafting and telling of stories about consumers—diffuse marketing ideology. We have shown that local advertising and marketing executives maintain and propagate many deep-seated assumptions about the future that reinforce a hierarchy in which consuming subjects are at the very top of a global pyramid, and where Western consumers are at the end of development and poorer, non-Western people are at the beginning.

Discussions about cake mixes in Indian corporate boardrooms and the lessons of international marketing textbooks have in fact much in common. They reflect and repeat the underlying vision of the future that dominates marketing scholarship and practice: a future of more consumption that is equated with human emancipation. In his chapter for this volume, Kalman Applbaum observes that not all our fears, hopes, and passions "are reducible or even translatable to that one component of our experience described by the word 'consumer'" (p. 293). We would add that not all visions of modernity equate it with more consumption and a model of development that is linear and preordained. Other paths and futures can be imagined.

For managers, the type of reflexivity we encourage is not only a moral necessity, but a strategic and pragmatic one. In addition to relegating third-world consumers to an anachronistic space (e.g., Indian consumers are from "before"), the linear logic of market development that is found in modernization theory and in the stories many managers told us is inherently unable to respond to market dynamics and future developments that are by definition uncertain. Plotting consumers and countries along a preordained temporal axis of development prevents companies from imagining another future for consumers and other ways of interacting with them.

For social scientists in general and marketing scholars in particular, there is an opportunity here to reflect upon the conceptualization of modernity which we perpetuate in textbooks, conferences, and journal articles. If the sight of small, barefooted Indian boys carrying copies of the *Harvard Business Review* proves anything, it is that academics may live in ivory towers, but their values and credo take life on the streets and in the boardrooms and meeting halls of many cities around the world. It is only when marketing and business scholars become truly reflexive in their vision of the world and of humanity that we can start imagining other forms of market relations.

Notes

1. The term "middle class" is problematic in the Indian context. As Dwyer (2000) argues, the middle class is a category that originates in Western countries where the socio-economic class pyramid actually bulges in the middle. When we employ the term "middle class" in this chapter, we usually refer to an expression used by the executives we interviewed and observed.

2. A long shirt and a pair of pants, often complemented by a rather large scarf, called a dupatta.
3. A loose, collarless shirt.

References

Aaker, D.A. (1996) *Building Strong Brands*. New York: The Free Press.

Appadurai, A. (1988) "How to Make a National Cuisine: Cookbooks in Contemporary India." *Comparative Studies in Science and History*, 30(1): 3–24.

Applbaum, K. (2009) Personal communication.

Barry, D., and Elmes, M. (1997) "Strategy Retold: Toward a Narrative View of Strategic Discourse." *Academy of Management Review*, 22: 429–52.

Boje, D. (1991) "The Storytelling Organization: A Study of Story Performance in an Office Supply Firm." *Administrative Science Quarterly*, 36(1): 106–26.

Boyacigiller, N., and Adler, N.J. (1991) "The Parochial Dinosaur: Organizational Science in a Global Context." *Academy of Management Review*, 16(2): 262–90.

Cateora, P., and Graham, J. (2002) *International Marketing*. Burr Ridge, IL: McGraw-Hill/ Irwin.

Chatterjee, P. (1993) *The Nation and Its Fragments: Colonial and Postcolonial Histories*. Princeton: Princeton University Press.

Cronon, W. (1992) "A Place for Stories: Nature, History, and Narrative." *Journal of American History*, 78: 1347–76.

Derne, S. (2008) *Globalization on the Ground: New Media and the Transformation of Culture, Class, and Gender in India*. New Delhi: Sage Publications.

Dornfeld, B. (1998) *Producing Public Television, Producing Public Culture*. Princeton, NJ: Princeton University Press.

Dru, J.M. (1996) *Disruption: Overturning Conventions and Shaking Up the Marketplace*. New York, NY: Wiley and Sons.

Dwyer, Rachel (2000) *All You Want is Money, All You Need is Love*. London: Cassell.

Easterly, William (2000) The Elusive Quest for Growth: Economists' Adventures and Misadventures in the Tropics. Cambridge, MA: MIT Press.

Feldman, M. Sköldberg, K., Brown, R.N., and Hunter, D. (2004) "Making Sense of Stones: A Rhetorical Apporach to Narrative Analysis." *Journal of Public Administration Research and Theory*, 14(2): 147–70.

Ferguson, J. (2005) "Decomposing Modernity: History and Hierarchy after Development." In Ania Loomba, Suvir Kaul, Matti Bunzl, Antoinette Burton, and Jed Esty, eds. *Postcolonial Studies and Beyond*. Duke: Duke University Press, pp. 166–82.

Firat, F., and Venkatesh, A. (1995) "Liberatory Postmodernism and the Reenchantment of Consumption." *Journal of Consumer Research*, 22(3): 239–67.

Gaonkar, D.P. (2001) *Alternative Modernities*. Durham, NC: Duke University Press.

Ger, G., and Belk, R.W. (1996) "I'd Like to Buy the World a Coke: Consumptionscapes of the 'Less Affluent World'." *Journal of Consumer Policy*, 19(3): 271–304.

Inkeles, A., and Smith, D.H. (1974) *Becoming Modern*. Cambridge, MA: Harvard University Press.

Kemper, Steven (2001) *Buying and Believing: Sri Lankan Advertising and Consumers in a Transnational World*. Chicago: University of Chicago Press.

Leichty, M. (2002) *Suitably Modern: Making Middle-Class Culture in a New Consumer Society*. Princeton, NJ: Princeton University Press.

Lofland, J., and Lofland, L.H. (1995) *Analyzing Social Settings: A Guide to Qualitative Observation and Analysis* (3rd ed.). Belmont, CA: Wadsworth Publishing.

Luqmani, M., Yavas, U., and Quraeshi, Z.A. (1994) "A Convenience-oriented Approach to Country Segmentation: Implications for Global Marketing Strategies." *Journal of Consumer Marketing*, 11(4): 29–40.

Manning, P., and Uplisashvili, A. (2007) "'Our Beer': Ethnographic Brands in Postsocialist Georgia." *American Anthropologist*, 109(4): 626–41.

Mazzarella, W. (2003) *Shoveling Smoke: Advertising and Globalization in Contemporary India*. Durham, NC: Duke University Press.

Mbembe, A. (2002) "African Modes of Self-Writing." *Public Culture*, 14(1): 239–73.

McKee, R. (2003) "Storytelling That Moves People." *Harvard Business Review*, June: 51–5.

Mehmet, O. (1999) *Westernizing the Third World: The Eurocentricity of Economic Development*. London: Routledge.

Morgan, G. (1989) "The Role of Stories." In Gareth Morgan ed. *Creative Organization Theory: Á Resource Book*, Beverly Hills: Sage Publications, pp. 297–8.

Nerhu, J. (1946) *The Discovery of India*. Calcutta: The Signet Press.

Polkinghorne, D.E. (1988) *Narrative Knowing and the Human Sciences*. Albany: State University of New York Press.

Prahalad, C.K. (2004) *The Fortune at the Bottom of the Pyramid*. Upper Saddle River: Wharton School Publishing.

——and Hammond, A. (2002) "Serving the World's Poor, Profitably." *Harvard Business Review*, 80(9): 48–58.

——and Lieberthal, K. (1998) "The End of Corporate Imperialism." *Harvard Business Review*, 76 : 69–79.

Ramarapu, S., and Timmerman, J.E., and Ramarapu, N. (1999) "Choosing Between Globalization and Localization as a Strategic Thrust for Your International Marketing Effort." *Journal of Marketing Theory & Practice*, 7(2): 97–105.

Rosaldo, R. (1989) *Culture and Truth: The Remaking of Social Analysis*. Boston: Beacon Press.

Rostow, W.W. (1960) *The Stages of Economic Growth: A Non-Communist Manifesto*. Cambridge: Cambridge University Press.

Samli, Coskun (1965) "Exportability of American Marketing Knowledge." *MSU Business Topics*, 13(Autumn): 34–42.

Usunier, J.C., and Lee, J. (2005) *Marketing Across Cultures*. New York: Financial Times/ Prentice-Hall.

Wade, R.H. (2003) "The Invisible Hand of the American Empire." *Ethics and International Affairs*, 17(2): 77–88.

Weick, K. (1995) *Sensemaking in Organizations*. Thousand Oaks, CA: Sage.

Zaltman, G. (2003) *How Customers Think*. Boston: Harvard Business School Press.

Afterword

The Marketing Reformation Redux

John F. Sherry Jr.

In several recent essays (Sherry, 2008*a*, 2008*b*), I have confessed my ambivalence as an ardent critic and willing concelebrant of consumer culture, and professed my dual allegiance to disciplines that are at once pure and applied. I chair a department that has adopted a marketing-and-society positioning. A proponent of the consumer culture theoretics (Arnould and Thompson, 2007) represented in this volume, I have taught my students how to accommodate and resist both the globalization of markets and the marketization of life. I have trained managers and been an active industry consultant for almost three decades. I have practiced and researched social and commercial marketing as an insider and an outsider. Working both sides of several streets, I have cultivated the same sense of skepticism our authors bring to bear upon the fundamentals of our discipline, as theorized and practiced. That skepticism has been sharpened in the reading of their insightful work, and I look forward to deploying it in my next projects, whether teaching, research, or consulting. With these biases in mind, the reader may take the following remarks with a grain of salt.

The contributors to this volume have explored the terrain on the frontier between critical and reflexive marketing. They are concerned to revise marketing's understanding of itself, not just as a technology of influence but as a means of apprehending and recreating the world. They address marketing as an ideological screen and a cultural force, a well-intended but impoverished philosophy with egregiously unanticipated consequences. The unexamined assumptions embedded in our theorizing and the unreflective translation of theory into managerial practice compromise comprehension and intervention alike. Wholesale employment of methodologies ill-suited either to intellectual or practical challenge further compounds the confusion. To prevent marketing from becoming a juggernaut, remaking experience in its image, our authors have recommended a re-engineering by insiders, sensitive to the shortfalls and promise the discipline embodies. In savoring the fruits of their labor, I have tried to extract just a few seeds from which the hybrid vigor of our enterprise might be improved.

In the following few paragraphs, I parse the collective wisdom (and, in many cases, borrow the language) of the volume's contributors into the convenient categories of ontology, epistemology, axiology, and praxis. The nature of what we know, the manner of our knowing, the values underlying our knowing, and the implementation of that knowing are treated separately for expositional convenience, even though they are ineluctably interconnected. They pervade the chapters of this book in different combinations and measures, and will be familiar to the reader. I begin by hectoring the insiders with a summary question in each domain that has arisen in my engagement with the ideas the authors have furnished.

Ontology

Can we discern and harmonize the interpenetrating ideologies, relationships, inter-actions, and material that direct life to prevent a cultural hijacking?

The dethroning of grand narratives in the postmodern moment has done little to discourage pretenders in the present era. Sacred and secular world-views, once presumed consecutive and discrete, are revealed to be fused in our era (Latour, 1993) and profoundly shaped by the political at all levels of operation (Foucault, 1970). The corruption of religion and science are equally likely as ideologies are translated into practice.

We seem to be leaving an epoch that has witnessed a shift from what sociologists have called the medicalization of deviance to the medicalization of life (Szasz, 2007), and entering another in which theorists (Heath and Potter, 2004; Moore, 2007) claim to be increasingly unable to disentangle marketing from culture. Public and commercial forces are not simply collid-ing, they are being interwoven in a common fabric. The consequences of this weaving are contested by our authors.

Marketing is both a barometer and a pressure front in respect of cultural ethos. All elements of the marketing mix shape and reflect culture, society, and personality. Marketing is thoroughly imbricated in everyday life. Given this fundamental enmeshment, and both the unanticipated and unintended consequences of the marketization of life, it is imperative that we learn to think systemically about marketing, using as many holistic frameworks— without automatic recourse to the still useful Marxian infrastructure/struc-ture/superstructure model latent in our authors' efforts—as we can muster in the enterprise. Whether we call it marcology (Levy, 1976), agorology (Mit-tlestaedt, 2006), or cultural ecology (Sherry, 2008*b*), understanding all the ramifications of the interrelations between stakeholders and (im)material in the aggregate marketing system (Wilkie and Moore, 2006) must become a priority for theorists and practitioners.

The relentlessly adaptive radiation of brands to ever newer niches requires renewed consideration. As brands become magnets and beacons (McCracken, 1988, 2006), totems and fetishes (Sherry, 2005), and, ultimately, pilgrimage sites (Diamond et al., 2009), life appears to become absorbed into their auras and orbits. It is clearly time to rethink our conception of the consumer, insofar as the notion obscures both the extensive productive and extra-economic activity in which the actor is engaged.

And let us rethink "community" too. Especially the kinds of moral community that exist at the intersection of economy, ecology, and cultural ethos. It is here that the moral philosophies of hazard, panic, and accountability arise and interact, forcing us to reconsider fundamentally our notions of obligation. Our overlooking of the environment both natural and built—in conceptualizing and implementing marketing has returned to haunt us. Renewed attention to infrastructure and material culture, and to sources rather than resources, promises to help us reform marketing in a radical fashion.

Epistemology

How can we encourage a habit of inquiry that matches methodology to research question rather than vice versa, recognizes the inherently interdisciplinary and hermeneutic nature of understanding, and promotes respect across paradigmatic boundaries?

While the tyranny of paradigms is no longer the scourge it was even a decade ago, the academic discipline of marketing is still hampered by a disproportionate reverence for positivist methods. Our managerial kin have been more pragmatic, adopting most of the approaches advocated by the paladins of the postmodern moment of the late 1980s, further refining many of the tools and creating new ones as well.

With the flourishing of consumer culture theoretics, and the discovery of consumer behavior across an array of disciplines (social sciences as well as humanities) contiguous to marketing, the hegemony of economics and psychology as dominant discourses is being vigorously challenged. In an ironic turn, the rise of "behavioral economics"—at once a legitimate, if belated hybridization of social sciences and a defensive retrenchment in service to the status quo—promises to affirm much of the so-called "interpretive" work that has preceded it. It is time, as Grant McCracken (2009) has proclaimed, for a Chief Culture Officer to ascend to the C-suite, for academic counterparts to edit more marketing journals (in the tradition of *Culture, Markets and*

Consumption), and for marketing adepts to influence social science outlets (such as the *Journal of Consumer Culture*).

Our authors draw upon an impressive assortment of methods and perspectives in their inquiries. Archival analysis, historiography, ethnography, and survey are each employed to enlightening effect. The disciplines of anthropology, cultural studies, history, sociology, semiotics, and logistics are brought to bear upon the re-conceptualization of marketing. The sampling frames employed are also quite distinctive in comparison to conventional marketing inquiry. A wide selection of temporal eras and cultures is represented in the book, which is another pleasant contrast with the tempo- and America-centric foci that orient the field.

The essay format observed by the authors is itself an interesting and impactful departure from the journal article template that acts as a constraint on creative discovery, a kind of straitjacket ensuring formulaic conformity, ostensibly in the service of efficiency. The essay permits greater recognition of and ethical exploitation of the awesome power of rhetoric in the creation of meaning. That writing is a foundational dimension of knowing, that the text is not merely a vessel of knowledge conveyance but a method of generating insight and understanding, is too infrequently acknowledged in our field. While there is a vibrant subaltern tradition of scholarly book publishing (and a brisk one in text and trade books) in academic marketing, this effort has been lost to most of the field, even if it has inspired some path-breaking research on the margins. Ironically, much marketing insight has diffused to contiguous disciplines through books rather than journal articles, given both differing reward structures and misperceptions at work beyond our field.

Axiology

Given that the legal is not always (or often) the ethical, should needs (vs. wants) be placed beyond the reach of the market, in some restricted sense?

Oscar Wilde once observed: "A map of the world that does not include Utopia is not worth even glancing at, for it leaves out the one country at which Humanity is always landing. And when Humanity lands there, it looks out, and seeing a better country, sets sail. Progress is the realisation of Utopias" (1910: 27). Wildean cynicism might hold that marketers know the price of everything and the value of nothing. The chapters in this volume are shot through with the moral significance of marketing. From the apparently perversely self-defeating ideology of marketing humanism, to the shift toward a stakeholder- and service-dominant perspective of marketing, even our most benign efforts to relieve the discontents of everyday life with a spoonful of strategic planning are fraught with peril. As an intellectual discipline and a managerial practice, marketing is the envisioning of, and questing for, Utopia (Maclaran and Brown, 2005). It is arguably the paramount utopian force at work in the world today. If marketers are the chief cartographers of this enterprise, such misplaced pre-eminence exacts a moral toll. Whether it involves something as massive and exteroceptive as retheorizing our conception of nonethnocentric development (the promotion of appropriate local utopias), or as primal and intraceptive as articulating an authentic self, moral geography demands to be renegotiated. These choices stem from the values the discipline embraces.

Value polarity between competing world views (marketing, science, religion, politics, etc.) is exceedingly difficult to reconcile. Polarity that may exist within a world view may be impossible to resolve without significant compromise. For example, our ostensibly honorable consumer-centric philosophy of marketing seems to conflict with an apparently more generative and sustainable socio-centric orientation. Giving the consumer what s/he really wants (pace Levitt) may ultimately be harmful both to consumer and society. Giving social considerations priority over individual ones seems paternalistic in the best case, and autocratic in the worst. If marketing humanism is to be rehabilitated, the "debate" between private gain and public good must be staged in every venue of enculturation and cultural production. Debate must be as pervasive as the influence it enshrines; we must "commit to the seminar as a way of life, so teaching moments don't go unrealized" (Sherry, 2008*b*: 93). This means moving the discussion beyond seminar rooms, lecture halls, and the research pods of cubicle land, and into the precincts of everyday life. We might begin with conversations around the electronic hearth, in all its manifestations, as we all lead super-mediated lives. The yoking of any cultural cynosure such as play (the heir to the sacred in commerce) to marketing should always be a cause for deep reflection and public discussion.

Perhaps all marketing must become social marketing, and the template imposition reversed. Demarketing? Yes, demarketing (Kotler and Levy, 1971), via re-envisioned marketing (Sherry, 2000). Before profitable brands enter their conservative financial phase, perhaps they should be held accountable for producing social value in their dynamic creative phase. Both centipedal and centrifugal forces should comprise the brand's energy (Mish and Scammon, 2010). As marketers discover/create segments, a social impact assessment might be demanded, and social permission marketing enforced. Viewing research simply as a proprietary exercise in exploration or confirmation is so idealistic as to be naïve.

Praxis

How can we best negotiate beyond constraints (or low expectations) placed upon us by clients (commercial and noncommercial) to deliver uncommon value?

Our authors make it abundantly clear that slippage occurs across all stakeholder activities, and, in those cases where it can actually be said to be motivated, may spring from either benign or malign intent. Marketers can further corrupt an already compromised science, compounding the felony. Marketers can ignore consumer agency, disingenuously discover an experience economy that has always existed, and then appropriate consumer creativity in service to the brand. Marketers can inexpertly apply a one-size-fits-all commercial template to social concerns for which it is ill-suited, rather than attend to nuance and selectively modify models to engage challenge more effectively. These decisions arise from the latitude marketers are given in matching the goals of consumer and corporate satisfaction.

We learn from the volume's contributors that marketing rhetoric shapes not only positioning decisions but cultural evolution as well. Marketing becomes a cognitive and visceral way of knowing that reinforces and alters social structure (class, ethnicity, gender, life course, core/periphery relations) over time. Stakeholder snafu is often the order of the day, and, as with sausage, spicy succulence may be the end result, but consumers (perhaps especially students) are not encouraged to watch how marketing is actually made.

Reformation

It is interesting to speculate whether or not the current economic meltdown, coupled with the escalating threat of environmental degradation, will have a significant lasting effect on consumer behavior. Will frugality and involuntary simplicity become hazy memories if the economy rebounds and the ice caps remain visible in the next few years? Will a revitalization movement depose the culture of consumption and readjust our relationship to the world of goods? Will the global transformation the Mayan calendar predicts for 2012 be catalyzed by these synchronous economic and ecological calamities? It appears there has never been a more propitious time (aside, perhaps, from Stephen Brown's millenarian Belfast trilogy of conferences) to reconsider the roots and fruits of marketing. A re-conceiving of the marketing imagination (again, pace Levitt) would seem to be a moral imperative for our field. I offer a mythopoeic injunction. Just as the universe is danced into being, so the dance of death will close it out. We will need to separate the dancer from the dance, if just for awhile, to improve and prolong the quality of life. To the extent that marketing calls the tune, marketing ought to be reformed.

The ambitious agenda of *Inside Marketing*, like that of its predecessor *Philosophical and Radical Thought in Marketing*, and its contemporaries *Critical Marketing: Defining the Field* and *Critical Marketing: Issues in Contemporary Marketing*, challenges us to understand more comprehensively and apply more humanely one of the most powerful forces on the planet. Taming and harnessing this force requires that its theoretical assumptions and practical consequences be inventoried and assessed on a regular basis, so that dysfunctional conventional wisdom is not perpetually recycled. Critical analysis is the first step, and the questions it raises comprise the platform from which practical answers can be sought. A cultural perspective must guide this analysis, if the reformation is to be comprehensive.

It is time for marketing to be rocked by the reflexive revolution that has unmoored the identities of its neighboring disciplines (Sherry, 2008a). And that revolution should be televised. Our authors have revealed a host of flashpoints from which to commence: Pre-commercial marketing. Branditization. Segment caricaturization. Social engineering. Latent theories-in-use. Upstream ethics. Researcher activism.... Let us hope that this new wave of reflexivity will sustain and deepen the marketing reformation, and lead to a new era (Applbaum, 2004) of more elegant theorizing and humane practice.

References

Applbaum, Kalman (2004) *The Marketing Era: From Professional Practice to Global Provisioning.* New York: Routledge.

Arnould, Eric, and Thompson, Craig (2007) "Consumer Culture Theory (And We Really Mean Theoretics): Dilemmas and Opportunities Posed by an Academic Branding Strategy." In Russell Belk and John F. Sherry, Jr. eds. *Consumer Culture Theory*, Vol. 11 of *Research in Consumer Behavior*. Oxford: Elsevier, pp. 3–22.

Diamond, Nina, Sherry Jr., John F., Muñiz Jr., Albert M., McGrath, Mary Ann, Kozinets, Robert V., and Borghini, Stefania (2009) "American Girl and the Brand Gestalt: Closing the Loop on Sociocultural Branding Research." *Journal of Marketing*, 73(3): 118–34.

Firat, A. Fuat, Dholakia, Nikhilesh and Bagozzi, Richard, eds. (1987) *Philosophical and Radical Thought in Marketing*. Lexington, MA: Lexington Books.

Foucault, Michel (1970) *The Order of Things: An Archaeology of the Human Sciences.* New York: Pantheon.

Heath, Joseph, and Potter, Andrew (2004) *Nation of Rebels: Why Counterculture Became Consumer Culture*. New York: Harper Collins.

Kotler, Philip, and Levy, Sidney J. (1971) "Demarketing, Yes, Demarketing." *Harvard Business Review*, 49(6): 74–80.

Latour, Bruno (1993) *We Have Never Been Modern* (Trans. Catherine Porter). Cambridge, MA: Harvard University Press.

Levy, Sidney (1976) "Marcology 101, or the Domain of Marketing." In Kenneth Bernhardt, ed. *Marketing 1776–1976 and Beyond*. Chicago: American Marketing Association, pp. 577–81.

Maclaran, Pauline, and Brown, Stephen (2005) "The Center Cannot Hold: Consuming the Utopian Marketplace." *Journal of Consumer Research*, 32(September): 311–23.

McCracken, Grant (1988) *Culture and Consumption*. Bloomington: Indiana University Press.

——(2006) *Culture and Consumption II*. Bloomington: Indiana University Press.

——(2009) *Chief Culture Officer: How to Create a Living, Breathing Corporation*. New York: Basic Books.

Mish, Jennifer, and Scammon, Debra (2010) "Principle-Based Stakeholder Marketing: Insights from Private Triple-Bottom-Line Firms." *Journal of Public Policy and Marketing* 29(1): 12–26.

Mittlestaedt, John (2006) "Macromarketing as Agorology: Macromarketing Theory and the Study of the Agora." *Journal of Macromarketing*, 26(2): 131–42.

Moore, Anne Elizabeth (2007) *Unmarketable: Brandalism, Copyfighting, Mocketing and the Erosion of Integrity*. New York: New Press.

Saran, Michael, Maclaran, Pauline, Golding, Christina, Elliott, Richard, Shankar, Avi, and Catterall, Miriam, eds. (2007) *Critical Marketing: Defining the Field*. New York: Elsevier.

Sherry, John F., Jr. (2000) "Distraction, Destruction, Deliverance: The Presence of Mindscape in Marketing's New Millennium." *Marketing Intelligence and Planning*, 18 (6–7): 328–36.

——(2005) "Brand Meaning." In T. Calkins and A. Tybout, eds. *Kellogg on Branding*. New York: John Wiley, pp. 40–69.

——(2008a) "Ethnography Goes to Market." *American Anthropologist*, 110(1): 73–6.

——(2008b) "The Ethnographer's Apprentice: Trying Consumer Culture from the Outside In." *Journal of Business Ethics*, 80: 85–95.

Szasz, Thomas (2007) *The Medicalization of Everyday Life: Selected Essays*. Syracuse, NY: Syracuse University Press.

Tadajewski, Mark, and Douglas, Brownlie, eds. (2008) *Critical Marketing: Issues in Contemporary Marketing*. Chichester, UK: John Wiley.

Wilde, Oscar (1910) *The Soul of Man under Socialism*. Boston: Luce.

Wilkie, William, and Moore, Elizabeth (2006) "Macromarketing as a Pillar of Marketing Thought." *Journal of Macromarketing*, 26(2): 227–32.

Index

Pictures and diagrams are given in italics.

Index

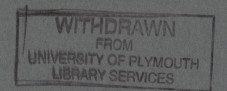

Fracture Mechanics of Cementitious Materials

Fracture Mechanics
of Cementitious Materials

BRIAN COTTERELL
Professor of Mechanical & Production Engineering
Nanyang Technological University
Singapore

and

YIU-WING MAI
Professor of Mechanical Engineering
University of Sydney
Australia

BLACKIE ACADEMIC & PROFESSIONAL
An Imprint of Chapman & Hall
London · Glasgow · Weinheim · New York · Tokyo · Melbourne · Madras

Published by
Blackie Academic & Professional, an imprint of Chapman & Hall,
Wester Cleddens Road, Bishopbriggs, Glasgow G64 2NZ

Chapman & Hall, 2–6 Boundary Row, London SE1 8HN, UK

Blackie Academic & Professional, Wester Cleddens Road, Bishopbriggs,
Glasgow G64 2NZ, UK

Chapman & Hall GmbH, Pappelallee 3, 69469 Weinheim, Germany

Chapman & Hall USA, 115 Fifth Avenue, Fourth Floor, New York,
NY 10003, USA

Chapman & Hall Japan, ITP-Japan, Kyowa Building, 3F,
2-2-1 Hirakawacho, Chiyoda-ku, Tokyo 102, Japan

DA Book (Aust.) Pty Ltd, 648 Whitehorse Road, Mitcham 3132, Victoria,
Australia

Chapman & Hall India, R. Seshadri, 32 Second Main Road, CIT East,
Madras 600 035, India

First edition 1996

© 1996 Chapman & Hall

Typeset in 10/12pt Times by Academic & Technical Typesetting, Bristol
Printed in Great Britain by St Edmundsbury Press Ltd, Bury St Edmunds, Suffolk

ISBN   0 7514 0036 X

A catalogue record for this book is available from the British Library
Library of Congress Catalog Card Number: 95-81444

∞ Printed on permanent acid-free text paper, manufactured in accordance
with ANSI/NISO Z39.48-1992 (Permanence of Paper).

Preface

Since the early works of Griffith (1921), Orowan (1948) and Irwin (1957) linear elastic fracture mechanics (LEFM) has been successfully used by many researchers and engineers not only to obtain methodologies for the safe design of engineering materials and structures but also to develop new advanced materials by identifying the critical parameters in the fracture energy–microstructure relationship. Many high strength metals and ideally brittle ceramics and polymers have been adequately characterised by a single linear elastic fracture mechanics parameter such as the critical potential energy release rate G_c or the critical stress intensity factor K_c. However, the application of classical LEFM to cementitious materials like pastes, mortars and concretes (Higgins and Bailey, 1976; Kaplan, 1961; Kesler et al., 1972) has not been as successful and critical failure cannot be defined by G_c or K_c alone. As it is understood now this is because of the large localised tension-softening or damage zone at the notch tip. Cementitious materials are therefore 'quasi-brittle'. Provided the damage zone can be modelled appropriately LEFM can still be used to characterise the fracture process and predict the failure loads of structrues. However, this requires a fundamental understanding of the stress-displacement relationship of the tension-softening zone in cementitious materials.

Cementitious materials are often assumed to have negligible strength in tension. As will be shown in this book this assumption has prevented the efficient use of these materials for many years. Fibres are therefore usually added to improve the tensile properties and the capacity for impact energy absorption. These fibres can be long (continuous) or short (discontinuous) and may be asbestos, steel, carbon, glass, polypropylene, polyethylene, nylon, Kevlar and many other natural fibres like cellulose, cotton, sisal, jute, bamboo etc. In fibre reinforced cementitious materials there is a large fibre bridging zone (FBZ) in addition to the matrix fracture process zone (FPZ) intimately associated with the tension-softening characteristic of the cement matrix. Fracture mechanics description of the failure of fibre reinforced cementitious materials has to include both the FPZ and the FBZ. Naturally, the constitutive relationship of the FBZ will depend on the geometric dimensions of the fibres and the nature and physico-mechanical properties of the fibre–matrix interphase.

Whilst several books have been written on the application of fracture mechanics to polymers (Williams, 1984), ceramics (Lawn, 1993), metals (Knott, 1973) and materials in general (Atkins and Mai, 1985) there is no single book that is devoted to the fracture mechanics of *both* cementitious materials and their fibre reinforced composites. The necessity for a consistent fracture mechanics approach to the failure of cementitious materials and its implications to design codes have been quite succinctly covered in the two Reports (ACI 446.1R–91 and 446.2R–92) by the ACI Committee 446 on Fracture Mechanics. Over the last 15 to 20 years there have been many research papers and reports on the fracture mechanics and fracture mechanisms of cementitious materials; and we have made our own contributions. Many of these papers however, appear in different mechanics and materials journals and various conference proceedings. This makes it very difficult for the postgraduate students, the practising engineers and the beginners in the field to seek the required information. We believe the time is ripe for a systematic introduction to the application of fracture mechanics for the failure of cementitious materials including their fibre composites. However, in writing this book we are very much guided by our own research experience; and in the choice of subjects and presentation we seek a balance of theories, experiments and applications. The mechanics and materials aspects are very much emphasised. The book should be of interest, as a reference text, to professional engineers, research scientists and concrete technologists who have little knowledge of fracture mechanics and who want to enter this fast developing field. It will be of particular interest to civil, structural and materials engineering postgraduate research students and their supervisors in universities and institutions.

The book contains eight chapters. Chapter 1 presents the fundamentals of both linear elastic and non-linear fracture mechanics theories to the readers and their potential application and limitation to characterise the fracture propagation of cementitious materials. In Chapter 2 the development of the FPZ in the cementitious matrices due to the phenomenon of tensile-softening and the FBZ due to fibre bridging across the crack faces is introduced. The associated fracture mechanisms are also discussed and the role of the interphase between the paste and aggregates and that between the fibre and matrix material are explained. Particularly, the strengthening and toughening mechanisms for the new inorganic material—*macro-defect-free cement*—invented by ICI (UK) Ltd in the 1980s have been clearly identified as due to the presence of the polymer. Chapter 3 gives an account of the many experimental techniques appropriate for the measurement of the FPZ and FBZ. It is shown that the two most important parameters in these two zones are the fracture strength f_t and the fracture energy G_{If}. The precise stress–displacement relationships are unimportant if these two parameters are correct.

Theoretical models for fracture in cementitious materials are developed in Chapter 4. Such models must consider the effect of the FPZ and be able to reproduce the load–displacement curves as in experiments. These include the equivalent crack model, the crack band model and the fictitious crack model. It is suggested that the most convenient model is the fictitious crack model with the LEFM K-superposition principle. Size and notch effects as well as the 'energy brittleness number' are also discussed here within the framework of fracture mechanics. In Chapter 5 fracture mechanics models are presented for crack growth in fibre reinforced cementitious composites. It is not necessary to model the matrix FPZ provided the fracture toughness of the reinforced matrix is used. The most important fracture parameters are K_{Ic}, f_t, E (Young's modulus), and G_{If}. Once determined they enable the load-displacement and crack-resistance curves for any geometry and size of specimens and structures to be predicted. Because of the large FBZ the crack-resistance curve is both geometry and size dependent. A unique crack-resistance curve can be obtained only if the FBZ is fully developed. This means prohibitively large specimens or structures.

Statistics is seldom considered in the fracture mechanics of cementitious materials although it is fully recognised that they are quasi-brittle and not very homogeneous. In Chapter 6 statistical fracture mechanics theories of ideally brittle solids and two-phase materials are given. It will be shown that the Weibull distribution cannot predict the strength dependence on size because of the non-proportional scaling of the localised tension-softening zone. Fibre reinforcement reduces the scatter of the strength distribution and increases the structural reliability. Even low stiffness fibres can improve the tensile strength of cementitious matrices. Chapter 7 presents the strength characteristics of cementitious materials under time-dependent loading from the viewpoints of both the deterministic single crack theory and the probabilistic statistical multiple crack approach. Cracks in these materials are susceptible to environment-assisted slow crack growth under static, dynamic and cyclic stresses. However, the mechanical fatigue due to cyclic stresses is still an unresolved problem. Under certain circumstances it is demonstrated that the statistical time-dependent fracture theories developed for single phase materials can be empirically used for two-phase materials with reasonable success.

Finally, in Chapter 8, the application of fracture mechanics to the design of concrete structures is demonstrated with known case studies in the literature. This shows how far fracture mechanics has now been adopted by the concrete community. It is expected that over the next few years the practical design rules will be modified to take into account the research results on the fracture mechanics of cementitious materials and their fibre composites.

We began work on fibre cements in the late 1970s for James Hardie & Coy. Pty. Ltd. looking for replacement fibres for asbestos and we quickly realised that fracture mechanics was scarcely used then to characterise the failure of fibre reinforced cements. There were many opportunities for making significant contributions on the fracture mechanics of these quasi-brittle materials. So when this project was finished our fundamental fracture mechanics work for cementitious materials was continued with funding from the Australian Research Council. Many of the experimental results and theoretical models of the FPZ and FBZ contained in this book are taken from past students and colleagues who worked on these projects during those times. In this regard, we thank both James Hardie & Coy. Pty. Ltd. and the Australian Research Council for their financial support. To R. Andonian, B.G. Barakat, R.M.L. Foote, Y.C. Gao, M.I. Hakeem, X.Z. Hu, J.K. Kim, M.V. Swain and L.M. Zhou we acknowledge their many contributions. Also, T.J. Chuang and B.R. Lawn of NIST and K.Y. Lam of National Singapore University have made numerous other contributions which are incorporated in one form or another in this book.

The concept of writing this book first came from Professor Narayan Swamy of Sheffield University in the late 1980s and to him we express our sincerest gratitude. We must apologise that it has taken so long to see the book in print and the fault is all ours. Finally, we thank our wives, Maureen and Louisa, for the patience and understanding when the book was written over several years in Sydney, Singapore and Hong Kong.

Brian Cotterell
Yiu-Wing Mai

Singapore and Sydney
September 1995

Foreword

Linear elastic fracture mechanics has been developed since the early twenties of this century but essentially for brittle materials. This theoretical concept proved to be a powerful tool to predict failure of materials such as glass, ceramics or high strength metals in a realistic way and under various given loading conditions. No wonder that this approach is now widely used for many years to solve practical problems. New and sophisticated experimental techniques and theoretical concepts have been elaborated continuously and most standards in this field are based on fracture mechanics. A number of excellent textbooks are available.

Already the first attempts to apply linear fracture mechanics to describe failure of concrete and concrete structures have shown clearly that crack growth in this type of composite material is not well represented by linear elastic fracture mechanics. Even modifications introduced in order to overcome obvious discrepancies have had little or no success. Therefore design rules for concrete structures are most often still based on predominantly empirical rules rather than being developed systematically within a wider and generally accepted theoretical concept.

It took a considerable time before a rational basis for a non-linear fracture mechanics approach was formulated for application to concrete; a material with pronounced strain softening. For the time being we live in a split situation. On one side we are able to predict failure of concrete and concrete-like materials by means of advanced numerical methods in great detail and with astonishing precision. In addition relevant material parameters are available for many practical applications. On the other side traditional standards still use the unrealistic strength criterion with a whole series of necessary correction factors. The fact that there is no comprehensive textbook on the theoretical basis and potential applications of non-linear fracture mechanics is certainly one major reason for this obvious gap.

Even at university level the relevant concepts of non-linear fracture mechanics are hardly taught and research activities are still widely diverging. A closer look into the relevant technical literature tells us immediately that some research groups take a lead and further improve the underlying theoretical concepts as well as the experimental and numerical methods while others continue to apply simplifying approaches which had long ago proved to be of little or no real meaning. Sometime it is very difficult to understand this unfortunate situation which may be characterized by 'le dialogue des sourds'.

At last, a book on fracture mechanics of cementitious materials written by two widely acknowledged expers Yiu-Wing Mai and Brian Cotterell has appeared. This book is written in a rigorous way and access to the corresponding original literature is made easy by an extensive list of references. It can be used as a textbook for students and at the same time as an appropriate introduction for engineers already active in practice. After the publication of this volume there is no more excuse for engineers not being informed on most recent developments in fracture mechanics of concrete and its consequences for design of concrete structures as well as for the analysis of concrete failures.

It is hoped that in the future research will be streamlined and progress will be accelerated. Implementation of relevant results into codes and practice of civil engineering will now be facilitated. It is rare that a textbook is so definitely needed as in the present case.

Folker H. Wittmann
Zürich, December 1995

Contents

Nomenclature

a	Crack length, or total length of true plus fictitious crack lengths.
a_0	Reference crack size.
a_e	Equivalent crack length.
a_i	Initial crack length.
A	Crack area or fibre area.
b	Ligament length.
B	Thickness. Risk of rupture.
c	Pore size.
c_f	Same as Δa_e.
C	Compliance.
C_m	Machine compliance.
C_p	The compliance of a specimen after saw-cutting through part of the FPZ.
C^*	Unloading compliance containing an FPZ.
d_a	Aggregate size.
d_f	Diameter of fibre or length of the FBZ.
d_p	Length of the FPZ.
$D = \begin{bmatrix} D_{nn} & D_{nt} \\ D_{tn} & D_{tt} \end{bmatrix}$	Instantaneous moduli matrix.
E	Young's modulus.
E'	Young's modulus of damaged material in the FPZ.
$E^* = E$ $= E/(1 - \nu^2)$	Young's modulus for plane stress for plane strain.
E_c	Young's modulus of composite.
E_f	Young's modulus of fibre.
E_m	Young's modulus of matrix.
E_t	Tangent softening modulus.
$f(a)$	Flaw size distribution function.
f_c	Compressive strength.
f_t	Tensile strength.
F, F_f	Load carried by fibre bundle. Fibre bridging force.
F_f	Fibre force.
g_{If}	Specific fracture energy.
G	Shear modulus. Crack extension force.
G_m	Shear modulus of matrix.

G_I, G_{II}, G_{III}	Rate of release of potential energy, or crack extension force, for the three modes of fracture.
G_{IIb}	The interfacial fracture energy between the fibre and matrix.
G_{If}, G_{IIf}	Mode I and II fracture energies.
G_i	Initiation fracture energy.
G_{Im}	The mode I fracture energy of the matrix.
$G_R(\Delta a)$	Crack growth resistance in terms of work of fracture.
G_u	Upperbound crack extension force.
h	Width of FPZ or depth of beam.
h_c, h_t	Depths of tensile and compressive zones.
h_y	Distance of first cracking strain from neutral axis.
H	Beam height.
J, J_R	Line integral. Crack growth resistance in terms of J.
k_I	Stress intensity factor for unit force.
K_a	Applied stress intensity factor.
K_e	Effective stress intensity factor.
K_F	Stress intensity factor due to fictitious force.
K_I, K_{II}, K_{III}	Mode I, II, III stress intensity factors.
K_i	Initiation fracture toughness.
K_{If}	Fracture toughness of cementitious material. If there is crack growth resistance, the plateau value of the mode I fracture toughness.
K_{Ic}	The plane strain fracture toughness or fracture toughness of reinforced matrix.
K_{Ic}^*	Reference fracture toughness of reinforced matrix.
K_{Ic}^e	Equivalent stress intensity factor.
K_m	Stress intensity factor due to stress in FPZ.
K_p	Fracture toughness of particle.
K_r	Stress intensity factor due to stress in the FPZ.
K_{ref}	Reference stress intensity factor.
$K_R(\Delta a)$	The crack growth resistance in terms of fracture toughness.
K_t	Crack tip total stress intensity factor.
l	Total length of real plus fictitious crack. Fibre length.
l_c	Critical length for fibre pull-out.
$l_{ch} = EG_{If}/f_t^2$	Characteristic length of the first kind.
$l_{ch}^* = l_{ch}(f_t/E)^2$ $= G_{If}/E$	Characteristic length of the second kind.
L	Length of specimen.
L_m	Spacing of multiple cracks.
m	Weibull modulus.
$m(a, x)$	Weight function.

M_c, M_u	Critical and ultimate bending moment.
n	Power law exponent, or number of fibres.
N	Number of cycles to failure, or number of intact fibres in a bundle.
p	Hydrostatic stress.
P	Load. Probability of failure.
P_m	Maximum load.
q_0	Initial clamping stress at fibre-matrix interface.
q_{th}	The threshold interfacial pressure at which the interfacial contact pressure between a fibre and the matrix just falls to zero before debonding.
r_p	Distance from the tip of the equivalent crack to the edge of the FPZ.
R	Stress ratio or radius of curvature.
s_E	Stress brittleness number.
$S(\sigma)$	Probability of survival at stress σ.
S	Shear strength or loading span.
t	Thickness of FPZ or time.
t_f	Lifetime.
T_i	Traction vector.
T_n, T_s	Normal and shear tractions at crack faces.
v	Volume fraction of fibres.
v_c	Critical volume fraction of fibres. For volume fractions greater than v_c the fibres alone can withstand a higher load than the composite before the matrix cracks completely.
v_m	Volume fraction of matrix.
v_p	Volume fraction of pore or second phase particle.
V	Volume.
V_p	Volume of PFZ.
w	Half-width of FPZ.
w_f	Specific fracture work.
w_s	Work of fracture per unit thickness of plate.
w_p	Specific fracture work of fibre pull-out.
W	Specimen width or a characteristic specimen dimension. Strain energy density function.
$\bar{W}$	Non-dimension specimen size of the first kind.
$\bar{\bar{W}}$	Non-dimension specimen size of the second kind.
W_f	Work of fracture.
β	Shear retention factor, $(\pi/2)(\sigma/f_t)$, or an angle.
ϵ^{co}	Strain due to elasticity of the uncracked material.
ϵ^{cr}	Strain due to opening of microcracks.
ϵ_{nn}, ϵ_{tt}	The strain referred to local coordinates, n and t.

ϵ_f	The mode I strain at complete tensile failure.
ϵ_t	The strain at the onset of mode I strain-softening.
ϵ_u	The ultimate strain in the matrix.
$\delta(x)$	The COD at a general position on a crack face.
δ_f	The CTOD at the tip of the true crack at the initiation of real crack growth in a cementitious material or final fibre pull-out in a fibre reinforced composite.
δ_m	The CTOD at the tip of the true crack at the moment of the formation of a continuous *cmatrix* crack in a composite.
δ_{ref}	Reference COD.
δ_t	The CTOD at the tip of the true crack.
Δ	Deflection.
Δ_i	Indicated deflection.
Δ_m	Machine deflection.
Δ_r	Residual displacement.
γ	Shear strain.
γ_u	Ultimate shear strain.
γ_s	Specific surface energy.
Γ	Surface energy.
λ	Ratio of mode II to mode I stress intensity factor.
Λ	Strain energy.
$\eta, \eta_1, \eta_\theta$	A parameter for determining J from Λ. Efficiency factors for fibre reinforcement.
θ	Angle.
ν	Poisson's ratio.
μ	Frictional coefficient, or mean fibre bundle stress.
ν_m, ν_f	Poisson's ratio of the matrix and fibre respectively.
Π	Potential energy of system.
Π_l	Potential energy of external loads.
ρ	Flaw density.
ρ_c	Density of concrete.
ρ_f	Fibre density.
ρ_p	Particle density.
ρ_w	Density of water.
σ	Normal stress.
σ_0	Reference stress.
σ_c	Cyclic stress amplitude, or critical fracture stress.
σ_{cmc}	The composite stress at which the matrix cracks.
σ_f	Fibre stress in a cementitious composite.
σ_{fb}	Fibre stress at debonding.
σ_{fbi}	Initial fibre stress at debonding.
σ_{fc}	Fibre fracture stress.
σ_{fp}	Fibre pull-out stress.

σ_{nn}, σ_{nt}	Normal stress and shear stress referred to local coordinates n, t.
σ_m	Matrix stress in a cementitious composite.
σ_{mc}	Critical matrix cracking stress for a cementitious composite.
σ_N	Nominal fracture strength.
σ_Y	Yield strength of a metal.
τ	Shear stress.
τ_b	Bond strength between fibre and matrix.
τ_u	Ultimate shear stress.
τ_f	Interfacial frictional shear stress.

1 Fundamentals of fracture mechanics

1.1 Introduction

Much of the design of structures is about scaling. In conventional strength of materials, prior to the development of fracture mechanics, the maximum stress level alone was thought to determine fracture and there were various stress-based criteria of failure. In very many design cases, such as small ductile metal components, the strength of materials approach is sufficient and designs can be based on stress alone. The concept of stress enabled the formulation of rational scaling laws. Galileo (1638) devoted a considerable portion of his book, *Dialogues concerning two new sciences,* to a discussion on the strength of materials and had a very clear understanding of the concept of stress and gave an early discussion on scaling.[1] Galileo deduced that the maximum bending moments sustainable by geometrically similar beams are proportional to the cube of a characteristic dimension whereas the bending moment due to the self-weight of a beam is proportional to the fourth power of a characteristic dimension. This size effect places a limit on the size of structures, both man-made and natural, which makes it impossible to build 'ships, palaces, or temples of enormous size in such a way that all their oars, yards, beams, iron bolts... will hold together; nor can nature produce trees of extraordinary size because their branches would break down under their own weight' (Galileo, 1638). Until Griffith (1921) wrote his famous classic paper, *The phenomenon of rupture and flow in solids*, the strength scaling laws remained basically the same as Galileo's.

1.2 Griffith's theory of fracture

Griffith (1921) showed that the tensile strength of aged glass fibres was not constant, as is predicted by conventional strength of materials, but that fine glass fibres are stronger than thicker ones. Griffith's theory accounted for the size effect he observed.

There are two basic aspects to Griffith's innovative approach to fracture. First he realized that the relatively low strength of bulk glass was due to the presence of crack-like flaws and secondly he saw that a static crack in

[1] The Alexandrian Greeks, in the third century BC devised a very much earlier scaling law. They gave the correct equation to scale the size of torsion catapults to give the same range (Marsden, 1969; Cotterell and Kamminga, 1992).

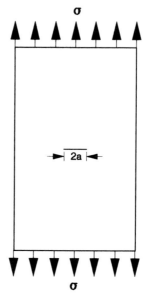

Figure 1.1 The classic Griffith crack.

an ideal elastic-brittle material could be modelled as a reversible thermo-dynamic system. The energies associated with a cracked ideal elastic-brittle solid, under static conditions, are the potential energy of the external loads, Π_l, the strain energy stored, Λ, and the surface energy, Γ. It can easily be shown that the potential energy of the system, $\Pi = \Pi_l + \Lambda$, decreases as a crack extends. If this decrease in potential energy is equal to or greater than the necessary increase in surface energy $d\Gamma$, then the crack can grow. Griffith (1921, 1925) used the solution of Inglis (1913) to show that the rate of release of potential energy, or crack extension force as it is often called,[2] G_I, with respect to the crack area, $2aB$, in an infinite plate loaded by a normal stress, σ, is given by[3] (see Figure 1.1)

$$G_I = -\frac{1}{B}\frac{d\Pi}{d(2a)} = \frac{\sigma^2 \pi a}{E^*} \tag{1.1}$$

where B is the thickness of the plate. For plane stress, $E^* = E$, the Young's modulus, and for plane strain, $E^* = E/(1 - \nu^2)$, where ν is Poisson's ratio. If the specific surface energy is γ_s the necessary work to produce a unit area of fracture surface is $2\gamma_s B$. If the crack extension force is equal to or greater

[2] The unit of the rate of release of potential energy is J/m^2 which is the same as N/m. Hence G_I can be conceived as a force per unit length of the crack front in a similar fashion to how the work required to move a dislocation line of unit length through a unit distance is conceived as a force per unit length of a dislocation.
[3] In his original paper, Griffith (1921) made an error in proceeding to the limit which he corrected in his second paper (Griffith, 1925).

than this rate of fracture work, then the crack can propagate. So that the necessary condition gives the critical fracture stress, σ_c, as

$$\sigma_c = \sqrt{\frac{2\gamma_s E^*}{\pi a}} \qquad (1.2)$$

Most materials do not even approximate to an ideal elastic-brittle material and much more work than the surface energy is required to produce fracture. In general there will be a zone at the crack tip where the material is behaving non-elastically. Dissipative work has to be performed in this zone in addition to the surface energy. Orowan (1948) and Irwin (1948) saw that a plastic zone forms at the tip of a crack in high strength metals and, provided this zone is small, the plastic work required to create a unit area of fracture surface is a material constant that can be added to the surface energy. Since the surface energy is in most cases orders of magnitude less than the plastic work, it can be neglected. It has become normal practice to relate the plastic work to the fracture area of one surface, and if the specific fracture energy is G_{If} then the critical stress is given by

$$\sigma_c = \sqrt{\frac{E^* G_{\text{If}}}{\pi a}} \qquad (1.3)$$

In the case of high strength metals, the fracture energy associated with the plastic particle is a material constant. It is unnecessary to separate the continuum plastic work from the total work performed within the plastic zone, to obtain the essential non-continuum work of fracture, because each work component separately is a constant. The concept of including all the work performed within the plastic zone in the fracture energy has been generalized to other materials. In this generalization, the plastic zone is called the fracture process zone (FPZ) which can be defined as the smallest zone where the specific work performed, or fracture energy, is reasonably constant in a large specimen. In cementitious materials the FPZ is the strain-softened zone at the tip of the notch or crack where microcracking and debonding between the cement and the aggregate causes the stress to decrease with further straining (see Figure 1.2). However, whereas in high strength metals the fully developed plastic zone or FPZ can be much less than a millimetre in size, in cementitious materials the fully developed FPZ is usually large. Although the FPZ for cement paste is quite small, of the order of a millimetre (Higgins and Bailey, 1976), the FPZ in mortar is around 30 mm (Hu and Wittmann, 1989), and for concrete up to 500 mm (Chhuy *et al.*, 1981). Outside the FPZ the cementitious material is essentially elastic, but the large FPZ makes the application of classic elastic fracture mechanics impossible in most laboratory size specimens.

In classic elastic fracture mechanics, the nominal fracture strength, σ_N, is, for a notched geometrically similar specimen, a function of the fracture energy, G_{If}, Young's modulus, E, and a representative length of the

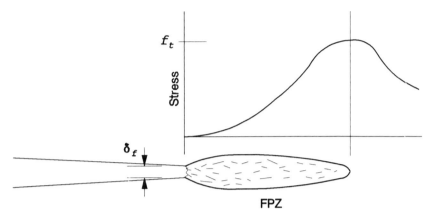

Figure 1.2 The fracture process zone and strain-softening.

specimen, W. Dimensional arguments show that the nominal stress is given by

$$\sigma_N \propto \left(\frac{G_{If} E}{W} \right)^{1/2} \tag{1.4}$$

Hence, whereas the strength according to conventional strength of materials is constant, if there is a notch or crack in an essentially elastic material that is large compared with the size of the FPZ, then the strength scale is inversely proportional to the square root of a characteristic dimension. If the FPZ is not small then there is an extra parameter to be considered, the tensile strength f_t of the material which is the maximum stress in a strain-softening FPZ. Introducing this extra term into a dimensional argument it is found that the strength also depends upon a characteristic length, l_{ch}, defined by Hillerborg *et al.* (1976) as

$$l_{ch} = \frac{EG_{If}}{f_t^2} \tag{1.5}$$

(a typical value of l_{ch} for concrete is 200 mm). The nominal fracture strength for a material with a finite FPZ is therefore, by dimensional arguments given by,

$$\sigma_N = F_1(\bar{W}) \left(\frac{G_{If} E}{W} \right)^{1/2} \tag{1.6}$$

where $\bar{W} = W/l_{ch}$ is the non-dimensional size of the specimen, and $F_1(\bar{W})$ is a function of $\bar{W}$. Equation 1.6 is an appropriate form of scaling if $\bar{W} > 1$. If $\bar{W} \ll 1$, then the FPZ only partially develops before the nominal fracture strength is attained, and a more appropriate characteristic length is given by

$$l_{ch}^* = \frac{G_{If}}{E} = \left(\frac{f_t}{E} \right)^2 l_{ch} \tag{1.7}$$

which we will call the characteristic length of the second kind to distinguish it from the more familiar characteristic length defined by Hillerborg *et al.* (1976). This second characteristic length is small and for concrete is of the order of $10^{-8}l_{ch}$. If $\bar{W} \ll 1$ then a more appropriate scaling equation is based upon the non-dimensional length of the second kind $\bar{\bar{W}} = W/l_{ch}^*$ and is

$$\sigma_N = f_t F_2(\bar{\bar{W}}) \tag{1.8}$$

where $F_2(\bar{\bar{W}})$ is a function of $\bar{\bar{W}}$. As the non-dimensional size of the second kind of a specimen, $\bar{\bar{W}}$, tends to zero so the nominal strength will tend to a constant value that is dependent on the geometry. For small plain tensile specimens, the FPZ can spread quickly across the specimen before complete fracture. The fracture strength in this case is close to f_t, the maximum sustainable tensile strength. For plain bend specimens, the limiting nominal bending stress is much larger than f_t. The nominal strength of small specimens where $\bar{W} \ll 1$ can be scaled according to conventional strength of materials. It is, of course, not necessary to use two different characteristic lengths, and the characteristic length of the second kind is only introduced here to emphasize the nature of the scaling of small specimens and throughout the rest of the book only the more usual definition of characteristic length, given by eqn 1.5, is used.

The size effect law (SEL), or relationship between the nominal fracture strength and the non-dimensional size, $\bar{W}$, of the specimen was first discussed for cementitious materials by Bažant (1984). The logarithmic variation of σ_N/f_t with $\bar{W}$ for a geometrically similar notched specimen is schematically illustrated in Figure 1.3a.

The SEL, as illustrated in Figure 1.3a, only applies to geometrically similar notched specimens or specimens where there is a high stress concentration. In very large specimens of this type, the FPZ is fully developed at final fracture. Smooth bend specimens, with no large stress concentration, do not develop a full FPZ before fracture except in the largest specimens. The SEL for smooth geometrically similar specimens is illustrated in Figure 1.3b. Only in the limit as the size tends to infinity, does fracture occur when the maximum stress in the FPZ reaches the tensile strength, f_t.

1.3 The compliance method of calculating the elastic potential energy release rate

This method enables the crack extension force, G, to be calculated from the compliance, whether obtained numerically, for example from a finite element solution, or experimentally. The compliance, C, of a cracked body increases with the crack size. In a perfectly elastic body there is no residual displacement on unloading (see Figure 1.4a) and under an equilibrium increase in fracture

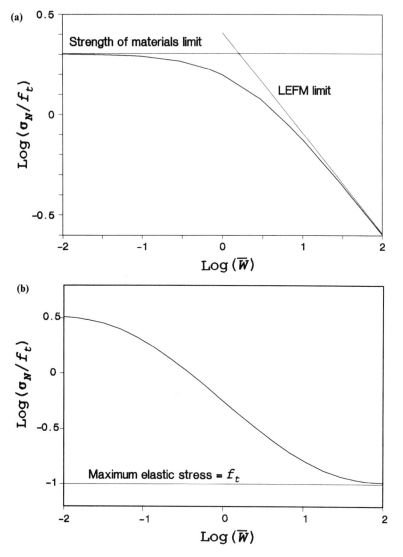

Figure 1.3 The size effect law: (a) geometrically similar notched specimens, (b) geometrically similar smooth specimens.

area, dA, the release in energy that is available for fracture is given by

$$\frac{d\Pi}{dA} = -\left[\frac{d\Pi_1}{dA} + \frac{d\Lambda}{dA}\right] \tag{1.9}$$

which is the area OAB. The strain energy stored, Λ, is given by

$$\Lambda = \frac{P\Delta}{2} = \tfrac{1}{2}P^2C \tag{1.10}$$

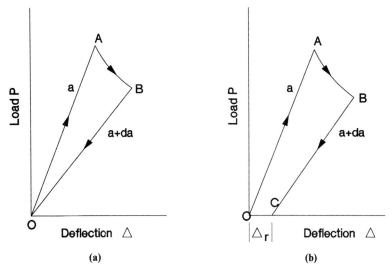

Figure 1.4 The compliance method: (a) ideal perfect elastic material, (b) real material.

and the rate of increase in strain energy with fracture area, dA, is given by

$$\frac{d\Lambda}{dA} = PC\frac{dP}{dA} + \frac{P^2}{2}\frac{dC}{dA} \tag{1.11}$$

At the same time the rate of change in potential energy of the load is

$$\frac{d\Pi_l}{dA} = -P\frac{d\Delta}{dA} = -\left[P^2\frac{dC}{dA} + PC\frac{dC}{dA}\right] \tag{1.12}$$

Hence the crack extension force, G, is given by

$$G = -\frac{d\Pi}{dA} = \frac{P^2}{2}\frac{dC}{dA} \tag{1.13}$$

which is independent of the load-deflection path.

In a real material there will be some non-elastic deformation at the crack tip, and on unloading some residual strain energy will remain locked in the specimen (see Figure 1.4b). The work done in extending the fracture area by dA will be less than the area OABC, but greater than the area OAB. Therefore, in the presence of residual displacements an upper bound to the crack extension force, G_u, is given by

$$G_u = \frac{P^2}{2}\frac{dC}{dA} + P\frac{d\Delta_r}{dA} \tag{1.14}$$

The lower bound to G is then given by eqn 1.13. Similar expressions for the crack extension force have been given by Wecharatana and Shah (1982) and Mai and Hakeem (1984).

In cementitious materials the behaviour is essentially elastic. The main contribution to residual displacements comes from two sources. One source is the residual dilatation of the FPZ, caused by microcracks failing to close perfectly and aggregate pull-out not being reversed. The other source is wedging open of the crack by debris. There may be some energy dissipated on unloading through friction between the aggregate and the matrix. However, for cementitious materials, crack extension force is probably better given by the lower than the upper bound.

1.4 Energetic stability

Fracture in elastic-brittle materials is often unstable and catastrophic, but inherent stability depends upon geometry (Atkins and Mai, 1985). Obviously all specimens are more likely to be stable under fixed grip than constant load conditions, because the compliance increases with crack growth. For stable fracture of a material whose fracture energy is constant, the crack extension force must decrease with crack growth. Thus from eqn 1.13 the condition for stable crack growth is given by

$$\frac{\mathrm{d}G}{\mathrm{d}A} = P\frac{\mathrm{d}C}{\mathrm{d}A} + \frac{P^2}{2}\frac{\mathrm{d}^2C}{\mathrm{d}A^2} < 0 \qquad (1.15)$$

Therefore for stable crack growth under constant load $(\mathrm{d}P/\mathrm{d}A = 0)$ $\mathrm{d}C^2/\mathrm{d}A^2 < 0$, but under fixed grips $(\mathrm{d}\Delta/\mathrm{d}A = \mathrm{d}(PC)/\mathrm{d}A = 0)$, only the less difficult condition, $\mathrm{d}C^2/\mathrm{d}A^2 < 2(\mathrm{d}C/\mathrm{d}A)^2/C$, has to be satisfied. In general tensile loads cause instability under both constant load and fixed grip conditions; bending loads (as in the double cantilever beam specimen) cause instability under constant load conditions, but the specimen may be stable under fixed grip conditions; specimens loaded in compression are usually stable under both fixed grips and constant load conditions.

Fixed grip conditions can never be achieved precisely, because there must be some stiffness associated with any loading arrangement. If C_m is the machine stiffness, then the deformation of the fracture specimen and machine can be schematically represented by a spring of compliance C_m and a specimen of compliance C stretched between two rigid abutments (see Figure 1.5). The indicated deflection, Δ_i, is given by

$$\Delta_i = \Delta + \Delta_m = P(C + C_m) \qquad (1.16)$$

where Δ_m is the machine displacement. The condition for fixed indicated deflection is $\mathrm{d}[P(C + C_m)]/\mathrm{d}A = 0$, and eqn 1.15 shows that stability is ensured if $\mathrm{d}C^2/\mathrm{d}a^2 < 2(\mathrm{d}C/\mathrm{d}a)^2/(C + C_m)$.

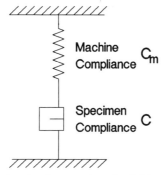

Figure 1.5 Equivalent load situation for a specimen loaded in a machine whose compliance is non-zero.

1.5 Linear elastic fracture mechanics (LEFM)

Although historically linear elastic fracture mechanics was first formulated in terms of energy, a stress approach has become more usual. Irwin (1957, 1958) and Williams (1957) realized that near a crack tip the stresses are inversely proportional to the square root of the distance from the crack tip. Under a pure opening mode, where near the crack tip the only displacements are normal to the crack surfaces, the only non-zero stresses near the crack tip (see Figure 1.6) can be written as

$$\left.\begin{aligned}
\sigma_x &= \frac{K_\text{I}}{\sqrt{2\pi r}}\cos(\theta/2)[1 - \sin(\theta/2)\sin(3\theta/2)] \\
\sigma_y &= \frac{K_\text{I}}{\sqrt{2\pi r}}\cos(\theta/2)[1 + \sin(\theta/2)\sin(3\theta/2)] \\
\tau_{xy} &= \frac{K_\text{I}}{\sqrt{2\pi r}}\sin(\theta/2)\cos(\theta/2)\cos(3\theta/2)
\end{aligned}\right\} \tag{1.17}$$

where K_I, the stress intensity factor, has the units of MPa$\sqrt{\text{m}}$ and depends upon the geometry, applied stress, and crack length. For the classic Griffith

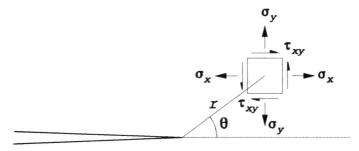

Figure 1.6 Stresses near a crack tip.

crack, the stress intensity factor is given by

$$K_I = \sigma\sqrt{\pi a} \qquad (1.18)$$

For other geometries the stress intensity factor can be written as

$$K_I = \sigma_N \phi \sqrt{\pi a} \qquad (1.19)$$

where σ_N is the nominal stress at the crack and ϕ is a geometric factor that depends upon the geometry of the specimen. The geometric factor, ϕ, is usually of the order of unity and can be found in stress intensity handbooks such as Tada *et al.* (1973) and Rooke and Cartwright (1976).

The pure crack opening mode (mode I), where the displacement is normal to the crack surfaces, is not the only possible opening mode. In general the displacement of the crack surface can be in any direction, and there are two other archetypal shearing modes: mode II where the only displacements near the crack tip are in the plane of the crack surface and normal to the crack front, and mode III where the only displacements are in the plane of the crack surface but parallel to the crack front. The three archetypal crack opening modes are schematically illustrated in Figure 1.7. The non-zero stresses near a crack tip under mode II and mode III opening are:

Mode II:

$$\left.\begin{aligned}
\sigma_x &= \frac{K_{II}}{\sqrt{2\pi r}}\sin(\theta/2)[2 + \cos(\theta/2)\cos(3\theta/2)] \\[2mm]
\sigma_y &= \frac{K_{II}}{\sqrt{2\pi r}}\sin(\theta/2)\cos(\theta/2)\cos(3\theta/2) \\[2mm]
\tau_{xy} &= \frac{K_{II}}{\sqrt{2\pi r}}\cos(\theta/2)[1 - \sin(\theta/2)\sin(3\theta/2)]
\end{aligned}\right\} \qquad (1.20)$$

where K_{II} is the mode II stress intensity factor;

Mode III:

$$\left.\begin{aligned}
\tau_{xz} &= -\frac{K_{III}}{\sqrt{2\pi r}}\sin(\theta/2) \\[2mm]
\tau_{yz} &= \frac{K_{III}}{\sqrt{2\pi r}}\cos(\theta/2)
\end{aligned}\right\} \qquad (1.21)$$

where K_{III} is the mode III stress intensity factor.

One of the attractions of the stress approach to LEFM is that it enables the principle of superposition to be used, provided the stress intensity factor is separated into its archetypal modes. An apparent problem with the stress approach is that the stresses right at the crack tip are infinite. Barenblatt (1959, 1962) discussed this problem and formulated the necessary hypotheses for the strict application of classic LEFM. Considering an ideal elastic-brittle

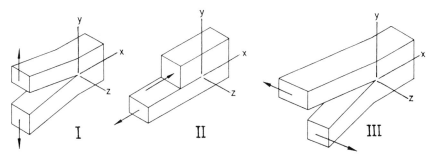

Figure 1.7 The three crack opening modes.

material, Barenblatt argued that very near the tip of a crack, where the separation of the crack faces is of the order of the equilibrium intermolecular distance, b, the forces of cohesion are important. These cohesive forces pull the two faces together in a similar fashion to the forces in the macroscopic FPZ shown in Figure 1.2. The cohesive forces cause a stress intensity factor K_r at the crack tip, which is negative, and adds to the stress intensity factor, K_a, due to the applied loads. Thus by the principle of superposition, the total stress intensity factor is given by

$$K_t = K_a + K_r \tag{1.22}$$

The infinite stress at the crack tip is removed if the total stress intensity factor is zero. In this case the stresses at the crack tip are continuous with the stresses in the FPZ and the faces meet in a cusp (see Figure 1.8). Barenblatt

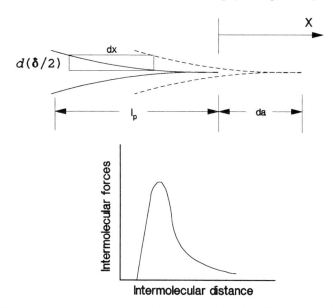

Figure 1.8 Crack in an ideal elastic-brittle material and the forces of cohesion.

(1959, 1962) showed that Griffith's theory of fracture and classic LEFM depends on two hypotheses: (i) the size of the FPZ is small compared with the size of the crack and other dimensions of the specimen; (ii) the shape of the crack surface in the FPZ (and consequently the cohesive forces) is the same for a given material during equilibrium crack growth.

The first of these hypotheses is well recognized but the second, which is very important for cementitious materials because they have large macroscopic FPZs, is often forgotten. During a crack extension of da, the work done against the forces of cohesion, dw_s, per unit width of the plate is given by

$$dw_s = \int_{-l_p}^{0} \sigma \frac{d\delta}{da} \, da \, dx \tag{1.23}$$

where the integral is taken from a point where the forces of cohesion are negligible. From Barenblatt's second hypotheses

$$\frac{d\delta}{da} = -\frac{\partial \delta}{\partial x} \tag{1.24}$$

and hence

$$\frac{dw_s}{da} = \int_{0}^{\infty} \sigma \, d\delta = 2\gamma_s = G_{If} \tag{1.25}$$

Irwin (1957) showed that the mode I crack extension force, G_I, and stress intensity factor, K_I, are related by[4]

$$G_I = \frac{K_I^2}{E^*} \tag{1.26}$$

Hence for equilibrium crack growth

$$G_{If} = \frac{K_a^2}{E^*} = \frac{K_r^2}{E^*} \tag{1.27}$$

which formally shows that at equilibrium crack growth, the critical applied stress intensity, or plane strain fracture toughness, $K_{Ic} = K_a$, is a material constant and is related to the fracture energy, G_{If}, through eqn 1.26.

If Barenblatt's (1959, 1962) hypotheses are satisfied for a cementitious solid, then the fracture energy is given by eqn 1.25 as

$$G_{If} = \int_{0}^{\delta_f} \sigma \, d\delta \tag{1.28}$$

---

[4] The mode I and mode II stress intensity factors are related to the respective crack extension forces by (Paris and Sih, 1965)

$$G_{II} = \frac{(1 - \nu^2)}{E} K_{II}^2$$

$$G_{III} = \frac{(1 + \nu)}{E} K_{III}^2$$

The crack extension forces for the three modes can be simply added to give the total energy release rate, because there is no interaction between the modes.

where δ_f is the crack tip opening displacement (CTOD) across the FPZ at the initiation of a continuous crack.

1.5.1 Weight functions of Bueckner and Rice

Very often in the analysis of the fracture behaviour of cementitious materials it is necessary to calculate the stress intensity factor due to stresses acting over the crack faces. In this case the concept of the weight function introduced by Bueckner (1970) and Rice (1972) can be used. If the stress on the crack face is $\sigma(x)$ then the stress intensity factor is given by

$$K_I = \frac{1}{\sqrt{W}} \int_0^a \sigma(x)m(a, x)\, dx \qquad (1.29)$$

where W is a characteristic dimension of the specimen and $m(a, x)$ is the weight function and

$$k_I = \frac{1}{\sqrt{W}} m(a, x) \qquad (1.30)$$

is the stress intensity factor for unit point forces, per unit thickness of the specimen, acting on both faces of the crack at position x. However, the weight function can be found by use of the reciprocity theorem from any known stress intensity factor for a particular geometry. The weight function method of calculating stress intensity factors is well described by Wu and Carlsson (1991) who show that eqn 1.29 is applicable to mixed boundary problems as well as static boundary problems. The general expression for the weight function is

$$m(a, x) = \frac{E^*\sqrt{W}}{2K_{ref}(a)} \frac{\partial \delta_{ref}(a, x)}{\partial a} \qquad (1.31)$$

where K_{ref} and δ_{ref} are the reference stress intensity factor and COD, respectively, whose geometry, including the boundary composition of the static and kinematic boundaries, is the same as the new load case.

1.5.2 Measurement of the fracture toughness

Provided the material is brittle enough the fracture toughness can be measured using any geometry for which the stress intensity factor is known. ASTM E399 (1990) describes the measurement of the plane strain fracture toughness, K_{Ic}, of metallic specimens. It will be seen that, for valid measurement of K_{If} in cementitious materials, specimens generally have to be very large and probably the most appropriate standard test geometry is the three-point-bend specimen (see Figure 1.9a). In large bend specimens tested with the notch downwards, either the bending moment at the notch due to the self-weight must be made zero by making the length of the

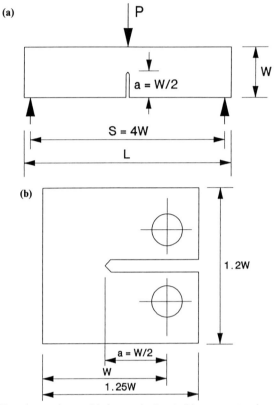

Figure 1.9 Fracture specimens: (a) three-point-bend, (b) compact tension specimen.

beam twice its span (or by providing counter-balancing weights) or allowance must be made for the stress intensity factor due to the self-weight. The other appropriate standard geometry is the compact tension specimen (see Figure 1.9b). Again large cementitious compact tension specimens must be counter-balanced to eliminate the effect of self-weight.

It is appropriate to record the load against the crack mouth opening displacement (CMOD) measured by a clip gauge, though in the case of the three-point-bend specimen an alternative would be to record the central displacement. The load-displacement curve can take on two forms (see Figure 1.10). It may be possible to calculate a valid K_{If} if the behaviour is brittle (Type I) using the procedure given in ASTM E399 (1990). For a cementious material it is appropriate to take the maximum load as an indication of crack initiation. However, it is impossible to calculate a valid K_{If} if the behaviour is ductile (Type II), because such a curve indicates that the FPZ is large.

For a valid measurement of fracture toughness the FPZ must be embedded in a K-stress field so that Barenblatt's (1959, 1962) first hypothesis applies.

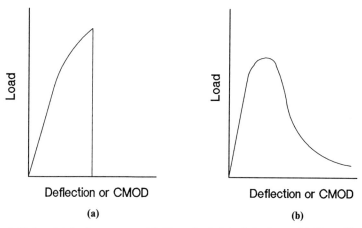

Figure 1.10 Load-deflection curves: (a) Type I—brittle behaviour, (b) Type II—ductile behaviour.

For common test geometries, the K-stress field is accurate to within 7% over a distance of 2% of the crack length ahead of the crack tip (Wilson, 1966). For metals the length, d_{p}, of the plastic zone or FPZ has been shown by Irwin (1960) to be approximately given by

$$d_{\mathrm{p}} = \frac{1}{p\pi}\left(\frac{K_{\mathrm{I}}}{\sigma_{\mathrm{Y}}}\right)^2 = \frac{l_{\mathrm{ch}}}{p\pi} \tag{1.32}$$

where $p = 1$ for plane stress and $p = 3$ for plane strain. The difference in the size of the plastic zone (FPZ) in metals, depending upon the stress state, is because plastic flow depends upon the degree of constraint which is low in thin metal sheets under essentially plane stress conditions and high in thick metal plates under essentially plane strain conditions. There are no constraint effects with cementitious materials and, if the FPZ is modelled as a region of constant stress (as Irwin (1960) did), the appropriate value in eqn 1.32 is $p = 1$ with the yield strength σ_{Y} replaced by the tensile strength of the cementitious material f_{t}. The requirement for a valid measurement of the plane strain fracture toughness, K_{Ic}, according to ASTM E399 (1990) is that the plastic zone is smaller than about 4% of the crack length which on substitution from eqn 1.32 gives

$$a > 2.5\left(\frac{K_{\mathrm{Ic}}}{\sigma_{\mathrm{Y}}}\right)^2 \tag{1.33}$$

Similar requirements necessary for the application of classic LEFM to cementitious materials are discussed in section 4.3.

In plane strain fracture toughness testing of metals, there is also the additional requirement that the thickness of the specimen shall also satisfy the inequality given in eqn 1.33. This requirement is to ensure that the fracture is essentially plane strain and the shear lips on the fracture edges are small. A limitation on thickness is not necessary for cementitious materials.

1.6   Crack opening displacement (COD)

Crack surfaces open under load and Wells (1961) suggested that in metals, fracture occurs when the crack tip opening displacement (CTOD) reaches a critical value. Such a criterion of fracture is attractive because it is independent of whether LEFM applies or not and has been tacitly assumed to apply to cementitious materials by many researchers. The concept is most readily applied in conjunction with the fictitious crack model of Hillerborg *et al.* (1976), which is discussed in detail in section 4.5. Although he did not call it a fictitious crack, the concept was first applied by Dugdale (1960) to the problem of a Griffith crack in an elasto-plastic solid. In thin plates the plastic zone is in the form of a thin flame-like zone that Dugdale assumed could be modelled as an infinitely narrow line zone extension, or fictitious crack extension, to the true crack across which a closing stress equal to the yield strength existed (see Figure 1.11). By these assumptions, Dugdale turned an elasto-plastic problem into a simpler elastic one. At the end of the plastic fictitious line crack, the elastic stresses must be continuous with the plastic ones. The problem is similar to Barenblatt's (1959, 1962) analysis of the

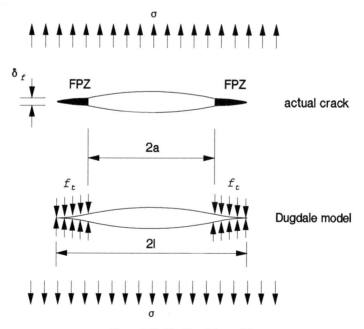

Figure 1.11 The Dugdale model.

cohesive forces at a crack tip. The stresses equal to the yield strength acting across the fictitious crack cause a stress intensity factor, K_r, that is negative. The applied stress, σ, causes a positive stress intensity factor, K_a, at the tip of the fictitious crack. For continuity in the stresses at the tip of the fictitious crack the total stress intensity factor $K_a + K_r$ must be zero as in eqn 1.22. The Dugdale model can be applied to cementitious materials if it is assumed that the stress within the FPZ is constant and equal to the tensile strength, f_t.

The stress intensity factor for a central crack loaded over its centre by a normal stress f_t is given by (Tada *et al.*, 1973)

$$K_I = 2f_t \left(\frac{l}{\pi}\right)^{1/2} \sin^{-1}\left(\frac{a}{l}\right) \tag{1.34}$$

Combining this equation with that for a Griffith crack of length l closed by a stress $(f_t - \sigma)$ the stress distribution for the Dugdale model is obtained, and the total stress intensity factor is given by

$$K_I = -(f_t - \sigma)\sqrt{\pi l} + 2f_t \left(\frac{l}{\pi}\right)^{1/2} \sin^{-1}\left(\frac{a}{l}\right) = 0 \tag{1.35}$$

Thus

$$\frac{l}{a} = \sec \beta,$$

$$\tag{1.36}$$

where

$$\beta = \frac{\pi}{2}\left(\frac{\sigma}{f_t}\right)$$

Hence the extent of the FPZ, $d_p = l - a$, is given by

$$d_p = a[\sec \beta - 1] \tag{1.37}$$

If σ/f_t is small

$$\sec \beta \approx \frac{1}{(1 - \beta^2/2)} \tag{1.38}$$

and

$$\frac{d_p}{a} = \frac{\pi^2}{8}\left(\frac{\sigma}{f_t}\right)^2 \tag{1.39}$$

which is very similar to the estimate of Irwin (1960) for plane stress ($p = 1$) given in eqn 1.32.

The crack tip opening displacement, δ_t, can be calculated from the elastic field (Goodier and Field, 1963) and is

$$\delta_t = \left(\frac{8f_t a}{\pi E}\right) \ln(\sec \beta) \tag{1.40}$$

If δ_f is the critical crack opening displacement the specific fracture energy, G_{If}, is given by

$$G_{If} = \int_0^{\delta_f} \sigma \, d\delta = f_t \delta_f \tag{1.41}$$

However, the specific fracture work is only equal to G_{If} if σ/f_t is very small because during crack growth, at constant applied stress, the size of the FPZ increases with crack length as given by eqn 1.37. In general the specific fracture work, w_f, is given by

$$w_f = -f_t \int_{x=a}^{x=l} \frac{\partial \delta(x, a)}{\partial a} \, dx \tag{1.42}$$

Goodier and Field (1963) have evaluated eqn 1.42 and obtained

$$w_f = G_{If} \left[\frac{\beta \tan \beta}{\ln(\sec \beta)} - 1 \right] \tag{1.43}$$

The normalized specific fracture work, w_f/G_{If}, is shown as a function of the normalized FPZ d_p/a, in Figure 1.12. Since the size of the FPZ increases with crack growth the specific fracture work, w_f, is always greater than the fracture energy G_{If} and the discrepancy increases with the size of the FPZ relative to the crack length.

This example of an approximate analysis of the fracture of cementitious materials using the Dugdale model demonstrates how the specific fracture work, w_f, is only identical to the fracture energy, G_{If}, if both of the

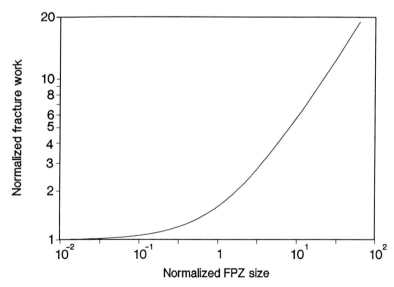

Figure 1.12 The specific fracture work as a function of the relative size of the FPZ.

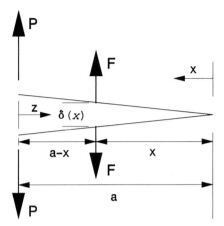

Figure 1.13 Calculation of the crack face displacements using Castigliano's theorem and a fictitious force.

hypotheses of Barenblatt (1959, 1962) are true. Thus, in general, G_{If} cannot be measured from the rate of fracture work.[5]

Fracture must occur when the CTOD reaches its critical value δ_f. In infinitely big specimens, such as presented in the Dugdale model, unstable fracture does initiate when the CTOD reaches its critical value, δ_f, but it will be seen in Chapter 4 that in finite specimens, if the FPZ is large, unstable fracture occurs before the critical value of the CTOD is reached.

1.6.1 The use of Castigliano's theorem to calculate the COD

If a more realistic stress-displacement relationship is used in the FPZ, instead of a constant stress, it is necessary to calculate the COD along the fictitious crack faces. The COD can be easily calculated from the stress intensity factor, which can be found in handbooks such as Tada *et al.* (1973) and Rooke and Cartwright (1976), by use of Castigliano's theorem (Tada *et al.*, 1973; Foote *et al.*, 1986a). Suppose the displacement $\delta(x)$ is required at a distance x from the crack tip due to the applied forces. Applying a fictitious force F at x (see Figure 1.13) the displacement is given by the application of Castigliano's theorem by

$$\delta(x) = \left[\frac{\partial \Lambda}{\partial F} \right]_{F=0} \tag{1.44}$$

---

[5] Although the rate of fracture work is not equal to the fracture energy, in a finite width specimen that fractures in a stable fashion the total work of complete fracture must equal the fracture energy multiplied by the fracture area if the stress-displacement relationship in the FPZ is unique for a particular material.

The strain energy stored, Λ, can be found from the crack extension force, G, and is given by

$$\Lambda = \int_0^A G \, dA + \Lambda_0 = \int_0^a \frac{K^2}{E^*} B \, da + \Lambda_0 \qquad (1.45)$$

where Λ_0 is the strain energy stored in the uncracked body and K is the sum of the stress intensity factor due to the applied forces, K_a, and the stress intensity factor, K_F, due to the fictitious force, F. Thus the displacement is given by

$$\delta(x) = \frac{2B}{E^*} \int_{(a-x)}^a K_a(z) \left[\frac{\partial K_F(z-a+x)}{\partial F} \right]_{F=0} dz \qquad (1.46)$$

A similar expression obtained if the applied force is a point force acting between x and the crack tip is

$$\delta = \frac{2B}{E^*} \int_{x-a}^x K_a(z-x+a) \left[\frac{\partial K_F(z)}{\partial F} \right]_{F=0} dz \qquad (1.47)$$

By integration the displacement due to a continuous distribution of stress $\sigma(x)$ along the crack faces can be found.

1.6.2   Measurement of the CTOD

For ductile metals the CTOD can be measured in deep notch bend specimens that yield completely before fracture from measurement of crack mouth opening displacements (CMOD), because the deformation is essentially the rotation of the halves of the specimen about a rigid hinge. Attempts have been made to measure the CTOD of fibre reinforced concrete by this method (Brandt, 1980). However, at best, this method can only give a rough approximation to the CTOD of cementitious materials, because the stress-strain relationship does not approximate to the rigid-plastic behaviour necessary for an accurate measurement of the CTOD.

1.7   The T-stress and higher order stress terms

The stress fields given by eqns 1.17, 1.20 and 1.21, give the singular part of the stress field at the tip of a crack. Williams (1957) showed that the stresses near a crack tip can be written in terms of the ascending power series

$$\sigma_{i,j} = \sum_{n=1}^{n=\infty} a_n f_{i,j}^n(\theta) r^{(n-2)/2} \qquad (1.48)$$

The first terms give the singular stress fields given by eqns 1.17, 1.20 and 1.21. These singular terms are the most important but the higher order terms, especially the second, also control some of the aspects of fracture (Cotterell,

1966). The most important of the higher order terms is the second, which under mode I opening gives what is called the T-stress. This stress field is simply $\sigma_x = T$, a constant, all the other in-plane stresses are zero. Under mode II crack opening, the second constant term is identically zero.

1.7.1 Mixed-mode fracture and crack paths

So far the discussion of fracture mechanics has been to mode I, though expressions for K and G for the other modes have been given. The direction for continuous crack growth in an ideal elastic-brittle material where one of the principal applied stresses is tensile, is such that the local stress field at the tip is mode I, which is often referred to as the criterion of local symmetry (Gol'dstein and Salganik, 1974). This result is consistent, in the sense that it follows by contradiction, with the various proposed mixed mode fracture criteria. However, the FPZ, if large, can have a significant effect on the crack and make it deviate from the ideal path. Rubinstein (1991) examined the experimental data on the propagation of a crack under tensile loading near to a hole in a polystyrene sheet (Chudnovsky et al., 1987). Only near to the hole was the crack path affected (see Figure 1.14). The experimental

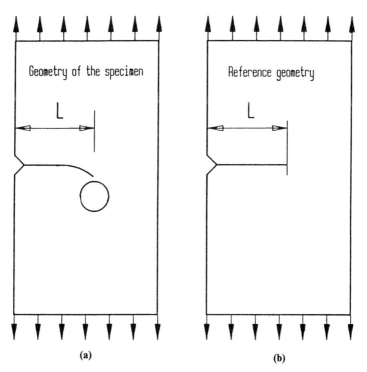

Figure 1.14 Crack propagation near a hole. (a) Actual specimen. (b) Definition of the reference crack. (After Rubinstein, 1991.)

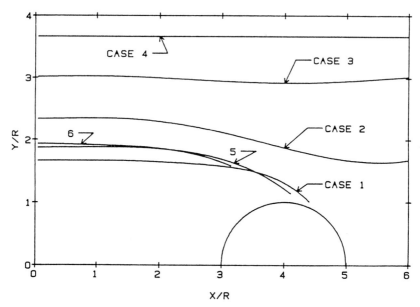

Figure 1.15 Experimental crack paths. (After Chudnovsky *et al.*, 1987.)

crack paths of cracks initiated near to a hole are shown in Figure 1.15. These crack paths are close to satisfying the criterion of local symmetry ($K_{II} = 0$) as Rubinstein (1991) showed by calculating the mode II stress intensity factor at the crack tip (see Figure 1.16). Although the maximum value of K_{II} is small,

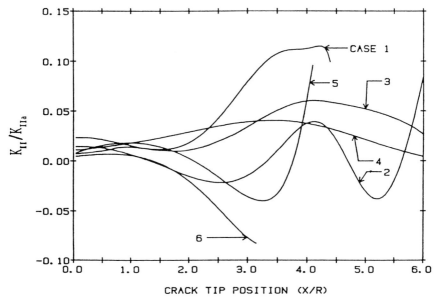

Figure 1.16 K_{II} variation along the crack paths near the hole. (From Rubinstein, 1991.)

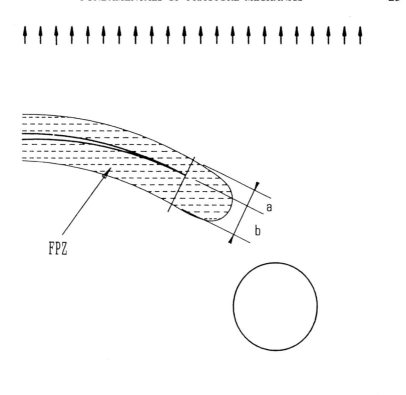

Figure 1.17 The FPZ surrounding the tip of a tightly turning crack. (After Rubinstein, 1991.)

only a little more than 10%, it is significant. The maximum deviation from the condition of local symmetry occurs in Case 1 which shows the greatest curvature. Rubinstein (1991) argues that the reason for the deviation in the crack path from the ideal is the FPZ surrounding the crack tip. While the crack path curvature is slight the FPZ is nearly symmetrical but, if the path turns sharply, the FPZ becomes asymmetrical and makes the path deviate from the ideal (see Figure 1.17). In polystyrene, the FPZ size is only of the order of 0.5 mm (Berry, 1964). In cementitious materials the FPZ is very much larger and even more significant deviations from ideal paths can be expected. One example of strong deviation from the ideal crack path is provided by the 'shear specimen' of Bažant and Pfeiffer (1986) which will be discussed further in Chapter 4. Melin (1989) has compared the crack path in a PMMA specimen, whose FPZ size is only of the order of 25 μm, with that obtained by Bažant and Pfeiffer in a concrete specimen (see Figure 1.18). Real crack paths can be expected to deviate from the ideal crack path if the radius of curvature of the ideal crack path is comparable with the size of the FPZ.

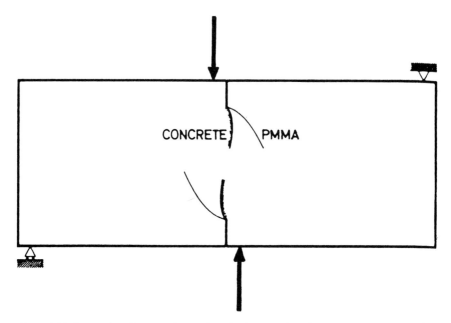

Figure 1.18 Comparison between the crack paths in PMMA and concrete specimens. (After Melin, 1989.)

While the criterion of local symmetry is accepted as the criterion for the crack path in an ideal elastic-brittle material, there is still controversy over the initial direction of crack growth from a crack tip under mixed mode loading conditions. This controversy almost certainly is due to the very small, but finite, FPZ of the brittle polymers that are used to model an ideal elastic-brittle material. The original criterion for crack direction is the maximum tangential stress (MTS) criterion proposed by Erdogan and Sih (1963). In this criterion crack growth is assumed to occur in a radial direction perpendicular to the direction of maximum tension. The stress intensity factor at the tip of a kink formed according to the MTS criterion has, to a first order, a pure mode I stress intensity factor (Cotterell and Rice, 1980). It was quickly realized that the FPZ could affect the crack direction and a better fit to the experimental data was obtained by taking, not just the singular stress field, but also the T-stress. In this modification of the MTS criterion the direction of crack propagation is taken as the maximum tangential stress at a critical distance, which can be identified with the tip of the FPZ (Williams and Ewing, 1972; Finnie and Saith, 1973; Ewing and Williams, 1974; Ewing *et al.*, 1976; Streit and Finnie, 1979). Wu (1978) assumed that the maximum tangential strain controlled the crack path. Palaniswamy and Knauss (1978) postulated that a crack would grow in the direction of maximum energy release. To obtain the direction of maximum energy release rate, Palaniswamy and Knauss (1978) calculated the energy

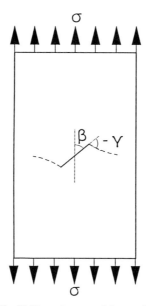

Figure 1.19 The CNT specimen used for crack path studies.

release rate for a kinked crack in terms of the length of the kink, and then let the length of the kink tend to zero. Sih (1973a) proposed that a crack develops in the radial direction of the minimum strain energy density. However, Sih (1973a) then goes on to state that propagation occurs when the strain energy density reaches a critical value which is self-contradicting. With the strain energy density criterion the crack extension direction is a function of Poisson's ratio. Finnie and Weiss (1974) conducted experiments on cross-rolled beryllium sheets that effectively had a Poisson's ratio of zero and found that the MTS criterion gave the better prediction than the strain energy density criterion.

The most common geometry used to examine the criteria of crack direction is the centre notched tension geometry (CNT) with the crack at an angle, β, to the applied load (see Figure 1.19). Using the mode mixity parameter, $\lambda = K_{II}/K_I$, the MTS criterion gives the crack direction as

$$\sin\gamma + (3\cos\gamma - 1)\lambda = 0 \qquad (1.49)$$

where for the geometry shown in Figure 1.19, $\lambda = \cot\beta$. Mahajan and Ravi-Chandar (1989), in their excellent review of mixed-mode fracture, point out that there is considerable similarity between the various criteria if $\lambda < 0.37$ or $\beta > 15°$. The CNT specimen is not really suitable for studying larger mode mixities, because as $\beta \to 0°$, $\lambda \to \infty$, but both K_I and K_{II} tend to zero and hence the general stress level is high for $\beta < 15°$. A better geometry for studying crack directions at high mixities is the compact shear specimen

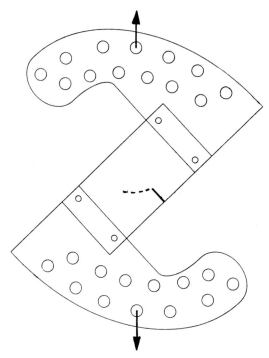

Figure 1.20 Schematic illustration of the CTS specimen. (After Mahajan and Ravi-Chandar, 1989.)

(CTS) shown in Figure 1.20. With this specimen the mode mixity needs to be measured directly at the crack tip by photoelasticity or the method of caustics. Experiments by Mahajan and Ravi-Chandar (1989) on PMMA and a birefringent brittle polymer, Hormalite-100, using the CTS geometry clearly showed that the crack direction was accurately predicted by the MTS criterion. However, none of the criteria gave a good prediction of the critical load because of strain rate effects and changes in fracture mode.

Mode II crack propagation in a brittle material is possible if both principal stresses are compressive (Melin, 1986; Broberg, 1987). However, even if both principal stresses are compressive a kink can occur with a tensile K_I providing the ratio between the principal stresses is large enough. Under a combined hydrostatic pressure, p, and a shear stress, τ, the direction of maximum shear stress is given by (see Figure 1.21)

$$\theta = 0 \qquad \qquad \text{if } p/\tau \leq 0$$

$$\theta = \tfrac{1}{2}\sin^{-1}(p/\tau) \quad \text{if } 0 < p/\tau \leq \mu/(1+\mu^2)^{1/2} \qquad (1.50)$$

$$\theta = \tfrac{1}{2}\tan^{-1}\mu \qquad \text{if } \mu/(1+\mu^2)^{1/2} < p/\tau < (1+\mu^2)^{1/2}/\mu$$

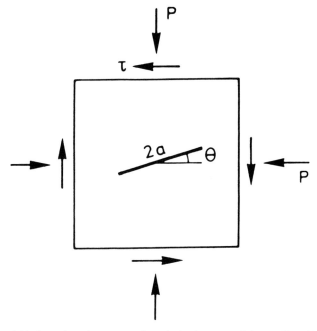

Figure 1.21 A crack under compressive principal stresses. (After Melin, 1986.)

where μ is the coefficient of friction between the closed crack surfaces (Melin, 1987). There are two options for crack propagation: the crack can propagate under mode II in the direction of the crack, or a kink can form with a tensile mode I stress intensity factor. The kink angle for maximum K_I occurs at about 70° but the maximum value is only weakly dependent on the angle. Melin (1986) has calculated the maximum mode II stress intensity factor at the tip of a favourably aligned crack, K_{IImax}, and the maximum mode I stress intensity factor at a kink making an angle $\alpha = 70°$. The ratio $\kappa = K_{IImax}/K_{Imax}$ is plotted in Figure 1.22 as a function of p/τ. If $p/\tau < 2.4$, K_I is tensile, which is quite close to the limit for all crack growth at $p/\tau = 2.69$ when friction prevents all motion between the crack faces. However, the ratio, κ, increases rapidly if $p/\tau > 2$. Broberg (1987), experimenting with cracks in PMMA, found that the crack could be made to propagate in mode II without kinking if $p/\tau > 2$, the experimentally determined coefficient of friction being 0.46. Thus pure mode II fracture is possible if the ratio, $\kappa = K_{IImax}/K_{Imax}$, is large enough. It must be noted that in these compression experiments, PMMA was quite ductile and that substantial plastic flow occurred. In concrete and rock, mode II type fractures are possible under compressive load even without any confining pressure because of the development of a large FPZ.

If a crack is under mixed mode I and III, the crack front cannot advance smoothly because it wants to rotate about an axis perpendicular to the crack front to achieve a mode I fracture. The crack front as a whole cannot

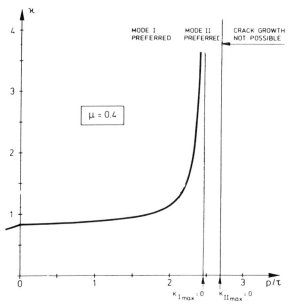

Figure 1.22 The ratio $\kappa = K_{IImax}/K_{Imax}$ as a function of p/τ for $\mu = 0.4$. (After Melin, 1986.)

accomplish this rotation and breaks up into a series of sub-fronts. Broberg (1987) shows that pure mode III fracture is possible, in PMMA, if there is sufficient compressive stress perpendicular to the crack surface. However, in these experiments he did not use closed cracks, but open notches and, therefore the compressive stress could generate a negative K_I, which would effectively eliminate the possibility of mode I fracture.

The ideal mode I crack path is not always stable. The crack trajectories from fracture of a biaxially loaded PMMA containing a central Griffith crack are shown in Figure 1.23 (Radon *et al.*, 1977). When the transverse stress parallel to the crack is less than the stress normal to the crack, the trajectory is almost identical to the ideal path normal to the maximum stress. However, if the transverse stress is equal to or greater than the normal stress, then the crack deviates from the line of symmetry. Cotterell and Rice (1980) showed that the stability of a mode I crack path in an ideal elastic-brittle material is determined by the T-stress. If the T-stress is negative the crack path is stable, that is, after any small deviation from the mode I direction, the crack tends to return to its original path. For a classic Griffith crack under normal tension, the T-stress is negative and equal to the applied stress, hence the fracture path is very close to the ideal path.[6] The transverse stress simply adds to the T-stress, so that if the transverse stress

---

[6] This statement is true for slowly propagating cracks. If the crack velocity approaches about one-third of the speed of shear wave propagation, the fracture can branch. The dynamic effects on fracture will not be discussed.

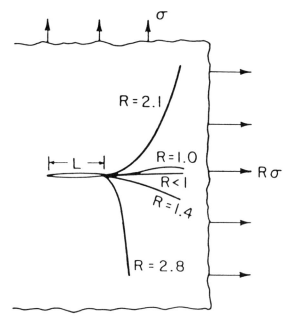

Figure 1.23 Crack trajectories from a biaxially loaded Griffith crack. (After Radon *et al.*, 1977.)

is greater than the normal stress, the T-stress is positive and the crack path is unstable. Naturally in real materials the presence of a FPZ can modify the criterion stated above. In Cotterell and Rice's (1980) analysis, an infinitesimal deviation was considered. Sumi *et al.* (1985) have considered terms higher than the T-stress and finite deviations. The net result is that there is a grey area around a zero T-stress where, in a real material, the crack path stability cannot be determined from the T-stress alone.

The nominal stresses near a crack tip under mode I loading can be used as a practical guide to crack path stability. For example, in the compact tension specimen simple engineer's theory of bending can be used to calculate the nominal stresses parallel and normal to the crack, if the nominal stress normal to the crack is greater than the stress parallel to the crack, then the crack path is likely to be stable (Cotterell, 1970). The double cantilever bend specimen has the disadvantage that its crack path is inherently unstable because of the high bending stress parallel to the crack and symmetrical crack propagation can only be achieved by providing guiding grooves or super-imposing a longitudinal compressive stress.

1.8 Crack growth resistance

So far it has been assumed that the fracture toughness of a material is a constant independent of crack growth, but that is the exception. In general, resistance to fracture and the fracture toughness increase with crack growth. Kraft *et al.* (1961) originated the concept of crack growth resistance to explain the fracture behaviour of thin ductile metal sheets. In this case the crack growth resistance is due to the development of shear lips. However, there are many mechanisms whereby crack growth resistance develops (Mai, 1988). With cementitious materials, the crack growth resistance is due to the development of the FPZ and the bridging of the crack by aggregate. Fibre reinforced cementitious materials have a very large-scale crack growth resistance due to the pull-out of the fibres. In this section only the general mechanical consequences of crack growth resistance will be discussed; the details of the fracture resistance mechanisms will be left until the next chapter.

The fracture toughness of a material exhibiting crack growth resistance increases with crack growth. If the FPZ, and any trailing bridging zones caused by fibres not pulled out completely, is small compared with the crack length and the remaining ligament, then the fracture toughness is only a function of the crack growth, Δa, and can be considered a material property. Under these circumstances FPZ is in a K-stress field, and the crack growth resistance, $K_R(\Delta a)$, is defined as the value of the applied stress intensity factor, K_a, calculated at the tip of the continuous crack,[7] that causes a stable crack extension of Δa. The crack growth resistance, K_R, increases from its initiation value, K_i, with crack growth, to a plateau value, K_{If}. A schematic crack growth resistance curve is shown in Figure 1.24. In smaller sized specimens, where the FPZ is not in a K-stress field, the crack growth resistance is both size and geometry dependent and the concept of a crack growth resistance curve is not particularly useful.

Crack growth resistance curves can also be based on the energetic concept of fracture. In this case the fracture resistance, $G_R(\Delta a)$, is defined as the value of the applied crack extension force, G, that causes a stable crack extension of Δa. The fracture resistance rises from an initiation value, G_i, to a plateau value, G_{If}, if the FPZ is small compared with the specimen dimensions and Barenblatt's (1959, 1962) hypotheses hold. The plateau value in this case is the true fracture energy and K_{If} is given by

$$G_{If} = \frac{K_{If}^2}{E^*} \tag{1.51}$$

However, since Barenblatt's second hypothesis cannot hold while the crack growth resistance is developing, because the crack shape must change with crack growth, in general the fracture resistance, G_R, is not exactly the same as the energy required to produce a unit area of fracture surface. However, from a practical viewpoint the distinction between G_R and the true fracture energy is unimportant.

---

[7] The definition of the crack tip varies according to the material. In cementitious materials the crack tip is usually defined as the tip of the visible continuous matrix crack. If there is fibre reinforcing, fibres will bridge the crack behind the crack tip.

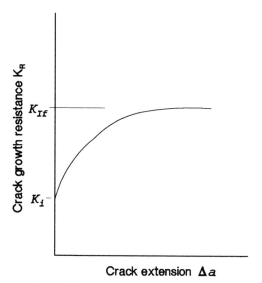

Figure 1.24 Crack growth resistance curve.

Crack growth resistance confers extra stability to crack growth. However, the maximum plateau value can only be utilized in very large specimens. Consider the fracture of a classic Griffith specimen with crack growth resistance (see Figure 1.25). The crack extension force is given by eqn 1.1 and increases linearly with the crack length, a. Hence, in Figure 1.25, G_I is

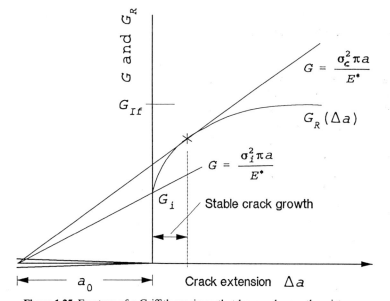

Figure 1.25 Fracture of a Griffith specimen that has crack growth resistance.

represented by a straight line whose slope is proportional to σ^2. When the stress increases to a value, σ_i, a crack can start to grow, but if the material has a crack growth resistance, the crack growth is stable because the work requirement for fracture increases with crack growth. Therefore, unstable fracture does not occur immediately. As the stress is increased the crack can propagate stably so that

$$G(a) = G_R(\Delta a) \tag{1.52}$$

However, when the crack extension force curve makes a tangent to the crack growth resistance curve, the stress reaches a critical value, σ_c, and the potential energy released is greater than that required for further growth. Unstable fracture occurs at this critical stress. The critical condition is given by

$$\frac{\partial G(\sigma, a)}{\partial a} = \frac{dG_R(\Delta a)}{d\Delta a} \tag{1.53}$$

The critical crack growth, Δa_c, increases with the size of the initial crack and the critical fracture resistance increases correspondingly. The energy approach was chosen to illustrate the concept of stable crack growth because, for a Griffith crack, G_I is a linear function of a, but the argument is similar for the stress approach using K and K_R.

A crack growth resistance confers stability to all geometries and its modifications to the stability discussed in section 1.4 are dealt with by Atkins and Mai (1985).

1.9 Non-linear fracture mechanics (NLFM)

In theory LEFM can be applied to any material provided the specimen is large enough, but for many materials the size of the specimen is larger than can be tested in a laboratory, or the component, whose strength prediction is required, is too small. NLFM was originally developed to cope with medium and low strength metals where the plastic zone is too large to be dominated by the K-stress field. In this case it is argued that there is an inner FPZ within the plastic zone where the essential fracture work is performed. Hence, NLFM is really about separating the essential work of fracture, which is a material property, from the larger plastic work which depends upon the size and geometry of the specimen. In cementitious materials, though the FPZ is large, there is no inner kernel that can be separated because by definition the material is linearly elastic outside of the FPZ. Hence, the basic rationale for NLFM does not really apply to cementitious materials, but the computational and experimental procedures of NLFM can be useful. The fundamentals of NLFM have been well reviewed by Hutchinson (1983).

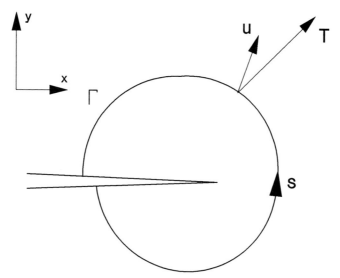

Figure 1.26 The J-integral.

1.9.1   The J-integral

For a non-linear elastic solid the line integral

$$J = \int_\Gamma W \, dy - T_i \frac{\partial u_i}{\partial x} \, ds \qquad (1.54)$$

taken anticlockwise around a crack tip (see Figure 1.26) along a path Γ that starts on one crack surface and ends on the other, where W is the strain energy density function, T_i are the components of the traction vector, u_i are the components of the displacement vector, and ds is an element along the path of the integral, is a constant independent of the path taken provided it is outside of the FPZ (Rice, 1968). The J-integral can be applied to metals deforming plastically if the loading is near proportional so that a deformational theory of plasticity which is indistinguishable from a non-linear elastic deformation, provided there is no unloading, approximates to the exact incremental theory. The J-integral applies exactly to cementitious materials that are essentially elastic outside of the FPZ.

If the FPZ is narrow and the J-integral is taken around its edge of the FPZ at the tip of a crack under mode I loading, then the first term in eqn 1.54 is small and can be neglected. Along the bottom of the FPZ, $ds = dx$ and the displacement vector $v = -\delta/2$, and along its top, $ds = -dx$ and $v = \delta/2$. The stress vector, $T_i = \sigma$, is the stress at the edge of the FPZ. Thus the J-integral at fracture initiation reduces to

$$J = J_{Ic} = \int_0^{\delta_f} \sigma \, d\delta = G_{If}, \qquad (1.55)$$

where δ_f is the crack opening displacement across the FPZ at crack initiation and the critical value of the J-integral, J_{Ic}, is identical to the fracture energy, G_{If}. The expression given in eqn 1.55, unlike that of eqn 1.28, apparently does not have the limitation placed upon it that the length of the FPZ must be small compared with the crack and remaining ligament lengths. However, if the FPZ is restricted in its length because the specimen is small, then the FPZ is short and fat and the first term in the J-integral, eqn 1.54, will not be negligible. Hence, the J-integral is also subject to the limitations imposed by Barenblatt's (1959, 1962) hypotheses.

An alternative interpretation of the J-integral is that it is the rate of change in potential energy of the system with crack growth (Begley and Landes, 1972). Consider a crack extension da (see Figure 1.27). The change in potential energy within the contour is

$$\frac{d\Pi}{dA} = \iint_s \frac{\partial W}{\partial a}\, dS - \oint_c T_i \frac{\partial u_i}{\partial a}\, ds \qquad (1.56)$$

where the double integral is taken over the area S enclosed by the contour Γ. Providing the crack propagation is self-similar

$$\frac{\partial}{\partial a} = -\frac{\partial}{\partial x} \qquad (1.57)$$

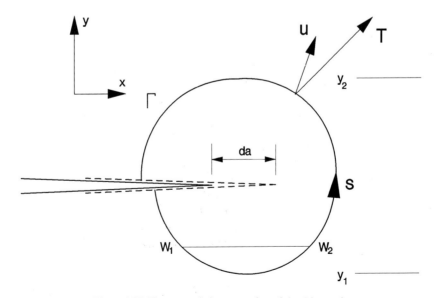

Figure 1.27 The energetic interpretation of the J-integral.

Hence

$$-\frac{d\Pi}{dA} = \iint_s \frac{\partial W}{\partial x}\, dx\, dy - \oint_\Gamma T_i \frac{\partial u_i}{\partial x}\, ds$$

$$= \int_{y_1}^{y_2} (W_2 - W_1)\, dy - \oint_\Gamma T_i \frac{\partial u_i}{\partial x}\, ds$$

$$= \oint_\Gamma W\, dy - T_i \frac{\partial u_i}{\partial x}\, ds \tag{1.58}$$

and

$$J = -\frac{d\Pi}{dA} \tag{1.59}$$

For a linear elastic material $G = J$. The derivation of eqn 1.59 clearly shows that Barenblatt's (1959, 1962) hypotheses are applicable to NLFM. Thus there is a minimum specimen size for determination of a valid fracture toughness J_{Ic}. For metallic specimens of high constraint (such as deep notch bend specimens) the ligament, b, at the notched section should satisfy the inequality

$$b > 25 \frac{J_{Ic}}{\sigma_Y} \tag{1.60}$$

but for low constraint (such as centre notch tension specimens) the condition is more onerous (Hutchinson, 1983)

$$b > 175 \frac{J_{Ic}}{\sigma_Y} \tag{1.61}$$

There is no constraint effect with cementitious materials and discussion of the appropriate limitation for these materials is deferred until Chapter 4.

The J-integral can also be expressed in terms of the complementary strain energy, Ω, under constant load conditions or the strain energy, Λ, under fixed grips by

$$J = -\frac{d\Pi}{da} = \left(\frac{\partial \Omega}{\partial A}\right)_P = -\left(\frac{\partial \Lambda}{\partial A}\right)_\Delta \tag{1.62}$$

1.9.2 Measurement of J_{Ic}

There are three methods that are commonly used to evaluate J_{Ic}, all of which are based on the energetic interpretation of J:

(i) A direct application of eqn 1.59 can be made if the fracture is stable. Two specimens with slightly different crack lengths are loaded up to crack initiation and record the load and load-line deflection (see Figure 1.28). J_{Ic} is then given directly by $-\Delta\Pi/\Delta A$, where $-\Delta\Pi$ is the area OAB in Figure 1.28.

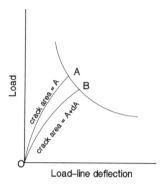

Figure 1.28 Direct calculation of J from stable load-deflection curve.

(ii) A number of specimens of different crack lengths are loaded to various displacements and the strain energy, Λ, plotted against the crack length for constant values of the displacement, u (see Figure 1.29). J is then given by the slope of the lines of constant displacement (see Figure 1.29a) through eqn 1.62 and J can be plotted against the deflection Δ (see Figure 1.29b). J_{Ic} is the value of J at the displacement at which a crack initiates.

(iii) The third method enables J to be determined from a single $P - \Delta$ plot and is the basis of the ASTM standard methods for determination of J_{Ic} for metals (ASTM, 1989). In this method, J is related to the work done on the specimen through the equation (Turner, 1979)

$$J = \frac{\eta\Lambda}{Bb} \tag{1.63}$$

where Λ is the strain energy stored (which is the same as the work done), b is the remaining ligament and η is a function of the geometry. The values of η

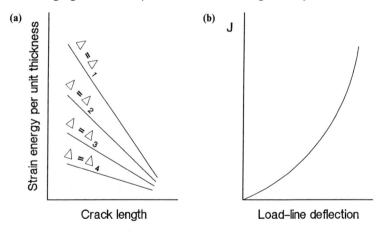

Figure 1.29 Calculation of J from multiple specimens. (a) Strain energy as a function of crack length for constant deflection. (b) J-integral as a function of deflection.

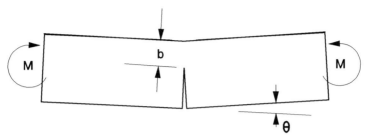

Figure 1.30 The deformation of a deeply notched bend specimen.

for deep notched specimens where the deformation is dominated by the deformation at the notch are particularly easily obtained. For a deep notched bend specimen (see Figure 1.30) $\eta = 2$, this result was first obtained by Rice *et al.* (1973) from dimensional arguments. If the deformation is confined to the ligament then the bending moment, M, at the notched section is a function of the rotation, θ, of the halves of the beam given by

$$M = Bb^2 f(\theta) \tag{1.64}$$

where B is the width of the beam and b is the ligament length. Thus,

$$\Lambda = \int_0^\theta M \, d\theta = \int_0^\theta Bb^2 f(\theta) \, d\theta$$

and

$$J = -\left(\frac{\partial \Lambda}{\partial A}\right)_\theta = 2 \int_0^\theta bf(\theta) \, d\theta \tag{1.65}$$

Substituting for $f(\theta)$

$$J = \frac{2}{Bb} \int_0^\theta M \, d\theta = \frac{2\Lambda}{Bb}, \tag{1.66}$$

since up to initiation b is constant. For general geometries η is given reasonably accurately by the linear elastic value (Turner, 1973)

$$\eta = \frac{b\phi^2 a}{\int_0^a \phi^2 a \, da} \tag{1.67}$$

1.9.3   Crack growth resistance J_R

The crack growth resistance of a material can be measured in terms of $J_R(\Delta a)$ the value of the applied J that produces a crack extension of Δa. Provided the FPZ is small compared with the remaining ligament, the crack growth resistance $J_R = G_R$ may be obtained from eqn 1.63. However, if there is appreciable crack growth, then eqn 1.63 is inaccurate because b

is not constant and should be replaced by (Hutchinson and Paris, 1977)

$$J = \frac{\eta}{Bb} \int_0^\Delta P \, d\Delta - \int_0^a \frac{\gamma J}{b} \, da$$

where

$$\gamma = \eta - 1 - \frac{b}{\eta W} \frac{d\eta}{d(a/W)} \tag{1.68}$$

There is a problem in applying the J-integral to the crack growth of metallic specimens because the material behind the crack tip must unload during crack extension and this unloading is completely non-proportional. Therefore, the J-integral can only be applied where the loading due to the increase in J_R dominates the unloading due to crack extension (Hutchinson and Paris, 1977; Hutchinson, 1983). However, there is no such problem with cementitious materials and the restrictions on the measurement of a valid J_R are the same as those for a valid J_{Ic} discussed in section 1.9.2.

1.10   Summary

The fracture of cementitious materials can only be characterized by a single parameter if the FPZ is small and embedded in a stress field dominated by the singularity at the crack tip. In this case LEFM is sufficient because outside of the FPZ a cementitious material is essentially elastic. However, since the FPZ of a cementitious material is usually large, laboratory sized specimens are in general too small for the valid application of classic LEFM. Small cementitious specimens fracture before the FPZ is fully developed and the fracture stress is not a direct function of the fracture energy, G_{If}.

Outside the FPZ, a cementitious material is essentially an elastic material. Thus it is possible to use LEFM if the FPZ is adequately modelled. In this case the simplest criterion for crack initiation is that the CTOD reaches a critical value, δ_f. This application of LEFM to cementitious materials is discussed in Chapter 4.

It is not strictly necessary to use the J-integral concept for cementitious materials, because they are essentially linear elastic and J is hence identical with G. However, there are situations where the J-integral is useful.

2 Fracture mechanisms in cementitious materials

2.1 Introduction

In the microscopic sense most engineering materials are not homogeneous but have domains with different microstructures. The properties, whether physical, chemical or mechanical, measured on these materials are no more than the average of these domains. Thus, cementitious materials, such as pastes, mortars and concretes, are heterogeneous materials with very complex microstructures that increase in complexity from cement pastes to concretes. In cement pastes, hydrated cements form from the reaction of cement particles with water, and the microstructure consists of both unhydrated cement and hydrated products (see Figure 2.1). The hydrated cement consists of a hierarchy of needle-like colloidal particles of calcium silicate hydrate (C–S–H) surrounding and intergrowing with calcium hydroxide (CH) crystals (see Figure 2.2). In mortars and concretes there is an additional phase of aggregates of various sizes and shapes which becomes bounded by the cement paste matrix as it hardens. Many of these aggregates are chemically stable rock materials such as river gravels or crushed particles. Whilst the shapes and sizes of the aggregates do affect the mechanical properties they are not as important as the interfacial bond strength between the paste and the aggregates.

For material modelling, Zaitsev and Wittmann (1981) consider cementitious materials as a four-level system: the nano, micro, meso and macro levels. At the nano-level, typical of the hardened cement paste with capillary pores, the characteristic size is about 500 nm. The micro-level refers to cement paste with large pores as the main inhomogeneity and the characteristic size is about 0.5 mm. The size of the meso-level, characterized by the structure of mortar, is taken as typically 10 mm. Finally, at the macro-level of concrete, the coarse aggregates are the main inhomogeneities and the characteristic size is at least four times the aggregate size which for a typical concrete is about 100 mm. Wittmann (1983) has argued that the appropriate structural, materials engineering and science models are different for each microstructural level. However, this rather complicated characterization may not be strictly necessary. Modeer (1979) suggested that it is simpler to consider all cementitious materials as a two-phase composite with a homogeneous phase and a particle phase. Thus, in cement paste the matrix is the hydrated cement gels and the unhydrated cement particles the reinforcement; in mortar the two phases are cement paste and fine aggregates, while in concrete the matrix is mortar and the reinforcement is

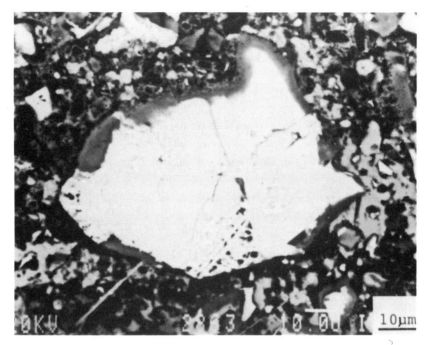

Figure 2.1 Large anhydrous core. BEI polished surface. (After Baldie, 1985.)

the coarse aggregates. In this way the properties of concrete, mortar and paste can be considered as the averages of the individual properties of the phases and the interfacial bonds between the phases.

When fibres are added to reinforce a cementitious matrix the interphases formed between the fibre and matrix are significant in determining the effective stress transfer between them. Various types of fibres have been used and these include both high and low Young's modulus fibres such as steel, asbestos, glass, synthetic (e.g. aramid, polyethylene, polypropylene, acrylic, nylon, poly-vinyl alcohol, carbon) and natural fibres (e.g. cellulose, sisal and coconut). Strengthening of the matrices occurs not only because the fibres are able to take up the applied load transferred from the matrix material, but more impor-tantly because the fibres can bridge the pre-existing matrix pores or micro-cracks thus delaying critical failure. This latter aspect means that even low modulus fibres (and not necessarily high modulus fibres as required by conven-tional composite mechanics) can strengthen brittle cementitious materials.

2.2 Cementitious materials

When a plain cementitious specimen is loaded in tension a FPZ forms right across the section at maximum load (see section 1.2). A similar FPZ also

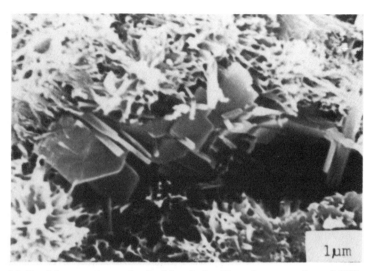

Figure 2.2 Small hexagonal crystals of calcium hydroxide and outer product of CSH needles. SEI fracture surface. (After Baldie, 1985.)

develops at the tip of a notch or a crack. The critical size of the FPZ is dependent upon both the material properties and the geometry and size of the specimen. Only in extremely large specimens can the FPZ develop to its full extent. The most important material property that determines the size of the FPZ is the stress-displacement relationship for the FPZ. The width of the FPZ is reasonably constant except in very small specimens, and the stress-displacement relationship of the strain-softened FPZ is very nearly a material property independent of geometry and size. The magnitude and shape of the stress-displacement curve depends upon: the size and shape of the aggregates, the matrix properties, the interfacial bond between the matrix and reinforcing phase, as well as on the failure mechanism. Because it is difficult to identify precisely where the FPZ ends, various methods have been proposed in the past decade to measure the extent of the FPZ. These experimental methods are discussed in section 3.2.

2.2.1 Fracture process zone (FPZ) and strain-softening characteristics

The development of the FPZ in concrete during a direct tensile test and the associated stress-displacement relationship has been obtained by Petersson (1985) using a very stiff testing machine and a short-gauged tensile specimen. These requirements must be satisfied, otherwise the fracture process is unstable. The development of the FPZ in such a direct tension test is shown in Figure 2.3 and the corresponding stress-displacement curve is shown in Figure 2.4. Widening of the FPZ begins from photograph 3 where the width is about 15 μm and increases to about 170 μm in

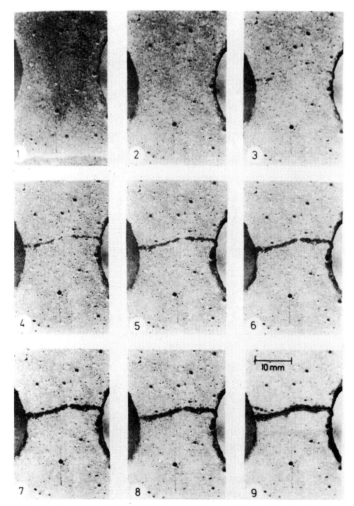

Figure 2.3 The development of a FPZ during a tensile test. The surface has been cast against a steel mould. (After Petersson, 1985.)

photograph 9. Up to the maximum stress f_t there are no signs of a FPZ; in fact the first visible signs of the FPZ appear in photograph 3 where the stress carried is already very much less than f_t. The reason for the delayed appearance of a FPZ is because in a plain tension specimen there is no focus for the formation of a FPZ and at first microcracking occurs over a diffuse area. In the presence of a notch or crack, this initial diffuse development does not occur and a concentrated FPZ forms directly. Although there is some curvature in the stress-displacement curve up to the maximum stress, it is usually assumed that the displacement up to this point is elastic and uniform over the entire gauge length. Since the FPZ is narrow compared with

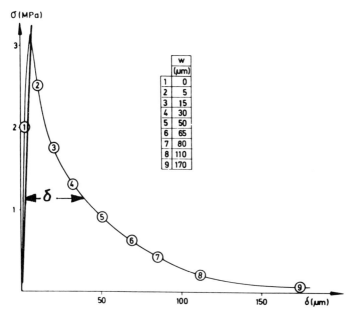

Figure 2.4 The stress-displacement curve. The numbers on the graph correspond to the photographs in Figure 2.3. w is widening of the FPZ. (After Petersson, 1985.)

the gauge length, the elastic contribution from the pupative FPZ can be neglected and the opening of the FPZ, δ, measured from the elastic loading line as shown in Figure 2.4. The stress-displacement curve is shown schematically in Figure 2.5. There are three regions in this schematic stress-displacement curve. Up to about 60% of the ultimate strength, f_t, the specimen is elastic (Region A). In Region B the deformation is non-linear because of dispersed cracking. At a critical stress the damage in a cementitious material becomes localized and a FPZ starts to form. It is only from this point that the displacement becomes virtually independent of the gauge length. Hence, in Figure 2.5 the displacement is measured from the elastic loading line passing through the point of maximum load. There is elastic recovery in the body of the specimen as the stress decreases in Region C where the FPZ strain softens as the bridges pull out or fracture. A visible continuous crack forms when the local displacement across the FPZ reaches a critical value, δ_f. The stress-displacement relation for the FPZ is obtained by subtracting the elastic displacement of Region A from the total displacement as shown in Figure 2.4. Of note is the long tail to the stress-displacement curve where locked bridging aggregates are pulled out against frictional forces. The long tail makes accurate measurement of the fracture energy, G_{If}, difficult (see section 3.5).

It may be noted that in cementitious materials the FPZ, albeit analogous to the plastic yielding zone in ductile materials, is not affected by the state of

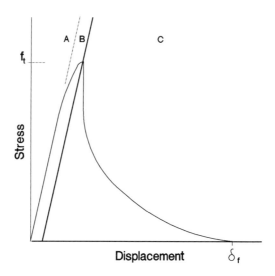

Figure 2.5 Schematic stress-displacement curve for a cementitious material.

stress and is therefore independent of the thickness of the specimen provided the specimen is more than three or four times the thickness of the aggregate. The reason is that the loss of strength is caused by microcracking and the pull-out of interlocking aggregates and there is little shear deformation. Hence, there is very little difference in the FPZ between plane stress and plane strain.

2.3   Cementitious fibre reinforced composites

When fibres, whether continuous, or discontinuous, are added to the brittle cement matrix materials, the fracture toughness and strength of the resultant composites are significantly improved. The fibres alone are capable of sustaining a stress greater than that which causes the matrix to crack if the volume fraction of the reinforcing fibres is greater than a critical value, v_c (Aveston *et al.*, 1971). In this case the matrix breaks up into a number of parallel cracks, the spacing being determined by the distance over which the stress transferred from the fibre to the matrix builds up to the critical value (Aveston *et al.*, 1971). The critical volume fractions are in the range of 0.3–0.8% for aligned continuous steel, glass and polypropylene fibres (Hannant, 1978). The stress-strain behaviour for this kind of cementitious composite we term Type I and Figure 2.6 shows the curves for carbon fibre and steel wire reinforced composites of this type. A schematic stress-displacement curve for Type I composites is shown in Figure 2.7; note that since the deformation is not confined to a single FPZ or FBZ, the displacement is not separated into deformation across the FPZ/FBZ and the bulk

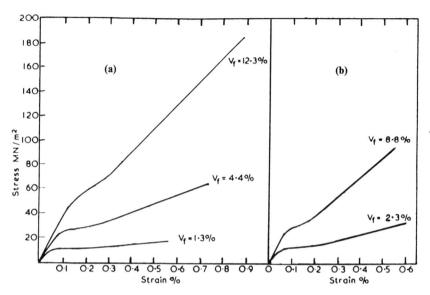

Figure 2.6 Stress–strain curves for (a) carbon fibre reinforced cement, (b) steel wires. (After Aveston *et al.*, 1974.)

elastic displacement. In Region A the behaviour is essentially elastic though there is some diffuse microcracking. A defined FPZ forms in Region B, causing non-linearity. If the fibres have a higher elastic modulus compared with the matrix, Region B may not be detectable. At a critical composite stress, σ_{cmc}, the matrix cracks and a continuous matrix crack forms in the FPZ. Since the volume fraction is greater than the critical value, the stress carried by the bridging fibres increases with further straining and leads to the development of multiple cracks (Region C) until the spacing reaches a minimum distance depending upon the bond strength between the fibres and the matrix (Aveston and Kelly, 1973; Hannant *et al.*, 1983). The stress in Region C may remain constant or increase (as discussed below). In Region D further straining causes the stress to increase almost linearly with a less steep slope than in Region A, but greater slope than in Region C, as the fibres stretch. Region D ends in either the fibres breaking,[1] or if the fibres are shorter than the critical length at which the fibres can just develop their fracture strength, the fibres gradually pull out (Region E). The ultimate strength of cementitious matrices reinforced with continuous wires or fibres of steel carbon or polypropylene can be very much greater than the stress, σ_{cmc}, at which the matrix first cracks (Aveston *et al.*, 1974; Keer, 1984; Majaumdar and Walton, 1984; Swamy and Hussin, 1989; Li *et al.*, 1993).

---

[1] If the Weibull distribution for the strength of the fibres has a high modulus there can be no significant fibre pull-out. However, if the Weibull modulus is low, fibres can break away from the matrix crack causing some fibre pull-out.

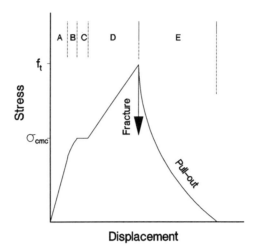

Figure 2.7 Schematic stress-displacement curve for a Type I composite with multiple matrix cracking.

There is some controversy as to whether the stress in Region C is constant or increases. The stress during multiple cracking of the matrix can rise for two reasons:

(i) There is a significant variation in the strength of the matrix. Since the Weibull modulus for cementitious materials is of the order of 10 (see Chapter 6), comparatively large matrix strength variations are possible.
(ii) The fibres debond easily so that there is no longer strain compatibility between the fibres and the matrix and the fibres take more than their fair share of the load. Hence, the load has to rise before more matrix cracks can be generated. Few fibres bond well to cementitious matrices.

Examination of the stress-strain curves of a variety of Type I composites suggests that the stress in Region C is more nearly constant if the volume fraction of the fibres is close to the critical value for multiple cracking and that Region C becomes less distinguishable from Region D as the volume fraction increases.

The stress-strain curve for a cementitious composite is also difficult to measure and some of the experimental techniques used may introduce errors. Li $et\ al.$ (1993) report a stress-strain curve for steel fibre reinforced cementitious composite ($v = 1.53\%$, $d_f = 0.4\,\text{mm}$) where the change in slope from Region C to Region D is very small (see Figure 2.8) and the test method may have affected the curve. They aligned 30 steel wires and cast epoxy resin at the ends to form the anchorages and then cast the

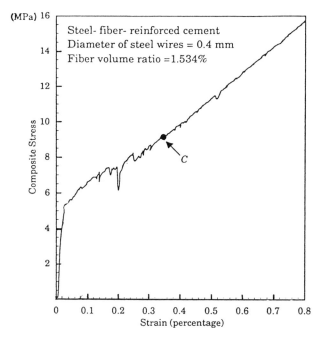

Figure 2.8 Stress–strain curve for steel wire reinforced cement, $v = 1.53\%$, $d_f = 0.4\,\text{mm}$, C marks the end of multiple cracking. (After Li *et al.*, 1993.)

Portland cement in the test section. By this method the wires were very securely anchored in the epoxy resin which bonds well to steel and poorly bonded in the test section. It is suggested that under these circumstances the wires might have been more highly stressed than would be expected from the rule of mixtures even before the matrix cracked so that the deformation of the specimen may have been very much controlled by the steel wires throughout the experiment with some slippage taking place between the wires and the cement matrix even before the matrix cracked. Composites that are Type I behave in many ways like elastic-plastic materials and fracture mechanics as such is not needed to describe the behaviour of structures made from these materials. Type I fracture behaviour is most common for cementitious materials reinforced with continuous fibres or networks. If the volume fraction of the fibres is less than v_c then the stress sustainable by the composite drops either when the matrix cracks or, if there is some stable debonding, just after the matrix cracks. This kind of composite we term Type II. Most Type II composites are reinforced by discontinuous fibres which usually pull out rather than fracture. Multiple cracking does not occur in Type II composites and fracture in a tension specimen occurs essentially on a single narrow FPZ. The behaviour of Type II composites can be best described in terms of a stress-displacement curve where the bulk elastic displacement is separated from that acting

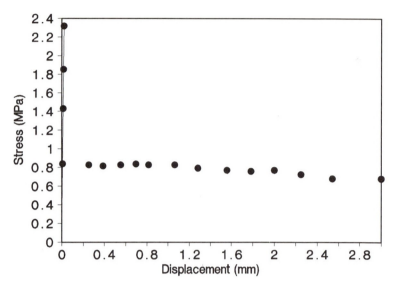

Figure 2.9 Stress-displacement curve for a steel–fibre–concrete reinforced with straight wires 0.565 mm in diameter and 30 mm long; fibre volume fraction 1.5%. (After Lim *et al.*, 1987b.)

across the FPZ/FBZ. There are two sub-types. In Type IIA composites the fibres are long and the fibre pull-out stress is virtually constant for large CODs. The stress-displacement curve for a steel–fibre–concrete reinforced by smooth steel wires with a volume fraction of 1.5%, shown in Figure 2.9 is typical of a Type IIA composite. A Type IIB composite has short fibres and the stress drops more sharply with fibre pull-out. Typical Type IIB composites are shown in Figure 2.10.

A schematic stress-displacement curve for Type IIA composites is shown in Figure 2.11. The initial behaviour is elastic (Region A). At higher stresses the load-deflection curve becomes non-linear (Region B) primarily because of microcracking in the FPZ. The microcracks are partially stabilized by the fibres and the maximum strain achieved before the FPZ becomes localized is larger than the corresponding strain in the unreinforced matrix. This increase in matrix strain can occur even if the modulus of the reinforcing fibres is less than that of the matrix. The fibre debonding can be either completely unstable or the fibres may debond stably at first in which case the partial debonding can contribute to the non-linearity of Region B and a continuous matrix crack forms before the tensile strength, f_t, is reached. On reaching the fracture strength, f_t, of the composite the stress drops as friction takes the load. There can be a slight recovery in load (Region C) as fibres that are debonded in the vicinity of the matrix crack stretch elastically before pulling out against friction. If the fibres are long, the stress remains almost constant over COD of the order of 5 mm or more.

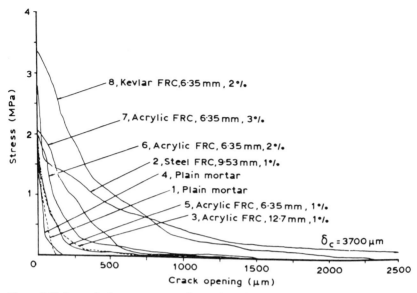

Figure 2.10 Stress-displacement curves for various fibre reinforced cementitious materials. (After Li and Ward, 1989.)

With short fibres (Type IIB) the schematic stress-displacement curve superficially looks the same as that for an unreinforced cementitious material (Figure 2.5), but the COD, δ_f, which is of the order of 0.1 mm for unreinforced material is equal to half the fibre length for fibre reinforced composites. After the essentially elastic Region A, diffuse microcracking

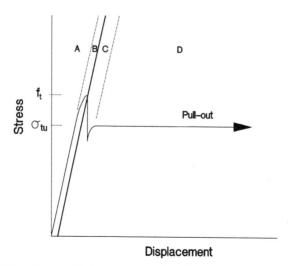

Figure 2.11 Schematic stress-displacement curve for a Type IIA composite with long fibres.

and possibly stable partial debonding of fibres causes the non-linearity in Region B. If there is some stable debonding, the matrix cracks completely at a stress, σ_{cmc}, which is less than the strength of the composite. Once debonding becomes unstable the stress drops. If the fibres are poorly bonded so that friction provides the main shear transfer from the fibres to the matrix, the drop in stress, though steep has a finite slope, whereas for well bonded fibres there is a sudden drop in stress as friction takes over. In Region C the fibres pull out against friction and the stress decreases.

2.3.1 The crack tip fibre bridging zone (FBZ)

When a Type II cementitious structure containing a notch is loaded, a FPZ initially forms at its tip. With increase in load the CTOD reaches the critical value, δ_m, of the matrix and a fracture bridging zone (FBZ) starts to grow. When the FBZ is fully developed the bridging fibres either pull out or fracture (see Figure 2.12). The division between the FPZ and the FBZ is the tip of the continuous matrix crack which is often difficult to locate exactly and the measurements of the sizes of the two zones can be inaccurate. Generally, the FBZ in cement composites depends on the aspect ratio of the fibres and

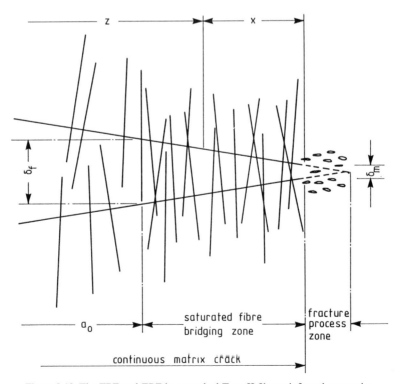

Figure 2.12 The FPZ and FBZ in a notched Type II fibre reinforced composite.

on the geometry and size of the specimen and the loading configuration. The magnitudes of the FBZ in common cement composites can vary considerably: in asbestos cement with a fibre length of about a couple of millimetres the FBZ is of the order of 30 mm in a double-cantilever-beam (DCB) specimen (Lenain and Bunsell, 1979); in a steel fibre reinforced concrete with a fibre length of 6.35 mm the FBZ, in a DCB specimen, is more than 600 mm long (Visalvanich and Naaman, 1983); in a glass fibre cement with chopped strand glass mat the FBZ is about 15 mm (Patterson and Chan, 1975).

2.4 Fracture mechanisms in cementitious materials and fibre composites

In this section the micro-failure mechanisms of cementitious materials and their fibre composites are discussed. Emphasis is placed on the role of interfaces on strength and fracture energy absorption. The development of macro-defect-free (MDF) cement pastes in the last 10 years by ICI in the UK, which give both high strength and high toughness, and the mechanisms involved in this new class of material, are described.

2.4.1 The micromechanisms of failure in concretes and the new cement pastes

The micro-failure mechanisms in cement paste, mortar and concrete have been studied with great detail by Diamond and Bentur (1985) using a scanning electron microscope equipped with a chamber that permits saturated specimens to be observed in a wet environment by detecting back-scattered electrons. Similar studies have also been conducted by Tait and his co-workers (1986, 1990) using the same technique but with a double-torsion specimen which allows stable crack growth to occur. In mortar and concrete, failure is characterized by crack deviation, branching and multiple cracking. Crack deviation, where the crack meanders in the paste matrix between aggregates or propagates around the aggregates and along debonded paste/aggregate interfaces, is shown in Figure 2.13. Branches are more predominant in concrete than in mortar and multiple subdivision into three or more branches is not uncommon as is shown in Figures 2.14–2.16. In the case of mortar, multiple cracking occurs where the crack leaves a debonded aggregate or around an air void (see Figure 2.17). In concrete, multiple cracking often occurs between adjacent sand grains rather than around isolated ones as in mortar. The interaction of the propagating crack with the inhomogeneities is of particular interest. In dried mortar specimens the crack runs along the interface between the sand grain and the paste matrix resulting in debonding. However, in undried specimens the crack always avoids the interface even though it may run along it for some distance. In concrete the interaction of the crack tip with sand

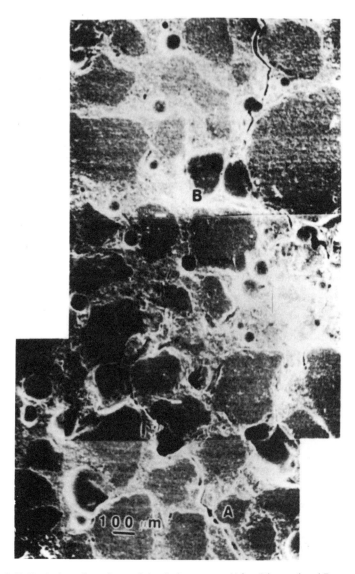

Figure 2.13 Typical portion of a crack in air dry mortar. (After Diamond and Bentur, 1985.)

grains is much the same as in mortar but, in addition, multiple radial cracks are often found between adjacent grains caused by shrinkage misfit (see Figure 2.18). However, the presence of large coarse aggregates produces some interesting features. Occasionally, the cracks run into the large aggregates but more often they are arrested in front of these aggregates thus activating another main crack in a new path. In more recent work where the crack was made to propagate stably in a double-torsion specimen,

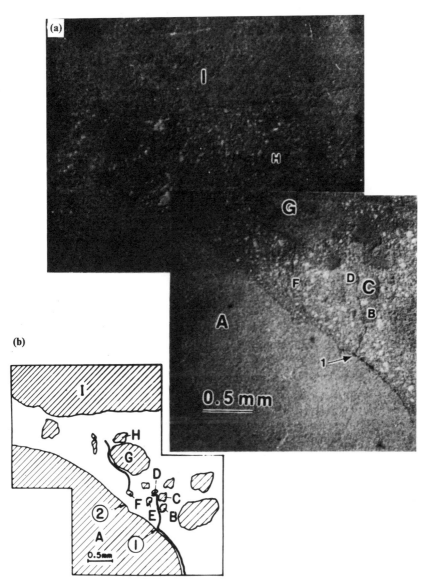

Figure 2.14 The crack tip zone in concrete during the first stage of loading. (After Diamond and Bentur, 1985.)

Tait *et al.* (1990) found that for mortar there was a substantial microcrack zone at the main crack tip much like 'tree branches'. Eventually one of these branches becomes the main crack with its own system of microcracks. In so doing the previously formed microcracks are unloaded and a good illustration of this feature is given in Figure 2.19.

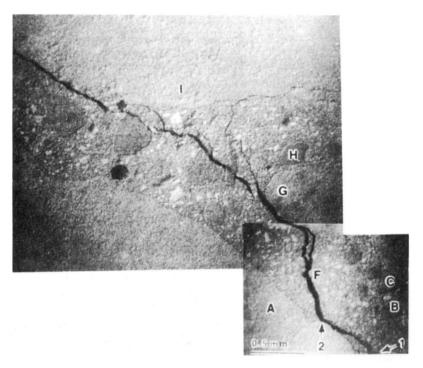

Figure 2.15 The same zone as in Figure 2.14 after the second loading stage. (After Diamond and Bentur, 1985.)

The failure processes are complicated. The high fracture energy absorptions, which are associated with crack deviations, crack branching, and multiple microcracking, make concrete a much tougher material than paste. Whilst the microcracking zone can be reasonably treated as a FPZ it is very difficult to distinguish a traction-free main crack behind this region. Furthermore, the main crack is never straight and the FPZ is somewhat diffused. All these features seem to cast some doubts on the fracture mechanics modelling of concrete and mortar using a single equivalent traction-free crack (Tait *et al.*, 1990). Hillerborg's fictitious crack model (Hillerborg *et al.*, 1976; Petersson, 1985) and Bažant's crack band model (Bažant and Cedolin, 1979; Bažant and Oh, 1983; Bažant and Lin, 1988; Bažant *et al.*, 1988; Bažant and Ozbolt, 1990), which is discussed in Chapter 4, are better equipped to deal with these materials.

In ordinary Portland cement paste, Bailey and his co-workers (Higgins and Bailey, 1976; Bailey *et al.*, 1986) have used a 'diffuse illumination' optical microscopy technique to reveal a small FPZ at the notch tip. They show that the FPZ is synonymous with a discontinuous or tied-crack, within which the silicate hydrate fibrils are pulled apart. Unfortunately, this model is inconsistent with recent microstructural observations on polished

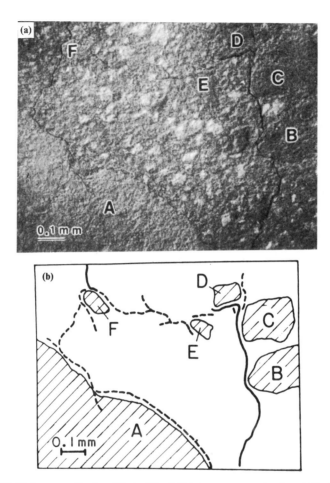

Figure 2.16 Higher magnification (75×) of the field between aggregates A and F in Figure 2.14 during the first stage of loading, showing a network of cracks of width 1 μm or less between the aggregates and along the aggregate surfaces. (After Diamond and Bentur, 1985.)

epoxy-impregnated cement paste carried out by Struble *et al.* (1989) using SEM with back-scattered electron imaging. They show quite conclusively that the crack-resistance curve behaviour in cement paste is primarily due to the discontinuous crack path in which the gaps between offset segments form crack bridges behind the advancing crack front. These unbroken gaps across the offsets behave similarly to the localized grain bridging in coarse-grained alumina (Swanson *et al.*, 1987). It is these bridging unfractured segments rather than the interlocking silicate hydrate fibrils that provide the microstructural basis for the so-called 'tied-crack' model. *In-situ* studies in the SEM show that the main crack is generally straight but higher magnification reveals that it is composed of many linked short

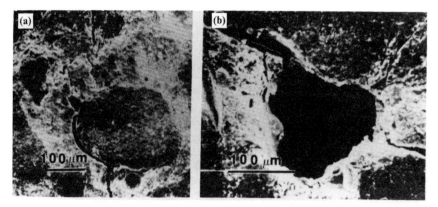

Figure 2.17 Debonding and multiple cracking in air-dry mortar, (a) around a sand grain, (b) around a void. (After Diamond and Bentur, 1985.)

segments about 60 μm in length. Restricted crack branching is visible and more importantly the crack is discontinuous in several places near its tip as shown in Figure 2.20. This observation confirms the comment of Struble *et al.* (1989) that unbroken segments exist in the wake of the propagating crack tip. Higgins and Bailey (1976) found that the fracture toughness, K_c,

Figure 2.18 Multiple radial cracks between adjacent sand grains in concrete. (After Diamond and Bentur, 1985.)

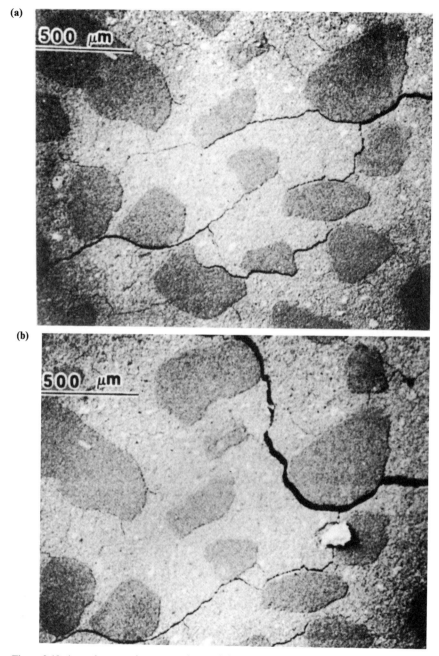

Figure 2.19 A crack system in mortar, the crack has propagated from top right to bottom left. (a) A crack bridge has developed. (b) On increasing the load, the main crack has propagated upwards allowing the initial cracks to close. (After Tait *et al.*, 1990.)

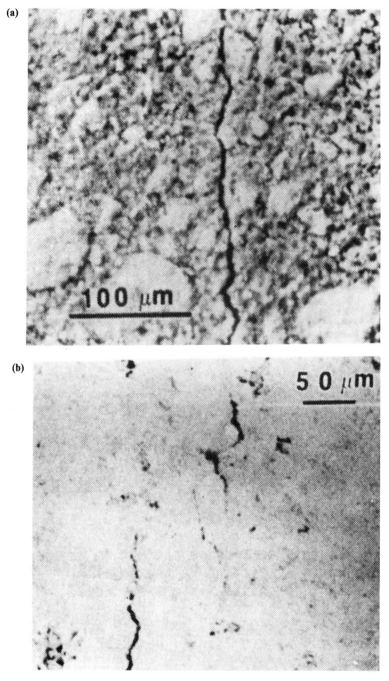

Figure 2.20 Typical cracks in cement paste. (a) Continuous crack. (b) Discontinuous cracks. (After Struble *et al.*, 1989.)

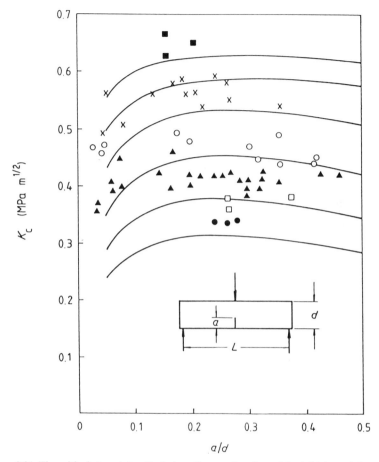

Figure 2.21 The critical stress intensity factor, K_c, as a function of the initial notch length for various cement paste specimen sizes with $L = 5d$ (experimental data from Higgins and Bailey, 1976; d (mm) $= 5$ ●, 8 □, 14 △, 28 ○, 56 ×, 110 ■: theoretical curves from Cotterell and Mai, 1987).

for their Portland cement pastes was not a constant but increased with the size of the notched beam specimens. They concluded that the Griffith fracture criterion is invalid without realizing that the 'tied-crack' dimension is much larger than the very small zone of silicate hydrate fibrils and is of the order of the unbroken ligaments. Cotterell and Mai (1987) have actually shown that these K_c results are in good agreement with the predictions of a crack-resistance curve model (see Figure 2.21). It was further shown that the FPZ is dependent on the size of the beam. Thus the crack-resistance is size dependent as is shown in Figure 2.22, and there is no unique crack-resistance curve. The R-curve is only unique if the size of the beam is much larger than the FPZ.

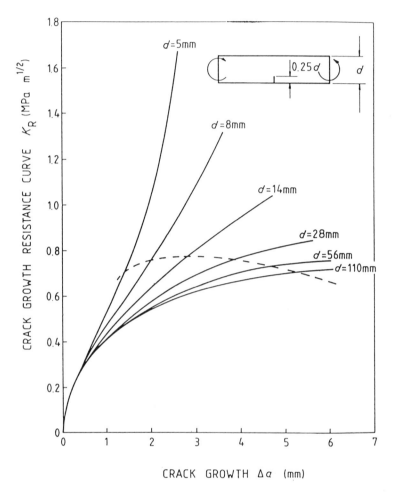

Figure 2.22 Crack growth resistance curves for different size cement paste specimens with $a/d = 0.25$, instability locus - - - -.

The source of weakness in cement pastes is associated not with the total porosity but with the size and shape of the largest pore. Thus, by reducing the size and amount of these large pores the strength of cement pastes can be improved. Birchall and co-workers (Birchall *et al.*, 1981, 1982; Kendall *et al.*, 1983, 1985) have made use of this concept to develop what is commonly called macro-defect-free (MDF) cement paste. The MDF paste was prepared using calcium aluminate cement premixed with a polyvinyl alcohol–acetate copolymer which are passed through a two-roll mill with a high shearing rate to reduce the size and level of porosity in the pastes. Typical properties of these MDF cement pastes in 2–3 mm thicknesses are: bending strength (three-point bend and span 100 mm) of 145 ± 5 MPa with a Weibull modulus of between 20 and 30, Young modulus, E, of 52 ± 1 GPa, fracture toughness, K_{Ic}, of 3.3 ± 0.1 MPa$\sqrt{m}$ and fracture energy, G_{If}, of 400 ± 60 J/m^2. According to Birchall and his co-workers, the improved tensile strength of the new pastes is entirely caused by the reduction in pore size ($2c$) according to the equation

$$\sigma_c = \left[\frac{E_0 G_{If0}(1 - v_p)^3 \exp(-\alpha v_p)}{\pi c} \right]^{1/2} \qquad (2.1)$$

where E_0 and G_{If0} are values for the Young's modulus and the fracture energy when the volume fraction, v_p, of the porosity is zero; α is a constant. In this view the polymer largely acts as a rheological aid to reduce the pore size, though it is understood that there is a chemical interaction between polymer and cement (Sinclair and Groves, 1985; Roger *et al.*, 1985) which alters both E_0 and G_{If0}. Poon and Groves (1987) confirm that E_0 and G_{If0} are strength limiting factors. A totally different argument for the strength improvement in polymer-modified cement pastes was presented by Eden and Bailey (1984a,b, 1985a,b). They did not agree with the pore size reduction theory and suggested that the polymer must have played a significant role in the strength development in these polymer-modified pastes. For the Portland (calcium silicate) MDF cements they proposed a 'tied-crack' model in which the tensile strength is controlled by the pulling apart of the hydrate fibrils with the polymer acting as an adhesive interface (Eden and Bailey, 1984b, 1988). It is the variation of the interfacial shear strength with polymer content and water absorption that determines the magnitude of the fracture stress according to the Griffith equation. This is a physically attractive model which relates the macroscopic tensile strength to the microscopic interfacial shear strength properties. However, Bailey and co-workers realized that the 'tied-crack' model could not be applied to the calcium aluminate MDF cements because they could not detect the development of an FPZ (akin to the tied-crack) ahead of the machined notch. Consequently, they believed that the high strength and high fracture toughness obtained in these MDF cement pastes must have come from the large deformation of the polymer. But again there is no experimental evidence to support this proposed mechanism for calcium aluminate MDF cements.

Recently, Mai *et al.* (1990) have shown that in the ICI calcium aluminate MDF cements a crack-resistance curve behaviour does exist similar to that observed for unmodified paste. The saturated FPZ in these MDF cements is about 3 mm long in a double-cantilever-beam specimen. Toughening mechanisms giving rise to the R-curve have been identified, using both optical and scanning electron microscopy, in the crack wake. The predominant mechanism is due to unbroken cement ligaments bridging the crack faces. The evolution and break-up of these bridges are shown in Figure 2.23.

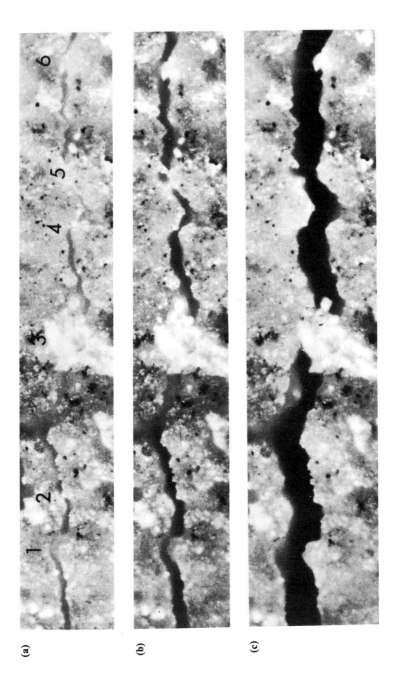

Figure 2.23 Evolution and break-up of crack bridges in MDF paste, ×500.

Similar bridges by untorn ligaments are shown in Figure 2.24e, and by isolated grains in Figure 2.24f. Other less significant contributions are due to frictional interlocking of adjacent grains on the fracture plane (see Figures 2.24a, 2.24b) and tearing of polymer fibrils (see Figure 2.24g). It is concluded from these results that the much enhanced total fracture energy of the polymer modified cement paste comes equally from the improved intrinsic fracture toughness G_{If0} and from the fracture work necessary to pull the crack bridges apart. The role of the polymer is, therefore, more than just a rheological processing aid.

2.4.2 *The micro-fracture mechanisms in fibre reinforced cements*

The total fracture energy of a Type II fibre reinforced cement composite comes from many different energy absorbing mechanisms. It is the understanding of these micromechanisms and the material parameters that control them that will enable the design of stronger and tougher fibre cements. There have been many studies on the fracture micromechanisms in resin-based fibre composites (e.g. Harris, 1980; Kim and Mai, 1991). Such mechanisms include fibre–matrix interface debonding, stress relaxation caused by fibre failure, fibre pull-out, and fractures of fibre and matrix. Because the failure strain of the reinforcing fibres is usually larger than that of the cementitious matrix material, the matrix cracks before the fibres fracture and the major contribution to the total fracture energy comes from work involved in pulling out the fibres from the matrix. An example of fibre reinforced cementitious composites is the high strength steel fibre reinforced concretes. The total fracture energy in this case is given by the sum of the fibre pull-out work and the matrix fracture work including the fibre–matrix debonding work. The work of fibre pull-out gives by far the largest contribution to the fracture energy. For many glass and polymeric fibre reinforced cementitious materials the fibre length is often longer than the critical value l_c so that those fibres which are embedded to a depth of more than $l_c/2$ will break first before they are pulled out; those fibres embedded to a depth of less than $l_c/2$ are simply pulled out. The total fracture energy is now the sum of the work of pulling out of fibres over a length of l_c, the energy absorbed by stress redistribution, the work of fracture of the matrix and fibres, and the work of fibre debonding. Generally, the stress redistribution term is small and can be ignored. Also the fracture work for high strength brittle fibres such as glass, asbestos, carbon, etc. is negligible. However, for ductile fibres like Kevlar and polypropylene, both of which are used for reinforcing cementitious matrices, the work of fracture can be quite substantial.

Fibre reinforcement in cementitious matrices is usually randomly orientated and this affects the fibre pull-out contribution to the fracture work. The pull-out term will have to be multiplied by an orientation efficiency

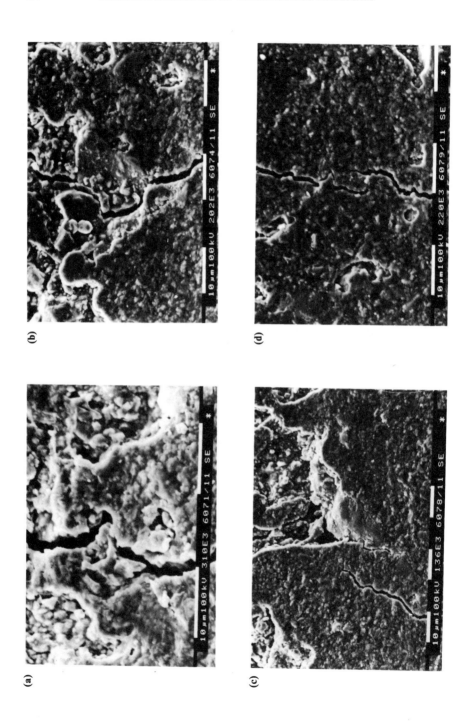

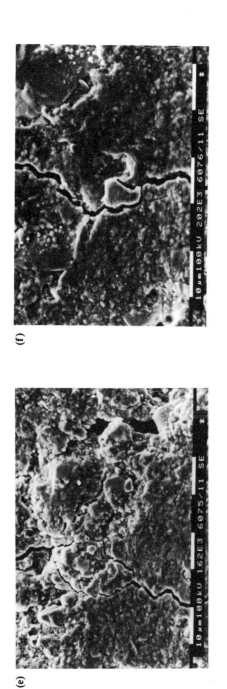

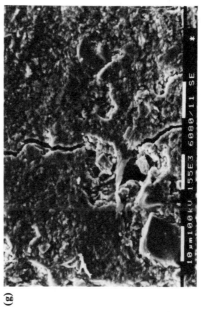

Figure 2.24 Crack bridging mechanisms in MDF paste showing (a) and (b) frictional interlocking; (c) and (d) offset cracks bridged by untorn ligaments; (e) and (f) grain-localized bridging; and (g) polymer fibril bridging.

factor depending on the degree of randomness. While this has an adverse effect of reducing the pull-out work the fact that the fibres are randomly orientated across a fracture plane can introduce some toughness enhancement in certain types of fibre cements such as steel fibre concretes where the fibre length is less than l_c. The toughness enhancement occurs because the steel fibres lying at an angle to the fracture plane are plastically sheared and extra work is dissipated (Harris et al., 1972). A number of investigators have commented on the beneficial toughening effect due to fibre orientation in steel fibre concretes (Helfet and Harris, 1972; Naaman and Shah, 1975; Morton, 1979). Unfortunately, there is no such toughness enhancement in more flexible fibres such as glass, asbestos and cellulose. However, there can be a snubbing effect (Li, 1990) with these fibres.

2.4.3   The role of interfaces in controlling strength and toughness

In all types of composites, the strength and toughness are largely controlled by the interfacial properties. Generally, a strong bond is required for high composite strength and a weak bond is needed to achieve large composite toughness. The nature of the interface is such that there is a physical transition zone or what is commonly called an interphase layer between the cement paste and the reinforcement. The microstructural features of this zone are different from those of the bulk matrix material away from it. For mortars and concretes, this interface layer is less compact with a higher amount of calcium hydroxide crystals oriented with their c-axis normal to the aggregate surface (Larbi, 1993). The interphase layer is the weakest link in those cementitious composites that have a high density of fractures and microcracks. This interphase is also affected by the water–cement ratio. The heterogeneity and microstructural defects increase with the amount of water leading to reduced compressive strength. Larbi (1993) has shown that by adding silica fume, fly ash and metakaolinite to cement paste produces a denser and thinner interphase layer with a smaller amount of calcium hydroxide crystals. This in turn enables a better stress transfer between paste and aggregate particles so that the strength is improved.

In fibre cements there is also an interphase region which is sufficiently distinct from the bulk matrix material. The interphase region for a steel fibre reinforced cement consists of a thin duplex film $1-2\,\mu m$ thick in direct contact with the steel fibre and a $10-30\,\mu m$ thick layer of calcium hydroxide crystals surrounded by a highly CSH porous layer (Diamond and Bentur, 1985) as shown in Figure 2.25. Cracks propagate in this porous layer parallel to the fibre. During the pull-out of the fibres this porous layer can densify causing the frictional stress to drop (Bentur et al., 1985). The weak porous layer also acts as the source for the well known Cook–Gordon (1964) debonding mechanism in deflecting a propagating

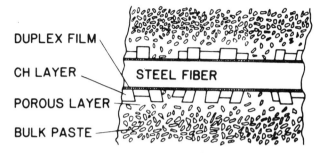

Figure 2.25 Schematic description of the microstructure of a steel fibre-cement paste interface. (After Diamond and Bentur, 1985.)

crack along the porous layer (see Figure 2.26). The crack will eventually fracture the fibre before being arrested again in another porous layer. In principle this mechanism should increase the fracture toughness of the steel fibre cement composite.

The role of the interface on the mechanical properties of glass cements is more striking than that in steel fibre cements. At an early stage under normal cure conditions the bond at the interface is predominantly mechanical (Vekey and Majumdar, 1970). Pores gather at the interface and the bond strength is very low. Kim *et al.* (1993) have inferred from pull-out

Figure 2.26 Arrest of a crack near the cement paste/steel fibre interface by the Cook–Gordon mechanism. (After Diamond and Bentur, 1985.)

Figure 2.27 Pulled out glass filaments bridging a crack in a glass fibre reinforced cement prepared with Cem FIL-2 glass fibre strand, cured for 14 days in lime water. (After Majaumdar and Walton, 1984.)

tests on single fibres that the interfacial fracture energy, G_{IIb}, after a 3 day normal cure is only $0.03 \, J/m^2$. Even after 14 days in lime water, there is true debonding along the interface exposing the clean surfaces of the fibre (see Figure 2.27). With age the CH layer forming at the interface, when the cement is hydrated, becomes progressively more crystalline and less porous. The interfacial bond strengthens as a result of the chemical reaction and also because of an increase in fibre/matrix contact area. Accelerated ageing in lime water at elevated temperatures gives the same result.[2] When the interface is completely mature the interfacial bond energy is about $20 \, J/m^2$ (Kim *et al.*, 1993). The fracture surface of a glass fibre reinforced cement paste that has been subject to accelerated ageing is shown in Figure 2.28. The fibres are broken and there are cement hydration products between the empty spaces of adjacent fibres.

[2] One day of accelerated curing at 50°C in lime water is equivalent to 100 days in water at 10°C.

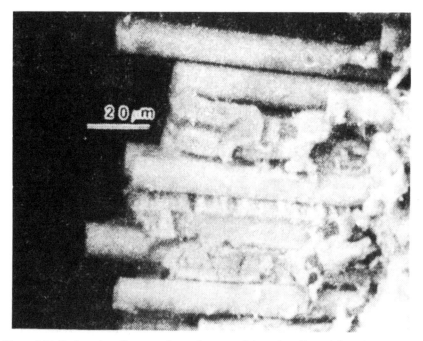

Figure 2.28 Broken glass filaments observed at a crack in a glass fibre reinforced cement prepared with Cem FIL-1 glass fibre strand, after accelerated ageing. The spaces between the filaments are filled with hydration products. (After Majaumdar and Walton, 1984.)

2.5   Summary

The fracture of cementitious materials is typified by the presence of a fracture process zone (FPZ) in which all kinds of micro-failure mechanisms take place. Such processes include microcracking, crack deviation, crack branching and cement-aggregate interface debonding which all contribute to the fracture energy.

The realization that the sizes and shapes of the pores in cement pastes are strength-limiting factors has led to the development of polymer modified cement pastes using the polymer both as a processing aid to reduce the sizes of the pores and a toughening agent to enhance its specific work of fracture. These new MDF cement pastes have rising R-curve characteristics. An effective way to make high strength cements is to engineer the interfacial properties between the paste and the aggregates. The addition of silica fume and fly ash, etc., is useful in changing the structure and properties of the interphase layer to increase the strength of concrete.

The fracture of cementitious fibre composites is characterized by the development of a fibre bridging zone (FBZ) in the wake of the continuous tip of the matrix crack and matrix FPZ. The precise position of the crack tip that divides these two zones is hard to identify. There are many micro-failure mechanisms that take place in the FBZ including fibre–matrix interface debonding, fibre fracture, fibre pull-out, and shear yielding of the fibre. Many of these processes depend on the nature and properties of the fibre–matrix interfaces that can vary between different composites. Design of new tough and strong cement composites therefore depends on optimal control of the interfacial properties.

3 Fracture parameters for cementitious materials

3.1 Introduction

In the previous chapter it is shown that the failure of unreinforced cementitious materials is characterized by the development of a fracture process zone (FPZ) at the notch tip. For fibre reinforced composites, there is an additional fibre bridging zone (FBZ) formed immediately behind the FPZ. The dimensions of the fracture process zone and the fibre bridging zone are difficult to determine precisely and it is also difficult to distinguish between the two zones. Consequently, many experimental methods have been developed to enable the sizes of the FPZ and the FBZ to be measured in cementitious materials and fibre reinforced composites.

To predict the crack-resistance behaviour and the fracture strength of cementitious structures it is necessary to know the constitutive relationships of material in the FPZ and the FBZ. For the unreinforced cementitious materials this constitutive relationship is best described by a strain-softening characteristic in terms of a closure stress and a crack opening displacement (or strain) in the FPZ. Experimental techniques to determine these relationships for mode I and mixed mode fractures and models for these relationships are discussed.

The most important parameter to define the mechanical behaviour of cementitious materials is the fracture energy. This parameter is usually assumed to be a material constant, but does vary slightly with size. The standard RILEM (1985) method of measuring the fracture energy is presented. The stress-displacement relationship of fibre reinforced cement composites, both Type I composites, whose fibre volume fraction is greater than the critical value and whose fibres alone can bear a higher stress than that necessary to crack, and Type II where the stress sustained at matrix cracking is the maximum value, are discussed.

3.2 Experimental techniques for measurement of the FPZ and FBZ

3.2.1 Measurement of fracture process zone in cementitious materials

A comprehensive review of the experimental techniques and methodologies to detect the shape and size of the fracture process zone at the notch tip in unreinforced cementitious materials has been given by Mindess (1991a,b). For convenience, these may be classified into direct and indirect methods. The direct methods involve either surface measurements such as (a) optical microscopy, (b) scanning electron microscopy, (c) resistance strain gauges, and (d) interferometry techniques, or measurements through the specimen interior which include (a) X-ray techniques, (b) mercury penetration measurements, (c) dye penetrants, (d) ultrasonic pulse velocity, (e) infrared vibrothermography, and (f) acoustic emission. The indirect methods are those of (a) compliance measurements and (b) multi-cutting techniques.

Numerical methods can also be used to estimate the FPZ as a function of specimen size and geometry and crack growth, if the closure stress–crack face separation relationship (or strain-softening) is known, based on fracture mechanics analysis (for example, see Cotterell and Mai, 1987). Similar numerical techniques can be applied to fibre reinforced cements. For both analyses it is necessary to know the stress–crack opening relationships for the FBZ and the FPZ. The fracture mechanics procedure for the prediction of the FPZ and FBZ as a function of specimen geometry and size as well as crack length is also given by Cotterell and Mai (1988b).

Not all of the experimental techniques mentioned above are useful to detect the size of the FPZ in cementitious materials. For example, X-ray (Slate and Hover, 1984), mercury penetration measurements (Schneider and Diederichs, 1983), dye penetrants (Swartz and Go, 1984) and resistance strain gauges (John and Shah, 1986) are not always sensitive enough to define the process zone. Mixed results have also been reported with a variety of techniques based on both optical and scanning electron microscopy. Some investigations confirm the existence of the FPZ but others do not, even though the same technique is used. In optical microscopy these methods include diffuse illumination (Eden and Bailey, 1986), thin sections with impregnated epoxy containing a fluorescent dye (Knab et al., 1984, 1986; van Mier, 1989). In scanning electron microscopy, in-situ observations of specimens in the chamber of the SEM (Mindess and Diamond, 1982a,b; Diamond and Bentur, 1985; Tait and Garrett, 1986), back-scattered electron imaging (Baldie and Pratt, 1986; Knab et al., 1986), and replica technique (Ringot et al., 1987; Bascoul et al., 1989a,b) have also been used. Similarly, averaging techniques based on total damage such as the infrared vibro-thermography (Luong, 1986) and ultrasonic pulse velocity (Alexander and Blight, 1986; Chhuy et al., 1986; Alexander, 1988; Reinhardt and Hordijk, 1988; Berthaud, 1989; Alexander et al., 1989) have also yielded mixed results in measuring the size of the FPZ.

Mindess (1991a,b) has also suggested that the compliance measurement technique is not a good method to determine either the 'total' (Kobayashi et al., 1985) or the 'effective' crack length (Karihaloo and Nallathambi, 1989). Although the laser holographic and speckle interferometry techniques are the most sensitive, the definition of the FPZ is often in terms of some limiting strain and it is not always possible to specify the FPZ

(Ferrara and Morabito, 1989). However, Moiré interferometry has been used successfully to measure the FPZ of concrete by Du *et al.* (1987, 1989) and Raiss *et al.* (1989) though the values seem rather large. Acoustic emission measurements can detect the growth of the FPZ and the evolution of damage in a specimen during loading. Berthelot and Robert (1987) found a microcracked zone (i.e. FPZ) ahead of the continuous crack and that this zone grew with crack extension. Maji and co-workers (Maji and Shah, 1988; Maji *et al.*, 1990) also observed acoustic emission events, after the maximum load, to occur both ahead of (which indicates a frontal process zone) and behind (which confirms the existence of ligament bridging) the visible crack tip.

3.2.2 The multi-cutting technique to measure the FPZ in cementitious materials

A simplified view of a critical or saturated FPZ in an unreinforced cementitious material is shown in Figure 3.1. The continuous crack is traction-free. Within the FPZ the effective Young's modulus is reduced from that of the undamaged material E to E' due to the presence of the microcracks. The closure stress associated with the bridging grains and the localized damage is a maximum f_t at the tip of the FPZ and decreases to zero at the continuous crack tip where the crack opening displacement is δ_f. For the same continuous crack length, a, the compliance of a saw cut specimen $C(a)$ is smaller than that

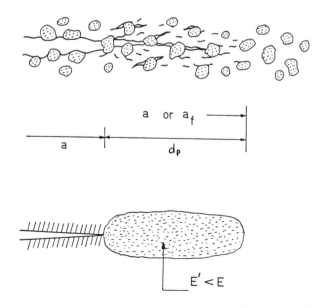

Figure 3.1 Schematic representation of a fracture process zone (FPZ) in a cementitious material. (After Wittmann and Hu, 1991.)

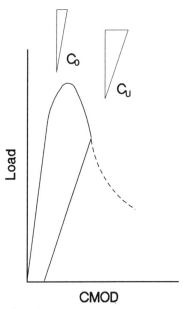

Figure 3.2 Increase in compliance from C_0 for the initial crack length to C_u with the growth of the crack and FPZ. (After Hu and Wittmann, 1989.)

of a natural crack containing an FPZ, $C_u(a)$ (see Figure 3.2). The compliance for a saw cut notch can be obtained experimentally using small loads or obtained from elastic solutions. In the latter case the compliance is readily obtained from the stress intensity factor by the method of Castigliano as described in section 1.6.1.

The multi-cutting technique was first used by Knehans and Steinbrech (1982) to determine the crack wake bridging effect in a coarse-grained alumina. Similar methods have been employed to estimate the FPZ size of mortars and cement pastes (Hu and Wittmann, 1989, 1990, 1991, 1992a; Wittmann and Hu, 1991). Essentially, the bridging zone is consecutively removed by a small amount by saw cutting and the compliances measured after each removal step. Before any bridges are removed there is no change from the original compliance, C_u. However, the compliance, C_p, will increase if any bridging ligaments are removed by cutting. When the whole FPZ has been cut through the compliance, C_p, is equal to the elastic compliance. A schematic illustration is shown in Figure 3.3, where d_p is the size of the saturated bridging zone or critical FPZ.

Compliance measurements made on wedge-opening-loaded (WOL) mortar specimens after saw cutting along the FPZ by Hu and Wittmann (1992a) are shown in Figure 3.4. The WOL specimen dimensions were $200 \times 197 \times 15$ mm with $a/W = 0.4$. Grooves 2 mm deep were machined on both sides to guide the fracture. The water/cement and sand/cement

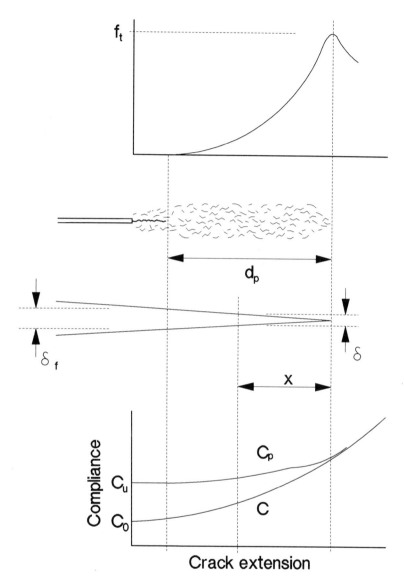

Figure 3.3 Schematic distribution of stress in the FPZ and the change in compliance due to saw cutting into the FPZ. (After Hu and Wittmann, 1989.)

ratios for the specimens were 0.4 and 1.5, respectively. The specimen was loaded to increase the initial compliance from 0.15 to 0.9 m/MN. There was no change in the saw cut compliance until the saw cut was greater than about 32 mm. Hence the continuous crack was about 32 mm long. With longer saw cuts there was an increase in compliance. A curve fitted to the saw cut compliances for $\Delta a > 32$ mm intersects with the

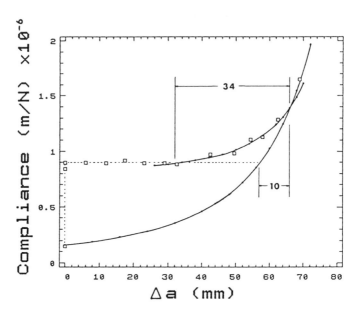

Figure 3.4 Use of saw cutting technique to determine FPZ in a WOL mortar specimen. (After Hu and Wittmann, 1989.)

theoretical compliance at a crack length of 66 mm giving the FPZ length as 34 mm.

The size of the FPZ depends upon the specimen size and geometry as well as on the material properties of the cementitious material as can be seen from the multi-cutting experiment shown in Figure 3.5 for the same mortar specimen used in the experiment shown in Figure 3.4. The initial a/W was again 0.4. In the first experiment the length of the FPZ was found to be 43 mm. After the first saw cutting experiment the specimen was reloaded to extend the FPZ. The compliance curve for the second saw cutting experiment intersects the elastic compliance with the theoretical compliance curve to give a much smaller FPZ of 12 mm. The shortening of the FPZ as the continuous crack grows can be predicted theoretically (see, for example, Cotterell and Mai, 1987, 1988b).

In using the multi-cutting technique, some precautions are required to avoid any additional damage or crack growth due to saw cutting and subsequent reloading. For concretes and mortars with relative large FPZs, a fast cutting speed and a slow feeding rate plus reloading to only half the critical level required for further crack extension are sufficient. However, for cement pastes with much less pronounced FPZs, although the saw-cutting technique may, in principle, be applied, in practice it is not easy because the accuracy of removal of the bridging zone has to be within a millimetre. The same difficulty is experienced in the case of FPZs in quasi-brittle ceramics.

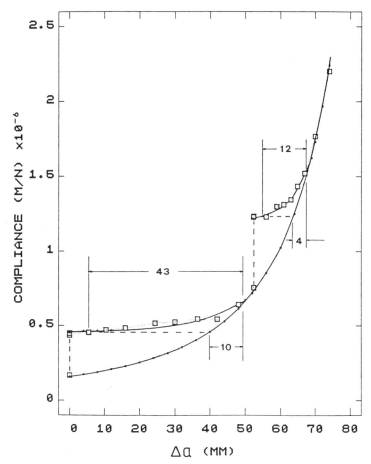

Figure 3.5 Repetition of saw cutting on one specimen after the previous FPZ has been removed. (After Hu and Wittmann, 1992.)

3.3 Measurement of the mode I strain-softening relationship for cementitious materials

The strain-softening relationship for cementitious materials can be expressed in terms of either a stress-strain relationship or a stress-displacement relationship measured at the edge of the FPZ. For mode I fracture these two approaches are very similar because the width, w, of the FPZ is a quasi-material constant. Since the FPZ is narrow it can usually be assumed that the elastic contribution to the displacement is negligible.

The stress-displacement relationship for the FPZ of a cementitious material can in theory be obtained directly from a tension test because, though the initial microcracking activity is dispersed, the deformation becomes localized in a FPZ after the maximum load has been reached. The most important parameter that can be obtained from the mode I stress-displacement curve is the mode I fracture energy, G_{If}, which is the specific work of fracture necessary to develop and completely fracture the FPZ. Thus the mode I fracture energy is given by

$$G_{If} = \int_0^{\delta_f} \sigma \, d\delta \qquad (3.1)$$

3.3.1   The direct tension method

In the direct tension method the specimens used to obtain the stress-displacement curves can either be plain (Petersson, 1985; Guo and Zhang, 1987) or have shallow notches on both edges to locate the FPZ (Reinhardt, 1984; Gopalaratnam and Shah, 1985; Reinhardt *et al.*, 1986; Hordijk *et al.*, 1987; Rots, 1988). The tensile area of the specimens must be large enough to contain a reasonable number of aggregates. Testing can be performed in a servo-hydraulic machine driven by LVDTs mounted on the specimens (Reinhardt, 1984; Gopalaratnam and Shah, 1985; Reinhardt *et al.*, 1986; Hordijk *et al.*, 1987) or in a universal testing machine with heavy springs in parallel with the specimen to stabilize the fracture (Petersson, 1985; Guo and Zhang, 1987). Apart from the problem of stabilizing the fracture, the main problem in making direct tensile tests is that the FPZ does not establish itself instantaneously right across the specimen. Hordijk *et al.* (1987) have made a detailed study of the mode of failure in the direct tension test and found that the deformation was often asymmetrical especially if the specimen was long. If the deformation was asymmetrical a 'bump' was introduced in the stress-displacement curve which was partly associated with local instability referred to as 'snap-back'. This behaviour has been modelled using finite elements (Rots, 1988).

Because the direct tension test is not as simple as first appears, indirect methods of obtaining the stress-displacement curve have been proposed.

3.3.2   The J-integral method

The *J*-integral can be used to obtain the stress-displacement curve from a compact tension test (Li, 1984; Li *et al.*, 1987). If in the *J*-integral the integration is performed around the edge of the FPZ, which has a thickness t, the integral reduces to

$$J \approx \int_0^a \sigma \frac{\partial \delta}{\partial a} \, dx + \tfrac{1}{2} f_t \epsilon_e t = -\int_0^a \sigma \frac{\partial \delta}{\partial x} \, dx + \tfrac{1}{2} f_t \delta_e \qquad (3.2)$$

where ϵ_e and δ_e are the elastic strain and displacement in the FPZ at the ultimate strength of the material which yields

$$J(\delta) = \int_0^\delta \sigma \, d\delta \qquad (3.3)$$

When a continuous crack forms, $\delta = \delta_f$ and $J(\delta_f) = J_{Ic}$ can be identified with G_{If}. J can be calculated experimentally using the energy interpretation given by eqn 1.59. If the load/load-line deflection $(P - \Delta)$ for two compact tension specimens of slightly different crack lengths a and $a + da$ are obtained (see Figure 1.28) the J-integral for a given deflection, Δ, is given by

$$J(\Delta) = \frac{\text{Area}\,(OAB)}{B \, da} \qquad (3.4)$$

The stress-displacement relationship is given by

$$\sigma(\delta) = \frac{\partial J(\delta)}{\partial \delta} \qquad (3.5)$$

and hence combining eqns 3.4 and 3.5

$$\sigma(\delta) = \frac{1}{B \, da} \frac{\partial \,\text{Area}\,(OAB)}{\partial \delta} \qquad (3.6)$$

Since in the experimental method only finite differences are measured, the CTOD, δ, measured simultaneously with the load-point deflection, is taken as the average of the CTODs obtained from the two specimens. The CTOD has to be measured from two points on the specimen a finite distance apart and thus an elastic displacement not associated with the FPZ is included in the measurement. This elastic component can be subtracted from the measured COD to give the true CTOD across the FPZ.

The main problem with Li's (1984, 1987) method is that the stress-deflection curve has to be obtained from two specimens. Since cementitious materials are very inhomogeneous and no two supposedly identical specimens behave identically the same, there can be considerable scatter in the stress-displacement curves. Rokugo *et al.* (1989) have proposed using a single specimen for the determination of the J-integral. However, the details of their proposition are not very clear. The similarity arguments used to obtain J for a deep notched bend specimen (see section 1.9.2) rely on the FPZ being small compared with the ligament. If the FPZ is not small compared with the ligament length, as is usually the case with cementitious materials, the similarity argument fails. The η factor used by Rokugo *et al.* (1989) is not stated explicitly.

3.3.3 Indirect method using a notch bend specimen

An alternative indirect method that uses a load-deflection curve obtained from a notched bend test has been suggested by Chuang and Mai (1989). In this method the strain distribution across the notched section is assumed to be linear and global equilibrium of forces and moments are satisfied. A dis-advantage of this method, which is discussed in more detail in section 4.2, is that the width of the FPZ as well as the stress-strain relationship affects the load-deflection curve. However, the width of the FPZ can be inferred from the fracture energy G_{If}.

3.3.4   Compliance methods

Hu and Wittmann (1989, 1990, 1991, 1992a) have developed a compliance method, combined with cutting through the FPZ, to determine the stress-displacement relationship. The method is explained using the compact tension specimen, which is a suitable geometry, but other geometries may be used. An elastic compliance calibration curve, C, is obtained as a function of the crack growth from some datum crack length, either experimentally from a lightly loaded specimen with saw-cut cracks, or from theoretical compliance expressions and an effective Young's modulus that normalizes the compliance for the datum crack length. The specimen is then loaded to produce a FPZ. In this illustration of the method, it is assumed that the specimen is loaded until the FPZ is fully developed. The crack line is now sawn through to increase the datum crack length in stages, measuring the new compliance C_p at every stage, as described in section 3.2.2. If the first cutting stages do not cut into the FPZ, the compliance remains constant at its initial uncut value, C_u. On further cutting the compliance increases as the FPZ is penetrated. It is assumed that the crack faces remain straight.[1] Thus, at a distance x from the tip of the FPZ (see Figure 3.3), the COD, δ, is given by

$$\frac{x}{d_p} = \frac{\delta}{\delta_f} \tag{3.7}$$

and the fracture energy, G_{If}, is given by

$$G_{If} = \int_0^{\delta_f} \sigma \, d\delta = \frac{\delta_f}{d_p} \int_0^{d_p} \sigma \, dx \tag{3.8}$$

If the FPZ translates with no change in shape the second of Barenblatt's (1959, 1962) hypotheses is valid. This restriction, which is not mentioned by Hu and Wittmann (1991), means that strictly the method is only accurate for large specimens. The problem would not be nearly as accurate with the double-cantilever-beam specimen (see section 4.5.2). Consider the load-crack mouth opening (P-CMOD) relationship schematically illustrated in Figure 3.6, where P_u is the load without cutting into the FPZ and P_x is the load after part of the FPZ has been cut away keeping the CMOD constant.

---

[1] This assumption has been shown to be quite accurate (Foote *et al.*, 1986; Cotterell *et al.*, 1988, 1992; Cotterell and Mai, 1988a) and is discussed in section 4.5.2.

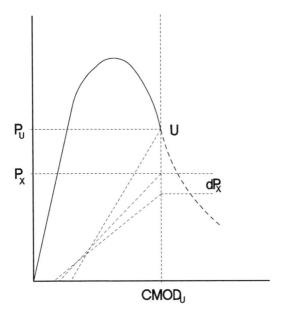

Figure 3.6 Load-CMOD during partial removal of the FPZ. (After Hu and Wittmann, 1991.)

If the residual deflection is neglected the load, P_x, after cutting into the FPZ leaving a length x intact, is given by

$$P_x = \frac{CMOD_u}{C_p} \tag{3.9}$$

The change in the load due to cutting, dP_x, depends upon the bridging stress, σ, removed. Hu and Wittmann (1991) introduce a coefficient $k(a, x)$, dependent on the length, a, of the combined true crack and FPZ and x, the remaining uncut FPZ, defined by

$$k(a, x) = \frac{\sigma(x)}{\left(\dfrac{1}{B}\dfrac{dP_x}{dx}\right)} \tag{3.10}$$

Using eqns 3.8 and 3.9, Hu and Wittmann (1991) obtained the expression

$$G_{If} = k\frac{\delta_f CMOD_u[C_p(0) - C_p(d_p)]}{Bd_p C_p(0)C_p(d_p)} \tag{3.11}$$

for the fracture energy, G_{If}, by assuming that dk/dx is small and can be neglected. Solving for k and substituting in eqn 3.10 yields the expression for the bridging stress

$$\sigma(x) = G_{If}\left(\frac{d_p}{\delta_f}\right)\frac{C_p(0)C_p(d_p)}{[C_p(0) - C_p(d_p)]}\frac{d}{dx}\left(\frac{1}{C_p}\right) \tag{3.12}$$

the tensile strength, f_t, is given by

$$f_t = G_{If} \left(\frac{d_p}{\delta_f} \right) \frac{C_p(d_p)}{C_p(0)} \frac{1}{[C_p(0) - C_p(d_p)]} \frac{dC}{da} \qquad (3.13)$$

because

$$\left[\frac{dC(a)}{da} \right]_a = - \left[\frac{dC_p(x)}{dx} \right]_0 \qquad (3.14)$$

The difficulty with eqn 3.14 is that the absolute magnitude of the bridging stresses depends upon the critical CTOD, δ_f, which is difficult to measure (Hu and Wittmann, 1992a). However, the ratio of the bridging stress to the tensile stress does not depend upon δ_f and is given by

$$\frac{\sigma}{f_t} = - \frac{d}{dx} \left(\frac{1}{C_p(x)} \right) \Big/ \frac{d}{da} \left(\frac{1}{C(a)} \right) \qquad (3.15)$$

If the tensile strength, f_t, is obtained from an independent tensile test then eqn 3.15 can be used to give the absolute bridging stresses. The closure stress in the FPZ of a WOL specimen obtained by their multi-cutting technique and eqns 3.13 and 3.15 are shown in Figure 3.7. The average values of the important parameters are: $G_{If} = 21.8$ N/m, $\delta_f = 0.02$ mm, and $f_t = 3.71$ MPa. Even though the FBZ varies from 12 to 43 mm, Figure 3.7 shows that there is a reasonable small scatter in the curve for the bridging stress. The accuracy of the method has been demonstrated by Alvaredo et al. (1989) who used this stress-displacement relationship to calculate the theoretical

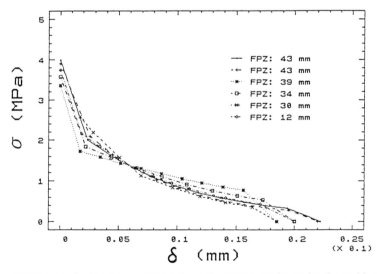

Figure 3.7 Strain-softening curves derived from six mortar specimens by the multi-cutting technique. (After Hu and Wittmann, 1992.)

load-deflection curve which was in good agreement with the experimental results.

To avoid the cumbersome procedure of multi-cutting, Hu and Mai (1992a,b) have extended the method described above so that saw cutting is not required. The method hinges on the realization that the unloading compliance, C^*, of a partially grown FPZ is equivalent to a saturated FBZ that has been partly cut through. The argument leads to the same expression as eqn 3.15. Hu and Mai (1992a) derived a function, ϕ, given by

$$\phi = \frac{C(a)}{C^*(a)} \frac{[C(a) - C^*(a)]}{dC/da} \tag{3.16}$$

where Δa is the size of the partial FPZ. Assuming that the stress-displacement relationship can be modelled by the power law

$$\frac{\sigma(x)}{f_t} = \left[1 - \frac{\delta(x)}{\delta_f}\right]^n \tag{3.17}$$

where $n > 0$, Hu and Mai (1992a) showed that the function, ϕ, can be expressed in terms of the size of the fully developed FPZ, d_p, the size of the partially developed FPZ, Δa, and the exponent, n, by

$$\phi = \frac{d_p}{(n+1)} \left[1 - \left(1 - \frac{\Delta a}{d_p}\right)^{n+1}\right] \quad \text{for } \Delta a < d_p$$

$$= \frac{d_p}{(n+1)} \quad \text{for } \Delta a > d_p \tag{3.18}$$

A plot of ϕ against Δa can be constructed using eqn 3.16, because the compliance is easily obtained from experiment. A schematic relationship of ϕ against Δa is shown in Figure 3.8. The plateau value of the curve in

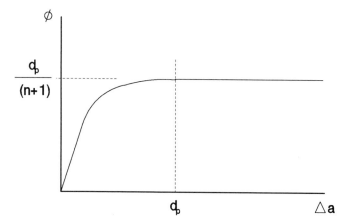

Figure 3.8 Schematic variation of ϕ with Δa.

Figure 3.8 gives the ratio $d_p/(n+1)$, and the size of the fully developed FPZ, d_p, is the crack extension necessary to reach the plateau value. Hence, the exponent n can be determined and, if f_t is determined separately, the bridging stress is known. An application of this method to a fibre cement composite is given in section 3.8.

3.3.5   Comment on the methods of determining the stress-displacement relationship

All of the methods of determining the stress-displacement relationship for the FPZ described above have their limitations and the best method is to assume a suitable form for the relationship as described in section 3.4 and then to model the load-deflection curve and find the stress-displacement parameters that give the best fit to the experimental data. This method is described in section 4.5.

3.4   Modelling the mode I strain-softening relationship for cementitious materials

Under symmetrical loading the principal stresses in the FPZ are essentially aligned to the line of symmetry. It is often useful to consider the strain as composed of two parts: an elastic strain, ϵ^{co}, derived from the uncracked material and a cracked component, ϵ^{cr}, due to the micro-cracking activity within the FPZ. It is assumed that strain-softening does not produce a strain parallel to the FPZ. In modelling the behaviour of the FPZ local cracked-strains cannot be used or localization will occur when the model is used to predict load-deflection curves for cementitious specimens. For this reason the cracked strain is usually taken as the average through the thickness of the FPZ though other non-local definitions of the cracked strain are discussed in section 4.4. Provided the width of the FPZ is constant, the stress-displacement relationship measured at the edge of the FPZ is equivalent to the stress-strain relationship.

The simplest approximation to the stress-displacement curve is the linear approximation

$$\frac{\sigma}{f_t} = 1 - \frac{\delta}{\delta_f} \tag{3.19}$$

This approximation is sufficiently accurate for many purposes, but cannot accurately predict the post-ultimate load behaviour of laboratory specimens, and a variety of more complicated expressions have been suggested.

The power law expression given by eqn 3.17, which gives zero slope at final separation or alternatively the power law

$$\frac{\sigma}{f_t} = 1 - \left(\frac{\delta}{\delta_f}\right)^k \tag{3.20}$$

with the index k in the range $0.2 < k < 0.4$, has been suggested by Reinhardt (1984) for concrete. However, a problem with the power law of eqn 3.20 is that it has a finite slope at final separation which makes its use to numerically simulate the load-deflection curve for notched concrete beams little better than the simpler linear law (Rots, 1986). Exponential relationships (Reinhardt, 1984; Gopalaratnam and Shah, 1985; Reinhardt *et al.*, 1986) are better at modelling the load-deflection curves of specimens. Since the exponential expressions are asymptotic to zero at infinity, they are either truncated or have an additional linear term to bring them to zero at a finite critical crack opening displacement. A typical expression (Reinhardt *et al.*, 1986) is

$$\frac{\sigma}{f_t} = \left[1 + \left(\frac{C_1\delta}{\delta_f}\right)\right]^3 \exp\left(-\frac{C_2\delta}{\delta_f}\right) - (1 + C_1^3)\left(\frac{\delta}{\delta_f}\right)\exp(-C_2) \qquad (3.21)$$

Ingraffea and his coworkers (Ingraffea and Gerstle, 1984; Ingraffea and Saouma, 1984; Ingraffea *et al.*, 1984; Ingraffea and Panthaki, 1985) have used a semi-reciprocal expression with a linear term to make the stress zero at a finite displacement. However, the bilinear stress-displacement relationship, shown in Figure 3.9, has the advantage of simplicity and has enough parameters to enable the load-deflection curve to be accurately predicted by numerical simulation. The bilinear curve is, in the authors' opinion, the best expression if high accuracy is required. Petersson (1985) found that the parameters that gave a good fit to the stress-displacement curve for a range of concretes were $s = 0.33$ and $v = 0.22$. Wittmann and his co-workers (Roelfstra and Wittmann, 1986; Wittmann *et al.*, 1987) found that with the parameters $s = 0.12-0.19$ and $v = 0.16-0.22$ they obtained the best fit to

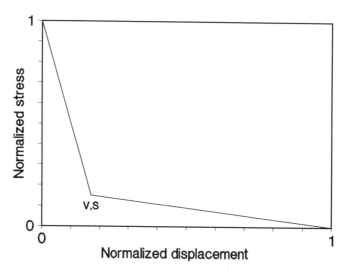

Figure 3.9 Bilinear stress-displacement relationship.

the load-deflection curves for notched concrete beams under three-point loading. The new draft CEB-FIP Model code (1990) recommends $s = 0.15$ (see section 8.1). For mortar, v is in the same range as it is for concrete, but s appears to be much smaller and in the range 0.02–0.11. With a bilinear stress-displacement curve the mode I fracture energy is given by

$$G_{If} = \tfrac{1}{2} f_t \delta_f (s + v) \qquad (3.22)$$

Liaw *et al.* (1990) have proposed a trilinear stress-displacement curve where for very small crack opening displacements the stress in the FPZ remains constant at the ultimate strength f_t. However, with regard to the inherent scatter in results obtained from fracture tests on cementitious materials this refinement, which makes the stress-displacement curve more complicated, is not justified.

Smith (1994) has suggested that the stress-displacement relationship can be approximated by two regions of constant stress (see Figure 3.10). This simple stress-displacement relationship captures the essential features of strain-softening and only the crack displacement at two points is needed to determine the stress in the FPZ. The stress-displacement of Smith (1994) suggests an even simpler relationship. It is the long tail to the stress-displacement curve that causes the large FPZ. Thus there may be situations where the high stresses that can be sustained at small CTOD are modelled by a critical stress intensity factor, K_{Ic}, at the tip of the FPZ and the long tail in the stress-displacement relationship is modelled by a constant stress region. Then in the terms of Smith's stress-displacement relationship

$$K_{Ic} = \sqrt{E f_t v} \qquad (3.23)$$

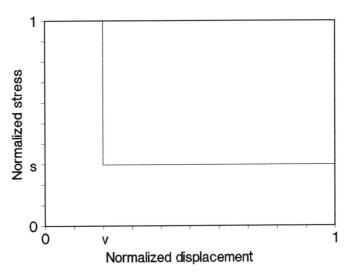

Figure 3.10 Piece-wise softening law.

A very similar technique is suggested for fibre reinforced cementitious materials in section 3.9.5 where the FPZ is modelled by a fracture toughness of the reinforced matrix and only the bridging fibre stress is modelled explicitly.

3.5 Measurement of mode I fracture energy

Although the most direct way of determining the mode I fracture energy is by means of a uniaxial tension test, the test is not easy because of stability problems. It is much easier to perform bending tests on notched specimens because these are stable in reasonably stiff testing machines. If the mode I fracture energy is a material property then it is simply given by the total work required to fracture a notch bend specimen divided by the ligament area. For these reasons a three-point notch bend test has been chosen by RILEM (1985) as a draft recommendation for measuring fracture energy.

The RILEM standard specimen is a rectangular bar notched at its centre to half the depth of the beam. The depth of the beam is at least six times the aggregate size. The beam is tested under three-point bending either under closed-loop servo control or in a stiff testing machine to ensure that the fracture is stable with the notched surface downwards. For the 100 mm deep beam, which is the smallest recommended, the required machine stiffness to ensure stability is about 10 kN/mm. To obtain the work done the load is plotted against the load-point deflection. The work done by the beam's own weight may not be negligible and the work measured from the load-deflection curve has to be corrected before the fracture energy can be calculated. In theory a correction to the work done by the applied load could be avoided if the weight of the beam is compensated by using a beam whose length is twice the span or by using weights applied to the ends of the beam. However, as Petersson (1985) has stated, there will then be a long tail to the load deflection curve and a small discrepancy in the balancing system can give rise to a significant error in the work done. Hence, a beam only slightly longer than the span is used and a correction is applied. The load-deflection curve for an uncompensated beam can be constructed from that for a compensated beam (see Figure 3.11), by shifting the zero load of the uncompensated beam to a load P_0 on the compensated beam's curve where the load P_0 gives rise to the same bending moment at the notched section as does the self-weight of the beam. Hence, if Mg is the weight of the beam between the supports then

$$P_0 = \frac{Mg}{2} \tag{3.24}$$

If Δ_0 is the deflection at fracture in the uncompensated beam then the area A_2 of Figure 3.11 is given by

$$A_2 = \frac{Mg\Delta_0}{2} \tag{3.25}$$

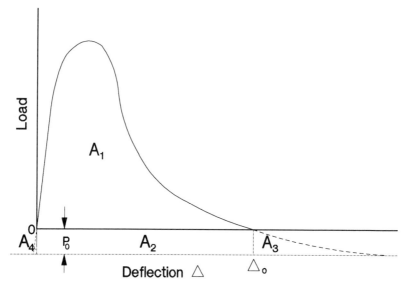

Figure 3.11 Compensated load-deflection diagram for a three-point bend test to measure the fracture energy, G_{If}.

A continuous crack will have propagated and the FPZ will have nearly reached the back surface of the beam by the time that specimen is finally broken by its own self-weight. Petersson (1985) assumed that the compression zone had degenerated almost to a point on the back surface of the specimen during the final stages of fracture, so that the halves of the beam effectively rotate about that point as rigid bodies (see Figure 3.12). During propagation the CTOD at the tip of the continuous crack is δ_{f}, and the angle of rotation of the beam, θ, is approximately δ_{f}/b, where b is the

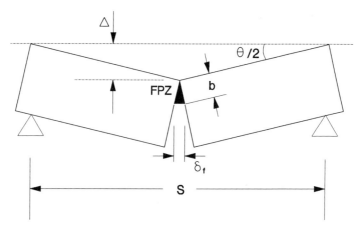

Figure 3.12 Beam during the last stages of fracture.

remaining ligament. Consequently the remaining ligament in the beam, b, is inversely proportional to the deflection, Δ, of the beam. Both the closing force in the FPZ and its moment arm about the point of rotation are proportional to the ligament length, b. Therefore, in the tail of the load-deflection curve, the load is given by

$$P = P_0 \left(\frac{\Delta_0}{\Delta} \right)^2 \tag{3.26}$$

The work done in the tail of the compensated specimen (area A_3 in Figure 3.11) is given by

$$A_3 = \int_{\Delta_0}^{\infty} P \, d\Delta \tag{3.27}$$

which on substituting from eqn 3.26 gives

$$A_3 = \frac{Mg\Delta_0}{2} \tag{3.28}$$

The small elastic work performed by the beam's self-weight, A_4, is negligible and hence the corrected expression for the mode I fracture energy is

$$G_{If} = (A_1 + Mg\Delta_0)/Bb \tag{3.29}$$

Hilsdorf and Brameshuber (1984) examined the effect of size on the fracture energy testing concrete and mortar beams 100, 400 and 800 mm deep. There was very little difference in the mean value of G_{If} between the two smaller concrete beams, but the fracture energy for the largest beam was 20% larger (see Table 3.1). There is much less difference in the fracture energy for the mortar beams and in fact the largest beam has the smallest value, but this value is doubtful because there may have been some instability in the fracture. For the 32 mm aggregate of the concrete used by Hilsdorf and Brameshuber (1987), the recommended minimum specimen depth (RILEM, 1985) is 300 mm. Apart from the obvious requirement that the specimen size shall be significantly larger than the aggregate, a more fundamental gauge of the size is given by the non-dimensional size, $\bar{W} = W/l_{ch}$. The mortar results seem to indicate that the maximum value of G_{If} is obtained for a relative size of 0.65 or less, but the fracture energy for the concrete does not appear to have reached its limiting value until $\bar{W} > 0.65$. A summary of a wide range of tests shows similar dependence on size (Hillerborg, 1985a).

Elices, Planas and Guinea have made a study of the errors involved in the RILEM fracture energy test to determine whether the size effect in the fracture energy is real. The sources of error examined were: (a) hysteresis in the testing equipment and energy dissipated in the lateral supports (Guinea et al., 1992); (b) energy dissipated in the bulk of the specimen away from the fracture plane (Planas et al., 1992); (c) underestimation of the work in the tail of the load-deflection curve. The first error (a) is very minor contributing an

Table 3.1 Size effect on fracture energy and characteristic length (data from Hilsdorf and Brameshuber, 1984)

(i) Tensile strength and Young's modulus

	f_t (MPa)	E_c (GPa)
Concrete	2.7	32.3
Mortar	3.0	25.7

(ii) Fracture energy and characteristic length

Beam depth W (mm)	G_{If} (J/m²)	$K_{If} = (G_{If}E)^{1/2}$ (N/mm$^{-3/2}$)	l_{ch} (mm)	$\bar{W} = W/l_{ch}$
(a) Concrete				
100	141	67.5	625	0.16
400	141	67.3	621	0.64
800	176	75.3	777	1.03
(b) Mortar				
100	53.8	37.2	154	0.65
400	48.4	35.2	138	2.9
800	(34.5)	(29.8)	(98)	8.61

error of less than 1% in the measurement of the fracture energy. The second error (b) is not negligible. The local compressive deformation under the centre load can absorb up to 10% of the energy and increases with size. The bulk energy absorbed away from the fracture plane is only up to 2% of the fracture energy. These errors while contributing to a size effect are far too small to account for the size effect. The energy absorbed under the centre load could be eliminated if the beam was indented by the loading head up to the maximum load expected in the fracture energy test while the beam was supported over its entire length prior to the fracture energy test. Elices *et al.* (1992) claim it is the third error (c) that is the largest error and one which, if allowances are made for it, gives a fracture energy that is independent of size.

Elices *et al.* (1992) used weight compensation in their tests rather than make a correction for the weight. For the smaller sizes they accomplished the weight compensation by testing beams that were twice as long as the span, while prestressed springs were used to take the weight of the beam for the larger specimens. They argue that it is impossible to fracture the specimen right through stably, which is Petersson's (1985) objection to this method of testing. Hence, they argue that there is a tail to the load-deflection curve that is neglected. The angle of bend, θ, is given by $4\Delta/S$, where S is the loading span. Hence during the final stages of fracture the load, P, is given by

$$P = \frac{4\xi B}{S\theta^2} = \frac{\xi BS}{4\Delta^2} \tag{3.30}$$

where ξ is the first moment of the stress-displacement curve given by

$$\xi = \int_0^{\delta_f} \sigma(\delta)\delta \,\mathrm{d}\delta \tag{3.31}$$

Elices *et al.* (1992) assume that the deflection, Δ_f, recorded as that at final fracture occurs at the same angle of beam rotation, θ_f, independent of the size. The work done, $\Delta W_{f(tail)}$, in what would be the tail of the load-deflection curve if the fracture were completely stable is therefore given by

$$\Delta W_{f(tail)} = \int_{\Delta_f}^{\infty} P \,\mathrm{d}\Delta = \frac{\xi BS}{4\Delta} = \frac{\xi B}{\theta_f} \tag{3.32}$$

This correction to the work done in fracturing the beam appears reasonable. However, Elices *et al.* (1992) also assume that, since the final fracture occurs at a small value of the load, P_f, there is an additional work term, $P_f\Delta_f$, which is equal to $\Delta W_{f(tail)}$. This additional work term is unreasonable since it would have already been included in the area under the load-deflection curve, W_f, obtained during the test. Thus the measured work of fracture is

$$W_f = G_{If}Bb - \Delta W_{f(tail)} = G_{If}B\left(b - \frac{\xi}{G_{If}\theta_f}\right) \tag{3.33}$$

in which the correction term differs from that of Elices *et al.* (1992) by a factor of two. The problem is how to estimate ξ. There are two alternative methods: ξ can be estimated from an assumed form of the stress-displacement relationship for the FPZ, or it can be obtained from the relationship given in eqn 3.31. It is not too clear how Elices *et al.* (1992) obtain ξ and seem in fact to adjust it so that they show that the true fracture energy is independent of size. The adjustment amounts to only about 10% so that is not too important, but if the correction to the work of fracture is only $\Delta W_{f(tail)}$, and not twice that value as argued by Elices *et al.* (1992), the correction cannot explain the apparent size effect in the fracture energy as measured by the RILEM method. Hence we believe that Elices *et al.* (1992) have not demonstrated that the size effect is an artifact of the test method. The size effect on the fracture energy is real. Hu and Wittmann (1992b) have given an explanation of the cause of the size effect.

The fracture energy increases with size because the width of the FPZ increases with ligament size. Since the deformation of cementitious material is relatively independent of the strain path, the specific fracture energy decreases during crack propagation in a notch bend test and also decreases with notch to width (a_0/W) ratio for the same beam size. In the RILEM (1985) method the fracture energy is an average of the specific fracture energy, g_{If}, necessary to completely fracture a unit area of the specimen at a particular position on the notched ligament. Hu and Wittmann (1992b) have used multiple specimens to obtain the distribution of specific fracture energy across a compact tension specimen and have shown for mortar that

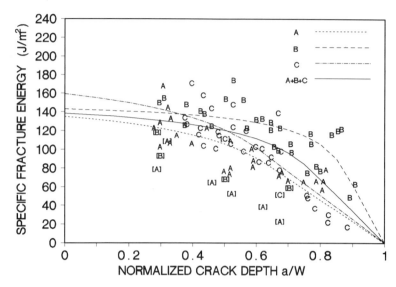

Figure 3.13 Specific fracture energy as a function of a/W (A, B and C are precracked specimens with $W = 102$, 203 and 305 mm, respectively; [A], [B] and [C] are notched specimens with same Ws. (Data from Swartz and Refai, 1987.)

g_{If} is approximately given by

$$g_{\mathrm{If}} = g_{\mathrm{Ifm}} \qquad \text{for } a_0/W < \alpha$$

$$g_{\mathrm{If}} = \frac{g_{\mathrm{Ifm}}(1 - a_0/W)}{1 - \alpha} \quad \text{for } a_0/W > \alpha \qquad (3.34)$$

where $\alpha \approx 0.7$. Swartz and Refai (1987) give the fracture energies for a large range of a_0/W ratios for three sizes of beams mainly precracked rather than notched (see Figure 3.13). The scatter in the results for the precracked specimens is perhaps considerably induced by the irregular crack front, but it appears that the specific energy is larger for the precracked specimens. The increase in fracture energy is perhaps caused by the FPZ being wider with a precrack. Curves have been fitted to the results shown in Figure 3.13, using eqs 3.34; the best values of the parameters are shown in Table 3.2.

Table 3.2 Specific fracture energy as a function of position obtained from curves of best fit, using eqns 3.34, from the data of Swartz and Refai (1987) shown in Figure 3.13

Series	W (mm)	g_{Ifm} (J/m²)	α	g_{If} ($a/W = 0$) (J/m²)	g_{If} ($a/W = 0.5$) (J/m²)
A	102	165	0.64	135	106
B	203	153	0.88	143	134
C	305	198	0.61	160	124
A + B + C	—	157	0.77	139	121

There does seem to be an increase in fracture energy with specimen size, but the curve obtained by pooling all the results is reasonable.

The standard specimen size in the RILEM (1985) draft standard for the measurement of fracture energy is 100 mm, with an increase to 200 mm if the aggregate is 16–32 mm and a further increase to 300 mm for larger aggregates. This simple rule may not be adequate to ensure that the fracture energy reaches its maximum value. Practically the effect of testing a specimen that is too small to achieve the maximum fracture energy is probably not that significant. A small specimen will give conservative predictions of the maximum sustainable loads, but the difference may not be significant. A 20% difference in the fracture energy affects the maximum load predictions by less than 7% (Hillerborg, 1985b). Hence for practical design purposes the mode I fracture energy, G_{If}, can be considered a material constant. If the fracture energy is assumed to be a constant, that presupposes that the stress-displacement relationship in the FPZ is also an autonomous material property.

3.6   Modelling the mixed mode strain-softening relationship for cementitious materials

As discussed in section 1.7.1, fractures propagate under mode I conditions unless asymmetry in the FPZ forces the fracture to propagate under mixed mode conditions. Hence, mixed mode strain-softening is not as important as mode I. The mixed mode constitutive equations can be discussed either in terms of a stress-displacement relationship at the edge of the FPZ or a stress-strain relationship within the FPZ. There is much less consensus on the appropriate constitutive equations for a mixed mode FPZ than for pure mode I. The discussion here is limited to two-dimensional problems.

3.6.1   The mixed mode stress-strain relationship

In mixed mode analysis it has been more common to represent the FPZ as a zone of finite width and to specify stress-strain constitutive equations. In the FPZ an increment in strain referred to global coordinates can be decomposed into that due to the elasticity of the uncracked material $d\epsilon^{co}$, and that due to the opening up of microcracks in the FPZ $d\epsilon^{cr}$ so that

$$d\epsilon = d\epsilon^{co} + d\epsilon^{cr} \qquad (3.35)$$

Even if the FPZ extends to maintain local symmetry at its tip, shear stress can develop behind the crack tip as the principal stresses rotate. If it is assumed that once a crack is formed it remains fixed in direction, then the matrix that transforms the local strains into global strains is fixed. In symmetrical problems there can be no rotation of the principal axes in a FPZ modelled by a single element and only slight rotation if it is modelled by a number of elements using a non-local crack strain. However, in mixed mode fracture, there can be a significant rotation of the principal axes. In this case the fixed smeared crack concept can be modified by allowing new microcracks to form according to the new principal stress directions. The decomposition of the strain into cracked and uncracked strain then has the advantage that the cracked strain can be further decomposed to give separate contributions from a number of multi-directional cracks (Bažant and Gambarova, 1983; Rots and de Borst, 1987; Rots, 1988). An alternative approach is the so-called rotating crack where the axes of material orthotropy are rotated with the principal directions (Rots and de Borst, 1987; Bažant and Lin, 1988). The rotating crack concept is related to the multi-directional concept and Rots (1988) notes that the two are the same providing that:

(i) The threshold angle for the initiation of new cracks is zero.
(ii) Previous cracks are made inactive.
(iii) The local strain-softening law of the active crack is such that the memory of the previous cracks is maintained and the overall shear modulus ensures that the principal axes of strain and stress coincide.

The crack strain increment referred to the local coordinates (n, t) aligned with the cracks only has two non-zero components, $d\epsilon_{nn}^{cr}$, $d\epsilon_{nt}^{cr}$, since it is assumed that a microcrack does not induce any strain parallel to itself. In general the constitutive relations for the FPZ are given by:

$$\left\{ \begin{array}{c} d\sigma_{nn} \\ d\sigma_{nt} \end{array} \right\} = \left[\begin{array}{cc} D_{nn} & D_{nt} \\ D_{tn} & D_{tt} \end{array} \right] \left\{ \begin{array}{c} d\epsilon_{nn}^{cr} \\ d\epsilon_{nt}^{cr} \end{array} \right\} \qquad (3.36)$$

where σ_{nn}, σ_{nt} are the normal and shear stress referred to local coordinates and D is the instantaneous moduli matrix that describes the strain-softening relationship. The instantaneous moduli must satisfy (Bažant and Gambarova, 1980):

$$\frac{\partial D_{nn}}{\partial \epsilon_{nt}^{cr}} = \frac{\partial D_{nt}}{\partial \epsilon_{nn}^{cr}}$$

$$\frac{\partial D_{tn}}{\partial \epsilon_{nt}^{cr}} = \frac{\partial D_{tt}}{\partial \epsilon_{nn}^{cr}} \qquad (3.37)$$

It is usually assumed that there is little interaction between shear and normal stress so that the off-diagonal terms in eqn 3.36 are taken as zero (Rots and de Borst, 1987; Bažant and Lin, 1988; Rots, 1988). The mode I strain-softening relationships, discussed in section 3.4, can be used for D_{nn}. If the simplest linear stress-strain relationship is used and the strain is constant over the thickness h of the FPZ, then

$$D_{nn} = -\frac{f_t^2 h}{3G_{If}} \qquad (3.38)$$

There is less agreement over the mode II modulus. Bažant and Lin (1988) have suggested that an empirical shear retention factor, β, similar to that proposed for sudden cracking by Schnobrich co-workers (Suidan and Schnobrich, 1973; Yuzugullu and Schnobrich, 1973; Hand *et al.*, 1973) could take into account the reduced shear stiffness in the FPZ by expressing the shear stress as

$$\sigma_{nt} = G\beta\epsilon_{nt}$$

or

$$D_{tt} = \frac{G\beta}{1 - \beta} \tag{3.39}$$

where G is the shear modulus. Such a formulation is probably adequate if the shear strains are moderate, but may lead to unrealistically high shear stresses and mode II fracture energies. If a constant shear retention factor is used, the fracture energy becomes infinite for a pure mode II fracture. It is probable that the mode II fracture energy can be very much larger than the mode I value. Bažant and Pfeiffer (1987), using their size effect law (see section 4.6), obtained values about 25 times that of the mode I fracture energy in tests where the fracture was close to mode II. Also the measurement of the fracture energy by Swartz *et al.* (1988) from three-point notched beam specimens, where the notches were located at different positions along the beam, indicated a large increase in the fracture energy as the fracture's mode II component was increased.

Rots and de Borst (1987) have suggested that there will be an ultimate shear stress τ_u and that for large strains there will be shear stress-softening which can be approximated by linear behaviour shown in Figure 3.14,

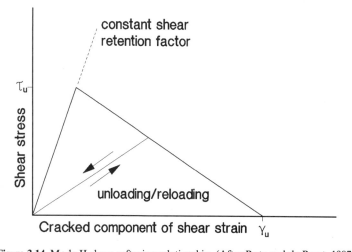

Figure 3.14 Mode II shear-softening relationship. (After Rots and de Borst, 1987.)

where the ultimate cracked shear strain γ_u is related to a mode II fracture energy G_{IIf} by

$$\gamma_u = \frac{2G_{IIf}}{h\tau_u} \tag{3.40}$$

The main objections to such a proposal are that the ultimate shear stress must surely be related to the mode I damage. Elsewhere, Rots (1988) has given an alternative expression for the instantaneous strain-softening modulus where the shear retention factor, β, depends not on the cracked shear strain, but on the cracked normal strain. The linear version of this proposal is expressed by

$$\beta = \left[1 - \frac{\epsilon_{nn}^{cr}}{\epsilon_u^{cr}}\right] \tag{3.41}$$

and D_{tt} is given by eqn 3.39. The degradation from full interlock to zero strength corresponds to a degradation of β form 1 to 0. It should be noted that since D_{tt} is infinite when ϵ_{nn}^{cr} is zero that this expression for the mode II modulus can only be used if it is assumed that the FPZ propagates to maintain local symmetry so that at the tip of the FPZ the shear stress τ_u, and hence the cracked shear strain ϵ_{nt}^{cr}, is zero. Provided the assumption of local symmetry is accepted, this proposal seems more reasonable than the other proposal of Rots and de Borst (1987), because surely when a continuous open crack is established, the shear stress in the FPZ must be zero. Continuous cracks can resist shear stress only when there is a normal compressive stress acting between the two surfaces. The mechanism of shear resistance across a continuous crack is one of interlock, which like friction, can only operate if there is a compressive force between the two surfaces. The proposal is open to the objection that in the absence of a large mode I component the shear stress may be very large, but in most situations the mode I component will effectively limit the shear stress. The proposal agrees qualitatively with the results of Swartz et al. (1988) that indicate that the mode II fracture energy is not a material constant, but increases as the mode II component increases. A more serious problem is that since the mode II instantaneous modulus depends on the mode II strain there must be a mixed mode modulus, D_{tn}, which is given by eqn 3.39

$$D_{tn} = -G\frac{\epsilon_u \epsilon_{nt}}{\epsilon_{nn}^2} \tag{3.42}$$

There is more work needed before the most suitable form of the mixed mode constitutive equations for the FPZ are established.

3.6.2 The mixed mode stress-displacement relationship

Stress can be transmitted across even a continuous crack if the stress normal to the crack is compressive. Studies of the stress-displacement relationships for precracked bodies were undertaken before the constitutive equations for a mixed mode FPZ were considered (Fenwick and Pauley, 1968; Pauley and Loeber, 1974; Fardis and Buyukzturk, 1979; Bažant and Gambarova, 1980; Bažant and Tsubaki, 1980; Divaker et al., 1987). At a fixed crack opening displacement, crack slip will cause both a shear stress and a normal stress to be developed causing a strong relationship between the crack sliding, δ_t, and the normal crack opening, δ_n. Thus

$$\sigma_{nn} = F_n(\delta_n, \delta_t)$$
$$\sigma_{tt} = F_t(\delta_n, \delta_t)$$

(3.43)

where Bažant and Gambarova (1980) have given empirical expressions for the functions on the basis of data obtained by Pauley and Loeber (1974). Although both Ingraffea and his co-workers (Ingraffea and Saouma, 1984; Ingraffea et al., 1984; Ingraffea and Panthaki, 1985) and Liaw et al. (1990) apply an expression for the shear stress obtained from similar data to the propagation of a mixed mode crack, there is no justification and the direct application of such equations to a FPZ can at best be only very approximate. Because of the frictional nature of the shear transfer between crack surfaces, a shear stress can only be developed if there is a corresponding compressive normal stress acting across the crack surfaces. It is possible that behind the FPZ a compressive normal stress could occur and shear be transferred across the continuous crack, but usually the crack faces behind the FPZ will not be compressed together and there will be no shear transfer behind the FPZ.

The stress-strain constitutive equations for the FPZ discussed in section 3.6.1 can be converted into stress-displacement relationships by multiplying by the thickness of the FPZ.

3.7   Experimental techniques for the measurement of the FPZ and FBZ in fibre reinforced cementitious materials

In fibre cements it is necessary to distinguish between the FPZ ahead of the continuous matrix crack and the FBZ behind it. Many of the above-mentioned techniques have been employed to measure the size of these two zones, for example optical and scanning electron microscopy, photography, staining and Moiré interferometry, replicas, electrical potential difference methods, acoustic emissions and compliance measurement. However, difficulties are considerable; Foote (1986) has given a review of these techniques.

The multi-cutting technique is recognized as a more direct method of determining the size of the FPZ in both unreinforced cementitious materials and fibre cements (Mindess, 1991a). It is a variant of the compliance method and it makes use of the compliance difference of an unbridged and a bridged crack of the same crack length (Mai and Hakeem, 1984). The multiple cutting technique described for the unreinforced cement matrices in section 3.2.2 cannot be readily applied to fibre cements to separate and measure the FPZ and the FBZ. An estimate of the size of the FBZ is the more important for the purpose of modelling as in many theoretical analyses the FPZ can be replaced by a critical matrix fracture toughness.

Foote *et al.* (1987) developed a computer-aided method of crack length measurement using a conductive grid whereby cracking can be sensed by the breaking of the lines of the grid. In this method a grid pattern of conductive ink, consisting of fine carbon particles dispersed in a vinyl resin binder and a butyl cellosolve acetate solvent, is screen printed onto the specimen. The grid pattern, used for a compact tension (CT) specimen (see Figure 3.15), has 64 bars in eight blocks of eight allowing the crack to be measured over a distance of about 140 mm. The bars were nominally 1 mm in width and 2.14 mm apart. A schematic diagram of the computerized method is shown in Figure 3.16. The computer scans each bar on the grid serially and tests for continuity. When a bar is broken, indicating cracking at that location, a corresponding voltage is sent to a plotter, and a graphic display of the grid on a monitor shows that the bar is broken. With each scan the latest broken bar detected is plotted and displayed. This technique has made visible the whole crack growth process,

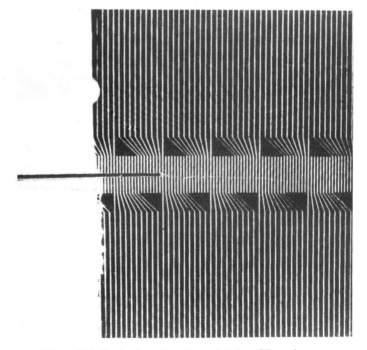

Figure 3.15 Conductive grid pattern printed on CT specimen.

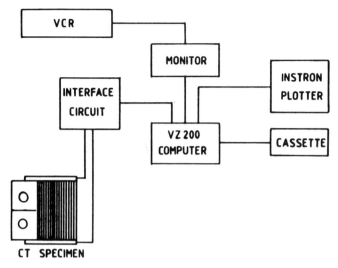

Figure 3.16 Computer-aided crack growth monitoring system.

and both crack extension-time and load-time records can be simultaneously and continuously obtained until final failure. The experimental results for a CT wood fibre cement composite are shown in Figure 3.17. They reveal a complex picture of crack growth in which the bars record breaks and closures followed by second breaks. The region of bars breaking, or the activity zone, corresponds closely with the FPZ and was approximately 20 mm throughout the crack growth. Table 3.3 compares the continuous matrix crack length obtained by optical microscopy and that determined with the present computer-aided method. The leading edge of the activity zone is a good indication of the front of the FPZ and the trailing edge represents the tip of the continuous matrix crack and the leading edge of the FBZ.

An alternative method of locating the extent of the FPZ and the FBZ is to measure the bending stiffness of narrow strips cut from the specimen perpendicular to the crack (Foote *et al.*, 1987). This technique was applied to the CT specimen whose cracking, monitored using the computerized system, is shown in Figure 3.18. The bending stiffness of the strips was measured in pure bending and the location of failure noted. Strips were also cut at the back of the specimen in the relatively unstressed region to represent the undamaged material so that the bending stiffnesses could be normalized by that of the undamaged material. For strips cut within the FBZ the failure sites were the prolongation of the machined notch, but the failure sites for strips cut from the FPZ were scattered randomly about the prolongation of the machined notch. In the FBZ the fracture of the strips takes place close to the prolongation of the machined notch. The bending stiffness in the FBZ is not zero though the matrix is completely cracked because the strips can support a bending moment since their rotation about

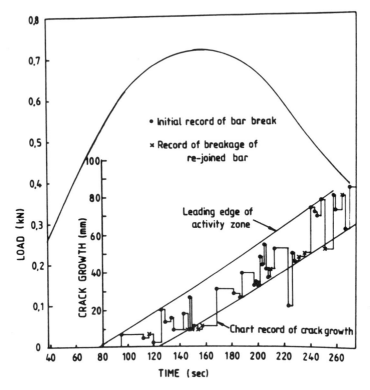

Figure 3.17 Crack growth and load-time traces recorded by the computer-aided system. The leading edge of the activity zone gives a measure of the continuous matrix crack length.

one surface can be resisted by the bridging fibres. Within the FBZ the bending stiffness increases in an orderly fashion from the trailing edge but in the FPZ, though there is an increase in stiffness, there is considerable scatter in the results. Thus from Figure 3.18 the leading edge of the FPZ is at about $a = 80$ mm. Figure 3.18 is poor for evaluating the size of the FPZ because the crack has extended too close to the back face of the CT specimen. In another series of experiments (see Figure 3.19), free of boundary effects, the size of the FPZ can be bounded between 30 and 40 mm.

Table 3.3 Crack growth measurement using the computer aided method, optical microscope and the section and bending stiffness test

Specimen No.	Crack length (mm)		
	Computer-aided	Optical	Bending stiffness
1	62–86	78	77
2	56–88	83	83
3	70–105	99	112

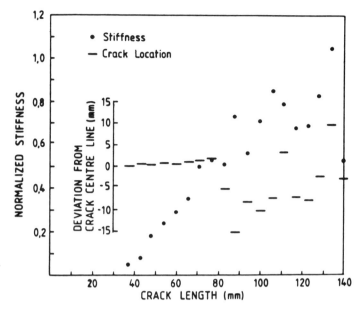

Figure 3.18 A plot of normalized stiffness *versus* crack length. Failure sites of sectioned strips are indicated by horizontal bars.

The estimates of the tip of the continuous crack obtained from optical, computerized grid and stiffness methods are compared in Table 3.3.

3.8 Measurement of the mode I strain-softening relationship for fibre reinforced cementitious materials

Because fibres greatly increase the toughness and crack growth resistance of cementitious materials, fracture is more stable. Thus a direct tension test to determine the stress-displacement relationship is more practical for composites than unreinforced cementitious materials. The other methods of measuring the stress-displacement relationship for unreinforced cementitious materials can be applied to composites, but there are problems with the very large size of the FBZ.

The compliance method of Hu and Mai (1992a) that uses the compliance of a partially developed FPZ or FBZ, described in section 3.3.4, has been applied to wet and dry cellulose cement composites using DCB specimens. The plot of the function, ϕ, against crack extension is shown in Figure 3.20. The size of the FBZ obtained from the crack extension to reach the plateau value of ϕ is 50 mm and 57 mm for the wet and dry composites, respectively. Using the plateau values of the curves in Figure 3.20 and eqn 3.18, the exponent for the stress-displacement relationships, given by eqn 3.17, are

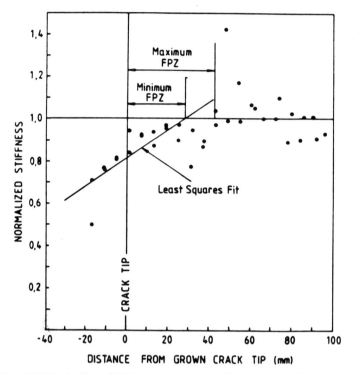

Figure 3.19 Evaluation of FPZ using normalized stiffness-crack tip distance plot.

1.4 and 3.8, respectively. The normalized stress-displacement curves are shown in Figure 3.21.

3.9 The stress-strain relationship for fibre reinforced cementitious materials

3.9.1 Uncracked composites

Prior to matrix cracking a fibre reinforced cementitious material is elastic. For aligned continuous fibres the Young's modulus of the composite, E_c, in the direction of the fibres can be found from the condition of equality of strain, assuming good bonding, and is given by the rule of mixtures

$$E_c = vE_f + (1 - v)E_m \qquad (3.44)$$

where v is the volume fraction of the fibres, and E_f, E_m are the Young's modulus of the fibres and the matrix, respectively.

In discontinuous fibre reinforced composites, the stress in the matrix has to be transferred to the fibre. At low stress levels, this transfer will take place elastically. The stress transfer can be modelled using shear lag theory which was first applied to fibre reinforced composites by Cox (1952). If the

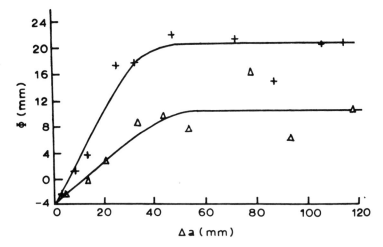

Figure 3.20 $\phi - \Delta a$ curves for wet (+) and dry (Δ) cellulose-fibre reinforced mortar.

fibre is relatively long, the interfacial shear stress, τ, decays exponentially as the stress in the fibre, σ_f, builds up to a plateau value equal to that carried by continuous fibres which is $\sigma_c(E_f/E_c)$, where σ_c is the stress applied to the composite and the stresses[2] are (see Figure 3.22a)

$$\left.\begin{aligned} \tau(x) &= \sigma_c \frac{E_f}{E_c} \frac{\beta d_f}{4} \exp(-\beta x) \\[2mm] \sigma_f(x) &= \sigma_c \frac{E_f}{E_c} [1 - \exp(-\beta x)] \end{aligned}\right\} \tag{3.45}$$

where

$$\beta = \left[\frac{16 G_m}{E_f d_f^2 \ln(2\pi/3v)}\right]^{1/2}$$

for hexagonal packing (Piggott, 1980), where G_m is the shear modulus of the matrix and d_f the fibre diameter. Often fibres in cementitious composites are poorly bonded and debond at low stress levels. Under these circumstances it is usually assumed that the frictional interfacial shear stress, τ_f, is constant and then for long fibres the stresses (see Figure 3.22b) are given by

$$\left.\begin{aligned} \tau &= \tau_f \\[2mm] \sigma_f &= \tau_f \frac{4x}{d_f} \end{aligned}\right\} \tag{3.46a}$$

for $x < l^*/2$, and

---

[2] It is usually assumed that the ends of the fibre are stress free, because either they are poorly bonded or, if the modulus of the fibre is much larger than that of the matrix, the stress in the matrix is small compared with the stress in the fibre.

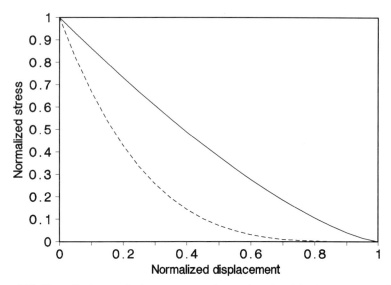

Figure 3.21 Normalized stress-displacement curves for wet (———) and dry (– – –) cellulose-fibre reinforced mortar.

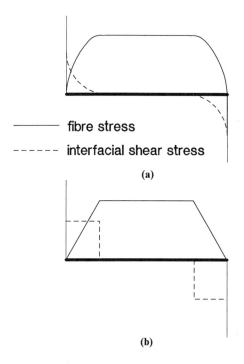

Figure 3.22 Stress transfer to a fibre (a) elastically, (b) constant interfacial shear stress.

$$\left.\begin{array}{c} \tau = 0 \\[2mm] \sigma_f = \sigma_c \dfrac{E_f}{E_c} \end{array}\right\} \tag{3.46b}$$

for $x > l^*/2$, where

$$l^* = \frac{d}{2} \frac{\sigma_c}{\tau_f} \frac{E_f}{E_c}$$

If the fibres are shorter than a critical length, l_c, defined by

$$l_c = \frac{\sigma_{fc}}{\tau_f} \frac{d}{2} \tag{3.47}$$

where σ_{fc} is the fibre fracture stress, then the fibres can never break, but must pull out during fracture.

The Young's modulus of composites reinforced with aligned discontinuous fibres is given by

$$E_c = \eta_1 v E_f + (1 - v) E_m \tag{3.48}$$

where η_1 is an efficiency factor defined by (for poorly bonded fibres)

$$\begin{aligned} \eta_l &= \frac{l}{2l_c} & l < l_c \\[3mm] &= 1 - \frac{l_c}{2l} & l > l_c \end{aligned} \tag{3.49}$$

If the fibres are not aligned, then the contribution of the fibres to the Young's modulus must be multiplied by a further orientation efficiency factor η_θ, which depends slightly on whether deformation perpendicular to the stress is constrained or not (Krenchel, 1964), and are given in Table 3.4.

3.9.2 Matrix cracking stress and the critical volume fraction

The matrix of cementitious composites usually cracks before the fibres break and the stress in the composite at first matrix cracking, σ_{cmc}, is given by

$$\sigma_{cmc} = E_c \epsilon_{mc} \tag{3.50}$$

Table 3.4 Orientation efficiency factors for composites; μ is the coefficient of friction (from Cox (1952) and Krenchel (1964))

Fibre orientation factor η_θ	Random 2-D	Random 3-D
Uncracked:		
unconstrained	0.333	0.167
constrained	0.375	0.20
Cracked matrix:		
without snubbing	$2/\pi$	0.50
with snubbing	$2[1 + \mu\exp(\mu\pi/2)]/\pi[1 + \mu^2]$	$[1 + \exp(\mu\pi/2)]/[4 + \mu^2]$

where ϵ_{mc} is the matrix cracking strain. If the volume fraction of the fibres is greater than a critical value, v_c, given by

$$v_c = \frac{E_c \epsilon_{mc}}{\sigma_{fc}} \tag{3.51}$$

where σ_{fc} is the smaller of the fibre strength or pull-out stress, σ_{fp}, then the fibres alone can withstand the stress at first matrix cracking and the composite is Type I. It should be noted that for randomly orientated fibres, the efficiency factor after matrix cracking is not the same as in the uncracked composite. After the matrix cracks the orientation efficiency factor depends upon the number of fibres per unit area that cross the matrix fracture and there can be an increase in the factor due to snubbing. If the fibres are flexible, the snubbing effect is similar to pulling a rope over a corner. For steel wires of relatively large diameter, there is an additional plastic bending and unbending term. Snubbing increases the pull-out stress for a fibre by a factor $\exp(\mu\theta)$ where θ is the orientation angle of the fibre and μ is the coefficient of friction. For polypropylene and nylon μ is approximately 0.7 and 1.0, respectively (Li *et al.*, 1990). The orientation efficiency factors for randomly orientated fibre reinforced composites are given in Table 3.4.

3.9.3   Fibre pull-out

The mechanics of fibre debonding and pull-out in a composite is complex and most studies have focused on a single fibre. There have been two different criteria of debonding: a maximum shear bond strength (Takaku and Arridge, 1973; Lawrence, 1980) or a critical specific work of debonding (Gurney and Hunt, 1967; Atkinson *et al.*, 1972; Bowling and Groves, 1979; Stang and Shah, 1986; Gao *et al.*, 1988). The simplest fracture mechanics approach is that of Gurney and Hunt (1967). If the fibre volume fraction is small, the change in matrix stress during fibre debonding is small and hence the rate increase in strain energy stored during debonding, which is numerically equal to the decrease in potential energy of the system, is given by

$$\frac{d\Lambda}{dl} = -\frac{d\Pi}{dl} = \frac{1}{2}\frac{\sigma_f^2}{E}\frac{\pi d_f^2}{4} \tag{3.52}$$

Hence if G_{IIb} is the interfacial debond energy, the debond stress, σ_{fbo}, is given by

$$\sigma_{fbo} = \left[\frac{8E_f G_{IIb}}{d_f}\right]^{1/2} \tag{3.53}$$

When a fibre is partially debonded, compressive stresses due to shrinkage of the matrix act on the fibre causing friction between the fibre and the matrix in the debonded zone. Because of Poisson's effect, the pressure between the fibre and the matrix in the debonded zone is reduced and the frictional force is not constant.[3] The Gao–Mai–Cotterell (1988) model assumes a Coulomb friction and takes account of the Poisson effect. If the embedded length of the fibre is long then the initial debond stress is independent of the fibre length and the initial fibre debond stress, σ_{fbi}, is given by

$$\sigma_{fbi} = \sigma_{fbo} \left[\frac{(1+\beta)}{(1-2kv)} \right]^{1/2} \tag{3.54a}$$

$$\text{where } k = \frac{\nu_f \dfrac{E_m}{E_f} + \nu_m \dfrac{v}{1-v}}{(1+\nu_m) + (1-\nu_f)\dfrac{E_m}{E_f} + \dfrac{2v}{1-v}} \tag{3.54b}$$

$$\beta = \frac{(1-2k\nu_m)}{(1-2k\nu_f)} \left(\frac{v}{1-v} \right) \left(\frac{E_f}{E_m} \right) \tag{3.54c}$$

where ν_f and ν_m are the Poisson's ratio of the fibre and matrix, respectively. This model gives a good prediction of the debond stress for long embedded lengths, but overestimates σ_{fbi} for short lengths; Zhou et al. (1992) give the corresponding theory for finite embedded lengths. For fibres with higher moduli than the cementitious matrix, such as steel wires,

$$k \ll 1$$

$$\beta \approx \frac{v}{1-v} \frac{E_f}{E_m} \tag{3.55}$$

$$\sigma_{fbi} \approx \sigma_{fbo} \left[1 + \frac{v}{1-v} \frac{E_f}{E_m} \right]^{1/2}$$

and since the maximum practical fibre volume fraction is of the order of 10%, the initial fibre debond stress is less than 5% greater than σ_{fbo}. For low modulus fibres like polypropylene, $\beta \ll 1$, and the initial fibre debond stress is less than 6% smaller than σ_{fbo}. Hence, the initial fibre debond stress for cementitious composites is reasonably well given by eqn 3.53.

If under load the interfacial clamping pressure is reduced to zero by contraction of the fibres before the initiation of debonding, then the debonding is unstable and complete debonding takes place at σ_{fbi}. The critical interfacial threshold clamping pressure, q_{th}, at which debonding takes place unstably is given by

$$q_{th} = \frac{k\sigma_{fbi}}{1 + \dfrac{E_f \nu_m}{E_m \nu_f} \dfrac{v}{1-v}} \tag{3.56}$$

---

[3] The interfacial contact pressure decreases if there is significant slip due to compaction of the cement near the wire surface (Pinchin and Tabor, 1978).

and if the initial clamping pressure, q_0, is greater than q_{th}, then the critical pull-out stress for long fibres is $(q_0/q_{th})\sigma_{fbi}$. For a steel wire ($d_f = 0.5\,mm$; $v \approx 10\%$) reinforced mortar the approximate threshold clamping pressure $q_{th} = 10\,MPa$. The shrinkage of mortar is strongly dependent on the curing details and also on the volume fraction of the steel wires (Malmberg and Skarendahl, 1978) and is of the order of 0.1% which, assuming $E_m = 25\,GPa$ and $\nu_m = 0.2$, implies an interfacial pressure of some $30\,MPa$. Thus in theory such steel wires should debond stably. However, in practice the debond strength is not so simple. Pinchin and Tabor (1978) found that the debonding load for steel wires embedded in water-cured specimens was two to four times that for specimens sealed during curing, despite the fact that water-cured mortar expands by about 40 microstrain, whereas sealed mortar shrinks by 400 microstrain.

Once debonded the fibres pull out against friction and for a single fibre the pull-out stress, σ, for a fibre embedded over a length x is given by

$$\sigma = \sigma_{fbi} \frac{q_0}{q_{th}} [1 - \exp -\lambda x] \qquad (3.57)$$

where

$$\lambda = \frac{4\mu}{k d_f}$$

Kim et al. (1993) have analysed the pull-out tests of Li et al. (1991) on glass fibres embedded in cement paste using both a normal 3 day cure and an accelerated cure of 1 day at 50°C in lime water using the theory for fibres embedded by a finite length (Zhou et al., 1992). The maximum debond stress and the initial frictional pull-out stress immediately after debonding are compared in Figure 3.23 with the theoretical predictions using the parameters in Table 3.5 that gave the best fit. The theoretical predictions are reasonably convincing. Note that the accelerated cure produces a higher clamping stress, q_0, confirming the comments made in section 2.4.3. Kim et al. (1993) also analysed the results from a wide range of steel–fibre–mortar composites. However, with steel fibres a good fit for both the debond and the frictional pull-out stress could not be obtained using the same clamping stress, q_0. For the debond stress, the value of the clamping stress that gave the best fit was $50\,MPa$, but this had to be reduced to $24\,MPa$ to obtain a good fit to the frictional pull-out stress. The reduction in the clamping stress can be due to the compaction of the mortar (Pinchin and Tabor, 1978) or by the densification of the porous CSH transition zone between the fibre and the bulk mortar (Bentur et al., 1985).

In practice the friction between a debonded fibre and the matrix is not necessarily controlled by Coulomb friction. If the fibres are not perfectly

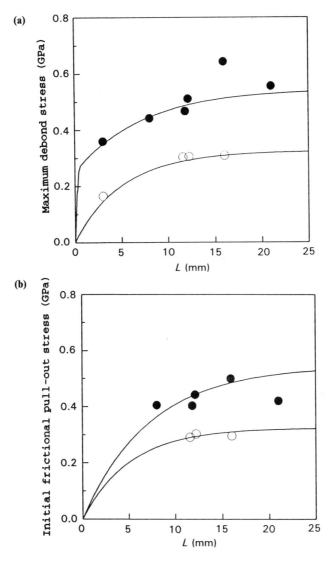

Figure 3.23 Glass-fibre cement paste pull-out tests, comparison of experiment with theory: (a) maximum pull-out stress; (b) initial frictional pull-out stress: O, normal cure, ●, accelerated cure. (After Kim *et al.*, 1993.)

straight and smooth the effects of fibre curvature and roughness dominate and the simpler assumption of a constant frictional shear stress can be more appropriate. The interfacial frictional stress can fall during pull-out not because of Poisson's contraction, but because of compaction of the less dense interphase layer between the fibre and bulk matrix. With the assumption of a constant frictional interfacial shear stress, the pull-out

Table 3.5 Fibre pull-out properties for glass-fibre–cement-paste

	Normal cure	Accelerated cure
Initial debond stress σ_{fbi} (MPa)	10	274
Frictional decay factor λ (mm^{-1})	0.193	0.138
Critical debond stress for very long fibres		
$(q_0/q_{th})\,\sigma_{fbi}$ (MPa)	325	545
Interfacial energy G_{IIb} (J/m^2)	0.03	22.8
Coefficient of friction μ	0.14	0.1
Initial clamping pressure q_0 (MPa)	20.1	33.8

stress, σ, on a fibre embedded to a depth x is given by

$$\sigma = \frac{4\tau_f}{d_f}x \tag{3.58}$$

3.9.4   Stress-strain curve for Type I composites

Multiple cracking Type I composites have a fibre volume fraction greater than the critical value given by eqn 3.51. The matrix reaches its ultimate strength, σ_{mc}, at a strain, ϵ_{mc}, which can be greater than the fracture strain in the unreinforced matrix. Using energy arguments (the ACK model), Aveston et al. (1971) have estimated the fracture strain for a reinforced matrix to be

$$\epsilon_{mc} = \left[\frac{24\tau_b G_{Im} E_f v^2}{E_c E_m^2 d_f (1 - v)} \right]^{1/3} \tag{3.59}$$

where τ_b is the shear bond strength and G_{Im} is the specific work of fracture of the matrix. This prediction of the fracture strain of the reinforced matrix has been refined by considering the spacing of the fibres (Hannant et al., 1983). In this refinement, which is not expressible analytically, it is assumed that the matrix fracture strain is only enhanced if the fibre spacing is less than the size of the inherent flaw. Thus if the fibre spacing is large, as in the case of steel fibre reinforced cementitious materials, there is no enhancement of the fracture strain. However, both the ACK model and its refinement assume that the specific fracture work is a material constant, whereas there will undoubtedly be an R-curve effect so that the inherent flaw size will not directly control the fracture strain of the reinforced matrix. Aveston et al. (1971) assume that multiple cracks form at an essentially constant stress, $E_c \epsilon_{mc}$, with a spacing of between x and $2x$ where x, the distance over which the matrix strain builds up to its critical value ϵ_{mc}, is given by

$$x = \left(\frac{1 - v}{v} \right) \frac{\sigma_{mc} d_f}{4\tau_f} \tag{3.60}$$

The matrix breaks down into blocks of length between x and $2x$. When this process is complete, the strain in the composite, ϵ_c, is between the limits

(Aveston *et al.*, 1971)

$$\left[1 + \frac{E_m}{2E_f}\left(\frac{1-v}{v}\right)\right] < \frac{\epsilon_c}{\epsilon_{mc}} < \left[1 + \frac{3E_m}{4E_f}\left(\frac{1-v}{v}\right)\right] \quad (3.61)$$

On further straining the fibres stretch until they break or slip through the matrix blocks. In the latter case the modulus of the composite becomes $E_f v$.

The theory of multiple cracking can be extended to cover short fibres (Aveston *et al.*, 1974). Most short fibres pull out, except weak fibres such as aged glass fibres (Hannant *et al.*, 1983) or bleached cellulose fibres (Mai *et al.*, 1983), rather than fracture. If the average stress sustainable on first matrix cracking is greater than $E_c \epsilon_{mc}$ then multiple cracking will occur. If the fibres are well bonded, the stress sustainable by the fibres alone once the matrix cracks can drop suddenly as some of the fibres debond, so that there is only frictional shear between the fibre and the matrix. On further straining the fibres stretch and, provided sufficient fibres remain well bonded, the stress can again rise to the first cracking stress causing multiple cracking.

Consider the crack spacing for aligned short fibres. Let x_d be the distance from the crack face that the strain in the matrix can build up to the matrix cracking strain, ϵ_{mc}, then $N(1 - 2x_d/l)$ fibres per unit area have both ends at a greater distance from the crack plane than x_d and therefore fully transfer their portion of the load carried by the matrix prior to failure. The remaining $2Nx_d/l$ fibres only transfer half of the load. Therefore, the total load per unit area, P, transferred is (Aveston *et al.*, 1974)

$$P = \pi d_f \tau_f x_d N \left[1 - \frac{x_d}{l}\right] = \sigma_{mc}(1 - v) \quad (3.62)$$

and substituting from eqn 3.60, x_d is given by the smaller root of

$$\frac{x_d}{l} = \frac{1 - [1 - 4(x/l)^2]^{1/2}}{2} \quad (3.63)$$

Multiple cracks form with a spacing of between x_d and $2x_d$ at an essentially constant stress. After multiple cracking is complete, the stress will increase until it reaches the maximum pull-out stress, σ_{cp}. The deformation will then localize on a single matrix crack and the stress will decrease as the fibres pull out. This phase in the stress-strain behaviour will be identical to the pull-out behaviour of Type II composites.

3.9.5 Stress-strain curve for Type II composites

With Type II composites the first cracking stress represents the maximum stress sustainable. For Type IIA composites with long fibres it is sufficient to assume that composite is elastic up to the first matrix cracking strain at which the stress drops to a constant pull-out stress, σ_{tu}, which for straight fibres is given by eqn 3.58 (Lim *et al.*, 1987). The stress-displacement curve for Type IIB composites is similar to that for unreinforced cementitious materials. The COD at which a continuous matrix crack occurs will be larger than the value for an unreinforced material, and the COD at which the last fibre pulls out is half the fibre length.

The average embedded length is $l/4$ of the fibres, hence the maximum fibre pull-out stress is obtained by $x = l/4$ in eqns 3.57 and 3.58. After the matrix crack has opened by δ, a fraction $2\delta/l$ will have pulled out and the average embedded length, of the fibres that remain embedded, is $(l/2 - \delta)/2$. The number of fibres bridging the crack when the COD is δ is therefore $(4\eta_\theta v/\pi d_f^2)(1 - 2\delta/l)$. Thus, under the assumptions of Coulomb friction the pull-out stress, σ_{cp}, based on the area of the composite is given by

$$\sigma_{cp} = \eta_\theta v \sigma_{fbi} \frac{q_0}{q_{th}} \left[1 - \frac{2\delta}{l} \right] \left[1 - \exp - \frac{\lambda l}{4} \left(1 - \frac{2\delta}{l} \right) \right] \qquad (3.64)$$

and under the assumption of a constant interfacial friction the pull-out stress is given by

$$\sigma_{cp} = \eta_\theta v \tau_f \left(\frac{l}{d_f} \right) \left[1 - \frac{2\delta}{l} \right]^2 \qquad (3.65)$$

The limits to the stress-displacement relationship obtained if Coulomb friction is assumed are linear if λ is very large (i.e. the pull-out stress on each fibre remains constant); parabolic if λ is very small (i.e. a constant interfacial friction stress). In practice the stress-displacement curve for fibre reinforced composites can be parabolic, such as the results obtained by Wecharatana and Shah (1983) for smooth steel wires; can agree with eqn 3.64 as is the case for wet cellulose fibres; or to have an exponent to the power law given in eqn 3.17 greater than 2 which does not conform to either the model using Coulomb friction or a constant interfacial frictional stress, such as dry cellulose fibres (Hu and Mai, 1992).

There is not much loss in accuracy of load-deflection predictions if the stress-displacement curve is assumed to be linear. As with unreinforced cementitious materials, the two most important fracture parameters are the fracture energy and the fracture strength, the actual form of the curve being comparatively unimportant. The strain-softening of the matrix before it cracks completely can also be assumed to be linear with little loss of accuracy provided the fracture work is the same. Hence, the bilinear curve used for unreinforced cementitious materials (see Figure 3.9) is also appropriate for composites, but now the break points are quite different. If the fibres are well bonded the stress at the formation of a continuous matrix crack can be greater than the stress at the initiation of a FPZ. An even simpler strain-softening relationship can be obtained if the FPZ is modelled by the fracture toughness of the reinforced matrix, K_{Ic}, and the fibre pull-out by a linear relationship. Although K_{Ic} is not exactly a material constant, because Barenblatt's hypotheses are not satisfied (see section 1.5), it can in practice be considered constant.

3.10 The toughness of fibre reinforced composites

The concept of fracture energy based upon an area of fracture surface is not appropriate for Type I composites that do not fail on a single fracture plane. However, with Type II composites, apart from minor energies associated with dispersed microcracking activity before the development of a FPZ, the fracture work is concentrated in a thin layer on either side of the single fracture. The major contribution to the total fracture energy comes from the work of fibre pull-out. The fracture of the matrix obviously contributes to the fracture energy, but the work necessary to fracture any fibres[4] and the work of debonding are usually negligible. The fracture energy of the reinforced matrix, G_{Im}, which is approximately given by K_{Ic}^2/E^*, can be significantly larger than the fracture energy of the unreinforced matrix. The specific fracture work of pull-out, w_p, can be obtained from the expression for the stress–displacement relationship given in eqn 3.65 and is

$$w_p = \int_0^{1/2} \sigma_{cp} \, d\delta = \frac{\eta_\theta v}{6} \frac{\tau_f l^2}{d_f} \tag{3.66}$$

This equation, derived by another method, is given by Kelly and Macmillan (1986).

Because of the well-developed crack growth resistance in fibre reinforced cementitious materials fracture in tension is much more stable than in unreinforced materials. Hence the direct tension method can be used to measure the fracture energy as well as the fracture strength. It is difficult to use the RILEM (1985) method for cementitious composites, because the fibres in a bend specimen cannot be easily pulled out completely. Because of the difficulties in measuring a fundamental toughness for Type I composites, a variety of practical toughness indices have been proposed. All these indices are obtained by taking the ratio of the work of deformation in a beam test up to some specified deflection greater than that necessary to cause first cracking. Barr and Hasso (1985) have reviewed the various toughness indices that have been proposed. The ACI Committee 544 method relies on a standard size (100 × 100 × 300 mm) bend test and defines the toughness index as the ratio of the work done up to a deflection of 1.9 mm to the work done up to first cracking. The toughness index is dependent on the size and geometry of the specimen. The ASTM Standard specifically warns that the toughness index can be size dependent (Rokugo et al., 1989). The ACI method with its arbitrary deflection is one of the least attractive methods. The ASTM method (Rokugo

---

[4] The fracture of some more ductile fibres such as Kevlar and polypropylene can contribute significantly to the fracture energy.

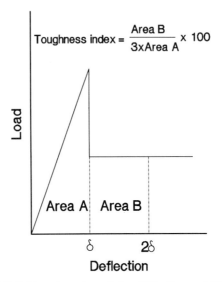

Figure 3.24 Definition of toughness index. (After Barr and Hasso, 1985.)

et al., 1989) and the proposals of Barr and Hasso (1985) all use multiples of the deflection to cause first cracking. Barr and Hasso (1985) show that the same toughness index can be obtained from notched beams of the same size but different notch depths. This result is explained by the fact that K_R curves are not very dependent of the notch depth in beams (see section 5.4.2). The toughness index proposed by Barr and Hasso (1985) seems the best. In their definition (see Figure 3.24) the toughness index, I, is defined as

$$I = \frac{\text{Area } B}{3 \times \text{Area } A} \times 100 \qquad (3.67)$$

where Area A is the area under the load-deflection curve up to first matrix cracking and Area B is the area from first matrix cracking to a deflection equal to twice the first matrix cracking deflection. Thus, if the matrix cracking had no effect, the toughness index would be 100% and if after the matrix cracked the load remained constant, giving a pseudo elastic-plastic behaviour, the toughness index would be 67%.

The toughness index can provide a means of judging the effectiveness of a fibre reinforcement, providing specimens of the same size and geometry are used, but it is of little use in predicting the behaviour of fibre reinforced structures.

3.11 Summary

The most important feature of cementitious materials is their large FPZ and FBZ. Consequently, many methods have been devised to measure the sizes of these zones and their properties. The most basic property is the stress-strain or the stress-displacement relationship. An inherent characteristic of materials that strain-soften is the formation of a single fracture. Strain-softening leads to localization of the deformation which makes it difficult to determine the stress-strain relationship. It is easier to determine the displacement across the FPZ than the strain within it. The analysis of Type I composites that do not strain-soften is analogous to the ductile deformation of metals and it is plastic collapse or large deformations that are the limits rather than fracture. Consequently, Type I composites are outside the scope of this book.

The two most important parameters in the strain-displacement relationship either for the FPZ or the FBZ are the fracture strength, f_t, and the fracture energy, G_{If}. The particular form of the model used to describe the stress-displacement relationship is relatively unimportant provided these two parameters are correct. Consequently, complicated stress-displacement relationships are not necessary and simple linear or bilinear curves are sufficient. The mode I properties are far more important than mixed mode because only in a few cases does the FPZ cause the fracture to propagate as a mixed mode fracture.

The fracture energy, G_{If}, is easier to measure than the fracture strength, f_t. The RILEM (1985) standard method is suitable for measurement of the fracture energy; there is some size effect but for practical purposes the fracture energy can be considered a constant. The fracture strength cannot be measured directly in a bend test and is difficult to measure in a direct tension test. Fibre reinforced composites are more easily tested in tension because of their large crack growth resistance.

4 Theoretical models for fracture in cementitious materials

4.1 Introduction

Cementitious materials are only quasi-brittle. A load-deflection curve obtained from a notch bend test on a small cementitious beam looks very similar to that of a ductile metal. This possibility of ductile behaviour in an apparently brittle material is paradoxical. Not only are small beams ductile but they also have a larger modulus of rupture. Some of the apparent increase in strength can be explained by statistics (see Chapter 6), but the difference is too great for this explanation to be the complete answer. To understand these paradoxes we must model the fracture process.

The flexural behaviour of beams can be modelled approximately using simple beam theory and assuming that plane sections remain plane, even if the beam is notched, and just satisfying global equilibrium (Chuang and Mai, 1989). However, fracture mechanics is needed for accurate modelling. Classic Griffith fracture mechanics cannot generally be used to model fracture in cementitious materials because the FPZs are too large. Even in hardened cement paste where the FPZ is relatively small (of the order 1–4 mm) notch bend specimens need to be deeper than 100 mm before Griffith theory can be used (Cotterell and Mai, 1987). Equivalent crack concepts have been applied to the fracture of cementitious materials where the real crack is replaced by a larger stress free crack (Jenq and Shah, 1985; Nallathambi and Karihaloo, 1986; Shah, 1988; Karihaloo and Nallathambi, 1988, 1989a,b; Alvaredo *et al.*, 1989; RILEM, 1990), but fracture does not occur at the same critical fracture toughness independent of geometry and size as is assumed in these concepts. The two physically sound approaches to modelling the FPZ are the fictitious crack model (Hillerborg *et al.*, 1976; Petersson, 1985) and the crack band model (Bažant and Cedolin, 1979; Bažant and Oh, 1983; Bažant and Lin, 1988; Bažant *et al.*, 1988; Bažant and Ožbolt, 1990). Since the FPZ in cementitious materials is narrow, it can be approximately modelled by a fictitious crack extension to the true stress free crack that carries a stress. The fictitious crack model assumes that there is a unique stress-displacement softening relationship for the FPZ. In the crack band model the FPZ is assumed to have a finite width. Within the FPZ the material is strain softening. The width was, in the original formulation, assigned a somewhat arbitrary value dependent on the aggregate size; but in a subsequent development of the theory, where the fundamental instability of a strain-softened zone is inhibited by using a non-local approach (Bažant and Lin, 1988), the width of the FPZ is determined theoretically. However, unless one is specifically interested in very deep notches or in the last stages of crack propagation, the added preciseness of the crack band model over the fictitious crack model is largely illusory because the heterogeneity of cementitious materials gives rise to a large scatter in results from even supposedly identical specimens. As Bažant and Cedolin (1979) remark "the choice of either [the line crack or the crack band] is basically a question of computational effectiveness".

The approximate method based on the engineers' theory of bending is presented first. The effective crack length models are then reviewed before treating the crack band and the fictitious crack models. Comparison of the various theoretical models with experimental data is difficult for a number of reasons. Firstly, it is almost impossible to produce specimens of differing size that have the same material properties. Secondly, most research workers have concentrated on the three-point notch bend geometry and so there are very few experiments that enable the geometric independence of fracture parameters to be assessed. Where data exist they are often not sufficient to enable other models to be examined because experimenters are usually interested in justifying their own models.

4.2 The flexure of strain-softening materials

Chuang and Mai (1989) have discussed how the engineers' theory of bending can be applied to strain-softening materials. Lim et al. (1987) present a similar method for long fibre reinforced cementitious materials for a restricted class of strain-softening materials (Type IIA). The method does not depend on the particular strain-softening relationship chosen. Chuang and Mai (1989) used the power law

$$\sigma = f_t \left[1 - \left(\frac{\epsilon - \epsilon_t}{\epsilon_f - \epsilon_t} \right)^n \right] \tag{4.1}$$

where f_t is the tensile strength of the material, ϵ_t is the strain at the onset of strain softening $(\epsilon_t = f_t/E)$, ϵ_f is the strain at which the material fails completely, and $0 < n < 1$. The width of the FPZ, $2w$, is assumed to be constant across the beam. Plane sections are assumed to remain plane and there are three regimes. In regime I the strain ϵ_s at the surface of the beam is less than ϵ_t so that the entire beam is elastic. If $\epsilon_t < \epsilon_s < \epsilon_f$ (regime II), an FPZ develops spreading from the surface of the beam towards the centre. When the surface strain ϵ_s exceeds the maximum strain that can be sustained without complete failure, ϵ_f, a crack develops. The stress distributions in the three regimes are shown schematically in Figure 4.1. The position of the neutral axis, the size of the FPZ and the depth of the crack can be determined from force and moment equilibrium. The curvature $1/R$ within the FPZ is

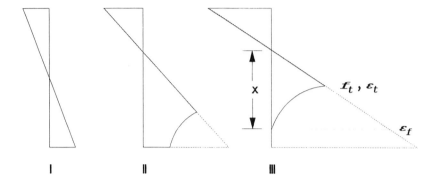

Figure 4.1 Schematic diagram of the strain (----) and stress (——) distribution across the beam for the three regimes. (Chuang and Mai, 1989.)

given by

$$\frac{1}{R} = \frac{\epsilon_t}{x} \tag{4.2}$$

where x is the distance from the neutral axis to the tip of the FPZ. The contribution of the FPZ to the deflection of a beam under three-point load is calculated from the assumption that the beam has constant curvature over the width $2w$ of the FPZ, i.e. $2w$ is much smaller than the span of the beam. The normalized load-deflection curves for a beam whose properties were deduced from the experiments of Krause and Fuller (1984) are shown in Figure 4.2. The shape of the curve depends on the width of the FPZ. Since the width of the FPZ determines the fracture work within the FPZ the correct width can be determined from the condition that the total work of fracture is equal to the fracture energy, G_{If}, multiplied by the area of the fracture surface. A narrow FPZ implies that the fracture energy is small and hence the material is brittle which leads to the 'snap back' instability shown by curve (a) in Figure 4.2. Snap back will be discussed further in section 4.6. Chuang and Mai (1989) suggest that this approximate method of analysis can be used to solve the inverse problem of knowing the load-deflection curve for a beam to infer the strain-softening behaviour. However, the fictitious crack line model discussed in section 4.5 is more accurate since local rather than global equilibrium and compatibility are satisfied.

4.3 Equivalent crack models

Provided the FPZ is small relative to the size of the specimen or structure, the actual crack and FPZ can be replaced by an equivalent elastic crack as is done in the fracture of metals. To determine the size of the equivalent crack, the

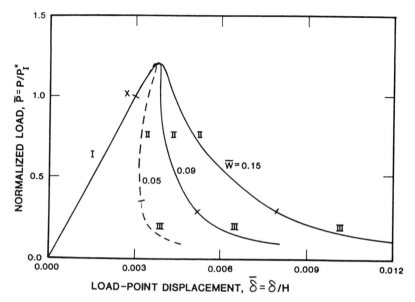

Figure 4.2 Load-deflection for three different FPZ widths; the load is normalized by the maximum elastic load and the deflection and FPZ width by the beam depth. (Chuang and Mai, 1989.)

actual crack and the FPZ can be replaced by a fictitious crack that extends to the end of the FPZ. That portion of the fictitious crack that models the FPZ is subjected to closure forces equal to the forces that exist at the edge of the FPZ. In section 4.5.3 it will be shown that the fictitious crack faces remain almost straight over the FPZ so that when the FPZ is fully developed

$$\frac{x}{d_p} = \frac{\delta}{\delta_f} \tag{4.3}$$

where x is measured from the tip of the fictitious crack and d_p is the size of the FPZ. If the stress field is K-dominated, then equating the equivalent elastic stress at the edge of the FPZ to the ultimate strength of the material yields

$$f_t = \frac{K_{If}}{\sqrt{2\pi d_p(1-\alpha)}} \tag{4.4}$$

where α is the fraction of the FPZ that is included in the equivalent crack. As in Irwin's (1958) analysis to ensure that the same load is carried by the equivalent elastic system as in the actual one

$$\int_0^{d_p(1-\alpha)} \frac{K_{If}}{\sqrt{2\pi r}} \, dr = -\int_0^{d_p} \sigma \, dx \tag{4.5}$$

where r is measured from the tip of the equivalent crack and σ is the actual stress in the FPZ. Assuming the crack faces remain straight and a bilinear stress-displacement relationship for the FPZ, eqns 4.4 and 4.5 can be solved to give the non-dimensional size of the FPZ, $\bar{d}_p$:

$$\bar{d}_p = \frac{d_p}{l_{ch}} = \frac{2}{\pi(s+v)} \tag{4.6a}$$

and

$$\alpha = 1 - (s+v)/4 \tag{4.6b}$$

Hence

$$\Delta\bar{a}_e = \alpha\bar{d}_p = \frac{1}{2\pi}\left(\frac{4}{s+v} - 1\right) \tag{4.6c}$$

and the equivalent crack length, a_e, is given by

$$a_e = a + \Delta a_e \tag{4.7}$$

Taking typical values of s and v for concrete as 0.16 and 0.19, respectively, the size of a fully developed FPZ in concrete is about 1.8 l_{ch}. Thus, for concrete the size of a fully developed FPZ is huge. Typically, the characteristic lengths of concrete with aggregate sizes of 8 and 32 mm are 250 and 800 mm, respectively; hence, d_p ranges from 450 to 1400 mm and about 90% of the FPZ is included in the equivalent crack length. The distance from the tip of the equivalent elastic crack to the edge of the FPZ, r_p, is given by

$$r_p = (1 - \alpha)d_p = \frac{l_{ch}}{2\pi} \tag{4.8}$$

and is independent of the stress-displacement relationship. As discussed in section 1.5.2, a K-dominated stress field is ensured if the crack and ligament lengths are at least $50r_p$. Hence, for cementitious materials, the crack and remaining ligament lengths should be greater than about eight times the characteristic length, l_{ch}, which implies immense specimens.

The above calculations give the size of a fully developed FPZ. However, the FPZ can only develop to its full extent in a very large specimen. An alternative approach to the estimation of the equivalent elastic crack is to determine the size of the elastic crack that has the same compliance as the secant compliance of the actual crack. This is the method used by the equivalent crack approaches for the analysis of notch bend tests (Jenq and Shah, 1985; Nallathambi and Karihaloo, 1986; Shah, 1988; Karihaloo and Nallathambi, 1988, 1989a,b; Alvaredo et al., 1989; RILEM, 1990).

In the effective crack model (Nallathambi and Karihaloo, 1986; Karihaloo and Nallathambi, 1988, 1989a,b) the Young's modulus is obtained from the linear portion of the load-deflection curve using LEFM expressions with the initial crack length, a_i. Using the same expressions an effective crack length, a_e, is found by iteration that gives the measured deflection at maximum load. It is then postulated that the stress intensity factor, calculated using the effective crack length, attains a critical value K_{Ic}^e at the maximum load that is a material constant independent of geometry and size, with the proviso that the ligament must be more than five times the aggregate size (Karihaloo and Nallathambi, 1988). The approach given in the draft RILEM (1990a) recommendation is somewhat different. In this approach the unloading compliance of the load-crack mouth opening displacement (CMOD) is used. Young's modulus is obtained from the initial linear part of the curve and an effective crack length calculated from the unloading compliance just after the attainment of maximum load (95% of maximum). If the deformation within the FPZ was purely due to the elastic opening of microcracks, the two approaches would give the same effective crack length. However, if there is significant non-elastic deformation such as aggregate slippage within the FPZ or if debris falls into the cracks decreasing the unloading compliance, the RILEM (1990a) method underestimates the effective crack length. In the RILEM (1990a) method not only is a critical stress intensity factor calculated (denoted by K_{Ic}^s) but also the CTOD at maximum load (denoted by CTOD$_c$) is calculated from LEFM analyses using the effective crack length. It is not at all clear why two critical parameters are needed in the RILEM (1990a) method. It is assumed that in the three-point notched bend test, and in those test geometries where the stress intensity factor increases monotonically with crack length, both K and CTOD attain their critical values at maximum load (Jenq and Shah, 1985) which can only be interpreted as meaning that true crack growth starts when the load reaches a maximum. However, Karihaloo and Nallathambi (1989) allow that some true crack growth may occur before the maximum load is reached. In fact, the point at which true crack growth starts is dependent on the size of the specimen and the FPZ is not necessarily fully developed at maximum load. In test geometries where the rate of change in the stress intensity factor with crack length reaches a minimum at some particular crack length for constant load, Jenq and Shah (1985) recognize that the critical values of K and CTOD will be attained prior to the maximum load. In experiments on a panel with a central notch with the load applied at the centre of the notch (K at constant load decreases monotonically with increase in crack length) the critical value, K_{Ic}^s, is taken as the plateau value of a plot of K against effective crack growth and the CTOD at that point is taken as CTOD$_c$ (Alvaredo et al., 1989). The main criticism of these equivalent crack models is that the maximum load is not generally attained when the fracture toughness reaches a critical value. Only in very large specimens will the maximum load occur when the stress intensity factor is equal to K_{If}.

Karihaloo and Nallathambi (1988) have given a comprehensive review of the equivalent crack models. They conclude that the two equivalent crack models are in good agreement and state that the critical stress intensity factor at the tip of the equivalent crack is essentially independent of beam depth apart from the size proviso already mentioned, but their conclusions

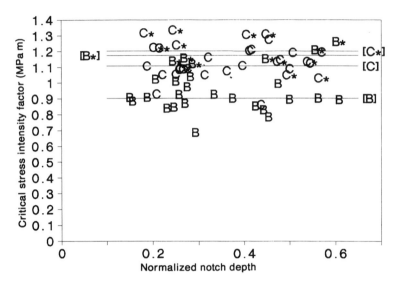

Figure 4.3 The variation of critical stress intensity factor with normalized notch depth, based on results of Swartz and Refai (1987) (K_{Ic}^e: B, $W = 203$ mm and C, $W = 305$ mm; K_{Ic}^s: B*, $W = 203$ mm and C*, $W = 305$ mm).

are worth re-examining. From the limited data available it appears that the critical stress intensity factor is independent of the relative notch depth, a/W. The results of Swartz and Refai (1987) who tested a wide range of a/W ratios, albeit using pre-cracked rather than notched beams, are presented in Figure 4.3 (except for results that fell outside the size limitation suggested by Karihaloo and Nallathambi (1988)). Although there is considerable scatter the critical stress intensity factors are essentially independent of a/W. There does seem a trend for the critical stress intensity factor to increase with beam depth, but since the difference in size is not great, one could not be certain that this difference is significant. There are two sets of data that cover a much wider range of beam size: those of Alexander reported by Karihaloo and Nallathambi (1988) and those of Hilsdorf and Brameshuber (1984). Although the data of Alexander come from three different series of beams, the concrete has the same mix and there does not seem to be any consistent difference between the series and it is assumed that they have identical material properties. An approximation to the characteristic length l_{ch} has been calculated from the mean value of K_{Ic}^e for the largest beams ($W = 800$ mm) and an estimate of the tensile strength f_t of the concrete obtained from the compressive strength of the concrete. The critical stress intensity factor K_{Ic}^e is plotted against the non-dimensional beam depth ($\bar{W} = W/l_{ch}$) in Figure 4.4; the a/W ratios in these tests varied from 0.2 to 0.4, but it is assumed that this variation does not have a significant effect. Although there is some scatter in the results, there is a definite trend for K_{Ic}^e to increase with the non-dimensional beam depth.

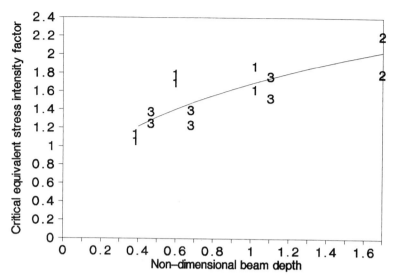

Figure 4.4 The variation of the critical stress intensity factor K_{Ic}^e (in MPa$\sqrt{m}$) with non-dimensional beam depth ($\bar{W}$), based on results of Alexander as reported by Karihaloo and Nallathambi (1988) (numbers represent the series and give a standard deviation on either side of the mean).

A power law

$$K_{Ic}^e = 1.68\,\bar{W}^{0.354} \qquad (4.9)$$

gives a good fit to the experimental data. The results of Hilsdorf and Brameshuber (1984) encompass an even greater range in beam depths for concrete and mortar beams. When these results are plotted against the non-dimensional depth, power laws with exponents of 0.202 and 0.227 fit the results for concrete and mortar, respectively. Since these exponents are so similar and not that very much different to that obtained for the results of Alexander, the results for both cementitious materials have been pooled in Figure 4.5 by plotting the critical stress intensity factor, K_{Ic}^e, relative to its value for a beam whose non-dimensional depth is 1. These relative critical stress intensity factors lie on a single curve that is given empirically by

$$\frac{K_{Ic}^e}{[K_{Ic}^e]_{\bar{W}=1}} = \bar{W}^{0.214} \qquad (4.10)$$

By combining the results for concrete and mortar specimens, a 20-fold range in $\bar{W}$ is obtained where the relative critical stress intensity factor nearly doubles and does not seem to have reached a plateau value even for the 800 mm deep mortar beams. The reason for the increase in the critical stress intensity factor with beam depth is that the maximum load only approaches the plateau value of the K_R-curve for extremely large specimens. The equivalent crack length models only give an approximately constant

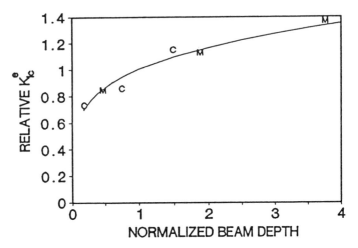

Figure 4.5 The variation of relative critical stress intensity factor with non-dimensional beam depth (based on results by Hilsdorf and Brameshuber (1984); C and M are results for concrete and mortar specimens, respectively).

value for the critical stress intensity over a very limited size range for notch bend specimens and the results cannot be applied to other specimen geometries.

Apart from the fact that the critical stress intensity factor is not a material constant, the equivalent crack models lack a real predictive capability. Karihaloo and Nallathambi (1988) do give an empirical expression for the equivalent crack length as a function of the nominal stress, notch depth, and aggregate size for notch bend specimens, but such a relationship cannot be relied upon outside of the range of the data for which it was obtained and cannot be used for any other geometries. Even if sufficient empirical data are accumulated to enable the equivalent crack length to be estimated, the equivalent crack models are only capable of calculating the maximum load and cannot predict whether a specimen or structure will fail in a comparatively gentle ductile manner with further external work necessary to complete the fracture after the maximum load has been reached, or whether it will fail in a brittle manner with all the energy coming from stored elastic energy without the need for additional external work.

4.4   The crack band model

Bažant and his co-workers (Bažant and Cedolin, 1979; Bažant and Oh, 1983; Bažant et al., 1984; Bažant and Lin, 1988; Bažant and Ožbolt, 1990; Jirásek and Bažant, 1994) have taken an early smeared crack concept used in finite element studies of reinforced concrete for simulating the microcracking and consequent strain softening behaviour of concrete, and made it objective for notched or cracked specimens so that it is not sensitive to the mesh size. Here the theory is presented for specimens where the fracture forms along the line of symmetry, though the method can be used for asymmetrical situations.

In the simplest form of the crack band theory, the FPZ is modelled by a band of width, $w = nd_a$, where d_a is the aggregate size and n a constant greater than 1, which is equal to or less than the element mesh size h. It is assumed that when the maximum principal stress σ_z exceeds the tensile strength f_t of the cementitious material, micro-cracks form which induce a strain-softened FPZ. In the original presentation (Bažant and Oh, 1983) the strain-softening was assumed to be linear and given by:

$$\epsilon^{cr} = f(\sigma) = \frac{(f_t - \sigma)}{D} \tag{4.11}$$

where ϵ^{cr} is the additional strain caused by the microcracks and D is the unloading stiffness. Although in principle any strain-softening relationship could be used, in a later paper (Bažant and Lin, 1988) it is suggested that a truncated exponential relationship is more realistic. A local definition of strain cannot be used in the FPZ and ϵ^{cr} is interpreted as the average strain over the thickness w of the FPZ. Within the FPZ the strain is given by:

$$\begin{Bmatrix} \epsilon_x \\ \epsilon_y \\ \epsilon_z \end{Bmatrix} = \begin{bmatrix} E^{-1} & -\nu E^{-1} & -\nu E^{-1} \\ -\nu E^{-1} & E^{-1} & -\nu E^{-1} \\ -\nu E^{-1} & -\nu E^{-1} & E_t^{-1} \end{bmatrix} \begin{Bmatrix} \sigma_x \\ \sigma_y \\ \sigma_z \end{Bmatrix} + \begin{Bmatrix} 0 \\ 0 \\ \epsilon_0 \end{Bmatrix} \tag{4.12}$$

where $1/E_t = 1/E - 1/D < 0$, E_t is the tangent softening modulus, and $\epsilon_f = f_t/D$ is the strain at which a complete fracture occurs and the stress in the FPZ falls to zero. The use of a total strain relationship implies that path independence is assumed; provided the loading is near proportional this assumption is justified. Objectivity is assured by requiring the specific work performed in separating the faces of the FPZ to be equal to the fracture energy, G_{If}, whether the finite element mesh size h is equal to or larger than the width w of the FPZ. Hence, the tangent softening modulus E_t must be negative, which limits the mesh size to

$$h = \frac{2G_{If}E}{f_t^2} \tag{4.13}$$

In practice the mesh size should be less than about half this limit.

Fracture of a notched or cracked body is solved by an incremental step by step increase in deflection or the crack opening displacement in the case of very large specimens (Rots, 1988). When the principal strain in a certain element exceeds the strain, ϵ_t, for the initiation of microcracking, the compliance switches to eqn 4.12. When the strain exceeds ϵ_f, the material in the element is completely fractured. Bažant and Oh (1983) analysed test data from many sources considering G_{If}, f_t, n and $h = w = nd_a$, as variables to find the values that gave the optimum fits. In these analyses n varied from 1.5 to 4. However, there is little difference in the solutions if n is always taken as 3.

The crack band model described above is quite suitable in many cases, but it does suffer from a number of limitations. Refinement of the mesh so that h is less than w, which may be necessary to model crack growth accurately under asymmetrical conditions, is impossible and the variations in width along the FPZ which occur in practice cannot be modelled. The stress-strain relationship given in eqn 4.12 can be rewritten as (Bažant and Lin, 1988)

$$\begin{Bmatrix} \epsilon_x \\ \epsilon_y \\ \epsilon_z \end{Bmatrix} = \begin{bmatrix} E^{-1} & -\nu E^{-1} & -\nu E^{-1} \\ -\nu E^{-1} & E^{-1} & -\nu E^{-1} \\ -\nu E^{-1} & -\nu E^{-1} & [E(1-\hat{w})]^{-1} \end{bmatrix} \begin{Bmatrix} \sigma_x \\ \sigma_y \\ \sigma_z \end{Bmatrix} \tag{4.14}$$

where $\hat{w}$ represents the damage and may be regarded as the cracked area fraction; for no damage $\hat{w} = 0$, and for complete fracture $\hat{w} = 1$. Under monotonic loading if $\epsilon_z > \epsilon_t$ and $\Delta\epsilon_z > 0$,

$$\frac{1}{(1-\hat{w})} = F(\epsilon_z) \tag{4.15}$$

With a linear strain-softening relationship, the damage function is given by

$$\left. \begin{aligned} F(\epsilon_z) &= 1, & \epsilon_z < \epsilon_t \\ F(\epsilon_z) &= \frac{E\epsilon_z}{E_t(\epsilon_f - \epsilon_z)}, & \epsilon_t < \epsilon_z < \epsilon_f \\ F(\epsilon_z) &= 0 & \epsilon_z > \epsilon_f \end{aligned} \right\} \tag{4.16}$$

In a subsequent paper an exponential damage function is suggested (Bažant and Prat, 1988).

The variable that determines the strain-softening must be non-local and this condition is indicated by a chara over the variable. In the earliest versions of the non-local model, the non-local variable is the average strain across the FPZ, but a non-local variable can be obtained by spatial averaging that can be applied to whole continuum rather than just to the FPZ (Bažant and Lin, 1988; Bažant and Ožbolt, 1990). The spatial average strain normal to the FPZ, ϵ_z, is defined by:

$$\hat{\epsilon}_{ij}(\mathbf{x}) = \int_V \alpha(\mathbf{x}, \boldsymbol{\xi}) \langle \epsilon_{ij}(\boldsymbol{\xi}) \rangle \, \mathrm{d}\xi \tag{4.17}$$

in which

$$\int_V \alpha(\mathbf{x}, \boldsymbol{\xi}) \, \mathrm{d}V = 1 \tag{4.18}$$

the integral is taken over the volume V of the specimen, $\mathbf{x}$ and $\boldsymbol{\xi}$ are general coordinate vectors, $\alpha(\mathbf{x}, \boldsymbol{\xi})$ is a weighting function assumed to be a material property, and the angle brackets, $\langle \ \rangle$, indicate that only the positive values of ϵ are considered. In the original presentation the weighting function is effectively taken as 1 for over the crack band and 0 elsewhere. Bažant and Lin (1988) proposed a Gaussian weighting function. The spatial average strain is used to determine the damage function.

In the latest work from Bažant and co-workers (Bažant, 1994; Bažant and Jirásek, 1994; Jirásek and Bažant, 1994) it is suggested that a non-local inelastic stress increment vector, $\Delta \hat{\mathbf{S}}$, leads to a simpler finite element approximation. The increments in the strain tensor, $\Delta \epsilon$, are decomposed into an elastic component, $\Delta \epsilon'$, and an inelastic component due to strain-softening, $\Delta \epsilon''$, so that the stress increment vector, $\Delta \boldsymbol{\sigma}$, is given by the inelastic increment in stress vector defined by

$$\Delta \boldsymbol{\sigma} = \mathbf{E} : (\Delta \epsilon - \Delta \epsilon'') = \mathbf{E} : \Delta \epsilon - \Delta \mathbf{S} \qquad (4.19)$$

where $\mathbf{E}$ is the elastic modulus tensor of the uncracked material. During unloading $\Delta \mathbf{S}$ is zero and the unloading modulus is the initial modulus, $\mathbf{E}$. In their latest non-local continuum formulation the inelastic stress increment in eqn 4.19 is replaced by a non-local inelastic stress increment, $\Delta \hat{\mathbf{S}}$, which can be defined by an equation similar to eqn 4.17. However, Bažant (1994) has generalized the non-local formulation based on the interaction between microcracks. If only the interactions between dominant microcracks forming in planes perpendicular to the maximum principal stress are considered, the increment in the non-local principal stress component $\Delta S^{(1)}$ is in the generalized formulation given by (Jirásek and Bažant, 1994)

$$\Delta \hat{S}^{(11)}(\mathbf{x}) = \int_V \alpha(\mathbf{x}, \boldsymbol{\xi}) \Delta S^{(1)}(\boldsymbol{\xi}) \, \mathrm{d}\xi + \int_V \Lambda^{(11)}(\mathbf{x}, \boldsymbol{\xi}) \Delta \hat{S}^{(1)}(\boldsymbol{\xi}) \, \mathrm{d}\xi \qquad (4.20)$$

where $\Lambda^{(11)}$ is a crack influence function.

A problem using a spatially averaged strain to calculate the damage function has to be solved incrementally with iterations at each step to determine the size of the FPZ. A global stiffness matrix is assembled using, for every finite element, the non-local material compliance from the previous iteration (at the start of the iteration procedure for each load step, the compliances from the previous step are used) for the current load step. With the prescribed load and displacement increments the nodal displacement increments are calculated. An estimate of the strains at the end of the load increment is then found. Each integration point is checked to see if cracking has initiated; if it has not, the principal strain directions are calculated but for cracked elements the principal directions are kept the same. The strains in the new principal directions are then calculated. The spatial average strain and the damage function are found from the principal strains. The

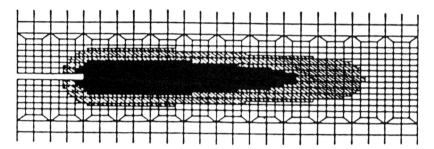

Figure 4.6 The FPZ for a notch bend specimen obtained from the non-local smeared crack model: the softened region is cross-hatched and the completely cracked zone is black. (After Bažant and Lin, 1988.)

non-local compliance matrices for each element are then updated and the nodal forces recalculated. The iteration process is continued until the difference between successive iterations is small. The FPZ for a notch bend specimen obtained by this method is shown in Figure 4.6.

4.5   The fictitious crack model

The fictitious crack has been modelled by finite elements by many researchers (Hillerborg *et al.*, 1976; Ingraffea and Gerstle, 1984; Ingraffea and Saouma, 1984; Petersson, 1985; Rots, 1986; Roelfstra and Wittmann, 1986; Carpinteri *et al.*, 1986, 1987; Wittmann *et al.*, 1988; Liaw *et al.*, 1990; Alfaite *et al.*, 1994) and boundary elements (Harde, 1991; Liang and Li, 1991; Cen and Maier, 1992; Salih and Aliabadi, 1994). However, it can be modelled more simply, if a specimen has a standard geometry, by use of known stress intensity factors and the K-superposition principle (Foote *et al.*, 1986; Cotterell and Mai, 1991; Cotterell *et al.*, 1992).

4.5.1   The finite element method

In the finite element method applied to symmetrical specimens with symmetrical loading, the crack and its fictitious prolongation are represented by pairs of finite element nodes. If the true crack tip is represented by the kth pair of nodes and the end of the fictitious prolongation, that represents the FPZ, by the nth pair of nodes, then the loads p at nodes numbers less than k must be zero and for numbers greater than n the crack opening displacement δ must be zero (see Figure 4.7). Along the fictitious prolongation the displacement is given in terms of the compliance $C(i)$ due to the external load P and the influence coefficients $K(i, j)$ that give the displacement at the ith node due to a unit load at the jth node. Hence, the boundary

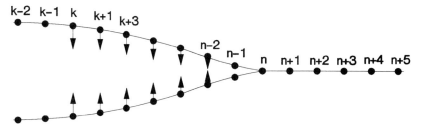

Figure 4.7 The finite element idealization of the fictitious crack in a symmetrical case.

conditions along the line of symmetry are:

$$\left.\begin{array}{ll} p(i) = 0 & i < k \\ \delta(i) = \sum_{j=k}^{n} [K(i,j)p(j) + C(i)]P & k < i < n \\ \delta(i) = 0 & i > n \end{array}\right\} \qquad (4.21)$$

The compliances $C(i)$ and the influence coefficients $K(i, j)$ can be determined by finite element calculations. The closing forces $p(i)$ can be expressed in terms of the nodal displacements if the stress-displacement law is known. For a given load, P, the n displacements can then be found by solving the system of $2n$ equations defined by eqn 4.21.

In the original finite element analyses of the fictitious crack model a linear strain-softening relationship was used (Hillerborg et al., 1976). However, with a linear relationship it is not possible to duplicate the deep belly that is obtained in the load-deflection curve for notch bend specimens and a variety of stress-displacement relationships have been used to obtain a better description of the load-deflection curve. All the analyses assume that the stress-displacement relationship is a unique material property. The bilinear stress-displacement relationship (see Figure 3.9) is the simplest curve that can accurately model the load-deflection curve of notch bend specimens. Some methods of determining the strain-softening relationship have been discussed in section 3.3, but the most straightforward method is that used by Wittmann and his co-workers who determine the bilinear curve that gives the best fit to the load-deflection curve (Roelfstra and Wittmann, 1986; Wittmann et al., 1987, 1988). In addition to determining the strain softening parameters by optimization, Wittmann and his co-workers also allow the Young's modulus E to be a variable so that in all five parameters $E, G_{\mathrm{If}}, f_{\mathrm{t}}, v$ and s are optimized. Experimental and theoretical load-deflection curves for a concrete notch bend specimen are compared in Figure 4.8. The fit between experiment and theory is good but not surprising, since it was obtained from five independent parameters. The fracture energy obtained by curve fitting was $90.5\,\mathrm{J/m^2}$ as compared with the RILEM (1985) method which gave $112.5\,\mathrm{J/m^2}$. Wittmann et al. (1987) argue that the

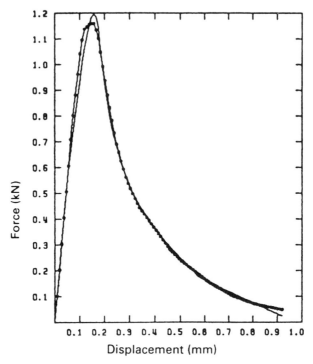

Figure 4.8 The comparison of experimental (curve with circular dots) and theoretical load-deflection curves for a notch bend specimen (After Wittmann *et al.*, 1987).

RILEM method is inaccurate, because it depends on the accurate determination of the deflection at which final instability occurs in the notch bend test. Although it is difficult to determine G_{If} accurately by the RILEM method we are not convinced that Wittmann's method gives any better accuracy because a curve fitting exercise does not ensure that the total work of fracture is exactly the area under the load-deflection curve. What is apparent is that the size restrictions imposed by the proposed RILEM (1985) method are not restrictive enough. Wittmann and his co-workers (1988) have performed a series of tests on compact tension specimens of different size (ligaments 150, 300 and 600 mm). Using their curve fitting technique they found that whereas there was little difference in any of the optimum fracture parameters between the three sizes except that G_{If} for the smallest specimen was significantly less than the values for the two larger specimens. According to the RILEM (1985) method a notch beam only 100 mm deep could be used to obtain a valid fracture energy. However, the load-deflection curve for the largest specimen could only be predicted from the specimen with a 300 mm ligament, as presumably could the load-deflection curves for larger specimens or specimens of different geometry providing they were big enough.

4.5.2 The boundary element method

The use of the boundary element method to the analysis of the fracture of cementitious materials is comparatively new (Harde, 1991; Liang and Li, 1991; Cen and Maier, 1992; Salih and Aliabadi, 1994). The simplest way to use boundary elements is to use the dual boundary element method (DBEM) (Portela et al., 1992). The dual equations on which the DBEM is based are the displacement and the traction boundary integral equations (Salih and Aliabadi, 1994). The boundary integral representation of the displacement components, u_i, in terms of a boundary point is

$$c_{ij}(x')u_i(x') + P \int_\Gamma T_{ij}(x',x)u_j(x)\,d\Gamma(x) = \int_\Gamma U_{ij}(x',x)t_j(x)\,d\Gamma(x) \quad (4.22)$$

where $P \int$ is the Cauchy principal value, $T_{ij}(x',x)$ and $U_{ij}(x',x)$ are the Kelvin traction and displacement fundamental solutions at a boundary point x, and the coefficient $c_{ij}(x')$ is given by the Kronecker delta for a smooth boundary at x'. The boundary integral representation of the traction components is

$$\frac{1}{2}t_j(x') + n_i(x')H \int_\Gamma S_{ijk}(x',x)u_k(x)\,d\Gamma(x)$$

$$= n_i(x')P \int D_{ijk}(x',x)t_k(x)\,d\Gamma(x) \quad (4.23)$$

where $H \int$ is the Hadamard principal value integral, n_i is the component of the outward normal to the boundary, and S_{ijk} and D_{ijk} are linear combinations of the derivatives of $T_{ij}(x',x)$ and $U_{ij}(x',x)$. On the fictitious crack continuity in the tangential displacement and self-equilibrium of the forces acting across it are enforced. If a linear stress-displacement relationship is assumed, then a direct solution of the boundary integral equations can be obtained since the equations can be simplified to (Salih and Aliabadi, 1994)

$$\begin{bmatrix} A & [H_f] & [G_f] \\ 0 & [C_f] & [D_f] \end{bmatrix} \begin{Bmatrix} X \\ \{u_f\} \\ \{t_f\} \end{Bmatrix} = \begin{Bmatrix} F \\ \{S_f\} \end{Bmatrix} \quad (4.24)$$

where $[H_f]$ and $[G_f]$ are coefficients at the nodes on the fictitious crack, $[C_f]$ and $[D_f]$ are the fictitious crack boundary conditions corresponding to the vectors on the fictitious crack $\{u_f\}$ and $\{t_f\}$, and $\{S_f\}$ is a vector of the material parameters. The efficiency of the DBEM as compared with an FEM method is not discussed. It should be noted that the simplified method cannot be used with a more general stress-displacement relationship for the FPZ.

4.5.3 The K-superposition method

The simplest method of analysing specimens with standard symmetrical geometries is by the K-superposition method (Foote et al., 1986; Cotterell *et al.*, 1988; Cotterell and Mai, 1991). This method was originally proposed by Lenain and Bunsell (1979) for asbestos reinforced cement sheet and developed for fibre reinforced cementitious materials (Foote *et al.*, 1980, 1986; Cotterell and Mai, 1988; Cotterell *et al.*, 1988). As in the finite element method, the FPZ is replaced by a fictitious prolongation of the true crack over which bridging stresses exist, but the problem is solved by superposition of the stress system due to the bridging stresses on the stress system caused by the applied loads. If the stresses at the tip of the fictitious crack are to be finite and continuous then the total stress intensity factor (see eqn 1.22) must be zero. The stress intensity factor, K_a, due to the applied loads can be found for standard specimen geometries from handbooks of stress intensity factors (Tada *et al.*, 1973; Rooke and Cartwright, 1976) and the stress intensity factor, K_r, due to the closing bridging stresses can be found by integration of standard K expressions for point loads on a crack face. The crack opening displacements and specimen deflections can be found from Castigliano's theorem (see section 1.6.1). The problem is non-linear because K_r depends on the crack opening displacement which is not known explicitly. However, the problem can be solved quite quickly by iteration because under load the faces of the fictitious prolongation to the crack remain reasonably straight (Foote *et al.*, 1986; Cotterell and Mai, 1988; Cotterell *et al.*, 1988, 1992). The fictitious crack tip must meet in a cusp, but this cusp is very sharp. The crack faces show most deviation from a linear profile when the FPZ is small, but then the stress in the FPZ is close to the ultimate strength of the material and the exact form of the crack opening is comparatively unimportant. Thus, the load-deflection curve can be determined to an accuracy of about 5%, if it is assumed that the fictitious crack faces remain straight. The method of solution is described for a three-point notch bend specimen, but can be applied to any geometry for which expressions for the stress intensity factors are known.

The solution of crack propagation and fracture is driven by the CTOD until the CTOD (δ_t) reaches its critical value δ_f at which the true crack starts to propagate; from this point the solution is driven by the true crack length (a_0). Thus this method can be used even where the behaviour is brittle and the load-deflection curve 'snaps-back' (Biolzi *et al.*, 1989; Carpinteri, 1990). For a particular value of the driving variable, the load P and the normalized length of the fictitious crack a/W can be found by iteration. A flow-chart of the sub-program that carries out this iteration is shown in Figure 4.9. The input into this subroutine is the driving parameter (δ_t, or a_0) the depth of the beam (W), and an initial estimate of the depth of the fictitious crack (a) . The subroutine first calculates the load P that satisfies $K_t = 0$ and then calculates the beam depth (w) that gives the required CTOD. Iteration is performed to find the value of a that gives the required beam depth (W). The subroutine can be used whether the faces of the fictitious crack are assumed to be straight or if the true shape is found by

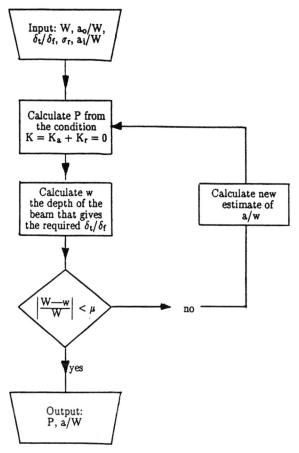

Figure 4.9 Subroutine LOAD: flow chart for determination of P and a/W.

iteration. During the running of subroutine LOAD it is assumed that the relative shape of the crack faces does not change. That is

$$\delta = \delta_t f(\bar{x}) \tag{4.25}$$

where $\bar{x}$ is the distance from the tip of the fictitious crack normalized by the length of the FPZ and the function $f(\bar{x})$ is kept constant. The bridging stress along the fictitious prolongation of the crack is calculated from δ and the strain-softening relationship.

If the actual profile of the fictitious crack is used in calculating the bridging stresses instead of assuming that the faces are straight, subroutine PROFILE is used (see Figure 4.10). The starting point for this iteration routine is a linear profile, where $f(\bar{x}) = \bar{x}$. Subroutine PROFILE uses subroutine LOAD to determine P and a, it then calculates the crack profile determined by the previous estimate of the bridging stresses in the FPZ. The new profile

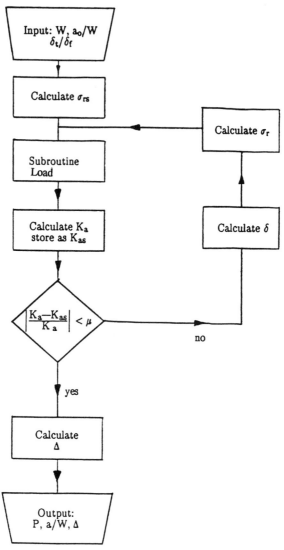

Figure 4.10 Subroutine PROFILE: flow chart for iterative calculation of the fictitious crack profile.

then becomes the input to subroutine LOAD and the process continues until the difference between the current value of K_a and the previous value is small. Since the profile is never very much different to the initial linear one, the convergence is swift. An accuracy of 0.2% is obtained in about three iterations.

To perform the foregoing analysis, assuming a bilinear softening relationship it is necessary to know the parameters G_{If}, f_t, v and s, as well as the Young's modulus E. The load-deflection curve can be modelled with accuracy if the fracture energy is obtained by the RILEM (1985) method so that the number of parameters that need to be optimized is reduced to four. The optimization process makes use of the fact that the maximum load (P_m) of most laboratory sized concrete NB specimens occurs at a relatively small CTOD. Under these conditions the bridging stresses are close to the ultimate strength, f_t, and hence, for a given G_{If}, the maximum load is mainly controlled by f_t. The beam deflection Δ_m at maximum load is largely controlled by the Young's modulus E because the FPZ is only just developing. Thus, for a given break point (v, s) in the bilinear curve, iteration can be used to find the values of f_t and E that give the experimental values of P_m and Δ_m. The break points (v, s) can then be determined by finding values that give the best fit to the rest of the load-deflection curve.

To compare the K-superposition with the finite element method of solving the fictitious crack model the results of Wittmann et al. (1987) shown in Figure 4.8 have been analysed (Cotterell et al., 1992). In this analysis the value of $G_{If} = 112.5 \, \text{J/m}^2$ obtained by the RILEM method (1985) has been used and the other material parameters found as described above. The values of these parameters obtained from the K-superposition method are compared with those obtained from the finite element method in Table 4.1, and the theoretical load-deflection curve obtained from the K-superposition method is compared with the experimental results of Wittmann et al. (1987) in Figure 4.11. The material parameters, apart from G_{If}, are very similar and the K-superposition modelled curve fits the experimental data as well as the finite element model (cf. Figure 4.8). Thus, there is little difference in fracture solutions to the fictitious crack model whether the finite element or the K-superposition method is used. The advantage of the K-superposition method is that it is simple and the program can be run on a personal computer. However, it cannot be used for mixed mode fractures.

The profile of the fictitious prolongation to a notch in the NB specimen analysed above is shown in Figure 4.12. Only when δ_t/δ_f is small, is the profile significantly different from a linear profile. The load-deflection curve obtained from the assumption that the fictitious crack faces remain straight is compared with the 'exact' curve in Figure 4.13. The difference between these two curves is much less than the scatter between supposedly identical specimens and there seems little point in finding the 'exact' crack

Table 4.1 Computed parameters for experiments of Wittmann et al. (1987)

Parameter	Wittmann et al. (1987)	Cotterell et al. (1992)
G_{If} (J/m^2)	90.5	112.5
E (GPa)	27.1	32.8
σ_t (MPa)	4.76	4.79
δ_f (mm)	0.132	0.150
s	0.150	0.140
v	0.137	0.174

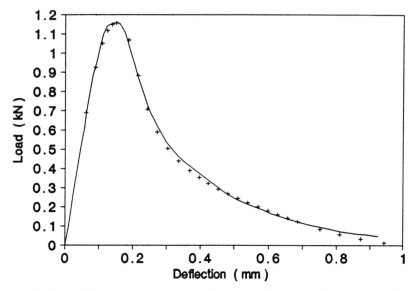

Figure 4.11 Load-deflection curve for a concrete NB test performed by Wittmann *et al.* (1987): (----) experimental data, (+) *K*-superposition modelling.

profiles. However, the discrepancy between 'exact' load-deflection curves and those obtained from the assumption that the crack faces remain straight is a little more for the double cantilever beam geometry and may be greater for other geometries.

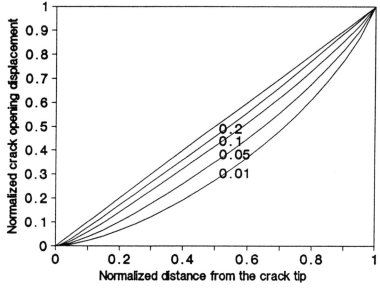

Figure 4.12 Theoretical fictitious crack profiles for the Wittmann *et al.* (1987) NB specimen. The curves for $\delta_t/\delta_f = 0.01, 0.05, 0.1, 0.2$ are compared with a linear profile.

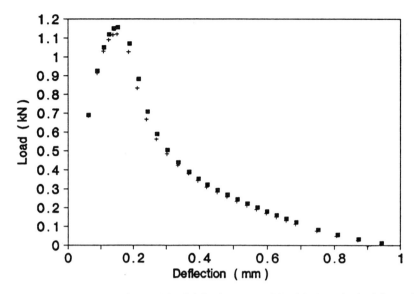

Figure 4.13 Comparison of 'exact' load-deflection curve (■) with that obtained from the assumption that the fictitious crack faces are straight (+).

An essential feature of any fracture model is its predictive capability. The load-deflection curves for two sizes of beam ($W = 100$ and $150\,$mm) are given in Figures 4.14 and 4.15 (Cotterell *et al.*, 1992). There is significant difference in the experimental curves of supposedly identical specimens, but no more

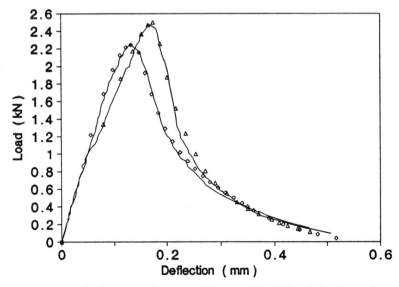

Figure 4.14 Load-deflection curves for mortar NB tests ($W = 150\,$mm): (----) experimental, ($\Diamond, \triangle$) modelled curves for beams 1 and 2, respectively.

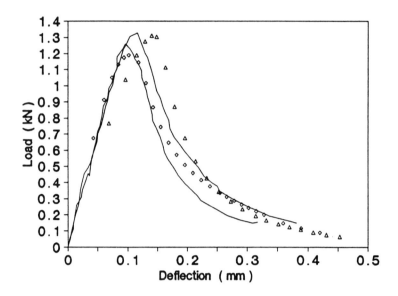

Figure 4.15 Load-deflection curves for mortar NB tests ($W = 100$ mm): (----) experimental, ($\Diamond$, $\triangle$) modelled curves using parameters from beams 1 and 2, respectively.

than that observed by other workers (Hillerborg *et al.*, 1976; Kormeling and Reinhardt, 1981). The fracture energies, obtained by the RILEM (1985) method for the two large beams, are very similar. The theoretical curves given in Figure 4.15 were constructed from the parameters found by the optimization procedure explained above using the load–deflection curves for the larger beams shown in Figure 4.14. The maximum load for the smaller beam predicted from the two sets of material parameters effectively bound the experimental values, but the deflection at maximum load is overestimated somewhat by one set of the parameters. Thus the predictive capabilities shown by these tests are reasonable.

The main characteristics of the stress-displacement relationship that determine the load-deflection curves of cementitious specimens apart from the fracture energy, G_{If}, are the stress, f_t, at which strain-softening initiates and the long tail caused by the pulling-out of interlocking aggregates. Smith (1994) has suggested that these characteristics could be modelled by a simple piece-wise softening law (see Figure 3.10) consisting of two constant stress sections. Such a strain-softening relationship is attractive because it is only necessary to determine the COD at the end of each constant stress section. However, an even simpler strain-softening relationship that will give accurate load-deflection predictions is obtained by a combination of the classic LEFM approach and the fictitious crack model. In this simpler model, the FPZ near the tip of the true crack where the stress is close to the tensile strength, f_t, is modelled by a critical stress intensity factor, K_c, and the remainder of the FPZ by a constant stress region where the bridging stress is $f_{tt} < f_t$. The three parameters defining strain-softening are then K_c, f_{tt} and δ_f. A similar scheme is discussed in section 5.4.1 for fibre reinforced cementitious materials.

4.6 Size and notch effects

If the specimen is large in comparison with the characteristic length l_{ch}, the FPZ will develop to its full extent before the maximum load P_m is reached, and the nominal strength σ_n can be obtained by equating the stress intensity factor at the tip of the crack

$$K = \sigma_n \sqrt{W} F(a/W) \qquad (4.26)$$

to the plateau value of the fracture toughness, K_{If}. Thus

$$\frac{\sigma_n}{f_t} = \frac{1}{F(a/W)\sqrt{\bar{W}}} \qquad (4.27)$$

where $\bar{W}$ is the non-dimensional size $\bar{W} = W/l_{ch}$ and for a three-point bend specimen σ_n is defined by

$$\sigma_n = \frac{1.5 P_m (S/W)}{BW(1 - a/W)^2} \qquad (4.28)$$

The nominal strength normalised by f_t for three-point notch bend specimens of different non-dimensional size $(S/W = 8)$ obtained from classic LEFM are compared in Figure 4.16, with the strength obtained from the fictitious

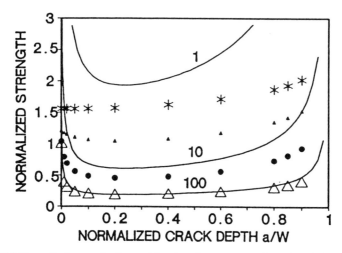

Figure 4.16 Normalised strength of a notch bend specimen—comparison of predictions of classic (——— $\bar{W} = 1, 10, 100$) LEFM and the fictitious crack model ($\bar{W} = 0.1$, *; 1.0, ▲; 10, ●; 100, △).

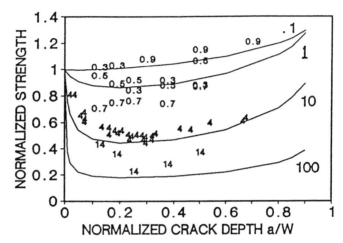

Figure 4.17 Experimental results of notch sensitivity for hardened cement paste, mortar and concrete normalised by the strength of an un-notched beam: the numbers refer to approximate non-dimensional beam depth; the sources of the data are $\bar{W} = 0.3$, 0.5, 0.7, 14 (Shah and McGarry, 1971); $\bar{W} = 4$ (Higgins and Bailey, 1976); $\bar{W} = 0.9$ (Malvar and Warren, 1988).

crack model using the K-superposition method for a bilinear strain-softening material whose properties are given in Table 4.1 (Cotterell and Mai, 1991). A beam whose non-dimensional depth is unity has a physical depth equal to its characteristic length, which for the concrete whose properties are given in Table 4.1 is 160 mm. Hence, it is seen that only for extremely large specimens does classic LEFM give a good approximation to the nominal strength. Over quite a wide range of notch depths the nominal strengths of the notch bend specimens are reasonably constant. Thus, when considering size effect, results in the range $a/W = 0.167$–0.5 can be lumped together. The solution given by the fictitious crack model is not strongly dependent on either the span to depth ratio or the break point (v, s) in the bilinear curve and is therefore compared with experimental results drawn from a variety of sources in Figures 4.17–4.19.

The notch sensitivity of cementitious materials ranging from hardened cement paste to concrete is shown in Figure 4.17, where the strength is normalized by the modulus of rupture for the un-notched specimens. The determination of G_{If} and f_t is not the same in all the references used in Figure 4.17. Often the ultimate tensile strength of the material f_t is not given and it has been necessary to estimate its value from compression tests or to assume a value based on the bend tests. In view of these difficulties in accurately determining the material parameters, the notch sensitivity is reasonably well predicted by the theory.

The size dependence of the nominal strength for plain and notched beams is shown in Figures 4.18 and 4.19. Here, apart from the variety of methods of determining G_{If} and f_t, there is the difficulty of ensuring that specimens of

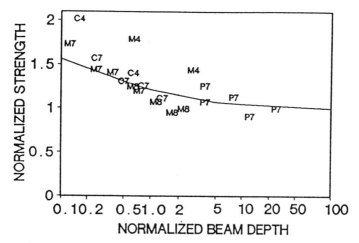

Figure 4.18 Size effect on un-notched beams normalised by f_t: P, M, C refer to cement paste, mortar and concrete, respectively; 4, Hilsdorf and Bramshuber (1984); 7, Strange and Bryant (1979); 8, Ward and Li (1989).

different size have the same material properties, and it is unsurprising that there is considerable scatter in the experimental data. However, the experimental results broadly follow the trends predicted by the theory.

The size effect predicted on the basis of classic LEFM can be modified to take account of the size of the FPZ by using the equivalent crack concept (Cotterell and Mai, 1991), defining a nominal stress σ_N in the same way as

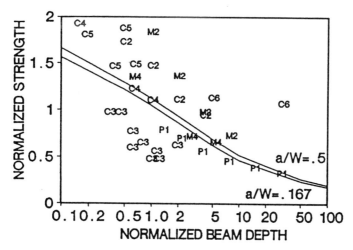

Figure 4.19 Size effect on notched beams normalised by f_t: $a/W = 0.167$–0.5, P, M, C refer to cement paste, mortar and concrete, respectively, data from: 1, Higgins and Bailey (1976); 2, Bažant and Pfeiffer (1987); 3, Mindess (1984); 4, Hilsdorf and Bramshuber (1984); 5, Jenq and Shah (1986); 6, Malvar and Warren (1988).

Bažant et al. (1986) by

$$\sigma_N = \frac{P_m}{BW} \tag{4.29}$$

Since it already has been noted that $F(a/W)$ is not very sensitive to a/W, and provided the FPZ is relatively small, $F(a_e/W) \approx F(a/W)$. Hence

$$\frac{\sigma_N}{f_t} \approx \frac{(1 - a_e/W)^2}{1.5\sqrt{\bar{W}}(S/W)F(a/W)} \tag{4.30}$$

If the proportion of the FPZ that has to be added to the crack length to obtain its equivalent length is small then to a first order

$$\frac{\sigma_N}{f_t} = \frac{(1 - a/W)^2}{1.5(S/W)F(a/W)\sqrt{\bar{W}\left(1 + \dfrac{4\Delta \bar{a}_e/\bar{W}}{1 - a/W}\right)}} \tag{4.31}$$

If the FPZ is fully developed, $\Delta a_e = \alpha d_p$, and is a material property. Hence, for geometrically similar specimens the first order size effect law is given by

$$\frac{\sigma_N}{f_t} = \frac{A}{\sqrt{(1 + \lambda W)}} \tag{4.32}$$

where (A, λ) are constants that depend on the geometry and the material properties. Equation 4.32 is the size effect law (SEL) for geometrically similar specimens originally obtained from dimensional arguments by Bažant (1984). In a later paper (Bažant and Kazemi, 1991), an argument similar to that given above was developed. Bažant et al. (1994) have recently reviewed the application of the SEL to a wide range of specimen geometries. If the SEL is valid, a linear relationship is obtained when $(1/\sigma_N)^2$ is plotted against W with an expected slope m given by

$$m = \frac{[1.5(S/W)F(a/W)]^2}{EG_{If}(1 - a/W)^4} \tag{4.33}$$

The SEL forms the basis of a RILEM draft standard for the determination of the fracture energy (G_{If}) from the above plot (RILEM, 1990b). A SEL plot of data obtained by Bažant and Pfeiffer (1987) is shown in Figure 4.20.

The SEL as originally stated only applies to a single specimen geometry but it can be generalized to include all geometries by a suitable definition of the nominal stress. Following the notation of Bažant and Kazemi (1991), the energy release rate (G) of any notched specimen can be written as

$$G = \frac{P^2 g(\alpha)}{E^* b^2 d} \tag{4.34}$$

where bd^2 is proportional to the volume of the specimen, and $g(\alpha)$ is a function of the crack length normalized by the characteristic dimension d.

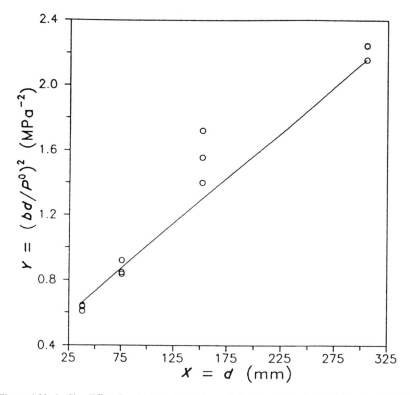

Figure 4.20 A 'Size Effect Law' plot of data from Bažant and Pfeiffer (1987) (After RILEM 1990b).

If it is assumed that the FPZ is fully developed at the maximum load, then the first order approximation to the nominal stress σ_N is given by

$$\sigma_N = \left(\frac{E^* G_{If}}{g'(\alpha)c_f + g(\alpha)d}\right)^{1/2} \tag{4.35}$$

where $g'(\alpha)$ is the differential of $g(\alpha)$ (it is assumed here that $g'(\alpha) > 0$; Bažant and Kazemi (1991) discuss the implications if $g'(\alpha) < 0$), and c_f is the same as Δa_e. It is tacitly assumed by Bažant and Kazemi (1991) that the extension c_f necessary to the real crack to obtain the equivalent crack is always equal to the limit value for an infinitely large specimen. Redefining the nominal stress as

$$\sigma_N = \frac{\sqrt{g'(\alpha)}P_m}{bd} \tag{4.36}$$

and introducing a 'brittleness number' (β) defined by

$$\beta = \frac{g(\alpha)d}{g'(\alpha)c_f} \tag{4.37}$$

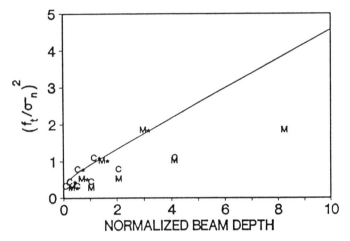

Figure 4.21 A replot of the size effect law of Bažant *et al.* (1986); (---) theoretical curve from the fictitious crack model; C, M experimental data points for concrete and mortar using G_{If} obtained by Bažant's method; C^*, M^* experimental points obtained by choosing the l_{ch} that gives the best fit with the theoretical curve.

Equation 4.35 can be rewritten as

$$\sigma_N = \left(\frac{(E^* G_{If})/c_f}{(1 + \beta)} \right)^{1/2} \tag{4.38}$$

This equation looks like a very attractive way of dealing with the vexatious question of size effect. Unfortunately, both eqns 4.31 and 4.38 are only first order approximations and only hold for extremely large specimens.

A plot of $(1/\sigma_N)^2$ against the beam depth W for NB specimens is approximately linear, but the fracture energy obtained from the slope is significantly underestimated. Using the earlier definition of nominal stress, σ_n, the experimental data of Bažant *et al.* (1986) (with G_{If} corrected for the weight of the beams and f_t obtained by extrapolating the notch tension results to zero ligament length) have been replotted in Figure 4.21 in the form of $(f_t/\sigma_N)^2$ against W (Cotterell and Mai, 1991). The theoretical results obtained from the fictitious crack model by the K-superposition method are also given in Figure 4.21. The experimental data based on the values of l_{ch} (74 mm and 37 mm for concrete and mortar, respectively) estimated from the value of G_{If} obtained from the SEL, do not agree well with the theoretical results. The theoretical curve is quite linear except near the origin, but the slope at $\bar{W} = 8$ is about 4, whereas the asymptotic slope obtained from classic LEFM is only 0.275. Thus, unless unrealistically large specimens are tested, G_{If}, obtained by the RILEM (1990b) method is significantly underestimated. If we assume l_{ch} is 200 mm and 100 mm, respectively, for the concrete and mortar specimens, which are far more reasonable values than those given above, then the experimental data fit the theoretical curve (the data

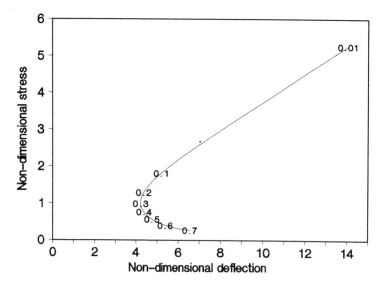

Figure 4.22 The equilibrium fracture stress as a function of the load point deflection (the values of a/W are indicated).

points obtained using these new estimates of l_{ch} are marked with an asterisk in Figure 4.21). This re-analysis of the data of Bažant *et al.* (1986) gives some confirmation to the contention that the RILEM (1990b) draft method for obtaining the fracture energy from the SEL significantly underestimates its value.

The stability during fracture of a flawed structure depends on its material properties, geometry and size of the structure. If the FPZ is small compared with the structure then the stability of the structure can be determined from classic LEFM and its geometry alone. For example, a large tension specimen is unstable whether fracture occurs under force or deflection control, but in other structures may be stable if the loading is controlled by deflection. Beams always fracture unstably under load control; the fracture is stable under deflection control if the notch is deep no matter how brittle the material is. To investigate the inherent stability of a structure we only need to know the stress intensity factor in terms of the notch or crack depth and the load-point deflection in terms of the load and notch depth. Tada *et al.* (1973) give the stress intensity factor and the load-point deflection (Δ) for a three-point notch bend specimen with a span four times the depth of the beam, in terms of the nominal stress

$$\sigma_0 = \frac{1.5PS}{BW^2} \tag{4.39}$$

that would be at the surface of the beam if there were no notch. Equating the stress intensity factor to the fracture toughness K_{Ic} for an ideal brittle material, we obtain an expression for the equilibrium nominal stress σ_0 as a function of the relative crack depth a/W. Knowing the equilibrium nominal stress, the non-dimensional load-point deflection, $E\Delta/(K_{Ic}W^{1/2})$, can be calculated and is shown in Figure 4.22. To maintain equilibrium the load point deflection must decrease as the crack grows if the initial relative crack depth is less than about 0.3. Carpinteri (1989a,b, 1990, 1991) calls this behaviour 'catastrophic'. Hence, notched beams of a brittle material loaded under deflection control fracture initially in an unstable manner if the relative crack depth a/W is less than 0.3, but are stable if the relative crack depth is greater than 0.3. A fracture that is initially unstable may arrest. The possibility of arrest cannot be completely determined from the equilibrium solution because in unstable fracture there is an excess of energy released over and above that needed to create the fracture. Arrest can only be predicted accurately from a dynamic analysis, but arrest is guaranteed if the elastic energy stored is less than the fracture energy required to complete the fracture. In Figure 4.23 the ratio of the energy stored to the energy required to complete the fracture (defined by Carpinteri (1989a) as the 'global brittleness') is shown as a function of the relative crack depth. It can be seen that provided the relative crack depth is greater than about 0.1, a fracture in a three-point notch bend specimen $(S/W = 4)$, though it may be initially unstable, will arrest. As the slenderness ratio (S/W) increases so the behaviour of a beam becomes more brittle. In the above treatment it is assumed that the fracture is not limited by the stress the material is able to sustain, which leads to the impossibility of a plain

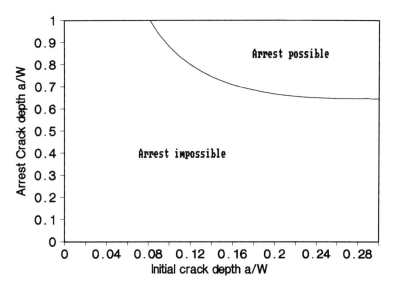

Figure 4.23 The ratio of the elastic energy stored at fracture initiation to the energy required to complete the fracture in a three-point notch bend specimen $(S/W = 4)$.

un-notched specimen being able to sustain infinite load without failure.[1] If the FPZ is small then the global brittleness or 'energy brittleness number' can be expressed as (Carpinteri, 1989a, 1991)

$$\text{Global brittleness} = \frac{\epsilon_t}{18 s_E} \left(\frac{S}{W} \right) \qquad (4.40)$$

where ϵ_t is the elastic strain at the critical stress, f_t, and s_E is the 'stress brittleness number' defined by

$$s_E = \frac{G_{If}}{f_t W} \qquad (4.41)$$

Equation 4.40 under-predicts the slenderness ratio at which catastrophic or snap back fractures occur. Assuming that in the limit situation at complete fracture, the beam effectively rotates about a hinge in the upper face of the beam,[2] an approximate condition for catastrophic or snap back behaviour is given by

$$\frac{s_E}{\epsilon_t} \leq \left(\frac{S}{3W} + \frac{4W}{S} \right) \qquad (4.42)$$

In cementitious materials the FPZ is usually not small compared with the specimen dimensions, and to determine the overall stability one must consider the strain-softening relationship. A finite FPZ implies that a material has a K_R-curve but, if the FPZ is large, it is not independent of the specimen geometry or size. The K_R-curves (normalized by K_{If}) obtained from the concrete parameters given in Table 4.1 for three beams of depth 0.1, 1 and 10 m are shown in Figure 4.24. In the largest beam, the FPZ develops to a length of 730 mm and is almost entirely in a K-dominated stress field. The K_R-curve for this beam has the classic shape and rises to a non-dimensional plateau value of unity. During the very early stages in the development of the FPZ the K_R-curve is unique, but unless the beam is very large it curves concave upwards to non-dimensional values far in excess of unity. The reason why small cementitious bend specimens behave in a ductile fashion is because of the size effect on the K_R-curve. A K_R-curve that curves upwards confers stability, because instability can only occur if the applied stress intensity factor curves upwards even more steeply. It should be noted that the size effect on the K_R-curve is not necessarily always as marked as it is for notched bend specimens. The K_R-curves for DCB and CT specimens have a far smaller size effect

---

[1] The inability of classic LEFM to describe fracture when a crack is very small is one of its drawbacks. However, if the FPZ is modelled, the fracture of a body with the smallest flaw, or even no flaw at all, can be described. Thus, conventional strength of materials and fracture mechanics can be combined into a single theory.
[2] Rather appropriately this assumption is similar to that made by Carpinteri's fellow Italian, Galileo (1638), in his analysis of the bending stresses in a beam. Although the assumption does appear to give results that agree approximately with more exact theory, the beam is not in global equilibrium which was also Galileo's error, and the agreement must be partly fortuitous.

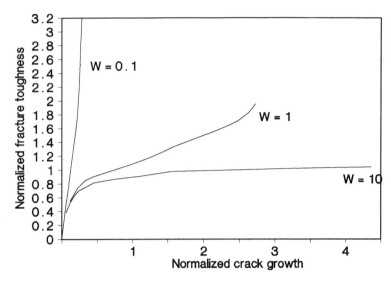

Figure 4.24 K_R-curves for concrete beams of depth $W = 0.1$, 1 and 10 m.

(Cotterell and Mai, 1988). Carpinteri (1991) also discusses the effect of crack growth resistance on the transition from brittle to ductile fracture for a general material. However, the J_R-curve assumed, though appropriate for metals, does not represent the behaviour of cementitious materials.

4.7 Asymmetrical fracture

If the specimen or the load is asymmetrical the crack follows a curved path and the fracture is often referred to as 'mixed-mode'. However, there is debate as to whether such fractures are truly mixed-mode. In isotropic elastic materials with very small FPZ, fractures do not generally propagate under mixed-mode conditions, but propagate so that the fracture is pure mode I as discussed in section 1.7.1.

The Iosipescu geometry shown in Figure 4.25 has been used in a round-robin test series by RILEM TC 89-FMT in an investigation of asymmetrical fracture. In this geometry the bending moment is zero at the notch and a maximum under the central loading points. There are four possible failure modes with this specimen (Ballatore *et al.*, 1990):

(a) Fracture from the notches with the crack path following essentially that predicted by LEFM (referred to as 'mixed mode' crack propagation).
(b) Flexural failure initiated away from the notches opposite the supports.
(c) 'Shear failure' between the central supports.
(d) A Brazilian-like splitting failure in the middle of the specimen.

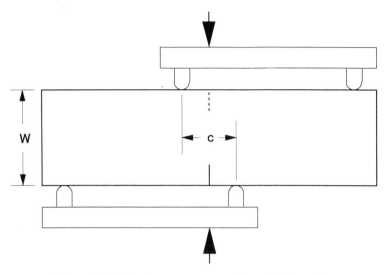

Figure 4.25 The Iosipescu geometry—single or double notches.

The mode of failure is determined by the loading configuration through c/W and is shown in Table 4.2. When the mode of failure is 'mixed mode', the fracture path can be reasonably well predicted by either LEFM (Swartz and Taha, 1990) assuming the crack propagates in the direction of the maximum circumferential stress, or the fictitious crack model (Swartz and Taha, 1990; Ballatore *et al.*, 1990) assuming that the crack grows in the direction of the maximum strain energy density. The fracture energy in these so-called 'mixed-mode' fractures is very similar to G_{If} (Biolzi, 1990; Boca *et al.*, 1990; Ballatore *et al.*, 1990) and one can conclude that the crack propagates so that there is local symmetry at the tip of the FPZ. However, the crack propagation in the specimen where $c/W = 0.167$ (Bažant and Pfeiffer, 1987) is very different (see Figure 1.18). In this case the crack propagates almost vertically along a path that is quite different

Table 4.2 Mode of failure in Iosipescu geometry specimens

Loading configuration c/W	Mode of failure	Reference
0.167	'shear'	Bažant and Pfeiffer (1987)
0.2	'mixed mode'	Ballatore *et al.* (1990)
0.333	'mixed mode'	Bažant and Pfeiffer (1987)
0.4	'mixed mode'	Ballatore *et al.* (1990)
		Rots and de Borst (1987)
0.5	'mixed mode'	Swartz *et al.* (1988)
0.8	11/12 'mixed mode'	Ballatore *et al.* (1990)
	1/12 'flexural'	
1.2	'flexural'	Ballatore *et al.* (1990)
0.24, with axial compression	Transition between splitting and mixed mode	Swartz and Taha (1990)

to the theoretical LEFM path, which predicts that the path deviates sharply away from the vertical, and is the path observed in a brittle polymethyl methacrylate specimen (Melin, 1989). The fracture energy observed in the test with $c/W = 0.167$ is very large, approximately 25 times that of the mode I fracture energy (Bažant and Pfeiffer, 1987). The crack band model was used to analyse specimens with $c/W = 0.167$ and 0.333; in these finite element studies, the crack band was advanced into the element that released the maximum energy, and the simulations indicated that the crack propagated vertically when $c/W = 0.167$ and sideways when $c/W = 0.333$ (Bažant and Pfeiffer, 1987). Although this result for small c/W and large shear indicates a 'shear fracture', Bažant and Pfeiffer (1987) suggest that microscopically, the 'shear fracture' is likely to have formed as a series of isolated inclined tensile microcracks in the region of high stress that stretches between the two notches. When c/W is not small and the shear/normal stress ratio not so high, there is much less difference between the principal stress direction and the direction of high tensile stress. In this case there is little difference between the direction of microcracking and the direction for a mode I fracture and the fracture follows essentially the path predicted by LEFM. Although it is convenient to lump the microcracks into a FPZ, only if the microcracks form essentially the direction in which the FPZ grows will the fracture be able to be predicted from a universal fracture energy. The prime example of the direction of FPZ growth and the direction of microcrack formation being completely different is in a compression fracture. As Hoek and Bieniawski (1965) showed, it is impossible to make a series of small cracks in a homogeneous brittle material link up to form a compression fracture. Hence, the conclusions are that provided the direction of high stress is essentially normal to the maximum principal stress direction, a fracture will propagate so that local symmetry is maintained with a fracture energy of G_{If}; but if the two directions differ significantly, then the fracture will propagate in the direction of high stress and the fracture energy will be greater than G_{If}.

Since there has been some uncertainty in the direction of crack growth in cementitious materials some workers have used a hybrid method of analysis where the crack path has been obtained from experiment and the fracture modelled by the fictitious crack model (Ingraffea and Gerstle, 1984; Ingraffea and Saouma, 1984; Liaw et al., 1990). Provided the crack path can be predicted 'mixed-mode' fractures can be analysed by either smeared or discrete representations of the FPZ. The K-superposition method is inappropriate for the mixed mode problem.

4.7.1   The smeared crack model for mixed mode fracture

Rots and de Borst (1987) have analysed an asymmetrically loaded beam with the Iosipescu geometry used by Arrea and Ingraffea (1982) without imposing any prior conditions on the direction of cracking. The incremental finite element solutions were driven by the crack mouth sliding displacements (CMSD) in a similar manner to the experiments. A non-linear mode I stress-softening relationship proposed by Cornelissen et al. (1986) was used with the crack band width taken as 20.3 mm. The mode I fracture energy was assumed to be 75 J/m^2. Three different assumptions were made about the mode II behaviour. In the first a constant shear retention factor of 0.2 was assumed. The other two assumed a linear shear-softening diagram with the same initial shear retention factor and an ultimate shear strength of 0.5 MPa; two mode II fracture energies were assumed, 10 and 75 J/m^2. There is considerable scatter in the experimental load-CMOD results of Arrea and Ingraffea (1982), but the triangular softening relationship with a mode II fracture energy of 75 J/m^2 fitted the data best. Rots (1988) also analysed the same experimental data of Arrea and Ingraffea (1982), assuming that the fracture is pure mode I and a fracture energy $G_{If} = 100 \text{ J/m}^2$, and obtained very similar results. Thus, it can be concluded that the simpler assumption that the fracture is pure mode I is to be preferred.

One of the problems with the smeared crack approach, that is not encountered by either the crack band or the fictitious crack model, is that geometric discontinuities in the real crack are not modelled. This leads to the problem called 'stress-locking' by Rots (1991). Stress-locking is not important until a true crack has extended significantly. Since the ultimate strength is usually reached before true crack growth, the maximum load can be predicted accurately by the smeared crack model. However, with the smeared crack model the load does not drop to zero, but to a relatively large positive value (Rots, 1991).

4.7.2   The fictitious crack model for mixed mode fracture

The analyses of mixed mode fracture by the fictitious crack model have been made by both the hybrid method of using the experimentally determined crack path (Ingraffea and Gerstle, 1984; Liaw et al., 1990) and without any prior assumptions of the crack path (Ingraffea and Saouma, 1984; Ingraffea et al., 1984; Ingraffea and Panthaki, 1985; Ballatore et al., 1990; Boca et al., 1990; Rots, 1991). Ingraffea and Gerstle (1984) calculated the load-displacement using the experimentally determined crack path and the theoretical mode I path. In the first method they used a shear retention factor that is a function of the CTOD. With this method the maximum load was predicted with a fair accuracy, but the post maximum load-deflection curve was not so well modelled. In the second method and in subsequent papers (Ingraffea and Saouma, 1984; Ingraffea et al., 1984; Ingraffea and Panthaki, 1985) the criterion for the crack path was $K_{II} = 0$ even though at the tip of a fictitious crack both the stress intensity factors must be zero. Starting from the previous iteration step that uses a singular element at the tip, the 'load' is increased which creates small non-zero stress intensity factors at the fictitious crack tip. The position of a new crack tip is now determined on the basis that $K_{II} = 0$ at the new crack tip. Iteration is then performed to determine the value of the 'load' increment that also makes $K_I = 0$. The theoretical crack path agrees well with the experimental one.

The crack paths, in compact tension specimens with a superimposed diagonal compression, are approximately straight, which has enabled their analysis by the hybrid method to be simple (Liaw *et al.*, 1990). Analysis using a trilinear normal stress-displacement softening relationship on its own and combined with an empirical shear-softening relationship showed that there was little difference in the two sets of results (Liaw *et al.*, 1990).

4.8 Summary

Cementitious laboratory specimens are usually too small to enable fracture loads to be predicted from the fracture energy, G_{If} and classic LEFM. The FPZ is also too large to enable the concept of an equivalent stress-free crack to be used. For symmetrical loading the load-deflection curve can be predicted if the stress-displacement softening relationship is known. Because of the inhomogeneous nature of cementitious materials, there is considerable scatter in the stress-displacement curve. The most important fracture parameter is the fracture energy G_{If}, which must be equal to the integral of the stress-displacement curve. The bilinear stress-displacement relationship is sufficiently accurate for all purposes and often even a simpler linear relationship will suffice. The engineers' theory of bending can be used to give a simple approximate prediction of the load-deflection curve for beams once the width of the FPZ is established. An accurate analysis of symmetrically loaded specimens can be made using either the crack band theory or the fictitious crack model. However, the easiest way of modelling the fracture process is with the fictitious crack model and the K-superposition principle.

The analysis of mixed mode fractures can be performed using either crack band models or the fictitious crack model. This latter method requires remeshing at each step. Unless the shear/tensile stress ratio is high, the crack path can be determined from any theory giving local symmetry. The exception is at initiation where there may be a kink in the fracture path. At kinks the criterion of maximum energy release is the most appropriate. More work needs to be done on 'mixed-mode' fracture where the shear/tensile stress ratio is high before it becomes clear how best to treat the problem.

5 Theoretical models for fracture in fibre reinforced cementitious materials

5.1 Introduction

Although high modulus fibres, and to a lesser extent low modulus fibres, can increase the strength of a cementitious material, the main effect of fibres is to increase the toughness by bridging cracks in the matrix. Beams manufactured from Type I composites which form multiple cracks can be analysed by standard elasto-plastic methods (Kalisky, 1989) and are not considered. Type II cementitious composite beams reinforced with long fibres, such as steel wires or polypropylene, where the pull-out length is so large that the maximum load is attained with little loss in fibre bridging stress, can be analysed approximately using the engineers' theory of bending (Nishioka *et al.*, 1975; Babut and Brandt, 1978; Swift and Smith, 1978; Lim *et al.*, 1987a; Naaman *et al.*, 1993a,b). However, for more accurate analysis of all Type II composites fracture mechanics is essential. The analysis of Type II composites using the engineers' theory of bending is considered first.

5.2 Engineers' theory of bending analysis of Type II composites

The analysis using the engineers' theory of bending is simplest for Type IIA composites where, after first cracking, the pull-out stress is almost constant (see Figure 2.11). The tensile elastic modulus, E_{ct}, for strains less than the first cracking strain can be calculated from the rule of mixtures (see section 3.9.1). After the critical stress, σ_{mc}, for first cracking is reached the stress drops to σ_{tu} and, providing the fibres are long, the stress during fibre pull-out is reasonably constant. The compressive stress-strain curve has been idealized by Lim *et al.* (1987a) as elastic up to a critical compressive strain, γ_{cc}, and perfectly plastic for greater strains as shown in Figure 5.1. The composite has a compression elastic modulus, E_{cc}, which is somewhat larger than the tensile modulus, E_{ct}. The effective ultimate compressive strength of the composite is assumed to be $\alpha\sigma_{cu}$, where σ_{cu} is the compressive strength of a standard cylinder test and α is a constant. For steel fibre reinforced concrete, the value of α is not critical, and Lim *et al.* (1987a) suggest that a value of 0.9 is appropriate.

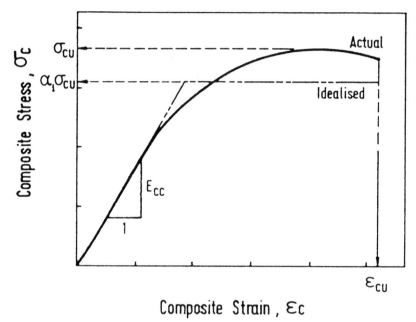

Figure 5.1 Idealized compressive stress-strain relationship for Type IIA composites. (After Lim *et al.*, 1987.)

In the elastic range, the position of the neutral axis can be located by a parameter μ (see Figure 5.2a)

$$\mu = \frac{h_t}{h_c} = \sqrt{\frac{E_{cc}}{E_{ct}}} \qquad (5.1)$$

where h_t and h_c are the depths of the tensile and compressive zones. Integration of the moments of the elastic stresses gives the moment curvature relationship

$$M = \frac{E_{ct}h^3}{3R} \left[\frac{\mu}{1+\mu} \right]^2 \qquad (5.2)$$

where R is the radius of curvature of the beam. Equation 5.2 holds until the tensile strain reaches the first cracking strain, ϵ_{mc}. The critical curvature is given by

$$\frac{1}{R_c} = \frac{\epsilon_{mc}}{h} \left[\frac{1+\mu}{\mu} \right] \qquad (5.3)$$

and the corresponding critical moment, M_c, can be found from eqn 5.2.

The stress distribution after first cracking, shown in Figure 5.2b, can be defined by a parameter, λ, where

$$\lambda = \frac{h_y}{h_t} \qquad (5.4)$$

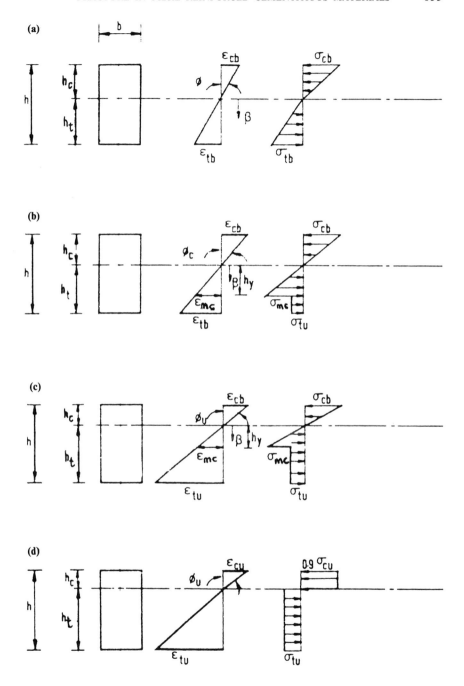

Figure 5.2 Stress-strain relationship in bending (a) elastic range, (b) after first cracking, (c) ultimate condition—case 1, (d) ultimate condition—case 2. (After Lim *et al.*, 1987a.)

and h_y is the distance of the first cracking strain from the neutral axis. The parameter λ can be obtained in terms of the first cracking strain, ϵ_{mc}, from its definition given in eqn 5.4, and is

$$\lambda = \epsilon_{mc} \frac{R_c}{h} \left[\frac{1 + \mu}{\mu} \right] \tag{5.5}$$

The moment-curvature relationship can be obtained by integration and is given by

$$M = \frac{1}{3R} \left[\frac{h}{1 + \mu} \right]^3 [E_{cc} + E_{ct}(\lambda\mu)^3] - \frac{\sigma_{tu}}{2} \left[\frac{h\mu}{1 + \mu} \right]^2 [\lambda^2 - 1] \tag{5.6}$$

Ultimate tensile failure can occur either (1) without crushing in the compressive zone (see Figure 5.2c), or (2) after crushing in the compressive zone (see Figure 5.2d). In case (1) the ultimate moment is given by eqn 5.6 with μ_u and λ_u given by

$$\mu_u = \left[\frac{E_{cc}\epsilon_{tu}}{E_{ct}\epsilon_{mc}^2 + 2\sigma_{tu}(\epsilon_{tu} - \epsilon_{mc})} \right]^{1/2}$$

$$\lambda_u = \frac{\epsilon_{mc}}{\epsilon_{tu}} \tag{5.7}$$

where ϵ_{tu} is the ultimate tensile strain. The ultimate curvature is given by

$$\frac{1}{R_u} = \frac{\epsilon_{tu}}{h} \left[\frac{1 + \mu}{\mu} \right] \tag{5.8}$$

For case (2) the ultimate moment can be calculated with little loss of accuracy if the stress in the tension and compression sides of the beam are assumed to be constant and equal to σ_{tu} and $\alpha\sigma_{cu}$, respectively (see Figure 5.2d). The ultimate moment is then given by

$$M_u = \tfrac{1}{2}\sigma_{tu}hh_t \tag{5.9}$$

where

$$\frac{h_t}{h} = \frac{\alpha\sigma_{cu}}{\alpha\sigma_{cu} + \sigma_{tu}} \tag{5.10}$$

and the ultimate curvature is given by the smaller of

$$\frac{1}{R_u} = \epsilon_{tu} \frac{1 + \mu_u}{h} \quad \text{or} \quad \frac{\epsilon_{cu}}{h - h_t} \tag{5.11}$$

There are two types of moment-curvature relationship for long steel wire reinforced cementitious materials: (a) when $M_u < M_c$ and (b) when $M_u > M_c$. Lim et al. (1987a) suggest that the two types of behaviour can be idealized by the straight line relationships shown in Figure 5.3. With type (a) behaviour there will be only a single crack, but with type (b) behaviour,

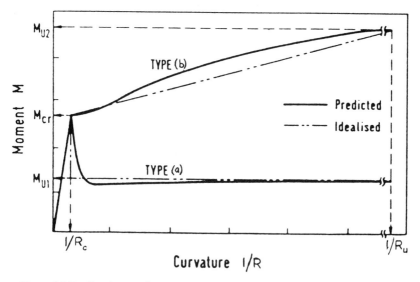

Figure 5.3 Predicted $M - 1/R$ curves and their idealizations. (After Lim *et al.*, 1987a.)

though in tension only a single crack will form, under bending, multiple cracks occur. The load-deflection relationship for type (b) beams loaded by three- or four-point bending can be obtained by double integration of the moment-curvature relationship. The predicted load-deflection curves have been compared with experimental data by Lim *et al.* (1987a). They tested two series of steel fibre reinforced concrete specimens one using hooked and the other straight fibres of diameter 0.5 mm and 30 or 50 mm long. The volume fraction of the fibres varied from 0.5 to 1.5%. All the straight fibre reinforced specimens showed a drop in load at first cracking, whereas those reinforced with hooked fibres showed either type (a) or (b) behaviour depending upon the fibre length and volume fraction. The predictions were generally good and an example of type (a) and type (b) behaviour are shown in Figure 5.4, which also contains predictions from K-superposition which will be discussed in section 5.4.1.

The idealized moment-curvatures were used by Lim *et al.* (1987a) to obtain simple expressions for the toughness index. Using the toughness index, I, defined by eqn 3.67 (Barr and Hasso, 1985), the toughness index for type (a) composites is given by

$$I = \frac{1}{4} + \frac{1}{2}\left(\frac{M_u}{M_c}\right) \tag{5.12}$$

For type (b) composites the toughness index is given by

$$I = \frac{3}{4} + \frac{1}{4}\left(\frac{M_2}{M_c}\right) \tag{5.13}$$

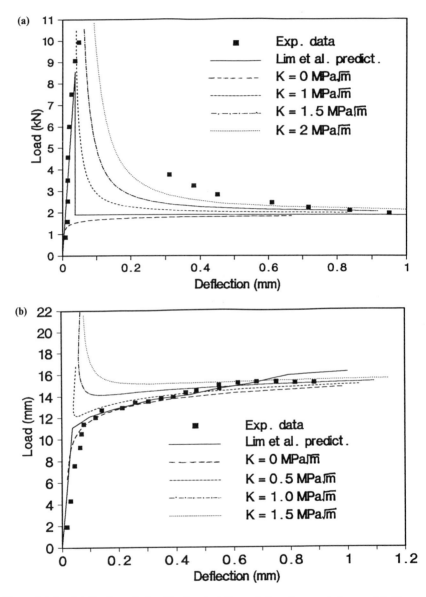

Figure 5.4 Load-deflection relationship for steel fibre reinforced concrete beams, (a) 30 mm straight fibres, 0.5% volume fraction; (b) 30 mm hooked fibres, 1.5% volume fraction. Theoretical curves from Lim *et al.* (1987a) and from application of fracture mechanics.

where M_2 is the moment at a curvature twice the critical curvature, $1/R_c$, for first cracking.

SIFCON, slurry infiltrated fibre concrete, can have a higher fibre fraction ratio than conventional fibre reinforced concrete manufactured by mixing

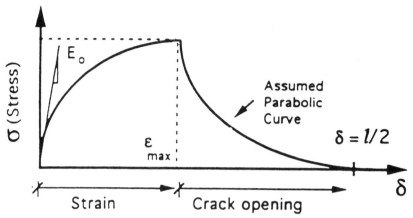

Figure 5.5 Schematic representation of the stress-elongation curve for SIFCON in tension. (After Naaman *et al.*, 1993.)

the fibres into the concrete mix and the stress does not drop suddenly on first cracking. A schematic representation of the stress-strain-displacement relationship for SIFCON in tension is shown in Figure 5.5. Because localization must take place with strain-softening, the descending portion of the curve cannot be related directly to strain and can only be expressed in terms of the crack opening. Localization is, of course, a major problem in the analysis of cementitious materials and prevents a straightforward finite element solution. In section 4.2 a strain-softening solution based on the engineers' theory of bending was presented in which a finite width FPZ was introduced to cope with the problem of localization. Naaman *et al.* (1993) have attempted a somewhat similar analysis for reinforced concrete beams using a SIFCON matrix. The reinforcing bars simplify the problem somewhat because they are a constraint to strain localization. A length scale is still needed to convert displacements in the strain-softening part of the stress-displacement relationship to strains, but the choice of that length scale is not quite so critical. Naaman *et al.* (1993) found that they could get good load-deflection predictions for reinforced SIFCON beams by taking the length scale equal to the depth of the beam. Knowing that in pure bending plane sections must remain plane, Naaman *et al.* (1993) solved the non-linear problem of reinforced SIFCON iteratively. The maximum loads were predicted reasonably accurately, but there was less success in predicting the load-deflection relationship. The load dropped after the maximum load was obtained in their experiments, but the analysis of Naaman *et al.* (1993) failed to predict any load drop. Probably the experimental load drop was not predicted because the tensile localization behaviour was not modelled well. Also, all the beams tested by Naaman *et al.* (1993) had depths in a rather narrow range from 18.75 to 26.25 mm. For much larger beams it is questionable whether the assumption that the length scale for converting displacement to strain would be equal to the beam depth.

Hence, while the engineers' theory of bending approach is suitable for Type IIA cementitious materials, reinforced with a low volume fraction of long fibres, that show a drop in strength at first cracking and little change in stress with further straining, its suitability for general Type II cementitious materials is doubtful.

5.3 Fracture behaviour of short fibre Type II reinforced cementitious composites

Although the work of fibre pull-out provides a major contribution to the fracture energy of short fibre composites, the load carrying capacity of beams and other structures cannot be determined accurately without fracture mechanics consideration of the propagation of cracks in the matrix. When a crack propagates a FBZ develops behind the matrix crack tip. The load taken by the bridging fibres impedes the growth of the crack in a similar way to the bridging grains that impede crack propagation in an unreinforced cementitious material. However, the fibres can span a very much larger crack opening, and hence the FBZ is much bigger than the FPZ and the crack growth resistance of fibre reinforced cementitious materials is much greater than that of unreinforced ones. Because of the large size of the FBZ, the crack growth resistance curves are generally both geometry and size dependent (Cotterell and Mai, 1988a). Only in very large specimens, where the FBZ is small compared with the overall size of the specimen, can the crack growth resistance curve be considered a material constant. Thus the concept of the crack growth resistance curve, which is very useful for materials such as fibre reinforced ceramics that have a relatively small FBZ, is inappropriate for most fibre reinforced cementitious materials except in its asymptotic form for very large specimens.

5.4 Crack growth models for fibre reinforced Type II cementitious composites

Most theoretical models for crack growth in fibre reinforced cementitious materials are based on the fictitious crack model of Hillerborg *et al.* (1976). The main problem in analysing the fictitious crack model for reinforced cementitious materials is the same as those discussed in Chapter 4 for unreinforced materials, namely the non-linearity caused by the crack closure stresses being dependent on the crack opening displacement. Hillerborg (1980, 1983) has solved this problem using the finite element method described in section 4.5.1 and this method will not be discussed further.

Jenq and Shah (1984, 1986a,b) proposed that the two-parameter model they developed for concrete could be applied to fibre reinforced composites. The two parameters are a critical stress intensity factor, K_{Ic}^s, at the tip of the effective crack and a critical crack tip opening displacement, $CTOD_c$, measured at the tip of the original crack (RILEM, 1990a). For what Jenq and Shah (1986a) call type G specimens,[1] it is assumed that K_{Ic}^s and $CTOD_c$ are the values of the applied stress intensity factor at the tip of an effective crack and the crack opening displacement at the tip of the original crack at maximum load. Some crack growth may occur at lower loads, but once the maximum load is achieved, it is assumed that the crack propagates so that the total stress intensity factor remains constant at K_{Ic}^s. In their earlier papers, Jenq and Shah (1984, 1986a,b) attempted to partition the total load P so that

$$P = P^M + P_k^f + P_s^f \qquad (5.14)$$

where P^M is the contribution due to the matrix and is related to the applied stress intensity factor, P_k^f accounts for the effect of the bridging fibres, and P_s^f satisfies global equilibrium due to the fibre bridging forces. However, in later works Shah and his co-workers (Ouyang et al., 1990; Mobasher et al., 1991) appear to have abandoned their earlier method and instead partition the stress intensity factor in a more readily understood fashion that is similar to the original suggestion of Lenain and Bunsell (1979). Their earlier method will not therefore be discussed.

Fracture of Type II composites usually occurs by the formation of a single crack. Multiple cracking can occur in some small un-notched specimens, such as the bend specimen, where there are stress gradients. The discussion here is limited to single cracks. For symmetric geometries, where the expressions for the stress intensity factors are known, the simplest method of analysis is to use the K-superposition principle which was first introduced for fibre reinforced cementitious materials by Lenain and Bunsell (1979). The total stress intensity factor K_t at the tip of a continuous matrix crack is given by

$$K_t = K_a + K_r \qquad (5.15)$$

where K_a is the stress intensity factor due to the applied loads, and K_r is the stress intensity factor due to the bridging fibres. K_r is negative, since the fibre forces tend to close the crack. Lenain and Bunsell (1979) assumed that, for equilibrium crack growth, the total stress intensity factor must be equal to

[1] In type G specimens, later identified as 'positive geometry' specimens, the applied stress intensity factor increases monotonically with crack length (Ouyang et al., 1990). The notch bend specimen is of type G and the measurement of K_{Ic}^s and $CTOD_c$ in such specimens is the subject of a draft RILEM recommendation (RILEM, 1990a). In type N, or 'negative geometry' specimens, the second derivative of the applied stress intensity factor is positive, but for small crack lengths the derivative is negative, so that there exists a minimum applied stress intensity factor.

the fracture toughness of the reinforced matrix, K_{Ic}. This value is greater than the fracture toughness of the unreinforced material because the strength of the reinforced matrix in the FPZ and the critical crack tip opening displacement are both larger than the corresponding values for the unreinforced material. For example, Lenain and Bunsell (1979) measured K_{Ic} at crack initiation for an asbestos reinforced mortar to be 1.7 MPa√m as compared to 0.6 MPa√m for the unreinforced mortar. At the initiation of a continuous crack, K_r is zero and the applied stress intensity factor, K_a, is equal to K_{Ic}. As the load is increased the matrix crack extends so that $K_t = K_{Ic}$ and the relationship between the applied stress K_a and the crack extension Δa gives what is known as the K_R-curve. However, as noted previously, crack growth resistance curves obtained from reinforced cementitious materials are geometry and size dependent (Cotterell and Mai, 1988a).

The use of the K-superposition principle does not remove the problem of non-linearity. The closing stress in the FBZ is in general dependent on the crack opening displacement. However, this problem can be solved by a simple iteration routine as discussed in section 4.5.3. What is not so clear is whether the FPZ of a fibre reinforced cementitious material can be modelled by a critical stress intensity factor K_{Ic} for the toughness of the matrix and the effective crack tip taken as the tip of the continuous matrix crack, or whether it is necessary to model the FPZ as a fictitious crack and take the effective crack tip at the tip of the FPZ. Hillerborg (1980, 1983) does not distinguish the FPZ as a separate entity and so effectively uses the latter model. If the FPZ is treated as a separate zone, then the equation for the total stress intensity factor K_t (eqn 5.15) has to be replaced by

$$K_t = K_a + K_r + K_m = 0 \qquad (5.16)$$

where the stress intensity factors are calculated at the tip of the fictitious crack tip, and K_m is the stress intensity factor due to the stress in the FPZ.

5.4.1 The K-superposition method applied to fibre reinforced Type II composites using a critical stress intensity factor

Type IIA composites, where the fibre pull-out stress after first cracking is practically constant, are the simplest to analyse because, since the fibre bridging stress does not depend upon the COD, the problem is linear. The load-deflection curves for the steel wire reinforced concrete three-point bend specimens tested by Lim et al. (1987a) have been calculated from the tensile pull-out data (Lim et al., 1987b). Since Lim et al. (1987a,b) do not give the fracture toughness of the reinforced concrete, the load-deflection curves have been calculated for a range of toughnesses, K_{Ic}, ranging from 0 to 2 MPa√m, which cover the expected range in values for concrete (Pak and Trapeznikov, 1981) and are shown in Figure 5.4. Modelling the FPZ by assigning a critical stress intensity factor for first cracking is only valid if the crack is large compared with the FPZ and cannot be used to obtain initiation accurately. For specimen reinforced with smooth wires (Figure 5.4a), the load drops suddenly after the matrix cracks. It is not surprising that the model overestimates the load for small deflections. The K-superposition method should give an accurate load-deflection curve once the matrix crack is deep, but it appears to underestimate the load as does the simpler theory developed by Lim et al. (1987a). There is an increase in the load after first cracking in the specimens reinforced with hooked wires (Figure 5.4b) and in these specimens two closely spaced parallel matrix cracks formed near the centre of the beam. For both the smooth and hooked ended wires the load at large deflections is little affected by the fracture toughness of the matrix, because the crack has already penetrated almost to the back surface of the beam and most of the tensile stresses are being resisted by the fibres with the matrix carrying the compressive stresses. At loads greater than the first cracking load, K_{Ic} needs to be greater than $2\,MPa\sqrt{m}$, which is unrealistically high, to give a good prediction of the load-deflection curve for smooth wires (see Figure 5.4a), but for the hooked ended wires the more reasonable assumption that $K_{Ic} = 0.5\,MPa\sqrt{m}$ gives an accurate prediction of the load-deflection curve apart from the initiation of the matrix crack (see Figure 5.4b).

Mobasher et al. (1991) also suggest that in the absence of knowledge of the actual stress-displacement relationship, the fibre bridging stress should be considered basically constant during the growth of a matrix crack. However, they complicate their analysis by assuming that the bridging stress builds up to the constant value from zero over a distance proportional to the critical crack length. This assumption is unrealistic. After a continuous matrix crack forms in a Type II composite the stress carried drops, not rises. Mobasher et al. (1991) are confused by the fact that in a pull-out test, the stress does first rise with displacement as the fibres stretch elastically before pull-out is initiated, but in a Type II composite, the fibre volume fraction is less than the critical value, and the stress carried drops. At the tip of a crack in a matrix there is considerable strain in the FPZ, which in the fictitious crack model is equivalent to a CTOD, δ_m, and the fibres are already stressed before a continuous matrix crack forms. The initial build-up in fibre bridging stress makes the problem of Mobasher et al. (1991) non-linear.

For a general Type II composite the fibre bridging stress is a function of the COD and the problem is non-linear. Solutions can be found by the use of Muskhelishvili's (1953) method. The method has been applied to a specimen with a semi-infinite crack (Foote et al., 1980). In this solution the closing stress on the crack face was represented by a fifth order polynomial which enabled the displacements of the crack face to be found analytically. Iteration was then used to obtain the fibre bridging stresses that matched the crack face displacements. A similar method was used for the stress intensity factor for a double cantilever beam specimen (Foote *et al.*, 1986b). Although the analysis of the semi-infinite crack by this means was comparatively simple, there were problems in convergence with the DCB specimen. A simpler approximate method gives results that are sufficiently accurate for practical purposes.

In the FBZ, the crack faces are very nearly straight except for a theoretically necessary parabolic opening right at the crack tip (Foote *et al.*, 1986b; Cotterell *et al.*, 1988). The approximate method makes use of the fact that the crack faces in the FBZ remain reasonably straight as they also do in the FPZ of unreinforced cementitious materials. Llorca and Elices (1993) use the same approximation to analyse the fracture of fibre reinforced ceramic matrix composites. If the crack faces are assumed to remain straight and the general stress-displacement curve is represented by

$$\frac{\sigma}{f_t} = F\left(\frac{\delta}{\delta_f}\right) \tag{5.17}$$

where f_t is the maximum stress resisted by the bridging fibres, the stress in a fully developed FBZ is given by

$$\frac{\sigma}{f_t} = F(1 - x/d_f) \tag{5.18}$$

where d_f is the length of the FBZ and x is measured from the tip of the matrix crack. The problem of calculating the load for a fully developed bridging zone knowing K_{Ic}, E, f_t and δ_f, then reduces to finding by iteration the length of the saturated bridging zone d_f while satisfying the condition for equilibrium growth that the total stress intensity factor at the continuous crack tip, K_t, is equal to the fracture toughness of the reinforced matrix, K_{Ic}. It is often sufficient to model the stress-displacement relationship for fibre pull-out by the linear expression

$$\frac{\sigma}{f_t} = \left[1 - \frac{\delta}{\delta_f}\right] \tag{5.19}$$

though the theoretical relationship is given by either eqn 3.64 or 3.65, depending upon whether a Coulomb or a constant interfacial frictional stress is assumed and in practice by eqn 3.17 with the exponent n greater than 1. The crack profile calculated from the external load and the fibre bridging stresses is reasonably linear (see Figure 5.6) which justifies the use of eqn 5.18. A similar iteration procedure can be used if the FBZ is only partially developed. However, a simplified method that requires no further iteration once the saturated length of the FBZ d_f is known is often sufficient (Foote *et al.*, 1986). This method assumes that the fibre bridging stress is given by eqn 5.19, even when the FBZ is only partially developed. The approximate method differs little from an 'exact' method where the actual crack profile is used, as can be seen from the comparison of crack growth

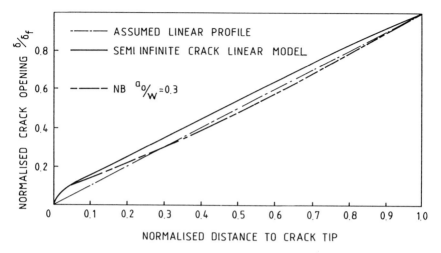

Figure 5.6 Shape of the crack faces in a fully developed FBZ for a semi-infinite and a notch bend specimen.

resistance curves for a DCB specimen calculated by the two methods shown in Figure 5.7. Once the length of the FBZ is known, the load-point displacement can be obtained by the method described in section 1.6.1.

For fibre reinforced cementitious materials it is possible, in theory, to model the debonding and pull-out of the fibres and predict the stress-displacement

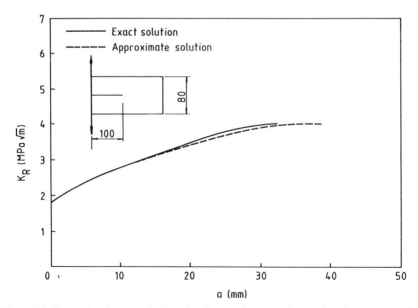

Figure 5.7 Comparison between the 'exact' and approximate crack growth resistance curves for a DCB specimen ($E = 6\,\text{GPa}$, $f_t = 6\,\text{MPa}$, $\delta_f = 0.8\,\text{mm}$, $K_{Ic} = 1.8\,\text{MPa}\sqrt{m}$).

relationship as has been discussed in section 3.9.5. At a less fundamental level one could start from an experimentally determined stress-displacement relationship, but the best method is to use an experimentally determined load-deflection curve and find the parameters that give the best fit to the curve. If a linear relationship is assumed for the stress-displacement curve, the fracture parameters required are: E, K_{Ic}, f_t and δ_f. In this case the post-ultimate load-deflection curve will probably not be modelled precisely but all the other essential features can be accurately modelled. The effective Young's modulus can be found from the initial slope of the load-deflection curve. The fracture toughness of the reinforced matrix, K_{Ic}, can be found from the load to cause first cracking. The maximum pull-out stress, f_t, can be estimated from the maximum load. The final pull-out displacement, δ_f, mainly controls the shape of the post-ultimate load-deflection curve and ensures that the fracture energy, G_{If}, is given by

$$G_{If} \approx \frac{K_{Ic}^2}{E} + \tfrac{1}{2} f_t \delta_f \qquad (5.20)$$

An optimization program to determine the fracture parameters from these initial estimates will converge with little difficulty. Once the fracture parameters are determined the load-deflection curve or the crack growth resistance can be predicted for any geometry or size of specimen.

Mobasher *et al.* (1991) propose a method that is somewhat similar to that outlined above. They obtain K_{Ic}^s and $CTOD_c$ from notch bend tests performed according to the RILEM (1990a) draft recommendation. As with the above method, Mobasher *et al.* (1991) assume that the stress intensity factor at the tip of the matrix crack, calculated according to eqn 5.15, is K_{Ic}^s. It is difficult to understand the other criterion for equilibrium crack growth of Mobasher *et al.* (1991), which is that the CTOD at the tip of the original crack should be equal to $CTOD_c$. Since the value of the $CTOD_c$ is obtained at maximum load, it cannot be the same as the critical COD, δ_f, at which the crack surfaces are stress free. However, the logical use of a critical COD seems to be limited to determining the extent of the bridging fibre free crack after a fully developed FBZ has been formed. Mobasher *et al.* (1991) use an iterative routine to obtain the applied load that results in a bridging stress determined from fibre pull-out tests for a particular matrix crack using the two criteria given above. Instead of calculating the load-deflection curve directly, Mobasher *et al.* (1991) use an energy balance to calculate an R-curve[2] which is then used to obtain the load-deformation response. It is difficult to form an opinion of the validity of their method but it is in any case a very indirect method of predicting the load-deflection curve.

---

[2] Shah and his co-workers recognize that the R-curve is geometry dependent (Ouyang *et al.*, 1990), but it is not clear whether they consider the R-curve to be size dependent.

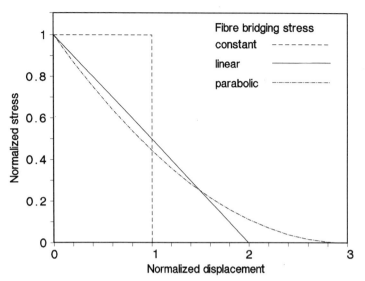

Figure 5.8 Constant, linear, and parabolic stress-displacement curves giving the same work of pull-out.

5.4.2   Crack growth resistance curves

The exact shape of the stress-displacement relationship for the FBZ has only a comparatively small effect on the analysis, providing the fracture energy is the same, as can be judged from a study of the crack growth resistance curves for a semi-infinite crack. These resistance curves are the limiting curves for all geometries as the size increases and are particularly easy to obtain by the approximate method given above because the non-linearity is in the form of a quadratic equation. The theoretical K_R curves have been constructed for three FBZ stress-displacement relationships: (i) a constant stress, (ii) a linear variation, and (iii) a parabolic variation. Thus, the stress-displacement relationship is assumed to be given by

$$\frac{\sigma}{f_t} = \left[1 - \frac{\delta}{\delta_f}\right]^n \tag{5.21}$$

where $n = 0$, 1, or 2. The three different stress-displacement relationships that give the pull-out work are given in Figure 5.8. Assuming that the crack faces remain almost straight, the stress in a fully developed FBZ, of length d_f, is given by

$$\frac{\sigma}{f_t} = [1 - x/d_f]^n \tag{5.22}$$

The stress intensity factor due to a unit point load a distance x from the crack tip is given by

$$K = \sqrt{\frac{2}{\pi x}} \tag{5.23}$$

Hence, for a bridging stress given by eqn 5.22, the stress intensity factor due to the bridging forces in a fully developed FBZ is

$$K_r = f_t \alpha_n \sqrt{\frac{2d_f}{\pi}} \qquad (5.24)$$

where $\alpha_0 = 2$, $\alpha_1 = 1.333$, and $\alpha_2 = 1.067$. For a semi-infinite crack with a fully developed FBZ, both of Barenblatt's (1959, 1962) hypotheses hold (see section 1.5) and hence the plateau value of the fracture toughness, K_{If}, is given by

$$K_{If}^2 = K_{Ic}^2 + \frac{E^* f_t \delta_f}{n+1} \qquad (5.25)$$

The crack opening displacement at the tip of the crack has two components; that due to the applied stress intensity factor, K_a, and that due to the closing stresses exerted by the bridging fibres. The crack opening displacement, δ_a, due to the applied load is given by

$$\delta_a = \frac{4K_a}{E^*} \sqrt{\frac{2x}{\pi}} \qquad (5.26)$$

The crack opening displacement due to the bridging fibres can be found by Castigliano's method (section 1.6.1) and for a fully developed FBZ is

$$\delta_r = -\frac{4\alpha_n f_t d_f}{\pi(n+1)E^*} \qquad (5.27)$$

Hence, the equation that determines the length of the fully developed FBZ, d_f, is given by

$$\delta_f = \delta_a + \delta_r$$

$$= \frac{4}{E^*} \left[K_{Ic} \left(\frac{2d_f}{\pi} \right)^{1/2} + \frac{\alpha_n f_t}{2} \left(\frac{2n+1}{n+1} \right) \left(\frac{2d_f}{\pi} \right) \right] \qquad (5.28)$$

This equation can be best expressed by introducing the non-dimensional terms:

$$\bar{K}_{Ic} = \frac{K_{Ic}}{K_{If}}$$

$$\bar{a} = \frac{a}{l_{ch}} \qquad (5.29)$$

where the characteristic length, l_{ch}, is defined by

$$l_{ch} = \left(\frac{K_{If}}{f_t} \right)^2 \qquad (5.30)$$

Using eqn 5.23 the length d_f of the fully developed FBZ can be found as a function of K_{Ic} from eqn 5.28. Assuming that the closing bridging stress for

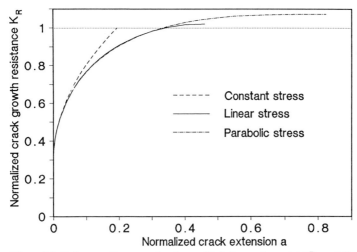

Figure 5.9 Reference K_R-curves for the semi-infinite crack model ($\bar{K}_{Ic} = 0.3$).

a partially developed FBZ is also given by eqn 5.22, enables the K_R-curves, shown in Figure 5.9 for $\bar{K}_{Ic} = 0.3$, to be obtained directly. The K_R-curve for case (i), constant stress, is exact and reaches the exact non-dimensional plateau value of unity. The slight discrepancy between the plateau value, $\bar{K}_{If}$, and unity, for the other stress-displacement relationships, is caused by the assumption of straight crack faces. There is little difference between the K_R-curves for the linear and parabolic stress-displacement relationships, which shows that the shape of the stress-displacement curve is relatively unimportant providing it gives the same fracture energy and justifies the use of a linear relationship.

The crack growth resistance curves for all specimen geometries tend to that for the semi-infinite crack as their size increases and it is only this curve that can be considered as a reference crack growth curve independent of geometry. If the FBZ is not small compared with the specimen's dimensions then the crack growth resistance curve can be very much different to the reference curve. The non-dimensional crack growth resistance curves have been calculated for two different specimen geometries: the double cantilever beam (DCB) and the notch bend (NB) specimen under pure bending (Cotterell and Mai, 1988a). A non-dimensional reinforced fracture toughness $\bar{K}_{Ic} = 0.3$ has been chosen that is representative of asbestos and cellulose reinforced mortars. The non-dimensional crack growth resistance curves for DCB specimens of varying size, but constant notch to height ratio $a_0/H = 0.3$, are shown in Figure 5.10. All the curves reach a plateau value $\bar{K}_{If}$ close to unity, the only difference being the size of the fully developed FBZ. The ratio a_0/H has little effect on the crack growth resistance curve (Foote *et al.*, 1986). The NB specimens behave quite differently to the

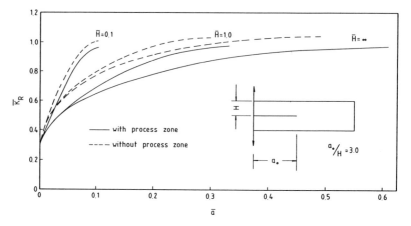

Figure 5.10 Crack growth resistance curves for the DCB geometry, with and without modelling of the FPZ ($a_0/H = 3$).

DCB specimens, as can be seen from Figure 5.11, which gives the K_R-curves for NB specimens of varying size, but constant notch to depth ratio a_0/W. Only for very large beams does the crack growth resistance curve reach a plateau close to that of the reference crack growth resistance curve of the semi-infinite crack model. For small beams, the K_R-curve increases with crack growth and never attains a plateau. Similar shaped crack growth

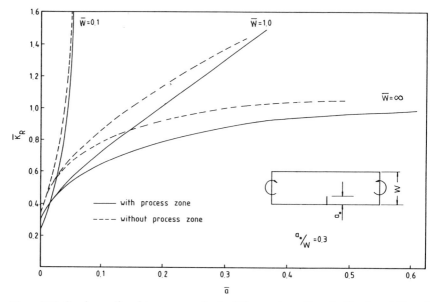

Figure 5.11 Crack growth resistance curves for the NB geometry, with and without modelling of the FPZ ($a_0/W = 0.3$).

resistance curves have been obtained by Llorca and Elices (1993) for ceramic-matrix composites by the same method, the only difference between the behaviour of the ceramic and the cementitious matrix is due to the very different characteristic lengths. For the LAS glass-ceramic reinforced with 50% SiC fibres the characteristic length is about 4 mm as compared with 250 mm for the asbestos/cellulose reinforced mortar considered here. Llorca and Elices (1993) also show that the centre notch tension, and the single edge notch tension specimens exhibit similar crack growth resistance curves that increase sharply as the crack, in a small specimen, approaches a free edge. The reason for the difference in behaviour of the DCB specimen to the other geometries is that the compliance in the DCB specimen increases relatively gradually, in proportion to the square of the crack length, whereas in the other geometries the compliance increases without limit as a crack approaches the free surface. Hence in the NB geometry, the notch to depth ratio has a large effect on the K_R-curve for small specimens (see Figure 5.12). The crack growth resistance curve for crack extensions greater than that necessary to develop the full FBZ can be obtained by joining the values for the fully developed zones. If the solutions were exact, then all the curves in Figure 5.12 would be smooth. 'Exact' solutions can be obtained

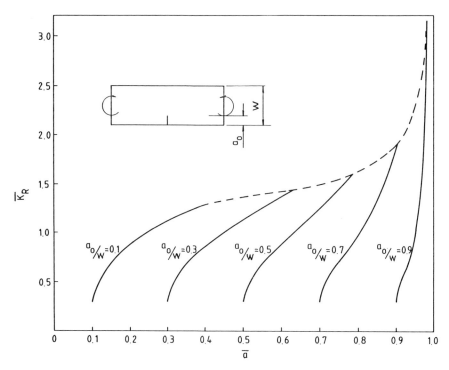

Figure 5.12 Crack growth resistance curves for the NB geometry ($\bar{W} = 1$).

Table 5.1 Properties of asbestos/cellulose reinforced mortar

	Asbestos	Cellulose
(a) *Fibre properties*:		
Fibre length	2 mm	3.5 mm
Aspect ratio	80	135
Volume fraction	8%	7%
Bond strength	0.8 MPa	0.35 MPa
(b) *Composite properties*:		
Young's modulus (E)		6 GPa
Tensile strength (f_t)		10 MPa
Reinforced matrix toughness (K_{Ic})		1.9 MPa√m
Plateau value of fracture toughness (K_{If})		5 MPa√m

by iteration to obtain the true crack profile, as described for unreinforced materials in section 4.5.3, but the gain in accuracy is slight.

Experimental crack growth resistance curves obtained from asbestos/ cellulose/mortar NB specimens (whose properties are shown in Table 5.1) are compared with the predicted crack growth resistance curves in Figures 5.13 and 5.14. The bond strengths shown in Table 5.1 are only estimates and were selected to give reasonable agreement between theoretical and experimental fracture strengths (Mai *et al.*, 1980). The fibres in the mortar sheet, which was manufactured by the Hatschek process, were not randomly aligned. The crack growth resistance curves were obtained for cracks propagating in the weak direction for which the efficiency factor was estimated to be

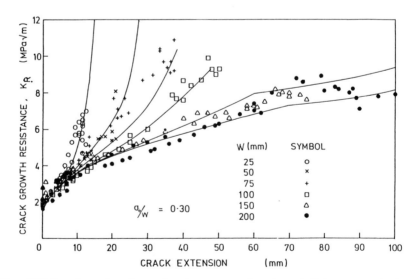

Figure 5.13 Experimental crack growth resistance curves for asbestos/cellulose mortar obtained from NB specimens, $a_0/W = 0.3$. Parameters used to calculate the predicted curves: $f_t = 10$ MPa, $K_{If} = 5$ MPa√m, $K_{Ic} = 1.9$ MPa√m.

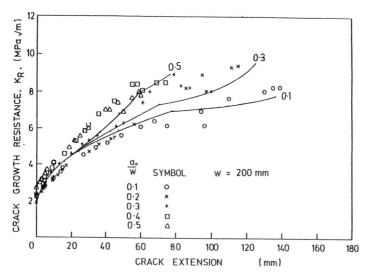

Figure 5.14 Experimental crack growth resistance curves for asbestos/cellulose mortar obtained from NB specimens, $W = 200$ mm. Parameters used to calculate the predicted curves: $f_t = 10$ MPa, $K_{If} = 5$ MPa$\sqrt{m}$, $K_{Ic} = 1.9$ MPa$\sqrt{m}$.

0.31 (Mai *et al.*, 1980). Using the data given in Table 5.1, the plateau value of the reference crack growth resistance curve was estimated to be 8.4 MPa$\sqrt{m}$. This value is very similar to the plateau value for the largest specimen ($W = 200$ mm). However, this agreement is, to some extent, fortuitous because the non-dimensional length of the largest beam is close to unity and for this case the plateau value is significantly larger than that of the reference curve, as Figure 5.11 shows. The parameters for the predictions of the crack growth resistance curves were those which gave the best fit to the experimental data for the largest specimen ($W = 200$ mm, $a_0/W = 0.3$). The agreement with the smaller beams and the other a_0/W ratios is good and gives justification to the approximate model.

5.4.3 The K-superposition method applied to fibre reinforced Type II composites modelling the FPZ as a fictitious crack

The FPZ for fibre reinforced cementitious composites are not generally small and may not always be accurately modelled by assuming that equilibrium crack growth occurs when the stress intensity factor at the tip of the matrix crack is equal to the fracture toughness of the reinforced matrix. The FPZ can be more exactly modelled by replacing the FPZ by a fictitious extension to the continuous matrix crack (Cotterell and Mai, 1988b). It can be difficult to separate that part of the stress-displacement curve that is due to the formation of the FPZ from that due to the development of an FBZ; it is for this reason Hillerborg and his co-workers do not distinguish the FPZ

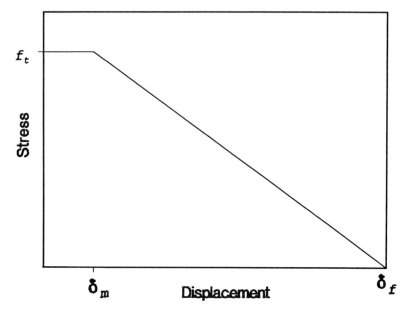

Figure 5.15 Idealized stress-displacement relationship for the FPZ and FBZ.

from the FBZ in their analysis (Hillerborg *et al.*, 1976; Hillerborg, 1980, 1983). However, such a division can be useful especially if there is a large drop in strength when the matrix cracks. In the analysis presented here it is assumed that the strength of the FPZ is constant until the crack opening displacement reaches the critical value, δ_m, at which a continuous matrix crack forms and there is no drop in strength at first cracking. A linear stress-displacement is assumed for fibre pull-out. The idealized stress-displacement relationship is illustrated in Figure 5.15. For a semi-infinite crack with a fully developed FBZ, the reference fracture toughness of the reinforced matrix, K_{Ic}^*, is given by

$$K_{Ic}^* = \left[E \int_0^{\delta_m} \sigma \, d\delta \right]^{1/2} \tag{5.31}$$

Because Barenblatt's two hypotheses are not satisfied, generally the fracture toughness, K_{Ic}, of the reinforced composite is only approximately equal to its reference value—the fracture toughness of a specimen which is large compared with the characteristic length and propagating under self-similar conditions.

In this analysis the crack faces in both the FBZ and the FPZ are assumed to be straight, but the crack opening angle is allowed to be different in each region. The first stage in the solution is to determine the lengths d_f of the FBZ and d_p of the FPZ when they are both fully developed. The lengths of these zones are found from the three conditions: (i) the total stress intensity factor at the tip of the fictitious crack is zero, (ii) the crack opening displacement at the tip of the continuous matrix crack is δ_m, and (iii) the crack opening displacement at the tip of the FBZ is δ_f. The applied force necessary to develop full FPZ and FBZ can be found and the crack growth resistance calculated. For crack growths less than that necessary to produce a fully developed FBZ, it is assumed that the crack opening angle in the FBZ remains the same, but the size of the FPZ changes with crack propagation and its current size is found from the condition that the crack opening displacement at the tip of the continuous matrix crack is δ_m. Three specimen geometries have been analysed: a semi-infinite crack (SIC), a double cantilever beam (DCB), and a notched beam under pure bending (NB). A hypothetical cementitious composite where the non-dimensional reference matrix crack stress intensity factor, $\bar{K}_{Ic}^* = 0.3$, which implies for the idealized behaviour illustrated in Figure 5.15 that $\delta_m/\delta_f = 0.047$, has been used so that the results can be compared with section 5.4.1. The non-dimensional sizes of the FPZ and the FBZ at the initiation of a matrix crack and when the FBZ is fully developed are shown in Figures 5.16 and 5.17 for the DCB and NB specimens. There can be a significant difference between the size of the FPZ at the initiation of a matrix crack and when the FBZ is fully developed,

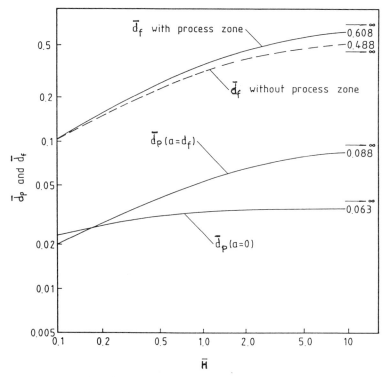

Figure 5.16 Size effect on the FPZ and FBZ for DCB specimens ($a_0/H = 3$).

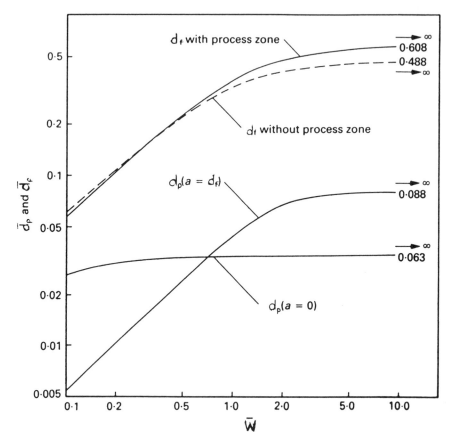

Figure 5.17 Size effect on the FPZ and FBZ for NB specimens ($a_0/W = 0.3$).

especially for small NB specimens, where the crack growth occurs well before the FBZ is fully developed. There is not a large difference between the size of the fully developed FBZ calculated by the alternate methods of modelling the FPZ. The crack growth resistance curves for DCB and NB specimens are compared with the curves given by the method of section 5.4.1 in Figures 5.10 and 5.11. The main difference in the crack growth resistance curves is caused by the difference in the size calculated for the FBZ by the two methods. One feature of the more exact modelling of the FPZ is the prediction that the fracture toughness of the reinforced matrix of small NB specimens is less than that for large ones; this variation in toughness has been observed experimentally (Mai *et al.*, 1980). The same experimental data presented in section 5.4.1 were analysed by this method, but gave no better agreement (Cotterell and Mai, 1988b).

In the practical application of crack growth models the prediction of the maximum load is more important than the crack growth resistance curve.

The nominal bending stress as a function of crack growth is given for three different sizes of NB specimen in Figure 5.18. There is reasonable agreement between the predicted maximum bending stresses for the two larger specimens obtained by either modelling the FPZ or replacing it by a singularity. However, there is a significant difference for the smallest specimen. The difference in the two predictions is mainly caused by the reduction in the effective fracture toughness of the reinforced mortar for small specimens.

5.5 Size effect and the R-curve

The strength of a fibre reinforced cementitious material is size dependent. In the limit for very large notched structures the strength can be determined from LEFM and the plateau value of the K_R-curve or the total fracture energy of the composite, G_{If}. However, the size required before LEFM becomes applicable is much larger than that for unreinforced cementitious materials because the characteristic length of fibre reinforced materials can be very large as can be seen from the characteristic lengths given in Table 5.2 for a range of fibre reinforced mortars. Bažant and his co-workers (Bažant et al., 1986; Bažant and Kazemi, 1991) have suggested that the SEL can be used to obtain an R-curve for unreinforced cementitious materials, since the fracture strength gives the slope of the R-curve at that point. However, the premise upon which the construction of the R-curve is based is that it is independent of size. As has been shown in this chapter, the R-curve is very size dependent

Table 5.2 Fracture energy, Young's modulus, tensile strength, and characteristic length of a number of fibre reinforced mortars (Ong and Ohgishi, 1989)

	Fracture energy G_{If} (J/m^2)	Young's modulus E (GPa)	Tensile strength f_t (MPa)	$l_{ch} = G_{If}E/f_t^2$ (mm)
Plain mortar	44	24	3.4	91
PAN-carbon	860	25.5	6.45	530
Vinylon (RMS182E)	6840	23.6	4.57	7730
Tyrano (Si-Ti-C-O)	6890	25.5	5.34	6160
Al- resist. glass	4310	24.2	6.89	2200
Mild steel	8890	25.6	7.86	3860
Alumina	5580	25.6	8.64	1910
Silicon carbide	10050	25.6	8.64	3450
Aramid (Kevlar 49)	13370	24.8	10.3	3130
Polyacrylate	22340	24.2	10.1	5300
Amorphous metal	48670	24.7	12.7	7453

Fibre fraction 3%, except for amorphous metal fibres which were 2%; fibre length 25 mm; Young's modulus estimated by rule of mixtures assuming a two-dimensional randomness; tensile strength obtained from split tests.

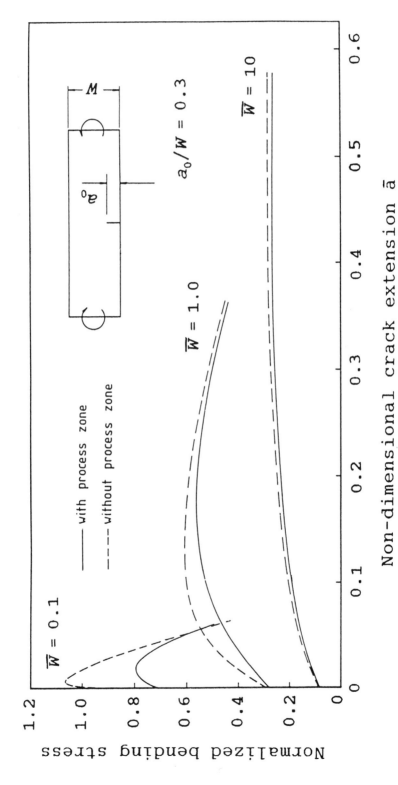

Figure 5.18 Nominal bending stress as a function of crack growth for three sizes of NB specimens.

and only if the size is large compared with the characteristic length does it approach a limiting form. What Bažant and his co-workers obtain is a composite R-curve for the whole range in specimen sizes that approximates to the limiting or reference R-curve. Tarng *et al.* (1991) apply Bažant's method to concrete reinforced with Fibercon 19 mm steel fibres. The expected general trend that the plateau value and the range of the R-curve increase with the fibre volume fraction is obtained, but curiously for small crack extensions, the R-curve for reinforced concrete is less than that for concrete unreinforced with 2% fibre volume fraction. Also the plateau value of the R-curve of $120 \, \text{J}/\text{m}^2$ is very low.

5.6 Summary

Fibre reinforced cementitious materials are important as structural materials because of their post-cracking ductility. Typically fibre reinforced cementitious matrix structures develop their ultimate loads after the matrix cracks. The fracture behaviour of such materials can be modelled by the K-superposition principle as outlined in section 5.4, assuming that for crack growth the stress intensity factor at the tip of the matrix crack is equal to the fracture toughness, K_{Ic}. It is not necessary to model the FPZ other than by the fracture toughness of the reinforced matrix unless the specimen is very small ($\bar{W} < 1$). In most cases a linear stress-displacement relationship can be assumed with little loss of accuracy. It is also sufficient to assume that the crack faces in the FPB remain straight. The fracture parameters that are necessary for predicting the ultimate strength of a structure are K_{Ic}, f_{t}, E, and K_{If}, or G_{If} or δ_{f}. These are best found by optimization of the fit to an experimentally determined load-deflection curve for a particular specimen, such as a three-point notch bend specimen. Once obtained these fracture parameters can be used to predict the fracture behaviour of any other specimen or structure. Other stress-displacement relationships can easily be used and it is possible to find the exact crack profile by iteration in a similar manner to that described in section 4.5.3 for unreinforced materials, but these refinements do not usually affect the load-deflection curve significantly.

Crack growth resistance curves, though useful for the analysis of the fracture behaviour of high strength metals and fibre reinforced ceramics which have small characteristic lengths, cannot usually be assumed to be material constants for fibre reinforced cementitious materials. In most relatively small specimens with geometries that lead to a very large increase in compliance as the crack approaches a free edge, the crack growth resistance does not tend to a plateau value. Hence, in general the concept of the crack growth resistance curve is not useful for prediction of the ultimate strength. However, the reference crack growth resistance curve for large specimens can be used to compare the toughnesses of different fibre reinforced cementitious materials.

An approximate method that satisfies global equilibrium, but does not consider the fracture mechanics of matrix crack growth can be used with what we have termed Type IIA fibre reinforced cementitious materials where the fibres are long so that the pull-out force is essentially constant for large crack openings. However, the K-superposition principle can also be used in these cases. In fact, since, in these cases, the fibre-bridging stress does not depend on crack opening, the K-superposition method is particularly simple.

6 The statistical nature of fracture in cementitious materials

6.1 Introduction

The strength of brittle solids is governed by the fracture toughness and the flaw size distribution. Under uniform tensile stress, in such a material, catastrophic fracture will be initiated at the largest flaw. This is the concept of the weakest link originally proposed by Weibull (1939, 1951). Cementitious materials are not ideal brittle materials and cracks can be initiated that will grow stably under increasing stress. Fracture is even more stable for fibre reinforced cementitious materials. In the limit case cementitious materials, reinforced by long fibres whose critical strain to failure is greater than the matrix, behave like bundles of fibres which share the load. The statistical theory of bundles was first considered theoretically by Daniels (1945). The weakest link and the bundle theories bound the behaviour of all materials.

6.2 The strength distribution for ideal brittle solids

In Weibull's (1939) analysis it is assumed that a structure is composed of N small 'elements', ΔV. The strength of each of these 'elements' is assumed to be independent of the strength of any adjacent elements. Weibull defined the 'risk of rupture', B, of a component as

$$B = -\ln S(\sigma) \tag{6.1}$$

where $S(\sigma)$ is the probability of the survival of the component. Weibull assumed that the risk of rupture, ΔB, of a single element could be given as

$$\Delta B = -\ln(\Delta S) = (\sigma/\sigma_0)^m \tag{6.2}$$

where σ_0 is a reference stress. The probability of survival of the whole component is the joint probability that each element survives or

$$S(\sigma) = \prod_1^N \exp -\Delta B = \exp -\sum_1^N \Delta B \tag{6.3}$$

If it is assumed that the 'elements' can be made as small as one likes, the probability of failure $P(V)$ of a specimen of volume V can be expressed as

$$P(\sigma, V) = 1 - S = 1 - \exp\left\{-\int_V (\sigma/\sigma_0)^m \rho \, dV\right\} \tag{6.4}$$

where ρ has the dimension of $1/V$. Since a brittle fracture originates at a flaw, ρ can be interpreted as the density of the flaws. Although in practical terms this interpretation of ρ is satisfactory, it does cause some problems. Another slight problem is that the strength of the 'elements' is not bounded, which implies that the solid is a continuum down to an infinitesimal scale and the Weibull distribution implies that the fracture of a specimen is not certain except at infinite stress. The statistical strength distribution of most brittle materials is reasonably modelled by the Weibull distribution.

In a uniformly stressed tensile specimen of volume V the probability of failure at a stress σ or less is given by

$$P(\sigma, V) = 1 - \exp[-\rho V (\sigma/\sigma_0)^m] \tag{6.5}$$

and the probability density function is given by

$$p(\sigma, V) = \frac{dP(\sigma)}{d\sigma} = \frac{m\rho V}{\sigma_0} \left(\frac{\sigma}{\sigma_0} \right)^{m-1} \exp[-\rho V (\sigma/\sigma_0)^m] \tag{6.6}$$

The mean strength of the tensile specimen is given by

$$\bar{\sigma} = \int_0^\infty \sigma p \, d\sigma = \frac{\sigma_0}{(\rho V)^{1/m}} \Gamma(1 + 1/m) \tag{6.7}$$

There is little difference between the mean strength and the median strength, σ_m, given by

$$\sigma_m = \sigma_0 \left(\frac{0.693}{\rho V} \right)^{1/m} \tag{6.8}$$

for $m > 10$. The coefficient of variation of the strength of the uniform tensile specimens μ is given approximately by

$$\mu = 1.283/m \tag{6.9}$$

for $m \geq 10$ (Coleman, 1958).

Under three-point bending the stress, in a beam of rectangular cross-section with a span S and depth W, is given by the engineers' theory of bending as

$$\sigma = 4\sigma_{max} \frac{xy}{SW} \tag{6.10}$$

where σ_{max} is the maximum stress at the load point and (x, y) are the coordinates measured from the centre of one end of the beam. If it is assumed that failure only occurs on the tension side of the specimen, the probability of failure at a maximum stress of σ_{max} or less is found by integration of eqn 6.4 to be given by

$$P(\sigma_{max}, V) = 1 - \exp\left[-\frac{\rho V}{2(1 + m)^2} (\sigma_{max}/\sigma_0)^m \right] \tag{6.11}$$

Equation 6.11 can be refined by including the Seewald–Karman correction for the stress near the load point (Diaz and Kittl, 1988). If the median strength of a three-point bend specimen is compared to that for a tensile specimen of the same volume the ratio in strengths is given by

$$\sigma_{\text{bend}}/\sigma_{\text{tensile}} = [2(1+m)^2]^{1/m} \qquad (6.12)$$

This ratio is predicted to be independent of the size of the specimen. Other assumptions of risk of rupture do show a decrease in the ratio with an increase in the size as does the theory for two-phase brittle materials (Hu *et al.*, 1985). However, the major contribution to size effect in cementitious beams comes from the crack growth resistance of the material rather than from a statistical distribution of the strength (see section 4.6). There is no deterministic size effect under tension in cementitious materials since once the material reaches its maximum strength, at the onset of strain-softening, a tensile specimen must fail. Hence, for a deterministic cementitious material the ratio of bending to tensile strength must decrease as the size increases, tending to unity for very large beams.

The Weibull distribution as defined by eqn 6.5 is a two-parameter distribution where the Weibull modulus, m, defines the variance of the distribution. The Weibull modulus m is usually found from linear regression applied to a double logarithmic plot

$$\ln\ln\{1/[1 - P(\sigma)]\} = m\ln(\sigma/\sigma_0) + \ln(\rho V) \qquad (6.13)$$

To find the cumulative probability of failure a number of experiments N are performed on identical specimens. These experiments will give strengths that can be ranked in order of ascending values so that the ith strength is σ_i and the probability that the strength of a specimen is σ_i or less is $i/(N+1)$.[1] A double logarithmic plot of the bending strength of porcelain taken from Weibull's original 1939 paper is shown in Figure 6.1; the results conform to the Weibull distribution except for very high probabilities of failure greater than about 99.5%. However, in practice it is the low probabilities of failure that are important and here the Weibull distribution is excellent. For many other materials the Weibull distribution describes the variation in strength well, but for some materials the double logarithmic plot gives a curve rather than a straight line. To accommodate these materials, Weibull (1939, 1951) introduced a third parameter σ_u in his distribution so that

$$P(\sigma, V) = 1 - \exp{-\rho \int_V \left(\frac{\sigma - \sigma_u}{\sigma_0}\right)^m \mathrm{d}V} \qquad (6.14)$$

[1] It has been argued that this interpretation of the cumulative probability is based on erroneous assumptions of the weighting function and that a better estimate of the cumulative probability is given by $(i - 0.5)/N$ (Bergman, 1986). However, provided a sufficiently large sample size is tested there is little practical difference in the probability.

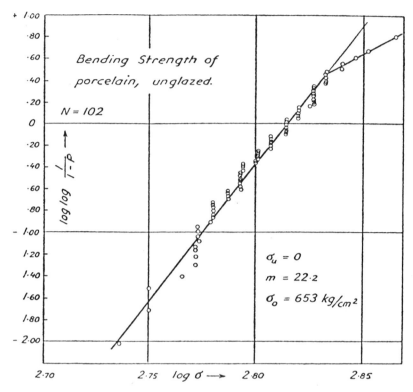

Figure 6.1 The bending strength of unglazed porcelain (Weibull, 1939).

An equation with three parameters that is of the right general form naturally gives a good fit to most data.

6.2.1 The fracture mechanics approach to strength distribution

Although Weibull's formulation of the statistical strength distribution of brittle materials has stood the test of time, it does not give a direct physical insight to the problem. More recent discussions have applied LEFM to the statistics of fracture (Jayatilaka and Trustrum, 1977; Hunt and McCartney, 1979; McCartney, 1979; Trustrum and Jayatilaka, 1983). In these analyses it is assumed that the brittle material possesses defects in the form of Griffith cracks that are sufficiently widely spaced so that there is no interaction between them. These crack-like flaws are not necessarily orientated so that they are normal to the maximum principal stress and some analyses have taken the orientation of the flaws into consideration (Jayatilaka and Trustrum, 1977; McCartney, 1979; Trustrum and Jayatilaka, 1983). However, since the exact distribution in flaw size is difficult to determine, there seems little point in this refinement and it is sufficient to describe a distribution of equivalent Griffith cracks that are orientated normal to the maximum principal stress. These equivalent cracks have the same critical stress for propagation as the real flaws. In the analysis of strength, the fracture toughness is usually considered to be a deterministic material property. McCartney (1979) does consider variations in the fracture toughness of the material, but such refinements seem unjustified because these variations can be absorbed into the equivalent Griffith crack distribution.

Here the argument of Hunt and McCartney (1979) is followed. Assume that the flaws can be replaced by equivalent penny shaped cracks of radius a and that the density of the flaws is sparse so that there is no interaction. If a tensile specimen has a strength σ and its fracture toughness is K_{Ic} its largest equivalent crack is given by

$$a = \left(\frac{K_{Ic}}{2\sigma} \right)^2 \pi \qquad (6.15)$$

Let $q(a)\,\mathrm{d}a$ be the expected number of flaws per unit volume in the size range a to $a + \mathrm{d}a$. If $f(a)\,\mathrm{d}a$ is the probability of a flaw having a size range a to $a + \mathrm{d}a$, and ρ is the density of the flaws, then

$$q(a) = \rho f(a) \qquad (6.16)$$

In a small element, $\mathrm{d}V$, the probability of finding more than one flaw must decrease to zero as the size of the element becomes infinitesimally small because the integral

$$\int_0^\infty f(a)\,\mathrm{d}a = 1 \qquad (6.17)$$

is bounded. The probability of finding no cracks in the volume element $\mathrm{d}V$ in the size range a to $a + \mathrm{d}a$ is

$$R(a) = [1 - q(a)\,\mathrm{d}a\,\mathrm{d}V] \qquad (6.18)$$

In the limit as the volume element becomes infinitesimal

$$R(a) = \exp[-q(a)\,\mathrm{d}a\,\mathrm{d}V] \qquad (6.19)$$

The probability that the equivalent cracks are all less than a in the elemental volume is given by

$$T(a, \mathrm{d}V) = R(a)R(a + \mathrm{d}a)R(a + 2\mathrm{d}a)\dots$$
$$= \exp\left[-\int_a^\infty q(a)\,\mathrm{d}a\,\mathrm{d}V \right] \qquad (6.20)$$

The probability that the largest equivalent crack in a specimen of volume V is less than a is the joint probability that each crack is less than a

$$T(a, V) = \exp\left[-\int_V \int_a^\infty q(a)\,\mathrm{d}a\,\mathrm{d}V \right] \qquad (6.21)$$

The probability that the strength of a specimen of volume V is less than or equal to σ is

$$P(\sigma, V) = 1 - T(a(\sigma), V) = 1 - \exp\left[-\int_V \int_{a(\sigma)}^{\infty} q(a)\, da\, dV\right] \qquad (6.22)$$

where $a(\sigma)$ is given by eqn 6.15.

Weibull's definition of the 'risk of rupture' interpreted in fracture mechanics terms implies a cumulative flaw size distribution

$$F(a) = \int_0^a f(a)\, da = 1 - \exp -\left(\frac{a_0}{a}\right)^{m/2} \qquad (6.23)$$

where the reference crack size, a_0, is given by

$$a_0 = \left(\frac{K_{Ic}}{2\sigma_0}\right)^2 \pi \qquad (6.24)$$

Hence, the probability that the strength of a tension specimen of volume, V, is less than or equal to σ is given by

$$P(\sigma, V) = 1 - \exp\{-\rho V[1 - \exp -(\sigma/\sigma_0)^m]\} \qquad (6.25)$$

This failure probability is not quite the same as Weibull's. If the expected number of flaws in the specimen, ρV, is large, or the stress small, then eqn 6.25 is the same as Weibull's (eqn 6.5). However, there is a difference if the expected number of flaws is small (Hu et al., 1988). The difference between the expression obtained by fracture mechanics considerations and that of Weibull arises, because if fracture only initiates at a flaw, the probability of there being no flaw in an element must be considered. Weibull in his analysis tacitly assumed that the number of flaws in a specimen is always equal to the expected number.

For tensile specimens under constant stress the expected number of flaws in a specimen has to be about 20 or less to cause a significant difference in the failure probability, but if the stress is not constant then the effective volume of the specimen is much smaller and the difference is more significant. For a three-point bend specimen of volume V with a rectangular cross-section the probability of failure at a stress σ or less is given by (Hu et al., 1988)

$$P(\sigma, V) = 1 - \exp\left\{-\frac{\rho V}{2}\int_0^1 \int_0^1 \{1 - \exp[-(\sigma/\sigma_0)^m]u^m v^m\}\, du\, dv\right\} \qquad (6.26)$$

The integral in eqn 6.26 has to be evaluated numerically unless the expected number of flaws is very large when the usual Weibull strength distribution given by eqn 6.5 is recovered.

The extension to Weibull's analysis presented above implies that if a straight line relationship is obtained for a double logarithmic plot (eqn 6.13), it may be curved for small specimens. If a straight line of best fit is forced through the

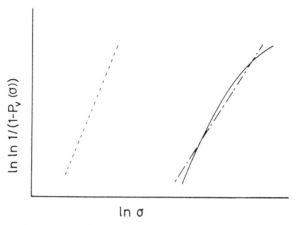

Figure 6.2 Schematic plot of $\ln\ln[1/(1 - P)]$ against $\ln\sigma$ for large and small specimens (small specimen —, best straight line through small specimen – — – —, large specimen – – – –).

data for a small specimen, as shown schematically in Figure 6.2, an effective Weibull modulus m^* that decreases with specimen size will be obtained. The effective modulus m^* partly depends on the sample size but reaches a limit when the sample size is greater than 50 (Hu *et al.*, 1988). The effective Weibull modulus is shown as a function of the number of flaws in Figure 6.3 for tensile, pure-bend, and three-point-bend specimens. The size effect on the Weibull modulus of tensile specimens is small and may not be observed, but the size effect for bend specimens is appreciable.

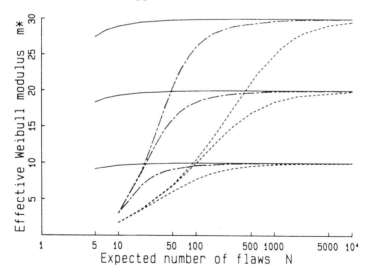

Figure 6.3 The effective Weibull modulus as a function of the expected number of flaws for: a tensile specimen —, a pure-bend specimen – — – —, a three-point-bend specimen – – – –; for three materials with a Weibull modulus of 10, 20 and 30.

Although Weibull's analysis is slightly at variance with fracture mechanics, the discrepancy is unimportant. Weibull's strength distribution can be obtained at all but the highest strengths if the flaw size distribution, $f(a)$, is assumed to be given by the Pareto distribution:

$$f(a) = 0 \qquad\qquad\qquad \text{for } a < a_0$$
$$f(a) = \frac{m}{2a_0}\,(a_0/a)^{(m/2+1)} \quad \text{for } a > a_0 \qquad (6.27)$$

This flaw size distribution gives exactly the same probability of failure as the Weibull probability function, provided the maximum stress is less than the reference stress, σ_0. For a tensile specimen of volume, V, and flaw density, ρ, the probability of fracture increases to $1 - \exp{-\rho V}$ at the reference stress, σ_0, which is the probability of finding no flaws in the specimen and is very small unless there are very few flaws expected. There will be a greater effect if the stress is not uniform. However, since one is usually more concerned with high survival rates, the probability of fracture at the higher stresses is relatively unimportant. For high survival rates the distribution in failure stress is insensitive to the flaw size distribution (Trustrum and Jayatilaka, 1983). This insensitivity partly explains the success of the Weibull distribution.

If the density of flaws is high, it cannot be assumed that there is no flaw interaction. On average flaw interaction causes a slight increase in the mean stress intensity factor, but the flaws need to be very close together before the increase is appreciable. Two-dimensional analyses (Lam *et al.*, 1991) show that the most probable nearest neighbour flaw must be closer than the average flaw size before the interaction causes an enhancement of more than about 10% in the stress intensity factor. The standard deviation in the stress intensity factor is about three times the mean enhancement in the mean stress intensity factor, so distortion in failure probability because of flaw interaction will only be very slight. Since it is impossible to divorce the flaw size distribution from the density of flaws, it is unnecessary to consider flaw interaction for static strength in an inert atmosphere. However, crack interaction can be significant in time dependent fracture where the rate of crack growth can be highly dependent on the stress intensity factor.

6.2.2 Strength distribution materials that exhibit R-curves

Cementitious materials have considerable crack growth resistance due to the pull-out of grains or aggregate behind a crack tip and do not fail when the first crack initiates. The effective Weibull modulus for such materials is enhanced (Kendall *et al.*, 1986). It is instructive to consider a simple model that demonstrates the enhancement in the Weibull modulus though a more rigorous model has been recently given by Duan *et al.* (1995).

As a crack propagates so generally its resistance to growth increases. The development of crack growth resistance from a flaw may not be the same as that measured with a long crack because the natural flaw is of the same dimension as the inhomogeneities causing the crack growth resistance. For the same reason there may be a variation in the crack growth resistance curve for different flaws. In this simple study of the effect of crack growth resistance it is assumed that the crack growth resistance is the same for all flaws and can be given by the power law

$$K_R = k(a - a_i)^{1/n} \qquad (6.28)$$

where a_i is the radius of the equivalent initial crack and a is its value after some crack growth and $n > 2$. The 'knee' in the K_R-curve sharpens as n increases and the limit is an ideally brittle material ($n = \infty$) that has no crack growth resistance. The general crack growth resistance expression implies that cracks start growing from flaws immediately load is applied. While in practice some stress can be sustained without crack growth the neglect of an initiation phase will not negate the qualitative conclusions. Using the criteria for unstable crack growth given in section 1.8 we obtain

$$2\sigma(a/\pi)^{1/2} = k(a - a_i)^{1/n} \qquad (6.29)$$

and

$$\frac{4\sigma^2}{\pi} = \frac{2k^2}{n(a - a_i)^{(n-2)/n}} \qquad (6.30)$$

Solving eqns 6.29 and 6.30 simultaneously gives the initial size of the equivalent crack a_i that causes instability at a stress σ

$$a_i = \left(\frac{2}{n}\right)^{2/(n-2)} \left[\frac{\pi}{4}\left(\frac{k}{\sigma}\right)^2\right]^{n/(n-2)} \left[1 - \frac{2}{n}\right] \qquad (6.31)$$

Comparing eqn 6.31 with eqn 6.15 it is seen that the strength follows the Weibull distribution with an increased modulus $m^* = mn/(n - 2)$. In the limit when $n = \infty$, $m^* = m$ and we have the Weibull distribution for an ideally brittle material. As n decreases the modulus of the distribution increases. In other words, the greater the range of the crack growth resistance curve the narrower is the range in strengths. This simple analysis demonstrates that crack growth resistance causes the strength of a material to be more reliable. Naturally, this analysis does not imply that all materials with a crack growth resistance are more reliable than those without, since the distribution of initial flaw sizes is independent of the crack growth resistance.

6.3 The statistics of heterogeneous brittle materials

In brittle homogeneous materials, fracture under uniform stress initiates at the largest flaw even if the material possesses a crack growth resistance.

Therefore failure is governed by the weakest link and can be modelled by the Weibull distribution. However, concrete and mortar are highly inhomogeneous. Many microcracks initiate before complete failure and the most severe flaw or defect in the highly stressed region is not necessarily the flaw that leads to final failure. Weibull's theory cannot therefore be applied directly to such materials (Bažant and Xi, 1991; Bažant et al., 1991). Because Weibull's theory is inappropriate, it does not necessarily follow that the probable strength of supposedly identical specimens will not be modelled approximately by the Weibull distribution. Zech and Wittmann (1977) found that the tensile strength of concrete specimens followed a Weibull distribution with a modulus, $m = 12$. However, where Weibull theory fails is in predicting the size effect (Bažant and Xi, 1991; Bažant et al., 1991; Mazars et al., 1991).

6.3.1   The fracture of two-phase brittle materials

Wittmann (1983) has pointed out that in inhomogeneous materials such as concrete, fractures can be arrested at stronger second phase particles. Under these conditions the final fracture does not necessarily initiate at the weakest link. The arrest and reinitiation of a crack in a real three-dimensional material is extremely complex. A micro-fracture nucleated at an internal flaw under tensile stress will grow as a penny-shaped flaw until it meets a second-phase particle. The propagation as a penny-shaped crack will then cease, but it may be able to continue propagation around the particle or in another direction. Here a simple two-dimensional model (Hu et al., 1985) based on an extension of the theory of Hunt and McCartney (1979) is discussed.

Consider a two-phase material in the form of a plate of unit thickness, where the second phase particles are modelled by prisms with square cross-sections with sides of length D and are randomly distributed throughout the matrix with a density, ρ_p. The elastic constants of the two phases are assumed to be similar so that the particles do not affect the stress distribution significantly. The flaws are randomly distributed in the matrix, and their size can be characterized by the length a of the equivalent Griffith crack lying normal to the maximum principal stress. It is assumed that the distribution of second phase particles and flaws are independent. The density of the flaws in the range a to $a + da$ is $q(a)\,da$. Although the density of the flaws is assumed to be sparse, there is no restriction on the density of second phase particles. Overlapping of particles is permitted. In the model a flaw may intersect a particle. Two models of the intersection have been considered: in one the flaw is bridged by the particle and in the other the particle is intersected by the flaw. Since there is little difference in these two models only the bridging model will be presented in detail.

It is assumed that a crack initiates at a flaw when the stress intensity factor at its tip reaches the fracture toughness of the matrix, K_m. When both tips of a crack meet tougher second phase particles, the crack is arrested if the stress intensity factor is less than the effective fracture toughness, K_p, of the particle. If the distance between particles is s, a crack will be arrested if

$$s < k^2 a \tag{6.32}$$

where $k = K_p/K_m$. Failure occurs when either a micro-fracture initiated at a flaw is not arrested or when an arrested crack is reinitiated. To avoid confusion, the term flaw is used for the original defect and the term crack is used for an arrested micro-fracture spanning two particles. The inequality (6.32) enables the flaws to be separated into two groups. The first group contains flaws that satisfy the inequality and are arrested, whereas the second group are not arrested. As the density of the second phase particles is reduced or if the fracture toughness of the second phase particles approaches that of the matrix, the number of flaws falling into the second group increases and the failure is governed by the weakest link. On the other hand, if the second phase particles are dense or their toughness high most flaws will be arrested and failure will be governed by the largest crack which again implies a weakest link theory. Hence, in a two-phase material, most deviation from weakest link theories will be expected for moderate densities of second-phase particles whose fracture toughness, while being higher than that of the matrix, is of the same order.

Assume that flaws are bridged by any intersecting second-phase particles. Failure can initiate from either a flaw or a crack spanning two particles. Consider first the probability of fracture initiation from a crack. Fracture occurs at the largest crack. The probability that a crack whose length is between s and $s + ds$, and which lies within a strip of width dy, has a particle centred within the small elements shaded in Figure 6.4 is $(\rho_p D \, ds)^2$, and the probability that there are no other particles intersecting the crack is $\exp[-\rho_p D(s + D)]$. Hence, the joint probability $F(s, D) \, ds^2$ that there are

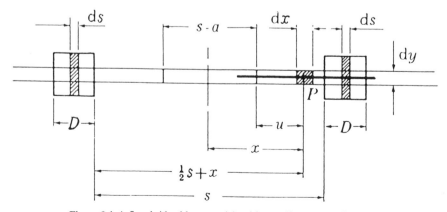

Figure 6.4 A flaw bridged by a particle with an adjacent arresting particle.

just two particles, of distance $s + D$ apart, that just touch the crack is given by

$$F(s, D) = (\rho_p D)^2 \exp[-\rho_p D(s + D)] \tag{6.33}$$

The shortest flaw centred at P (see Figure 6.4) that just intersects both particles to form a crack is $s + 2x$. Therefore, the probability that a crack is formed by a flaw centred within the element $dx\,dy$ at P which intersects both particles is

$$\int_{s+2x}^{\infty} q(a)\,da(dx\,dy) \tag{6.34}$$

and the probability $H(s)\,dy$ that a flaw centred anywhere along the thin strip of width dy intersects both particles is given by

$$H(s) = 2 \int_{0}^{\infty} \int_{s+2x}^{\infty} q(a)\,da\,dx \tag{6.35}$$

A fracture initiated at a flaw smaller than s, but larger than s/k^2, will be arrested by the two particles to form a crack. A flaw of length a will not touch either particle if its centre is within a median strip of length $(s - a)$ (see Figure 6.4). Hence, the probability of finding a flaw whose length is in the range a to $a + da$ and which does not touch either particle is

$$q(a)(s - a)\,da\,dy \tag{6.36}$$

In addition, a flaw centred within a small element $dx\,dy$ at P can be bridged, by the particle on the right, to form an effective flaw of length between a and $a + da$ if x is greater than $(s - a)/2$. The probability of finding such a flaw in the element $dx\,dy$ at P is

$$q(a + 2u)\,da(dx\,dy) \tag{6.37}$$

and the probability of finding one in both strips of width dy extending to infinity is

$$2 \int_{0}^{\infty} q(a + 2u)\,du(dx\,dy) \tag{6.38}$$

Therefore, the probability $Q(a, s)\,da\,dy$ of finding a flaw whose effective size is in the range a to $a + da$ in the total strip of width dy, is given by

$$Q(a, s) = \left[q(a)(s - a) + 2 \int_{0}^{\infty} q(a + 2u)\,du \right] \tag{6.39}$$

and the probability $E(s)\,dy$ that a micro-fracture initiated from such a flaw can be arrested to form a crack is given by

$$E(s) = \int_{s/k^2}^{s} Q(a, s)\,da \tag{6.40}$$

The probability $f(s)\,ds$ of finding a crack of length between s and $s + ds$ within a unit area of the plate is given by

$$f(s) = F(s, D)[E(s) + H(s)] \tag{6.41}$$

The derivation of the probability of fracture from a crack at a given stress level follows directly from Hunt and McCartney (1979) as outlined in section 6.2.2. A fracture will be initiated from a crack if s is greater than a critical value given by

$$s(\sigma) = \frac{2}{\pi}\left(\frac{K_p}{\sigma}\right)^2 \tag{6.42}$$

Hence, the probability $P_c(\sigma)$ that failure will occur at a stress σ or less is given by

$$P_c(\sigma) = 1 - \exp\left[-V\int_{s(\sigma)}^{\infty} f(s)\,ds\right] \tag{6.43}$$

The last step is to consider the probability of failure by a fracture initiated at a flaw that is not arrested by adjacent particles. A fracture initiated at a flaw will continue to propagate through the second phase particle if the inequality (6.32) is not satisfied. Hence, the probability $b(a)\,da$ of finding a flaw (within a unit area of the plate) of size between a and $a + da$ that is not arrested is given by

$$b(a) = \int_{k^2a}^{\infty} P(s, D)Q(a, s)\,ds \tag{6.44}$$

The probability $P_f(\sigma)$ of failure by fracture from a flaw at a stress σ can be obtained in the same manner as the probability $P_c(\sigma)$ of failure by fracture from a crack and is given by

$$P_f(\sigma) = 1 - \exp\left[-V\int_{a(\sigma)}^{\infty} b(a)\,da\right] \tag{6.45}$$

where $a(\sigma) = (2/\pi)(K_m/\sigma)^2$.

The probability $P(\sigma)$ of failure by either mechanism can be obtained from the joint probabilities of survival of the two modes of failure and is given by

$$P(\sigma) = 1 - [1 - P_c(\sigma)][1 - P_f(\sigma)]$$

$$= 1 - \exp\left\{-V\left[\int_{s(\sigma)}^{\infty} f(s)\,ds + \int_{a(\sigma)}^{\infty} b(a)\,da\right]\right\} \tag{6.46}$$

The calculation of the probability of failure assuming flaws cut any intersecting particle is similar to the above analysis (Hu et al., 1985). The probability of failure has exactly the same form as eqn 6.46 except that in the cutting case

$$b(a) = q(a)\{[\rho_p D(k^2 - 1)a - 1]\exp(-\rho_p D^2) + 2\}$$
$$\times \exp\{-\rho_p D[(k^2 - 1)a + D]\} \quad (6.47)$$

The failure probability for two phase materials has been calculated (Hu et al., 1985) assuming that the flaw size is given by the Pareto distribution (eqn 6.27). If it is assumed that the flaws cut the second-phase particles, then the Weibull distribution is recovered as the limiting case when the fracture toughness of the particles approaches that of the matrix. The bridging case has a slightly different limit, because the bridging particles alter the effective flaw size distribution.

Results are presented for two different particle densities of 250 and 1500 per unit volume each with a sparse distribution of flaws of 10 per unit volume. The flaw size has a Pareto distribution with $m = 10$, and $a_0 = 0.064$; the size of the second phase particles is taken as $D = 0.02$. Typical flaw and particle distributions generated randomly by computer are shown in Figure 6.5. Considerable overlapping of the particles occurs at the higher density, and the volume fraction is considerably less than the indicated 0.6. The probability that no particles occupy the volume of a particle is $\exp(-\rho D^2)$. Hence, the probable volume fraction of the matrix in the two-phase material is

$$v_m = \exp(-\rho_p D^2) \quad (6.48)$$

and the volume of the second-phase particles is

$$v_p = 1 - v_m = 1 - \exp(-\rho_p D^2) \quad (6.49)$$

Therefore, the actual volume fractions of the second-phase particles in the two materials shown in Figure 6.5 are 0.095 and 0.45, compared with the indicated values of 0.1 and 0.6, respectively.

The failure probability for a material with a density of 250 second-phase particles per unit volume is shown in Figure 6.6 for a specimen 20 times the unit volume for a matrix with unit fracture toughness with the ratio $K_p/K_m = 4$. The strong second-phase particles significantly increase the strength of the material. Because few flaws are intersected at the comparatively low density of flaws, the results for the model that assumes the flaws cut through the intersecting particles are very similar to the bridging model. At higher flaw or second-phase particle densities there is more difference between the two models, with the bridging model giving the highest strengths. For example, the mean strength for the bridging model of a 20-volume specimen ($K_p/K_m = 4$), with a density of particles of 1500, is 19% greater than a similar specimen where it is assumed that the flaws cut through the intersecting particles.

There is no synergistic coupling between the flaws and the particles in the model and the increase in mean strength of the two-phase material is

(a)

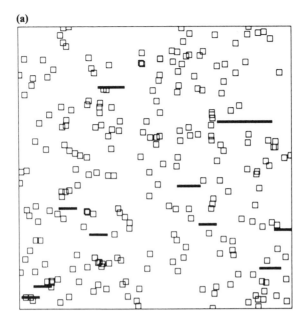

(b)

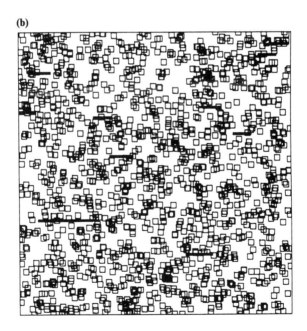

Figure 6.5 Computer simulation of a unit volume with two densities of particles: (a) $\rho_p = 250$, (b) $\rho_p = 1500$; $\rho = 10$, $m = 10$, $a_0 = 0.064$, and $D = 0.02$.

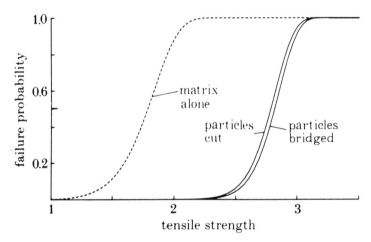

Figure 6.6 Failure probability of a two-phase material ($\rho_p = 250$, $\rho = 10$, $m = 10$, $a_0 = 0.064$, $D = 0.02$, $K_p/K_m = 4$, and $V = 20$).

very close to the value obtained from the rule of mixtures. Assuming that the specific work of fracture of the two-phase material is given by the rule of mixtures, the average fracture toughness K_c based on energy considerations is

$$K_c = [(1 - v_p)K_m^2 + v_p K_p^2]^{1/2} \tag{6.50}$$

The flaw size distribution for the model, where the particles are cut by the intersecting flaws, is unaffected by the second phase. In the bridging model, the distortion of the flaw size distribution only occurs at high particle/flaw ratios. Thus it can be assumed that the mean fracture strength is

$$\bar{\sigma} = K_c \sqrt{2/(\pi \bar{a})} \tag{6.51}$$

where $\bar{a}$ is the mean flaw size. Hence, according to the rule of mixtures,

$$\bar{\sigma}/\bar{\sigma}_m = [(1 - v_p) + v_p(K_p/K_m)^2]^{1/2} \tag{6.52}$$

where $\bar{\sigma}_m$ is the mean strength of the matrix. For a second-phase volume fraction of 0.95 and $K_p/K_m = 4$, the ratio in the strength of the two-phase material to the matrix, according to the rule of mixtures, is 1.56, which compares closely with the value 1.57 obtained from the statistical model for a 20-volume specimen where the intersecting particles are cut. Naturally, the maximum discrepancy between the rule of mixtures and the statistical model occurs at a second-phase volume fraction of about 0.5 when it is 13% for a 20-volume specimen. The discrepancy increases with specimen size, because as the size gets bigger it is the extreme of the flaw size distribution that dominates.

The rule of mixtures applies equally well to three dimensions as to two. Hence, the agreement between the rule of mixtures and the statistical model suggests that the model, while a two-dimensional one, has relevance for real three-dimensional materials.

Since failure does not generally occur until a number of cracks are formed, it is possible to calculate the expected number of cracks in a specimen. In counting the number of cracks, those formed because a flaw is bridged by two particles will be excluded. Cracks can only form from flaws that are bigger than the critical size $a(\sigma)$ for that stress level. The expected number of flaws $N_f(\sigma)$ that are bigger than this size and not touching two particles is given by

$$N_f(\sigma) = V \int_{a(\sigma)}^{\infty} q^*(a)\, da \qquad (6.53)$$

where $q^*(a)$ differs from $q(a)$, because some flaws are bridged to form smaller flaws and is given by

$$q^*(\sigma) = \int_{a}^{\infty} F(s, D) Q(a, s)\, ds \qquad (6.54)$$

if the flaws are bridged by intersecting particles and by

$$q^*(a) = q(a)\{1 - [1 - \exp(-\rho_p D^2)]^2\} \qquad (6.55)$$

if the flaws cut the bridging particles.

The first micro-fracture from a flaw not arrested would cause failure, and so we must exclude from our count of the number of flaws that are initiated those that would not be arrested, because we know *a priori* that these could not have existed in the specimen. The number of flaws M_f that would not be arrested is given by

$$M_f = V \int_{a(\sigma)}^{\infty} b(a)\, da \qquad (6.56)$$

Hence, the expected number of cracks, N_c, to be formed when a specimen is stressed is given by

$$N_c = V \int_{a(\sigma)}^{\infty} [q^*(a) - b(a)]\, da \qquad (6.57)$$

The number of cracks expected to form before failure in a 20-volume specimen is shown in Figure 6.7 as a function of the stress level. As is to be expected, more cracks form in the material where the flaws cut intersecting particles. The total number of flaws in the sample volume is 200. The ability of the model to predict the development of microcracks is probably more important than its ability to predict the probability of fracture, which can always be empirically modelled by the Weibull distribution.

The analysis for uniaxially stressed specimens can be extended to bending and other inhomogeneously stressed specimens. As before, the specimen is divided into small elements each small enough to contain at most a single

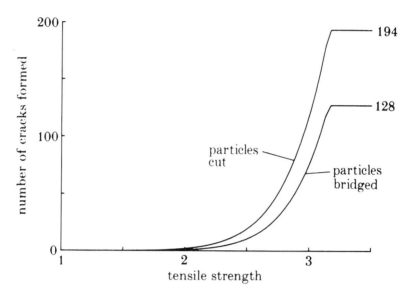

Figure 6.7 Number of cracks formed in a two-phase material ($\rho_p = 250$, $\rho = 10$, $m = 10$, $a_0 = 0.064$, $D = 0.02$, $K_p/K_m = 4$, and $V = 20$).

flaw. It is also assumed that the variation of stress across the average particle spacing is small.

The stress in a rectangular beam under pure bending at any element r, whose distance from the neutral axis line is given by

$$\sigma_r = \sigma_{\max} u \tag{6.58}$$

where $\sigma_{\max}$ is the maximum stress at the surface of the beam and $u = 2y/W$ is the non-dimensional position of the element. It is assumed that fracture only occurs in the tension half of the beam. The probability $P_y(\sigma_y)$ that the element at a distance y from the neutral axis fails at a stress less than or equal to σ_y is given by

$$P_r(\sigma_r) = 1 - \exp - \left[\int_{s(\sigma_r)}^{\infty} f(s)\,ds + \int_{a(\sigma_r)}^{\infty} b(a)\,da \right] dV \tag{6.59}$$

Hence, the probability of failure of the beam at a maximum stress equal to or less than $\sigma_{\max}$, $P(\sigma_{\max}, V)$, is given by

$$P(\sigma_{\max}, V) = 1 - \exp - \frac{V}{2} \int_0^1 \left[\int_{s(\sigma_r)}^{\infty} f(s)\,ds + \int_{a(\sigma_r)}^{\infty} b(a)\,da \right] du \tag{6.60}$$

The bending/tensile strength ratio for two-phase materials whose flaw size is given by the Pareto distribution is shown in Figure 6.8. The two-phase material shows a decrease in strength ratio as the specimen size increases, unlike a single-phase material. However, the decrease in strength ratio may not be entirely due to the presence of a second phase. The strength ratio

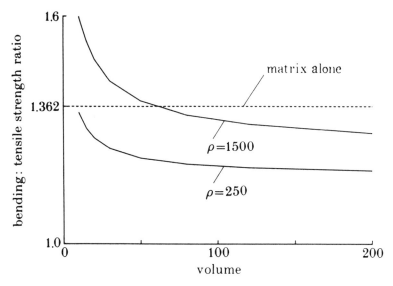

Figure 6.8 Bending-tensile strength ratio as a function of the size of a two-phase material $(\rho_p = 250, \rho = 10, m = 10, a_0 = 0.064, D = 0.02, K_p/K_m = 4)$.

for a single-phase material whose flaw size distribution has a faster rate of decay with size than an inverse power law also shows a ratio that decreases with specimen size. A single-phase material with a flaw size following the Laplacian distribution is shown in Figure 6.9, where the decrease in strength

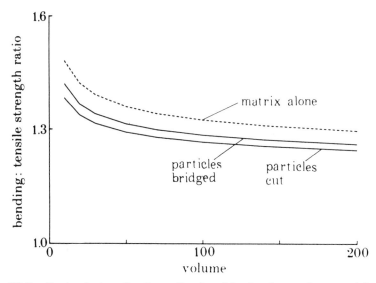

Figure 6.9 Bending-tensile strength ratio as a function of the size of a two-phase material where the flaws have a Laplacian size distribution $(\rho_p = 250, \rho = 10, m = 10, \bar{a} = 0.08, D = 0.02, K_p/K_m = 4)$.

ratio is similar to that for a two-phase material whose flaw size follows the Pareto distribution and where the mean flaw size is the same.

6.3.2 Computer simulation of fracture in concrete modelled as a two-phase material

The above analysis shows that when a second phase is introduced in a brittle material the first crack does not necessarily lead to immediate fracture. Many cracks may form in the specimen as the stress increases before final failure. However, in a large specimen when an arrested crack is reinitiated at a second-phase particle, the fracture is then completely unstable. In practice, small cementitious specimens tested in a stiff testing machine can fracture stably. However, microcracks can form unstably. A fracture formed by a succession of microcracks that propagate unstably and are then arrested, absorbs more energy than one that propagates stably, and hence it has a higher fracture toughness. The second phase need not be actually tougher than the matrix to arrest a microcrack. Weak interfaces normal to the expected crack path can form efficient crack arrestors by the Cook–Gordon (1964) mechanism. Tensile fractures in concrete initiate primarily from flaws in aggregate/mortar interfaces and propagate through the mortar matrix until they meet another aggregate/mortar interface, when they usually propagate around the interface rather than across the aggregate (Mindess, 1983). Concrete has a higher fracture toughness than the constituent parts of the fracture path. The fracture toughness of mortar is about $0.6\,\mathrm{MPa}\sqrt{m}$ and the toughness of the aggregate/mortar interface is only about $0.2\,\mathrm{MPa}\sqrt{m}$, whereas concrete has a toughness of about $1\,\mathrm{MPa}\sqrt{m}$ (Ziegeldorf, 1983). The fracture surface in concrete is very rough and the true surface area is greater than the projected area. Some of the toughness of concrete certainly comes from the additional fracture surface area, but a significant portion comes from unstable propagation of micro-fractures releasing energy in elastic waves.

In the analysis presented here (Hu *et al.*, 1986a) the growth of a fracture through the mortar and around the aggregate is followed by computer simulation similar to that used by Zaitsev (1983). The model is two-dimensional. The material parameters are based on the experimental results of Horvath and Petersson (1984). The concrete is composed of a matrix with a polygonal shaped aggregate of four to six edges whose Young's modulus is the same as that of the mortar. It is assumed that the corners of the aggregate lie on a circle that determines the size of the aggregate. The distribution in size between two limits d_{min} and d_{max} is assumed to be uniform, though any other distribution is possible. The number of sides is chosen randomly between four and six and the corners of the aggregate are positioned randomly. The centres of the aggregates are positioned randomly until the volume fraction reaches the required value; if two aggregates overlap a new choice is made for its centre. It is assumed that mortar/aggregate interface flaws dominate and that there is at most one interface on each aggregate. Every specimen is assumed to have the same number of flaws. When the number of aggregates in a specimen have been determined, the probability, p, that any aggregate has a flaw is calculated. To determine whether a particular aggregate has a flaw, a random number between 0 and 1 is generated and if this number is less than p, a flaw is assigned to the aggregate. The face on which the flaw appears is chosen randomly. A typical specimen of the two-dimensional model is shown in Figure 6.10(a).

Cracks are assumed to propagate either along the mortar/aggregate interface or in the mortar in a direction perpendicular to the applied stress. In an isotropic homogeneous brittle material a crack will grow so that there is local symmetry at its tip and the mode II stress intensity factor zero (see section 1.7.1). After being deflected by an aggregate the crack path will curve so that it becomes normal to the applied stress. Hence, the assumption that it always propagates normal to the applied stress will not

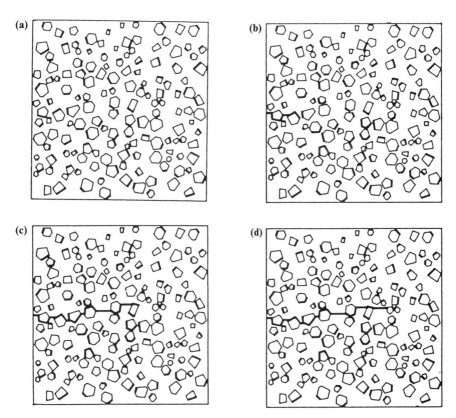

Figure 6.10 Crack development in a sample 100×100 mm two-dimensional concrete model: (a) before loading; (b) at maximum load; (c) after large load drop; (d) final failure.

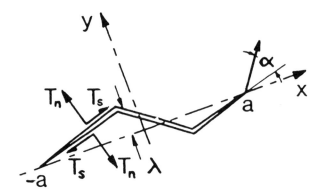

Figure 6.11 Crack configuration.

introduce a significant or systematic error. Since K_{II} is not necessarily zero, it is assumed that the crack grows when the modulus of the effective stress intensity factor, K_e, which is given by

$$K_e = (K_I^2 + K_{II}^2)^{1/2} \qquad (6.61)$$

is greater than the fracture toughness of either the mortar or the mortar/aggregate interface. It is assumed that there is no interaction between cracks and, since the mortar and aggregate have the same modulus, the aggregate does not disturb the stress distribution. The stress intensity factors are calculated from a first order solution for kinked or curved cracks (Cotterell and Rice, 1980) and for the tip at the right of the crack shown in Figure 6.11

$$K_I - iK_{II} = \frac{1}{\sqrt{\pi a}} \int_{-a}^{a} (q_I - iq_{II}) \left(\frac{a+t}{a-t}\right)^{1/2} dt \qquad (6.62a)$$

where

$$q_I = T_n - \tfrac{3}{2}\lambda'(a)T_s + \lambda(x)T_s + 2\lambda'(x)T_s \qquad (6.62b)$$

$$q_{II} = T_s + \lambda(x)T_n + \tfrac{1}{2}\lambda'(a)T_n \qquad (6.62c)$$

and T_n, T_s are the normal and shear tractions at the crack surfaces and $\lambda(x)$ describes the crack profile; the prime indicates a derivative with respect to x. This first order solution is accurate to within 5% if the slope $\lambda'(x)$ is less than 15°. The expression for the stress intensity factor at the left-hand tip is similar. For a small kink at the mortar/aggregate interface, the stress intensity factor is given by

$$\begin{bmatrix} K_I \\ K_{II} \end{bmatrix} = \begin{bmatrix} C_{11} & C_{12} \\ C_{21} & C_{22} \end{bmatrix} \begin{bmatrix} k_I \\ k_{II} \end{bmatrix} \qquad (6.63)$$

where k_I, k_II are the mode I and mode II stress intensity factors at the tip of the crack before it kinks, and

$$
\begin{aligned}
C_{11} &= \tfrac{1}{4}[3\cos\alpha/2 + \cos 3\alpha/2] \\
C_{12} &= -\tfrac{3}{4}[\sin\alpha/2 + \sin 3\alpha/2] \\
C_{21} &= \tfrac{1}{4}[\sin\alpha/2 + \sin 3\alpha/2] \\
C_{22} &= \tfrac{1}{4}[\cos\alpha/2 + 3\sin 3\alpha/2]
\end{aligned}
\tag{6.64}
$$

The expressions given above are for cracks in infinite plates and have been modified for cracks that are near to or intersect an edge, assuming that the geometrical correction factors applied to cracks normal to the applied stress in finite plates can be applied to the kinked cracks if the projected length of the crack a_p is used (Hu *et al.*, 1986a).

If the stress is increased incrementally the history of the crack development can be traced. When the stress intensity factor at any crack tip exceeds the fracture toughness, the crack will grow unstably until it meets an aggregate. At this stage the crack may be arrested if the aggregate/mortar interface is at a low angle to the applied stress, or it may propagate along the mortar/aggregate interface and into the mortar once more. Under these conditions the ultimate strength of the specimen will be reached when one crack propagates unstably right across the specimen. If the specimen is loaded in a rigid machine under fixed grip conditions, there will be a decrease in stress as a crack propagates. This reduction in stress can cause a crack to arrest that would have otherwise caused failure under constant stress and it is possible for failure to occur after the maximum load. Before the maximum load is reached there will be many growing cracks, but afterwards localization occurs. In this model, the size of the specimen is necessarily small and the fracture process localizes to a single crack.

The extension of the specimen can be calculated from the increase in strain energy due to the growing cracks. The strain energy stored per unit thickness in a specimen of width W and length L is

$$
\Lambda = \frac{\sigma^2}{2E}WL + \sum_{i=1}^{n}\int_0^{s_i} G_i\,\mathrm{d}s
\tag{6.65}
$$

where

$$
G_i = \frac{(1-\nu^2)}{E}K_\mathrm{e}^2
\tag{6.66}
$$

is the plane strain crack extension force for the ith crack and the integral is taken along the crack. For the purpose of calculating the stress-displacement relationship, it is sufficiently accurate to replace the real crack by a straight

Table 6.1 Mechanical properties of model aggregate

Young's modulus (GPa)	Poisson's ratio	Fracture toughness (MPa$\sqrt{m}$)	
		mortar	mortar/aggregate
27	0.25	0.6	0.2

crack equal in length to the projected crack length, a_p. Hence

$$G_i = \frac{(1 - \nu^2)}{E} F_i^2 \sigma^2 \pi a_{ip} \tag{6.67}$$

and the strain energy stored becomes

$$\Lambda = \frac{\sigma^2}{2E} WL + \frac{(1 - \nu^2)}{4E} \sigma^2 \pi \sum_{i=1}^{n} \bar{F}_i a_{ip}^2 \tag{6.68}$$

where $\bar{F}_i$ is the average value of the finite width correction factor for the ith crack. The stress-displacement $(\sigma - \Delta L)$ relationship

$$\sigma = \frac{E \Delta L}{L} \left[1 + \frac{(1 - \nu^2)}{2WL} \pi \sum_{i=1}^{n} \bar{F}_i^2 a_{ip}^2 \right]^{-1} \tag{6.69}$$

is obtained by equating the strain energy stored to the work done.

The fracture energy, G_f, can be calculated from the area under the stress-elongation curve. Some of the work of fracture goes into forming micro-cracks away from the pupative fracture plane. The work done away from the fracture plane, which is quite small in the small samples that have been modelled here, has been excluded by taking a line parallel to the initial linear response of the specimen through the point of maximum stress and calculating the fracture energy, G_F, from the area of the stress-displacement curve to the right of this line.

The material properties used in the computer simulation of fracture are given in Table 6.1. To study the statistical distribution in strength and toughness, 60 computer experiments were performed. A typical stress-displacement curve (based on the specimen shown in Figure 6.10a) is shown in Figure 6.12. The corresponding crack development is shown in Figure 6.10b–d. The distribution in fracture strength for a 100×100 mm specimen is shown in Figure 6.13. Because the distribution in initial flaw size is small, the distribution in the stress at which the first crack occurs is narrow. The aggregate almost doubles the mean strength of the concrete. The reduction in stress intensity factor caused by the deflection of the crack path by the aggregate causes arrest, despite the toughness of the interfaces being considerably less than the matrix. In the comparatively small specimens modelled here, there is a wide range in the tensile strengths. The fracture toughness of the concrete has been calculated from the fracture

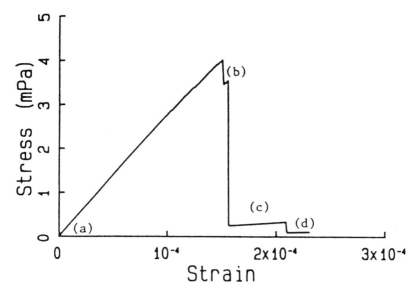

Figure 6.12 The stress-displacement curve for the specimen shown in Figure 6.10.

energy and is shown in Figure 6.14. The mean fracture toughness is 0.97 MPa$\sqrt{}$m which is very close to experimentally observed values. There is a large variation in fracture toughness in line with the large variation in strength. The excellent agreement between the calculated value and the experimentally determined value is to some extent fortuitous, but the

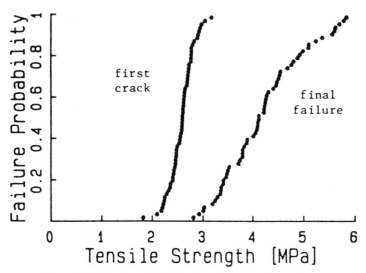

Figure 6.13 The strength distribution of the concrete specimens.

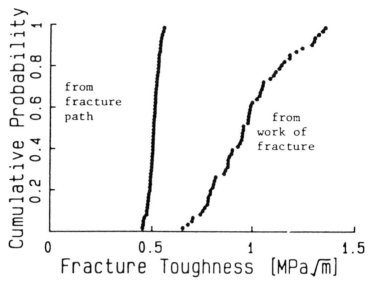

Figure 6.14 The fracture toughness distribution of the concrete specimens.

model does show that the arrest of unstable microcracks can be a significant source of toughness in concrete.

6.4 Statistics and size effect in cementitious materials

Fracture in cementitious materials is preceded by the formation of a localized strain-softened FPZ either at a notch, stress concentration, or defect. Since the size of the FPZ is large, a defect in an otherwise smooth component only locates the position for strain localization without significantly altering the strength. It is the condition of the material at the pupative FPZ that controls the fracture strength. Before the maximum load is reached, micro-cracking in a smooth component will occur outside the pupative FPZ, but such microcracking plays no significant part in the fracture process.

Mazars *et al.* (1991) have used the concept of damage to analyse the fracture of cementitious materials. In this concept, the stiffness of an element decreases from its virgin value to zero as the damage, D, increases from zero to unity. They assume that no damage occurs until the strain reaches a threshold value. After the threshold has been reached, it is assumed that damage increases with non-local strain. With a deterministic threshold for strain this approach gives similar results to other non-local damage models. However, Mazars *et al.* (1991) found that with a deterministic threshold to damage the strength of small beams was underestimated. By introducing a probabilistic threshold strain for damage that is based on

Weibull theory they obtain better agreement with experimental data. A probabilistic threshold for damage has little effect on the predicted strength variation for the larger beams.

Bažant and Xi (1991) have also considered the effect of statistical variation on the size effect law (Bažant et al., 1986). They argue that there are two asymptotic limits to the SEL for notched bend specimens: for large beams where the FPZ is small compared with the size of the beam, the variation in strength follows LEFM and $\sigma_N \propto W^{-1/2}$; for small beams where the FPZ dominates, the strength is according to the Weibull distribution and $\sigma_N \propto W^{-n/m}$, where n is the number of spatial dimensions. Bažant and Xi (1991) also give a simple empirical equation

$$\sigma_N = \frac{Bf_t}{\sqrt{\beta^{2n/m} + \beta}} \tag{6.70}$$

that has these limits. A more exact SEL can be obtained from the fictitious crack line model (Cotterell et al., 1995).

The FPZ has a narrow flame-like shape with a maximum width that is not very size dependent (Bažant and Lin, 1988). Hence, for the purpose of determining the statistical strain-softening characteristics, the FPZ is assumed to be a narrow zone, whose width is a material constant independent of the size of the specimen. Outside of the FPZ, it is assumed that the material is elastic and suffers no damage even in any region of high compressive stress. Once the strain-softening relationship is determined, the FPZ is modelled by a fictitious extension to the true crack. A simple linear stress-displacement relationship is chosen for the strain-softening behaviour of the FPZ. As the FPZ grows so its chance of encountering a zone of weakness increases and the average stress carried will diminish. To avoid using a stochastic method, it is assumed that the stress threshold, f_t, necessary to initiate strain-softening depends on the volume, V_p, of the FPZ, and is proportional to the Weibull mean strength so that

$$\frac{f_t}{f_0} = \left(\frac{V_{p0}}{V_p} \right)^{1/m} \tag{6.71}$$

where f_0 is the stress threshold for a standard FPZ of volume, V_{p0}. The fracture energy of cementitious materials, G_{If}, is usually assumed to be a material constant independent of size. Experiments indicate that in fact the fracture energy increases with specimen size (see section 3.5) and this increase in fracture energy with size must to some extent offset the decrease in f_t. However, here the fracture energy, G_{If}, is assumed to be a constant. Thus, combined with the assumption that the stress-displacement relationship is linear, the critical crack tip opening displacement δ_f is given by

$$\delta_f = \frac{2G_{If}}{f_t} \tag{6.72}$$

The statistical effect of size on the strength of three-point bend specimens has been obtained using the fictitious crack model and the K-superposition theory (Cotterell *et al.*, 1995). The faces of the fictitious crack are assumed to be straight, so that only the CTOD or the length of the fictitious crack, d_p, are unknown. Since the stress in the FPZ depends on its size, it is easiest to drive the program with the length of the fictitious crack, d_p. The values of the beam depth, W, initial notch depth, a_0, and, d_p, together with an initial guess of the crack tip opening displacement, δ_i, are used to calculate the load from the condition that the total stress intensity factor at the fictitious crack tip shall be zero, taking into account the variation in the mean ultimate strength of the cementitious material determined by eqn 6.71. An iterative routine similar to subroutine PROFILE shown in Figure 4.10 is used to find the actual value of the crack tip opening displacement, and then another subroutine calculates the corresponding load. A further subroutine finds the maximum load sustainable by the beam. In all cases maximum load occurs for $\delta_t < \delta_f$, though as the beam depth increases, so δ_t increases and approaches δ_f in the limit.

Since it has been argued that mortar and concrete do not follow Weibull's theory, supposed measurements of the Weibull modulus directly from a plot of eqn 6.13 cannot give the exact value for eqn 6.71. However, it is thought that Weibull moduli of 10 and 20 which bound the value measured by Zech and Wittmann (1977) are realistic bounds for cementitious materials. Three different classes of beams have been analysed:

(i) Beams with deterministic strain-softening characteristics ($m = \infty$).
(ii) Beams of constant width, $m = 20, 10$.
(iii) Beams whose width is proportional to their depth, $m = 20, 10$.

All the results have been normalized by the strength and size of the beams whose non-dimensional depth (W/l_{ch}) is unity.

Two sets of beams have been analysed. In the first beam the relative notch depth, a_0/W, is 0.3 and a logarithmic plot of the normalized strength against the normalized beam depth is shown in Figure 6.15. There is little statistical effect in large notched specimens because the FPZ is almost fully developed at final fracture and it is small compared with the notch size. Under these conditions it is the fracture energy, G_{If}, that controls the fracture not the stress-displacement relationship. In the limit for an infinitely large beam, the fracture occurs when

$$K_a = (EG_{If})^{1/2} \tag{6.73}$$

and the slope of the logarithmic plot tends to $-\frac{1}{2}$ as the beam size increases, as predicted by the size effect law (Bažant *et al.*, 1986). For small specimens fracture occurs before the FPZ has developed very much and the FPZ is comparable or even larger than the length of the notch. Under these conditions the actual strain-softening relationship is unimportant. Since

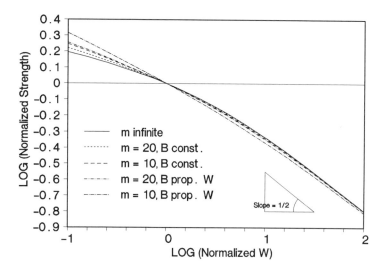

Figure 6.15 Normalized strength of notched beams $a_0/W = 0.3$.

physically the size of the FPZ must decrease as the specimens get smaller, the strength of small specimens is statistically greater than indicated from a deterministic model. Obviously, if the width of the specimens is in proportion to their depth then the increase in strength is greater than if the width of the specimens is kept constant, because the decrease in FPZ volume is greater.

These results are very similar to those given by the approximate relationship (see eqn 6.70) of Bažant and Xi (1991). However, here n is interpreted somewhat differently, and is taken as 2 for full geometric similarity and 1 for beams of constant width.

The second set of beams analysed is representative of plain, un-notched, beams. Because of a fundamental difference in the behaviour of notched and plain beams, a true un-notched beam cannot be analysed. In a notched beam, a FPZ starts to form immediately load is applied to the beam but, in a plain beam, a FPZ does not initiate until the maximum elastic stress attains the critical stress, f_t. If this stress is given by eqn 6.71, the critical stress is infinite at the initiation of a FPZ and the strength of the beam is infinite. In practice the inhomogeneity, inherent in cementitious materials, will lead to an early initiation of a FPZ. This early stage in the formation of a FPZ is not important and results have been obtained for beams that have a small defect or crack whose absolute size is the same for all beams. The non-dimensional defect size chosen is 10^{-2}, so that the smallest beam ($\bar{W} = 0.1$) has a defect whose relative size is $a_0/W = 10^{-1}$, and the largest beam ($\bar{W} = 100$) has a defect with $a/W = 10^{-4}$. A logarithmic plot of the normalized strength of such beams is shown in Figure 6.16. The beams whose strain-softening characteristics are deterministic tend to a non-dimensional strength of unity as they get larger. The slight dip in strength

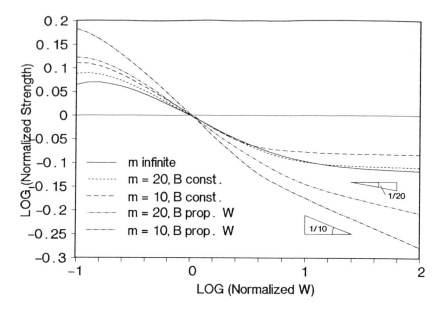

Figure 6.16 Normalized strength of 'plain' beams.

of these deterministic beams for $\bar{W} < 0.16$ is caused by the assumed defect, for a perfect beam the strength would continue to increase. The effect on the mean strength of the statistical strain-softening relationship is much more marked in these 'plain' specimens. The strength of the small specimens is increased by the statistical variation, as was the case for the notched beams shown in Figure 6.15. The size of the FPZ for 'plain' beams reaches its most developed state for near unit sized beams and then decreases to an asymptotic value as the beams increase in size. If the width of the beams is constant, the volume of the FPZ decreases causing the statistical mean strength of the large beams to be larger than the deterministic ones. However, the length of the FPZ decreases less slowly than the depth of the beam increases. Thus, if the width of the beam is kept in proportion to the depth of the beam, the FPZ increases in volume with size and the statistical strength is less than the deterministic value. For large beams the length of the FPZ is constant and the volume, therefore, in proportion to the depth of the beam. Thus, for beams whose width is in proportion to their depth, the slope of the logarithmic plot of strength against beam size tends to $-1/m$. This latter asymptotic trend was also noted by Mazars et al. (1991).

6.5 The statistics of fibre reinforced cementitious materials

Fibre reinforced cementitious materials form a diverse group from steel bar reinforced concrete, where in tension most of the load is taken by the reinforcement, through continuous fibre reinforced materials, where the fibres take a very significant portion of the load and cause multiple cracking, to short fibre reinforced materials, that do not greatly increase the strength of the cementitious material, but whose main purpose is to provide toughness as the fibres pull-out. Hence, the statistical behaviour is diverse. In the extreme case where there is a high density of strong continuous fibres, it is the strength of the fibres that determines the strength of the composite, so classic bundle theory is considered first.

6.5.1   The strength of bundles

In bundle theory it is usually assumed that the stress-elongation curve of each fibre is identical, but that the strength of each fibre is distributed according to some cumulative probability function $P(\sigma)$ (Daniels, 1945, 1989). The load F carried by the bundle of fibres, assuming that each fibre carries the same stress, σ, is given by

$$F = \sigma A N \tag{6.74}$$

where A is the cross-sectional area of each fibre and N is the number of fibres remaining intact. The expected number of fibres intact at a stress σ is given by

$$N = N_0[1 - P(\sigma)] \tag{6.75}$$

where N_0 is the number of fibres in the bundle. The expected strength of the bundle occurs when the differential of the force F sustained by the bundle is zero, or

$$\frac{\mathrm{d}F}{\mathrm{d}\sigma} = 0 = AN_0\{[1 - P(\sigma^*)] - \sigma^* P(\sigma^*)\} \tag{6.76}$$

The distribution in the actual number of fibres intact, at the fibre stress, σ^*, that gives the maximum bundle stress, is a binomial one which tends to a normal distribution as the number of fibres becomes large. However, the mean maximum strength only converges very slowly to the asymptotic value given by

$$\mu(\sigma^*) = \sigma^*[1 - P(\sigma^*)] \tag{6.77}$$

and Daniels (1989) has given a correction term for the asymptotic value that is correct within the $O(N^{-1/3})$. For large N the expected maximum strength, σ_b, is given by

$$\sigma_b = \mu(\sigma^*) + 0.99615N^{-2/3}[\mu(\sigma^*)]^{2/3}[-\mu''(\sigma^*)]^{-1/3} \tag{6.78}$$

where $\mu''(\sigma)$ is the second derivative with respect to σ. The standard deviation in the maximum strength has no distortion and is given by

$$s_b = \sigma^* \left\{ \frac{P(\sigma^*)[1 - P(\sigma^*)]}{N_0} \right\}^{1/2} \tag{6.79}$$

As is intuitively obvious, the variation in strength of a bundle decreases as the number of fibres is increased. If the strength of each fibre is assumed to be given by the Weibull distribution,

$$P(\sigma) = 1 - \exp - \frac{l}{l_0} \left(\frac{\sigma}{\sigma_0} \right)^m \tag{6.80}$$

the stress, σ^*, in each fibre at the expected strength of the bundle is given by

$$\sigma^* = \sigma_0 \left(\frac{l_0}{ml} \right)^{1/m} \tag{6.81}$$

Hence, the expected bundle strength for a large number of fibres is given by

$$\sigma_b = \sigma_0 \left(\frac{l_0}{ml} \right)^{1/m} [1 + 0.99615 N^{-2/3} \exp(2/3m)] \exp -(1/m) \tag{6.82}$$

The expected strength is always less than the average strength of an individual fibre and it is only when the Weibull modulus, m, becomes large that expected strength approaches the average strength of the fibres. Although the number of fibres in a bundle dominates the variation in the strength of the bundle, the standard deviation is also dependent on the Weibull modulus.

6.5.2   Type I continuous fibre reinforced cementitious materials

In Type I reinforced composites the fibres alone can more than withstand the load necessary to crack the matrix, and multiple matrix cracks form. The behaviour of these composites depends on the spacing, L_m (see eqn 3.61), of the multiple cracks. The spacing of matrix cracks is determined by two key parameters (Curtin, 1991; Phoenix, 1993)

$$\Delta_c = l_0^{1/(m+1)} \left[\frac{\sigma_0 d_f}{2\tau_b} \right]^{m/(m+1)}$$

$$\Sigma_c = \sigma_0^{m/(m+1)} \left[\frac{2\tau_b l_0}{d_f} \right]^{1/(m+1)} \tag{6.83}$$

These parameters define the expected fibre length, Δ_c, in which there will be exactly one flaw that will fail at a stress of Σ_c. The sub-Type I composites are: (1) Type IA, widely spaced multiple cracks: $L_m > \Delta_c$, $E_f \approx E_c$, $v_f \ll E_c/E_f$, and/or τ_b is small; (2) Type IB, closely spaced multiple cracks: $L_m \ll \Delta_c$, $v_f \gg v_{fc}$, $E_m \approx E_c$ and/or τ_b is large. The mechanical difference between Types IA and IB is in the variation in stress in the fibres (see Figure 6.17). In Type IA the stress transfer length is large and there is a relatively large variation in stress between the matrix cracks. After the matrix cracks in Type IB composites, the load is carried mainly by the fibres even away from the matrix cracks and there is little variation in fibre

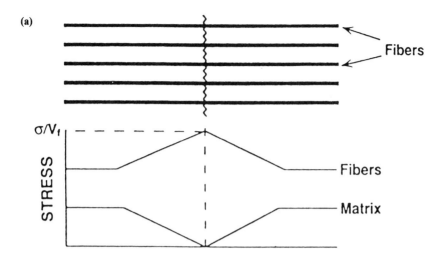

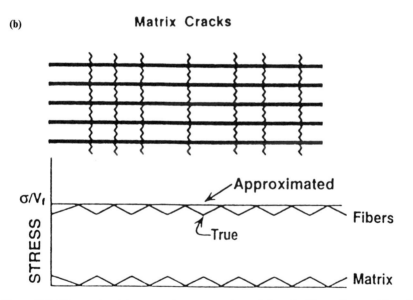

Figure 6.17 Fibre and matrix stress along composites reinforced with continuous fibres for (a) Type IA composites, $v_f \gg v_c$; (b) Type IB, $v_f \approx v_c$ (After Curtin, 1993).

stress. Since few cementitious composites would be of sub-type IB, which is more relevant to ceramic composites, this sub-type is not covered here and the reader is referred to the excellent review by Phoenix (1993).

The presentation of the statistics in this section assumes that there is equal load sharing across a composite in common with the classic bundle theory (Daniels, 1945, 1989). However, the 'characteristic bundle' does not occupy the whole length of the composite, but only a length over which there is load transfer between the fibres and matrix near a crack. In the most recent advances in the statistics of brittle matrix composites, the load is not considered to be shared equally across the composite and 'chain of bundles' both across and along the length of the composite are considered (Phoenix and Raj, 1992; Curtin, 1993b; Phoenix, 1993). However, in this discussion the characteristic bundle is assumed to encompass the width of the specimen.

The stress in the fibres is a maximum at the matrix crack and, if the strength of the fibres is deterministic, then failure occurs at this point. There is no fibre pull-out and the toughness of the composite comes from the work of debonding and the fracture energy of the matrix and fibres. For Type IA continuous fibre reinforced composites, fibre pull-out can only contribute to the toughness if there is a distribution in the strength of the fibres. Thus, it can be beneficial if the reinforcing fibres have a range of strengths. In contrast pull-out will occur in Type IB composites even if their strength is deterministic (Sutcu, 1989; Curtin, 1991).

Assuming a constant interface shear stress, τ_b, the stress in a fibre a distance z from a matrix crack decreases linearly and can be written approximately[2] as (Thouless and Evans, 1988; Sutcu, 1989)

$$\sigma_f(z) = \frac{4\tau_b}{d_f}[L_s - z] \tag{6.84}$$

where d_f is the diameter of the fibres and L_s is a sampling length defined by

$$L_s = \frac{\sigma_{fmax}d_f}{4\tau_b} \tag{6.85}$$

Broken fibres a distance greater than L_s from the matrix crack cannot be pulled out at the current stress level. The probability of a fibre failing under a maximum fibre stress, σ_{fm}, can be obtained from the Weibull distribution (eqn 6.80) and is given by (Thouless and Evans, 1988)

$$P(\sigma_{fm}) = 1 - \exp-\left[\frac{1}{m+1}\left(\frac{\sigma_{fm}}{\Sigma_c}\right)^{m+1}\right] \tag{6.86}$$

The mean overall bundle stress, $\mu(\sigma_{fm}) = \sigma_{fb}/v_f$, at the matrix crack as $N \to \infty$ is given by (Phoenix, 1993)

$$\mu(\sigma_{fm}) = \sigma_{fm}[1 - P(\sigma_{fm})] + \frac{\langle L(\sigma_{fm})\rangle}{L_s}P(\sigma_{fm}) \tag{6.87}$$

---

[2] Obviously the fibre stress does not decrease to zero, but to

$$\sigma_{fb} = \frac{\sigma_{fb}(0)}{\left[1 + \frac{E_m}{E_f}(1 - v_f)\right]}$$

However, the approximation leads to considerable simplification and does not significantly affect the results (Thouless and Evans, 1988).

where $L(\sigma_{fm})$ is the pull-out distance of a broken fibre and $\langle \rangle$ denotes the expected value. In eqn 6.87, the first term is the stress taken by the unbroken fibres and the second is the pull-out stress on the broken fibres. Phoenix (1993) shows that the mean bundle stress, $\mu(\sigma_{fm})$, is given approximately by

$$\mu(\sigma_{fm}) \approx \sigma_{fm}\left[1 - \frac{m+1}{m+2}P(\sigma_{fm})\right] \qquad (6.88)$$

The fibre stress, σ_{fm}^*, at which the mean bundle stress reaches its maximum value is given by

$$\sigma_{fm}^* = \Sigma_c\left(\frac{m+1}{m}\right)^{1/(m+1)} \qquad (6.89)$$

and an approximation to the maximum mean bundle strength, μ^*, is given by

$$\mu^* \approx \sigma_{fm}^*\left[\frac{1}{m+2} + \left(\frac{m+1}{m+2}\right)\exp-\frac{1}{m}\right] \qquad (6.90)$$

Equation 6.90 gives the asymptotic maximum mean bundle strength at $N = \infty$, as discussed in section 6.5.1, this asymptotic value is only approached very slowly. Phoenix (1993) gives the correction to this value that reduces the error to $O(N^{-1/3})$.

The average pull-out length at final failure, L_{pav}, at a single matrix crack is (using the definition of Δ_c) given by (Sutcu, 1989)

$$L_{pav} = \frac{\alpha}{2}(2\pi)^{1/(m+1)}\Delta_c \qquad (6.91)$$

where the coefficient α is given within $\pm 5\%$ for $2 < m < 60$ by the simple formula

$$\alpha = 1.1\frac{m}{(m+1)^2} \qquad (6.92)$$

The average pull-out length obviously decreases to zero as m becomes large. The work of fibre pull-out can be obtained by integrating the fibre force, as a function of the pull-out, over the pull-out length. The work of pull-out per unit area of composite fracture surface, for a single matrix cracking, is given by (Sutcu, 1989)

$$w_p = \frac{\beta v_f}{4}(2\pi)^{2/(m+1)}\Sigma_c\Delta_c \qquad (6.93)$$

A simpler non-dimensional version of eqn 6.93 can be obtained by non-dimensionalizing the work of pull-out of fibres, whose length L_{s0} is the sampling length of a fibre whose strength is σ_0 (see eqn 6.85) and is given by

$$\bar{w}_p = w_p \bigg/ \left(\frac{\sigma_0 L_{s0}}{2}\right) = \beta\left(\pi\frac{l_0}{L_{s0}}\right)^{2/(m+1)} \qquad (6.94)$$

The coefficient β is given within $\pm 2.5\%$ for $m > 3$ by the simple formula (Sutcu, 1989)

$$\beta = \frac{2.14(m-1)}{m^2(m+2)}[1 - \exp -0.387m] \qquad (6.95)$$

As already discussed, the pull-out contribution to the toughness decreases to zero as m tends to infinity. It should be noted that Sutcu's (1989) analysis of the work of pull-out, when closely spaced multiple cracking occurs in Type IB composites, does not appear to be as accurate as that given by Curtin (1991, 1993a).

6.5.3   Type II discontinuous fibre reinforced cementitious materials

In most practical cementitious composites reinforced with discontinuous fibres there is little fibre fracture and fibres simply pull out. The average post matrix cracking stress-displacement relationship for plain fibres during pull-out has already been discussed for both Coulomb and constant interfacial friction (see section 3.9.5).

Cementitious materials are often reinforced by fibres whose Young's modulus is less than that of the matrix, for example, cement mortar reinforced with cellulose or polypropylene fibres. The rule of mixtures predicts no increase in strength for a Type II composite reinforced by such fibres. However, some reinforcement does occur in materials that contain pores and other defects, because the fibres can bridge flaws in the mortar and reduce the effective stress intensity factors at the tips of the flaws (Andonian *et al.*, 1979). The fibres bridging flaws will have a higher strain than the nominal strain on the composite and so can carry higher stress even if they are of lower elastic modulus than the matrix. The fibres will also make the fracture more stable.

The possible statistical effects on fracture of fibre reinforced cementitious composites can be examined from a simple extension to Weibull's theory, as interpreted by Hunt and McCartney (1979) and presented in section 6.2.1 (Hu *et al.*, 1991). The statistics of the fracture of a cementitious composite are presented for a two-dimensional body loaded in simple tension. Flaws are assumed to be distributed randomly with an areal density, ρ, that can be modelled as equivalent through-the-thickness cracks whose length, a, has the Pareto distribution given by eqn 6.27. The matrix is assumed to be brittle and have a fracture toughness, K_{Ic}. Thus, the unreinforced strength of the matrix is given by the Weibull distribution. The fibres are assumed to be aligned, to have a fixed length, l, and to be randomly distributed with an areal density, ρ_{f}. It is assumed that the fibres pull-out rather than fracture. If the flaws are small, the fracture will be unstable after they have opened only slightly. Thus, the average force exerted by a bridging fibre is approximately its maximum value, F_f, given by

$$F_f = \frac{\pi l d_f \tau_b}{4} \qquad (6.96)$$

If the fibre density, ρ_f, is high, the number of fibres bridging a crack will be close to the expected number, $\rho_f \pi a l$. The average maximum stress exerted by the fibre stress to close a crack is given by

$$\sigma_{fb} = \frac{\rho_f \pi l^2 d_f \tau_b}{4} = v_f \tau_b \left(\frac{l}{d_f} \right) \qquad (6.97)$$

Thus, an upper bound to the average strength of the composite is given by

$$\sigma = \sigma_m + \sigma_{fb} \qquad (6.98)$$

where σ_m is the strength of the matrix alone. If the density of fibres is moderate, the number bridging any crack will vary. The largest crack may not be the most critical and there is the possibility of stable crack growth due to a statistical R-curve.

The number of fibres, n, bridging a crack will vary so that the bridging stress (assuming the fibres are smeared over the surface) can be written as

$$\sigma_{fb}(n, a) = \frac{nF_f}{at} \qquad (6.99)$$

where t is the thickness of the plate. The maximum number of bridging fibres that will enable a crack to propagate under a stress σ is given by

$$n_{max} = \frac{at}{F_f} \left[\sigma - K_{Ic} \left(\frac{2}{a\pi} \right)^{1/2} \right] \qquad (6.100)$$

The probability of finding n fibres bridging a crack is given by Poisson's distribution. If $q(a)\, da$ is the probability of finding a crack of length between a and da in the volume dV, the probability of finding such a crack that has less than n_{max} bridging fibres and can therefore propagate is given by

$$\sum_{n=0}^{n_{max}} q(a) \frac{(\rho_f la)^n}{n!} \exp(-\rho_f la)\, da\, dV \qquad (6.101)$$

Hence, the probability for first cracking is given by

$$P_{fc}(\sigma) = 1 - \exp\left[-V \int_{a(\sigma)}^{\infty} q(a) \sum_{n=0}^{n_{max}} \frac{(\rho_f la)^n}{n!} \exp(-\rho_f la)\, da \right] \qquad (6.102)$$

If there are less than n_{max} fibres bridging a crack of size a, the crack can grow. However, it may be arrested if the number of fibres, $n + \Delta n$, bridging the crack after an extension Δa, is greater than N_{max}, given by

$$N_{max} = \frac{(a + \Delta a)t}{F_f} \left[\sigma - K_{Ic} \left(\frac{2}{a\pi} \right)^{1/2} \right] \qquad (6.103)$$

that will cause the crack to arrest. Thus, for a given stress σ, the probability, $Q(a, \Delta a)\, da\, dV$, of finding a crack of size a in dV that can initiate and propagate further after it has grown to $a + \Delta a$, is given by

$$Q(a, \Delta a) = q(a) \exp[-\rho_f l(a + \Delta a)] \sum_{n=0}^{n_{\max}} \frac{(\rho_f la)^n}{n!} \sum_{\Delta n=0}^{N_{\max} - n} \frac{[\rho_f l \Delta a]^{\Delta n}}{\Delta n!} \quad (6.104)$$

It can be shown that there must be a finite non-zero value of Δa for which the integral

$$P(\sigma, \Delta a) = 1 - \exp\left[-V \int_{a(\sigma)}^{\infty} Q(a, \Delta a)\, da\right] \quad (6.105)$$

has a minimum. Hence, if Δa_c is that value, the probability of failure of the composite is given by

$$P(\sigma, \Delta a_c) = 1 - \exp\left[-V \int_{a(\sigma)}^{\infty} Q(a, \Delta a_c)\, da\right]$$

$$= P(\sigma, \Delta a)_{\min} \quad (6.106)$$

Since $P(\sigma, \Delta a)_{\min}$ gives the maximum stress level for a fixed failure probability, eqn 6.106 indicates the probability of the unstable fracture of a multiple crack system. Therefore, Δa_c is the statistically averaged maximum stable crack growth increment.

The most dubious assumption, in the above derivation of the strength of short fibre reinforced brittle matrices, is the smearing of the fibre bridging stresses over the crack surfaces. To test whether the assumption is justified, the theoretical strengths were compared with a computer simulation (Hu et al., 1986b, 1991). The composite chosen is representative of cellulose fibre reinforced cement mortar whose properties are given in Table 6.2. For comparison with computer simulation, a two-dimensional version of the above was used (Hu et al., 1991). A specimen $100 \times 100 \times 0.1$ mm was analysed. The median first crack strength was calculated from eqn 6.102. The median strength of the composite, for a particular value of Δa, is

Table 6.2 Properties of a short fibre reinforced mortar used in statistical analysis

	Fracture toughness of matrix	$K_{Ic} = 0.6$ MPa$\sqrt{m}$
Matrix properties:	Reference crack size	$a_0 = 2$ mm
	Weibull modulus	$m = 8$
	Flaw density	$\rho = 0.003$ mm^{-2}
Fibre properties:	Fibre diameter	$d_f = 0.1$ mm
	Fibre length	$l = 5$ mm
	Fibre bond strength	$\tau_b = 4$ MPa
	Fibre densities	$\rho_f = 0.1, 0.2$ mm^{-2}
	Fibre volume fraction	$v_f = 0.393, 0.785$

Table 6.3 Median strengths of short fibre reinforced mortar

Fibre density (mm^{-2})	Expected strength from eqn 6.98 (MPa)	Median first cracking strength (MPa)	Median ultimate strength (MPa)	Average stable crack growth (mm)
0	6.71	6.71	6.71	0
0.1	14.56	8.51	9.60	10
0.2	22.42	9.67	13.2	40

found by an iterative routine and Δa increased until the ultimate strength is obtained at Δa_c. The crack growth before the ultimate strength is reached is large, 10 mm for $\rho_f = 0.1$ mm^{-2} and 40 mm for $\rho_f = 0.2$ mm^{-2}, but the increase in strength over the first cracking strength is only moderate. Table 6.3 gives the median first cracking stress and ultimate strength of the simulated composite. Note that the ultimate strength of a composite reinforced with a moderate volume fraction of fibres is considerably less than that given by eqn 6.98 for high volume fractions.

Sixty computer experiments were also run for the composites given in Table 6.2 (Hu et al., 1986b). A typical flaw and fibre distribution (the actual number of fibres has been reduced by a factor of 10 for clarity) before loading is shown in Figure 6.18a. Finite width corrections for the cracks were used to calculate the stress intensity factors due to the applied stress. Finite length corrections were not used. The bridging fibres were modelled as point forces located symmetrically halfway along the shortest half of the fibre to avoid the problem of an infinite stress intensity factor when a fibre is at the crack tip. The stress intensity factors due to the bridging fibres have been calculated from the expression for point forces given by Tada et al. (1973) for cracks in infinite plates with a finite width correction (Hu et al., 1991). The cracks present at final failure are shown in Figure 6.18b. The distribution in first cracking and final failure for the two fibre densities are shown in Figure 6.19. The Weibull moduli for these distributions is shown in Table 6.4. The stable crack growth is caused by a statistical R-curve and, as discussed in section 6.2.2, this increases the effective Weibull modulus of the material. Since for high volume fractions of fibres there is little stable crack growth prior to fracture, the statistical R-curve is less pronounced at higher volume fractions. Thus, for $\rho_f = 0.2$ mm^{-2} the effective Weibull modulus for final fracture, while much larger than that of the matrix, is less than that for $\rho_f = 0.1$ mm^{-2}. The probabilities of failure for the two different fibre densities are compared with the theoretical predictions in Figure 6.20. The failure probability of the unreinforced mortar is indicated by the lines W_1 and the high density limiting probabilities are indicated by the lines W_2. The median strength of the composites is underestimated by the theory by about 15%. Nevertheless, the smeared fibre theoretical model does give a simple method that predicts the strength distribution reasonably well.

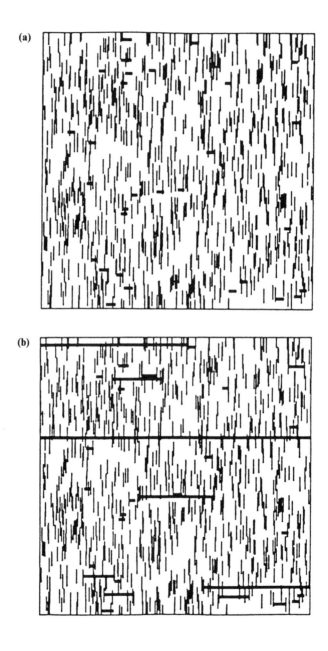

Figure 6.18 Crack development in a sample 100×100 mm two-dimensional fibre reinforced mortar: (a) before loading; (b) at final failure.

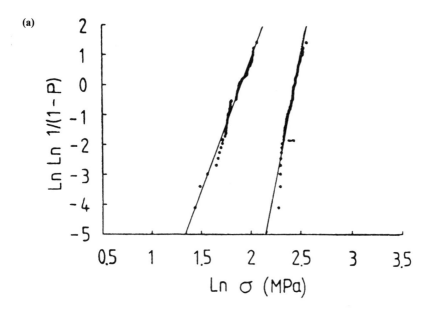

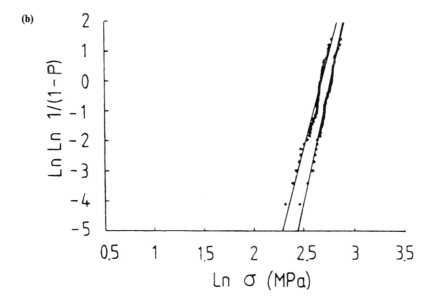

Figure 6.19 First crack and final failure strength distributions: (a) $\rho_f = 0.1\,\text{mm}^{-2}$; (b) $\rho_f = 0.2\,\text{mm}^{-2}$.

Table 6.4 Weibull moduli for short fibre reinforced mortar

Fibre density (mm^{-2})	Weibull modulus	
	First cracking	Final fracture
0.1	8.74	16.7
0.2	12.6	14.8

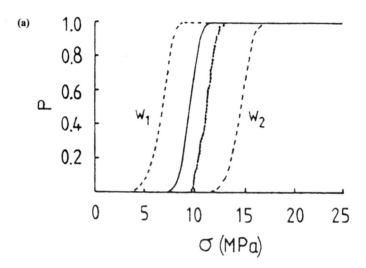

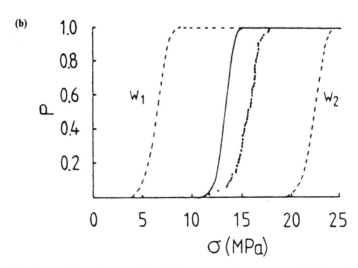

Figure 6.20 Comparison of strength distributions from theory —— (eqn 6.108), and computer simulation ⋯⋯: (a) $\rho_f = 0.1\,\text{mm}^{-2}$; (b) $\rho_f = 0.2\,\text{mm}^{-2}$.

6.6 Summary

Cementitious materials are only quasi-brittle and weakest-link statistics do not have a direct application. However, though the Weibull distribution was derived from a weakest-link concept, it can still be used in an empirical fashion for the reliability of supposedly identical components. What the Weibull distribution cannot do is predict the strength dependence on size in cementitious materials. The natural inhomogeneity of cementitious materials makes them somewhat crack tolerant. Random microcracking in cementitious materials is relatively unimportant, though eventually it does lead to localization of damage to the pupative fracture process zone. In practice the region of localization is more likely to be determined by design stress concentrations rather than material weaknesses. Therefore, the dominant volume is the region of localization, rather than the volume as a whole as is assumed in classic Weibull theory.

Reinforcement of cementitious materials with fibres makes them not only stronger but also more reliable which is often more important. Load sharing can occur between fibres as is assumed in classic bundle theory. For practical reasons useful fibre volume fraction that can be used with cementitious materials is relatively small. Thus, if the fibre bond strength or the fibre length is large and the fibres fracture before pulling out, it is paradoxically an advantage to have fibre strengths with a wide distribution in strength. Although reinforcing fibres can make the work of fracture large, such work can only be fully utilized in situations where there are large stress gradients, due to large fibre free cracks, stress concentrations, or, in small beams, bending stress. The development of an R-curve due to fibre pull-out from natural defects in uniformly stressed components is due only to the random distribution of the fibres. Thus, in fibre reinforced cementitious materials, a randomness in fibre distribution or strength can be an advantage.

7 Time-dependent fracture behaviour of cementitious materials

7.1 Introduction

It is well recognized that the strength degradation of cementitious materials and fibre cements is dependent on the loading rate as well as the time under which a sustained or cyclic load is applied (Mindess and Nadeau, 1977; Mindess, 1985; Hu et al., 1989). There are two main factors which control these time-dependent strength characteristics. One factor is the flaw statistics in terms of flaw density and flaw size distribution; the other factor is the slow crack growth process determined by the chemical reactive species at the flaw tip (Beaudon, 1986; Tait and Garrett, 1986). For slow loading rates both factors determine the strength characteristics of these materials. To avoid dealing with the statistics of pre-existing flaws the conventional approach is to consider the growth of a single crack only. This is acceptable for a uniform stress field since the largest flaw is the one that determines the strength according to the Weibull theory (1951). However, many cementitious structural applications have a non-uniform stress field and the single crack approach is not appropriate. A time-dependent statistical fracture mechanics theory is necessary and is given in the next section.

7.1.1 Slow crack growth in cementitious materials

Many glasses and brittle ceramics, such as aluminas and silicon nitrides, suffer slow crack growth as a result of attack by moisture or humidity in the air under the application of an external stress. Such environmental species effectively lower the surface energy of the material by chemically enhanced bond rupture (Evans, 1972; Atkins and Mai, 1985). In cementitious materials, such as cement paste, mortar and concrete, cracks grow from the flaws under stress in the presence of a wet environment (Mindess and Nadeau, 1977; Mindess, 1985; Wittmann, 1985). It is the rate or time-dependent fracture process at the flaw tip that determines the slow crack growth and hence the residual strength of the material.

The best way to describe the environmentally assisted slow crack growth is to relate the crack velocity (da/dt) to the applied stress intensity factor (K_a). A schematic log–log plot of da/dt versus K_a is shown in Figure 7.1 for ceramic materials. There are three regions of crack growth. In Region I the

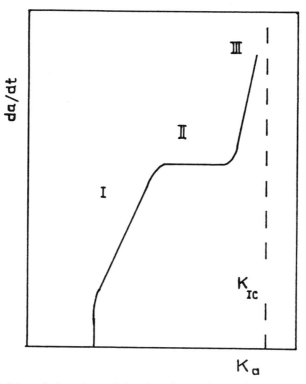

Figure 7.1 Schematic dependence of time-dependent crack growth on stress intensity factor.

crack velocity is a power law function of the crack tip stress intensity factor, that is,

$$\frac{\mathrm{d}a}{\mathrm{d}t} = AK_{\mathrm{a}}^{n} \tag{7.1}$$

where A and n, often called the corrosion exponent, are constants that depend on the environment-material system. In Region I crack growth is controlled by the stress enhanced chemical reaction rate. The crack velocity is independent of the applied stress intensity factor and dependent only on the rate of diffusion or mass transport controlled processes of the chemical species in Region II. The last region, Region III, has a similar power law function as in Region I, but crack growth is mechanically controlled with very little environmental effect (Atkins and Mai, 1985; Wiederhorn *et al.*, 1982).

In cementitious materials, only Region I has been observed with few reports of Regions II and III. Hence only slow crack growth in Region I is considered in this chapter. Since cementitious materials, and in particular concrete, are very heterogeneous in structure, as distinct from ceramics and glasses, the slow crack growth parameters, A and n, are not really constant. This phenomenon is seldom found in glasses and the more brittle ceramics. For example, the microscopic fracture path in hardened cement paste is tortuous both within the hydration products and around the unhydrated cement grains which effectively bridge the crack faces (Baldie and Pratt, 1986). The effects of crack tortuosity and grain bridging become more obvious in mortars and concretes and they exert a closure stress intensity K_r on the crack tip (van Mier, 1991). Hence, the applied crack tip stress intensity K_a is reduced by K_r to an effective crack tip stress intensity factor K_t. Since it is K_t and not K_a that drives the crack, it is not surprising that A and n are not true constants. However, if K_t is used instead of K_a the log–log plot is a straight line and A and n, referred to K_t, are constants.

7.2   Modelling time-dependent crack growth in brittle materials

The strength of brittle materials in glasses, ceramics and cementitious matrices varies with the stress rate ($\dot{\sigma}_a$), cyclic fatigue and the time under which a constant stress is applied. In the first case, the material is subjected to different constant stress rates often termed 'dynamic fatigue' by the ceramics community. Cyclic fatigue refers to experiments in which the material is under the application of a repeated stress of given magnitude and test frequency. Fracture that occurs with time under a constant stress is often called 'static fatigue' or 'delayed fracture'. All these tests involve an element of time and the strength results obtained simply reflect the time-dependent crack growth behaviour described by eqn 7.1.

7.2.1   Conventional single crack theory

The conventional approach to the prediction of the time-dependent strength of brittle materials neglects the flaw statistics and considers only the growth of a crack from a single flaw size, a_i, to a critical flaw size, $a_f = 1/\pi(K_{Ic}/\sigma\phi)^2$, whose rate is governed by the fundamental environment assisted crack growth law for the particular material concerned (Atkins and Mai, 1985). Assuming that there is no crack tip shielding effect eqn 7.1 becomes

$$\frac{da}{dt} = A(\sigma\phi\sqrt{\pi a})^n \qquad (7.2)$$

where σ is the nominal stress at the flaw and ϕ is a geometrical form factor. A flaw of size a_i will grow under uniform stress to a size a in a time, t, given by

$$\int_{a_i}^{a} \frac{da}{a^{n/2}} = A(\sigma\phi\sqrt{\pi})^n t \qquad (7.3)$$

so that

$$t = \frac{2}{(n-2)A(\sigma\phi\sqrt{\pi})^n} \left[\frac{1}{a_i^{(n-2)/2}} - \frac{1}{a^{(n-2)/2}} \right] \qquad (7.4)$$

If $(a_i/a_f)^{n/(2-1)} \ll 1$ the lifetime, t_f, for a specimen containing a flaw of size a_i under static fatigue is given by

$$t_f \sigma^n = \frac{2a_i^{(1-n/2)}}{(n-2)(\phi\sqrt{\pi})^n A} \tag{7.5}$$

Evans and Wiederhorn (1974) have combined the lifetimes given by eqn 7.5 with the Weibull inert strength distribution given by eqn 6.5, rewritten here as

$$P = 1 - \exp{-\left(\frac{\sigma}{\sigma_*}\right)^m} \tag{7.6}$$

where $\sigma_* = \sigma_0/\rho V$ is the normalizing parameter, to obtain the probability of finding a flaw bigger than a_i, on the assumption that the flaw that causes fracture in an inert environment also causes time-dependent fracture. Both m and σ_* can be determined from inert strength experiments. Hence, Evans and Wiederhorn (1974) obtained expressions for (a) static fatigue or constant applied stress, (b) dynamic fatigue or constant stress rate and (c) cyclic fatigue as follows.

Static fatigue or constant applied stress. The relationship between applied stress, σ_a, and the time to failure, t_f

$$t_f \sigma_a^n = \lambda_s^s \tag{7.7}$$

where

$$\lambda_s^s = \frac{2\sigma_*^{n-2}\left[\ln\left(\frac{1}{1-P}\right)\right]^{(n-2)/m}}{A(n-2)\phi^2\pi K_{Ic}^{n-2}} \tag{7.8}$$

The time to failure, t_f, is distributed according to the Weibull distribution with a modulus m_s^* given by

$$m_s^* = \frac{m}{n-2} \tag{7.9}$$

Dynamic fatigue or constant stress rate. Similarly the fracture strength, σ_f, under constant stress rate, $\dot{\sigma}_a$, experiments is given by

$$\sigma_f^{n+1} = \dot{\sigma}_a \lambda_d^s \tag{7.10}$$

where

$$\lambda_d^s = (n+1)\lambda_s^s \tag{7.11}$$

The strength probability for dynamic fatigue has the same form as a Weibull distribution and the failure probability, $P(\dot{\sigma}_a)$, for any particular stress rate can be written as

$$P(\sigma_f) = 1 - \exp - \left(\frac{\sigma_f}{\sigma_*^d}\right)^{m_d^*} \tag{7.12}$$

where

$$m_d^* = m\frac{(n+1)}{(n-2)} \tag{7.13a}$$

$$\sigma_*^d = (\dot{\sigma}_a C_T)^{1/(n+1)} \tag{7.13b}$$

and

$$C_T = \frac{2(n+1)}{(n-2)A\phi^2\pi}\left(\frac{\sigma_*}{K_{Ic}}\right)^{n-2} \tag{7.13c}$$

Clearly the effective Weibull modulus m_d^* is always bigger than m in the presence of slow crack growth. This dependence of the Weibull modulus on the stress rate has been reported widely. Physically, this implies that all the flaws will grow to a more uniform size distribution so that there is less scatter in the fracture strength and the Weibull modulus becomes larger.

Cyclic fatigue. The single crack approach to cyclic fatigue, both rotational bending and reversed bending, has also been given by Evans and Fuller (1974). It is assumed that the material does not suffer mechanical fatigue induced damage, and that crack growth is simply a time-dependent effect. In its original form the Weibull inert strength distribution eqn 7.6 was not included. However, this can be easily done as given in the following expressions. Thus, for rotational bending, where $\sigma_a(t) = \sigma_c \sin(\omega t)$,

$$t_f \sigma_{max}^n = \lambda_c^s \tag{7.14}$$

where σ_{max} is the maximum stress,

$$\lambda_c^s = \frac{\lambda_s^s}{\psi(n)} \tag{7.15}$$

and $\psi(n) = (1/\pi)\int_0^{\pi/2}\sin^n\theta\,d\theta$ is related to the gamma function by

$$\psi(n) = \frac{1}{\sqrt{4\pi}}\frac{\Gamma[(n+1)/2]}{\Gamma[(n+2)/2]}$$

For more general mechanical fatigue where $\sigma_a(t) = \sigma_0 + \sigma_c \sin(\omega t)$ and $\zeta = \sigma_c/\sigma_0$,

$$\lambda_c^s = \frac{\lambda_s^s}{G(n,\zeta)} \tag{7.16}$$

where

$$G(n,\zeta) = \frac{(1+\zeta)^n}{2\pi}\int_0^{2\pi}f(n,\zeta)\,d\theta$$

and

$$f(n, \zeta) = [1 + \zeta \sin \theta]^n \quad \text{if} \quad [1 + \zeta \sin \theta] > 0$$
$$f(n, \zeta) = 0 \quad \quad \text{if} \quad [1 + \zeta \sin \theta] < 0$$

The number of cycles to failure $N = ft_f$, where f is the frequency of loading, is distributed according to the Weibull distribution

$$P(N) = 1 - \exp - \left(\frac{N}{N_*} \right)^{m_c^*} \tag{7.17}$$

where

$$m_c^* = \frac{m}{n - 2} \tag{7.18a}$$

and

$$N_* = \frac{fC_T}{(n + 1)G(n, \zeta)\sigma_{max}^n} \tag{7.18b}$$

All these single-crack equations are applicable to all specimens with small flaws since the geometric factor ϕ is independent of the specimen geometry. The slow crack growth exponent, n, can be evaluated from simple static or dynamic fatigue. It is then possible to predict the lifetimes under static or dynamic and cyclic fatigue from the relationship for the parameter λ.

7.2.2 Statistical theory of time-dependent fracture

Since it is much easier to carry out flexural than uniaxial strength experiments, the statistical theory developed in this section will be for specimens subjected to pure bending only. However, the theory can be simply extended to other loading configurations. For simplicity, uniform specimens with rectangular cross-sections or circular cross-sections are considered. It is also assumed that the inherent flaws are distributed within the volume V of the material, whose size variation follows the Pareto distribution given by eqn 6.27. The density of the flaws is assumed to be small so that there is no interaction between flaws. For cementitious materials it is assumed that the environmental species will slowly diffuse through to interact with the flaws.

The single-crack theory predicts that fracture is independent of the specimen or loading conditions, but a statistical fracture mechanics approach shows that the flaw which causes instantaneous fracture is not necessarily the same as the flaw that causes time-dependent fracture except if the stress is constant. Thus, in this fuller treatment of the statistics of time-dependent fracture the growth of all flaws is studied rather than a single flaw, since crack growth alters the existing crack size distribution (Hu et al., 1988). The failure probability is obtained from the current crack size distribution

$q(a, t)$ which from eqn 6.22 is given by

$$P(\sigma_a, t) = 1 - \exp\left[-\int_V \int_{a(\sigma)}^{\infty} q(a, t)\, da\, dV\right] \qquad (7.19)$$

where $a(\sigma) = 1/\pi (K_{Ic}/\sigma\phi)^2$. Equation 7.19 can be solved by noting that if a_i is the flaw which grew to a size a in time t then

$$q(a, t)\, da = q(a_i)\, da_i \qquad (7.20)$$

Rearranging eqn 7.4, the crack of size a can be expressed in terms of the original flaw size a_i from which it grew, and the failure probability becomes

$$P(\sigma_a, t) = 1 - \exp\left[-\int_V \int_{a_i(a)}^{\infty} q(a_i)\, da_i\, dV\right] \qquad (7.21)$$

Hu *et al.* (1988) have used eqn 7.21 to obtain a more exact statistical strength of beams. Their results for static fatigue, dynamic fatigue and cyclic fatigue are summarized below. Details of the calculation together with other results are given by Hu *et al.* (1988).

Static fatigue or constant applied stress (rectangular cross-section). Under a constant stress, σ_a, the crack size, a, at any time, t, can be expressed in terms of the original flaw size a_i by

$$a = a_i\left[1 - \frac{n-2}{2} A(\sigma\phi\sqrt{\pi})^n t a_i^{(n-2)/2}\right]^{2/(2-n)} \qquad (7.22)$$

Thus, with the assumption $AK_{Ic}^{n-2}\sigma_a^2 t_f \gg 1$, the parameter λ_s for a true statistical theory is given in terms of the single crack parameter λ_s^s by

$$\lambda_s = t_f \sigma_a^n = \lambda_s^s\left[\frac{mn + n - 2}{(m+1)(n-2)}\right]^{(n-2)/m} \qquad (7.23)$$

Dynamic fatigue or constant stress rate (rectangular cross-section). Under a constant stress rate, $\dot{\sigma}_a$, the crack size, a, at any time, t, can be expressed in terms of the original flaw size a_i by

$$a = a_i\left[1 - \frac{n-2}{2(n+1)} A(\dot{\sigma}t\phi\sqrt{\pi})^n t a_i^{(n-2)/2}\right]^{2/(2-n)} \qquad (7.24)$$

Thus, the parameter λ_d for a true statistical theory, assuming that $AK_{Ic}^{n-2}\dot{\sigma}_a^2 t_f^3 \gg 1$, is given in terms of the single crack parameter λ_s^s by

$$\lambda_d = \frac{\sigma_f^{n+1}}{\dot{\sigma}_a} = (n+1)\lambda_s = (n+1)\lambda_s^s\left[\frac{mn + n - 2}{(m+1)(n-2)}\right]^{(n-2)/m} \qquad (7.25)$$

Cyclic fatigue (circular cross-section). Under a rotational bending, $\sigma_a = \sigma_c \sin\omega t$, assuming cracks only grow under the tensile half of the stress cycle, the crack size, a, at any time, t, can be expressed in terms of the original flaw size a_i by

$$a = a_i \left[1 - \frac{n-2}{2} A (\sigma \phi \sqrt{\pi})^n t \psi(n) a_i^{(n-2)/2} \right]^{2/(2-n)} \tag{7.26}$$

Assuming that $A K_{Ic}^{n-2} \sigma_c^2 \psi(n) t_f \gg 1$, the parameter λ_c for a true statistical theory is given in terms of the single crack parameter λ_s^s by

$$\lambda_c = t_f \sigma_c^n = \lambda_c^s \left[\frac{mn + 2n - 4}{2\pi(n-2)} \beta \left(\frac{m+1}{2}, \frac{3}{2} \right) \right]^{(n-2)/m}$$

$$= \frac{\lambda_s^s}{\psi(n)} \left[\frac{mn + 2n - 4}{2\pi(n-2)} \beta \left(\frac{m+1}{2}, \frac{3}{2} \right) \right]^{(n-2)/m} \tag{7.27}$$

where β is the beta function. It is commonly believed that glasses, ceramics and cementitious matrices do not suffer true cyclic-fatigue-induced damage because there is no associated plastic flow at the crack tip (Gurney and Pearson, 1948; Mai and Gurney, 1975; Tait and Garrett, 1986). However, it is not clear that there are no mechanical fatigue effects in these brittle materials. It has been found recently that ceramics and cementitious materials that possess crack-resistance curve characteristics do suffer mechanical fatigue in addition to the environment effect (Mai *et al.*, 1992). At present it is difficult to calculate the crack velocity component due to mechanical fatigue. Clearly, lifetimes predicted from the environment effect alone as given above will be longer than the experimental data if there is a genuine mechanical fatigue. If predictions and experiments agree then the mechanical fatigue is negligible.

The time-dependent strength predictions derived in this section differ from those obtained by earlier authors (Evans and Fuller, 1974; Jakus *et al.*, 1978; Helfinstine, 1980). These authors assumed that the flaw which causes failure in an inert atmosphere would also cause time-dependent failure in a hostile environment. This assumption is only true for uniformly stressed solids and not for non-uniformly stressed materials under bending. In the latter case the flaw which would cause failure in an inert atmosphere is not necessarily the same as the flaw that leads to time-dependent fracture. Therefore, although probability has been linked to the lifetime predictions by previous authors (Evans and Wiederhorn, 1974), the theory is essentially that for a single flaw and is not for multiple flaws.

7.2.3 Comparison of single crack and statistical fracture theories

The method of incorporating the failure probability into the single-crack based equations is empirical. It is useful therefore to compare the lifetime predictions for single crack theory, t_f^s, with the more rigorous statistical-fracture-based predictions, t_f, given in section 7.2.2. For constant applied stresses the predicted lifetimes from the single-crack approach are always smaller than the statistical theory—for large n and small m values the difference can be as much as 60%. In cyclic bending every flaw goes through tension and compression in each cycle and the predicted lifetimes from the statistical theory are orders of magnitude less than those obtained using the single-crack approach. The physical reason for this large difference is that in the statistical theory there are always flaws subjected to the cyclic stress at any time, and if n is large the time required to failure is small. In contrast, in the single-crack theory, the flaw is subjected to the cyclic stress and crack growth only occurs in the tension half of each cycle. Therefore, if rotation bending experiments are carried out on circular cross-sectional samples the data will provide a 'litmus test' for the relative accuracy of the two theories.

The prediction of lifetimes due to cyclic fatigue, t_{fc}, can be obtained from the lifetime data, t_{fs}, due to sustained stresses provided that there is no fatigue-induced damage at the flaw tip. In rotation bending of beams whose cross-section is circular the single crack theory (Evans and Fuller, 1974) gives

$$\alpha^s = \frac{t_{fc}^s}{t_{fs}^s} = \frac{1}{\psi(n)} \left(\frac{\sigma_a}{\sigma_c} \right)^n \tag{7.28}$$

From the more exact statistical theory the ratio is (Hu et al., 1988)

$$\alpha = \frac{t_{fc}}{t_{fs}} = \alpha^s \left[\beta \left(\frac{mn + n - 2}{2(n-2)}, \frac{3}{2} \right) \left(\frac{mn + 2n - 4}{2\pi(n-2)} \right) \right]^{(n-2)/m} \tag{7.29}$$

The lifetime ratios given by eqn 7.28 or 7.29 are the same whether the flaws are distributed over the surface or within the volume. Table 7.1 compares the ratio of lifetimes as given by eqns 7.28 and 7.29 when $\sigma_a = \sigma_c$. According to the

Table 7.1 Ratio of predicted lifetimes for rotation bending to constant sustained stress

m	n	Single-crack theory α^s	Statistical fracture theory α
5	10	8.13	4.15×10^{-1}
5	20	11.40	1.61×10^{-2}
5	40	16.00	1.87×10^{-5}
5	80	22.50	1.81×10^{-11}
10	10	8.13	1.40
10	20	11.40	2.39×10^{-1}
10	40	16.00	5.07×10^{-3}
10	80	22.50	1.63×10^{-6}
15	10	8.13	2.26
15	20	11.40	6.84×10^{-1}
15	40	16.00	4.53×10^{-2}
15	60	22.50	1.42×10^{-4}
20	10	8.13	2.94
20	20	11.40	1.22
20	40	16.00	1.50×10^{-1}
20	60	22.50	1.64×10^{-3}

single-crack theory the lifetime under cyclic loading is always larger than that under constant stress. The ratio of the lifetimes, α^s, only depends on the corrosion exponent n and is independent of the Weibull modulus m. On the other hand, the true statistical fracture theory shows that the lifetime under cyclic loading can be smaller than that under constant stress if the corrosion coefficient, n, is large or the Weibull modulus, m, is small. For many brittle materials such as glasses ($m \approx 5$, $n \approx 20$) and ceramics ($m \approx 20, n \approx 50$) the cyclic fatigue lifetimes are always less than the static fatigue lifetimes. The experimental results of Gurney and Pearson (1948) and Williams (1956) support the theoretical prediction of the true statistical theory for these materials.

7.2.4 Time-dependent creep strain

There are two components to the creep strain. One is caused by the homogeneous creep of the bulk material and the other is caused by the cumulative crack opening displacement of all the pre-existing flaws which extend during creep. The total creep is the sum of these two components. For practical purposes, in glasses, ceramics and cementitious materials at temperatures less than half the melting point, it is not necessary to consider the bulk material creep component. Only the component due to the growth of the pre-existing cracks has to be calculated. This concept of analysis is not new and has been applied to creep in polymers immersed in organic solvents (Wiedmann and Williams, 1975). In this case creep elongation is caused by the opening of the surface crazes which grow according to some time-dependent law similar to eqn 7.1.

Creep strain can be obtained from simple energy-balance consideration (Hu *et al.*, 1986, 1988). Consider a rectangular beam of length L and cross-section BW, containing volume-distributed flaws and subjected to a constant applied bending moment M_a. Only those flaws in the tensile half of the beam will grow and contribute to creep. Assuming that the cracks are penny-shaped with radius a, at time t the strain energy, $d\Lambda_c$, stored in an elemental volume $LB\,dy$ at a distance y from the neutral axis due to cracks whose size lies between a and $(a + da)$, is given by

$$d\Lambda_c = BL\,dy\,q(a, t)\,da \int_0^a \frac{G\pi a}{2}\,da$$

$$= BL\,dy\,q(a, t)\,da\frac{(1 - \nu^2)}{3E}\sigma^2(y)a^3 \tag{7.30}$$

where $\sigma(y) = 2\sigma_a y/W$ is the normal stress acting at a depth y below the neutral axis, and $G = (2\sigma^2(1 - \nu^2)a)/\pi E$ is the potential energy release rate. The total strain energy stored for all flaws from a to infinity is

$$\Lambda_c = \frac{BL(1 - \nu^2)}{3E} \int_0^{W/2} \left(\frac{2\sigma_a y}{W}\right)^2 \int_a^{a_c(y)} q(a, t)a^3\,da\,dy \tag{7.31}$$

where

$$a_c(y) = \frac{1}{16\pi} \left(\frac{K_{Ic} W}{\sigma_a y} \right)^2$$

is the size of the crack that will cause failure at time t. Cracks larger than a_c must be excluded from the calculation of the strain energy, because they would cause failure. Equation 7.31 can be solved numerically making use of the relationship given in eqn 7.20. The strain energy, Λ_{nc}, stored in the uncracked beam is

$$\Lambda_{nc} = \left(\frac{WBL}{6} \right) \left(\frac{\sigma_a^2}{E} \right) \tag{7.32}$$

and the total strain energy stored is

$$\Lambda = \Lambda_{nc} + \Lambda_c \tag{7.33}$$

The external work W_e performed by the bending moment M_a is given by

$$W_e = \tfrac{1}{2} M_a \theta = \frac{M_a L}{2R} = \left(\frac{WBL\sigma_a}{6} \right) \epsilon_a \tag{7.34}$$

where R is the radius of curvature of the beam and ϵ_a is the strain in the surface of the beam. Hence, the strain in the surface of the beam is given by

$$\epsilon_a(\sigma_a, t) = \Lambda \left(\frac{6}{WBL\sigma_a} \right) = \frac{\sigma_a}{E} + \Lambda_c \left(\frac{6}{WBL\sigma_a} \right) \tag{7.35}$$

Creep strain cannot be predicted from the single-crack theory.

7.2.5 Application to cementitious materials

The statistical fracture theory presented in section 7.2.3 to predict time-dependent strength characteristics of brittle materials is strictly valid only for single phase homogeneous materials. However, just as the Weibull strength theory, though strictly not applicable to heterogeneous materials, can be applied empirically to the fracture of cementitious materials, so too can the time-dependent theory for a brittle material. The extension of the time-dependent theory to two-phase materials is covered in section 7.2.6. To use the time-dependent statistical fracture theory it is necessary to determine the Weibull inert strength distribution and the environment-assisted slow crack growth law given by eqns 7.1 and 7.3 to determine the parameters σ_*, m, A and n. The fracture toughness K_{Ic} can be estimated from separate experiments.

A hardened cement paste is the most homogeneous cementitious material. The slow crack growth law

$$\frac{da}{dt} = 10^{16} K_a^{36} \quad (m/s, MPa\sqrt{m}) \tag{7.36}$$

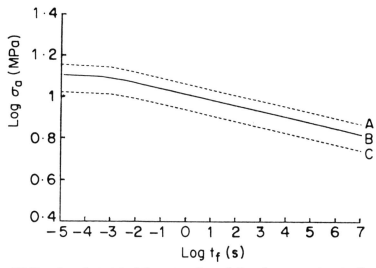

Figure 7.2 Time-dependent static fatigue strength predictions for a cement paste. Curve A: $P = 0.9$; curve B: $P = 0.5$; curve C: $P = 0.1$.

and fracture toughness, $K_{Ic} = 0.34\,\text{MPa}\sqrt{m}$, were obtained for a wet cement paste (water/cement ratio $= 0.5$, aged for 3–4 months) by Nadeau *et al.* (1974). No inert strength experiments were performed but the flexural strength was 12.7 MPa at 50% failure probability. Assuming $m = 10$ for cement paste (Hu *et al.*, 1985), σ_* is estimated from eqn 7.6 to be 13.17 MPa. Using these five parameters and assuming that $a_f/a_i \gg 1$, the time-dependent strength predictions for static fatigue and dynamic fatigue are shown in Figures 7.2 and 7.3 for rectangular cross-section specimens containing volume-distributed flaws subjected to pure bending. The curves shown are for three failure probabilities of $P = 0.1$, 0.5 and 0.9. For $t_f > 10^{-2}\,\text{s}$ and $\dot{\sigma}_a < 10^2\,\text{MPa/s}$, straight lines are obtained in the log–log plots because $a_f/a_i \gg 1$ and the predictions agree with those obtained from eqns 7.23 and 7.25. The plateaux shown in Figures 7.2 and 7.3 is because the size of the crack at failure is not large in comparison with the initial flaw size.

Creep curves can also be estimated by the method outlined in section 7.2.4, but, because of the large corrosion exponent, there is negligible creep strain due to flaw growth for this particular cement paste. The corrosion exponent for polymer modified cement paste is much smaller ($n \approx 8$) and for such pastes the creep strain is significant. In this case, the creep strain at failure at low applied stress can exceed that at high stress because cracks can grow to longer lengths at low stress final fracture.

7.2.6 Statistical time-dependent fracture in two-phase materials

Concrete and mortar can be modelled approximately as two-phase materials. There are two approximate ways to estimate the time-dependent strength

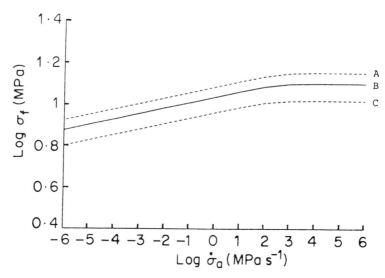

Figure 7.3 Time-dependent dynamic fatigue strength predictions for a cement paste. Curve A: $P = 0.9$; curve B: $P = 0.5$; curve C: $P = 0.1$.

behaviour of two-phase materials: one method is to develop an appropriate model to consider the effect of the second phase particles on the environment-assisted growth of the statistically distributed flaws in the matrix; the other method applies the theory developed in section 7.2.2 for a single-phase material to the two-phase material assuming equivalent slow crack growth parameters A and n for the latter material.

The analysis of the time-dependent strength of a two-phase material (Hu et al., 1992) derives from the time independent two-phase theory (Hu et al., 1985) presented in section 6.3.1. Only the behaviour of uniformly stressed specimens under static or dynamic fatigue are considered, but the analysis could be extended to cover non-uniformly stressed specimens. As in time independent statistics there are two models; the second phase particles are assumed to either bridge any intersecting matrix flaws or to be cut by any intersecting flaw. Only the bridging model is presented here; details of the cutting model can be found in Hu et al. (1992).

A number of simplified assumptions have been made in the analysis. The matrix and the particles are assumed to have the same elastic properties and the bond between them is perfect. Hence any stress variation due to the particles is neglected. The second phase particles are also assumed to be insensitive to slow crack growth. Thus when a crack meets a second phase particle it is arrested at that tip. If both crack tips meet a particle the crack is immobilized. The pre-existing flaws are assumed to have a low density so that there are no interactions between neighbouring flaws or cracks. The flaw sizes are distributed according to the Pareto distribution function (see eqn 6.27) in which the equivalent cracks are normal to the applied stress.

If the distance between two particles of size D is s, and k is the ratio of the fracture toughness of the particle K_p to that of the matrix K_m, then a crack is arrested according to eqn 6.32 where now the crack size is time-dependent. Thus, any crack that becomes unstable whose length is between s and s/k^2 will be arrested and is called a 'stabilized' crack. If one tip of a slowly growing crack encounters a second phase particle, that tip is arrested, but the other can still continue to grow. In the two-phase material, both the particles and the pre-existing cracks are assumed to be randomly distributed independently of each other. Let $f(s,t)$ denote the distribution function of the stabilized cracks formed by arresting matrix cracks, and $b(a(t),t)$ denote the distribution function of the cracks at time t. The failure probability of the two-phase material of volume V under a uniform tension at that moment is given by a time-dependent version of eqn 6.46

$$P(\sigma, t) = 1 - \exp\left[-V\left(\int_{s(\sigma)}^{\infty} f(s, t)\, ds + \int_{a(\sigma)}^{\infty} b(a, t)\, da\right)\right] \quad (7.37)$$

The first integral is obtained for the unstable fracture of the stabilized cracks, and the second integral is obtained for the unstable fracture of the non-arrested cracks. For a homogeneous material $f(s,t)$ is zero. If both $f(s,t)$ and $b(a,t)$ can be solved in terms of the initial pre-existing flaw distribution function $q(a_i)$, the failure probability $P(\sigma, t)$ and the lifetime under a given stress level or time-dependent strength for a given stress rate can be obtained.

Time-dependent fracture under a constant stress. The growth of the cracks touching less than two particles is given by eqn 7.4, where the initial flaw size a_i at $t = 0$ will extend to a at time t for a given applied stress σ_a. The expression for the crack size, a, at time t is given by eqn 7.22 and eqn 7.20 gives the relationship between the distribution of the current crack size as compared with the distribution of the initial flaw size. These two equations are required to evaluate the distribution functions $f(s,t)$ and $b(a,t)$ in eqn 7.37.

Because both particles and pre-existing cracks are randomly distributed, there are cases where they overlap. A crack is said to be bridged if it is intersected by a particle. As a result, the true crack distribution will be different to $q(a)$ as discussed in section 6.3.1. Consider a stabilized crack of size s at time t, which touches two particles. This crack can be formed by a pre-existing flaw intersecting the particles at $t = 0$; or by a flaw a_i, growing to s by time t, or by a crack growing to the range of s and s/k^2 and then propagating unstably under the applied stress until it meets two particles. The probability of finding such a crack of size s is given by the joint probability of finding a separation s for the particles and of finding a crack which satisfies eqn 6.32.

The probability that there are just two particles, of distance $(s + D)$ apart, that just touch the crack, is given by $F(s, D)$ in eqn 6.33. Similarly, the probability $H(s)\,dy$ that a pre-existing crack centred anywhere along a thin strip of width dy is obtained from eqn 6.35. Therefore, $F(s, D)H(s)$ is the probability of finding a pre-existing crack touching two particles with a distance s apart at $t = 0$. Also, the probability $Q(a_i, s)\,da_i\,dy$ of finding a crack whose size is in the range a_i to $a_i + da_i$ in the strip of width dy at $t = 0$ is given by eqn 6.39 with $a = a_i$. Further, the probability $E(s)\,dy$ that microfracture initiated from such a crack which can be arrested to form a stabilized crack of size s is given by eqn 6.40 with a replaced by a_i. Hence, $F(s, D)E(s)$ is the probability of finding a stabilized crack formed by arresting the fracture of a crack at $t = 0$.

A crack of length between s/k^2 and $a_i(s/k^2, \sigma, t)$ at $t = 0$ will extend to the range s and s/k^2 by the time t according to eqn 7.4. At time t, such a crack will be stabilized by two particles of distance s apart given by eqn 6.40. The crack will grow following eqn 7.2 and will not be affected by the encountered particles, unless both tips of the crack are touching particles, in which case, there is no slow crack growth. The probability $E^*(s, t)\,dy$ at time t that a microfracture initiated from a crack, which will be arrested by particles to form a stabilized crack of size s, is given by

$$E^*(s, t) = \int_{a_i(s/k^2, \sigma, t)}^{s/k^2} Q(a_i, s)\,da_i \tag{7.38}$$

$F(s, D)E^*(s, t)$ is therefore the probability of finding a stabilized crack formed by arresting fracture of a crack at time t. Note that at $t = 0$, $a_i = s/k^2 = a$ and $E^* = 0$.

From these three joint probabilities, the probability $f(s, t)\,ds$ of finding a stabilized crack of length between s and $s + ds$ within a unit area at time t is given by

$$f(s, t) = F(s, D)[H(s) + E(s) + E^*(s, t)] \tag{7.39}$$

The physical meaning of $H(s)$, $E(s)$ and $E^*(s, t)$ is straightforward. $H(s)$ is the contribution to stabilized cracks formed by flaws by touching the particles at $t = 0$. $E(s)$ is the contribution to stabilized cracks formed by arresting unstable microfractures at $t = 0$, and $E^*(s, t)$ is the contribution through arresting unstable microfracture by time t. Therefore, the failure probability $P_c(\sigma, t)$ of the two-phase material at time t under a tensile stress σ_a due to the final fracture of the stabilized crack is given by the time-dependent version of eqn 6.43, but with $f(s)$ replaced by $f(s, t)$ of eqn 7.39.

Now consider the failure probability of the two-phase material due to fracture initiated at cracks which are not arrested by the tougher particles. The probability $b(a_i, t)\,da$ of finding a crack of size between a_i and $a_i + da_i$

within a unit volume which is not arrested at time t is given by the time-dependent version of eqn 6.44

$$b(a_i, t) = \int_{k^2 a(a_i, \sigma, t)}^{\infty} F(s, D)Q(a_i, s)\, ds \qquad (7.40)$$

where $a(a_i, \sigma, t)$ is given by eqn 7.22. The failure probability $P_f(\sigma, t)$ of the two-phase material under tension caused by the propagation of the cracks is given by a time-dependent version of eqn 6.45. Finally, the failure probability $P(\sigma, t)$ of the two-phase material of volume V under tension by either mechanism at time t is given by

$$P(\sigma, t) = 1 - (1 - P_f)(1 - P_c)$$

$$= 1 - \exp -V\left[\int_{s(\sigma)}^{\infty} f(s, t)\, ds + \int_{a_i(\sigma, t)}^{\infty} b(a_i, t)\, da_i\right] \qquad (7.41)$$

which allows the failure probability to be calculated for a given stress, σ_a, and time t if the slow crack growth parameters, A and n, the Pareto distribution function $q(a)$, and the fracture toughness K_p and K_m are known.

Time-dependent fracture under a constant stress rate. The slow crack growth (eqn 7.1) can be evaluated for the condition that the stress rate, $\dot{\sigma}_a$, is a constant. The crack size, a, at time t can be represented in terms of the initial flaw size, a_i, at $t = 0$ by eqn 7.25. The analysis follows that given for the static fatigue case and the probability of failure is given by

$$P(\dot{\sigma}, t) = 1 - \exp\left[-V\left(\int_{s(\dot{\sigma}, t)}^{\infty} f(s, t)\, ds + \int_{a(\dot{\sigma}, t)}^{\infty} b(a_i, t)\, da_i\right)\right] \qquad (7.42)$$

7.2.7 Comparison of the time-dependent statistics of homogeneous and heterogeneous materials

In time-dependent fracture in a two-phase material the second phase particles can be crack arrestors for both unstable and environmentally assisted slow crack growth, whereas in a single phase material all the flaws grow until one becomes a critical size. To examine the effectiveness of tough second phase particles on the time-dependent behaviour, Hu et al. (1992) examined the statistics of fracture under simple tension in a hypothetical mortar where the matrix properties were based on the properties of hardened cement paste taken from Nadeau et al. (1974). The statistics were examined for the two-phase model where second phase particles are cut rather than bridged, but the results would not be very significantly different for a bridging model. There is a slight difference in the statistical theory for the matrix alone used in this section as compared with that presented in section 7.2.2. In this section the exact time for the growth of a flaw to a size a is used

Table 7.2 Material properties of hypothetical mortar (based on the properties of hardened cement paste) (Nadeau *et al.*, 1974)

Weibull modulus of matrix	$m = 8$
Flaw density	$\rho = 0.003 \, \text{mm}^{-2}$
Reference flaw size in $q(a)$	$a_0 = 2 \, \text{mm}$
Fracture toughness of matrix	$K_m = 0.34 \, \text{MPam}^{1/2}$
Volume of specimen	$V = LBW = 100 \times 100 \times 1 \, \text{mm}$
Crack growth law parameters	see eqn 7.36
Particle size	$D = 0.6 \, \text{mm}$
Fracture toughness of particle	$K_p = 0.68 \, \text{MPam}^{1/2}$
Density of particles $(v_p/V = 0.1)$	$\rho_p = 0.2778 \, \text{mm}^{-2}$
$(v_p/V = 0.2)$	$\rho_p = 0.5556 \, \text{mm}^{-2}$

instead of the approximation obtained if it is assumed that $a_f/a_i \gg 1$ to be consistent with the two-phase model.

The failure probability curves $P(\sigma_a, t)$ for a constant applied stress, $\sigma_a = 3.6$ MPa, are shown in Figure 7.4. Curve A gives the failure probability of the hardened cement paste matrix, and curves B and C are for the hypothetical mortars with particulate volume fractions of 10% and 20%, respectively. It can be seen that the failure probability of the two-phase material is much smaller than the matrix material. Also, with a two-phase material the probability can reach a plateau value, if the applied stress is below an inherent threshold value, at which there is no further increase in

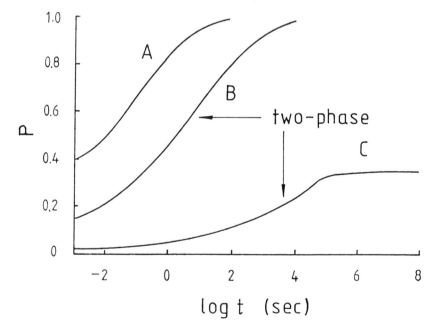

Figure 7.4 Failure probability for hypothetical mortars under static fatigue (applied stress 3.6 MPa: curve A, $v_p = 0\%$; curve B, $v_p = 10\%$; curve C, $v_p = 20\%$).

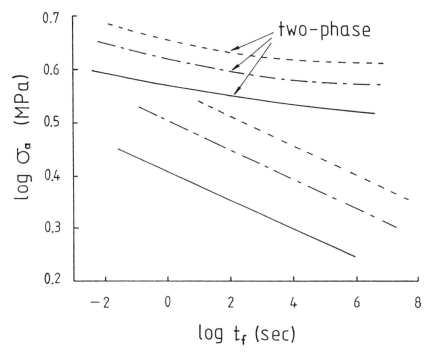

Figure 7.5 Time-dependent strength of hypothetical hardened paste, $v_p = 0$, and mortar, $v_p = 20\%$, under static fatigue, for failure probabilities of 10% ——, 50% — — — and 90% - - - - - -.

failure probability with time. The plateau occurs when all the matrix cracks have been arrested by particles. Naturally, in a real material the second phase particles could not completely arrest a crack, and in time, once a crack had met a particle it would either propagate around or through it. However, second phase particles can greatly reduce the rate of further crack growth.

The statistics of single phase materials given in section 7.2.2 show that in a $\log(\sigma_a)$–$\log(t_f)$ plot, the results for static fatigue should fall on a straight line. The results for the hardened cement paste and the hypothetical mortar with $v_p = 20\%$ are shown in Figure 7.5 for three levels of failure probability 0.1, 0.5 and 0.9. For the applied stress range considered, the matrix material follows the straight line relationship predicted, but the same cannot be said of the two-phase material. However, if a straight line relationship is forced to apply, then an effective slow crack growth exponent parameter n^* can be obtained which is larger than n. This result is in accordance with the larger n values reported for a range of two-phase materials.

The $\log(\sigma_f)$–$\log(\dot{\sigma}_a)$ plot for dynamic fatigue is a straight line according to the approximate theory for single phase materials. In Figure 7.6 the log–log plots for hardened cement paste and the hypothetical mortar with $v_p = 20\%$ are shown; the hardened cement paste has a straight line relationship for

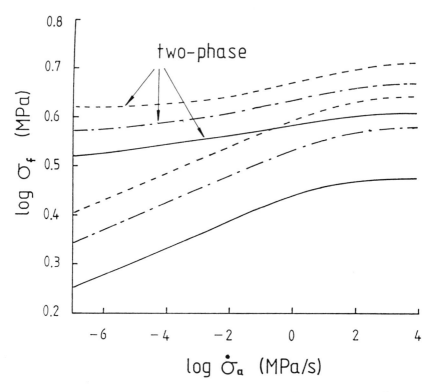

Figure 7.6 Time-dependent strength of hypothetical hardened paste, $v_p = 0$, and mortar, $v_p = 20\%$, under dynamic fatigue, for failure probabilities of 10% ——, 50% — – — and 90% - - - - - .

stress rate less than about 10 MPa/s when the assumption $a_f/a_i \gg 1$ is valid, but for larger stress rates the plot is curved. Even the plot for the hypothetical mortar is approximately straight for $\dot{\sigma}_a < 10$ MPa/s.

It is easier to perform a test at constant stress rate than one at constant stress and it has been shown that the static fatigue performance can be predicted from dynamic data using the single crack theory relationship of eqn 7.11 (which is identical to the relationship predicted by the fuller statistical treatment given in section 7.2.2). Hence, it is interesting to examine whether the same theoretical relationship applies to two-phase materials as is suggested by experimental evidence. If the best straight line is drawn through the theoretical dynamic fatigue predictions for 50% fracture probability (for stress rates less than 10 MPa/s), the single phase statistic predicts that

$$\sigma_a^{(n^*+1)} = \dot{\sigma}_a \lambda_d^*$$

or

$$\log \sigma = \frac{1}{n^*+1} \log \dot{\sigma} + \frac{1}{n^*+1} \log \lambda_d^* \qquad (7.43)$$

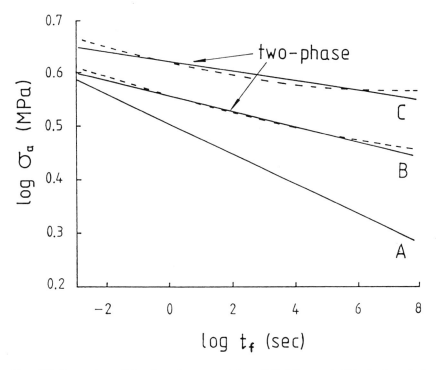

Figure 7.7 Comparison of time-dependent strength for a 50% failure probability for hypothetical two-phase materials: A, $v_p = 0\%$; B, $v_p = 10\%$; C, $v_p = 20\%$. (- - - -) exact solution; (———) single phase predictions from dynamic fatigue data.

Hence the effective corrosion coefficient n^* can be obtained from the slope and the effective dynamic fatigue parameter λ_d^* obtained from the intercept of the straight line. The effective static fatigue parameter, λ_s^*, can then be estimated from eqn 7.11. Thus, using the λ_s^* value obtained from the dynamic fatigue data, the single-phase lifetime predictions are compared with the theoretical two-phase results in Figure 7.7. The agreement is excellent. Thus, despite the fact that the tougher second phase particles interfere with the time-dependent slow crack growth and stabilize some unstable fractures of cracks, eqn 7.10 still holds over a wide range. The significance of the above results is that the lifetimes of a heterogeneous material under static fatigue can be predicted from the dynamic fatigue results which are easier to obtain experimentally.

The ability to apply the simple equations for single phase materials to predict static fatigue behaviour from dynamic fatigue data despite inhomogeneities leads to the assumption that the method may also be applied to cyclic fatigue, provided any mechanical fatigue effects are negligible. Evidence of the validity of this method comes from Tait (1984). He showed that in dry mortar the equivalent crack velocity under cyclic loading can be accurately predicted from crack velocity data obtained from static

Table 7.3 Cyclic fatigue stresses used in the tests by Saito and Imai (1983)

Series	Maximum stress (MPa)	$\zeta = \sigma_c/\sigma_0$
1	2.5	0.8072
2	2.582	0.8129
3	2.667	0.8182
4	2.748	0.8232
5	2.832	0.8280
6	2.916	0.8325

fatigue tests. Since the cyclic crack velocity is independent of cyclic frequency, provided the equivalent parameters A and n are obtained for the heterogeneous mortar, it can be treated as if it were a single-phase homogeneous material. With more complex structures, such as in concrete, it is interesting to determine if and under what conditions the single-phase statistical fracture theory can apply to predict the lifetimes.

According to the single crack statistical theory the failure probability, $P(\sigma_f)$, for dynamic fatigue is given by eqn 7.12 and the corresponding life probability $P(N)$ under general cyclic fatigue by eqn 7.17. If m_d^*, σ_*^d determined from constant stress rate tests using eqn 7.12 and m estimated from high rate inert strength experiments, the fatigue life N for a given cyclic stress can be predicted from eqn 7.17.

Direct tensile fatigue experiments were conducted by Saito and Imai (1983) on plain concrete (Portland cement, river sand, and crushed stone aggregate with a maximum size of 20 mm). A series of six fatigue tests were performed on specimens $160 \times 100 \times 70$ mm at a cyclic frequency of 40 Hz using the stresses given in Table 7.3. The plot of the probability of failure strength in fast direct tensile tests (inert strength), shown in Figure 7.8, can be fitted to the Weibull equation with a modulus $m = 20.3$. Because constant stress rate tests were not performed, a different technique has to be used to that outlined above. Equation 7.17 is first applied to the data obtained in the third test series (this series was chosen because it had the greatest number of tests). The effective Weibull modulus m^* obtained from this test series was 0.515. Knowing that $m = 20.3$, the corrosion exponent n can be calculated from eqn 7.18a to be 41.4. The reference number of cycles N^* can also be calculated. From the values of m^* and N^* obtained from series 3, the predicted lifetimes for the other series have been calculated. The experimental results, shown in Figure 7.9, are in good agreement with the predicted results.

As a further example of the prediction of cyclic lifetimes, the tensile fatigue experiments on lightweight concrete of Saito (1984), shown in Figure 7.10, are considered. The test specimens were similar to those used by Saito and Imai (1983) and the same cyclic frequency of 40 Hz was employed. The stresses used in these tests are shown in Table 7.4. Since no inert strength

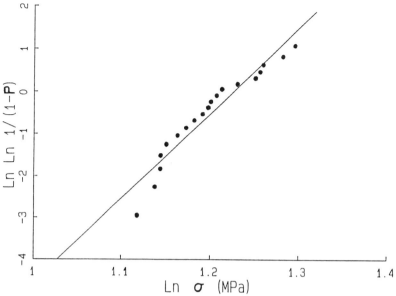

Figure 7.8 Inert strength probability for concrete. (After Saito and Imai, 1983.)

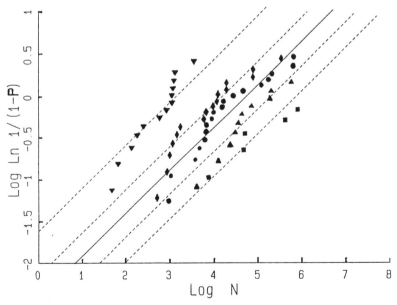

Figure 7.9 Comparison of single phase predictions of the cyclic fatigue of concrete with experimental results. (——) best fit; (- - - -) predictions. $S = $ (▼) 0.875, (◆) 0.825, (●) 0.8, (▲) 0.775, (■) 0.75 (after Saito and Imai, 1983.)

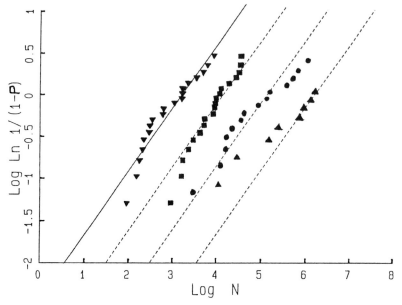

Figure 7.10 Comparison of single phase predictions of the cyclic fatigue of lightweight concrete with experimental results. (——) best fit; (- - - -) predictions. $S = $ (▼) 0.919, (■) 0.871, (●) 0.823, (▲) 0.774 (after Saito, 1984).

data are given for the lightweight concrete either the same corrosion coefficient as that for the previous concrete experiments has to be assumed, or two series analysed simultaneously to give both m and n. In either case m and n are approximately 30 and 40, respectively. The predictions of the lifetimes shown in Figure 7.10 in each case agree very well with experimental data.

Although the statistical fracture theory originally developed for the single-phase material predicts the lifetimes of the more heterogeneous plain and lightweight concretes subjected to cyclic stress reasonably well in the two examples given above, the approach is largely empirical because cracks in these latter materials are most likely stabilized by sands and aggregates. Hence, the Weibull parameters (m and σ_*) obtained are only statistical averages and so are the parameters (A and n) in the slow crack growth

Table 7.4 Cyclic fatigue stresses used in the tests by Saito (1984)

Series	Maximum stress (MPa)	$\zeta = \sigma_c/\sigma_0$
1	2.579	0.8126
2	2.744	0.8228
3	2.904	0.8318
4	3.062	0.8398

equation. This conclusion is consistent with the discussion of the relationship between dynamic and static fatigue.

It is not possible to infer from the above experimental results that the time-dependent fracture of plain and lightweight concrete under cyclic stress is purely caused by the environment-assisted crack growth. To do so it is necessary to be able to predict the cyclic fatigue results from either constant stress rate or constant sustained stress data. While Tait (1984) did exactly this for mortar, thus showing there was no true mechanical fatigue, the picture is not so clear for concrete. Murdock and Kesler (1958) have given some evidence that true mechanical fatigue did occur in bending tests on plain concrete beams (see Figure 7.11). For a given maximum stress it can be shown (Hu *et al.*, 1989) that, if there is no mechanical fatigue, the smaller the stress ratio, R, the longer the fatigue life. But the opposite trend is observed in Figure 7.11, indicating that the slow crack growth eqn 7.1 needs to be modified to account for the cyclic crack velocity component due to the true mechanical fatigue effect. Thus

$$\frac{da}{dt} = AK_a^n + A'\Delta K_a^{n'} \tag{7.44}$$

If the minimum stress in a cycle σ_{min} is fixed, then da/dt increases with the maximum stress σ_{max}. However, if σ_{max} is fixed and σ_{min} is reduced, the effect of the environment-assisted slow crack growth decreases and the effect of the

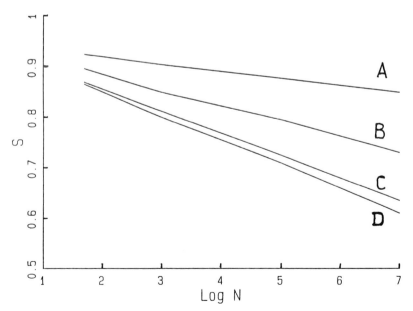

Figure 7.11 Effect of stress range ($S = \sigma_{max}/\sigma_{0.5}$) on the behaviour of plain concrete under bending fatigue at different stress ratio (R). A: $R = 0.75$, B: $R = 0.50$, C: $R = 0.25$, D: $R = 0.13$–0.18 (after Murdock and Kesler, 1958).

mechanical fatigue is enhanced. Whether the resultant da/dt increases or decreases depends on the relative magnitude of these two individual effects.

The parameter $G(n, \zeta)$ in the equation for cyclic fatigue life (see eqn 7.16) is essentially constant for $\zeta > 0.087$ ($R < 0.107$). It is shown by eqn 7.16 that for these low R values the fatigue lifetime only depends on the maximum stress σ_{max}. Hence the fatigue data in Figure 7.11 indicate that, if $R < 0.2$, N is independent of R because $G(n, \zeta)$ is practically constant. For $R > 0.25$ the lifetime N increases with R for any given maximum stress, showing that the mechanical fatigue effect is reduced. Even so, it is not accurate to use eqn 7.16 to predict the lifetime under cyclic stress. If the fatigue lifetime N only depends on σ_{max} such as at low R ratios, no matter whether mechanical fatigue occurs, the equivalent A^* and n^* values can be used to recast eqn 7.44 to an equivalent of eqn 7.1. However, for large R ratios the second term in eqn 7.44 depends on R and not σ_{max} or K_{max} alone. The tensile fatigue data in Figures 7.9 and 7.10 are for $R = 0.1$ and both slow crack growth and mechanical fatigue effects are operative. Thus, $n = 40$ determined from these data is actually the equivalent n^*. Lifetime predictions can hence be made for different maximum stresses using this value of n^* as already shown.

7.3 Summary

The strength of cementitious matrices is time-dependent being controlled by the slow crack growth induced by environmental effect and the statistics of flaw size and flaw distribution. The single crack approach which ignores the flaw statistics is found to be deficient, particularly in non-uniform stress situations, in predicting the time-dependent strength characteristics. Because of the large inhomogeneities in mortars and concretes that interfere with crack growth a more rigorous statistical fracture mechanics treatment than that applied to the 'pseudo'-homogeneous cement pastes is required. However, for practical purposes, such a distinction is not always needed provided the equivalent slow crack growth law of the statistically distributed flaws is determined. But this approximation approach cannot accurately predict the lifetimes of concrete under cyclic stress with high stress ratio because the mechanical fatigue effect has not been included.

Before leaving this chapter it is important to point out that at very fast loading rates not discussed here, slow crack growth is minimal as there is not enough time to permit chemically activated processes to take place. The time-dependent strength characteristics are then mainly determined by inertial effects and the original flaw size and density distributions. Because of the recent Kobe earthquake disaster (Sakamoto and Indrawan, 1995) studies on the dynamic effects or very high loading rates on the strength and fracture toughness of concrete structures have multiplied.

8 Application of fracture mechanics to the design of structures

8.1 Introduction

Until comparatively recently concrete was either assumed to have negligible tensile strength or to fail in a brittle manner at a low stress. As long as the stresses in a structure are small this assumption is reasonable. However, the trend is to use concrete more efficiently and to subject it to higher stresses. Also in many cases, such as un-reinforced beams, mass structures like dams, punching shear in concrete decks, reinforcement bonds and anchorages, and pipes, tensile failure can govern the strength. It has been shown in the preceding chapters that there is a size effect in strength that cannot be explained in terms of either strength of materials or classic LEFM. The application of fracture mechanics to concrete structures has therefore received considerable attention in the last few years, particularly by RILEM (Elfgren, 1989).

The realization of the importance of fracture mechanics to concrete design has seen the beginning of code-type formulation of fracture mechanics concepts (Hilsdorf and Brameshuber, 1991). The new draft CEB-FIP Model code (1990) includes a section 2.1, *Concrete—Classification and Constitutive Relations*, which gives some fracture mechanics properties. The key parameter for fracture mechanics, the mode I fracture energy, G_{If}, is given empirically in terms of the mean compressive strength, f_c, and a coefficient, a_d, that depends on the aggregate size, d_a (see Table 8.1) by

$$G_{If} = a_d f_c^{0.7} \quad (\text{J/m}^2, \text{MPa}) \tag{8.1}$$

This empirical relationship was largely based on a round robin test series (Hillerborg, 1985). Table 8.1 also gives the CTOD at fracture. The fracture energy is size dependent to a certain extent, but it has been shown that it reaches a plateau value at a remaining ligament of about 300 mm (Wittmann *et al.*, 1987). The mean tensile strength given empirically by

$$f_t = 0.3 f_c^{2/3} \quad (\text{MPa}, \text{MPa}) \tag{8.2}$$

The stress-strain relation is assumed to be linearly elastic up to a stress, $\sigma = 0.9 f_t$, with the Young's modulus given by

$$E = 10^4 f_c^{1/3} \quad (\text{MPa}, \text{MPa}) \tag{8.3}$$

At higher tensile stresses, the non-elastic deformation is assumed to decrease the stiffness and a strain of 0.00015 is assumed to be attained at the ultimate

Table 8.1 Coefficients for fracture parameters CEB-FIP (1990)

Aggregate size d_a (mm)	Coefficient a_d for G_{If}	Crack opening δ_f (mm)
8	4	0.12
16	6	0.15
32	10	0.25

strength of the concrete (see Figure 8.1). An empirical expression for the characteristic length, l_{ch}, can be found by combining eqns 8.1–8.3 and is given by

$$l_{ch} = \frac{G_{If} E}{f_t^2} = 110 a_d f_c^{-0.3} \qquad \text{(mm, MPa)} \qquad (8.4)$$

The stress-displacement strain-softening relationship is assumed to be bilinear (see Figure 3.8) with the break points (v, s) defined by

$$s = 0.15$$

$$v = \frac{G_{If}/\delta_f - 22(G_{If}/a_d)^{0.95}}{150(G_{If}/a_d)^{0.95}} \qquad (8.5)$$

The CEB-FIP Model Code 1990 is the first international concrete code that includes fracture mechanics data. However, the code-formulations

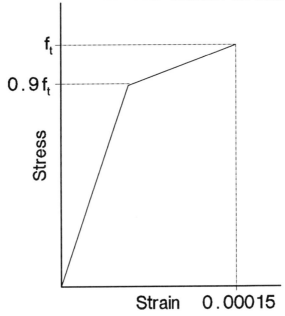

Figure 8.1 Stress-strain for uniaxial tension, $\epsilon < 0.00015$. (After Hilsdorf and Brameshuber, 1991.)

can be improved by experimental studies orientated towards practical engineering applications. In this chapter the application of fracture mechanics to practical engineering is discussed.

8.2 Application to monolithic structures

Although monolithic structures are mainly loaded in compression, it is usually cracks in local tension fields that cause problems. Dams are the largest monolithic structures and though the principal stresses are generally compressive, tensile stresses occur locally around openings and galleries. Reinforcement is usually provided in all areas where the tensile stresses exceed the allowable tensile stress and tensile cracks are more likely to be due to secondary rather than primary tensile stresses. Secondary tensile stresses can be caused by: temperature differences between the surface of the dam and the interior which can cause stresses as high as 4.5 MPa (Fanelli and Giuseppeti, 1990), abutment deformations exceeding that allowed for in the analysis, swelling of the concrete due to ageing or chemical processes, which can amount to 0.03% (Cervera et al., 1990), and earthquakes. Although tensile cracks have been observed in all types of dams, buttress dams seem more prone to cracks than other types (Fanelli and Giuseppeti, 1990).

Unfortunately, fracture mechanics is normally only used either to assess the effect of cracks that have been discovered in existing structures, or for studies of catastrophic failures, rather than as a design tool. Often fracture mechanics is seen as only relevant to older structures because it is assumed that new structures, designed using state-of-the-art finite element packages, will have only low tensile stresses that are unlikely to be a problem (Boggs et al., 1988). Classic LEFM can be applied in large monolithic structures whose dimensions and crack length are large compared with the characteristic length, l_{ch}. Here it must be noted that the characteristic length of the concrete used in dams is much larger than that of common concrete because of the large size of the aggregate (often up to 150 mm across) and l_{ch} can be as large as 1.7 m (Linsbauer, 1989a; Brühwiller and Wittmann, 1989b). Hence, the physical size of cracks in dams must be large before LEFM is applicable. Also, though dams are massive, the initial development of a crack cannot be modelled accurately by LEFM and the FPZ needs to be modelled by either the discrete or smeared cracks. In the case study of the fracture of a plinth in the Schoharie bridge, where there was no initial crack, modelling of the FPZ was essential (Swenson and Ingraffea, 1991). On the other hand, cracks discovered in dams are frequently very large and can be analysed using classic LEFM. The fracture mechanics applied to dams is described first.

8.2.1   The analysis of cracks in dams

Levy's rule is often used to determine the design profile of a gravity dam. According to this rule, the compressive stress on the upstream face of the dam must not be less than a threshold value, σ_u, to prevent water penetrating the dam face. The threshold value is given by (Linsbauer, 1989b)

$$\sigma_u = -\lambda \rho_w g h \tag{8.6}$$

where ρ_w is the density of water and λ is a reduction factor to allow for pore-water pressure. If it is assumed that the normal compressive stress has a linear variation across the base of the dam, it can be shown, for a dam with a triangular profile, that the ratio of the base (B) to height (h) must be given by (Linsbauer, 1989b)

$$\frac{B}{h} \geq \frac{1}{\sqrt{\rho_c/\rho_w - \lambda}} \tag{8.7}$$

where ρ_c is the density of concrete. Assuming that $\lambda = 0.85$, and $\rho_c = 2400 \, \text{kg/m}^3$, then according to Levy's rule, $B/h \geq 0.8$. Although fracture mechanics is not usually applied as such in dam design, the effects of cracks are considered in gravity and arch dams using a strength of materials approach similar to that described in section 4.2 (Rescher, 1990). It is assumed that cracks may form at the upstream face of a gravity dam and be penetrated by water to the point where the compressive stress is equal to the hydrostatic pressure. The variation of the compressive stress over the remaining ligament of the dam is assumed to be linear (see Figure 8.2). The crack is opened by the water pressure on the upstream face of the dam and closed by the weight of the dam. There will be a FPZ at the end of the crack which will be strained so that at its tip there will be a closing stress equal to the tensile strength of the concrete f_t. Water under hydrostatic pressure $\rho_w g h$ will penetrate right to the tip of the FPZ, so that here the tensile stress is $f_t - \rho_w g h$. Since the size of the FPZ would be small compared with a long crack the variation over the FPZ can be modelled by a discontinuous change in the stress from the hydrostatic pressure to a tensile stress $f_t - \rho_w g h$. Outside of the FPZ the stress must be continuous and could be modelled as a linear variation starting from a crack tip stress of $f_t - \rho_w g h$, as suggested by Saouma et al. (1987). However, Saouma et al. (1987) go on to assume that f_t is zero perhaps because of difficulties that are mentioned below. With the compressive stress assumed to be distributed as shown in Figure 8.2, it can be shown from equilibrium that the remaining uncracked ligament of the dam, b, is given by

$$\frac{b}{3} = \frac{M_0 - \rho_w g h B^2/2}{mg - \rho_w g h B} \tag{8.8}$$

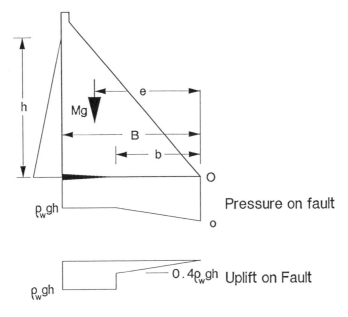

Figure 8.2 Forces acting on a section of a gravity dam.

where m is the mass (per unit width) of the dam above the particular horizontal section and M_0 is the moment (per unit width) of the weight of the dam about the toe (Corns *et al.*, 1988). For a dam of triangular profile, full with water, the remaining ligament is given by

$$\frac{b}{B} = \frac{2\left(\dfrac{\rho_c}{\rho_w}\right) - \left(\dfrac{h}{B}\right)^2 - 3}{\left(\dfrac{\rho_c}{\rho_w}\right) - 2} \tag{8.9}$$

The safety of the dam is then determined from the shear strength of the remaining ligament which must resist the hydrostatic thrust on the dam face. The dam is assumed to be subjected to a total uplift force, U, per unit width, due to the hydrostatic pressure in the cracked section and a reduced pressure varying from $0.4\rho_w gh$ at the crack tip to zero at the downstream face of the dam (see Figure 8.2). The shear strength, S, per unit width of the dam is then assumed to be

$$S = \tau_u b + \mu(Mg - U) \tag{8.10}$$

where τ_u is the shear strength of the concrete and μ is the coefficient of friction. Ingraffea (1990) gives a sample calculation for a generic gravity dam $(B/h = 0.8)$ at a depth of 100 m. The equilibrium crack length, 32.5 m, can be obtained from eqn 8.9. Assuming that $\mu = 0.7$ and $\tau_u = 2.75$ MPa, there is a factor of safety of 3.5 which would be less than the recommended value (Anonymous, 1976). A possible problem with the application of this method is the extreme sensitivity to the profile of the dam. Equation 8.6 predicts that crack penetration is impossible if $B/h > 0.845$ and that cracks will completely penetrate the dam when $B/h < 0.745$. If one attempts to improve on the approximate method by taking a representative tensile strength for the concrete instead of assuming that it is zero, as Saouma et al. (1987) did explicitly and every other author has done implicitly, then one finds that no equilibrium crack exists.[1] Similar strength of materials approaches have been used with arch dams (Rescher, 1990).

The effect of horizontal cracks initiated in the upstream face of gravity dams has also been considered using LEFM. A horizontal crack path is not a natural crack path for propagation under combined thrust on the upstream face of the dam by hydrostatic pressure in the crack, and gravity forces, because the stress intensity factor is a mixed mode. Linsbauer (1989b) has calculated the stress intensity factors at the tip of such a crack in a gravity dam with a triangular profile $(B/h = 0.8)$, using back face correction factors (Linsbauer and Rossmanith, 1984). Assuming that the appropriate fracture criterion is the maximum circumferential tensile stress criterion (Erdogan and Sih, 1963), Linsbauer (1989b) constructed curves of constant K_{Ic} as a function of the depth of the crack (see Figure 8.3). The 'strength of materials' approach could be considered equivalent to a LEFM criterion of $K_I = 0$, curves for which are given in Figure 8.3. At a depth of 100 m, the equilibrium crack length for $K_I = 0$ can be read from Figure 8.3 to be about 26 m. Ingraffea (1990) has used finite elements to analyse the same problem and obtained a crack length of 31 m. Both these crack lengths are similar to that obtained from the 'strength of materials' value of 32.5 m. However, though the agreement between the 'strength of materials' approach and LEFM is good, the sensitivity of the 'strength of materials' approach to the assumptions used creates the suspicion that the agreement might be fortuitous. There is also some doubt whether the limit criterion of $K_I = 0$ for the LEFM solutions is reasonable. Such a criterion does predict an increase in the critical crack length with depth in common with the 'strength of materials' approach. However, if either a constant K_I or constant K_{Ic} is used as a criterion, the solution of Linsbauer (1989b) predicts a decrease in critical crack length with depth, and Ingraffea's (1990) FEM solution predicts a maximum stable crack length at a particular depth (21 m at a depth of 40 m, using a criterion of $K_I = 2\,\text{MPa}\sqrt{m}$). Ingraffea (1990) also gives two other important qualifications to the comparison. If the elastic properties of the foundation and the concrete differ, then superposition cannot be used. Secondly the crack will not grow horizontally, but will propagate in a curvilinear manner downwards.

---

[1] The roots of the quadratic equation to determine the equilibrium crack length are imaginary.

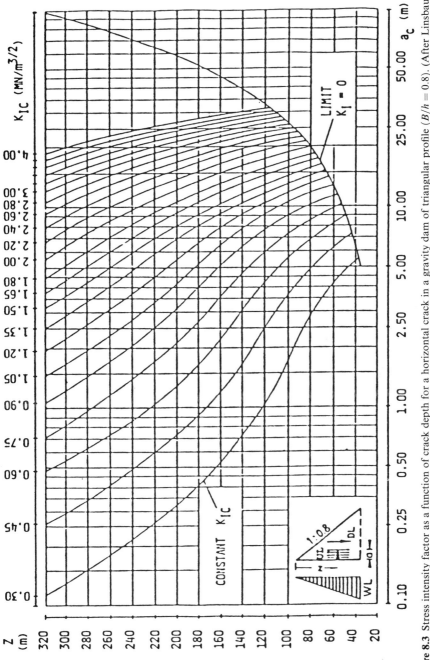

Figure 8.3 Stress intensity factor as a function of crack depth for a horizontal crack in a gravity dam of triangular profile ($B/h = 0.8$). (After Linsbauer, 1989b.)

The first application of LEFM to dams was made in 1981 in the USA to the Fontana gravity dam by Chappell and Ingraffea (1981), and in China to the investigation of thermally induced cracks in the Zhexi diamond head buttress dam by Yu (1981, 1989). Since then there have been a number of other LEFM analyses of other gravity and arch dams (Saouma et al., 1987; Linsbauer et al., 1989). The study of the Austrian Kölnbrein arch dam (Linsbauer et al., 1989) made use of a two-dimensional fracture element analysis code, FRANC, developed by Wawrzynek and Ingraffea (1987a,b). This code models both the initiation[2] and propagation of cracks by the discrete method. The maximum circumferential stress criterion of Erdogan and Sih (1963) is used to determine the crack path at each increment in crack extension and the code has automatic remeshing after each crack increment. The fracture in the Fontana dam was also re-analysed using FRANC (Ingraffea, 1990) and the predictions of the crack path are compared with the actual path in Figure 8.4 (the crack path predicted in the original analysis used a code that needed to be driven manually and a slightly different definition of the crack path direction was also used). Both of the theoretical predictions are in excellent agreement with the observed crack. Gravity dams and the buttresses of buttress dams are essentially two-dimensional. Arch dams are more inherently three-dimensional structures, but even here a two-dimensional analysis can be sufficient for practical purposes (Linsbauer et al., 1989). Full three-dimensional codes will no doubt be produced in the future, but the question of mixed mode propagation in three dimensions has not yet been completely answered.

In order to predict the safety of a dam, in which a crack is discovered or to calculate the safety factor of a dam design, it is necessary to know the material properties of the concrete. The concrete used in dams is characterized by a very large aggregate, which is often low strength gneiss. As a consequence fractures usually pass through the aggregate rather than around it and the tensile strength is smaller than that observed for normal concrete (Brühwiller and Wittmann, 1989b). In contrast the fracture energy, G_{If}, is two to three times that of common concrete (Brühwiller and Wittmann, 1989b), maybe because a large aggregate implies a wide fracture process zone and hence a large CTOD. The net result is that the characteristic length (up to about 1.7 m) is up to ten times that of common concrete. The large size poses problems for the measurement of G_{If} since it has a size dependence when the RILEM (1985) TC-50 method is used to determine it. However,

---

[2] On a smooth surface a crack is initiated when the modulus of rupture is exceeded with an immediate transition to LEFM by the insertion of a small crack. Thus, the initial stages of crack formation will not be highly accurate. However, since in dams cracks are usually long, the initiation phase is not critical.

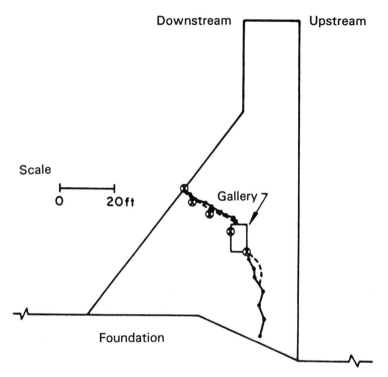

Figure 8.4 Comparison of predicted crack paths with that observed in the Fontana dam (- - - - - FEM, Chappel and Ingraffea (1981); - - - FEM, Ingraffea (1990); ⊗ Location of crack from drilling). (After Ingraffea, 1990.)

the wedge splitting test suggested by Brühwiller and Wittmann (1989a) is appropriate for concrete with large aggregate.

8.2.2   Case study of a fracture in a concrete bridge plinth

Swenson and Ingraffea (1991) have made a detailed fracture mechanics analysis of the fracture of the plinth of one of the piers in the Schoharie Creek Bridge (see Figure 8.5) which collapsed in 1987 killing ten people. The collapse of the bridge was due to the fracture of the plinth of Pier Three that had been undermined by scouring of its footing. The bridge was constructed in 1954. The plinth contained no structural reinforcement, but had some reinforcement against shrinkage and temperature. About a year after the bridge opened, vertical cracks were found in the upper surfaces of the plinths of all the piers. These cracks were attributed to excessive bending stresses in the plinths and they were reinforced with reinforced concrete beams dowelled to the plinth. The plinth of Pier Three fractured because of extensive scouring of its footing. The fracture did not initiate at

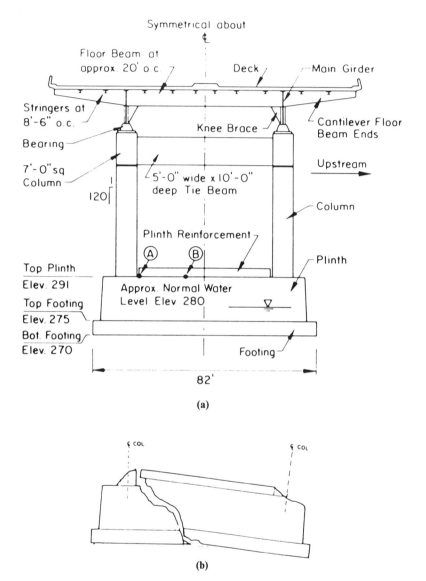

Figure 8.5 (a) Pier Three of the Schoharie Creek Bridge; (b) Fracture plinth of Pier Three. (After Wiss *et al.*, 1987.)

the pre-existing crack, location B in Figure 8.5, but at location A at the first set of dowels 0.5 m from the end of the reinforcing beam. The original failure report (Wiss *et al.*, 1987) used FEM to calculate the elastic stresses and found that at location A the tensile stress was 1.5 MPa (210 psi). Since the splitting tensile strength of the concrete was found to be 4.3 MPa (620 psi) the investigators looked around for a possible explanation of how the plinth failed when the calculated stress was so much less than the measured strength.[3] What was done illustrates the danger of non-fracture mechanists using fracture mechanics.[4] Bažant's size effect law (Bažant et al., 1986) was correctly used to argue that the modulus of rupture in the plinth would be smaller than the modulus of rupture measured in a small laboratory specimen, but the tensile splitting strength was confused with the modulus of rupture (Swenson and Ingraffea, 1991). It was not understood that the modulus of rupture does not represent the actual bending strength, but is the equivalent elastic bending stress at failure. Another problem with the original failure analysis was the failure to recognize that, near a singularity, the stresses calculated by FEM are mesh size dependent (Swenson and Ingraffea, 1991). A correct analysis of the problem has been given by Swenson and Ingraffea (1991), who modelled the development of the FPZ and crack at location A using the discrete model of Hillerborg et al. (1976). Not having the actual value of the fracture energy, G_{If}, Swenson and Ingraffea (1991) estimated its value from the size of the aggregate (25 mm) to be 241 J/m^2.[5] Since the fracture energy was not known accurately a linear stress-displacement relationship was assumed for the FPZ. Theoretically a FPZ must initiate, at the singularity at the re-entrant corner, for the smallest applied load, and to model accurately the early stages in the development of the FPZ the mesh size must be able to cope only with a high, but not infinite, stress gradient at the tip of the FPZ. Thus the analysis is objective and converges. Swenson and Ingraffea (1991) used quadratic triangular elements. With a mesh size of 3 inches, a FPZ of 4 inches was shown to form after a scour of 32 feet. The size of the zone does not increase rapidly with the length of scour, and was not much different after a scour of 36 feet. A scour of only 28 feet was assumed to have caused unstable crack propagation by Wiss et al. (1987). Even with a scour of 41 feet and equal column loads, unstable propagation was not predicted and the pier became kinematically unstable. Swenson and Ingraffea (1991) postulated that settlement in the piers led to a redistribution in the column loads so that scouring greater than 41 feet could take place without kinematic

---

[3] The authors of the original report on the failure should not be blamed too much for seeking to alter their material properties to give a satisfactory answer, since this is exactly what the father of fracture mechanics, Griffith, did himself. In his first paper, Griffith (1920) presented results from tests on glass to support his theory by annealing his specimens, arguing that it was necessary to anneal to remove the residual stresses. Unfortunately, there was an error in the theory of his first paper that caused a 44% error in fracture strength. In his second paper, Griffith (1925) argued that annealing had blunted his cracks in the glass; by reducing the annealing time he got agreement between his experiments and his theory. This very human failing in no way detracts from Griffith's genius.
[4] Alternatively, one could say it illustrates the failure of fracture mechanists to communicate their work to practising engineers.
[5] This value seems somewhat high. If the formula given by the CEB-FIB Model Code 1990 (see section 8.1) is used $G_{If} \approx 110$ J/m^2. Naturally the code is giving a lower bound to G_{If}, but it is unlikely that the most probable value will be more than twice this value.

instability. There was in fact direct evidence, from the disposition of the fractured plinth, that at least 44 feet of scouring had taken place before failure. At 44 feet of scour the analysis of Swenson and Ingraffea (1991) indicated that a true crack of greater than 4 inches would have formed with a FPZ of about 10 inches.[6] Calculation of the applied stress intensity factor at the tip of a true crack showed that instability would occur with a true crack less than 1 foot with a scour of 44 feet. Swenson and Ingraffea (1991) concluded that the plinth fractured after a scour of about 44 feet. They predicted the fracture path using LEFM and found good agreement with the actual fracture path. It should be noted that in inherently unstable geometries, that is those where the fracture of an ideal brittle material would be unstable, fracture always occurs before the FPZ is fully developed. The larger the component, the nearer to complete formation will be the FPZ at instability.

8.2.3   In situ *measurement of fracture properties*

The properties of concrete used in a structure are usually determined from field-cast specimens. However, there is a difference in properties between concrete cast and cured in test cylinders and the same concrete in a structure. Also, in the event of a structural failure many years after construction, the properties may not be available or suspect. For these reasons there is increasing interest in the *in situ* properties. The Break-Off (BO) test, reviewed by Naik (1991), was established as a method of measuring the *in situ* strength of concrete. In the BO test a cylindrical test specimen is separated from the concrete structure during pouring by a plastic cylinder. The test is performed using a special loading attachment that produces a transverse load (see Figure 8.6). Although the BO test is fundamentally a flexural test, the break-off load is usually correlated with the compressive strength of the concrete.

The BO test has been modified by Hashida *et al.* (1990) to enable the fracture toughness to be measured *in situ*. A pair of cores are drilled into the face of the concrete. A conventional BO test is performed on one of the cores, and a notch is then machined into the base of the other using a diamond saw (see Figure 8.7). The second core is broken off from the structure using the standard BO loading apparatus. A LVDT is used to measure the displacement during fracture and the acoustic emission is measured. The J-integral is calculated from the area (A) under the load-displacement curve; at the moment there is a sudden rapid increase in acoustic emission, from the

---

[6] For this degree of scouring, the condition of zero stress intensity factor was not met. In fact the stress intensity factor was about 80% of the fracture toughness. No reasons are stated for not determining the equilibrium condition but, since the finite element program was driven by the degree of scouring rather than the CTOD or true crack length, the program would encounter difficulties near instability.

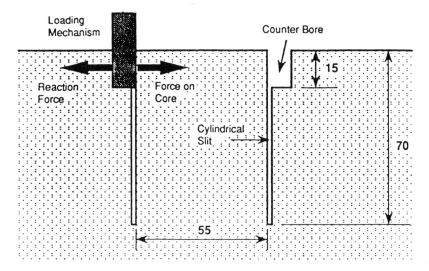

CROSS SECTION

Dimensions in millimeters

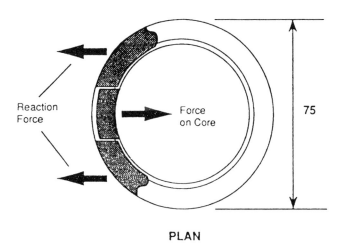

PLAN

Figure 8.6 The Break-Off Test. (After Naik, 1991.)

expression

$$J = \frac{\eta A}{Bb} \tag{8.11}$$

where b is the remaining ligament, B is the width of the notch, and η is estimated to be 2.5 for $a/D > 0.4$ from simple beam theory. The results from more standard fracture toughness specimens using the same technique

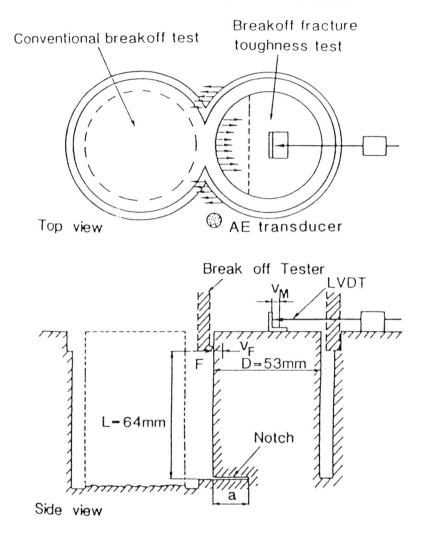

Figure 8.7 Break-off fracture toughness testing method. (After Hashida *et al.*, 1990.)

are used to suggest that the value measured in this way is independent of the specimen size. The break-off tests performed by Hashida *et al.* (1990) used core diameter of 53 mm and the concrete had a maximum aggregate size of 20 mm. The results from these tests gave similar fracture toughness values to those obtained from compact tension specimens with a ligament *b* of 110 mm. However, the use of fracture toughness for small size specimens is questionable and it would perhaps be preferable to measure the fracture energy by this method. Whether the fracture toughness or fracture energy is measured, there seems little point in performing *in situ* tests when the broken off core could be more easily tested in the laboratory using either the short rod or notch bend geometry.

A more interesting *in situ* test, suitable for massive structures such as dams, has been suggested by Saouma *et al.* (1991). In this test a borehole is drilled into the concrete and the borehole pressurized with a dilatometer probe which contains LVDTs to measure the hole dilatation. Acoustic emission sensors are mounted near the borehole on the surface to detect cracking. Initially, the borehole is subjected to cycles of pressure, too small to cause cracking, so that effective Young's modulus can be obtained from compliance measurements. The probe is then slowly pressurized until a large burst in acoustic emissions indicates the borehole has cracked. This pressure then gives the apparent tensile strength, f_{tapp}, of the concrete. The true strength cannot be determined directly because the state of stress at the position of the probe is not known exactly. The apparent strength of the concrete is given approximately by

$$f_{\text{tapp}} = f_{\text{t}} - 3\sigma_2 + \sigma_1 \qquad \text{if} \quad 3\sigma_2 > \sigma_1 > \sigma_2 \qquad (8.12a)$$

and

$$f_{\text{tapp}} = f_{\text{t}} - 3\sigma_1 + \sigma_2 \qquad \text{if} \quad \sigma_1 > 3\sigma_2 \qquad (8.12b)$$

where σ_1 is the maximum normal stress acting perpendicularly to the bore-hole and σ_2 is the minimum. In a dam, one or both of these normal stresses are usually compressive and this case f_{tapp} is greater than the true tensile strength.[7] It is possible, in theory, to estimate the maximum tensile stress that exists at the borehole from a measurement of the tensile strength of the core. However, the core is necessarily going to be quite small in diameter[8] and in practice the tensile strength obtained may not be accurate enough. The borehole is then subjected to larger and larger pressure cycles and compliance measurements used to determine the effective crack length at each cycle. The apparent fracture toughness, $K_{\text{Ic}}^{\text{app}}$, is then calculated from the effective crack length and the pressure. There are two reasons why Saouma *et al.* (1991) quote the fracture toughness as an apparent value. Firstly, the state of stress at the borehole is not known exactly and $K_{\text{Ic}}^{\text{app}}$ is calculated from only the pressure applied. Secondly, since the effective crack method of measuring fracture toughness is very approximate, $K_{\text{Ic}}^{\text{app}}$ depends upon the effective crack length. The results of the *in situ* measurements are given in Figure 8.8.

---

[7] In laboratory tests on blocks of concrete 910 × 910 × 1140 mm, which were compressed across one pair of faces with a compressive stress of 0.69 MPa, the differences between f_{tapp} and f_{t}, obtained from a standard splitting test, were 0.71, 0.63 and 0.13 for the three different aggregate sizes of 19 mm, 38 mm and 76 mm, respectively (Saouma *et al.*, 1991). Obviously the results from the concrete with the two smaller aggregates agree with eqn 8.7. The large discrepancy for the largest aggregate size may have been due to an inadequate size for the splitting test.
[8] In field tests by Saouma *et al.* (1991), the borehole was cored with a standard HWD4 core drill which has a 61 mm diameter barrel.

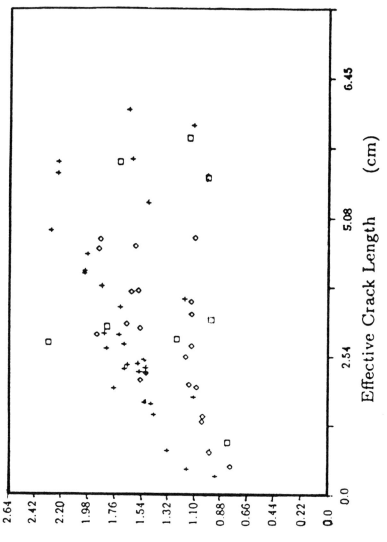

Figure 8.8 Apparent fracture toughness, measured *in situ* in a US dam, as a function of the effective crack length. □, 19-mm MSA; +, 39-mm MSA; ◊, 76-mm MSA. (After Saouma *et al.*, 1991.)

As might be expected, there is considerable scatter in the results, but there is a trend for the apparent fracture toughness to increase with the effective crack length. Such an increase in apparent fracture toughness is not surprising because the size of the FPZ must increase with the crack size and hence the apparent fracture toughness must also increase. However, the method pioneered by Sauoma *et al.* (1991) is worth pursuing, because it could very easily be modelled by the fictitious crack model to obtain a reasonable estimate of the fracture energy, G_{If}, if a suitable generic form of the strain-softening stress-displacement relationship is assumed.

8.3 Punching shear failure of slabs

One of the possible modes of failure for slabs is punching. This failure mode occurs when a slab is subjected to a concentrated load which eventually punches a slug from the slab. The current design approaches to punching are covered by a wide range of empirical formulae much derived from plastic limit analysis. These formulae have been reviewed by Stefanou (1993). The codes, though primarily strength based, defining nominal allowable stresses based on the concentrated load divided by a representative area of the concrete, do have allowances for size effect. For example, CP110 (1972) gives the effective shear strength, τ_u, as

$$\tau_u = \frac{0.27}{\gamma_m} \left(\frac{500}{d} \right)^{1/4} (100vf_c)^{1/3} \tag{8.13}$$

where d is the effective depth of the slab (measured from the compression surface to the centre of any reinforcement), γ_m is a constant ($= 1.25$, for $f_c < 40$ MPa), and v is the volume fraction of reinforcement. Bažant and Cao (1987) have discussed the size effect in punching from the concept of Bažant's (1984) SEL. The SEL applies to geometrically similar notched specimens. Since there is no notch in the punching test, it has to be assumed that a geometrically similar crack has developed stably at maximum load. Bažant and Cao's (1987) size effect plot (see Figure 8.9) shows that there is only a weak dependence of the shear strength on size and there is no sign of a trend to an asymptotic slope of $-1/2$ as the size gets larger which throws some doubt on the application of the SEL in punching. Gardner (1990) has compared the shear strength predicted by the codes and the prediction given by Bažant and Cao (1987) with the experimental results of others—the codes give a better prediction. In fact the size effect predicted by eqn 8.13 is stronger than that predicted by Bažant and Cao (1987).

There have been a few fracture mechanics analyses of punching using the smeared crack model (de Borst and Nauta, 1985; González-Vidosa *et al.*, 1988; Malvar, 1992). The analyses using the smeared crack model are aimed more at reproducing experimental results numerically rather than

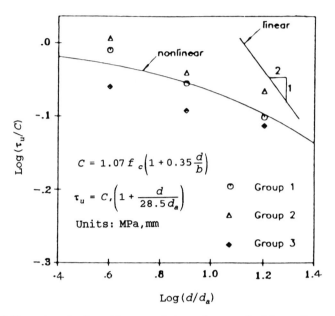

Figure 8.9 Shear strength of punching tests relative to the strength of the smallest specimen (d is the full slab thickness and d_a is the size of the aggregate). (After Bažant and Cao, 1987.)

establishing a more rational treatment of punching. The details of some of the numerical analyses are at best sketchy. Statements like 'a fracture energy of $100\,N/m$ was assumed' (Malvar, 1992) give rise to the suspicions that the parameters in this paper and the others may have been adjusted in order to give good agreement with the experimental results.

The smeared crack model would appear to be too complex to establish general equations for the predictions of shear strength in punching and the time may be right for simpler treatments. It would appear that the early analysis of Kinnunen and Nylander (1960) could be re-examined in light of the fictitious crack model as a possible method of obtaining a simple rational approach to the important phenomenon of punching.

8.4 Reinforcement bonding and anchorage to concrete

The difference between the reinforcement and anchor bolts is that reinforcement is continuous, so that the tensile load is transmitted mainly by the reinforcement and the prime function of the concrete is to provide shear strength, whereas in anchor bolts there is a direct transfer of tensile load to the concrete through shear over the shank and compression under the head. However, there are similarities between the behaviour of reinforcement and anchors. Even with continuous reinforcement some tensile load is taken

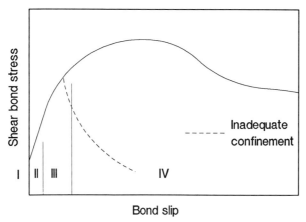

Figure 8.10 Schematic reinforcement bond stress-slip relationship. (After Gambarova *et al.*, 1989a.)

by the concrete between the cracks, resulting in what is known as tensile stiffening (Gilbert and Warner, 1978; Foegl and Mang, 1982; Gerstle *et al.*, 1982; Wu *et al.*, 1991). If anchor bolts are long, a considerable proportion of the load can be transferred to the concrete along the shank of the anchor. The reinforcement bond is considered first.

8.4.1 Reinforcement bond slip and tensile stiffening

Four stages (see Figure 8.10) have been characterized in the pull-out behaviour of reinforcement bar (Gambarova *et al.*, 1989a). At low shear stresses ($<0.5f_t$) the shear in stage I can be resisted by the chemical bond and no bond slip occurs (Gambarova and Karakoç, 1982). At higher shear stresses the chemical bond is broken by the wedging action of the ribs on the reinforcement and the bond becomes purely mechanical. In stage II, for bond shear stresses $0.7-1.5f_t$, secondary transverse cracks develop from the ribs. The stress at which the transverse cracks develop in this stage is dependent on the confining pressure. At higher shear stresses in stage III ($1-3f_t$), the concrete ahead of the ribs starts to crush and, under the hoop stress caused by the wedging action, longitudinal splits initiate (Gambarova and Karakoç, 1982). If the cover on the reinforcement is insufficient, primary transverse cracks can propagate from the outer surface of the concrete to the reinforcement bar (Gerstle *et al.*, 1982) and the longitudinal cracks extend to the surface. In the absence of transverse reinforcement the shear resistance drops to practically zero at this stage. However, if there is transverse reinforcement that provides a significant confining pressure, the shear resistance can increase to give stage IV. In this stage the bond shear stress can reach as high as $1/3$ to $1/2f_c$. There are two aspects of the problem: the

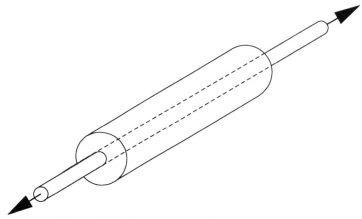

Figure 8.11 Pull–pull tension reinforcement specimen.

modelling of the bond-slip mechanisms and the incorporation of bond-slip interface elements in finite element programs.

The two main contributions to bond-slip up to stage IV are transverse cracking and crushing at the ribs. The mechanics of bond-slip have been modelled using either smeared cracks (Rots, 1985, 1988) or discrete cracks (Ingraffea *et al.*, 1984; Yao and Murray, 1993). The favoured geometry analysed is that of the pull–pull tension specimen (see Figure 8.11) which was the experimental geometry used by Goto and his co-workers (1971, 1979). The choice of this specimen geometry is perhaps unfortunate because it does not really correspond to the practical reinforcement situation. The cracking is confined to the loaded ends of the specimen and the secondary cracks here soon extend to the ends of the concrete confinement. Rots (1985, 1988) considers both the transverse and longitudinal cracks. The transverse cracks were modelled using the coaxial rotating crack concept and the longitudinal cracks treated as fixed cracks. In addition, potential discrete crack elements were placed mid-section so that a primary crack could be triggered. The crack formation just prior to primary crack formation is shown in Figure 8.12. In the discrete crack treatment of Ingraffea *et al.* (1984), only transverse cracks were modelled because axial symmetric elements were used. Yao and Murray (1993) have given a three-dimensional discrete crack solution that enabled longitudinal cracks to be studied. Ingraffea *et al.* (1984) remesh at each crack growth increment so that the crack could grow according to the condition of local symmetry, whereas Yao and Murray (1993) used a fixed element mesh and orientated the cracks along the element faces that most nearly corresponded to the principal stress trajectory. The cracking in a pull–pull tension specimen (Ingraffea *et al.*, 1984), at the moment the first secondary crack extends to the edge of the concrete confinement is shown in Figure 8.13. Ingraffea *et al.* (1984) give an empirical

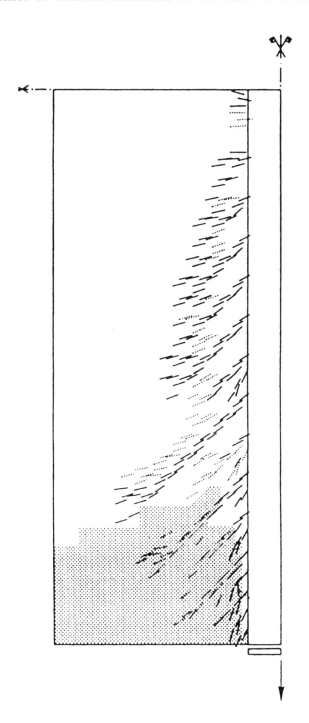

Figure 8.12 Crack formation in the pull–pull tension specimen at impending primary crack formation (– – – – active transverse cracks, · · · · · inactive transverse cracks, longitudinal cracks shaded). (After Rots, 1988.)

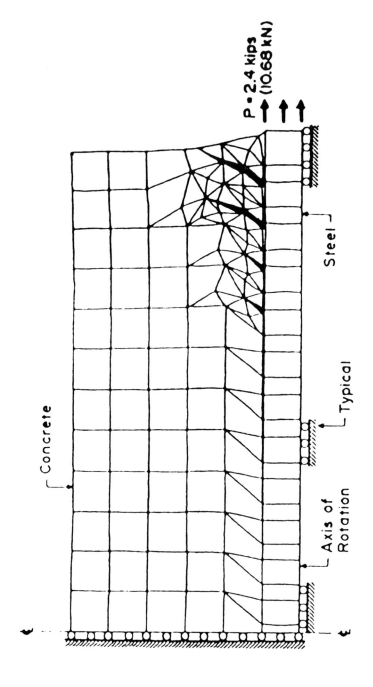

Figure 8.13 Crack formation in the pull–pull tension specimen showing four secondary transverse cracks. (After Ingraffea *et al.*, 1984.)

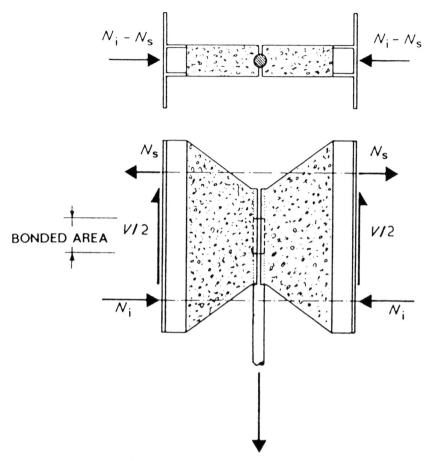

Figure 8.14 Specimen for measuring stage IV bond stress-slip relationship. (After Gambarova *et al.*, 1989a.)

expression for the slip at the end of the specimen that includes the effect of secondary cracking. Gambarova and Giuriani (1985) have criticized the analysis of Ingraffea *et al.* (1984) because they neglected crushing at the reinforcement ribs which becomes the dominant factor for a relatively small slip.

Stage IV of the shear bond-slip relationship has been less studied than the earlier stages, but is important for the proper design of stirrups in beams (Gambarova *et al.*, 1989a). A realistic test method for the study of stage IV reinforcement bond behaviour, shown in Figure 8.14, enables the effect of the confining pressure of transverse reinforcement to be examined (Gambarova *et al.*, 1989a,b). The longitudinal split is cast into the specimen by inserting plexiglass separators into the formwork. Typical bond stress-slip curves for 18 mm diameter round deformed reinforcing bar with crescent-shaped lugs are shown in Figure 8.15. In these tests the confining pressure

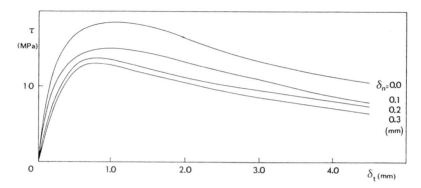

Figure 8.15 Bond stress-slip relationship for stage IV, split opening $\delta_n = 0$, 0.1, 0.2, 0.3 mm. (After Gambarova *et al.*, 1989a.)

was adjusted to allow the longitudinal splits to open by varying amounts. The bond stress-slip relationship can be idealized into a trilinear model (see Figure 8.16) where the first linear portion is stage I, the second linear portion stages II and III, and the final plateau value, stage IV. The drop in shear resistance with bond slip in stage IV need not be modelled since the drop is slight over a considerable slip if there is sufficient confining pressure.

Analytical estimates of the stiffening effect of the concrete have been made using idealized bond stress-slip relationships (Giuriani, 1982; Wu *et al.*, 1991). Wu *et al.* (1991) assumed that stage I was the most important in determining the tensile stiffening, whereas Giuriani (1982) assumed stage II to be more important (see Figure 8.17 for the idealizations). Since in both cases multiple cracking is assumed, Giuriani's (1982) idealization seems preferable. For moderate reinforcement the exponential decay in slip u_s from a crack face is given by

$$u_s = u_{0s} \exp(-\lambda x) \tag{8.14}$$

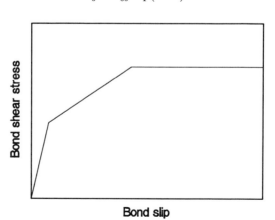

Figure 8.16 Idealized bond stress-slip relationship. (After Gambarova and Giuriani, 1985.)

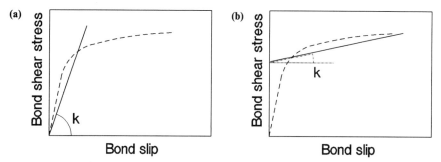

Figure 8.17 Idealized bond stress-slip relationships used to determine tensile stiffening: - - - - - experimental curve, ——— idealization. (a) Wu *et al.*, 1991; (b) Giuriani, 1982.

where u_{0s} is the slip at the crack face and $\lambda^2 = 4k/E_s d$, k being defined in Figure 8.17, E_s is the Young's modulus of steel and d is the diameter of the reinforcement. The transfer length, $1/\lambda$, is clearly much longer under Giuriani's (1982) assumption than that of Wu *et al.* (1991).

8.4.2 Anchorage to concrete

Anchoring elements are used to transmit local loads into reinforced concrete components. The load transmitted can be tension, shear or a combination of the two. Unless the anchorage is near the edge of a member, tensile loads are the most critical and it is anchorages transmitting tensile loads that will be discussed here. The anchors can be headed studs or undercut bolts, where the load transfer is mainly due to mechanical interlock, or expansion or grouted bolts, where the transfer is through the bond between the bolt and the concrete. The possible failure modes of anchors loaded in tension are:

(I) The anchor is pulled out of its hole with little concrete damage. This mode occurs in bonded anchors if the bond strength is too small and the bond stress-slip relationship will be similar to that discussed in section 8.4.1. Expansion anchor bolts will pull out if the expansion force is too small to give the required frictional force.

(II) The anchor is placed too near an edge or too close to each other and the concrete splits (Olsson, 1985).

(III) The bolt or the sleeve fails.

(IV) The full strength of the concrete is realized and a concrete failure cone is developed. If the anchor is too near an edge a partial cone will form at a lower load and if there are multiple anchors too close together a combined cone will form usually at a lower load. If the anchor is deeply embedded to a depth greater than the transfer length given by eqn 8.4, a series of failure cones will develop (Goto *et al.*, 1993).

It is failure mode IV, in which the maximum load is attained, that is of most interest. For a headed anchorage, where all the load is taken on the

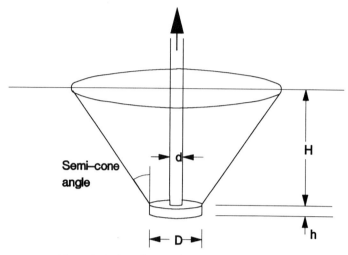

Figure 8.18 Cone fracture from a headed anchorage.

Table 8.2 Dimensions of headed anchor bolts (Eligehausen and Sawade, 1989)

Anchor size	h (mm)	d (mm)	D (mm)	H (mm)	$\bar{H} = H/l_{ch}$
1	10	22	35	120	0.236
2	10	30	45	250	0.492
3	20	50	80	500	0.985

head, failure is by the propagation of a cone fracture (see Figure 8.18). Provided the depth, H, to head diameter, D, is reasonably large, the initial development of a cone fracture is stable even in an ideally elastic-brittle material.[9] The semi-angle generally varies from 45 to 60° and it is assumed to be 45° in ACI 349 (1980). In a series of tests on headed anchor bolts of varying size, Eligehausen and Sawade (1989) found the semi-angle to be 52.5°. For very large embedded lengths LEFM can be used and assuming that the semi-cone angle is 52.5°, Eligehausen and Sawade (1989) have calculated that the cone fracture in an elastic-brittle material will grow stably until $a/L \approx 0.45$. At instability the nominal pull-out stress ($\sigma_N = P/H^2$) is given by (Eligehausen and Sawade, 1989)

$$\sigma_N = \frac{2.1 f_t}{\sqrt{\bar{H}}} \tag{8.15}$$

where $\bar{H} = H/l_{ch}$ is the non-dimensional depth of the anchor. Eligehausen and Sawade (1989) performed pull-out tests on a series of different size specimens (see Table 8.2). The properties of the concrete used in these tests

[9] Two-dimensional analysis by Ballarini *et al.* (1986, 1987) shows that a stable crack will be initiated if $H/D \geq 2$.

Table 8.3 Properties of concrete (Eligehausen and Sawade, 1989)

Compressive strength, f_c	22.9 MPa
Tensile strength, f_t	1.8 MPa
Young's modulus, E	23.5 GPa
Fracture energy, G_{If}	70 J/m^2
Characteristic length, l_{ch}	508 mm

are shown in Table 8.3, from which the characteristic length can be calculated to be 508 mm, and thus the non-dimensional embedment depths are as shown in Table 8.2. Eligehausen and Sawade (1989) found that LEFM predicted the nominal pull-out strengths reasonably well (see Figure 8.19). The accuracy of this prediction is surprising given the rather small non-dimensional embedment depth. For small embedment depths LEFM will not apply and the pull-out strength would be expected to tend to a finite value as $H \rightarrow 0$. The transition in behaviour from large embedment depths to small is similar to other size effects and could be expected to be covered by Bažant's (1993) size effect law. Assuming that the SEL given by eqn 4.32 applies and for very deep embedments the pull-out strength is given by eqn 8.15, we have taken the results of Eligehausen and Sawade (1989) for the shortest anchor to calculate the SEL

$$\sigma_N = f_t \frac{7.55}{(1 + 12.9\bar{H})^{1/2}} \tag{8.16}$$

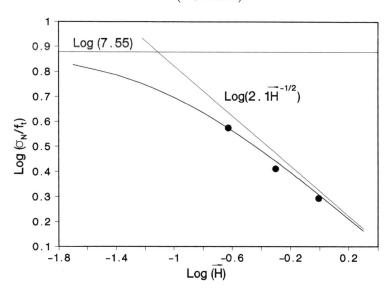

Figure 8.19 Normalized pull-out strength as a function of the non-dimensional embedment depth for headed anchor bolts (● experimental points from Eligehausen and Sawade, 1989; —— eqn 8.17).

The predictions of eqn 8.16 are shown in Figure 8.19. It is difficult to conclude that the SEL is more efficient than simple LEFM because one of the data points was used for the prediction. The SEL gives the limiting nominal pull-out strength as 13.6 MPa as $H \to 0$, which is equivalent to an average normal stress over the conical surface of 1.31 MPa. This stress value compares well with the tensile strength of 1.8 MPa given for the concrete in Table 8.3.

In an earlier series of tests the pull-out force for expansion bolts whose embedded depths varied from 20 to 150 mm were measured (Eligehausen and Pusill-Wachtsmuth, 1982; Eligehausen, 1987). The semi-angle of the pull-out cone was larger for this series at about 60°. The test results came from concrete whose compressive strengths, f_c, varied from 10 to 50 MPa, but most had a strength close to 20 MPa. The pull-out strengths shown in Figure 8.20 have been adjusted to a strength of 20 MPa by assuming that the strength is proportional to $f_c^{2/3}$. Evaluation of the data by regression analysis by Eligehausen and Pusill-Wachtsmuth (1982) yielded an empirical

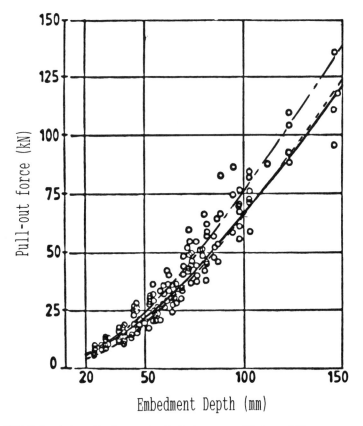

Figure 8.20 Pull-out strength of expansion bolts (- — - modified eqn 8.15; - - - - modified eqn 8.16; —— eqn 8.17). (After Eligehausen and Pusill-Wachtsmuth, 1982.)

equation

$$P = 7.4H^{1.54}f_c^{2/3} \qquad \text{(N, mm, MPa)} \qquad (8.17)$$

that gave a correlation coefficient of 0.97. Although the semi-angle of the pull-out cone is different in the analyses of the later results given above, it is interesting to examine their predictions. To correct for the different compressive strength and the different characteristic length, the pull-out force has been assumed to be proportional to $f_c^{2/3}$ and the characteristic length proportional to $f_c^{-0.3}$, in keeping with eqns 8.2 and 8.4. The LEFM prediction of Eligehausen and Sawade (1989), eqn 8.15, and the SEL derived by us, eqn 8.16, are superimposed on the earlier results of Eligehausen and Pusill-Wachtsmuth (1982) in Figure 8.20. The SEL prediction is extremely close to the empirical relationship (eqn 8.17). The LEFM prediction generally overestimates the pull-out force, but the overestimate is less than 13%. Eligehausen (1987) compares the failure loads measured in his tests on expansion bolts with the values predicted by ACI 349 (1980) and a number of other empirical predictions. ACI 349 (1980), in common with most other predictions, uses a strength of materials approach and assumes that failure occurs when the tensile stress σ_t over the projected area of a pull-out cone with a semi-angle of 45° is given by

$$\sigma_t = 0.33\phi\sqrt{f_c} \qquad \text{(MPa, MPa)} \qquad (8.18)$$

where ϕ is a strength reduction factor. ACI 349 (1980) under-estimates the strength of the expansion anchor bolts shown in Figure 8.20, even using a strength reduction factor of 1, but overestimates the strength of the anchor bolts shown in Figure 8.19, even when a strength reduction factor of 0.85 is used. Such are the dangers of using a strength of materials approach which does not give the correct scaling.

Elfgren et al. (1987) have analysed anchor pull-out using the fictitious crack model of Hillerborg et al. (1976). The most interesting case they analysed was where the crack followed a slightly curved path so that the opening was mode I. The initial direction of the crack was at 73° to the vertical. Unfortunately, only one case was analysed for a bolt embedded to a depth of 150 mm, the tensile strength was assumed to be 3 MPa and the fracture energy 100 J/m². The maximum load predicted from the finite element study was 340 kN. An experimental test on a bolt of similar geometry, but located only 300 mm from an edge, gave a failure load of 206 kN (the tensile strength of the concrete was 2.9 MPa). Using eqns 8.15 and 8.16, the predictions from LEFM and the SEL are 211 kN and 195 kN, respectively. It is surprising that these predictions should be more accurate than the prediction where the FPZ is modelled.

Standard pull-out tests are used to determine whether the in-place strength of concrete has reached a specified level and are reviewed by Carino (1991). The first such test to gain acceptance was the Danish LOK-TEST system

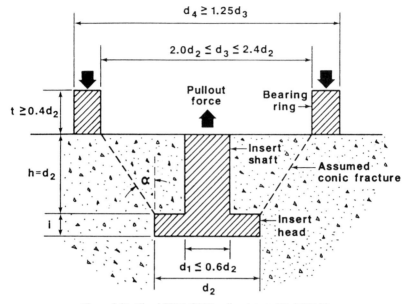

Figure 8.21 The ASTM C900 pull-out test. (© ASTM.)

which was based on the research of Kierkegaard-Hansen (1975). The ASTM standard pull-out test is covered by ASTM C900 (1987). In the standard method a bearing ring is used to react the pull-out force (see Figure 8.21) which to some extent controls the fracture path. Attempts have been made to relate the pull-out strength to the compressive strength of concrete. The correlation relationship originally proposed by the LOK-TEST system for aggregate up to 32 mm was

$$P = 9.48 + 0.829 f_c \qquad \text{(kN, MPa)} \qquad (8.19)$$

However, Bickley (1982) reported considerable differences from eqn 8.19 and proposed different coefficients for differing strength ranges. ACI Committee 228 (1988) recommends establishing an empirical relationship for a range of strengths in the particular concrete being used. Hellier *et al.* (1987) have analysed the pull-out test geometry using the fictitious crack model, assuming that local symmetry is maintained at the crack tip. They found that the primary crack followed an essentially conical path, but with a semi-angle somewhat less than the 35° determined by the test geometry. When the primary crack had grown along a little more than half of the conical surface, a secondary sub-surface crack was initiated under the influence of the reaction ring. This secondary crack grew both towards the free surface and the bolt head. The analysis was terminated shortly after the secondary crack broke through to the free surface, because the value of the maximum compressive stress at this point became sufficient to cause a direct shear failure of the remaining ligament. The same crushing failure mode was predicted in an earlier finite element model using smeared cracks (Ottosen, 1981). The pull-out load when the program was terminated was 22.2 kN which was close to the failure load obtained experimentally.

8.5 Concrete pipes

The failure of pipes would seem to be a fruitful area for the application of frac-ture mechanics, but there seems to have been no study since that of Gustafsson (1985) which was reported by Hillerborg (1989). In the absence of large defects, the strength of a pipe will tend to its 'strength of materials' value as the size increases. Un-reinforced pipes generally fail in either bending or local crushing. In bending of a thin walled pipe the FPZ will spread from the point of maximum stress around the circumference (see Figure 8.22a). The non-dimensional size will therefore depend upon the ratio of the pipe dia-meter to the characteristic length, l_{ch}, and the thickness to diameter ratio will be a weak variable. Four hinges must form under local crushing (see Figure 8.22b) as the FPZ spreads from the inside of the pipe to the outside under the local loads and from the outside of the pipe to the inside at the hinges located at the other quarter points. Hence, the non-dimensional size of the pipes under local crushing depends on the ratio of the thickness to characteristic length. Thus, thin walled pipes are non-dimensionally much smaller under local crushing than under bending. Therefore, concrete pipes can be expected to behave in a more ductile fashion under local crushing than under bending.

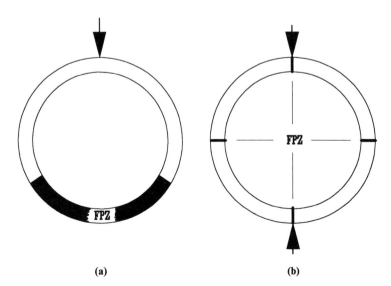

(a)   (b)

Figure 8.22 Failure of un-reinforced concrete pipes (a) in bending and (b) in local crushing.

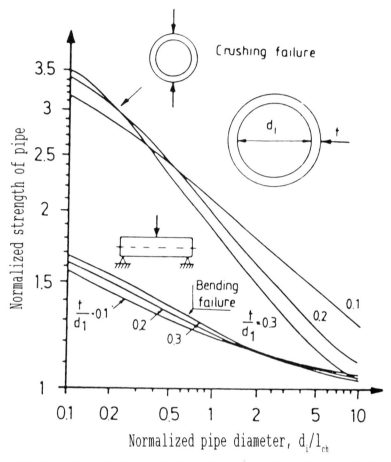

Figure 8.23 Conventional elastic strength of pipes in bending and crushing normalized by the tensile fracture strength of concrete. (After Gustafsson, 1985.)

The ratio of the conventional ultimate elastic strength, σ_u, to the tensile fracture strength, f_t, of the concrete, calculated by Gustafsson (1985) on the basis of the fictitious crack model assuming a linear stress-displacement relationship in the FPZ, is shown in Figure 8.23. The results for both bending and local crushing are presented in terms of the non-dimensional diameter. Not surprisingly then, the 'strength' in local crushing is much higher than the 'strength' in bending. It is reported by Hillerborg (1989) that Scandinavian pipe manufacturers have redesigned their pipes by means of Figure 8.23.

8.6 Summary

The strategy for the design of concrete structures needs to change to take advantage of the advances that have been made in fracture mechanics.

Naturally in an evolving discipline there is no one, universally accepted way of applying fracture mechanics. Some approaches seek to use empirical methods to extend the now well-established LEFM to account for the large FPZ. However, it will greatly impede the development of a rational approach to the design of concrete structures if such empirical approaches are accepted. Empirical methods will be found inadequate to deal with new situations and there will be a never ending need to update the various empirical expressions. Most importantly, such an approach fails to take account adequately of the size effect in concrete structures which is the major contribution of fracture mechanics to concrete design. The design method is not determined by the material properties of concrete alone, size is most important. Small concrete components behave in a ductile fashion and in the limit can be designed by conventional strength of materials. Very large structures with large cracks are brittle and their behaviour can be determined by classic LEFM. However, the ultimate strength of very large structures can only be determined by LEFM if a large crack can grow stably. In an inherently unstable geometry any crack will be small relative to the FPZ at the ultimate load, classic LEFM will not apply, and the FPZ will need to be modelled. The SEL can help in understanding some of the size effects, but only applies if the crack is relatively large at the ultimate load. The empirical approaches using LEFM do not show the true nature of the behaviour of concrete structures and can only be used within the limitations imposed by the data used to obtain them.

In the present chapter it has been shown that if the FPZ is modelled an accurate prediction of the failure modes can be predicted within the limitations imposed by the inherent inhomogeneity of concrete. Some of the advances that have been made in applying statistics to the variations in strength of concrete have been discussed in Chapters 6 and 7. Such work will enable rational factors of safety to be applied to calculations using average values to ensure a safe design.

There are two basic methods of modelling the FPZ: either it can be treated in a discrete fashion with the fictitious crack, or it can be treated as a smeared crack providing the strain-softening relationship is based on a non-local strain. There seems to be no more need to choose one of these two methods of describing the FPZ as 'the Method' than there does between using finite elements or boundary elements in general stress analysis. Each method has its uses and different people will be more confident of using one or the other. Where codes will be called to play their part will be in specifying the material properties of the concrete and, as has been seen in this chapter, the CEB-FIP model code has already gone some way in this regard.

Concrete structures of the future can be more efficiently designed using fracture mechanics, especially if the FPZ is modelled.

References

ACI 349 (1980) Code Requirements for Nuclear Safety Related Concrete Structures.

ACI 228 (1988) *ACI J.*, **85**, 446.

ACI Committee 446 (1989) Fracture of Concrete: Concepts, Models and Determination of Material Properties, Report ACI 446-1R 91.

ACI Committee 446 (1992) Fracture Mechanics: Application to Concrete Structures and Implications with Regard to the Code, Report ACI 446-2R.

Alexander, M.G. (1988) *J. Cem. Concr. Aggregates*, **10**, 9.

Alexander, M.G. and Blight G.E. (1986) In: *Fracture Toughness and Fracture Energy of Concrete* (ed. F.H. Wittmann), p. 323, Elsevier Science Publishers, Amsterdam.

Alexander, M.G., Tait, R.B. and Gill, L.M. (1989) In: *Fracture of Concrete and Rock: Recent Developments* (eds. S.P. Shah, S.E. Swartz and B. Barr), p. 317, Elsevier Applied Science, London.

Alfaiate, J., Pires, E.B. and Martins, J.A.C. (1994) In: *Localized Damage Computer-Aided Assessment and Control III* (eds. M.H. Aliabadi, A. Carpinteri, S. Kalisky and D.J. Cartwright), p. 185, Computational Mechanics Publications, Southampton.

Alvaredo, A.M., Hu, X.Z. and Wittmann, F.H. (1989a) In: *Fracture of Concrete and Rock: Recent Developments* (eds. S.P. Shah, S.E. Swartz and B. Barr), p. 51, Elsevier Applied Science, London.

Alvaredo, A.M., Shah, S.P. and John, R. (1989b) *ASCE J. Eng. Mech.*, **115**, 366.

Andonian, R., Mai, Y.W. and Cotterell, B. (1979) *Int. J. Cem. Composites*, **1**, 151.

Anonymous (1976) *Design of Gravity Dams*, p. 30, US Dept. of the Int., Bureau of Reclamation, Water Resources Technical Publication.

Arrea, M. and Ingraffea, A.R. (1982) *Mixed-Mode Crack Propagation in Mortar and Concrete*, Rpt. 81-13, Dept. Struct. Eng., Cornell Univ., Ithaca, N.Y.

ASTM C900 (1987) *Standard Test Method for Pullout Strength of Hardened Concrete.*

ASTM E399 (1990) *Method of Test for Plane Strain Fracture Toughness of Metallic Materials.*

ASTM E813 (1989) *Standard Test Method for J_{Ic}, a Measure of Fracture Toughness.*

ASTM E1152 (1989) *Standard Test Method for Determining J-R Curves.*

Atkins, A.G. and Mai, Y.W. (1985) *Elastic and Plastic Fracture: Metals, Polymers, Ceramics, Composites, Biological Materials*, Ellis Horwood Ltd., Chichester.

Atkinson, C., Avila, J., Betz, E. and Smelser, R.E. (1972) *J. Mech. Phys. Solids*, **30**, 97.

Aveston, J., Cooper, G.A. and Kelly, A. (1971) In: *Proceedings National Physical Laboratory*, p. 15, IPC Science and Technology Press, London.

Aveston, J. and Kelly, A. (1973) *J. Mater. Sci.*, **8**, 352.

Aveston, J., Mercer, R.A. and Sillwood, J.M. (1974) *Composites—Standards, Testing and Design*, Conference Proceedings, p. 93, National Physical Laboratory, Teddington.

Babut, R. and Brandt, A.M. (1978) In: *Testing and Test Methods of Fibre Cement Composites* (ed. R.N. Swamy), p. 479, The Construction Press, Lancaster.

Bailey, J.E., Chanda, S. and Eden, N.B. (1986) *Fracture Mechanics of Ceramics* (eds. R.C. Bradt *et al.*) Vol. 7, p. 157, Plenum Press, New York.

Baldie. K.D. (1985) PhD Dissertation, University of London.

Baldie, K.D. and Pratt, P.L. (1986) In: *Cement-Based Composites: Strain Rate Effects of Fracture, MRS Symposia Proc.* (eds. S. Mindess and S.P. Shah), Vol. 64, p. 61, Materials Research Society, Pittsburgh.

Ballarini, R., Shah, S.P. and Keer, L.M. (1984) *Eng. Fract. Mech.*, **20**, 433.

Ballarini, R., Keer, L.M. and Shah, S.P. (1986) *Proc. R. Soc. London*, **A404**, 35.

Ballarini, R., Keer, L.M. and Shah, S.P. (1987) *Int. J. Fract.*, **33**, 75.

Ballatore, E., Carpinteri, A., Ferrara, G. and Melchiorri, G. (1990) *Eng. Fract. Mech.*, **35**, 145.

Barenblatt, G.I. (1959) *J. Appl. Math. Mech.*, **23**, 622.
Barenblatt, G.I. (1962) In: *Advances in Applied Mechanics*, **7**, 55, Academic Press, New York.
Barr, B.I.G. and Hasso, E.B.D. (1985) *Mag. Concr. Res.*, **37**, 162.
Bascoul, A., Detriche, C.H., Ollivier, J.P. and Turatsinze, A. (1989a) In: *Fracture of Concrete and Rock: Recent Developments* (eds. S.P. Shah, S.E. Swartz and B. Barr), p. 327, Elsevier Applied Science, London.
Bascoul, A., Ollivier, J.P. and Poushanchi, M. (1989b) *Cem. Concr. Res.*, **19**, 81.
Bažant, Z.P. (1984) *ASCE J. Eng. Mech.*, **110**, 518.
Bažant, Z.P. (1993) *ASCE J. Eng. Mech.*, **119**, 1828.
Bažant, Z.P. (1994) *ASCE J. Eng. Mech.*, **120**, 593.
Bažant, Z.P. and Cao, Z. (1987) *ACI Struct. J.*, **84**, 44.
Bažant, Z.P. and Cedolin, L. (1979) *ASCE J. Eng. Mech.*, **105**, 297.
Bažant, Z.P. and Gambarova, P. (1980) *ASCE J. Struct. Div.*, **106**, 819.
Bažant, Z.P. and Gambarova, P. (1983) *ASCE J. Struct. Eng.*, **110**, 2015.
Bažant, Z.P. and Jirásek, M. (1994) *J. Eng. Mater. Tech.*, **116**, 256.
Bažant, Z.P. and Kazemi, M.T. (1991) *Int. J. Fract.*, **51**, 121.
Bažant, Z.P. and Lin, F.B. 1988 *ASCE J. Struct. Eng.*, **114**, 2493.
Bažant, Z.P. and Oh, B.H. (1983) *Mater. Struct.*, **16**, 155.
Bažant, Z.P. and Ožbolt, J. (1990) *ASCE J. Eng. Mech.*, **116**, 2485.
Bažant, Z.P. and Pfeiffer, P.A. (1987) *ACI Mater. J.*, **84**, 463.
Bažant, Z.P. and Prat, P.C. (1988) *ASCE J. Eng. Mech.*, **114**, 1672.
Bažant, Z.P. and Tsubaki, T. (1980) *ASCE J. Struct. Div.*, **106**, 1947.
Bažant, Z.P. and Xi, Y. (1991) *ASCE J. Eng. Mech.*, **117**, 2623.
Bažant, Z.P., Belytschko, T.B. and Chang, T.P. (1984) *ASCE J. Eng. Mech.*, **110**, 1666.
Bažant, Z.P., Kim, J.K. and Pfeiffer, P.A. (1986) *ASCE J. Struct. Eng.*, **112**, 289.
Bažant, Z.P., Xi, Y. and Reid, S.G. (1991) *ASCE J. Eng. Mech.*, **117**, 2609.
Bažant, Z.P., Ožbolt, J. and Eligehausen, R. (1994) *ASCE J. Struct. Eng.*, **120**, 2377.
Beaudon, J.J. (1986) In: *Fracture Toughness and Fracture Energy of Concrete* (ed. F.H. Wittman), p. 11, Elsevier, Amsterdam.
Begley, J.A. and Landes, J.D. (1972) In: *Fracture Toughness*, ASTM STP 514, p. 1, American Society for Testing and Materials, Philadelphia.
Bentur, A., Diamond, S. and Mindess, J. (1985) *J. Mater. Sci.*, **20**, 3610.
Bergman, B. (1986) *J. Mater. Sci. Letters*, **5**, 611.
Berry, J.P. (1964) In: *Fracture Processes in Polymeric Solids* (ed. B. Rosen), p. 236, Wiley and Sons, New York.
Berthaud, Y. (1989) In: *Fracture of Concrete and Rock* (eds. S.P. Shah and S.E. Swartz), p. 644, Berlin, Springer-Verlag.
Berthelot, J.M. and Robert, J.L. (1987) *J. Acoustic Emission*, **6**, 43.
Bickley, J.A. (1982) *Concr. Int.*, **4**, 44.
Biolzi, L. (1990) *Eng. Fract. Mech.*, **35**, 187.
Biolzi, L., Cangiano, S., Tognon, G. and Carpinteri, A. (1989) *Mater. Struc.*, **22**, 429.
Birchall, J.D., Howard, A.J. and Kendall, K. (1981) *Nature*, **289**, 388.
Birchall, J.D., Howard, A.J. and Kendall, K. (1982) *Proc. Br. Ceram. Soc.*, **32**, 25.
Boca, P., Carpinteri, A. and Valenti, S. (1990) *Eng. Fract. Mech.*, **35**, 159.
Boggs, H.L., Jansen, R.B. and Tarbox, G.S. (1988) In: *Advanced Dam Engineering* (ed. R.B. Jansen), p. 493, Van Nostrand Reinhold, New York.
Bowling, J. and Groves, G.W. (1979) *J. Mater. Sci.*, **14**, 443.
Brandt, A.M. (1980) *Int. J. Cem. Comp.*, **2**, 35.
Broberg, K.B. (1987) *Eng. Fract. Mech.*, **28**, 663.
Brühwiller, E. and Wittmann, F.H. (1989a) *Eng. Fract. Mech.*, **35**, 117.
Brühwiller, E. and Wittmann, F.H. (1989b) *Eng. Fract. Mech.*, **35**, 563.
Bueckner, H.F. *Z. Angew. Math. Mech.*, **50**, 529.
Carino, N.J. (1991) In: *Handbook on Non-Destructive Testing of Concrete* (eds. V.M. Malhotra and N.J. Carino), p. 39, CRC Press, Boca Raton.
Carpinteri, A. (1989a) *ASCE J. Eng. Mech.*, **115**, 1375.
Carpinteri, A. (1989b) *Mater. Struc.*, **22**, 429.
Carpinteri, A. (1990) *Int. J. Fract.*, **44**, 57.

Carpinteri, A. (1991) *Int. J. Fract.*, **51**, 175.

Carpinteri, A., Columbo, G., Ferrara, G. and Guiseppetti, G. (1987) In: *Fracture of Concrete and Rock* (eds. S.P. Shah and S.E. Swartz), p. 131, Springer-Verlag, Berlin.

Carpinteri, A., DiTommaso, A. and Fanelli, M. (1986) In: *Fracture Toughness and Fracture Energy of Concrete* (ed. F.H. Wittmann), p. 117, Elsevier, Amsterdam.

CEB-FIP Model Code 1990, First Predraft 1988, Bulletin d'Information, 190a,b Comité Euro-International du Béton, Lausanne.

Cen, Z. and Mier, G. (1992) *Fatigue Fract. Eng. Mater. Struc.*, **15**, 911.

Cervera, M., Oliver, J., Herrero, E. and Oñate, E. (1990) *Eng. Fract. Mech.*, **35**, 573.

Chappell, J.F. and Ingraffea, A.R. (1981) *A Fracture Mechanics Investigation of the Cracking of Fontana Dam*, Rpt. 81-7, School of Civil and Environmental Engineering, Cornell University, Ithaca.

Chhuy, S., Baron, J. and François, D. (1981) In: *Advances in Fracture Research* (ed. D. François), **4**, 1507.

Chhuy, S. Cannard, G. Robert, J.L. and Acker, P. (1986) In: *Brittle Matrix Composites* (eds. A.M. Brandt and I.H. Marshall), Vol. 1, p. 341, Elsevier Applied Science, London.

Chuang, T.J. and Mai, Y.W. (1989) *Int. J. Solids Struct.*, **25**, 1427.

Chudnovsky, A., Chaoui, K. and Moet, A. (1987) *J. Mater. Sci. Lett.*, **6**, 1033.

Coleman, B.D. (1958) *J. Mech. Phys. Solids*, **7**, 60.

Cook, J. and Gordon, J.E. (1964) *Proc. R. Soc.*, **A282**, 508.

Cornelissen, H.A.W., Hordijk, D.A. and Reinhardt, H.W. (1986) *Heron*, **21**, 45.

Corns, C.F., Tarbox, G.S. and Schrader, E.K. (1988) In: *Advanced Dam Engineering* (ed. R.B. Jansen), p. 466, Van Nostrand Reinhold, New York.

Cotterell, B. (1965) *Int. J. Fract. Mech.*, **1**, 96.

Cotterell, B. (1966) *Int. J. Fract. Mech.*, **2**, 526.

Cotterell, B. (1970) *Int. J. Fract. Mech.*, **6**, 189.

Cotterell, B. and Kamminga, J. (1992) *Mechanics of Pre-Industrial Technology*, Cambridge University Press, Cambridge.

Cotterell, B. and Mai, Y.W. (1987) *J. Mater. Sci.*, **22**, 2734.

Cotterell, B. and Mai, Y.W. (1988a) *Mater. Forum*, **11**, 341.

Cotterell, B. and Mai, Y.W. (1988b) *Adv. Cem. Res.*, **1**, 75.

Cotterell, B. and Mai, Y.W. (1991) In: *Fracture of Engineering Materials and Structures* (eds. S.H. Teoh and K.H. Lee), p. 348. Elsevier Applied Science, London.

Cotterell, B. and Rice, J.R. (1980) *Int. J. Fract.*, **16**, 155.

Cotterell, B., Mai, Y.W. and Foote, R.M.L. (1988) In: *Engineering Applications of New Composites* (eds. S.A. Paipetis and G.C. Papanicolaou), p. 186, Omega Scientific, Wallingford, UK.

Cotterell, B., Paramasivan, P. and Lam, K.Y. (1992) *Mater. Struct.*, **25**, 14.

Cotterell, B., Mai, Y.W. and Lam, K.Y. (1995) *Cem. Concr. Res.*, **25**, 408.

Cox, H.L. (1952) *Br. J. Appl. Phys.*, **3**, 72.

CP110 (1972) *The Structural Use of Concrete, Part 1. Design Materials and Workmanship*, London.

Curtin, W.A. (1991) *J. Am. Ceram. Soc.*, **74**, 2837.

Curtin, W.A. (1993a) *J. Mech. Phys. Solids*, **41**, 35.

Curtin, W.A. (1993b) *J. Mech. Phys. Solids*, **41**, 217.

Daniels, H.E. (1945) *Proc. R. Soc.*, **A186**, 405.

Daniels, H.E. (1989) *Adv. Appl. Prob.*, **21**, 315.

de Borst, R. and Nauta, P. (1985) *Eng. Comp.*, **2**, 35.

de Vekey, R.C. and Majumdar, A.J. (1970) *J. Mater. Sci.*, **5**, 183.

Diamond, S. and Bentur, A. (1985) In: *Application of Fracture Mechanics to Cementitious Composites* (ed. S.P. Shah), p. 87, Martinus Nijhoff, Dordrecht.

Diaz, G. and Kittl, P. (1988) *Int. J. Struct. Mech. Mater. Sci.*, **24**, 209.

Divaker, M.P., Fafitis, A. and Shah, S.P. (1987) *ASCE J. Struct. Eng.*, **113**, 1046

Du, J.J., Kobayashi, A.S. and Hawkins, N.M. (1987) In: *Fracture of Concrete and Rock* (eds. S.P. Shah and S.E. Swartz), p. 199, Springer-Verlag, Berlin,.

Du, J.J., Hawkins, N.M. and Kobayashi, A.S. (1989) In: *Fracture of Concrete and Rock: Recent Developments* (eds. S.P. Shah, S.E. Swartz and B. Barr), p. 297, Elsevier Applied Science, London.

Duan, K., Mai, Y.-W. and Cotterell, B. (1995) *J. Mater. Sci.*, **30**, 1405.

Dugdale, D.S. (1960) *J. Mech. Phys. Solids*, **8**, 100.

Eden, N.B. and Bailey, J.E. (1984a) *J. Mater. Sci.*, **19**, 150.

Eden, N.B. and Bailey, J.E. (1984b) *J. Mater. Sci.*, **19**, 2677.

Eden, N.B. and Bailey, J.E. (1985a) *J. Mater. Sci.*, **20**, 1137.

Eden, N.B. and Bailey, J.E. (1985b) *J. Mater. Sci.*, **20**, 3419.

Eden, N.B. and Bailey, J.E. (1986) In: *Proc. 8th Int. Congress on the Chemistry of Cement*, Vol. 3, p. 382, Rio de Janeiro.

Eden, N.B. and Bailey, J.E. (1988) *Adv. Ceram.*, **22**, 249.

Eden, N.B. and Bailey, J.E. (1989) In *Fracture Mechanics of Concrete Structures: from Theory to Applications* (ed. L. Elfgren), RILEM Report 90-FMA, Chapman and Hall, London.

Elfgren, L. Ohlsson, U. and Gylltoft, K. (1987) In: *Fracture of Concrete and Rock* (ed. S.P. Shah and S.E. Swartz), p. 269, Springer-Verlag, Berlin.

Elices, M., Guinea, G.V. and Planas, J. (1992) *Mater. Struct.*, **25**, 327.

Eligehausen, R. and Pusill-Wachtsmuth, P. (1982) *IABSE Periodica*, No. 1.

Eligehausen, R. and Sawade, G. (1989) In: *Fracture Mechanics of Concrete Structures: from Theory to Applications* (ed. L. Elfgren) p. 281, Chapman and Hall, London.

Erdogan, F. and Sih, G.C. (1963) *J. Basic Eng.*, **85** 507.

Evans, A.G. (1972) *J. Mater. Sci.*, **7**, 1137.

Evans, A.G. and Fuller, E.R. (1974) *Metall. Trans. A*, **5**, 27.

Evans, A.G. and Wiederhorn, S.M. (1974) *J, Mater. Sci.*, **9**, 270.

Ewing, P.D. and Williams, J.G. (1974) *Int. J. Fract.*, **10**, R135.

Ewing, P.D. Swedlow, J.L. and Williams, J.G. (1976) *Int. J. Fract.*, **12**, 85.

Fanelli, M. and Giuseppeti, G. (1990) *Eng. Fract. Mech.*, **35**, 525.

Fardis, M.N. and Buyukzturk, O. (1979) *ASCE J. Eng. Mech. Div.*, **105**, 255.

Fenwick, R.C. and Pauley, T. (1968) *ASCE J. Struct. Div.*, **94**, 2325.

Ferrara, G. and Morabito, P. (1989) In: *Fracture of Concrete and Rock: Recent Developments* (eds. S.P. Shah, S.E. Swartz and B. Barr), p. 377, Elsevier Applied Science, London.

Finnie, I. and Saith, A. (1973) *Int. J. Fract.*, **9**, R484.

Finnie, I. and Weiss, H.D. (1974) *Int. J. Fract.*, **10**, R136.

Foegl, H. and Mang, H.A. (1982) *ASCE J. Struct. Div.*, **108**, 2681.

Foote, R.M.L. (1986) PhD Dissertation, University of Sydney, Sydney, Australia.

Foote, R.M.L., Cotterell, B. and Mai, Y.W. (1980) In: *Advances in Cement Composites* (eds. D.M. Roy, A.J. Majumdar, S.P. Shah and J.A. Manson), p. 135, Materials Research Society, Pittsburg.

Foote, R.M.L., Cotterell, B. and Mai, Y. W. (1986a) In: *Fracture Toughness and Fracture Energy of Concrete* (ed. F.H. Wittmann), p. 91, Elsevier, London.

Foote, R.M.L., Mai, Y.W. and Cotterell, B. (1986b) *J. Mech. Phys. Solids*, **34**, 593.

Foote, R.M.L., Mai, Y.W. and Cotterell, B. (1987) In: *Fibre Reinforced Concrete Properties and Applications*, SP-105 (eds. S.P. Shah and G.B. Batson) Vol. 2, p. 55, American Concrete Institute, Detroit.

Galileo, G. [1638] (1914) *Dialogues Concerning Two New Sciences*, Trans. H. Crew and A. de Salvico, Macmillan, New York.

Gambarova, P.G. and Giuriani, M. (1985) *ASCE J. Struct. Div.*, **111**, 1161.

Gambarova, P.G. and Karakoç, C. (1982) In: *Bond in Concrete* (ed. P. Bartos), p. 82, Applied Science Publishers, London.

Gambarova, P.G., Rosati, G.P. and Zasso, B. (1989a) *Mater. Struct.*, **22**, 35.

Gambarova, P.G., Rosati, G.P. and Zasso, B. (1989b) *Mater. Struct.*, **22**, 347.

Gao, Y.C., Mai, Y.W. and Cotterell, B. (1988) *J. Appl. Maths. Phys.*, **39**, 550.

Gardner, N.J. (1990) *ACI Struct. J.*, **87**, 66.

Gerstle, W., Ingraffea, A.R. and Gergely, P. (1982) In: *Bond in Concrete* (ed. P. Bartos), p. 97, Applied Science Publishers, London.

Gilbert, R.I. and Warner, R.F. (1978) *ASCE J. Struct. Div.*, **104**, 85.

Giuriani, E. (1982) In: *Bond in Concrete* (ed. P. Bartos), p. 107, Applied Science Publishers, London.

Gol'dstein, R.V. and Salaganik, R.L. (1974) *Int. J. Fract.*, **10**, 507.

González-Vidosa, F., Kotsovos, M.D. and Pavlovic, M.N. (1988) *ACI Struct. J.*, **85**, 241.

Gopalaratnam, V.S. and Shah, S.P. (1985) *ACI Mater. J.*, **82**, 310.

Goto, Y. (1971) *J. Am. Concr. Inst.*, **68**, 244.

Goto, Y. and Otsuka, K. (1979) *Technology Report Tohoku University*, **44**, 49.

Goto, Y., Obata, M., Maeno, H. and Kobayashi, Y. (1993) *J. Struct. Eng.*, **119**, 1168.
Griffith, A.A. (1921) *Trans. R. Soc. London, Ser. A*, **221**, 163.
Griffith, A.A. (1925) *Proc. 1st Int. Conf. Appl. Mech.* (eds. C.B. Biezeno and J.M. Burgers) Delft, Technische Boekhandel en Drukkerij, 55.
Guinea, G.V., Planas, J. and Elices, M. (1992) *Mater. Struct.*, **25**, 212.
Guo, Z.H. and Zhang, X.Q. (1987) *ACI Mater. J.*, **84**, 278.
Gurney, C. and Hunt, J. (1967) *Proc. R. Soc. London*, **A299**, 508.
Gurney, C. and Pearson, S. (1948) *Proc. R. Soc. London*, **A192**, 537.
Gustafsson, P.J. (1985) *Fracture Mechanics Studies of Non-Yielding Materials Like Concrete*, Report TVBM-1007, Div. Building Materials, University of Lund, Lund.
Hand, F.R., Pecknold, D.A. and Schnobrich, W.C. (1973) *ASCE J. Struct. Eng.*, **99**, 1491.
Hannant, D.J. (1978) *Fibre Cements and Fibre Concretes*, John Wiley and Sons, Chichester.
Hannant, D.J., Hughes, D.C. and Kelly, A. (1983) *Phil. Trans. R. Soc. London*, **A310**, 175.
Harde, N.A. (1991) *Computer Simulated Crack Propagation in Concrete Beams by Means of Fictitious Crack Method and Boundary Element Method*, Dept. of Building Tech. and Struct. Engn., University of Aalborg, Denmark.
Harris, B. (1980) *Metal Sci.*, **14**, 351.
Harris, B., Varlow, J. and Ellis, C.D. (1972) *Cem. Concr. Res.*, **2**, 447.
Hashida, T., Takahashi, H., Kobayashi, S. and Fukagawa, Y. (1990) *Cem. Concr. Res.*, **20**, 687.
Helfet,T.L. and Harris, B. (1972) *J. Mater. Sci.*, **7**, 494.
Helfinstine, J.D. (1980) *J. Am. Ceram. Soc.*, **60**, 113.
Hellier, A.K., Sansalone, M., Carino, N.J., Stone, W.C. and Ingraffea, A.R. (1987) *Cem. Concr. Aggregates*, **9**, 20.
Hibbert, A.P. and Hannant, D.J. (1982) *Composites*, **13**, 105.
Higgins, D.D. and Bailey, J.E. (1976a) *J. Mater. Sci.*, **11**, 1995.
Higgins, D.D. and Bailey, J.E. (1976b) In: *Proc. Conf. on Hydraulic Cement Paste*, p. 283, E & FN SPON, New York.
Hillerborg, A. (1980) *Int. J. Cem. Comp.*, **2**, 177.
Hillerborg, A. (1983) In: *Fracture Mechanics of Concrete* (ed. F.H. Wittmann), p. 223, Elsevier, Amersterdam.
Hillerborg, A. (1985a) *Mater. Struct.*, **107**, 407.
Hillerborg, A. (1985b) *Mater. Struct.*, **107**, 291.
Hillerborg, A. (1989) In: *Fracture Mechanics of Concrete Structures: from Theory to Applications* (ed. L. Elfgren), p. 314, Chapman and Hall, London.
Hillerborg, A., Modeer, M. and Petersson, P.E. (1976) *Cem. Concr. Res.*, **6**, 773.
Hilsdorf, H.K. and Brameshuber, W. (1985) In: *Application of Fracture Mechanics to Cementitious Materials* (ed. S.P. Shah), p. 361, Martinus Nijhoff, Dordrecht/New York/Lancaster.
Hilsdorf, H.K. and Brameshuber, W. (1991) *Int. J. Fract.*, **51**, 61.
Hoek, E. and Bieniawski, Z.T. (1965) *Int. J. Fract. Mech.*, **1**, 137.
Hordijk, D.A., Reinhardt, H.W. and Cornelissen, H.A.W. (1987) In: *Proc. SEM-RILEM Int. Conf. on Fracture of Concrete and Rocks* (eds. S.P. Shah and S.E. Swartz), p. 138, Springer-Verlag, New York.
Horvath, R. and Petersson (1984) *The Influence of the Size of the Specimen on the Fracture Energy of Concrete*, Rpt. TVBM-5005, Division of Building Materials, University of Lund, Lund.
Hu, X.Z. and Mai, Y.W. (1992a) *J. Mater. Sci.*, **27**, 3502.
Hu, X.Z. and Mai, Y.W. (1992b) *J. Am. Ceram. Soc.*, **75**, 848.
Hu, X.Z. and Wittmann, F.H. (1989) In: *Fracture of Concrete and Rock: Recent Developments* (eds. S.P. Shah, S.E. Swartz and B. Barr), p. 307, Elsevier Applied Science, London.
Hu, X.Z. and Wittmann, F.H. (1990) *J. Mater. Civil Eng.*, **2**, 15.
Hu, X.Z. and Wittmann, F.H. (1991) *Cem. Concr. Res.*, **21**, 1118.
Hu, X.Z. and Wittmann, F.H. (1992a) *Cem. Concr. Res.*, **22**, 559.
Hu, X.Z. and Wittmann, F.H. (1992b) *Mater. Struct.*, **107**, 407.
Hu, X.Z., Cotterell, B. and Mai, Y.W. (1985) *Proc. R. Soc. London*, **A410** 251.
Hu, X.Z., Cotterell, B. and Mai, Y.W. (1986a) In: *Fracture Mechanics of Concrete* (ed. F.H. Wittmann), p. 91, Elsevier, New York.
Hu, X.Z., Cotterell, B. and Mai, Y.W. (1986b) In: *Proc. 3rd Int. Symp. Development of Fibre Reinforced Cement and Concrete* (eds. R.N. Swamy *et al.*), Paper 6.4, Sheffield, Cement & Concrete Association, UK.

Hu, X.Z., Cotterell, B. and Mai, Y.W. (1988a) *Phil. Mag. Lett.*, **57**, 69.

Hu, X.Z., Mai, Y.W. and Cotterell, B. (1988b) *Phil. Mag.*, **58**, 292.

Hu, X.Z., Mai, Y.W. and Cotterell, B. (1989) *J. Mater. Sci.*, **24**, 3118.

Hu, X.Z., Mai, Y.W. and Cotterell, B. (1991) *Phil. Mag.*, **64**, 1265.

Hu, X.Z., Mai, Y.W. and Cotterell, B. (1992) *Phil. Mag.*, **66**, 173.

Hunt, R.A. and McCartney, L.N. (1979) *Int. J. Fract.*, **15**, 365.

Hussain, M.C., Pu, S.L. and Underwood, J. (1973) In: *Fracture Analysis*, ASTM SP560, p. 2.

Hutchinson, J.W. (1983) *J. Appl. Mech.*, **50**, 1042.

Hutchinson, J.W. and Paris P.C. (1977) In: *Elastic-Plastic Fracture*, ASTM STP 668, p. 37, American Society for Testing and Materials, Philadelphia.

Inglis, C.E. (1913) *Trans. Inst. Naval Archit.*, **55**, 219.

Ignacio, C., Prat, P.C. and Bažant, Z.P. (1992) *Int. J. Solids Struct.*, **29**, 1173.

Ingraffea, A.R. (1990) *Eng. Fract. Mech.*, **35**, 553.

Ingraffea, A.R. and Gerstle, W.H. (1985) In: *Applications of Fracture Mechanics to Cementitious Composites* (ed. S.P. Shah), p. 247, Martinus Nijhoff, Dordrecht/Boston/Lancaster.

Ingraffea, A.R. and Panthaki, M.J. (1985) *US–Japan Seminar on Finite Element Analysis of Reinforced Concrete Structures*, Vol. 1, p. 71, ASCE, New York.

Ingraffea, A.R. and Saouma, V. (1984) In: *Application of Fracture Mechanics to Concrete Structures* (eds. G.C. Sih and A. Di Tommaso), Martinus Nijhoff, Holland.

Ingraffea, A.R., Gerstle, W.H., Gergely, P. and Saouma, M. (1984) *Struct. Eng.*, **110**, 871.

Irwin, G.R. (1948) In: *Fracturing of Metals*, ASM, Cleveland, p. 147.

Irwin, G.R. (1957) *J. Appl. Mech.*, **24**, 361.

Irwin, G.R. (1958) In: *Handbuch der Physik*, Vol. VI (ed. W. Flugge), p. 551, Springer-Verlag, Berlin.

Irwin, G.R. (1960) In: *Structural Mechanics, Proc. 1st Symp. on Naval Structural Mechanics*, p. 557.

Isida, M. (1973) In: *Methods of Analysis and Solution of Crack Problems* (ed. G.C. Sih), p. 56, Noordhoff, Amsterdam.

Jakus, K., Coyne, D.C. and Ritter, J.E. (1978) *J. Mater. Sci..*, **13**, 2071.

Jayatilaka, A. De S. and Trustrum, K. (1977) *J. Mater. Sci.*, **12**, 1426.

Jenq, Y.S. and Shah, S.P. (1985) In: *Application of Fracture Mechanics to Cementitious Composites* (ed. S.P. Shah), p. 319, Martinus Nijhoff, Dordrecht/Boston/Lancaster.

Jenq, Y.S. and Shah, S.P. (1985) *ASCE J. Eng. Mech. Div.*, **111**, 1227.

Jenq, Y.S. and Shah, S.P. (1986a) *ASCE J. Struct. Eng.*, **112**, 19.

Jenq, Y.S. and Shah, S.P. (1986b) In: *Fracture Toughness and Fracture Energy of Concrete* (ed. F.H. Wittmann), p. 499, Elsevier, Amsterdam.

Jenq, Y.S. and Shah, S.P. (1988) *Int. J. Fract.*, **38**, 123.

Jirásek, M. and Bažant, Z.P. (1994) *ASCE J. Eng. Mech.*, **120**, 1521.

John, R. and Shah, S.P. (1986) *J. Cem. Concr. Aggregates*, **8**, 24.

Johnston, C.D. (1982) *Cem. Concr. Aggregates*, **2**, 53.

Kalisky, S. (1989) *Plasticity Theory and Engineering Applications*, Elsevier, Amsterdam.

Karihaloo, B.L. and Nallathambi, P. (1988) *A Notched Beam Test: Mode I Fracture Toughness*, Final Report to RILEM TC89-FTM.

Karihaloo, B.L. and Nallathambi, P. (1989a) *Mater. Struct.*, **22**, 185.

Karihaloo, B.L. and Nallathambi, P. (1989b) *Cem. Concr. Res.*, **19**, 603.

Keer, J.G. (1984) In: *New Reinforced Concretes, Concrete Technology and Design* (ed. R.N. Swamy) Vol. 2, p. 52, Surrey University Press.

Kelly, A. and Macmillan, N.H. (1986) *Strong Solids*, 3rd Edition, Claredon Press, Oxford.

Kendall, K. and Birchall, J.D. (1985) *Mater. Res. Soc. Symp. Proc.*, **42**, 143.

Kendall, K., Howard, A.J. and Birchall, J.D. (1983) *Phil Trans. R. Soc.*, **A310**, 139.

Kendall, K., Alford, N.McN., Tan, S.R. and Birchall, J.D. (1986) *J. Mater. Res.*, **1**, 120.

Kesler, C., Naus, D. and Lott, J. (1972) In: *Proc. Int. Conf. on Mechanical Behaviour of Materials*, Vol. 4, p. 113, Soc. Mater. Sci. Japan, Kyoto.

Kierkegaard-Hansen, P. (1975) *Nordisk Betong*, **3**, 19.

Kim, J.K. and Mai, Y.W. (1991) *Comp. Sci. Techn.*, **41**, 333.

Kim, J.K., Zhou, L.M. and Mai, Y.W. (1993) *J. Mater. Sci.*, **28**, 3923.

Kinnunen, S. and Nylander, H. (1960) Punching of Concrete Slabs Without Reinforcement, *Meddelande* no. 38, Institutionen för Byggnadsttik Kungliga Tekniska Högskolan, Stockholm.

Kormeling, H.A. and Reinhardt, H.W. (1981) *Determination of the Fracture of Normal Concrete and Epoxy Modified Concrete*, RPT 1 5-83-18, Steven Laboratory, Delft University of Technology.

Knab, L.I., Walker, J.N., Clifton, J.R. and Fuller, E.R. (1984) *Cem. Concr. Res.*, **14**, 339.

Knab, L.I., Jennings, H., Walker, J.N., Clifton, J.R. and Grimes, J.W. (1986) In: *Fracture Toughness and Fracture Energy of Concrete* (ed. F.H. Wittmann), p. 241, Elsevier Science Publishers, Amsterdam.

Knehans, R. and Steinbrech, R. (1982) *J. Mater. Sci. Lett.*, **1**, 327.

Knott, J.F. (1973) *Fundamentals of Fracture Mechanics*, Butterworths, London.

Kobayashi, A.S., Hawkins, N.M., Barker, D.B. and Liaw, B.M. (1985) In: *Applications of Fracture Mechanics to Cementitious Composites* (ed. S.P. Shah), p. 25, Martinus Nijhoff Publishers, Dordrecht.

Krafft, J.M., Sullivan, A.M. and Boyle, R.W. (1961) In: *Proc. Symp. Crack Propagation, Cranfield*, p. 8, College of Aeronautics, Cranfield.

Krause, R.F. and Fuller, E.R. (1984) *ASTM STP 855*, 309.

Krenchel, H. (1964) *Fibre Reinforcement*, Akademisk Forlag, Copenhagen.

Lam, K.Y., Cotterell, B. and Phua, S.P. (1991) *J. Amer. Ceram. Soc.*, **74**, 2527.

Landes, J.D. and Begley, J.A. (1974) In: *ASTM STP 560* p. 170, American Society for Testing and Materials, Philadelphia.

Larbi, J.A. (1993) Microstructure of the Interfacial Zone around Aggregate Particles in Concrete, *Heron*, **38**(1), 69.

Lawn, B.R. (1993) *Fracture of Brittle Solids*. Cambridge University Press, Cambridge.

Lawrence, P.J. (1980) *J. Mater. Sci.*, **7**, 351.

Lenain, J.C. and Bunsell, A.R. (1979) *J. Mater. Sci.*, **14**, 321.

Li, S.H., Shah, S.P., Li, Z.J. and Mura, T. (1993) *Int. J. Solids Struct.*, **30**, 1429.

Li, V.C. (1985) In: *Application of Fracture Mechanics to Cementitious Materials* (ed. S.P. Shah), p. 431, Martinus Nijhoff, Dordrecht/Boston/Lancaster.

Li, V.C. and Ward, R. (1988) In: *Proc. Int. Workshops on Fracture Toughness and Fracture Energy: Test Methods for Concrete and Rock* (ed. H. Mihashi), p. 139, Tohoku University, Japan.

Li, V.C., Chan, C.M. and Leung, K.Y. (1987) *Cem. Concr. Res.*, **17**, 441.

Li, V.C., Wang, Y. and Backer, S. (1990) *Composites*, **21**, 132.

Li, V.C., Ward, R. and Hamza, A.M. (1992) In: *Applications of Fracture Mechanics to Reinforced Concrete* (ed. A. Carpinteri), p. 503, Elsevier Applied Science, London.

Liang, R.Y.K. and Li, Y.-N. (1991) *Comp. Mech.*, **7**, 413.

Liaw, B.M., Leang, F.L., Du, J.J., Hawkins, N.M. and Kobayashi, A.S. (1990) *ASCE J. Eng. Mech.*, **116**, 429.

Lim, T.Y., Paramasivam, P. and Lee, S.L. (1987a) *ACI Struct. J.*, **84**, 524.

Lim, T.Y., Paramasivam, P. and Lee, S.L. (1987b) *ACI Mater. J.*, **84**, 286.

Linsbauer, H.N. (1989a) *Eng. Fract. Mech.*, **35**, 541.

Linsbauer, H.N. (1989b) In: *Fracture Mechanics of Concrete Structures: from Theory to Applications* (ed. L. Elfgren), p. 329, Chapman and Hall, London.

Linsbauer, H.N. and Rossmanith, H.P. (1984) *Eng. Fract. Mech.* **19**, 195.

Linsbauer, H.N., Ingraffea, A.R., Rossmanith, H.P. and Wawryzynek, P.A. (1989) *J. Struct. Eng.*, **115**, 1599.

Llorca, J. and Elices, M. (1993) *Eng. Fract. Mech.* **44**, 341.

Luong, M.P. (1986) In: *Fracture Toughness and Fracture Energy of Concrete* (ed. F.H. Wittmann), p. 249, Elsevier Science Publishers, Amsterdam.

McCartney, L.N. (1979) *Int. J. Fract.*, **15**, 477.

Mahajan, R.V. and Ravi-Chandar, K. (1989) *Int. J. Fract.*, **41**, 235.

Mai, Y.W. (1979a) *J. Mater. Sci.*, **14**, 2091.

Mai, Y.W. (1979b) *Int. J. Cem. Composites*, **1**, 151.

Mai, Y.W. (1988) *Mater. Forum*, **11**, 232.

Mai, Y.W. (1992) In: *Applications of Fracture Mechanics to Reinforced Concrete* (ed. A. Carpinteri), p. 201, Elsevier Applied Science, London.

Mai, Y.W. and Gurney, C. (1975) *Phys. Chem. Glasses*, **16**, 70.

Mai, Y.W. and Hakeem, M.I. (1984) *J. Mater. Sci.*, **19**, 501.

Mai, Y.W. and Lawn, B.R. (1987) *J. Amer. Ceram. Soc.*, **70**, 290.

Mai, Y.W., Foote, R.M.L. and Cotterell, B. (1980) *Int. J. Cem. Comp.*, **16**, 155.

Mai, Y.W., Hakeem, M.I. and Cotterell, B. (1983) *J. Mater. Sci.*, **18**, 2156.

Mai, Y.W., Barakat, B., Cotterell, B. and Swain, M.V. (1990) *Phil. Mag.*, **62**, 347.

Mai, Y.W., Hu, X.Z., Duan, K. and Cotterell, B. (1992) In: *Fracture Mechanics of Ceramics* (eds. R.C. Bradt, D.P.H. Hasselman, D. Munz, M. Sakai and V.Ya. Shevchenko), Vol. 10, p. 387, Plenum Press, New York.

Majaumdar, A.J. and Walton, P.L. (1985) In: *Application of Fracture Mechanics to Cementitious Composites* (ed. S.P. Shah), p. 157, Martinus Nijhoff, Dordrecht/Boston/Lancaster.

Maji, A. and Shah, S.P. (1988) In: *Bonding in Cementitious Materials, MRS Symp. Proc.* (eds. S. Mindess and S.P. Shah) Vol. 114, p. 55, Materials Research Society, Pittsburg.

Maji, A., Ouyang, C. and Shah, S.P. (1990) *J. Mater. Res.*, **5**, 206.

Malmberg, B. and Skarendahl, H. (1978) In: *Testing and Test Methods of Fibre Cement Composites* (ed. R.N. Swamy), Proc. RILEM Symp., The Construction Press, Lancaster.

Malvar, L.J. (1992) *ACI Struct. J.*, **89**, 569.

Malvar, L.J. and Warren, G.E. (1988) *Exp. Mech.*, **28**, 266.

Marsden, E.W. (1969) *Greek and Roman Artillery—Historical Development*, Clarendon Press, Oxford.

Mazars, J., Pijaudier-Cabot, G. and Saouridis, C. (1991) *Int. J. Fract.*, **51**, 159.

Melin, S. (1986) *Int. J. Fract.*, **30**, 103.

Melin, S. (1987) *Int. J. Fract.*, **32**, 257.

Melin, S. (1989) *Mater. Struct.*, **22**, 23.

Mindess, S. (1983) In: *Fracture Mechanics of Concrete* (ed. F.H. Wittmann), p. 1, Elsevier, New York.

Mindess, S. (1984) *Cem. Concr. Res.*, **14**, 431.

Mindess, S. (1985) In: *Application of Fracture Mechanics to Cementitious Composites* (ed. S.P. Shah), p. 617, Martinus Nijhoff Publishers, Dordrecht/Boston/Lancaster.

Mindess, S. (1991a) In: *Fracture Mechanics Test Methods for Concrete* (eds. S.P. Shah and A. Carpinteri), p. 231, Chapman and Hall, London.

Mindess, S. (1991b) In: *Toughening Mechanisms in Quasi-Brittle Materials* (ed. S.P. Shah), p. 271, Kluwer Academic Publishers, Dordrecht.

Mindess, S. and Diamond, S. (1982a) *Mater. Struct.*, **15**, 107.

Mindess, S. and Diamond, S. (1982b) *Cem. Concr. Res.*, **12**, 569.

Mindess, S. and Nadeau, J. (1977) *Bull. Am. Ceram. Soc.*, **54**, 478.

Mobasher, B., Ouyang, C.S. and Shah, S.P. (1991) *Int. J. Fract.*, **50**, 199.

Modeer, M. (1979) *A Fracture Mechanics Approach to Failure Analysis of Concrete Materials*, University of Lund, Report TVBM-1001.

Morton, J. (1979) *Mater. Struct.*, **12**, 393.

Murdock, J.W. and Kesler, C.E. (1958) *J. Am. Concr. Inst.*, **55**, 221.

Muskhelishvili, N.I. (1953) *Some Basic Problems of the Mathematical Theory of Elasticity*, Noordhoff, Groningen.

Naik, T.R. (1991) In: *Handbook on Non-Destructive Testing of Concrete* (eds. V.M. Malhotra and N.J. Carino), p. 83, CRC Press, Boca Raton.

Nallathambi, P. and Karihaloo, B.L. (1986) *Eng. Fract. Mech.*, **25**, 315.

Naaman, A.E. and Shah, S.P. (1975) In: *RILEM Symposium Fibre-Reinforced Cement and Concrete*, p. 171, The Construction Press, Lancaster.

Naaman, A.E., Reinhardt, H.W., Fritz, C. and Alwan, J. (1993a) *Mater. Struct.*, **26**, 522.

Naaman, A.E., Reinhardt, H.W., Fritz, C. and Alwan, J. (1993b) In: *Structural Engineering in Natural Hazards Mitigation*, p. 1396, ASCE, New York.

Nadeau, J.S., Mindess, S. and Hay, J.M. (1974) *J. Am. Ceram. Soc.*, **57**, 51.

Nishioka, K., Kamimi, N., Yamakawa, S. and Shirakawa, K. (1975) In: *Fibre Reinforced Cement and Concrete*, p. 425, The Construction Press, Lancaster.

Olsson, P.-A. (1985) *A Fracture Mechanics and Experimental Approach on Anchorage Splitting*, Nordic Concrete Research Publication No. 4, The Nordic Concrete Federation.

Ono, H. and Ohgishi, S. (1989) In: *Fracture Toughness and Fracture Energy* (eds. H. Mihashi, H. Takahashi and F.H. Wittmann), p. 73, Balkema, Rotterdam.

Orowan, E. (1948) *Rept. Prog. Phys.*, **12**, 185.

Ottosen, N.S. (1981) *J. Struct. Div. ASCE*, **107**, 591.

Ouyang, C.S. and Shah, S.P. (1992) *Cem. Concr. Res.*, **22**, 1201.

Ouyang, C.S., Mobasher, B. and Shah, S.P. (1990) *Eng. Fract. Mech.*, **37**, 901.

Pak, A.P. and Trapeznikov (1981) In: *Adv. Fract. Res.* (ed. D. Francois), **4**, 1531.

Palaniswamy, K. and Knauss, W.G. (1978) In: *Mechanics Today* (ed. S. Nermat-Nasser), Vol. 4, p. 87, Pergamon Press, New York.

Paris, P.C. and Sih, G.C.M. (1965) In: *Fracture Toughness Testing and its Application*, ASTM STP 381 (ed. W.F. Brown), p. 30, American Society for Testing and Materials, Philadelphia.

Patterson, W.A. and Chan, H.C. (1975) *Composites*, **6**, 102.

Pauley, T. and Loeber, P.J. (1974) *SP 42*, American Concrete Institute, 1.

Petersson, P.E. (1985) *Crack Growth Development of Fracture Zones in Plain Concrete and Similar Materials*, Rpt. TVBM-1006 Div. Bldg. Mats., Lund Institute of Technology.

Phoenix, S.L. (1993) *Composites Sci. Techn.*, **48**, 65.

Phoenix, S.L. and Raj, R. (1992) *Acta Metall. Mater.*, **40**, 2813.

Piggott, M.R. (1980) *Load Bearing Fibre Composites*, Pergamon Press, Oxford.

Pinchin, D.J. and Tabor, D. (1978) *J. Mater. Sci.*, **13**, 1261.

Planas, J., Elices, M. and Guinea, G.V. (1992) *Mater. Struct.*, **25**, 305.

Poon, C.S. and Groves, G.W. (1987) *J. Mater. Sci.*, **22**, 2148.

Portela, A., Aliabadi, M.H. and Rooke, D.P. (1992) *Int. J. Num. Meth. Eng.*, **33**, 1269.

Radon, J.C., Lever, P.S. and Culver, L.E. (1977) In: *Fracture*, **3**, 113, University of Waterloo Press, Waterloo, Canada.

Raiss, M.E., Dougill, J.W. and Newman, J.B. (1989) In: *Fracture of Concrete and Rock: Recent Developments* (eds. S.P. Shah, S.E. Swartz and B. Barr), p. 243, Elsevier Applied Science, London.

Reinhardt, H.W. (1984) *Heron*, **2**, No. 2.

Reinhardt, H.W. and Hordijk, D.A. (1988) In: *France–US Workshop on Strain Localisation and Size Effect Due to Cracking and Damage*, Cachan, France.

Reinhardt, H.W., Cornelissen, H.A.W. and Hordijk, D.A. (1986) *ASCE J. Struct. Eng.*, **112**, 2462.

Reinhardt, H.W., Cornelissen, H.A.W. and Hordijk, D.A. (1989) In: *Fracture of Concrete and Rock* (eds. S.P. Shah and S.E. Swartz), p. 117, Springer-Verlag, Berlin.

Rescher, O.J. (1990) *Eng. Fract. Mech.*, **35**, 503.

Rice, J.R. (1968) In: *Fracture* (ed. H. Liebowitz) **2**, p. 191, Academic Press, New York.

Rice, J.R. (1972) *Int. J. Solids Struct.*, **8**, 751.

Rice, J.R., Paris, P.G. and Merkle (1973) In: *Progress in Flow, Growth and Fracture Toughness Testing*, ASTM STP 536, p. 231, American Society for Testing and Materials, Philadelphia.

RILEM (1985) *Mater. Struct.*, **18**, 285.

RILEM (1990a) *Mater. Struct.*, **23**, 457.

RILEM (1990b) *Mater. Struct.*, **23**, 461.

Ringot, E., Ollivier, J.P. and Maso, J.C. (1987) *Cem. Conc. Res.*, 17, 411.

Roelfstra P.E. and Wittmann, F.H. (1986) In: *Fracture Toughness and Fracture Energy* (ed. F.H. Wittmann), p. 163, Elsevier Applied Science, London.

Rokugo, K., Iwasa, M., Seko, S. and Koyangi, W. (1989) In: *Fracture of Concrete and Rock* (eds. S.P. Shah, S.E. Swartz and B. Barr), p. 513, Elsevier Applied Science, London.

Roger, S.A., Brooks, S.A., Sinclair, W., Groves, G.W. and Double, D.D. (1985) *J. Mater Sci*, **20**, 2853.

Rooke, P.P. and Cartwright, D.V. (1976) *Compendium of Stress Intensity Factors*, H.M. Stationery Office, London.

Rots, J.G. (1985) *Bond-Slip Simulations using Smeared Cracks and/or Interface Elements*, Research RPT., 85-01, Struct. Mech., Dept. Civil Eng., Delft University of Technology.

Rots, J.G. (1986) In: *Fracture Toughness and Fracture Energy of Concrete* (ed. F.H. Wittmann), p. 137, Elsevier Applied Science, London.

Rots, J.G. (1988) *Computational Modelling of Concrete Fracture*, Dissertation, Delft Univ. of Technology.

Rots, J.G. (1991) *Int. J. Fract.*, **51**, 45.

Rots, J.G. and de Borst, R. (1987) *ASCE J. Eng. Mech.*, **113**, 1739.

Rubinstein, A.A. (1991) *Int. J. Fract.*, **47**, 291.

Saito, M. (1984) *Int. J. Cem. Comp. Lightweight Concr.*, **6**, 143.

Saito, M. and Imai, S. (1983) *Am. Concr. Inst. J.*, **67**, 431.

Sakamoto, M. and Indrawan, B. (1995) *Preliminary Report of the January 17, 1995 Great Hanshin Earthquake*, Kajima Corporation, Kabori Research Complex, Inc., Tokyo.

Salih, A.L. and Aliabadi, M.H. (1994) In: *Localized Damage Computer-Aided Assessment and Control III* (eds. M.H. Aliabadi, A. Carpinteri, S. Kalisky and D.J. Cartwright), p. 185, Computational Mechanics Publications, Southampton.

Saouma, V.E., Ayari, M.L. and Boggs, H. (1987) In: *Fracture of Concrete and Rock* (eds. S.P. Shah and S.E. Swartz), p. 311, Springer-Verlag, Berlin.

Saouma, V.E., Broz, J.J. and Boggs, H. (1991) *J. Mater. Civil Eng.*, **3**, 219.

Schneider, U. and Diederichs, U. (1983) In: *Fracture Mechanics of Concrete* (ed. F.H. Wittmann), p. 207, Elsevier Science Publishers, Amsterdam.

Shah, S.P. (1988) *Mater. Struct.*, **21**, 145.

Shah, S.P. and McGarry, F.J. (1971) *ASCE J. Eng. Mech. Div.*, **97**, 1663.

Sih, G.C. (1973a) *Eng. Fract. Mech.*, **5**, 365.

Sih, G.C. (1973b) *A Special Theory of Crack Propagation in Mechanics of Fracture, Methods, Analysis and Solutions of Crack Problems*, Noordhoff, Groningen.

Sih, G.C. (1974) *Int. J. Fract.*, **10**, 305.

Sinclair, W. and Groves, G.W. (1985) *J. Mater. Sci.*, **20**, 2846.

Slate F.O. and Hover, K.C. (1984) In: *Fracture Mechanics of Concrete: Material Characterisation and Testing* (eds. A. Carpinteri and A.R. Ingraffea), p. 137, Martinus Nijhoff Publishers, The Hague.

Smith, E. (1994) *Mech. Mater.*, **17**, 369.

Stang, H. and Shah, S.P. (1986) *J. Mater. Sci.*, **21**, 21.

Stefanou, G.D. (1993) *Eng. Fract. Mech.*, **44**, 137.

Strange, P.C. and Bryant, A.H. (1979) *ASCE J. Eng. Mech Div.*, **105**, 337.

Streit, R. and Finnie, I. (1980) *Exp. Mech.*, **20**, 17.

Struble, L., Stuzman, P. and Fuller, E.R. (1989) *J. Am. Ceram. Soc.*, **72**, 2295.

Suidan, M. and Schnobrich, W.C. (1973) *ASCE J. Struct. Eng.*, **99**, 2109.

Sumi, Y., Nemat-Nasser, S. and Keer, L.M. (1985) *Eng. Fract. Mech.*, **22**, 759.

Sutcu, M. (1989) *Acta Metall.*, **37**, 651.

Swamy, R.N. and Hussin, M.W. (1989) In: *Fibre Reinforced Cements and Concretes* (eds. R.N. Swamy and B. Barr), p. 90, Elsevier Applied Science, London.

Swanson, P.L., Fairbanks, C.J., Lawn, B.R., Mai, Y.W. and Hockey, B.J. (1987) *J. Am. Ceram. Soc.*, **70**, 279.

Swartz, S.E. and Go, C.G. (1984) *Exp. Mech.*, **24**, 129.

Swartz, S.E and Refai, T.M.E. (1987) In: *Fracture of Concrete and Rock* (eds. S.P. Shah and S.E. Swartz), p. 242, Springer-Verlag, Berlin.

Swartz, S.E. and Taha, N.M. (1990) *Eng. Fract. Mech.*, **35**, 137.

Swartz, S.E., Lu, L.W. and Tang, L.D. (1988) *Mater. Struct.*, **21**, 33.

Swenson, D.V. and Ingraffea, A.R. (1991) *Int. J. Fract.*, **10**, 73.

Swift, D.G. and Smith, R.B.L. (1978) In: *Testing and Test Methods of Fibre Cement Composites* (ed. R.N. Swamy), p. 463, The Construction Press, Lancaster.

Tada, H., Paris P.C. and Irwin, G.R. (1973) *The Stress Analysis of Cracks Handbook*, Del Research Corp., Hellertown.

Tait. R.B. (1984) PhD Thesis, University of Cape Town.

Tait, R.B. and Garrett, G.G. (1986) *Cem. Concr. Res.*, **16**, 143.

Tait, R.B., Diamond, S., Askers, S.A.S. and Mindess, S. (1990) In: *Micromechanics of Failure of Quasi-Brittle Materials* (eds. S.P. Shah, S.E. Swartz and M.L. Wang), p. 52, Elsevier Applied Science, London.

Takaku, A. and Arridge, R.G.C. (1973) *J. Phys. D: Appl. Phys.*, **6**, 2038.

Tarng, K.-M., Chern, J.-C. and Chen, H.-W. (1991) *J. Chinese Inst. Eng.*, **14**, 173.

Thouless, M.D. and Evans, A.G. (1988) *Acta Metall.* **36**, 517.

Trustrum, K. and Jayatilaka, A. De S. (1983) *J. Mater. Sci.*, **18**, 2765.

Turner, C.E. (1973) *Mater. Sci. Eng.*, **11**, 275.

Turner, C.E. (1979) In: *Post Yield Fracture Mechanics* (ed. D.G.H. Latzko) Applied Science Publishers, Barking, UK.

Van Mier, J.G.M. (1989) In: *Micromechanics of Failure of Quasi-Brittle Materials* (eds. S.P. Shah, S.E. Swartz and M.L. Wang), p. 33, Elsevier Applied Science Publishers, London.

Van Mier, J.G.M. (1991) In: *Fracture Processes in Concrete, Rock and Ceramics* (eds. J.G.M. van Mier, J.G. Rots and A. Bakker), Vol. 1, p. 27, E&FN Spon, London.

Visalvanich, K. and Naaman, A.E. (1983) *J. Am. Concr. Inst.*, **80**, 128.

Ward, R.J. and Li, V.C. (1989) In: *Fracture of Concrete and Rock* (eds. S.P. Shah. S.E. Swartz and B. Barr), p. 645, Elsevier Applied Science, London.

Wawrzynek, P.A. and Ingraffea, A.R. (1987a) *Theor. and Appl. Fract. Mech.*, **8**, 137.

Wawrzynek, P.A. and Ingraffea, A.R. (1987b) *Engn. Comput.*, **3**, 13.

Wells, A.A. (1961) In: *Proc. Symp. Crack Propagation, Cranfield*, **1**, p. 210, College of Aeronautics, Cranfield.

Wells, A.A. (1963) *Brit. Weld. J.*, **11**, 35.

Wells, J.K. and Beaumont, P.W.R. (1985) *J. Mater. Sci.*, **20**, 97.

Weibull, W. (1939) *Ingen. Vetenskaps. Akad. Hand.*, No. 151.

Weibull, W. (1951) *J. Appl. Mech.*, **18**, 293.

Wecharatana, M. and Shah, S.P. (1982) *J. Struct. Div. ASCE*, **108**, 1400.

Wecharatana, M. and Shah, S.P. (1983) *Cem. Concr. Res.*, **13**, 819.

Weidmann, G.E. and Williams, J.G. (1975) *Polymer*, **16**, 921.

Weiderhorn, S.M., Freiman, S.W., Fuller, E.R. and Simmons, C.J. (1982) *J. Mater. Sci.*, **17**, 3460.

Williams, L.S. (1956) *Trans. Br. Ceram. Soc.*, **55**, 287.

Williams, M.L. (1957) *J. Appl. Mech.*, **24**, 109.

Williams, J.G. and Ewing, P.D. (1972) *Int. J. Fract. Mech.*, **8**, 441.

Wilson, W.K. (1966) In: *Plane Strain Fracture Toughness Testing of High Strength Metallic Materials*, ASTM STP 410, p. 75, American Society for Testing and Materials, Philadelphia.

Wiss, Janney Elstner Associates, Inc. and Musuer Rutledge Consulting Engineers (1987) Final Report: Collapse of the Thruway Bridge at Schoharie Creek, New York State Thruway Authority, Albany, New York.

Wittmann, F.H. (1983a) In: *Fracture Mechanics of Concrete* (ed. F.H. Wittmann), p. 43, Elsevier, New York.

Wittmann, F.H. (1983b) *Concr. J., Japan Concr. Inst.*, **21**, 19.

Wittmann, F.H. (1985) In: *Application of Fracture Mechanics to Cementitious Composites* (ed. S.P. Shah), p. 593, Martinus Nijhoof Publishers, Dordrecht.

Wittmann, F.H. and Hu, X.Z. (1991) *Int. J. Fract.*, **51**, 19.

Wittmann, F.H., Roelfstra, P.E., Mihahashi, H., Huang, Y.Y., Zhang X.H. and Noniwa, N. (1987) *Mater. Strut.*, **20**, 103.

Wittmann, F.H., Rokugo, K., Bruhwiler, E., Mihashi, H. and Simonin, P. 1988 *Mater. Struct.*, **21**, 21.

Wu, C.H. (1978) *J. Appl. Mechs.*, **45**, 553.

Wu, X.R. and Carlsson, A.J. (1991) *Weight Functions and Stress Intensity Factor Solution*, Pergamon Press, Oxford.

Wu, Z., Yoshikawa, H. and Tanabe, T. (1991) *ASCE J. Struct. Eng.*, **117**, 715.

Yao, B. and Murray, D.W. (1993) *ASCE J. Struct. Eng.*, **119**, 2813.

Yu, Y.Z. (1981) *J. Water Conservancy*, No. 6 (in Chinese).

Yu, Y.Z. (1989) In: *Fracture Mechanics of Concrete Structures, from Theory to Applications* (ed. L. Elfgren), p. 355, Chapman and Hall, London.

Yuzugullu, O. and Schnobrich, W.C. (1973) *ACI J.*, **70**, 1973.

Zaitsev, Y. (1983) In: *Fracture Mechanics of Concrete* (ed. F.H. Wittmann), p. 251, Elsevier, New York.

Zaitsev, Y.B. and Wittmann, F.H. (1981) *Mater. Struct*, **14**, 365.

Zech, B. and Wittmann, F.H. (1977) In: *Trans. 4th. Int. Conf. on Structural Mechanics in Reactor Technology* (eds. T.A. Jaeger and B.A. Boley), Vol. H, J1/11, p. 1, European Communities, Brussels.

Zhou, L.M., Kim, J.K. and Mai, Y.W. (1992) *J. Mater. Sci.*, **27**, 3155.

Ziegeldorf, S. (1983) In: *Fracture Mechanics of Concrete* (ed. F.H. Wittmann), p. 371, Elsevier, New York.

Index